EGO FUNCTIONS IN SCHIZOPHRENICS, NEUROTICS, AND NORMALS

WILEY SERIES ON PERSONALITY PROCESSES

IRVING B. WEINER, *Editor*
Case Western Reserve University

INTERACTION IN FAMILIES
by Elliot G. Mishler and Nancy E. Waxler

SOCIAL STATUS AND PSYCHOLOGICAL DISORDER: A Causal Inquiry
by Bruce P. Dohrenwend and Barbara Dohrenwend

PSYCHOLOGICAL DISTURBANCE IN ADOLESCENCE
by Irving B. Weiner

ASSESSMENT OF BRAIN DAMAGE: A Neuropsychological Key Approach
by Elbert W. Russell, Charles Neuringer, and Gerald Goldstein

BLACK AND WHITE IDENTITY FORMATION
by Stuart Hauser

THE HUMANIZATION PROCESSES: A Social, Behavioral Analysis of
Children's Problems
*by Robert I., Hamblin, David Buckholdt, Daniel Ferritor, Martin Kozloff,
and Lois Blackwell*

ADOLESCENT SUICIDE
by Jerry Jacobs

TOWARD THE INTEGRATION OF PSYCHOTHERAPY
by John M. Reisman

MINIMAL BRAIN DYSFUNCTION IN CHILDREN
by Paul Wender

LSD: PERSONALITY AND EXPERIENCE
*by Harriet Linton Barr, Robert J. Langs, Robert R. Holt,
Leo Goldberger, and George S. Klein*

TREATMENT OF THE BORDERLINE ADOLESCENT: A Developmental Approach
by James F. Masterson

PSYCHOPATHOLOGY: Contributions from the Biological, Behavioral, and
Social Sciences
edited by Muriel Hammer, Kurt Salzinger, and Samuel Sutton

ABNORMAL CHILDREN AND YOUTH: Therapy and Research
by Anthony Davids

PRINCIPLES OF PSYCHOTHERAPY WITH CHILDREN
by John M. Reisman

AVERSIVE MATERNAL CONTROL: A Theory of Schizophrenic Development
by Alfred B. Heilbrun, Jr.

INDIVIDUAL DIFFERENCES IN CHILDREN
edited by Jack C. Westman

EGO FUNCTIONS IN SCHIZOPHRENICS, NEUROTICS, AND NORMALS: A
Systematic Study of Conceptual, Diagnostic, and Therapeutic Aspects
by Leopold Bellak, Marvin Hurvich, and Helen K. Gediman

EGO FUNCTIONS IN SCHIZOPHRENICS, NEUROTICS, AND NORMALS

A Systematic Study of Conceptual, Diagnostic, and Therapeutic Aspects

LEOPOLD BELLAK, M.D.
*Visiting Professor of Psychiatry,
Albert Einstein College of Medicine
Research Professor of Psychology
Postdoctoral Training Program, New York University
Clinical Professor of Psychiatry and Behavioral Sciences
The George Washington University School of Medicine*

MARVIN HURVICH, Ph.D.
*Professor of Psychology, Long Island University
Research Psychologist, Department of Psychiatry, The Roosevelt Hospital*

HELEN K. GEDIMAN, Ph.D.
*Assistant Clinical Professor of Psychiatry,
Albert Einstein College of Medicine, Montefiore Hospital and Medical Center*

with the assistance of

PATRICIA CRAWFORD, M.A. and DAVID JACOBS, Ph.D.

A WILEY-INTERSCIENCE PUBLICATION

JOHN WILEY & SONS, New York • London • Sydney • Toronto

Library of Congress Cataloging in Publication Data

Bellak, Leopold, 1916-
Ego functions in schizophrenics, neurotics, and normals.

(Wiley series on personality processes)
"A Wiley-Interscience publication."
1. Schizophrenia. 2. Neuroses. 3. Ego
(Psychology) I. Hurvich, Marvin, joint author.
II. Gediman, Helen K., joint author. III. Title.
DNLM: 1. Ego. 2. Neuroses. 3. Psychoanalysis.
4. Schizophrenia. BF 698 B435e 1973
RC514.B42   616.8'982   73-3199
ISBN 0-471-06413-0

Printed in the United States of America

10 9 8 7 6 5 4 3 2

Series Preface

This series of books is addressed to behavioral scientists interested in the nature of human personality. Its scope should prove pertinent to personality theorists and researchers as well as to clinicians concerned with applying an understanding of personality processes to the amelioration of emotional difficulties in living. To this end, the series provides a scholarly integration of theoretical formulations, empirical data, and practical recommendations.

Six major aspects of studying and learning about human personality can be designated: personality theory, personality structure and dynamics, personality development, personality assessment, personality change, and personality adjustment. In exploring these aspects of personality, the books in the series discuss a number of distinct but related subject areas: the nature and implications of various theories of personality; personality characteristics that account for consistencies and variations in human behavior; the emergence of personality processes in children and adolescents; the use of interviewing and testing procedures to evaluate individual differences in personality; efforts to modify personality styles through psychotherapy, counseling, behavior therapy, and other methods of influence; and patterns of abnormal personality functioning that impair individual competence.

IRVING B. WEINER

Case Western Reserve University
Cleveland, Ohio

Preface

This book first reviews the literature on the structural model of psychoanalysis and discusses in considerable detail the conceptions of various ego functions.

The review establishes the necessary background for the ensuing report of research on the assessment of ego functions in schizophrenics and, for comparison, in neurotics and normals. The original intent of the research was to demonstrate that schizophrenics can be differentiated from neurotics and normals by a quantifiable difference in the adaptive level of ego functions. Another intent was to demonstrate that within a sample of schizophrenics there would be many individual differences in ego function profiles.

An attempt is made to demonstrate the usefulness of the individual ego function assessment for specific diagnosis and the rational planning of treatment and the formulation of a prognosis.

In the process of this work it was necessary to develop tools to serve as a basis for assessing ego functions and to construct a valid and reliable rating scale. For that purpose an extensive review of the relevant literature was made and is presented, together with interview guide, manual, and rating form.

Thus, this volume attempts to provide a report on the research study, some clinical guidelines, a review of relevant literature, and a tool for ego function assessment.

Ego function assessment, as we present it, should help deal with the so far extremely vexing problem of cross-cultural comparisons of diagnoses. Obviously, behavior considered pathological in one culture is often acceptable in another one. This fact has, among other things, made data collection very difficult.

If, however, a rating scale is established for a given culture, it is possible then to compare a person who rates a 4 on impulse control in Zürich with one who rates a 4 on impulse control in the Fiji Islands, if a scale is standardized for Zurichers and one for Fiji Islanders. Therefore, it is hoped that this scaling approach will be helpful to the World Health Organization as well as anthropologists, transcultural psychiatrists, and others.

One of our not quite fulfilled aims also remains a hope for future research: that subgroups of ego function clusters will be demonstrated to exist and will lead to the identification of etiological or pathogenic subgroups of the schizophrenic syndrome.

In view of the multifaceted application of our toil, and of the book itself, it is hoped, then, that it will serve many different kinds of people for many different purposes: for a study of the literature and for testing our hypotheses and extending them to groups larger than ours and to different groups. We hope that students, researchers, and clinicians alike will find something potentially useful in our labors.

Although this is a book about psychoanalytic concepts in research and clinical practice, it would be regrettable if it were seen only in that relatively narrow context. We hope indeed that the methodology and data will be found useful in areas far removed from psychoanalysis per se.

LEOPOLD BELLAK, M.D.
MARVIN HURVICH, Ph.D.
HELEN K. GEDIMAN, Ph.D.

New York, New York
May 1, 1973

Acknowledgments

We gratefully acknowledge the support of the research study which constitutes the core of this project by grants MH 14260-03, MH 18395-01, 02, and 02S1 of the National Institute of Mental Health (Leopold Bellak, M.D., Principal Investigator). Quite aside from the financial support, we appreciate the constructive and supportive role played by various members of NIMH.

Stanley Yolles, M.D., as the then relatively new director of the National Institute, created the atmosphere in which such a project had a chance to be supported; under his successor, Bertram Brown, M.D., a constructive attitude continues to prevail. Louis Wienckowski, Ph.D., as director, Division of Extramural Research Programs, and Martin Katz, Ph.D., as chief, Clinical Research Branch, were always interested. Hassan Tuma, Ph.D., as project officer, was continually helpful with knotty administrative problems, and Loren Mosher, M.D., and his newly created Schizophrenia Research Center were a valuable resource.

A large number of people have been associated with the project in the course of five years. Jacob Cohen, Ph.D., Professor of Psychology at New York University, served as methodological and statistical consultant. Nancy Israel Goldberger, Ph.D., has been extremely helpful in that same area, and also as interviewer, rater, and friendly supporter. The Psychology Department of New York University and Dr. Bernard Kalinkowitz, chairman of the Postdoctoral Program in Psychotherapy, as administrative sponsor, are others to whom we are indebted.

Roosevelt Hospital, Gracie Square Hospital, and Lincoln Institute for Psychotherapy kindly permitted us to use their facilities and to study some of their patients for this project.

We are also thankful to Ms. Liselotte Bendix and Ms. Phyllis Rubinton, librarians of the A. A. Brill Library of the New York Psychoanalytic Institute, and their staff, and to Ms. Winifred Lieber and Ms. Margaret Ritchie from the Roosevelt Hospital Libraries.

Lloyd Silverman, Ph.D., revised the Manual for Scoring Psychological Tests.

Muriel Fox, Ph.D., was kind enough to permit us to include her paper on the use of the ego function scheme for diagnosis and treatment of adolescents.

Mark Silvan, Ph.D., contributed significantly to the development of the experimental test series as well as to other phases of the project.

Leonard Small, Ph.D., was associated with the study for only a relatively short span of time but contributed significantly to some conceptions.

Jacob Arlow, M.D., Bernard Pacella, M.D., Robert Savitt, M.D., and Julian Stamm, M.D., were kind enough to read critically some chapters, without, of course, being in any way responsible for our formulations.

The following have also participated in the study as interviewers, raters, testers, and consultants, and in administrative and editorial capacities.

Suzette Annin B.A.	Susan Linzer, B.A.	Martin Rock, M.A.
Jack Chassan, Ph.D.	Frances Lippman, Ph.D.	Elizabeth Schackman
Patricia Crawford M.A.	Lynn Lustbader, M.A.	Jean Schimek, Ph.D.
Lucy Domkus, M.A.	Milton Malev, M.D.	Howard Schlossman, M.D.
Morris Eagle, Ph.D.	Eva Meyer	Steve Silverman, Ph.D.
Nancy Edwards, Ph.D.	Carol Michalov	Peter Smith, M.A.
Katherine Flanz, B.A.	Richard Miller	Donald Spence, Ph.D.
Maryl Gearhart, M.A.	Joan Nissenberg, M.A.	Nina Tkachuk, B.A.
Stanley Grand, Ph.D.	Ann Noll	Michael Varga, Ph.D.
Wayne Holtzman, Ph.D.	Wendy Noll, B.A.	Paul Wachtel, Ph.D.
Milton Kapit, Ed. D.	Gustavia Pagan	Paula Wieluns, M.A.
Rose Kent, Ph.D.	Roger Reuben, M.A.	

Ann Noll quite especially deserves our thanks for performing the myriad of tasks it took to get this work from a loose collection of manuscripts into the final shape of the book. She brought to it good editorial judgment, incredible patience, tact, devotion, and a cheerful spirit, without which the volume might well not have been published.

We would also like to express our appreciation to Robert Cancro, M.D., Mazel/Brunner, Inc., and the *International Journal of Psycho-Analysis* for permission to use material previously published by them.

Above all, we are very grateful to the patients and other subjects of the study who, by their own volition and with their explicit permission, provided us with the basic data for our work.

L. B.
M. H.
H. G.

Contents

EGO FUNCTIONS IN SCHIZOPHRENICS,
NEUROTICS, AND NORMALS

Introduction

According to a report from the National Institute of Mental Health, mental illness cost the United States $20 billion in 1966; Of this $2.5 billion was spent on inpatient care alone. In 1968 the cost of schizophrenia to the country was estimated at $14 billion annually. This involves the care of two to three million living Americans diagnosed as schizophrenic.

Schizophrenics still fill nearly one-half of all mental-hospital beds (i.e., state and county mental hospitals and not including general hospitals), or, in other words, one-quarter of all hospital beds in the country. Reckoning only the cost of caring for schizophrenic inpatients — surely the smallest part of the cost of schizophrenia to the economy — the amount was $1.25 billion in 1966 alone.

Factors other than the economic one also make it likely that schizophrenia is indeed the number one public health problem. It strikes early in life — much earlier than the mean age (33 years) of first hospitalization suggests — and surely much earlier than heart disease and malignancies. Despite recent discharge rates of encouraging proportions, the schizophrenic disability probably continues in most cases after discharge. It is true that during the last 15 years there has been a 30 percent decrease in the number of hospitalized schizophrenics. During 1968, for example, resident patients in state and county mental hospitals declined from 210,000 to 195,000. Over the same 15 years, however, admission rates continued to rise, and in 1968 alone there were more than 320,000 episodes of illness diagnosed as schizophrenia in the United States. The "revolving door" phenomenon refers to the fact that while patients are being hospitalized for shorter periods, they are more frequently being readmitted. Even more crucial is the fact that only from 15 to 40 percent of schizophrenics living in the community can be considered to adjust on an average level: psychotropic drugs have mostly suppressed symptoms that had previously made it difficult for the patient to live within the community, but they do not necessarily enable him to function well enough. To add to the problem schizophrenia poses, it must also be remembered that such epidemiological figures as are available suggest that from 2 to 10 times as many schizophrenics may be in the community as are hospitalized. The most reliable expectancy rates suggest that up to 6 percent of the population may be diagnosed schizophrenic sometime in their lives.

So far, no convincing single explanation of the etiology or pathogenesis of schizophrenia has been produced. Bellak's attempt to find an answer has been formulated in the "egopsychological *multiplefactor psychosomatic theory of schizophrenia,*" wherein schizophrenia is seen as a syndrome caused by different etiological factors and pathogenic pathways, all of them sharing as final common manifest paths severe disorders of the ego functions 1949a; 1952; 1955; 1958a.

The current research was predicated on this multiplefactor theory. The hope was to show that a sample of people diagnosed as schizophrenics on the basis of ordinary clinical criteria, by clinicians independent of our study, would demonstrate that all persons diagnosed as schizophrenic manifest serious disturbances or regression of some ego functions but that schizophrenics differ in regard to which functions are the most disturbed. We further hoped that it would be found useful to group patients on the basis of similarities of ego function patterns or subpatterns.

In order to establish ego function levels for schizophrenics it was necessary to be able to compare their functioning with that of nonschizophrenic persons. We therefore included groups of both neurotics and normals in our study. In the process of studying neurotics and "normals" (we soon came to speak of those whom we selected as not being hospitalized, not in treatment, and, for practical purposes, seemingly well functioning, as "community representatives"), we were increasingly impressed by what a useful means of personality assessment ego function profiling appears to be. During the five years of the study, various opportunities to use the profile for the assessment of progress in psychotherapy, drug effects, and the like presented themselves and seemed to be promising. At present, some researchers are attempting to use our technique for the assessment of patients with psychosomatic problems; others have started to assess test pilots, to extend it to the study of adolescent problems, to assess the profiles of psychiatric residents, and to carry out a variety of still other projects.

In order to investigate ego functions, we had to clarify their meaning and find definitions that would lend themselves to independent rating by judges. We have included a rather comprehensive review of the psychoanalytic literature in our presentation of each of the 12 ego functions defined in our study, showing the development and gradual evolution of each.

Having stated our hypothesis, set up experimental conditions for examining it, and defined the variables necessary for our study, we then tested schizophrenics, neurotics, and normals by an interview, a psychological test battery, and a set of laboratory procedures. In all these spheres, we were in uncharted territory: we not only had to devise our instruments but at the same time we had to try to verify their usefulness by construct validity in relation to the clinical criteria. In this initial effort, other validational criteria were not available.

We believe we have demonstrated that, using our standard interview and rating scales, independent observers can rate people on ego functions with a useful degree of reliability and validity, on characteristic and current levels, and can make inferences about their highest and lowest levels of performance. We have a number of observations to offer on the nature of ego functions in the range of the sample we observed that may be useful for some problems of assessment.

In addition, we are presenting some inferences from our data regarding the important clinical problems of the diagnosis of schizophrenia, its treatment, and its prognosis. We therefore hope that our volume will be useful for researchers and clinicians alike.

Psychoanalysts have sometimes held that evaluation interviews and behavioral observations cannot generate data comparable to what is available through prolonged explorations in a clinical psychoanalytic setting. In discussing the relevance of direct observational procedures with child subjects, Anna Freud (1965) found some behavioral items that can be reliably translated into "the unconscious counterpart from which they are derived."

With regard to various ego apparatuses, Anna Freud states that valid observations can be made outside a psychoanalytic setting:

Notwithstanding the fact that the result of their action is of the utmost importance for internalization, identification, and superego formation, i.e., for processes which are accessible only in analytic work, they themselves and the degree of maturation reached by them are measurable from the outside (1965, p. 22).

In order to demonstrate that our ego function assessment is useful and practical in a strictly clinical setting, we also include a brief study that shows the ability to rate ego functions in the course of regular psychoanalytic therapy sessions and to have these ratings correlate highly with those obtained independently from our standard interview (see Chapter 19).

Furthermore, there is empirical evidence that systematic, clinical assessment of ego functions may be useful for assessing the difficult problems of analyzability and generally help chart and predict the therapeutic process and response (Bellak, 1972).

In addition, systematic ego function assessment can be useful in a variety of other contexts: the evaluation of psychological test data* is much needed in therapeutic planning for patients in the community mental health setting** to avoid the revolving door phenomenon. Finally, peer reviews and data demanded increasingly from third parties such as insurance companies should make systematic, independently verifiable methods such as ours of considerable value.

---

*A Guide to the Interpretation of the Thematic Apperception Test by Leopold Bellak, M.D. (N.Y.: The Psychological Corporation, revised 1973).
**A Concise Handbook of Community Psychiatry and Community Mental Health edited by Leopold Bellak, M.D. (N.Y.: Grune & Stratton, 1974).

While we hope to demonstrate that ego functions and their assessment may be useful for the study of the whole spectrum of human behavior, we also strive to make clear that it does not obviate or take the place of all other ways of studying people.

Part I

A SURVEY OF THE STRUCTURAL MODEL

Psychoanalysis is a comprehensive theory of personality. Its most ambitious formulation is stated as the metapsychological theory. In its most expanded version, metapsychology implies that each psychic phenomenon and its behavioral manifestation can, and must, be stated and understood in genetic, dynamic, structural, economic, topographic, and adaptive terms; one is tempted to add to this list the cultural context as another essential factor.

This comprehensive view of man is the strength of classical psychoanalysis as a theory of personality. The model has a certain beauty of inner consistency and some faults in some lack of clarity of definitions of terms and concepts.

There has been a tendency to disregard much of the complexity and a predilection for raising egopsychology to special status at the cost of the other systems and hypotheses. This happened in part out of a need for reductionism almost as basic as the need for oversimplification in terms of black and white thinking. In part, egopsychology seemed so much cleaner and easier to accept than other psychoanalytic tenets.

The present volume deals mostly with ego functions and, hence, with the ego. It would be a mistake, though, to count the present authors among those who mean to disregard the rest of psychoanalysis. To do our research, we simply had to focus on a limited slice of behavior; also, we did our best to see ego functions in relation to id and superego and not lose sight of dynamic and other aspects. The ensuing brief review of the structural model and the chapters on the id and superego are meant to serve as reminders that the ego should not be seen in

5

isolation. It must suffice to say here once more that the structural model should also not be seen as a substitute for the whole of metapsychological consideration.

CHAPTER 1

The Ego Concept in Psychoanalysis

"The empirical foundations of analysis are manifold, its theories are complex, verification is difficult and time consuming; therefore the actual interrelation of its various parts on (chronologically speaking) the same level has not always been clearly realized. Despite incomplete attempts toward a more or less systematic presentation, we may say that even at present an understanding of analysis is hardly possible without a detailed knowledge of its history" (Hartmann, 1948).

Although it is not our goal to provide the basis for understanding all of psychoanalysis, we believe it is worthwhile to include a historical perspective to the ego functions. This requires a discussion of the topographical and of the structural theories of Freud. While both of these have been dealt with in detail (see Gill, 1963, and Arlow and Brenner, 1964), a brief resume here will provide the background for a consideration of the id, ego, and superego constructs, the major mental structures of the structural theory. Since each of these structures is defined by its functions, we will then be in a position to focus on ego functions, their characteristics, and their conceptualization in the psychoanalytic literature.

TOPOGRAPHIC AND STRUCTURAL THEORIES

The topographic theory was introduced in chapter 7 of Freud's *Interpretation of Dreams* (1900) and mainly discussed in that place and in two later papers, "The Unconscious" (1915), and "A Metapsychological Supplement to the Theory of Dreams" (1915). The term "topography," which we usually associate with terrain, refers to a region of the mind that Freud talked about in terms of spatial ordering (sensory and motor ends of the mental apparatus). But he also cautioned against taking this literally and stated that it involved processes of excitation and modes of discharge.

The topographic theory represents the mental apparatus or the mind as divided into three dynamic systems in accordance with their relationship to consciousness, their mode of operation (primary versus secondary process) and the condition of their energy (free versus bound) (Gill, 1963). These are the system unconscious (Ucs.), defining mental events that usually cannot be made conscious (by intention and attention) or only with difficulty; the system preconscious (Pcs.), which includes mental events easily made conscious; and the system conscious (Cs.), which encompasses what is in awareness at any given point in time.

The topographic theory was not so named by Freud, and it is most accurately characterized as a group of related ideas and hypotheses rather than as a complete theory (Arlow and Brenner, 1964). The topographic hypotheses were based on clinical observations that led Freud to the formulation that neurotic symptoms result from unconscious desires for pleasurable experiences that are not acceptable to the person from a moral or maturational standpoint. When he discovered what these wishes were and helped the patient bring them into conscious awareness, the symptom would often disappear. Freud found unconscious mentation also to be involved in the formation of dreams, in the humor of jokes, and in such common phenomena as slips of the tongue and momentary forgetting.

But he realized that classifying mental phenomena in terms of their relationship to consciousness was inadequate and insufficient, primarily because it entailed unacceptable theoretical ambiguities. As we have stated, he placed central significance on the opposition between what was conscious and what was dynamically unconscious ("the fundamental premise of psychoanalysis," 1923) in the production and alleviation of neurotic symptoms. The realization that not only repressed ideas but also the repressing forces themselves were unconscious constituted for him a major drawback of the topographic approach.

A second difficulty was based on his realization that a sense of guilt, which plays an important role in many neuroses and can be an obstacle to improvement, may be unconscious. While Freud had been aware of an unconscious sense of guilt much earlier, in 1923 he saw it as a theoretical problem of the topographic theory because the sense of guilt was an important source of opposition to instinctual drives. Thus, if instinctual drives, repressed conflicts, the repressing forces of the ego, and the sense of guilt are all unconscious, Freud concluded that the relationship to consciousness does not provide an adequate basis on which to differentiate between mental events. His clinical experience with character neuroses and some aspects of regression seen in psychotic individuals also were not readily understandable in terms of conscious and unconscious systems. As Kris sums it up, "A new concept of the psychic apparatus was needed in order to establish once more the link between clinical work and theoretical assumption" (1951, p. 158).

In 1923, Freud introduced what has come to be called the structural theory, although forerunners can be found in the "Project for a Scientific Psychology" (1895), *The Interpretation of Dreams* (1900), and the papers on "Instincts and Their Vicissitudes" (1915), "Repression" (1915), and "The Unconscious"

(1915). He proposed to substitute for the antithesis conscious-unconscious, that "between the coherent ego and the repressed which is split off from it" (1923, p. 17). Here Freud also described and discussed the superego, aspects of which had been introduced in earlier papers, including "On Narcissism" (1914), "Mourning and Melancholia" (1917) and "Group Psychology" (1921).

Each of these structures, systems, or centers of psychic functioning was to be defined by its functions. It is the functions of the ego that are our central concern in this study; but before focusing on functions, we will review some highlights of Freud's ego concept. Then we will cover the other two major aspects of the structural theory, the id and the superego.

A BRIEF REVIEW OF FREUD'S EGO CONCEPT

Freud's use of the term "ego" (*das Ich*) was somewhat ambiguous in his early writings, with two main meanings being singled out by Strachey (Editor's Introduction to *The Ego and the Id*): first, the person or self (including probably the body) as distinguished from other individuals, and, second, the part of the mind that involves particular attributes and functions.

In his "Project for a Scientific Psychology" (1895), which Freud never published, the ego was described as an organization that has a permanent cathexis rather than a changing one (p. 323) and whose function is to inhibit psychical primary processes (p. 324). Kris (1951) states that after the "Project," the idea of the ego as a coherent organization was not further developed for 20 years, during which Freud concerned himself with the instinctual drives. But as Kris also points out, Freud's focus on mental conflict resulted in his assuming repressing forces (even though his main interest was on what was repressed) and on a censor as part of his theory of dreams (1900).

Various ego functions, such as reality testing, judgment, thinking, impulse control, and defense, were discussed throughout Freud's writings, beginning with the "Project."

An historical account of Freud's discussions of the various ego functions is presented in a later section. Freud's papers on psychoanalytic technique from 1910 to 1919, including discussions of the dynamic function of resistance, the technical rule of working with material from the surface of the patient's awareness to more remote (deeper) aspects, and the suggestion to interpret the defensive aspect before interpreting what is being defended against, all implied egopsychological principles, as Kris (1951) notes.

An important basis for building up the ego stressed by Freud is through identification. He discussed the tendency to identify with objects or people who are highly cathected with libido (the parents especially but also teachers, physicians, and others) and to identify with lost objects (1916), either lost through death or long separation or who are given up as love objects. Anna Freud (1936) spells out the important mechanism whereby children tend to identify with parents who are aggressively perceived or aggressively cathected.

A forerunner of the ego concept was the notion of ego instincts, introduced in 1910. They were assumed to subserve self-preservation and to repress the sexual instincts. They appeared to include cognitive functions, personal ideals, self-protection, and moral and social restrictions (Munroe, 1955). Freud said that he hypothesized the sexual and ego instincts because clinical work with hysteria and obsessional neuroses led him to conclude that at their root was a conflict between "the claims of sexuality and those of the ego" (1915, p. 124). In 1923, in *The Ego and the Id,* when Freud presented his structural model of the mind, which included id, ego, and superego, the hypothesis of ego instincts was supplanted by the ego construct. Self-preservation, however, was retained by Freud as a characteristic and function of the ego (1940).

When he was using the topographic approach, Freud employed the Pcs. system at times to refer to what he had earlier termed the ego. In his paper "The Unconscious" (1915), for example, censorship, reality testing, the reality principle, and conscious memory are all listed as functions of the system Pcs. (p. 188). But the id, ego, and superego systems did not replace Ucs. and Pcs. systems precisely, since part of the Ucs. became the id, while the Pcs. and part of the Ucs. became the ego (Gill, 1963). Nevertheless, with the exception of the relationship of contents to consciousness, the structural systems were defined by the same criteria as the topographic systems had been, which is to say, by mode of functioning (id according to primary process and ego according to secondary process) and by conditions of energy (id with free energy and ego with bound energy).

In the 1923 paper, Freud defined the ego as follows:

... the ego is that part of the id which has been modified by the direct influence of the external world through the medium of the Pcpt-Cs. [perception-consciousness]; in a sense it is an extension of the surface differentiation. Moreover, the ego seeks to bring the influence of the external world to bear upon the id and its tendencies, and endeavors to substitute the reality principle for the pleasure principle which reigns unrestrictedly in the id. For the ego, perceptions play the part which in the id falls to instinct. The ego represents what may be called reason and common sense, in contrast to the id, which contains the passions (p. 25).

A number of ego functions are spelled out in this paper, although as already mentioned, Freud included various functions in a number of papers beginning with the "Project." In "Formulations on Two Principles of Mental Functioning" (1911), for example, Freud discussed attention, memory, judgment, and reality testing. It is the idea of a coherent organization, first mentioned in the

"Project," that is emphasized in 1923 and remains as a characteristic of the ego construct. The ego of the structural theory must be distinguished from the concept of self. Clarification of this point has followed Hartmann's emphasis on narcissism being best defined as the libidinal cathexis of the self, not of the ego, a point Sterba had made earlier (1942).

Freud's early idea of the ego as the force that opposed the instinctual drives and the importance of this opposition for mental conflict and psychopathology are the reasons for defense mechanisms being the most closely studied functions of the ego. An important advance was Freud's second theory of anxiety (1926), which spelled out how the ego mobilizes defensive activity in response to anxiety signals. In *New Introductory Lectures* (1933), Freud elaborated on various functions of the ego (in addition to defenses) that are important in adaptation. Further systematic understanding of the defensive aspects of ego functioning were elaborated by Anna Freud in 1936, when she underscored the importance of giving equal weight to the ego, superego, and drive (id) aspects of mental functioning and behavior. Freud's final summary of the characteristics and functions of the ego is found in *An Outline of Psychoanalysis* (1940), which we recap in the chapter on ego functions. (Chapter 4)

While Freud substituted the id, ego, and superego systems for the Ucs., Pcs., and Cs. systems because of conceptual difficulties already described, the structural theory involved other difficulties. Gill (1963) points out that because unconscious defenses (which are attributed to the ego) utilize primary process functioning, it cannot be maintained that the ego operates exclusively according to the secondary process. And, since the id concept includes ideas, memories, symbols, and mechanisms, it cannot be without some structure. Thus, ego and id can most accurately be characterized as on a continuum.

That the ego construct has many contrasting facets is underscored by the following statement of Hartmann (1950):

. . . the ego has from its start the tendency to oppose the drives, but one of its main functions is also to help them toward gratification; it is a place where insight is gained, but also of rationalization; it promotes objective knowledge of reality, but at the same time, by way of identification and social adjustment, takes over in the course of its development the conventional prejudices of the environment; it pursues independent aims, but it is also characteristic of it to consider the demands of the other substructures of personality, etc. Of course it is true that ego functions have some general characteristics in common, some of which I mentioned today, and which distinguish them from id functions. But many misunderstandings and unclarities are traceable to the fact that we have not yet trained ourselves to consider the ego from an intrasystemic point of view. One speaks of "the ego" as being rational, or realistic, or an integrator, while actually these are characteristics only of one or the other of its functions (p. 139).

Rapaport (1959) summarized the major developments of egopsychology in four phases. In the first phase (up to 1897) he underscored the introduction of the defense concept and the role attributed to external reality.

In the second phase, there was a de-emphasis on the importance of external reality and a focus on instinctual drives. The major contributions to egopsychology were the secondary process (1900), the reality principle (1911), and the analysis of the process of repression ("Repression," 1915; "The Unconscious," 1915).

The third phase (1923-1937) is when the ego was conceptualized (again) as a coherent organization of mental processes based on identification with abandoned objects and was organized around the system perception-consciousness. It includes unconscious structures from which resistances arise, has the ability to use neutral energies, and can also transform instinctual drive energies for its use. This conceptualization of the ego, Rapaport points out, has the following shortcomings:

(1) It appears to be a resultant of id, superego, and reality promptings.

(2) It is still subservient to the id.

(3) While it is assumed to have some independent genetic roots, it is still seen as differentiating out of the id.

(4) No conception of ego development comparable to the phases of libidinal development is postulated.

(5) There is no general theory of the role of defenses within the ego, although Freud does recognize the structure responsible for resistance in psychoanalysis to be the ego functions.

(6) The notion of consciousness as a superordinate sense organ has not yet been integrated into the structural theory, although the place of consciousness in the topographic theory has been dropped.

In "Inhibitions, Symptoms and Anxiety" (1926), Freud increased the power of the ego over the id in his formulation of how ego mobilizes defensive activity by initiating anxiety signals. In this, it curtails instinctual drives by using the pleasure principle to suit its own ends, has the availability of a variety of defenses, and is concerned with reality relationships and adaptation. This phase in the development of egopsychology was capped by Anna Freud's book *The Ego and the Mechanisms of Defense*, in which she systematizes the concepts of specific defenses, investigates the role of affects, and integrates the two main themes into this phase of egopsychology development, defenses, and reality relations. We would add that she also underscores the importance of giving equal weight to the ego, superego, and drive (id) aspects of mental functioning.

Rapaport sees the fourth phase in the development of egopsychology (from the late 1930's through the time of his paper, published in 1959) as being heavily influenced by the work of Hartmann and Erikson. The contribution of

Hartmann "centers on those innate roots of ego development which are independent of instinctual drives; on reality relationships, that is, adaptation; and on the integration of the theory of the secondary process (second phase) with the theory of autonomous defense (third phase)" (p. 12). The contributions of Erikson center "on the epigenesis of the ego, on the theory of reality relationships and especially on the elaboration of the theory of the role of social reality, and these are the core of his psychosocial theory of development which complements Freud's theory of the third phase and Hartmann's elaboration of it" (p. 14).

EGO DEVELOPMENT

As already mentioned, Freud assumed that the ego developed out of the id and was that part which had been modified as a result of its closeness to and influence by the external world (1923). In "Analysis Terminable and Interminable" (1937), however, Freud suggested that the ego has biological roots of its own (p. 240) and in a later paper (1940), he suggested an undifferentiated ego-id. Regarding approaches to the issues of ego development, Hartmann (1952) said the following:

Earliest stages of ego development can be described from several angles: as a process of differentiation that leads to a more complete demarcation of ego and id and of self and outer reality; as a process that leads from the pleasure to the reality ego; as the development of the reality principle; as the way leading from primary narcissism to object relationships; from the point of view of the sequence of danger situations; as the development of the secondary process, et. The important thing for a systematic study of the subject, which, as I said, is not intended here, would be to clarify the interrelatedness of all these aspects of ego development (pp. 165-166).

Aspects of ego development have been discussed by a number of authors. Ferenczi (1916) made an early attempt to specify the stages in the development of the sense of reality, and he related these to the stages of libidinal development. In his papers on the development of the phases of the libido, Abraham (1916, 1921, 1924, 1925) included ego functions that were found at each of these phases.

Glover (1932) offered an hypothesis of ego development that held that originally there are independent ego nuclei derived from memory traces of early experiences of scattered instinct derivatives. These cluster formations are only loosely strung together initially and, after being subjected to both condensation and displacement, gradually synthesize. He correlated the development of the ego nuclei with the various libidinal stages.

Melanie Klein (1932) emphasized the importance of internalized (introjected) images of the mother's breast and body and the affects associated with these in the development of the ego.

The notions of an undifferentiated phase of development and independent ego roots suggested by Freud were elaborated by Hartmann and are considered in more detail in the chapter on autonomous functioning. In addition to absence of the id-ego differentiation for the first few weeks after birth, psychoanalytic observers of infants such as Spitz have hypothesized no differentiation of conscious, preconscious, and unconscious; no thought, perception, or volition; and no clear separation between psychic and somatic realms.

In 1959, Spitz provided a theory of ego development in which the inception of each hypothesized stage is marked by specific affective behavior. Each stage involves an organizing process that integrates maturational and psychological developmental factors, which the author calls organizers of the psyche. Following the stage of nondifferentiation referred to above, the first organizer, the smiling response, appears around the age of three months, and it is assumed to establish the beginning of the ego. This is reflected in recognition of, and specific emotional responses to, other people, which also heralds the beginnings of structural perception and of reality testing.

Other authors have emphasized the importance of anticipation of the feeding at about three months (Kris, 1951). Anna Freud underscored the ability to wait at about six months, the latter reflecting the beginning of what will later come to be the reality principle, the beginning of a curtailing attitude toward the id drives. This "introduces into the personality a first break, id and ego serving different aims from then onwards, governed in their functioning by different principles" (1954, p. 14). And Hoffer (1949) signaled the birth of the ego by voluntary thumb-sucking, since it reflected an intentional attempt to use one part of the body to relieve tension arising in another part.

Returning to Spitz, the second organizer is eight-month anxiety (infant's tendency to cry or show distress when in the presence of strangers), which indicates that the infant recognizes his mother. This organizer Spitz sees as heralding the attainment of the libidinal object. It also indicates development of memory, thought processes, and judgment; some understanding of social gestures; and the emergence of some defenses, especially identification. This attainment of the libidinal object, about which we will expand further in the chapter on object relations, thus coincides with the development of major ego functions. Décarie (1965) surveys the development of five major ego functions at this time. The ability to distinguish the love object from all others reflects the development of perception. Motor activity is developed enough to allow intentional activity. There are sufficient and stable enough memory traces to provide the basis for judgment. Conformity to orders and prohibitions reflects greater influence by the reality principle, and the synthetic function of the ego provides the basis for integrating the good and the bad object, which corresponds to integrating (fusing) libido and aggression.

Spitz identifies a third organizer, the attainment of the No, both in word and in gesture, and the use of speech in a symbolic sense which goes beyond the global need — gratifying words. With this stage, the ego has attained the capacity for abstraction and reversibility. He uses the concepts of dependent development, critical periods, and the synchronicity of maturation and development to formulate his notions of deviant ego development.

Dependent development holds that each subsequent stage of development depends on, and is influenced by, the one that precedes it. The notion of critical periods is that if a given function does not develop during a certain critical time, it will be difficult or impossible for the person to attain it at a later time. This is because, according to Spitz, favorable maturational conditions for its establishment are optimal during the critical period. When this given factor is not available during the critical period, other factors that are available will be modified and distorted to fit maturational needs, and a deviant integration will result. Later, when the factor does become available, "it will find the maturational positions occupied by a compensating, though deviant, structure and unavailable for normal integration" (p. 78). The idea of synchronicity is that normal development requires synchronicity of maturational and developmental factors.

Applying these concepts, Spitz maintains that when a deficiency occurs, either in maturational or psychological developmental processes, a deviant integration will result, which creates a developmental imbalance. This will influence and change the configuration of the next major organizer. "Ego apparatuses, ego functions, ego systems will be out of balance — some inhibited, some emphasized" (p. 93).

Mahler (1968), whose work is also based on observation of psychotic and normal children, hypothesizes three main phases of development, which can be divided into subphases. These are an autistic phase, in which there is no separate awareness of self from others or from the environment and which occurs during approximately the first three months; the symbiotic phase, in which the infant perceives the mother as part of himself; and the separation-individuation phase, in which the infant develops a sense of identity separate from the mother. Fixations on, and regression to, these phases can occur.

In the first phase (normal autism), the infant is assumed to be in a state of "primitive hallucinatory disorientation," in which the main waking activities involve attempts to attain homeostasis. In the second subphase of autism, the body image begins to form as the infant gains a dim awareness of the "need satisfying agent."

In the symbiotic phase, Mahler holds that the beginnings of an ego are reflected in the perception of the symbiotic object and the ability to wait for gratification, based on expectations of satisfaction, which are the result of memory traces of previous activities of the mother that were associated with satisfaction.

The separation-individuation phase or process involves increasing amounts of outwardly directed attention and the comparing of various percepts with the mother's face as an orientation point. The increase in locomotion during this time (last quarter of the first year) results in more physical separation from the mother and a greater separation and differentiation of self-representations out of the previously fused self-object representations. Energy is shifted from the symbiotic orbit to the autonomous ego apparatus of locomotion, perception, learning, and the self.

Weil (1970) postulates a basic core of fundamental trends that the infant possesses when it enters the symbiotic phase, and these trends result from the interaction of the congenital equipment and early experiential factors. She considers individual variations in the basic core, precursors of ego development, and the balance between libido and aggression. The author hypothesizes and offers support for the notion that the basic core partially determines individual differences in character and in symptomatology.

Anna Freud's approach to the ego development is in terms of developmental lines, which include both libidinal and ego aspects. Examples of these are included in the section on the relationships between ego and id.

Erikson's work (1950, 1959) is an important contribution to knowledge of ego development, both his stages of psychosocial development and his work on ego development and historical change, healthy personality development, and problems of ego identity. His stages of development are briefly discussed in the section on libidinal drives.

In this cursory survey of works on ego development, only some of the important sources have been cited. A few more significant ones are *The Magic Years* (Fraiberg, 1959), which includes a synthesis of Piaget's theories of cognitive growth with psychoanalytic developmental notions, and Brody and Axelrad (1970), who have carefully studied the effects of maternal behavior as it interacts with infant development. Loevinger, Wessler, and Redmore (1970) have recently published a method for assessing the level of ego development from a sentence-completion test. Finally, considerations relevant to the development of the major ego functions have been discussed by Bellak (1958a).

CHAPTER 2

The Id Concept

The concept of the id was introduced by Freud in 1923 as part of the structural theory, the other two major structures being the ego and the superego. His formulation of the new tripartite model of the mental apparatus resulted from the difficulties presented by his earlier conceptualization of the mind in terms of conscious, unconscious and preconscious, as we have already discussed (the topographical model). It is accurate to say that, of the three divisions of the structural theory, the id is the least understood, and there are many unanswered questions with regard to it (Schur, 1966).

The instinctual drives are the major components of the id but do not constitute a definition of it. Many of the characteristics of the id are those that Freud earlier attributed to the system Ucs. A succinct summary of what Freud included under the id concept is provided in his *New Introductory Lectures* (1933):

"You will not expect me to have much to tell you that is new about the id apart from its new name. It is the dark, inaccessible part of our personality; what little we know of it we have learnt from our study of dream-work and of the construction of neurotic symptoms, and most of that is of a negative character and can be described only as a contrast to the ego. We approach the id with analogies: we call it chaos, a cauldron full of seething excitations. We picture it as being open at its end to somatic influences, and as there taking up into itself instinctual needs which find their psychical expression in it, but we cannot say in what substratum. It is filled with energy reaching it from the instincts, but it has no organization, produces no collective will, but only a striving to bring about the satisfaction of the instinctual needs subject to the observance of the pleasure principle. The logical laws of thought do not apply in the id, and this is true above all of the law of contradiction. Contrary impulses exist side by side, without cancelling each other out, or diminishing each other: at the most they may converge to form compromises under the dominating economic pressure towards the discharge of energy. There is nothing in the id that could be compared with negation; and we perceive with surprise an exception to the philosophical theorem that space and time are necessary forms of our mental acts. There is nothing in the id that corresponds to the idea of time; there is no recognition of the passage of time, and − a thing that is most remarkable and awaits consideration in philosophical thought − no alteration in its mental processes is produced by the passage of time. Wishful impulses which have never passed beyond the id, but impressions, too, which have been sunk into the id by

17

repression, are virtually immortal; after the passage of decades they behave as though they had just occurred. They can only be recognized as belonging to the past, can only lose their importance and be deprived of their cathexis of energy, when they have been made conscious by the work of analysis, and it is on this that the therapeutic effect of analytic treatment rests to no small extent.

Again and again I have had the impression that we have made too little theoretical use of this fact, established beyond any doubt, of the unalterability by time of the repressed. This seems to offer an approach to the most profound discoveries. Nor, unfortunately, have I myself made any progress here.

The id of course knows no judgements of value: no good and evil, no morality. The economic or, if you prefer, the quantitative factor, which is intimately linked to the pleasure principle, dominates the processes. Instinctual cathexes seeking discharge — that, in our view, is all there is in the id. It even seems that the energy of these instinctual impulses is in a state different from that in the other regions of the mind, far more mobile and capable of discharge; otherwise the displacements and condensations would not occur which are characteristic of the id and which so completely disregard the *quality* of what is cathected — what in the ego we should call an idea. We would give much to understand more about these things! You can see, incidentally, that we are in a position to attribute to the id characteristics other than that of its being unconscious, and you can recognize the possibility of portions of the ego and super-ego being unconscious without possessing the same primitive and irrational characteristics (1933, pp. 73-75).

The absence of logical laws, of negation, and of time are all aspects of the primary process (see Gill [1967] and Holt [1967]), a primitive mode of functioning in which wishful and irrational impulses from infancy press for immediate and total discharge (i.e., in accordance with the pleasure principle). The primary process mechanisms — displacement, condensation, and symbolization — are found especially in primitive mental functioning, in dream formation, symptom formation, and in other areas. Primary-process functioning is contrasted with secondary-process functioning, which characterizes logical thinking. What is being discharged, displaced, and condensed is the mental energy attached to the instinctual drives. The "cathexis of energy" mentioned by Freud defines a quantity of mental energy that can become invested in a mental representation (such as an idea, an image, a fantasy, or a concept). The cathexes of mental energy that operate according to the primary process are easily displaceable (or mobile) and easily condensable, and thus move easily from one idea to another; or the cathexes from many ideas are condensed into one idea or image, taking no account of the content involved, as Freud pointed out in the passage quoted above. What Freud refers to as "instinctual needs" are subsumed under the id construct. Also included are experiences, fantasies, and wishes from childhood that were repressed during development.

Much of what Freud attributes to the id he had earlier attributed to the topographic conception of the system Ucs. The Ucs. had other characteristics besides the quality of being unconscious, just as the id does. Another feature of the system Ucs. that Freud also ascribes to the id is that its memory traces are not verbal but rather are sensory — visual, olfactory, auditory, or tactile. This assumption was based on his clinical experience that when repressed wishes and forgotten memories were brought to awareness and verbalized in analysis, the symptoms disappeared (Arlow and Brenner, 1964).

Another definition of the id is summarized by Bellak (1959) in his paper on the unconscious; he reminds us that Freud borrowed the term "id" from Groddeck (1923) and that it originally stood for all that was ego alien. It became the hypothetical locus and mainspring of drives, and the psychoanalytic concept of the id is part of the psychoanalytic theory of motivation (see Abrams [1971] on the psychoanalytic unconscious).

In a panel on the concept of the id (Marcovitz, 1963), Karush defined it as "a collection of the earliest percepts of internal urges and their activities as well as the original objects which helped reduce the tension of the drives." Marcovitz pointed out that the contents of such ego processes as perception and consciousness often includes id material. Scott stated that the id should include primitive drive impulses and everything unconscious that has not been repressed. Beres defined the id as "that part of the mind whose function it is to express instinctual drives and needs." Beres further identifies need as being "a step beyond the pure biological drive and not yet the organized wish or fantasy which I would consider as the products of ego functions." Moore defined the id as "that abstraction which refers to the expression of drive representations which are manifestations of undifferentiated or unneutralized energies, which have been relatively unmodified by realistic self or object interest." Arlow, summarizing the panel discussion, found agreement that the id should be defined in terms of function rather than in terms of employment of primary-process modes of energy mobilization. There was disagreement about what to include under the id concept, for instance organized or formed elements, and on the necessity of separating the concept of the id from that of the unconscious.

In a paper on unconscious fantasies (1962) Beres has dealt with some of these issues. He accepts the notion that a wish is the mental representation of an instinctual drive and that a fantasy is a further developed mental representation through which the wish is gratified. But he emphasizes that while needs are unstructured biological manifestations and id functions, unconscious fantasies, which are considered as an aspect of the id, are organized and that the organizing activity is an ego function. It will be recalled that Freud assumed that the system Ucs. and later the id were characterized by primary-process functioning, while the ego (and earlier the Cs. and Pcs. systems) was characterized by the secondary process. Beres concludes that the primary process cannot be equated with unconscious mental activity nor the secondary process with consciousness. As he points out, an unconscious fantasy may press for immediate discharge (primary-process characteristic) but still be an organized mental representation (secondary-process characteristic).

Schur (1966) approaches this issue from a slightly different angle and underscores a central problem in defining the id that results from Freud's definition of an instinctual drive as the mental representation of somatic stimuli (1915). This is a problem because a mental representation must be based on a memory trace, and a memory trace can only result from perceptual activity, either of outer or of inner stimuli. Both memory and perception are considered ego functions, so the problem is whether these mental representations should be assigned to the id. One solution would be to restrict the id to energy considerations, but this approach has not been a popular one, and Schur has stated that such a solution would necessitate a radical reformulation of many psychoanalytic concepts.

Schur attempts to resolve the problem by assuming that the id undergoes development as the organism develops. In the above-mentioned panel discussion Marcovitz said that changes in the id accompany changes in the ego, that during the undifferentiated phase there is an interaction between the development of the id and the development of perception and memory, and that the id uses some primitive perceptions and memory traces. While Hartmann had stressed apparatuses of primary autonomy from the angle of ego development, Schur assumes that these apparatuses (especially those of memory and perception) contribute to id development. A corollary of this assumption is that the id may be said to become a separate structure out of the undifferentiated phase with the advent of the wish, which is the mental representation of an instinctual drive and is a developmental step up from being merely a somatic need.

Many other issues relevant to the id are discussed by Schur, including the history of the concept, ambiguities in the concept, id functions, and developmental factors in the id.

We turn now to a consideration of the instinctual drives and their mental representations, which are the major components of the id.

FREUD'S INSTINCT THEORY: INSTINCTUAL DRIVES

Freud's instinct concept was designed to account for causation of behavior by forces within the organism. In 1920 he said that the instincts were both the most important and the most obscure elements of psychological research. His working hypotheses about the classification of instincts changed from time to time, and he held them rather tentatively. As he said in 1933, "The theory of the instincts is so to say our mythology. Instincts are mythical entities, magnificent in their indefiniteness. In our work we cannot for a moment disregard them, yet we are never sure that we are seeing them clearly" (p. 95). In 1915, in "Instincts and Their Vicissitudes," he defined instinct in the following way:

If we now apply ourselves to considering mental life from a *biological* point of view, an "instinct" appears to us as a concept on the frontier between the mental and the somatic, as the psychical representative of the stimuli originating from within the organism and reaching the mind, as a measure of the demand made upon the mind for work in consequence of its connection with the body (pp. 121-22).

Strachey points out (S.E. I,*xxiv-xxv) that Freud used the term, *Trieb* to cover a number of different ideas. Strachey decided that the best compromise available was to render *Trieb* as "instinct." Other authorities have preferred the term "drive." Freud also used the term *Instinkte*, and a comparison of Freud's usage of *Trieb* and *Instinkte* shows that *Instinkte* is used to refer to inherited mental formations, while *Trieb* is a concept that lies in between the mental and the physical, as the above passage quoted shows. Hartmann (1939, 1948) noted that the instinct concept in regard to lower animals is much more comprehensive than the instinctual drive concept in regard to man. The former entails considerably more adaptiveness to the environment than does the latter: man's instinctual drives are more estranged from reality in general than are animal instincts. Waelder (1960) says that *Trieb* (instinctual drive) defines powerful strivings rooted in the physical nature of organisms; the strivings are goal directed, connected with somatic sources, persistent, and produce a feeling of compulsion when their action is thwarted. The English word "instinct" suggests merely innate as opposed to acquired characteristics, without any connotations of force. It also

... carries the implication of inherited unlearned behavior and usually also that of biological usefulness for the species — like the nest building of birds or the avian migration to warmer climates — the kind of things that make people speak of the unconscious wisdom of nature. It carries an implication of preformed (inherited) order while *Trieb* suggests a power that defies organization (1960, p. 99).

Freud's theory of the instincts may be seen as having developed in four steps or stages (Bibring, 1941). In the first stage, he assumed two sets of instincts, the sexual and the ego instincts, the latter having to do with self-preservation. These are correlated with the pleasure principle and the reality principle, respectively.

The second stage in Freud's instinct theory was necessitated by some aspects of his theory of narcissism, which implied that the sexual and ego instincts had a common libidinal origin. Thus, in the theory of narcissism the sexual and ego

*S.E. I, cited throughout this book refers to the Standard Edition, Vol. I of the complete works of Sigmund Freud.

instincts derived from the same source, and since source was the basis on which Freud was classifying the instincts, both classes now had to be seen as libidinal instincts differentiated only in terms of objects, a libidinal cathexis of the self (more precisely, of a mental representation of the self) rather than of an external object.

In order to maintain the independence of sexual and ego instincts, which he thought was justified from a biological standpoint, Freud divided the ego instincts into two components, a libidinal-narcissistic part (about which we have spoken above) and a nonlibidinal aspect which he called ego interest. Narcissism thus was seen as the libidinal complement to the egoism of the self-preservative instinct.

In the third step of the development of his theory of the instincts, Freud made changes on the basis of his realization that aggressiveness (which included both hatred and the tendency to dominate) differed with respect to source and aim. He now included aggressiveness under the ego instincts, partly on the basis of the observable fact that aggressiveness is found when the ego instincts are threatened. While sexual and aggressive trends (the latter as part of the ego instincts) could be opposed, they could also be fused, and it was the latter possibility that was exemplified by such manifestations as oral and anal aggression (see below).

This third step then, Bibring points out, established the aggressive instincts as independent entities, underscored the idea that sadism was not purely sexual and allowed the ordering of various examples of libidinal and nonlibidinal aggressiveness (1941, p. 113).

In the fourth and final step in the development of his instinct theory, Freud accorded aggressive instincts a separate and independent status (1920). He made them parts of the "vital strata of the mind," and, together with the sexual instincts, a central aspect of the id. This was based on his recognition (which he considered belated) that hatred and destructiveness, which may have no essential or noteworthy sexual aspect, also are not in the service of the self-preservative instincts. Some examples that impressed Freud were the self-directed hatred that he saw in depressions and in the need for self-punishment, neither of which could be plausibly explained as a result of the aggressiveness of the ego instincts.

Freud further postulated that the sexual and aggressive instincts were aspects of more primal phenomena, the life and death instincts (1920), a speculative biological extension of his instinct theory that is still controversial in psychoanalytic circles. In this dichotomy, self-preservation, narcissism (self-love), and object love are all included under the life instinct (Eros).

Bibring summarized Freud's instinct concept as follows:

Instinct, then, is an energy which arises from the vital stratum of the mind, which has a direction that is determined inherently, which presses forward towards a particular aim and is directed somewhat loosely towards things and persons as its object. It is linked to an organ as the site of its satisfaction. Its satisfaction consists in the removal of those changes in the zones of excitation which accompany the instinctual tension (1941, pp. 106-107).

We will now survey the sexual and aggressive instincts in more detail.

THE SEXUAL DRIVES: THE LIBIDO THEORY

The libido theory involves the idea of component sexual instincts, which are usually associated with erotogenic zones, and hypotheses concerning the ways in which the sexual instincts develop, beginning in infancy, in successive stages and in a fixed order and undergo various transformations (Bibring, 1941). Other hypotheses (Fine, 1962) are that object choice results from libidinal transformations, that a libidinal drive may be either gratified, repressed, turned around on the subject's own self, reversed into its opposite (later called reaction formation) with resulting shame, disgust, and morality or sublimated. These were first called instinctual vicissitudes and later were conceptualized as defensive functions of the ego. Character structure was assumed to be built up from the ways in which the component instincts were dealt with and examples were provided quite early of character traits of the anal personality, especially orderliness, parsimony, and obstinacy (1908). Freud's formulation was that permanent character traits were either "unchanged perpetuations of the original impulses, sublimations of them, or reaction formations against them" (p. 50).

Finally, neurosis was seen as a fixation* on, or regression to, one of the phases of infantile sexuality, and the earlier the phase, the more serious the psychopathology. This brings us to the component sexual instincts.

As already pointed out, Freud's early theory of psychopathology was that repressed ideas cause symptoms. He found that what was most frequently repressed was sexual content. He made a detailed study of sexuality, and especially and centrally infantile sexuality, his most comprehensive work on the topic being "Three Essays on the Theory of Sexuality," published in 1905 but revised more than any of his other papers. Freud held this classification of instincts as a tentative hypothesis, and expressed dissatisfaction with his endeavors (see Bibring paper: also Strachey's introduction to "Instincts and Their Vicissitudes").

Based especially on his psychoanalyses of patients with perversions, Freud hypothesized that the sexual instinct is a composite that involves component instincts that operate independently of each other in early childhood. Each

---

*Fixation is defined as the persistence of a libidinal cathexis of an object from early life into adulthood or, more generally, the tendency to cling to a given stage of development.

component instinct can be characterized (as can any instinct, libidinal or nonlibidinal) by its source, its pressure, its aim, and its object. The source of the component sexual instincts Freud saw as being from a number of somatic processes (of which he did not claim an exact knowledge) and erogenous areas of the skin or mucous membrane, which yield pleasurable sensations when they are stimulated. He singled out oral, anal, urethral, clitoral, and genital zones, which are stimulated as a result of their anatomical location and their function in vital body processes.* The zones could be differentiated on the basis of what kind of stimulation was necessary for the pleasurable sensations (viz., sucking for oral, the process of elimination for anal, urination for phallic, rubbing for clitoral and genital). Freud used the source as a major basis for classifying the sexual and other instincts.

The pressure has to do with the amount of force it entails. Here Freud (1915, p. 122) describes instinctual force as a measure of the demand for work that is involved. By libido, Freud meant a quantity of drive energy from the sexual instincts (which is not the same as conscious sexual desire). Freud later described the pressure of the instinctual drives as a constant stimulus that could not be avoided by flight, as could external stimuli, and this was the basis he proposed for distinguishing internal from external stimuli.

The general aim of all component aspects of the instinctual drives is always the attainment of satisfaction by "removing the state of stimulation at the source of the instinct" (1915, p. 122).** But the specific aim of a component instinct is influenced by, and associated with, the object. Freud had shown how the specific aim of the infant was the stimulation of erotogenic zones. Initially, pleasure is sought independently in the various zones, beginning with the oral, then the anal, and so on. At puberty, a new sexual aim emerges that is associated with orgasm, and the component instincts become subordinated to the genital zone, while some aspects are repressed (and may subsequently show up as symptoms). As already mentioned, they may also succumb to reaction formation or be sublimated. Subordinated or forepleasure aims define perversions, according to Freud, when they become the final aims rather than subsidiary ones. Instinctual drives may also be characterized as having active or passive aims. When the aim is active, the person attempts to find an object with whom to gratify the drive manifestation, whereas a passive aim involves a wish to have someone else gratify one's needs.

The object, the most variable aspect of the sexual instincts, may be a part of the person's own body, another person, something inanimate, an animal, or even a corpse. The object of component instincts forms a bridge to the theory of

*Some component instincts (such as looking and being looked at) do not have their source in erotogenic zones.

**A drive-reduction model of motivation.

object relations, which is discussed in more detail in the chapter on object relations.

The stages of development of infantile sexuality were delineated as the oral sucking and then the oral biting (roughtly first year and a half), the anal expulsive and then the anal retentive (until approximately age three), the phallic-oedipal phase (three to six years), the latency phase, and then, at puberty, the genital phase. Fixation on, and regression to, earlier phases of development were hypothesized by Freud (1905) to be major factors in neurosis. Freud acknowledged (1940) that these stages do not succeed one another in a clear-cut fashion and that there may be some overlap and simultaneity.

Abraham (1916, 1921, 1924, 1925), Ferenczi (1916-17, 1924), and Jones elaborated on these stages, and their implications for character development and for psychopathology. Sterba provided a good summary of the libido theory (1931), which has recently been reissued. Indeed, clinical and theoretical studies related to various aspects of the libido theory, such as its relationship to character formation and to neurosis, dominated the psychoanalytic literature up until the 1940's.

An important extension and elaboration of libido theory is found in the work of Erikson (1950). To the zones Freud had identified (oral, anal, etc.) Erikson added and systematically worked out a conception of the various modes of behavior associated with each: incorporative$_1$ (to get) and incorporative$_2$ (to take) with the two oral stages, retentive and eliminative with the two anal stages, and intrusive with the phallic stage. In addition, he specified the alternative basic attitudes that characterize each step of development: in the oral stage it is basic trust versus basic mistrust, in the anal stage it is autonomy versus shame and doubt, and in the phallic stage it is initiative versus guilt. Erikson goes on to specify basic attitudes for later stages of life up to and including old age. Rubin and Gertrude Blanck (1968) have discussed marriage as a developmental phase.

AGGRESSIVE DRIVES

In "Three Essays" (1905), cruelty was seen as a component sexual instinct, which, like exhibitionism and scopophilia (the wish to look), did not have any connection with erotogenic zones. Freud assumed that the biological significance of aggression was the need to subjugate the sexual object when wooing was unsuccessful (pp. 157-158). Sadism, too, was seen as a component of the sexual instincts, as was masochism, which was considered in 1905 as inwardly directed sadism, "the passive instinct of cruelty" (p. 193).

As an aspect of the major component instinctual drives, biting was hypothesized to be the pleasurable activity during the second oral phase and was called the oral-sadistic stage. Likewise, Freud found sadistic impulses to be associated with the anal stage, which he designated the anal-sadistic phase. Phallic penetration and vaginal retentiveness are aggressive manifestations associated with the phallic stage. Freud's ideas about the systematic place of sadism and masochism changed as he revised the classification of instincts, as did his understanding of the meaning of these terms. Masochism, for example, was defined in "Three Essays" in terms of "any passive attitude towards sexual life and sexual object" (p. 158). Masochism was at first seen as a phenomenon derived from sadism (1905-1919), later as a primary manifestation (1920), and still later as both primary and secondary, and differentiated into the subforms of erotogenic, feminine, and moral masochism (1924).

As Freud evolved and changed his classification of instincts, aggression was classified as an ego instinct, that is, an aspect of self-preservation. In 1915, the major antithesis was between the ego instincts and the sexual instincts, two groups that had originally been attached to each other. In his case history the "Rat Man" (1909), Freud took account of the importance of hostility in the patient under scrutiny, and in obsessional neurosis more generally.

In *Beyond the Pleasure Principle* (1920), Freud revised his views about the place of aggression in order to take into account evidence from traumatic war neuroses and the repetition of various activities that could not be understood as providing pleasure and were thus "*beyond the pleasure principle*." These were now seen as reflecting a group of destructive instincts, which Freud made the antithesis of the life instincts (a combination of the sexual and the self-preservative instincts). While many analysts have found fault with the notion of a death instinct, the formulation of aggressive and destructive trends as instinctual drives in addition to sexual instinctual drives has been widely accepted in psychoanalytic theory.

One hypothesis relevant to psychopathology is that the amount of free (unbound) aggression plays an important role in determining the amount of conflict that is likely to develop (Freud, 1937). Hartmann applied this hypothesis to the predisposition to schizophrenia, namely, that the development of schizophrenia is influenced by the inability to neutralize aggression (1950).

Despite the dichotomy between sexual and aggressive instinctual drives, the clinical material suggested that libido and aggression were always found together (alloyed or fused) but with different amounts of each in different situations. Destructiveness is assumed to be decreased or neutralized as a result of the fusion or mixing of libidinal with aggressive energy, or love with hate.

Considerable attention has been focused on the question of whether aggression needs to be considered as an instinctual drive. Of those who have recently written on this topic, Scott (1958) and Berkowitz (1962) hold that aggression is secondary, while Lorenz (1966) and Storr (1968) maintain that there is a primary aggressive instinct.

Waelder (1960) is of the opinion that the characteristics of sexual and aggressive drives are asymmetrical, not parallel. Thus, while the sexual drives have a clear pattern of maturation, a parallel maturation of the destructive drive does not take place: "Destructiveness is probably at its most perfect in early childhood, and all later manifestations are, for most people, dilutions or mitigations" (p. 151).

Anna Freud (1965) states that the correlation of specific aggressive manifestations with relevant libidinal phases is the way the development of the aggressive drive is currently being handled: biting, spitting, and devouring are correlated with orality; sadistic torturing, hitting, kicking, and destroying with anality; and overbearing, domineering, and forceful behavior with the phallic phase. Another possibility is that destructiveness may be an instinctual drive that can operate independently of libidinal and ego activities.

In his recent discussion of aggression Brenner (1971) points out that most psychoanalysts today believe that aggression as an instinctual drive can be separated from the question of whether there is a death drive. If they are separated, the origin of aggression remains an open and unanswered question. Freud had assumed that aggression operates on the compulsion to repeat, which is beyond the pleasure principle, and that aggressive drive derivatives underlie self-destructiveness, guilt, and self-imposed suffering. Today, aggressive derivatives are seen to be operative in the production of neurotic symptoms along with derivatives of sexual drives. This understanding is consistent with the assumption of Hartmann, Kris, and Loewenstein (1949) that both libido and aggression operate according to the pleasure principle (Brenner, 1971).

Even if it is assumed that there is an instinctual drive of destructiveness, it is possible to specify a number of ways in which the presence of hostility can be accounted for as a secondary reaction. Some of those enumerated by Waelder (1960) are as follows: a threat to self-preservation or to goal-directed activity of the person; the frustration of a libidinal drive; the byproduct of an ego activity such as attempts at mastery of the external environment or control of one's own body or mind; or, finally, as an aspect of a libidinal urge, which implies aggressiveness against the libidinal object, such as incorporation or penetration (pp. 139-140).

Stone (1971) maintains that, in most instances, aggression is externally motivated and that it involves an "aggregate of diverse acts, having diverse origins, and bound together, sometimes loosely, by the nature of their impact on objects rather than by a demonstrably common and unitary drive" (p. 195). He goes on to say that aggression may be seen as having an ego function aspect by serving an instrumental role in achieving various goals and playing a part in primitive exploration, manipulation, and reality mastery.

The theory of instinctual drives has engendered considerable controversy, both within psychology and psychiatry in general and within psychoanalysis specifically.* Brenner (1971) recently discussed the following problem areas, which he did not claim to be a complete list: vitalism and drive theory; evidence for a dual as opposed to a unitary instinctual drive theory; fusion and defusion of drives; the concept of mental energy, its relation to physical energy, and its heuristic value; transformation of mental energy, neutralization and instinctualization; cathexis and countercathexes; cathexis of mental functions as distinct from cathexis of a mental representation; economic point of view, especially, the relative usefulness and possible disadvantages of explanations based on economic or quantitative considerations.

RELATIONS BETWEEN EGO AND ID

Anna Freud stated (1952) that the interrelations between the ego and the id, including a metapsychological assessment of their interdependence, are topics that cover most of the psychoanalytic theory. We can thus only hope to deal with some general ways in which these two systems of psychic functioning relate. She also surmised that academic psychologists tended to see ego apparatuses as too independent of the drives, while psychoanalysts tended to attribute failures in ego functioning to disorders of the instinctual drives. A brief discussion of the interrelationships will serve as an introduction to some of the issues involved.

From the dynamic point of view, conflict between the id and ego functions would be the focus. A central way in which they are brought into conflict is when instinctual drive manifestations represent a danger to the person, and the ego initiates a danger signal to activate defense measures (Freud 1926). This kind of conflict is central for psychopathology.

Cooperation between ego and id is also noteworthy. The ego frequently serves id aims, for instance, in facilitating the discharge of instinctual-drive energies. This begins early in life and continues during adulthood whenever instinctual-drive manifestations are ego syntonic (Anna Freud, 1952). Indeed, one aspect of ego strength in relation to the id involves finding ways to make drive discharge possible. Another way the ego may cooperate with the id and vice versa is that ego aims may substitute for id aims and id energy may be available to ego aims.

*See, for example, Panel on Psychoanalytic Theory of Instinctual Drives in Relation to Recent Developments, reported by H. Dahl, Journal of the American Psychoanalytic Assn. *16* 613-637 (1968).

Economic (energic) considerations have received much discussion but remain controversial. Freud (1914) attributed independent energy to the ego instincts, as already pointed out and postulated an original libidinal cathexis of the ego. With the structural model spelled out in 1923, Freud focused on ways in which the ego derived its energy from the id by desexualizing libidinal energy as a result of identification. He assumed that the ego worked with desexualized energy, while the id worked with sexualized, the former being bound and the latter unbound (see Holt, 1962, for a detailed discussion of these concepts). Hartmann expanded the economic considerations with his hypotheses of the neutralization of sexual and aggressive drive (id) energies by the ego, which he assumed to begin when the ego becomes differentiated from the id-ego (see genetic aspects below). Thus, ego aims can substitute for id aims. While he assumed that the ego works with neutralized energy, he also assumed that various ego functions use energy that is neutralized to different degrees.

In the infant, it is assumed that the apparatuses of primary autonomy that underlie perception, motility, and other ego functions are activated by instinctual drives. But as Hartmann emphasized, they are not created by the drives: they are partly inborn. We will deal with them in more detail in the chapter on autonomous functioning.

He later assumed that at the beginning of life there is an undifferentiated ego-id (1950). Hartmann developed this concept of an undifferentiated phase with Kris and Loewenstein (1946). This accounts for some ego aspects being based on drive characteristics. While the hereditary aspects of the drives had always been stressed, the undifferentiated id-ego phase implies that aspects of the ego are also inherited, such as special strengths and weaknesses and its maturational course of development.

Another implication of the undifferentiated phase is that in childhood, when the differentiation between the two is weak, drive regression tends to induce ego regression more readily than it does in adults. In the latter, the drive regression tends to be more strongly opposed by the ego, and internal conflict develops, while the ego functions tend to retain their adaptiveness.

Another and more recent way in which ego and id aspects have been interrelated is in the concept of developmental lines put forth by Anna Freud (1963, 1965). With regard to these, she said, "What we are looking for are the basic interactions between id and ego and their various developmental levels, and also age-related sequences of them which, in importance, frequency, and regularity, are comparable to the maturational sequence of libidinal stages or the gradual unfolding of the ego functions" (1965, p. 63). The developmental lines she discussed are as follows: from dependency to emotional self-reliance and adult object relationships, from sucking to rational eating, from wetting and soiling to bladder and bowel control, from irresponsibility to responsibility in body management, from egocentricity to companionship, from the body to the toy, and from play to work.

Hartmann (1948) summed up the mutual dependence of drive and ego theory in this way: "Certainly no thorough insight into psychic structure and into psychic conflicts could have been gained without knowledge of the psychology of the drives" (p. 80). But the reverse of Hartmann's statement is also true, as he goes on to say, namely, that in order to understand the function of instinctual drives, one must take into account their place within the psychic structure.

While our focus in this book is on ego functioning, we also want to emphasize that differences in drive endowment and strength do exist and that these influence ego development and ego functioning.

Greenacre (1952) noted congenital id variations, especially in the strength of drives. Fries and Woolf (1953) identified congenital activity patterns that appear to influence ego activity. Alpert, Neubauer, and Weil (1956) described in detail the developmental history of three children, focusing on how unusual drive endowments (high oral, high aggressive, and insufficient libidinal and aggressive) interacted with ego development.

Bellak (1956) summarized the issue of drive strength in this way: "Thus, one person's ego may be predestined for a more difficult time, simply because that particular person starts out life with a more vigorous id than the next."

Ostow's ideas on ego libido, energy supplies, and depletion are all related to drive strength (1962). With respect to libidinal-drive strength, he refers to the pressure toward discharge that it builds up, which sometimes overrides the defenses specifically mobilized against it. This in turn alters many aspects of ego functioning.

CHAPTER 3

The Superego Concept

The superego is the third agency in the tripartite model of the mental apparatus put forth by Freud in 1923. As we mentioned earlier, one reason the structural model was introduced was to take account of the unconscious sense of guilt, which is an important aspect of superego functioning. Rapaport stated in 1957 that since Freud introduced the structural theory in 1923, theoretical interest has mostly been focused on the ego, with a comparative neglect of superego theory. In this 1957 paper, Rapaport discussed a number of unresolved theoretical issues related to the superego concept. While unresolved difficulties remain, there has been considerable theoretical interest in the superego during the past 15 years. In this chapter, we will review the concept and its forerunners in Freud's work and then cover some important issues related to it, ending with a consideration of some relationships between ego and superego.

Freud's earliest references to moral functioning occur before he developed the concept of the superego, among them his discussion of the role of self-reproach in obsessional neuroses. Obsessions were understood to be reproaches related to a sexual deed enjoyed in childhood that later reemerged in a transmuted form (1896).* Thus, one function that might be termed self-criticism, later attributed to the superego, is present in an undeveloped form in 1896. Further development of the concept of the superego in the context of a growing understanding of obsessional neurosis is found in "Obsessive Actions and Religious Practices" (1907). In this paper Freud's explicit recognition that self-reproaches may be unconscious foreshadows his later view that the superego is for the most part, unconscious.

The censor concept in Freud's theory of dreams may be regarded as a forerunner of the superego. The censor is the representative of civilized morality operating even under the condition of sleep. It is primarily a prohibiting agency, in that it opposes the expression of certain wishes of the dreamer.

In "Civilized Sexual Morality and Modern Nervous Illness" (1908), Freud discussed the notion that the excessive moral demands of civilization result in neuroses. However, there is no explicit mention of "the sense of guilt" that he

---

*Freud subsequently recognized that a sexual fantasy can perform a similar function.

later developed in *Totem and Taboo* (1912) and in *Civilization and Its Discontents* (1930).

Thus far, then, we find references to moral functioning stemming from three sources: self-reproach related to obsessions, the role of the censor in dream psychology, and the antagonism between civilization and instinctual life. The question of the mechanism and genesis of moral functioning in the individual was not explicitly dealt with until Freud discussed the formation of the ego-ideal in "On Narcissism" (1914). Here he formulated that the source of the ego-ideal is found in the narcissism of the child. Under the influence of ethical demands, the child represses his egoistic wishes and, in their place, erects an internal ideal that becomes the transformed basis for loving himself. In this paper, Freud introduced several functions that he later attributed to the superego: (1) self-evaluation, that is, the ego* measures itself against the ideal and, depending upon the degree to which it approximates the ideal, experiences high or low self-regard; (2) self-observation (we will later discuss the question of how self-observation as a superego function is related to self-observation as an ego function). The emphasis on the concept of the ego-ideal here is on the positive ideals that a person strives toward and measures himself against.

In *Totem and Taboo* (1912-1913), Freud's phylogenetic speculations anticipated his later theory of the development of the superego in the individual as a consequence of the resolution of the Oedipus complex. He stated that the origin of conscience was similar to the origin of taboo, in that both are based on an emotional ambivalence in which a negative feeling is kept unconscious through the domination of the opposite feeling.

A connection between the "sense of guilt" and the "need for punishment" can also be found in Freud's early work. An attempt to grapple with this problem is found in "Some Character Types Met with in Psychoanalytic Work" (1916). He formulated that the person suffering from a "sense of guilt" commits misdeeds in such a way as to be caught and punished for them in order that his guilt might be mitigated. This behavior, then, inferentially, is regarded as reflecting a "need for punishment." At this point, the "sense of guilt" appears developmentally before the "need for punishment." These terms were not clarified until *Civilization and Its Discontents* (1930) and in the work of psychoanalysts after Freud.

In "Mourning and Melancholia" (1917), Freud noted that in cases of depression, the ego incorporates the lost love object (i.e., its mental representation). This mechanism of incorporation accounts for the guilt as well as the self-reproaches (reproaches that were first generated against the lost love object). In *The Ego and the Id*, Freud described the process of identification as an

---

*What Freud here called the ego can more accurately be termed the self, as we pointed out in Chapter 2.

instance of a more general aspect of mental functioning. It should be noted that identification (with the parents, especially the father) is the major basis assumed by Freud to underlie superego development.

In Freud's clinical account of melancholia in 1917, the flavor of the final concept of the superego as an often cruel and irrational self-critical agency in the mind becomes clearer. Unlike the discussion of the ego-ideal in "On Narcissism" (1914), here there is an emerging synthesis of various earlier trends of thought about the critical agency in man. Freud elaborated on the concept of the ego-ideal in noting that the members of a group take the leader as their common ego-ideal and by their common attachment they can identify with each other. The leader also serves the function of setting standards or ideals for the group. Freud pointed out that the followers accept the standards of the leader without criticism, and he described the relationship in terms of an "hypnotic" effect the leader has on the followers and the irrational nature of the "love" they have for the leader.

Freud noted that the fear of loss of love (i.e., "social anxiety," fear of public opinion) operates as a strong factor in inducing moral behavior. Another idea developed in this work is that conceptions of social justice (i.e., social conscience, sense of duty) may be dynamically understood as a reaction-formation against competitive feelings of rivalry toward a sibling.

In 1921 Freud described "a differentiating grade in the ego," which is a direct forerunner of the structural concept of the superego.

The structural concept of the superego as a system in its own right, apart from the ego, is discussed in *The Ego and the Id* (1923), as we pointed out earlier. Rapaport stated that "the major impetus for the structural hypothesis came from Freud's desire to introduce the superego in order to account for the unconscious sense of guilt and the negative therapeutic reaction" (1957).

Freud presented there (1923) a view of the superego as a structure formed in consequence of the resolution of the Oedipus complex, the two main factors determining its resolution being "the triangular character of the Oedipus situation and the constitutional bisexuality of each individual" (p. 31).

Freud also integrated the positive (i.e., striving toward ideals) and the negative (i.e., prohibitive) aspects of the critical agency in the concept of the superego. In this work, Freud also discussed superego formation in relation to the aggressive drives. He increasingly discussed the superego in terms of the death instinct (aggressive drives) turned inward against the ego (or more accurately, against the self). Whereas in earlier works Freud regarded sexuality and its renunciation as the crucial factor in the development of the superego, he later came to find aggression and self-destructiveness as equally, if not more, important factors in its development and functioning.

In "The Economic Problem of Masochism" (1924), Freud shed more light on the "unconscious sense of guilt," a topic that was to become one of the central concerns of his later work. This refers to "a need for punishment at the hands of a parental power." The ego in this clinical syndrome is viewed as being feminine (i.e., castrated), and a description of the masochistic ego is offered. The masochism associated with the ego is viewed as complementing the sadism of the superego.

In "Inhibitions, Symptoms, and Anxiety" (1926), Freud revised his theory of anxiety as previously noted. Up to then, the role attributed to the superego in the defensive process was somewhat vague. In his earlier works Freud tended to regard the "moral agency" as the cause of, and the enforcement of defenses against, an impulse. In the revised theory of anxiety, however, it is the anxiety signal that mobilizes the defensive reaction to danger. The role of the superego is here seen to lie solely in influencing the evaluation of the danger situation and in prompting the ego to give the anxiety signal that mobilizes defense, but the superego does not enforce the defense.

In *Civilization and Its Discontents* (1930), Freud returned to one of his favorite themes — the antagonism between instinctual life and civilized morality, and he focused on the unconscious sense of guilt in man. He stated that it is his "intention to represent the sense of guilt as the most important problem in the development of civilization" (p. 81). It is in this work that Freud most clearly connects the death instinct and the superego. He viewed the individual as faced with the choice of self-destruction or the destruction of external objects. However, in fusions with Eros (life instinct), the death instinct may be diverted from its aim of self-destruction and put into the service of cultural ideals. He saw civilization as faced with the task of controlling man's destructiveness. The more the individual inhibits the expression of aggression outward, the more he will direct destructive impulses against himself. The superego's severity is seen primarily to be a result of the turning inward of aggressive impulses. Hartmann and others later developed the idea of neutralization of aggressive energy, which provides an alternative to either directing aggression outward or against oneself. We discuss the concept of neutralization in Chapter 15.

In *An Outline of Psychoanalysis* (1938), Freud presented the superego as the psychic agency that includes a representation of the external world that involves both the conscious and unconscious attitudes of the parents and the influences of society. The child's dependence upon the parents and his desire to retain their love are viewed as early sources of conscience. So long as the ego works in agreement with the superego, it is not easy to distinguish between their manifestations; but tensions and estrangements between them are very plainly visible. Several points are implicit in this statement: (1) that ego development and superego development are intricately related; (2) that the various "systems" of the mind are differentiated primarily by differing functions; and (3) that the attribution of separate functions to the different systems is accomplished primarily in the observation of situations of conflict between two or more systems.

Theodore Reik (1925), in his essay "The Compulsion to Confess," elucidated aspects of the unconscious sense of guilt, the need for punishment, and the unconscious compulsion to confess. In this early work, he stressed the role of the superego in all neuroses, a conclusion implied in Freud's propositions that the superego is heir to the Oedipus complex and that derivatives of the Oedipus complex are involved in every neurosis. Reik held that the compulsion to confess is a strong force leading to the return of the repressed and that guilt feelings find a partial satisfaction in the confession. Most symptoms imply an unconscious confession, which mitigates the pressure of guilt feelings.

Nunberg (1926) held that although the sense of guilt and the need for punishment both arise during superego formation and are intertwined, they should be seen as different. The sense of guilt involves an attempt to cancel the deed, while in the need for punishment, the deed is carried on in relation to the subject's own person.

The talion principle underscores another aspect of the unconscious sense of guilt and the need for punishment. Talion is the notion that the punishment fits the crime: an eye for an eye. Thus, when a person wrongs someone else, there is an underlying tendency to expect a consonant punishment. In addition, punishment may be expected for wishes to harm others (thought crimes), and there is frequently an attempt by the person to bring about a punishment upon himself.

Saul (1950) has shown how in some cases, the punishment fits the motive for the crime, and more generally, the self-inflicted punishment fits the source of the person's own underlying motive. Thus, a person who takes hostile revenge because of frustrated needs for love punishes himself by frustrating his own needs for love.

FUNCTIONS OF THE SUPEREGO

In "On Narcissism" (1914), Freud described the conscience as an aspect of the mind whose function it is to see that the ego (self) gains narcissistic gratification by fulfilling the demand to conform to an ideal standard. In *The Ego and the Id* (1923), he attributed the following functions to the superego: (1) self-judgment, (2) prohibitions and injunctions, (3) sense of guilt, and (4) social feelings. In *New Introductory Lectures on Psycho-Analysis* (1933), Freud discussed the superego as an inner agent that replaces parental authority and now dominates the ego. The psychoanalytic literature on the functions of the superego after Freud has clarified and elaborated this list.

Hartmann and Loewenstein (1962) distinguish between superego contents and superego functions. Superego contents are values, moral beliefs, and ideals considered from a substantive point of view. Superego functions are the activities or processes or moral functioning without regard for actual content. Our discussion will focus on the various functions ascribed to the superego.

Brenner's (1955) list of superego functions is relatively comprehensive.

(1) The approval or disapproval of actions and wishes on the grounds of moral considerations.
(2) Critical self-observation.
(3) Self-punishment.
(4) The demand for reparation or repentence of wrongdoing ("an eye for an eye").
(5) Self-praise or self-love as a reward for virtuous or desirable thoughts and actions.

Brenner lists two self-rewarding functions of the superego, but he does not distinguish between self-esteem and self-love. R. White (1963) proposes that self-esteem and self-love may be considered conceptually "as partly independent variables." Thus, in some instances, a person may experience one and be deficient in the other. White states that self-esteem is rooted in a person's sense of competence in coping with the demands of the external world. For example, a particular person may be concerned "much less with himself than with other people and objective tasks, and his object libido must be rated relatively high as against his narcissistic libido" (p. 130). Self-love, unlike self-esteem, is rooted in narcissistic libido. Thus, from the point of view of superego functions, we may infer that the superego bestows love on the ego for narcissistic reasons (libido is directed toward the self, rather than the object), whereas esteem is bestowed on the ego by the superego as a "reward" for the ego's competence in its interactions with the environment. This distinction is useful both clinically and theoretically and can be formulated in nonanthropomorphic terms.

Beres (1966) offers a broad and comprehensive definition of the system superego: "In broad terms, we may designate the superego as that group of functions, which, through internalization of the demands of society, makes possible human existence in a social setting, however this may differ in different cultures" (p. 211). Beres includes the function of the superego in increasing the ego's capacity to recognize danger situations through anticipatory pangs of conscience (discussed in the chapter on judgment). A measure of the mature superego is that "it is less susceptible to outside influences, with greater stability in the manifestations of esteem of the self and with less swings from one extreme to the other" (p. 285). The degree of dependence on outside sources for self-esteem is thus seen as related to the immaturity of the superego organization. Beres also pointed out that we may directly observe an ego function in behavior, but a superego function manifests itself only through an ego function – that is, we assume the operation of a superego function to account for the behavior of the ego. We, typically, cannot observe superego functioning directly; we only observe its effects in ego functioning. One must be aware of this source of conceptual confusion in describing the various superego functions.

Hartmann and Loewenstein (1962), in their discussion of the enforcing function of the superego, make a distinction between the strong superego and the severe superego. A person with a strong superego has internalized moral injunctions that effectively regulate his moral behavior. A person with a severe superego reproaches himself incessantly, but these reproaches do not effectively regulate consistent moral behavior. Rather, the severity of the superego indicates its failure to enforce its injunctions upon the ego.

Piers and Singer (1953) propose that failure to reach an ideal be distinguished from acting contrary to an injunction. This distinction aids in categorizing the functions of the superego. They attribute the function of setting goals for the ego to the ego ideal.

Jacobson (1964) discussed the superego functions of signal fears, self-criticism, self-reward, and self-evaluation, guiding, inspiring, enforcing, and direction giving.

THE SUPEREGO AND THE EGO-IDEAL

Several relationships between these concepts have been proposed. Freud distinguished the ego-ideal from the self-critical agency in 1914, but in 1921 ego-ideal covered both the rewarding and prohibitive aspects of the critical agency. In 1923 he used the terms "superego" and "ego-ideal" interchangeably, and in 1932 he viewed the superego as "the vehicle of the ego-ideal."

We will summarize some of the important statements on the relationship between the two.

Nunberg (1932) proposed a distinction between the ego-ideal and the superego on the basis of the two types of instincts involved. "Whereas the ego submits to the superego out of punishment, it submits to the ego-ideal out of love." He referred to the ego-ideal as "an image of the loved objects in the ego," in contrast to the superego, which is "an image of the hated and feared objects." Nunberg stated that in practice, it is difficult to separate the manifestations of these sharply from each other.

Piers and Singer (1953) conceived of the ego-ideal as deriving from feelings of narcissistic omnipotence and as representing the total of positive identification with parent imagos. They view the experience of shame as the result of the tension between ego and ego-ideal and the experience of guilt as the outcome of the tension between ego and superego.

A. Reich (1954) spoke of the superego as "the later and more reality-syntonic structure" and the ego-ideal as "the earlier, more narcissistic one." The ego-ideal is based on "identifications with parental figures seen in a glorified light," while the superego represents the "identifications resulting from the breakdown of the Oedipus complex." According to her, the "ego-ideal expresses what one desires to be; the superego, what one ought to be."

Jacobson (1954) regarded the ego-ideal as part of the superego system, as a pilot and guide for the superego and as a kind of guide for the ego. She also regarded the formation of the ego-ideal as a precursor to the establishment of the superego system proper. She described the transformation of magical self-images and images of love objects into an ego-ideal and showed how internalization of the parental prohibitions and demands, establish superego identifications and self-critical superego functions." She added, "This double face of the ego-ideal, which is forged from ideal concepts of the self and from idealized features of the love objects, gratifies indeed the infantile longing of which we said that is never fully relinquished: the desire to be one with the love object" (p. 107).

Novey (1955) regards the ego-ideal as a separate operative unit playing a separate part in character formation and functioning. He believes that the ego-ideal is related to the superego but that its different origins and functions justify a separate theoretical status. He states that the superego at times is ego alien but that the ego-ideal is always ego syntonic. Although relatively few writers propose a complete separation of the two structures, almost all are agreed that one must refer to two qualitatively different aspects of moral functioning, whether or not one chooses to consider the ego-ideal as distinct (structurally) from the superego.

Hartmann and Loewenstein (1962), like Jacobson, see the ego-ideal as an aspect of the superego, which arises from preoedipal self and object idealizations. Sandler, Holder, and Meers (1963) pointed out that a disadvantage of conceptualizing ego-ideal and superego under the same heading requires that a very wide spectrum of functions has to be included, and both theoretical and clinical imprecision may result. These authors also noted that the concept of ego-ideal has included both ideal object and ideal self and that the ideal self need not be a mirror image of the ideal object or introject. They define the ideal self as "the shape which would provide the highest degree of narcissistic gratification and would minimize the quantity of aggressive discharge on the self." Sandler et al. (1963) emphasized the importance of distinguishing ideal self-representations from ideal object representations, in order to understand the development and function of the ego-ideal.

Lampl de Groot (1962) proposed a clear differentiation of the ego-ideal and the superego. She stated that "the ego-ideal is originally and essentially a need-satisfying agency, whereas the superego (or conscience) is originally and essentially a restricting and prohibiting agency." Although the ego-ideal retains a degree of functional independence from the superego, the two agencies normally work together harmoniously. The content of the ego-ideal is "I am like my omnipotent parents," whereas the superego's content may be expressed as "I will live up to the demands of my parents."

In summary of this section, while there is disagreement as to whether the ego-ideal is best included under the superego construct, there is general agreement on the following:

(1) From the developmental standpoint, the origins of the ego-ideal are assumed to be in the preoedipal and narcissistic stages of infancy, whereas the superego is regarded as arising out of the resolution of the Oedipus complex.

(2) In terms of instinctual drives, the ego-ideal is viewed as drawing more on libidinal impulses and consequently the emphasis in the use of this concept lies in the self-rewarding function. The superego is viewed as related more to the aggressive drives and the turning inward of these drives against the self, and emphasis tends to be placed on the self-punitive functions of the superego.

(3) The ego-ideal contents are always ego syntonic, while the superego attitudes, identifications, and contents may or may not be ego syntonic.

We turn now to the related issues of shame and guilt.

SHAME AND GUILT

Freud never attempted a systematic comparison of shame and guilt. He referred to the occurrence of shame reactions in 1905 ("Three Essays on the Theory of Sexuality") in a general way, as a defensive maneuver that is employed against libidinal impulse. Specifically, he defined shame as the force that opposes the infantile scopophilic and exhibitionistic impulses. Freud discussed guilt, or the "sense of guilt," in numerous contexts, as we have illustrated, and in general he viewed the source of guilt as in the Oedipus complex.

Psychoanalytic writers after Freud have drawn a distinction between shame and guilt that has proved to be of value, clinically and theoretically. As Hammerman pointed out (1965), the importance of the distinction is particularly apparent in the psychoanalytic treatment of masochistic or psychotic character disorders as well as in the treatment of the negative therapeutic reaction. Anthropologists have noted that entire societies may be characterized by their relative emphasis upon either the positive or negative aspects of shame or guilt. Certain cultures (e.g., Maori) place great emphasis upon living up to lofty ideals; others (e.g., Zuñi) place emphasis upon not being caught behaving in a deficient manner.

We will first review some of what has been said about shame in the psychoanalytic literature.

Fenichel (1945) noted that shame is often a defense against urethral-erotic impulses. Hammerman (1965) pointed out that "shame is associated with failure of instinctual control, with physical defect, and with public failure." Fear of exposure and ridicule, expressed in impulses "to bury one's face," are associated with shame. Hammerman stated that "shame has a great deal to do with body function and unconscious concepts of the body image, related to very early feelings of smallness and helplessness."

Shame primarily concerns feelings of inferiority and is connected with conflicts over self-esteem rather than with moral conflicts. Shame is associated with early stages of ego development and will be present in those who have problems of identity.

Kaplan et al. (1963) have presented a graduated conception of shame in terms of failure or success in achieving the goals of the ego-ideal. They describe a series of affects that vary with the degree to which the ego has achieved the goals of the ego-ideal. At one extreme, there is complete achievement of the goals of the ego-ideal, accompanied by feelings of pride and triumph. In descending order, as achievement decreases, are the affects of satisfaction, tolerance, regret, disappointment, and shame. As the failure to achieve the goals of the ego-ideal increases, there is chagrin — an increasing admixture of shame plus self-directed anger — and then humiliation. At the extreme end of failure to achieve the goals of the ego-ideal, there is mortification or the wish to die of shame.

According to Piers and Singer (1953), the shame-driven person constantly compares himself with others. They suggest that the degree of ego autonomy the person achieves at the height of the phallic phase determines whether he will strive realistically toward the realization of ego-ideals or will resort to magical wish-fulfilling fantasy without realistic achievement in an attempt to reduce the tension between ego and ego-ideal.

In contrast to shame, the feeling of guilt is generated when there is some transgression against the precepts of the superego proper. Hammerman (1965) noted that "guilt particularly is concerned with hostility against others and object relations in general, with no feeling of loss of self or identity."

Psychoanalytic writers have attempted to distinguish shame and guilt in a variety of other ways. Piers and Singer (1953) drew a distinction between the two affects based on the structural point of view. They stated:

> Whereas guilt is generated whenever a boundary (set by the Super-Ego) is touched or transgressed, shame occurs when a goal (presented by the Ego-Ideal) is not being reached. It thus indicates a real "short-coming." Guilt anxiety accompanies transgression, shame goes with failure.

Levin (1967) discussed the relationship of shame and guilt to the instinctual drives. He added to the Piers and Singer formulation the additional factor of self-exposure or its equivalent as contributing to the cause of the experience of shame. Thus, "the individual must usually become aware of or at least imagine that others have perceived or will perceive his failures and are having or will have negative reactions to them" in order for a shame reaction to occur. The hallmark of shame is the fear of rejection by others. Levin maintains that those people who experience shame do not typically possess well-internalized ideals, and one must take into consideration the fear of rejection (ridicule, humiliation) by others that such people experience.

Helen Lewis (1971) presents a comprehensive analysis of shame and guilt and distinguishes between the two on the basis of multiple criteria. One of these is the position of the self in the field in the experience of shame and guilt. Lewis stated that

... since shame is about the self, while guilt is about something, the position of the self with reference to events is very different in the two states. In particular, the relation of the self to the internalized "other" is different. In shame, the "other" is not apparent as the instigator and may or may not be apparent as the object to whom guilt refers (p. 87).

Lewis also contrasted shame and guilt in terms of the stimuli that elicit each experience. In shame, the stimulus is disappointment, defeat, or moral transgressions; in guilt the stimulus is a moral transgression. In shame the stimulus is a deficiency of the self, and in guilt the stimulus is the event, act, or thing for which the self is responsible. In shame the stimulus is involuntary and the self is unable, and in guilt the stimulus is voluntary and the self is able. In shame the stimulus is an encounter with the other, whereas in guilt the stimulus arises from within the self. Shame has a specific connection with sex, whereas guilt is generally connected with aggression.

In an important integration with experimental personality psychology, Lewis relates shame and guilt to the cognitive style dimension of field-independence — field-dependence. With the general conclusion that shame is associated with field-dependence and guilt with field-independence, Lewis discusses symptom pictures, defense mechanisms, organization of the self, and sex differences in relation to these dimensions and cites experimental evidence from diverse sources linking guilt-related phenomena with field independence and shame-related items with field dependence.

PRECURSORS OF THE SUPEREGO

Hammerman (1965) stated that

... the eventual existence of the superego as a discrete, psychic structure ... requires the concomitant and coordinated development of a number of elements which eventually coalesce. To understand the eventual development of the superego proper requires study of the superego precursors, the processes of internalization, identification, ego maturation, the genesis of object relations, identity formation, and psychic structure formation (pp. 322-323).

We shall review the literature on several of the elements that have been cited as crucial to understanding the development of the superego.

Psychoanalytic writers (with some exceptions, notably M. Klein and her group) have followed Freud in reserving the term superego for the postoedipal period and have referred to early manifestations of morality as representing precursors of the superego. This practice is based on Freud's conception of the superego as the "heir of the oedipus complex" (1923, p. 36).

Hartmann and Loewenstein (1962) have attempted to clarify the nature of the relationship between the precursors of the superego and the superego proper. They proposed that early manifestations of moral behavior be considered as genetic (developmental) antecedents of the system superego and noted that these antecedents (or precursors) may, in certain instances, possess an "analogy of function" (often vague) with the functions of the superego proper. Thus, a distinction is proposed between the genetic determinants and the system superego and its functions.

Freud drew attention to the precursors of the superego in his discussion of the events of the oral and anal phases of psychosexual development, and later psychoanalytic writers have expanded and elaborated upon this basic groundwork.

Melanie Klein and her followers maintain a somewhat different position on the development of the superego. She conceives of a fully formed superego before the resolution of the Oedipus complex. On the basis of her psychoanalytic work with young children, she holds that oral frustrations release oedipal impulses and result in the early stages of superego formation, beginning around the middle of the first year of life. For Klein (1932, p. 195) the beginnings of the superego result from objects that have been introjected during the oral-sadistic (cannibalistic) phase and from the destructive impulses and anxiety aroused by these internalized objects. The nucleus of the superego is to be found in the partial incorporation that takes place during this phase of development, and the child's early imagos take the imprint of those pregenital impulses.

Guntrip (1961) summarizes Klein's notion of the early superego as characteristically being extremely sadistic and not implying any moral values in the nature of an ego-ideal:

The super-ego had now become, as a result of Mrs. Klein's work, a blanket-term covering the complexity of the whole endopsychic world of internalized objects, for the world of inner reality as Mrs. Klein presents it is a scene in which the ego seeks the aid of good objects in its struggle with its persecuting bad figures. We must now regard the super-ego as standing for the whole complex process whereby the pristine ego undergoes the beginnings of structural differentiation under pressure of the external environment. The resulting psychic development has two aspects which Freudian and even Kleinian terminology do not yet enable us to conceptualize clearly. An "internal environment" is created in which the ego feels to be living under the shadow of powerful parental figures who are cruel persecutors at the deepest mental levels but steadily take on the aspect of ruthless punishers and guilt-inducers in later stages of development. But at the same time this complex structural differentiation includes a function of self-persecution and self-punishment in which the ego identifies with its internal enemies. One may say that the bad objects who arouse our rage in outer reality then become necessary to us to enforce control on our impulses; we can then forestall their punishment-cum-persecution by taking over their repressive functions ourselves. This entire process is duplicated in inner reality. If, for the moment, we exclude this function of self-judgment which is properly called "conscience," whether primitive or matured, we may then say that the super-ego covers the whole world of internal objects, good and bad (p. 231).

Another attempt in the psychoanalytic literature to formulate hypotheses concerning early moral development by direct observation of infants is Spitz's (1958). Spitz describes three successive "primordia" of the superego. The first stage involves the inhibition of the child's motor or physical behavior. Spitz notes that when the infant is restrained by an external source in his attempts to execute motor behavior, he perceives that he must take the external environment into account by submitting. Spitz maintains that the incorporation of motor prohibitions (acquired between the ninth and twelfth months) precedes the incorporation of verbal prohibitions. The next primordium involves identification with the love object. The connection between this mechanism and the later superego is obvious. The last primordium is the familiar "identification with the aggressor" (described by A. Freud, 1936). Spitz notes that this mechanism is involved in the child's early attempts to cope with aggressive impulses toward his parents and is a genetic forerunner of the "turning inward of aggression."

In another publication, Spitz (1957) describes the development of the ability for negation and affirmation. The acquisition of this capacity implies the ability to oppose both the environment and internal demands. Thus, the development of the "no" is viewed as a precursor of superego development.

Hammerman (1965) noted that obedience and self-control (two aspects of the superego precursors cited, in one form or another, by most psychoanalytic writers) "are not yet the same as self-criticism derived from moral judgment, which is the hallmark of a discrete intrapsychic structure." He further stated that "it seems reasonable that initially the developing superego organization works only under the actual supervision of external objects."

It may be useful to compare the psychoanalytic view of the development of the superego with that of Piaget's. Nass (1966) specifically compared the theories of moral development of Freud and Piaget. According to Piaget (1932), the child goes through two stages of morality. The first stage, which he calls "the morality of constraint" or "heteronomous morality," is characteristic of the child up until the age of seven or eight years. This type of morality is a reflection of the child's egocentrism, a quality prevalent in the young child's thinking in all areas studied by Piaget, and it is characterized by moral realism. The older child, through peer interaction, learns a kind of cooperative morality, which involves both autonomy and mutual respect. Once he has attained the capacity for thought which is largely free from egocentrism, he can develop peer reciprocity through social interaction, and not by the imposition of sanctions.

A comparison of the two levels shows the following:

Egocentric	*Autonomous*
Objective responsibility	Responsibility judged by intent
Unchangeability of rules	Flexibility of rules
Absolutism of value	Relativism of values
Transgression defined by punishment	Moral judgments made independently of sanctions
Duty defined as obedience to authority	Duty defined in terms of peer expectations
Ignorance of reciprocity	Reciprocity
Expiative justice	Restitutive justice
Immanent justice	Naturalistic causality
Collective responsibility	Individual responsibility

Nass points out that while Piaget is more concerned with cognitive aspects of development and tends to be focused at a descriptive level, psychoanalytic theorists attempt to relate cognitive processes with drives and affective processes. But even though the two theories approach the subject from different viewpoints and gather different kinds of data, there are parallels in their findings about moral development. Thus, the early superego, described by Freud (1923) as cruel, harsh, and unyielding is close to Piaget's morality of constraint, where rules are obeyed unquestioningly. Nass also compared Piaget's view of the mature adult conscience with the psychoanalytic conception of the autonomous superego. Hartmann and Loewenstein (1962) described superego autonomy in terms of independence from the drives and from objects. Piaget described the mature stage of morality in terms of "freedom from egocentric influences, i.e., from the kind of magical imagery which psychoanalytic theory characterizes as primary process (which is less subject to influence by the mature ego)."

INTERNALIZATION, IDENTIFICATION, INTROJECTION, AND INCORPORATION

Psychoanalytic discussion of the development of the superego relies heavily upon the use of the terms: internalization, identification, introjection, and incorporation. These concepts have been used interchangeably and inconsistently in the literature. As these terms are crucial to any discussion of the development of the superego, attempts to clarify their meanings are important.

That the development and formation of the superego is a process of internalization of certain elements of the external world was stated by Freud (1932), who discussed the superego as an inner agent that replaces external parental authority and later dominates the ego. Beres (1966) stated that the internalization of self-criticism is the hallmark of superego development. It is clear that an understanding of the processes of internalization is necessary to an understanding of the superego.

Schafer (1968) proposed that internalization be regarded as the most general and comprehensive of the four terms under discussion. In a modification and adaptation of Hartmann and Loewenstein's (1962) definition, Schafer offered the following:

Internalization refers to all those processes by which the subject transforms real or imagined regulatory interactions with his environment, and real or imagined characteristics of his environment into inner regulations and characteristics (p. 9).

. . . Introjection should be used to refer to one kind of internalization only, namely, the processes whereby object representations are constituted as introjects or are changed into them (p. 16).

He differentiates identification from introjection as follows:

While often interwoven with introjection, and often following upon it, identification refers to modifying the subjective self or behavior, or both, in order to increase one's resemblance to an object taken as a model; it does not refer, as introjection does, to carrying on certain purely internal relations with an object represented as such (the introject) (p. 16).

. . . incorporation refers to a particular content of primary process ideation. In the primary process, owing to its concreteness and its wish-fulfilling character, the idea (thought) is not differentiated from the deed. In this light, incorporation may be said to refer to ideas that one has taken a part or all of another person (or creature, or thing) into one's self corporeally, and, further that this taking in is the basis of certain novel, disturbing and/or gratifying sensations, impulses, feelings, and actions of one's own and of correlated changes in one's experience of the environment (1968, p. 20).

In the most general way, superego development can be characterized as "the internalization of real or imagined regulatory interactions with the environment" when such interactions involve a "moral" or "evaluative" aspect.

Hartmann and Loewenstein (1962) and Sandler (1963) have pointed out the distinction between self-representations and object representations in superego development. The concept of introjection is particularly useful for describing instances in which "object representations are constituted as introjects" without involving complex transformations of the self-representation. Schafer states that introjects are more readily decomposed than are identifications and that an identification represents a higher degree of internalization than does an introject, as noted above.

THE LOVING Versus THE PUNITIVE SUPEREGO

Freud emphasized the punitive, critical, and sadistic qualities of the superego and said little about its benign, loving, and protective qualities. One of the few exceptions to this tendency is his discussion of humor. In "Jokes and Their Relation to the Unconscious" (1905), there are suggestions that the "critical agency" relaxes its vigilance over the ego in the humorous situation and permits the ego "forbidden" pleasure. In "Humour" (1927), Freud noted that the superego, by means of humor, consoles and protects the ego from suffering.

Schafer (1960), in an attempt to correct this one-sided view of the superego, analyzed the reasons that led Freud to maintain a view of the superego as exclusively punitive. Schafer gives four main reasons for Freud's focusing on the punitive aspects of the superego:

(1) The conception of the punitive superego helps to explain the negative therapeutic reaction. Moreover, a major task of psychoanalytic treatment has been to increase the ego's independence from the superego.

(2) In his last theory of the instincts, Freud viewed the death instinct and its control by the superego as analogous to the sublimation of sexuality by the ego.

(3) Given the power of the oedipal urges, Freud needed the conception of a hostile superego to account for the successful and lasting socialization that most human beings achieve.

(4) Freud arrived at his conception of the hostile superego by drawing heavily on cases of obsessional neurosis, depression, and paranoia.

Having analyzed the reasons for the persistence of a conception of a solely punitive superego in psychoanalytic theory, Schafer advanced his view of the loving or benign superego. In some ways, Schafer's argument revolves around a strikingly obvious, but nonetheless important, point. If the child internalizes his parents' critical attitudes toward him, why would he not also internalize their caring and protective attitudes toward him? Schafer noted that the superego draws on libidinal impulses as well as on aggressive ones and that the turning inward of aggressive impulses against the self does not exhaust the possibilities of relationship between the id and the superego. He suggests:

Ideal self-representations and ideal object-representations originate in the undifferentiated id-ego at the time of the earliest illusion formation (in Winnicott's sense) or mutuality exchanges (in Erikson's sense). . . . The development of these ideal representations continues in the differentiating ego and superego on behalf of id wishes and ego interests, functions, and standards, and of moral commandments and standards as well. They assume socially benevolent as well as asocial, antisocial forms, mixed and nonmoral forms. . . . These ideal images take much of their raw material from the surrounding world, and, under favorable maturational and social circumstances, they give back to the world new forms of aspiration and appreciation (p. 174).

SOME RELATIONSHIPS BETWEEN EGO AND SUPEREGO

If the system superego is defined by its functions and refers to the structuralization associated with the resolving of conflicts associated with the oedipal phase of development, a number of relationships between ego and superego systems can be seen. We will enumerate some of these and then illustrate how superego functioning can interfere with particular ego functions.

Hartmann and Loewenstein (1962) state that the particular details of ego development in a given child influence the formation of his (or her) superego functioning. Both the degree of overall ego maturity and the stages of intellectual and language development at the time of superego formation are seen to have effects on the latter. They hypothesize that the extent of ego autonomy achieved by the time the phallic phase is at its height influences superego development. They also point out that during the first few years of life, the ways in which the child deals with external and internal danger situations also affects the development of the superego system. And for some individuals, superego danger is regressively experienced in terms of earlier threats such as the threat of separation (Loewenstein, 1966), one of the basic danger situations that Freud discussed in relation to the ego (1926). Thus, superego formation is influenced by the maturation and development of the ego, the oedipal situation, the phallic phase, preoedipal development, and the prephallic (oral and anal) phases (Hartmann and Loewenstein, 1962, p. 147).

Ego functions that particularly influence superego development are reality testing, the capacity for self-observation, and the potential for sublimation and/or neutralization. Hartmann and Loewenstein (1962) hypothesize, for example, that superego functioning seen in some psychotic individuals, which is characterized by cruelty and overpunitiveness, can be partly explained by an impairment in the capacity to neutralize aggressive energy. (We discuss some issues related to neutralization in the chapter on autonomous functioning.) These authors hypothesize that various superego functions use different degrees of neutralized energy, which is parallel to the assumption that different ego functions operate with different degrees of neutralized (or neutral) energy.

The choice of defenses (and their interactions) is also relevant to superego formation, especially reaction-formation, identification, projection, and denial. And guilt feelings, which are central to the superego, can stimulate defensive activity of the ego and serve as a signal to inhibit action (Jacobson, 1964). (A discussion of superego signals and judgment is found in Chapter 7.)

Negative and critical superego reactions can affect the total self-picture and thereby lower the level of self-esteem. This creates mood vacillations and, as a result, affects all ego functions. In people with a pathological archaic superego structure, the signal function of the superego referred to above may be put out of action; the person then becomes depressed as a result of the critical superego reaction, but defenses to ward off and sublimate the forbidden strivings that triggered the depressive mood are not activated (Jacobson, 1964, p. 134).

Superego demands, like instinctual demands, may or may not be ego syntonic. If they are ego syntonic, they will be integrated without opposition, but if they are not, they may be opposed and defended against. Some superego demands parallel ego tendencies, such as the demand for truthfulness, the ego aspects involving a striving toward acceptance of reality. The acceptance of superego demands can sometimes be attributed to the synthetic-organizing-integrative function of the ego, although a compromise formation may result, rather than complete acceptance (Hartmann and Loewenstein, 1962). Ego and superego functions also overlap, such as in self-observation. (We discuss this issue in the chapter on reality testing.)

Relations between ego and superego can also be discussed in terms of superego autonomy or independence from the ego. With regard to specific ego functions, there is the degree of independence of moral motives from social anxiety or from self-interest. In general, the independence of the superego refers to the imperviousness of superego directives to particular sociocultural pressures. But in virtually all areas, the normal functioning of the superego is continuously dependent upon a number of ego functions (Hartmann and Loewenstein, 1962).

The influence of current sociocultural factors on superego development and aspects of ego development is emphasized by Lowenfeld and Lowenfeld (1970).

The core of the superego is determined by the earliest parental imagos; the later influence of parents is less on the superego and more on the ego. Thus today we have the following problems: the inhibiting, controlling and guiding function of the superego, which largely merges with the ego, is weakened through the weakness of the parents, through indulgent education which fails to train the ego, and through the general social climate of permissiveness. The sexual and aggressive instinctual drives are much less under the guidance of rules. But the severe superego of early childhood still lives in the individual. The result is restlessness, discontent, depressive moods, craving for substitute satisfactions (pp. 595-596).

Thus, ego and superego factors influence each other in a number of ways. We will now illustrate some kinds of interferences. When the superego is consistent and appropriate, it generally enhances the functioning of all aspects of the ego. If it is too severe or weak or inconsistent, it may interfere with ego functions in the following ways:

Reality Testing. Strong underlying hostility, in conjunction with a superego that prohibits hostility expression, can result in projection of the hostility and thereby interfere with reality testing. An oversevere superego can make one misinterpret reality in excessively moral terms. A lax or weak superego can contribute to underestimating the harmful nature of some forms of the person's behavior.

Judgment. When action is influenced by a severe or by a weak superego, judgment can be interfered with in a way similar to that described above for reality testing.

Sense of Reality. (1) Feelings of depersonalization, an important disturbance in the sense of self, can result from underlying guilt about strong hostility. (2) Both guilt and shame can affect the subject's sense of self, and superego formation often results in marked changes in the self-image (Hartmann and Loewenstein, 1962).

Object Relations. (1) Projection of severe superego attitudes (blaming, faultfinding, etc.) can vitally affect object relations. (2) A lax superego, associated with irresponsibility, unfairness, cheating, taking advantage of, and so on, also can vitally affect an individual's relations with others. (3) A superego response (prohibition) to experienced aggression can result in withdrawal from another person.

Thought Processes. (1) Superego prohibitions of aggressive- and/or sexual-drive derivatives may play an important part in the genesis of obsessive thought mechanisms. (2) Indecisiveness or obsessive doubt can result from the unconscious idea that decisiveness constitutes destructive aggressive behavior.

Arise. (Adaptive Regression in the Service of the Ego) This function requires awareness of quite primitive sexual, aggressive, and other forbidden contents. Some individuals with severe superegos would be expected to find controlled regressions difficult with resulting constriction and sterility.

Defensive Functioning. A severe superego often tends to be associated with excessive use of defenses. Some defenses are directed primarily against superego contents.

Stimulus Barrier. (1) Superego "disapproval" of strong voyeuristic trends can result in the symptom of headaches and in disturbance in vision (Greenacre, 1947), involving a lowering of the stimulus barrier for light. The auditory sphere appears to be subject to similar disturbances. (2) Great hostility in conjunction with superego prohibition can result in projection of hostility and consequent vigilance and sensitization as a form of lowered stimulus barrier. Depressives are often highly sensitive to noise. Insomniacs may also illustrate the lowered stimulus barrier: fear of aggression and of being attacked at night is often found.

Autonomous Functioning. Autonomous functioning may be interfered with by any number of parapraxes, and such interference may be caused, not by drives, but by the superego; forgetting, stuttering, accidents, involving motor behavior, and so on may be influenced by guilt.

Synthetic Functioning. To the extent to which synthetic-integrative functioning involves reconciling incompatabilities between reality, id, and superego, an inconsistent, oversevere, or inappropriately deficient superego would make synthesis and integration more difficult.

Mastery-Competence. An excessively high ego-ideal, as well as overstrict superego standards, seriously interferes with a sense of competence, while an insufficient superego is likely to interfere with actual mastery. If mastery is symbolically equated with aggression, effective behavior may be adversely affected by superego factors.

Now that we have reviewed the ego, id, and superego constructs, we will focus more specifically on ego functions.

CHAPTER 4

Ego Functions in Psychoanalytic Theory

THE CONCEPT OF EGO FUNCTIONS

Freud was concerned with an ego construct throughout his psychological writings. Following the manner in which physiological organ systems were traditionally described, he defined the ego — as well as the id and the superego — by its functions. His most general formulation concerning ego strength was that it is reflected in the ability to love and work.

Federn (1952) early employed the idea that the outstanding feature in schizophrenia is a weakness of the ego. Tausk also saw schizophrenics as suffering from a deficiency in ego strength. The conception of ego boundaries was Tausk's original formulation, and he emphasized that ego defects underlie schizophrenia (Roazen, 1969).

It was Hartmann who pointed out that while ego weakness is characteristic of schizophrenics, there was still a need to specify which ego functions are impaired in any given ego weakness. To quote his general position from an earlier paper: "All definitions of ego strength will prove unsatisfactory as long as they take into account only the relation to other mental systems and leave out of consideration the intrasystemic factors" (1950, p. 138). Hartmann's position on this matter as published over 20 years ago appears to be still widely accepted by psychoanalysts. In this chapter, we shall discuss some of the issues raised by Hartmann and others that relate to ego functions, including ego function characteristics and their interrelationships.

WHAT EGO FUNCTIONS?

In choosing a list of ego functions that was reasonably exhaustive and contained minimal overlap between functions, we benefited greatly from the work of those who attempted the task before us. Some of this foundation work is summarized below.

In chapter 1 of *An Outline of Psychoanalysis* (1940), Freud discussed the principal characteristics of the ego. He included self-preservation; becoming aware of, and dealing with, external stimuli; controlling voluntary movement;

and learning to influence the external world to our own advantage through activity. Other aspects he included are the seeking of pleasure and the avoidance of pain, taking external circumstances into account in deciding when to satisfy instinctual drives, and transmitting an unexpected increase in unpleasure by an anxiety signal. Finally, the ego attempts to avoid overly strong stimuli, has a memory function, and attempts to reconcile the demands from id, superego, and reality sources.

Ten years later Hartmann discussed the question of what functions are attributed to the ego (1950), but with the disclaimer that no analyst had ever attempted a complete list and specifying that he himself would include "only some of the most important ones." He began with those functions centered on the relation to reality, such as the organization and control of motility and perception, the latter involving external stimuli and also the self. The ego serves as a barrier against external and internal stimuli, tests reality, carries out action, and engages in thinking. Both action and thinking imply and require delay of discharge, and these ego activities, along with the ego's use of anxiety as an aid in anticipating danger, are part of the organism's internalization tendency, which decreases its dependence upon current stimuli and permits it to function autonomously. Those functions associated with internalization can also be characterized as inhibitory; the most carefully studied defenses have been the inhibitory processes. Finally, Hartmann includes the synthetic (coordinating, integrating) function, which, together with the ego's capacity for differentiating, he calls an organizing function. Hartmann comments that analysts had studied some of these functions more than others and that some are most accessible to study through observations during psychoanalytic treatment, others by direct observation, and still others by experimental methods.

Anna Freud (1936) listed as essential ego functions the testing of inner and outer reality, building up of memory, the synthetic function, and the ego's control of motility. Hartmann, Kris, and Loewenstein (1946) referred to thinking, perception, and action as the three main functions of the ego but pointed out that these functions are frequently in the service of the id or superego.

Bellak (1949a), in discussing his multiple-factor psychosomatic theory of schizophrenia, included (1) reality testing; (2) mediating the drives, reason, the internalized rules of society, and the external environment; (3) frustration tolerance; and (4) the ability to engage in detour behavior for the long-range achievement of pleasure. In his 1952 book on manic-depressive psychoses, Bellak stated that the ego can be defined by its functions but also by its development and the quantitative aspects of its performance (i.e., ego strength). He proposed that ego strength be appraised with a scale based on data from the person's life history and symptoms and that such a scale should resemble an intelligence test (p. 11). In a later paper (1955), he defined the ego by the following functions: it (1) organizes and controls motility and perception; (2) serves as a protective barrier against excessive external and internal stimuli, performing the function of self-exclusion; (3) tests reality, engages in trial action, and sends out danger signals; (4) is responsible for detour behavior in gratification; and (5) includes character, defenses, and the integrating aspects of the ego under organizing and self-regulating functions.

Beres (1956), in the context of a discussion of childhood schizophrenia, included seven functions and illustrated them through case material. They are (1) relation to reality; (2) regulation and control of instinctual drives; (3) object relationships; (4) thought processes; (5) defense functions of the ego; (6) autonomous functions of the ego; and (7) synthetic function of the ego.

Arlow and Brenner (1964) in their systematic presentation of the structural theory in psychoanalysis, preface their enumeration of ego functions with the statement that there is no complete list of these functions. They include the following: (1) consciousness; (2) sense perception; (3) perception and expression of affect; (4) thought; (5) control of motor action; (6) memory; (7) language; (8) defense mechanisms and defensive activity in general; (9) control, regulation, and binding of instinctual energy; (10) integration and harmonization; (11) reality testing; (12) inhibition or suspension of the operation of any of these functions and regression to a primitive level of functioning (p. 39).

SOME ATTEMPTS TO MEASURE EGO FUNCTIONS AND RELATED CHARACTERISTICS

Prelinger, Zimet, Schafer, and Levin (1964) discuss some important earlier approaches to assessment. These include *Explorations in Personality* (1938), a multifaceted, psychoanalytically oriented study by Henry Murray and the staff of the Harvard Psychological Clinic; *The Assessment of Men* (1948), which describes selection techniques for potential spies and saboteurs used by the United States Office of Strategic Services; *The Prediction of Performance in Clinical Psychology* (1951) by Kelly and Fiske; and *Personality Patterns of Psychiatrists* (1958) by Holt and Luborsky.

While the last three studies attempt to predict success in given areas of endeavor on the basis of assessments of personality aspects, Prelinger et al. point out that their assessment scales have the aim not of specific prediction but of comprehending individual personality.

An important study that has employed rating scales of personality functioning based on psychoanalytic principles is the Psychotherapy Research Project of the Menninger Foundation (Wallerstein, Robbins, Sargent, and Luborsky, 1956; Sargent, Modlin, Faris, and Voth, 1958; Luborsky, Fabian, Hall, Ticho, and Ticho, 1958; Robbins and Wallerstein, 1959; Luborsky, 1962; Wallerstein,

1968). Beginning in 1949, five years were spent in planning and constructing instruments, and these researchers have been collecting data and publishing interim reports for the past 15 years. They used the rich and varied intake information routinely collected on Menninger Foundation patients (psychiatric case summary, psychological tests, and social work history), plus detailed notes from psychotherapy and psychoanalytic sessions. Assessment indices were organized into three groups (patient variables, treatment variables, and situational variables) and were based on what the researchers felt would be relevant to the course and outcome of psychotherapy. While not aimed at a general description of personality, the patient variables are nevertheless relevant to a general assessment of ego functioning, as the labels of most of the main categories imply: (1) sex and age; (2) anxiety and symptoms; (3) nature of conflicts; (4) ego factors and defenses; (5) capacity factors; (6) motivational factors; (7) relationship factors; and (8) reality factors. The Menninger workers are using, in addition to carefully defined variables, three different techniques for rating the variables, and at three different times (viz., before treatment, at termination, and two years after termination).

A factor analysis (principal components method) was carried out on the pretreatment ratings of 24 patients using a form of paired-comparison assessment of 12 patient variables judged to be central to the course and outcome of treatment. Five factors accounted for 90 percent of the common variance, and the first factor (41 percent of the common variance) had high loadings on interpersonal relationships, psychosexual development, anxiety tolerance, and ego strength.

A more recent report of one extensively studied patient (Wallerstein, 1968) includes graphic profiling of these variables and others.

An early attempt to measure ego functions was made by Green (1954). He listed 10 ego functions, a short definition of each, and a scoring guide (0-4) based on approximate level of maturity and the degree of integration of the functions achieved. The scores reflect the child's or adult's ability to exercise a given function in relation to expectations for his age and social milieu. The ego functions are (1) somatic perception; (2) memory; (3) reality testing; (4) judgment; (5) control of motility; (6) frustration tolerance; (7) establishment of object relationships; (8) affectivity; (9) defense mechanisms; and (10) basic intellectual capabilities.*

Bibring and associates (1961) published a comprehensive outline of variables used in the assessment of psychological processes in pregnancy. On the basis of psychoanalytic theory, a wide range of personality dimensions are included, such as mood and affective state; characteristic ways of behaving; character of object relations; narcissistic position; self image; superego manifestations; and defenses

*Scales for measuring ego functions from manifest dreams were presented by Sheppard and Saul, Psychoanal. Quart. 27, 237-245 (1957).

and signs of unconscious conflict. In all, the outline consists of five sections with many major subheadings. Unfortunately, no definition of terms is included, with the exception of an appendix by Arthur Valenstein, which contains a most useful definition of 24 basic and 15 complex defense mechanisms. Also, no rating manual was developed as a guide for rating the interview material; instead, ratings were assigned according to a conference consensus. The research group had spent a year developing the categories and materials, and the definitions of the concepts were said to be fairly well agreed upon within the group (Huntington, personal communication).

Prelinger, Zimet, Schafer, and Levin (1964) have devised a comprehensive, psychoanalytically based series of rating scales for character assessment. The 8 major categories (which include 78 subcategories are (1) ideational styles; (2) prominent affects; (3) prominent defenses; (4) superego; (5) adaptive strengths; (6) sense of self; (7) psychosocial modalities; and (8) character elaborations. A five-point scale is employed for most of the subcategories (plus an additional "cannot say" choice) and a brief description of each level on the ordinal scale (e.g., minimum, low, moderate, considerable, and high). The categories were set up to be rated on the basis of interview material and/or psychological test responses, although other sources of data (such as group therapy sessions) could be employed. To illustrate how ratings could be made from clinical data, two protocols are included, one from a psychological test response and one of extended excerpts from two evaluation-type interviews. The authors then spell out the considerations from the clinical material that led to the particular rating assigned. Some reliability data are available for both the interview and the psychological test protocols. For 19 normal, volunteer Yale freshmen, overall mean agreement between two independent raters was 69 percent for the test data (with a range from 51 percent to 82 percent agreement on individual subjects) and 68 percent for the interview (with a range of 57 percent to 86 percent), where agreement was defined as a difference of no more than half a point on the given scale. When reliability on each of the scales was tested for statistical significance, 62 of the 78 scales showed agreement at the 5 percent level of significance or beyond for the psychological test responses. For the interview protocol, 46 of the 78 scales were judged reliable at the 5 percent level or beyond. The authors suggest that the greater reliability in judging the test data (especially with regard to certain ego functions) may be due to the latter having been worked out in greater detail. Half of the scales (39) were judged reliable at the 5 percent level or beyond for both test data and interview material. Twelve of these are in the adaptive strengths group, a number of the categories of which are quite similar to what are defined in the present report as ego functions. The Prelinger and Zimet scales have the merit of comprehensiveness and are based on an up-to-date version of psychoanalytic theory, especially the developments in the area of egopsychology. The examples of ratings from clinical material included in the report add considerably to the usefulness of the categories. While the authors intended the scales to provide the basis for a description of character, the validity of the ratings with regard to some outside criterion nevertheless remains unestablished.

Karush, Easser, Cooper, and Swerdloff (1964) reported a method for profiling ego strength. Beginning with the idea that ego strength can be assessed by the organism's ability to balance various adaptive efforts, the authors defined nine areas: (1) dependency; (2) pleasure-frustration (general and genital); (3) affective; (4) defense; (5) emergency; (6) emotion; (7) guilt; (8) pathology; and (9) social-interaction balances. Each of these is rated on a nine-point bipolar scale with intermediate half points, providing a total of 17 scores for each scale; the resulting adaptive-balance curve can then be used in various ways, such as to predict therapeutic outcome. Although no data are provided in this report, the authors state that they have found high reliability and "discriminatory precision" in their preliminary studies.

The Hampstead Clinic group in London has spent a number of years compiling indices of psychoanalytic case material (Sandler, 1960, 1962; Sandler and Rosenblatt, 1962). Thus far, 10 manuals have been constructed, all of which are still being expanded and revised. They are entitled (1) general case material; (2) ego (general); (3) ego (anxiety); (4) ego (defenses); (5) instructural; (6) object relationships; (7) fantasies; (8) superego; (9) symptoms, and (10) treatment situation and technique. The psychoanalytic case material of a two-year-old boy, indexed according to the Hampstead method, has been published (Bolland and Sandler, 1965). Many definitions of psychoanalytic constructs have been sharpened, and a number of incongruities have come to light as a result of the Hampstead indexing project. In addition, the detailed demonstration of how clinical material can be rated and organized with the use of the indices is a significant addition to the published literature on the Hampstead Clinic project.

Grinker, Werble, and Drye (1968) reported a study on the borderline syndrome. They assessed 51 patients on ego function rating scales from hospital behavior in the ward, in occupational therapy, and during psychotherapy. A total of 280 variables were rated on 10-point scales, but sufficient data for statistical treatment were available on only 93 of the categories. Inter-rater reliabilities are reported in percentage agreements: two raters agreed within one scale point on 70 percent or more of the comparisons, and within two scale points on 85 percent or more. From a preliminary cluster analysis and then a principal-components factor analysis, 14 components (accounting for 70 percent of the total variance) were extracted. Then, guided by the factor loadings and the cluster analysis, the authors used their clinical experience to derive four subgroups of borderline patients, which they describe. This is the largest study thus far completed in which an attempt is made to use ego function categories systematically to delineate a clinical syndrome. The absence of the ego function measures on control subjects from the study leaves open the question of the relative presence, absence, or strength of the described behavioral traits in groups other than the borderline patients in the sample. While the hospital behaviors recorded are certainly relevant to ego functioning and to clinical status, other measures (such as standard psychological test responses and psychological laboratory procedures) would have broadened and probably enriched the basis for classifying the subjects.

The Camarillo Dynamic Assessment Scales (May, 1968; Dixon and May, 1968) were based on the Health-Sickness Rating Scale and nine other scales (each with nine points), six of which were adapted from the Menninger Psychotherapy Project. The Scales are (1) anxiety level; (2) extent to which environment suffers as a result of patient's illness; (3) ego strength; (4) insight; (5) motivation; (6) object relation. They added three others: (7) sense of personal identity; (8) affective contact; (9) sexual adjustment. These nine concepts reflected the research group's clinical judgment about what areas are significant for healthy functioning and vulnerable to the schizophrenic process.

In the scoring manual provided, five of the nine points are defined and four intermediate ones are not defined. Scales are dimensionalized in terms of increasing levels of "health." An average of all the scale scores (excluding sexual adjustment) provides a global estimate of "psychodynamic psychopathology."

Each record was rated by five raters, entirely from the following data: social worker's narrative history and background material and the psychiatric resident's history and mental status examination. The authors do not say how long a time was required to obtain this information, but they do say that the amount of information varied from case to case.

Ratings for the highest level the patient had ever reached and the level at the time of hospital admission were made, but we are not told how long these took. Also, rate-rerate data were provided by giving each rater the same 21 cases to rate in a different order, with a mean time of 110 days between first and second ratings, and a range of from 7 to 277 days. Reliability data are presented in considerable detail, including both inter-rater and rate-rerate reliabilities, and are quite good in both categories.

Bellak and Rosenberg (1966) published a drug study which employed a Global Ego Strength Scale with psychological and behavioral characteristics for each of seven ego functions (the ones put forth by Beres in his 1956 paper and elaborated upon by Bellak in his 1958 book). Each ego function was rated for amount and for appropriateness on the relevant characteristics specified for each function. Reliability data were included for subjects in the psychotropic drug study. The scale used for the Bellak and Rosenberg study is a forerunner of the ego function scales developed in the context of the study reported later in this book.

An important measurement approach relevant to ego function formulations is the work on cognitive styles and cognitive controls (G. Klein, 1951; Gardner et al., 1959; Gardner and Moriarty, 1968).

Klein and his colleagues have been concerned with individual differences. They have emphasized and experimentally demonstrated that consistencies are found in the style of functioning for a given person across various cognitive (ego) functions. Since an act of perception is also an act of attention deployment and memory formation, distinctions between these functions are seen to be somewhat arbitrary. Instead of focusing on these cognitive functions, Klein, Gardner, and associates have proposed various system principles (leveling-sharpening, tolerance for unrealistic experiences, equivalence range, focusing, constricted-flexible control and field-dependence-independence) as fruitful dimensions for describing consistencies in cognitive functioning (Gardner et al., 1959). The specific relevance of the cognitive-style cognitive-control approach to ego function assessment will be pointed out in various places further on.

A number of the authors who have offered lists of ego functions stated that it was not then possible to specify all the functions of the ego. Of course, the question of how many ego functions there are is not the same as the question of how many chemical elements there are in physical matter. The latter would qualify as a natural classification (Hempl, 1952, p. 53), whereas the former is an artificial classification. It is a question of finding a useful number of distinctions, enough to include what are considered the major dimensions as currently recognized. The problem is analogous to such problems as how many traits adequately describe human personality and how many defenses there are. Another consideration has been underscored by Nagera, whose contributions are discussed in the next section of this chapter. He points out that because man strives for adaptive solutions, "there is no limit to the potential number of ego functions . . . that can be created within the ego organization to deal with new problems" (1967, p. 98). Thus, how many ego functions there are is a matter of agreement among workers in the field about how many and what concepts seem necessary and sufficient to embrace what are currently understood as the major manifestations of ego functioning. Other relevant considerations are historical precedent, (i.e., beginning with those ego functions specified by Freud, Hartmann, etc.) and attempting to employ formulations congruent with clinical psychoanalytic material and also with direct observation and relevant experimental findings.

But even after taking these considerations into account, it is important to recognize the circularity or question-begging implications of the notion that the ego is defined by its functions. In a personal communication, Robert Holt states:

The formulation is question-begging, since the term "its" assumes that you already know what "it" is or at least which functions belong to it. I believe that Rubinstein is right when he comments that this amounts to a decision to classify functions in a certain way, and to call a *class* of functions *ego*. It is thus adjectival rather than nominal and so if you are going to take this tack toward a definition, you shouldn't speak of "the ego" as an agent or even as an entity.

Additional related issues are discussed in the section on characteristics of ego functions.

STRUCTURE, APPARATUS, AND FUNCTION

Considerable discussion of the issues of the merits of speaking of structure, apparatus, and function has appeared in the literature. It seems sufficient for the current context to summarize the major considerations. As already noted, it has been assumed that when Freud defined his three major structural divisions of the mind by their functions, he was following the manner in which physiological organ systems have been traditionally described. Hartmann, beginning with his 1939 monograph, frequently refers to ego apparatuses, while Rapaport emphasized the conception of structure in explaining the stability and characteristic style of manifestations of various mental functions for any given person. As Rapaport put it:

We know from biology, and from social studies also, that functions once established, structuralize, i.e., they form steady states which are resistive to change. In psychological life too, we find such automatized functions, which behave as structures (1953, p. 518).

Rapaport discussed many facets of mental structures. Two important formulations in addition to the one just cited are that mental structures are characterized by a slow rate of change (1957) and that they are hierarchically ordered, the level of the hierarchy on which they occur influencing the quality of the processes involved (Rapaport, 1950; Rapaport and Gill, 1959). Holt (1967) points out that Rapaport fails to specify what constitutes a slow rate of change. For Holt, the central characteristic of a psychological structure is its organization, that is, "an arrangement of parts in a pattern," although with no particular ordering and no specified length of persistence (p. 350 f.n.). One criterion for assessing the slow rate of change is implied by Lewis (1965) when he says that a mental structure is an ordered arrangement of elements sufficiently stable to allow predictability.

Sandler and Joffe (1966, 1967), following Hughlings Jackson's approach to brain function, emphasize that in the course of development, structures are not lost (except as a result of organic brain damage and some psychoses) but that new ones are superimposed on older ones and that the resulting, more complex organization includes, in addition to means of discharge and control, ways of inhibiting the older structures. This point will be taken up again in relation to regression of ego functions. Mental structures can be assessed in terms of the number of elements involved and the complexity of their organization and may refer to a sequential, as well as a simultaneous, relation between parts (Nagera, 1967).

The concept of mental structure has been used in different contexts (Holt, 1967) to refer to (1) ego, id, and superego (the macrostructures, as Gill [1963] had called them); (2) defenses, discharge thresholds, controls, and identification; and (3) specific mental contents, such as thoughts or percepts. The term "apparatus" has also been used in a number of different ways in the psychoanalytic literature, but both Hartmann and Rapaport appear to use "apparatus" and "structure" synonymously (Nagera, 1968). Hartmann had underscored the dependence of ego functioning on the nature, quality, and characteristics of physiological organ systems. Early in life, ego functions and specific physical organs are closely related and damage to the physical structures results in a typical and deviant ego organization (Nagera, 1968, p. 228). A number of studies illustrate this point: Nagera and Colonna's on the effects of blindness (1965), Goldfarb's on the deficiencies of somatic equipment in schizophrenic children (1961), and Bergman and Escalona's on early individual differences in stimulus barriers (1949), to mention a few.

Although mental apparatuses depend upon physiological processes, they can be differentiated in that the effects of mental apparatuses can be conceptualized as ideas, visual images, memories, and so on, while the effects of physiological processes reach awareness as pleasure-pain sensations and cannot readily be translated into the terms of mental functioning. Nagera summarizes this point as follows:

What raises visual perception from the level of primitive sensory impressions conveyed by the somatic organ to the sophisticated, invaluable process that we know as vision is the existence of the psychological ego apparatus of perception. By this I mean an intangible nonmaterial organization, with a functional structure of its own, which regulates its own activities and those of the multiple somatic structures it utilizes according to a well-established (though largely unknown) hierarchy of regulating principles and laws; a preordained set of processes that has structured itself slowly and gradually through development; a functional structuralization that has been learned, partly perhaps through trial and error (though not exclusively) and whose basic regulating principle during its organization (and perhaps afterwards as well) was its adaptive value, even its survival value (1968, p. 234).

Now, what about function? Beres (1965) holds that the basis of the structural theory is "the grouping of psychic functions according to their alignment in conflict and in adaptation (p. 60) and that "a psychology concerned with adaptation must be functional," that is, be concerned with the how of behavior and the why (to what end). Although functional approaches have been criticized as being teleological, Beres points out the importance of distinguishing attempts to set final causes from approaches that attempt to show how an observation fits in with a coherent hypothesis. Beres stresses the applicability of the functional approach to clinical observation and argues for greater emphasis on it in theory construction. While Beres has questioned whether mental function can be found without mental structure, Holt has cautioned that risks are involved in assuming that some specific structure underlies each specific function (footnote in Rubinstein, 1967, p. 74). Gill (1963) pointed out Freud's implicit distinction between an agency (structure) and the function it carries out, especially in Freud's discussion of censorship, resistance, and repression in *The Interpretation of Dreams* (1900) and in later writings. Gill believes that recognition of this distinction has been delayed in psychoanalytic theory as a result of failure to differentiate clearly between functioning that is regulated by a structure and that which is not (i.e., ad hoc psychic functioning). When ad hoc functioning has become habitual and regular, a structure with a fixed organization may be assumed to have been formed, so that, according to Gill, "neither the structure nor the function it regulates undergoes any change" (p. 113). He cites as an example the repeated discharge of primary-process material by displacement in a phobia: the structure here is a primary-process structure. Rapaport reasoned that such primary-process mechanisms as displacement, condensation, and substitution qualify as structures because, despite the rapid drive discharge they permit, discharge is slower than it would be without them (1960, p. 844, f.n.).

Sandler and Joffe (1965) distinguish structure and function in terms of patterns of organization: schemata, agencies, apparatuses, and mechanisms characterize the former, and activities and processes characterize the latter. While the attained level of structural organization is lost only as a result of organic brain changes and some psychotic developments, the mode of functioning can fluctuate considerably and readily.

Modell (1968) developed the idea that the same structure can underlie different functions at different times and that it is not necessary to postulate a change of structure with each change of function. Thus, an identification or a self-representation can have a different function depending upon whether at a given time gratification is being sought from the external or from the inner world. Weisman (1965) holds that structure, function, and operation differ in terms of polarity and viewpoint rather than in terms of qualitative absolutes. Structures refer to relatively fixed substantives; functions are systematic variations within these, and operations "are the final common acts of combined processes that exercise practical influence upon the world" (p. 45).

To summarize this section, ego functions are theoretical constructs derived from observation of behavior and from patients' accounts of their experience. They have a developmental history, depending partly upon the maturation of anatomical-physiological structures and processes early on, but less so as

maturation, development, and personality differentiation proceed. We agree with
Beres (1966) that the structural theory of psychoanalysis could just as
accurately be characterized as the functional theory. It also seems that the major
ego functions (reality testing, defenses, thinking) qualify as structures in that
they show a slow rate of change and involve an organization of elements and a
characteristic style of response.

CHARACTERISTICS OF EGO FUNCTIONS

We will now consider further questions that have been raised in connection with
defining the ego in terms of its functions. George Klein (1970) asks whether the
ego is an entity or a classification and reviews the various ways in which the ego
concept has been used. He points out that it has been conceptualized as a system
of self-regulation, with implied causal or process characteristics but without the
development of a model specifying the operational nature of the system. The
ego construct has also been used as though it were a classification of motives and
as a classification of functions as well. As a classification of functions, Klein
remarks that there is little in theory that clarifies what is to be included or what
the hierarchy among the functions should be. Also, different and sometimes
contradictory meanings of function found in the literature imply the notion of
phylogenetic utility for survival, individual motivational aims, nonmotivational
capacities such as perception or memory, and, finally, the notion of a capacity,
faculty, or apparatus (viz., organizing function of the ego).

Klein points to ambiguities in the conception of the relation between ego and
drive and in the conception of drive itself. He maintains that Freud broadened
the ego concept to avoid the necessity of either recasting his motivational theory
or changing the libido theory (for a similar view, see Apfelbaum, 1962). Klein
opts for abandoning attempts to conceptualize behavior (or mental functioning)
in terms such as homeostasis, equilibrium, cathexis, energy, and its modifica-
tions. He suggests using constructs that are simultaneously ego-drive structures,
and he cites Erikson's configurational conception of psychosexuality as an
example. We could add that Anna Freud's developmental lines (1963, 1965) are
likewise constructs that include both drive and ego aspects. Klein's suggestion
constitutes an alternative to the approach of ego, id, and superego functions and
their interrelationships.

Schafer (1970) contends that from the viewpoint of psychical reality (i.e.,
subjectively speaking), the ego functions may be seen as dynamic processes with
aims and influence and that changes in them can be understood in terms of how

close their aims are to instinctual ones and the kinds and extent of conflicts these aims involve. Schafer also points out the contrast between formulations from the outside, which tend to be favored when the focus is on adaptation and a natural-science approach, and formulations from the inside, where the focus is on subjective meanings and psychic reality. This point is central to all attempts to define ego functions in adaptational terms. Schafer also shows how Hartmann's work demonstrates the complexity and heterogeneity of ego functions and the difficulty in assigning events to only one psychic system (id, ego, or superego).

If the attempt is made to conceptualize an ego construct in terms of a number of functions, the following considerations are relevant. The various functions are abstractions, which do not qualify as categories in a strict sense because they do not refer to events that occupy a specifically circumscribed space (Yankelovich and Barrett, 1970, p. 381). It may be added that no psychological constructs or personality attributes merit the designation "categories" in this sense. Naming these constructs "functions" does not imply that one mental operation underlies each function. Ego function constructs may refer to mental contents, processes, or outcomes, and one sound basis for understanding and classification is in terms of the process involved, as Siegel (1969) has suggested for defense mechanisms. Outcomes are underscored when it is stated that a person manifests serious adaptive failure in a given area of ego functioning. The usefulness of such a statement is increased when there is a specification of relevant drives, superego factors, external circumstances, conflicts associated with the disturbance, and the extent of the ego function disruption. Ego functions may be discussed from all the metapsychological points of view.

Hartmann made some general statements about the characteristics of ego functions. Some of the major ones are as follows:

Ego function deficits are discrete rather than global (1950).

Ego functions can vary in the extent to which they are subject to regression and instinctualization (1955).

Ego functions need different degrees of neutralization for optimal functioning in different activities (1955).

Ego functions can cooperate or interfere with each other's functioning in the process of adaptation (1939).

The various ego functions have a rank order of biological purposiveness, and the particular order in a given person has much to do with his ego strength (1939).

Each of these general assumptions is in need of careful consideration, both with regard to how many and what kinds of qualifications limit its generality and with regard to the possibility of spelling out its implications and finding ways of assessing its correlates.

ADAPTATION AND EGO STRENGTH

The concepts of ego strength, ego weakness, and adaptation are most relevant to an understanding of ego functions and need to be considered. Some reference to psychological stress, characteristics of the external environment, and regression will be necessary to the discussion.

Nunberg, in his contribution to the 1938 symposium on ego strength, provided a comprehensive summary of the area. He stressed the level of synthetic functioning (reducing tensions, settling conflicts, reconciling contradictions, and mediating them) as central for ego strength or weakness. Other correlates of ego weakness included by Nunberg are oversensitivity to pain (unpleasure), high readiness to experience anxiety, proneness to develop guilt feelings, and the presence of neurotic or psychotic symptoms. Nunberg saw these factors as causes within the ego itself, while excessive strength of instincts and increased narcissism were labeled as causes of ego weakness emanating from the id. He recognized that factors that reflect ego strength, such as the capacity to expose oneself to danger while withstanding the anxiety, can also be indications of ego weakness (e.g., in a person with masochistic tendencies who seeks out danger and pain). Similarly, the synthetic function of the ego, the relatively unhampered operation of which is a main factor in ego strength, increases in paranoid conditions and in some cases of schizophrenia. Thus each of the factors that indicates ego strength in particular conditions may be correlated with ego weakness under other conditions. Nunberg assumed that weakness of the ego could result from different causes, such as developmental arrest with more or less strong fixations, persistence of infantile defensive methods, and physical factors including organic illness and exhaustion. While his criteria of ego strength and weakness would probably be considered generally valid today, Nunberg's focus was heavily on the intrapsychic situation, and he appears to have assumed that environmental adaptation is virtually defined by ego strength. Thus, he stated that the mastery of pain and the ability to endure tensions generally covers the meaning of adaptation to reality, since ego weakness or strength will influence one's reaction to the outer as well as to the inner world (p. 289).

Fenichel (1938) considered ego strength in relation to the external world, as well as in relation to id and superego and stated that a strong ego is able to make correct judgments about reality and carry out its intentions even when there are external obstacles. Zetzel pointed out (1963) that adaptive aspects of mental functioning are implicit in Freud's early writings and gradually became more integrated into the rest of his conceptions. A passage from *The Question of Lay Analysis* (1926) illustrates how important adaptation to the external environment was seen to be by Freud then: "A neurosis is thus the result of a conflict between the ego and the id, upon which the ego has embarked because, as careful investigation shows, it wishes at all costs to retain its adaptability in relation to the real external world" (pp. 203-204).

It nevertheless seems that up to, and including, the 1938 Nunberg and Fenichel papers, important implications of the adaptation issue had not been adequately explored in psychoanalytic theory. Hartmann (1939) stressed that adaptation involves a reciprocal relationship between organism and environment and is central for mental health. He granted that the concept of adaptation has various connotations and no precise definition in biology or psychoanalysis, nevertheless, it refers to the mastery of reality. Its hallmarks are productivity, ability to enjoy life, and an undisturbed mental equilibrium. The degree of adaptiveness can be determined only in relation to typical (i.e., average expectable) or atypical environmental situations. Hartmann pointed out that adaptation must be considered separately from its origins. This led him to the idea of change of function, a biological conception that he applied to psychological phenomena in a parallel way and to the concept of secondary autonomy that was developed in his later writings. While adaptation is influenced by constitution, external environment, and the organism's developmental phase, he stressed the importance of learning in human adaptation because of the long period of helplessness that human beings experience in infancy. A central and crucial aspect of man's adaptation is the social structure of his society, which specifies the adaptive potentialities of various behaviors by defining what functions are essential and useful. Superego factors are important in adaptation to the environment, especially as transmitters of values and traditions from one generation to the next.

Hartmann contrasts progressive and regressive attempts at adaptation. The former are the more well known, straightforward ones, the direction of which "coincides with that of development" (p. 36). Concerning the latter, he underscores the important notion that successful adaptation sometimes uses "pathways of regression" where the adaptive behavior is based on processes that are not intrinsically adaptive (i.e., fantasy) but may on occasion be detours to adaptation. This point is spelled out in Kris's notion of regression in the service of the ego. Hartmann further elaborated the complexities of the problem of adaptation in his paper on psychoanalysis and the concept of health (1939), showing the limitations of all the available criteria that analysts and others had employed to distinguish healthy from pathological states. In pointing out how successful adaptation may lead to maladaptive outcomes — as in the development of an overly-strong superego — Hartmann seems to be making the same point about adaptation that Nunberg had earlier made about ego strength. But he goes one step beyond Nunberg in stating that criteria for ego strength, such as the potential for achievement and enjoyment, can shed light on a person's capacity for adaptation only when his relationships with the external world have been assessed. Hartmann implies a close relationship between ego strength and adaptation in his statement that disturbances in mental harmony are often found in conjunction with disturbances in adaptation (1939, p. 17).

That a role in adaptation is played by the external environment as well as by personality structure is implied in Hartmann's (1947) statement that adaptations are appropriate for only a restricted range of situations and that an adaptation that is good in one set of circumstances may be unsuccessful in another. He also reemphasizes, however, the link between personality development and adaptation when he points out that psychoanalysis assumes adaptation in the adult is best in those who have attained the genital stage of libidinal development (p. 50).

With regard to Hartmann's emphasis on the importance of a society's social structure for the individual's adaptation, it can be asked what experiences the culture must provide to ensure optimal psychological development and environmental adaptation in its members. Developmental and maturational processes differ in the extent to which they are dependent upon specific experiences. Yankelovich and Barrett (1970) replace the notion of average expectable environment with the concept of dependency on experience. They hold that the issue is not what constitutes an average expectable environment but rather what particular experiences are needed for maturational potential to be realized (p. 329).

One author who has spelled out environmental requirements is Lois Murphy (1964), who specified seven basic adptational tasks that children in the United States are expected to have mastered by the age of three. She discusses cultural expectations for older children as well. While her paper includes an excellent summary of ego and drive development, in the present context it is her focus on environmental expectations and task requirements, such as what is demanded of the child in terms of ego and emotional development to enter school successfully, that we want to underscore.

Rosenwald (1968) emphasized that the adaptive point of view involves a change of focus from the central aspects of personality (unconscious instinctual factors that are least influenced by reality considerations) to the person's surface behavior, how it transforms external reality and is in turn, changed by it. This does not mean that adaptational is equated with behavioral, since the central (drive) factors are assumed to influence surface behavior, and are themselves seen as being subject to taming, modification, and individuation in part as a result of the organism's contact with external reality.

Sandler and Joffe (1969) maintain that adaptation is the superordinate metapsychological point of view, and includes adaptation not only to the external environment but also to inner forces and states. The most important of these inner states is the feeling of safety and well-being (Sandler, 1960) that results from smooth and integrated psychological functioning. The feeling of safety is not equated with energic and drive equilibrium, and a pleasure-producing activity that would decrease the feeling of safety may be inhibited on that account. These authors see the concept of autonomy as important for adaptation in that a high degree of autonomy provides the person with a greater number of opportunities for adaptive response. To autonomy from the drives (Hartmann) and from the environment (Rapaport), Joffe and Sandler (1968) add (relative) autonomy from superego introjects.

The adaptational point of view as used in Freudian egopsychology differs from Rado's adaptational psychodynamics in that Rado specifically rejects Freud's early work, especially his instinct theory (Zetzel, 1963). Zetzel points out that Rado's adaptational theory ignores drives (her paper includes an evaluation and critique of adaptational psychodynamics from the psychoanalytic point of view); Waelder similarly pointed out (1930) that Adler's theory concerned itself with attempted solutions of mastering the external world, while ignoring other relevant considerations, such as other drive and superego factors.

Phillips (1967) spelled out a number of dimensions relevant to adaptation, while stating that we do not yet have an adequate and comprehensive theory of human adaptation. He sees adaptation as the interaction of the person's achieved level of psychological development and the environmental support available (p. 7). Adaptive failure is most likely to occur when a relatively low level of psychological development is combined with a disorganization of the usual social milieu. He includes intellectual, social, and moral development under the rubric of psychological development, analyzing them in terms of social competence and societal expectations. He defines each of his major variables in terms of measurement scales and procedures, so that notions about the interrelationships of the variables can be assessed.

Psychological stress is another topic that is relevant to an understanding of ego functioning, ego strength, adaptation, and regression. In his formulation of ego strength Hartmann emphasized the ability of the autonomous ego functions to withstand impairment from defensive processes (1950, p. 140). Another way to formulate the issue is to assume that ego strength is reflected in ego function resistance to regressive impairment when the organism is faced with environmental stress. Only a few major aspects of psychological stress will be discussed; the topic has been well dealt with by Janis (1958), Bettelheim (1960), and Lazarus (1966), among others.

First, there are situations that are universally stressful. Loss, attack, restraint, and threats of these are emphasized by Levin (1966). Janis studied pre- and postoperative reactions to surgery, and found regressive effects in all the patients evaluated (1958). There were, however, large individual differences in patient reactions due both to constitutional factors and formative experiences and to specific situational factors and general environmental changes caused by hospitalization.

Personality factors can also play a crucial role in defining what is stressful for a given individual. Saul (1947) found that the World War II naval psychiatric casualties he examined and treated psychotherapeutically had developed symptoms in response to some generally stressful situations and not to others on the basis of their own specific emotional vulnerabilities, which in turn were related to nuclear emotional constellations developed in childhood.

Ego strength and weakness have proved to be fruitful psychoanalytic concepts. Their value is increased when they are considered in relation to adaptation, stress, and regression. Hartmann pointed out that the conception of ego weakness could be improved by a specification of which ego functions are being interfered with. While Hartmann's suggestion has gained wide acceptance, there does not appear to be adequate realization that not only is a detailed definition of what constitutes each ego function necessary to carry this out but also that the whole issue of the interrelationship of ego functions is involved.

REGRESSION, STABILITY, AND VARIABILITY OF EGO FUNCTIONING

Hartmann stated that ego functions differ in the degree to which they are subject to regression. As is true of many aspects of personality functioning, there is considerable stability in the level of ego functioning characteristic of a given individual. It is also true that the level of ego functioning varies more in some people than in others, and indeed the readiness with which fluctuations occur and their extent are important aspects of personality functioning. We shall summarize findings from studies that focus on three levels: transient lowering of some ego functions during psychoanalysis, severe regression during psychoanalysis, and the kinds of ego function deficits found in chronically psychotic persons. This summary will be followed by some consideration of the theory of ego regression.

A detailed report on temporary lowering of specific ego function levels in eight psychoanalytic patients has been published by members of the Kris Study Group from the New York Psychoanalytic Institute (Joseph, 1965). The report includes illustrations of disturbances in body image, perception, reality testing, time sense, distance judgment, and depersonalization observed during psychoanalytic sessions. In some of these cases, a number of ego functions were seen to be disturbed, but in others, only one function. The case material suggested to the authors, however, that lowering of the autonomous ego functions appeared to involve the ego's capacity to deal with all conflictual situations (pp. 92-93) and that even when the focus is on disturbance in one ego function, others are involved to some degree (p. 95).

In the cases included in the study, regression of the ego functions in question appeared to be precipitated by an anxiety-provoking situation, most frequently when a libidinal or aggressive wish had been stimulated and, once, by a superego command. Various kinds of anxiety (i.e., separation, castration) and a variety of defensive maneuvers were involved in bringing about the ego regressions. The general formulation here is that regressive alteration of ego functioning serves to decrease or minimize the development of anxiety, while also serving to discharge unconscious wishes from id and superego sources, such as to vent anger and to provoke punishment (Arlow and Brenner, 1964; Joseph, 1965).

In another formulation of the lowering of ego functioning introduced to fit the material from several cases, the lowering of the level of ego functioning is part of the reactivation of earlier ego states, in which the person may experience bodily sensations (and also memories, emotional reactions, and various ego function manifestations) similar to those he experienced at an earlier age in a conflictual or traumatic situation (Joseph, 1965, p. 96). The authors of this study suggest that a scale for the evaluation of ego regression would be useful. As already mentioned, Bellak had pointed out the value of an ego strength scale in 1952, and several such scales are currently available, some of them having been reviewed earlier in this chapter.

Interest in ego regression was spurred by reports in the literature of transference psychoses, that is, patients in psychoanalysis who were not known to be psychotic or borderline developed psychotic reactions during the treatment and within the transference relationship. The issue was discussed in an American Psychoanalytic Association panel on severe regressive states. In his presentation, Wallerstein (1967) reported finding six studies in the psychoanalytic literature. Parenthetically, the phenomenon of psychotic transference (displacement of psychotic symptoms into the psychotherapeutic situation) has been reported in many psychoanalytically oriented studies of the psychotherapy of psychotic individuals. Those six cases of transference psychosis found by Wallerstein were all transitory, most lasting a day or two, a few persisting for several weeks or several months. Formulations for understanding these cases were reviewed by Frosch (1967) and other panel members who also offered formulations of their own.

Romm (1959) had demonstrated that the severity of early traumatic experiences and the person's age and degree of ego weakness at the time of occurrence influence both the type and severity of regression during analysis. Reider (1957) proposed that temporary manifestations of transference psychosis were reenactments either of a childhood psychosis or of a previous identification with a psychotic person. Holtzman and Ekstein (1959) showed how a temporary psychosis reflected both the patient's attempt to solve a conflict from the past and his reliving of it in the present. One explanation proposed for the regression is that it is an attempt to master the earlier, dynamically similar situation.

In his summary of the panel on severe regressive states, Frosch noted that the ego function disturbances were similar to those regularly found in psychoses and allied conditions. The various bases for the regression, such as defensive reactions to a threatening transference situation, secondary gain, and attempts at belated mastery, were seen in relation to preexisting ego defects, for which Frosch found evidence in most of the cases discussed and which were assumed to provide the predisposition for the severe regression.

Concerning the stability and regression of ego functions in manifestly psychotic individuals, as opposed to the cases just reviewed, Freeman, Cameron, and McGhie (1966) provide much relevant material based on psychoanalytically sophisticated observations and case descriptions of hospitalized patients who are not in psychoanalytic treatment. They recorded patients' subjective experiences along with descriptions of the status of various ego functions and object relations. These authors find that in cognitive disorders perception, attention, and thinking may regress to different levels, that there may be substantial day-to-day differences in the degree of regression, and that the disorder can be manifested in different forms. While the depth of regression is one factor that affects the possibility of reversing the cognitive disorganization, other factors are also involved. The authors refer to Schilder's idea that organic impairment results in permanent loss of function, while psychological factors can also cause impairment, which, however, may be nullified if these factors become inoperative. However, as Schilder pointed out (1928), reversal of disorganization cannot always be taken as such an indicator of psychological causation, since observation reveals that psychological factors can temporarily reverse symptoms with an organic etiology: for instance, the speech difficulties of postencephalitics may improve when they are emotionally aroused.

Freeman, Cameron, and McGhie state that the shifts between disorganized thinking and normal cognition from one interview to another that they have observed many times are not easily explained on the basis of defense against anxiety. Granting that there is always the possibility that anxiety is responsible for the regression, these authors suggest that while the change in the level of cognitive function may have been initiated by interpersonal contact, no specific aim may be involved as is the case with a neurotic symptom. The complexity of regressive phenomena is illustrated in the Freeman, Cameron, and McGhie study, which demonstrates the importance of detailing the specific characteristics of the regressed ego functions – for example, whether a disturbance of attention is the result of passive assimilation replacing active attending or the result of a disorganization of the attention process. With regard to object relations (and transference), it is important to distinguish whether the patient's reaction to another person is an organized one or whether he is reacting in a diffusely emotional way.

One requirement here is that the processes underlying the ego function manifestations be analyzed, as Siegel (1969) had suggested for defenses. Twenty-five years ago Rapaport, Gill, and Schafer introduced process formulations in their approach to psychological test evaluation (1946). They showed how the same thought product can be arrived at by different routes, some of which are more efficient and adaptive than others. Thus, obsessive rumination may be employed when judgment is required, memory may be relied upon when the ability to conceptualize is decreased, and logic may be used to shore up defective memory functioning. A focus on the processes underlying ego function manifestations leads to aspects of the interrelationship of these functions, as well as to the issue of the relationships between drives, superego factors, and ego functions.

SUMMARY AND COMMENT

Freud defined the ego by its functions, and this approach has been widely accepted by psychoanalysts. Even so, there is no definitive answer to the question of how many ego functions there are; that is a matter of agreement among workers in the field on the basis of historical precedent, congruence of concepts and psychoanalytic observations, and a need to define criteria that are necessary and sufficient to characterize recognized, major dimensions of ego functioning.

Ego functions are theoretical constructs based on observations of behavior and on patients' reports of their experiences. Those behaviors and experiences to which ego function concepts refer are initially influenced to an important extent by anatomical and physiological structures and processes, less so as maturation, development, and personality differentiation proceed. Specific hereditary and experiential factors influence ego function manifestations, and the general outlines of ego function development are similar to those of drive development.

From a methodological standpoint, an attempt to define the ego by its functions involves a number of difficulties, including that of circularity. Moreover, the ego construct has been used in different and contradictory ways in the literature. Because of these difficulties, it has been suggested that ego-drive constructs (such as Erikson's modalities or Anna Freud's developmental lines) be used instead. The most widely held position is that it is fruitful to attempt to define the ego construct in terms of a number of functions that refer (among other things) to adaptively relevant actions and reactions of the individual person. Just how fruitful this approach will turn out to be depends in part on finding scientifically acceptable ways to specify the processes involved and to define relevant ego, drive, superego, and environmental variables.

Ego regressions have been studied less than drive regressions, but a number of formulations have appeared in the literature, ranging from very general to very specific. To summarize some clinical observations, ego regressions vary in depth and discreteness and in persistence. They are influenced by the degree of psychopathology, the status of defenses, nature of basic danger situations, character structure, and ego defects, the latter developing in response to a number of factors (probably including congenital ego weaknesses) and being associated with a range of disturbances. Formulations concerning the degree and kind of relationships possible between ego and drive regressions also vary, from the idea that they are quite separate to the idea that they are always related.

Part II
THE 12 EGO FUNCTIONS OF OUR STUDY

CHAPTER 5

General Considerations and Rationale for the Selection of the 12 Ego Functions

A degree of choice is always exercised when phenomena are categorized. As we pointed out in the last chapter, the number of ego functions is a matter of general agreement as to what concepts appear necessary and sufficient to encompass the data under consideration. We began with the seven ego functions proposed by Beres (1956) and elaborated by Bellak (1958a), which had been the basis for the Global Ego Strength Scale developed in a previous study on psychotropic medication (Bellak & Rosenberg, 1966). The scale includes psychological and behavioral characteristics relevant to each ego function, and these were rated on a six-point "amount" scale ranging from none to extensive, as well as on a six-point appropriateness scale. While this scale has been useful in the study of medication, we decided to revise it radically for the current schizophrenia research. It appeared that more-detailed descriptions would be necessary to insure adequate rater reliability. In addition, we decided to list the main component factors relevant to each ego function. Finally, we chose to dimensionalize each ego function in terms of the relative adaptive-maladaptive implications of the behavioral and other psychological manifestations relevant to it. Such an approach is in line with our interest in assessing ego strengths and the adequacy of ego functioning in the major areas germane to it; it allows a comparison of reality testing, for example, in a person who reports auditory hallucinations with someone who does not but who is subject to mild inaccuracies in perception. This handles the problem of comparing individuals who have symptoms such as hallucinations with people who do not, since many such symptoms are discontinuous (i.e., either present or absent). Wynne (1967) has underscored the discontinuity of symptoms as a difficulty in schizophrenia research.

Despite these advantages of dimensionalizing ego functions on an adaptive-maladaptive basis, we recognize that there are philosophical, moral, cultural, and logical problems that underlie this approach and the whole question of the definition of psychological health. We pointed out some of the complexities of ego strength-weakness and adaptation-maladaptation in the previous chapter. Jahoda (1958) and Offer and Sabshin (1966) have dealt in detail with problems in defining mental health and normality. In a paper on "The Discriminating

Function of the Ego" (to which we refer in the chapter on synthetic-integrative functioning), Hacker (1962) points out that certain forms of character disturbance illustrate that "a considerable, even extreme, degree of psychopathology is quite compatible with good and even excellent functioning maintained over long periods of time, or indefinitely."

These considerations emphasize the point that we are dimensionalizing according to degree of adaptiveness (and of ego progression-regression) as a tentative empirical-theoretical approach that does not presume to have solved the underlying problems inherent in the concepts of ego strength, adaptation, and mental health.

In addition, we decided on an ordinal scale that behaviors representing successive levels of adaptation would define. As we pointed out earlier (Bellak and Hurvich, 1969), there are other ways to measure ego functions. An example is a paired-comparison approach as was used in the psychotherapy-research project of the Menninger Foundation, in which two patients at a time were evaluated as to which one had the more adequate reality testing, judgment, and so on.* Each approach has both advantages and disadvantages.

While the paired-comparison approach is less subject to the halo effects and other rater biases, our ordinal point scale is more economical in terms of rating time and also allows one subject to be evaluated without having to compare him directly with a whole group of other subjects.

From the function relation to reality (one of the 7 discussed by Beres and elaborated by Bellak), we removed the subfunction of adaptation to reality, because, as already noted, we decided to dimensionalize all ego functions on this basis. We also developed separate scales for reality testing and sense of reality and added adaptive regression in the service of the ego (ARISE) and stimulus barrier. This totaled 10 functions, which we used in our early work (Hurvich and Bellak, 1968; Bellak, Hurvich, Silvan, and Jacobs, 1968). Soon after, we gave judgment a separate status (for reasons discussed in the chapter by that name) and later added mastery-competence. Having included the latter, we reflected that it was close to adaptation to reality (which we had earlier removed); but we felt this function added something unique to the list, justifying inclusion. This brought the number of functions up to a dozen.

As in the selection of ego functions, choice was exercised in the formulation and grouping of the various component factors. One of the considerations affecting the formulations was the degree of overlap of the functions. Inclusion of any particular component factor under more than one ego function was avoided, although interrelationship and some overlap of functions was assumed. Some behavioral manifestations would be pertinent to more than one function,

*This fact was called to our attention by Dr. Robert Wallerstein in a discussion of an earlier version of the above paper.

such as an hallucination. Reality testing, thought processes, defensive functioning, and autonomous functioning would all be affected but not necessarily to the same extent. We discuss interrelationships of ego functions in a separate chapter.

In selecting phenomena relevant to each ego function, we formulated general propositions about each function and then worked out what appeared to be major subfunctions, which we called component factors. Below is a listing of the component factors as used in this study. The *Manual for Rating Ego Functions from a Clinical Interview* includes an expansion and revision of component factors based on our experience in the study.

EGO FUNCTIONS AND COMPONENT FACTORS

1. Reality testing
   A. Distinction between inner and outer stimuli.
   B. Accuracy of perception and interpretation of external events including orientation to time and place.
   C. Accuracy of perception and interpretation of internal events. Includes reflective awareness or extent to which person is aware of accuracy or distortions of inner reality.
2. Judgment
   A. Anticipation of probable consequences of intended behavior (e.g., anticipating dangers, legal culpabilities, social censure, disapproval or inappropriateness, and physical harm).
   B. Extent to which manifest behavior reflects the awareness of its probable consequences, and the extent to which behavior expressing maladaptive judgment is repeated.
   C. Appropriateness of behavior, or extent to which person is able to attune himself emotionally to relevant aspects of external reality.
3. Sense of reality of the world and of the self
   A. Extent of derealization and related altered state of consciousness. The extent to which external events are experienced as real and as embedded in a familiar context.
   B. Extent of depersonalization and related altered states of consciousness. The extent to which the body (or parts of it) and its functioning and one's behavior are experienced as familiar and unobtrusive and as belonging to (or emanating from) subject.
   C. The degree to which subject has developed individuality, uniqueness, a sense of self, a stable body image, and self-esteem.
   D. The degree to which subject's self-representations are distinguished from object representations; that is, the extent to which other people are distinguished as independent entities and the extent to which subject

correctly ascribes which qualities are self-representative and which belong to others. Stated in another way, the extent to which ego boundaries between the self and the outside world are clearly demarcated.

4. Regulation and control of drives, affects, and impulses
   A. The directness of impulse expression, ranging from primitive and psychopathic acting out, through the activity of the impulse-ridden character, through neurotic acting out, to relatively indirect forms of behavioral expression. Maladaptiveness would be a function of the extent to which awareness of drive, affect, and impulse are experienced and expressed disruptively.
   B. The effectiveness of delay and control mechanisms (including both under- and overcontrol); the degree of frustration tolerance and the extent to which drive derivatives are channeled through ideation, affective expression, and manifest behavior.

5. Object relations
   A. The degree and kind of relatedness to others (taking account of narcissism, symbiosis, separation-individuation, withdrawal trends, egocentricity, narcissistic object choice or extent of mutuality, reciprocity, empathy, ease of communication); degree of closeness or distance and the degree of flexibility and choice in maintaining object relations.
   B. Primitivity-maturity of object relations, including the extent to which present relationships are adaptively or maladaptively influenced by, or patterned upon, older ones.
   C. The extent to which the person perceives and responds to others as independent entities rather than as extensions of himself.
   D. The extent to which he can maintain object constancy, that is, can sustain both the physical absence of the object and the presence of frustration or anxiety related to the object; degree and kind of internalization (the way subject perceives and responds to people who are not physically present).

6. Thought processes
   A. Degree of adaptiveness in memory, concentration, and attention.
   B. The ability to conceptualize. The extent to which abstract and concrete modes of thinking are appropriate to the situation.
   C. The extent to which language and communication reflect primary or secondary process thinking.

7. Adaptive regression in the service of the ego (ARISE).
   A. First phase of an oscillating process: degree of relaxation of perceptual and conceptual acuity with corresponding increase in ego awareness of previously preconscious and unconscious contents and the extent to which these "regressions" disrupt adaptation or are uncontrolled.

B. Extent of controlled use of primary process thinking in the induction of new configurations. Extent of increase in adaptive potential as a result of creative integrations produced by ultimately controlled and secondary process use of regressions.

8. Defensive functioning
   A. Extent to which defense mechanisms, character defenses, and other defensive functioning have maladaptively affected ideation, behavior, and the adaptive level of other ego functions.
   B. Extent to which defenses have succeeded or failed: for example, degree of emergence of anxiety, depression, and/or other dysphoric affects.

9. Stimulus barrier
   A. Threshold for, sensitivity to, or registration of, external and internal stimuli impinging upon various sensory modalities (corresponds to "receptive function").
   B. Degree of adaptation, organization, and integration of responses to various levels of sensory stimulation; the effectiveness of "coping mechanisms" in relation to degree of sensory stimulation, whether observed in motor behavior, affective response, or cognition.

10. Autonomous functioning
    A. Degree of freedom from impairment of apparatuses of primary autonomy (attention, concentration, memory, learning, perception, motor function, intention).
    B. Degree of freedom from impairment of secondary autonomy (disturbances in habit patterns, learned complex skills, work routines, hobbies, and interests).

11. Synthetic-integrative functioning
    A. Degree of reconciliation or integration of discrepant or potentially incongruent (contradictory) attitudes, values, affects, behavior, and self-representations (e.g., role conflicts).
    B. Degree of active relating together (i.e., integrating) of both intrapsychic and behavioral events. These events may or may not be conflict-ridden and are not necessarily limited to behavior.

12. Mastery-competence
    A. Competence, or how well the person actually performs in relation to his existing capacity to interact with and actively master and affect his environment.
    B. The subjective role, or subject's feeling of competence with respect to actively mastering and affecting his environment: subject's expectations of success on actual performance (how he feels about how he does and what he can do). Sense of competence is scored at face value: for example, higher than actual competence if there is an exaggerated sense of competence.

C. The degree of discrepancy between component A and component B: that is, between actual competence and sense of competence. It may be negative (-: actual competence exceeds sense of competence); it may be equal (=: actual competence and sense of competence are congruent); it may be positive (+: sense of competence exceeds actual competence, as in a grandiose, exaggerated sense of competence compared with performance).

In the chapters included in this section, we will review the literature on each of the 12 ego functions just listed. While much has been written about each of them, it is scattered and unsystematized, and reviews aimed at a detailed consideration of all of these functions have not previously appeared in one place. We hope this material will be of use to clinicians, researchers, and students. We have begun each chapter with a review of Freud's major statements on the topic; this is not meant to imply that Freud was the first to consider reality testing, judgment, and so on, but any review of these topics in a psychoanalytic framework logically begins with Freud, who had important things to say about all of them. We have not covered all the relevant papers and books in the psychoanalytic literature and may have missed some important contributions despite efforts to the contrary. We have mostly limited the reviews to work in the Freudian psychoanalytic tradition, and this inevitably results in some valuable contributions by neo-Freudians; Sullivanians; and followers of Horney, Rado, and others being omitted. The limitation was based primarily on practical considerations of time and space.

CHAPTER 6

*Reality Testing**

In this chapter we shall discuss Freud's major ideas about reality testing and then consider each of the component aspects of reality testing in detail. This will be followed by some notions regarding external reality and a few additional issues relevant to the understanding and study of reality testing.

FREUD'S MAJOR STATEMENTS ON REALITY TESTING

In the "Project for a Scientific Psychology" (1895), Freud was already concerned with the problem of how perceptions and ideas are distinguished. He concluded that the primary processes cannot make a distinction between perception and idea but that such a distinction becomes possible when they are inhibited from discharge by the secondary processes (pp. 324-327). In discussing the function of wishes, Freud (1900) assumed that in early life the infant who is hungry makes an hallucinatory attempt to reevoke an image of the need gratification previously experienced but that when this effort fails to result in satisfaction, the organism then is obliged to "seek out other paths which lead eventually to the desired perceptual identity being established from the direction of the external world" (p. 566).

Fantasy activity was early seen by Freud as antithetical to reality thinking. Thus, Breuer and Freud (1895) underscored daydreaming as one of the main activities that could lead to hypnoid states, which were assumed (particularly by Breuer) to be a necessary precondition for hysterical symptom development (p. 13). In his analysis of Jensen's *Gradiva* (1907), Freud characterized a delusion as a pathological state in which "fantasies have gained the upper hand—that is, have obtained belief and have acquired an influence on action" (p. 45). The next year Freud described fantasies as extensions of children's play and akin to dreams, built from wishes that depict possibilities not present in reality (1908). It was the problem of distinguishing conscious fantasies from memories of actual events (confessions of early childhood seductions that he found to be false) that led

*An earlier version of this chapter, by Marvin Hurvich, was published in *The International Journal of Psycho-analysis*, 51, 1970, and in *Psyche*, 26, 1972.

Freud to appreciate the importance of psychic reality in human psychology (1897, letter 69; 1914, pp. 17-18).

Freud amplified the concept of reality testing considerably in "Formulations on the Two Principles of Mental Functioning"(1911). After designating attention as the function of consciousness capable of meeting perceptions ("sense impressions") halfway by searching the external world and memory as the notational system for preserving a record of these perceptions, he assigned judgment a central role in reality testing, stating that an "impartial passing of judgment" was necessary to determine whether a given idea was consistent with reality by comparing it with memory traces of reality (p. 221).

In "Instincts and Their Vicissitudes" (1915), Freud provided a criterion for distinguishing internal from external stimuli originating outside the organism— namely, that external stimuli could be avoided by muscular action (i.e., flight), while drive (internal) stimuli could not. In "A Metapsychological Supplement to the Theory of Dreams" (1917), he placed reality testing among the major institutions of the ego and focused on its mechanics, in part by examining how it is that in both dreams and psychotic hallucinations the distinction between perceptions and ideas is not made. He concluded that reality testing need involve nothing more than that the system Pcpt.-Cs. have the opportunity to assess whether motor activity results in a disappearance of the impression (p. 233). Reality testing was seen as being put out of action when the ego withdrew cathexes from the "system of perceptions, thus allowing wishful fantasies access to consciousness, as in states of hallucinatory confusion" (p. 233). This explanation is similar to, and consistent with, Freud's view of withdrawal of cathexes from the system Cs. during sleep.

Reality testing was briefly attributed to the ego-ideal in 1921 (p. 114), but in *The Ego and the Id,* published two years later, Freud stated in a footnote that it is best seen as a task of the ego (p. 28).

In "Negation" (1925) Freud reiterated that reality testing consists of judgment being employed to rediscover in external reality that which corresponds to something previously perceived. The aspect of reality testing that can be designated as accuracy of perception is also discussed here:

Another capacity of the power of thinking offers a further contribution to the differentiation between what is subjective and what is objective. The reproduction of a perception as a presentation is not always a faithful one; it may be modified by omissions, or changed by the merging of various elements. In that case, reality testing has also to ascertain how far such distortions go (p. 238).

In *Civilization and Its Discontents* (1930) Freud again summarized his view of the mechanism of reality testing as a learned procedure of deliberate direction of attention and suitable motor action for the differentiation of internal from external. He referred, in his papers "Neurosis and Psychosis" (1924) and "The

Loss of Reality in Neurosis and Psychosis" (1924), to the ego detaching itself from the external world (p. 153), and he raised the question of what mechanism (analogous to repression) could bring about this cathectic withdrawal. In the latter paper, he stressed the loss of reality (p. 187).

We can identify three interrelated processes, or subfunctions, that summarize Freud's meaning of reality testing as discussed in the papers here reviewed. These are (1) the distinction between ideas and perceptions (1895), (2) the decision as to whether an idea was based on a memory-trace of reality (i.e., external perception) (1911, 1925), and (3) accuracy of perception (1925). Other mechanisms, processes, and functions involved in reality testing, and explicitly mentioned by Freud, are secondary process, or inhibition of immediate discharge (1895); attention (1911); memory (1911, 1925); and judgment (1911). From a genetic standpoint, Freud posited that reality testing could come about if the organism had the opportunity to determine whether an impression could be made to disappear following motor activity (1915, 1917, 1930).

COMPONENT ASPECTS OF REALITY TESTING

Balint (1942) distinguished four aspects of the process of reality testing: (1) the decision whether stimulation originates within or outside the organism, (2) drawing inferences from the stimuli or sensations about what is causing them, (3) discovering the stimuli's significance, and (4) finding "the correct reaction to the perceived sensations" (p. 211). He illustrated this scheme by classifying psychopathological conditions in relation to it. Thus, an incorrect decision or solution at step 1 would result in hallucinations; at step 2 ("faulty object formation"), in melancholia; at step 3 (ascribing an incorrect meaning), in phobias and paranoia; and at step 4 (incorrect reaction), in hysteria, obsessional, and anxiety neuroses (p. 213).

A review of Rapaport's writings reveals an interlocking and overlapping of reality testing, reflective awareness, and judgment. Reflective awareness (i.e., the awareness of being aware) plays a central role in reality testing, according to Rapaport. "It [i.e., reflective awareness] seems to be a subspecies of the function that distinguishes imagery from hallucination and percept, thought from reality" (1951, p. 302, n. 56). (We shall return to the relationship between reality testing and judgment in the next chapter.) In Rapaport's view, the safeguarding of reality testing once the motor differentiation of internal and external has been accomplished depends on the development of memory frames of reference (with conceptual, spatial, and temporal dimensions), which replace the drive organization of memories (1950, p. 32).

Rubinfine includes in reality testing the attributes pleasant versus unpleasant, veridical versus imaginary, inner versus outer, and purely memorial versus recoverable in reality (1961, p. 80). He points out that the distinction between inner and outer is more difficult when external perceptions are not available and when motility is restricted (the latter because motor movement will affect the perception of an outer event but not of an inner event). He cites sensory isolation studies as demonstration of the effect of perceptual (and sensory) restriction in the blurring of inner and outer spheres.

Weiss (1950) summarized relevant factors involved in the apprehension of external reality and its testing, in terms of direct perception (seeing, hearing, touching, tasting, smelling); indirect perception (information and facts about reality from parents, school, books); thinking (i.e., logical conclusions from direct perceptions or from memories); and experimentation and testing to affirm or refute the reality status of data (such as the origin of a sound heard in a dark room where one believes he is alone).

Linn's (1954) description of what he calls the discriminating function of the ego details what probably happens in the process of reality testing. In the perception of a stimulus, there is a focus on a group or cluster of related ideations, then a scanning of the cluster for the element or memory that most closely matches the external stimulus, the correct selection then possibly being accompanied by a feeling of recognition. If the cluster is scanned incompletely, primary process manifestations emerge (wish fulfillments, condensations, displacements) and errors in evaluating reality. This description is similar in many respects to the one advanced by Rapaport, Gill, and Schafer (1946) for the coming about of a Rorschach response (Vol. II, pp. 92-94). Linn further hypothesized that those units of the cluster that can result in the greatest pleasure are scanned first; then those likely to arouse the least pleasure; and last, those associated with anxiety, the latter not being scanned at all when the anxiety potential is high. The scanning is usually preconscious, Linn contends. Schafer (1968) points out that while they are ordinarily automatic and preconscious, various aspects of the reality testing process enter awareness under stressful or ambiguous circumstances when the person asks himself such questions as "Is it real, or did I only imagine it?"

Schafer (1968) sees reality testing as involving varying degrees of the processes of perceiving, feeling, remembering, anticipating, forming concepts, reasoning, paying attention, concentrating, and the directing of interest to internal events and the external world. For Schafer, the crucial factor in the maintenance of adequate reality testing is a self-awareness variable he terms reflective self-representation: the awareness by the person that he is the thinker of the thought. When such awareness is not present, there is no basis for distinguishing between a thought and the concrete reality to which it refers, resulting in a drop in the level of reality testing.

Modell (1968) concludes that the perceptual distortion in psychotics is usually a distorted perception of other people's feeling states. He believes that the need to disavow painful perceptions is the key factor in decreased reality testing and that the function is not lost in psychotics and borderlines but remains intact alongside the distortions.*

Frosch has proposed the concept of reality constancy, described by him as "a psychic structure which arises in conjunction with the establishment of stabilized internal representations of the environment" (1966, pp. 349-350). He sees reality constancy as genetically dependent on, and growing out of, libidinal object constancy, although more inclusive than the latter and in some instances relatively independent of it. Reality constancy develops in mutual interdependence with the ego functions of perception, delay, anticipation, intentionality, predictablity, and especially reality testing (p. 361).

Hartmann holds that different layers of reality testing can be distinguished and that these may be differentially affected or interfered with (1953, p. 201). He described the basic layer as the capacity to distinguish ideas from perceptions. Another layer or aspect is where perceptions are recognized as such, but an idiosyncratic (and objectively incorrect) meaning is attached to them. An additional facet is the presence (or elimination) of "subjective elements in judgments meant to be objective" (p. 201), or the ability to differentiate between what one believes to be so, and what one can objectively verify to be so (Rapaport, 1957, vol. IV, p. 255). Delusions would be one extreme outcome of this tendency. These last two "layers" appear to be related to the accuracy of perception. Still another aspect of reality testing was specified by Hartmann in 1953, namely, inner reality testing.

We shall now discuss some aspects of these major component factors of reality testing: the distinction between ideas and perceptions, the accuracy of perception, and inner reality testing.

Distinction between Ideas and Perceptions

The ability to distinguish between ideas and perceptions is most adversely affected in psychotic states and conditions. In his analysis of Schreber's psychotic delusions Freud (1911) hypothesized that when repression of instinctual derivatives occurred, there was a complete detachment of the libidinal cathexis from the external world and a withdrawal of the libido into the self, which was then used for "the aggrandizement of the ego" (p. 72). He further assumed that following the break with reality, delusions (and hallucinations) constitute an attempt to reestablish contact with the environment or external objects by reinvesting libido in them once more. These assumptions concerning the development of delusions and hallucinations have been questioned. Federn held that the withdrawal from reality followed, rather than preceded, the development of delusions and/or hallucinations (1948, p. 187).

---

*Freud expressed a similar idea (1940, pp. 201-202).

And Waelder (1960) did not find a breakdown in the sense of reality adequately explained by libidinal withdrawal from objects to the self and consequent overevaluation of the latter (pp. 207-208). In a later section, we summarize how Waelder sees such factors as leading to less severe inaccuracies of perception than are found in psychoses.

Hartmann, on the other hand, believes that the libido withdrawal described by Freud is correlated with reality loss but that it is not only because of the reattachment or hypercathexis of the libido to the ego (either the ego functions or the self) but also because ego functions (including reality testing), self-representations, and object-directed ego cathexes become flooded with nonneutralized libido (1953, p. 193).* Mahler is also in agreement with Freud that libidinal withdrawal from the human object world is the crucial factor in a psychotic break with reality (1968, p. 64).

Arlow and Brenner (1964) hold that Freud's later writings provide a more accurate and fruitful basis for understanding the loss of distinction between ideas and perceptions than the earlier notion of detachment of libido from objects and withdrawal to the ego or self. They maintain that while such disturbances in reality testing are multiply determined, they are most often brought about to decrease anxiety (i.e., for defensive reasons).

Frosch (1967) makes the additional point that a major reason for the persistence of a delusion is that the basic danger situation against which a psychotic person defends himself with the delusions is a feared disintegration and dissolution of the personality. In neurosis, the focal danger situation typically involves the instinctual drives, with defenses being arrayed against fears of separation, castration, and/or superego punishment.

From the standpoint of the structural theory, one could argue that reality testing might be interfered with from id, superego, or other ego function sources. The first alternate is exemplified by perceptions being distorted from unconscious wishes and/or fears, the second occurs when situations are misperceived as a result of (externally) unjustified anticipation of blame or punishment, and the third could be illustrated by defensive denial that an external event actually took place.**

Freud primarily emphasized the necessity of distinguishing between ideas and perceptions, but this formula can be expanded to include the distinction between images and perceptions, so as to account for visual hallucinations. Even

---

*Hartmann assumed that a defect in the ability to neutralize *aggression* is especially important in the predisposition to psychosis.

**In a recent paper, Arlow develops the position that the interaction between perception and unconscious fantasy determines the way reality is experienced. He holds that unconscious fantasy thinking is the strongest distorting factor on perception (1969). Beres, (1960) on the other hand, emphasized positive aspects of the relationships between fantasy and reality perception, and that the two processes are not basically antagonistic.

more comprehensive is the distinction between internal and external. But as Schafer has recently pointed out (1968), the term "internal" is ambiguous since it could include items within or outside the subjective self. He distinguishes three kinds of subjective self for clarification: the self as agent ("I"), the self as object ("me"), and the self as place (p. 80). With regard to external objects, the distinction between animate and inanimate is important in early childhood (Mahler, 1968). It will be recalled that Freud hypothesized the distinction between inside and outside the body to be based originally on the ability to avoid external stimuli, but not internal stimuli, by motor activity. Shevrin and Toussieng (1965) point out, however, that the infant cannot regularly get away from auditory stimuli and, on the other hand, can remove an internal stimulus by the muscular activity of defecation (p. 316). And Schafer (1968) reminds us that the image of the drive object, the main representative of instinctual tension in early infancy, cannot be escaped by motor activity, so that motor activity by itself is not an adequate basis for the inner-outer distinction.

Garma (1969) takes similar considerations into account and concludes that external perceptions are the ones the organism judges to be outside because they cannot be readily controlled, while endogenous perceptions are understood to be internal because they can be more readily handled.

There is general agreement among psychoanalytic writers that the distinction between self and not-self develops gradually and that at first the infant does not distinguish between his own sensations and the objects with which they are associated (such as positive feelings brought about by the mother's ministrations). Fusion and refusion of self images and object images or representations continually take place in early childhood and conscious fantasies of merging with love objects up to the age of three are considered by analysts to be normal (Jacobson, 1964, p. 41). This has been hypothesized to be caused by utilization of introjective and projective mechanisms whereby the self images take on attributes of object images and vice versa. The boundaries between self and object representations gradually become stronger, and both kinds of representations are progressively based more on perceptual and self perceptive data (i.e., on reality testing). The introjection of object images into self images or the projection of self images into object images in the adult characterize psychotic identifications (Jacobson, 1964, p. 47).

Developmentally, the two objects seen to play a central role in the process of self-external differentiation are the infant's own body and the mothering person (Provence and Ritvo, 1961). Freud had pointed out the body's importance in developing one's sense of self (1923), while Hoffer stressed the hand and mouth in this same process (1949, 1950) and Greenacre emphasized the importance of vision (1960). Defects in the inner-outer differentiation during early life have been attributed to insufficiently repeated experiences of timely relief of tensions by an outside source and/or the buildup of too much pain and distress. These findings are consistent with Mahler's contention that outwardly directed attention (the earliest manifestations being the periods of alert inactivity described by Wolff, 1966) gradually replaces inwardly directed attention when the prior symbiotic mother-infant relationship has been optimally pleasurable (1968, p. 16).

Provence and Ritvo (1961) demonstrated that institutionally-reared infants (who received adequate care but not the usual mothering of the home-raised infant) manifested a different response to inanimate objects than did the control home-reared infants. They showed less exploratory interest in toys, failure to search for a toy moved out of sight (Piaget's studies show normal children of this age will so search), and failure to develop an attachment to a specific toy, unlike the home-reared children who did develop such attachments.

Genetic psychologists have also focused on factors associated with the inner-outer distinction. Werner (1948) showed how mental development proceeds from syncretic (nondifferentiated), diffuse, indefinite, rigid, and labile functioning to more discrete, articulated, definite, flexible, and stable functioning. In primitive mental functioning (where Werner convincingly demonstrated formal parallels among higher animals, human children, primitive peoples, and schizophrenic and brain-damaged human adults) objects in the external environment are not apprehended as things with separate, fixed characteristics. Rather, objects tend to be understood in relation to their emotional and motor connection with the perceiver, animistic qualities are often imputed to inanimate objects, and there is an inability to distinguish separate parts or to discriminate between essential and nonessential characteristics.

While Werner spelled out the general principles of mental development, Piaget studied the evolution of thinking and intelligence in children, and systematized his observations into a theory of stages of intellectual development. How the human organism apprehends and deals with external reality constitutes a central aspect of Piaget's work. In the first stage of sensorimotor development (approximately the first month of life) evidence points to external objects having no separate existence for the infant, while in the third stage delineated by Piaget (approximately the fifth to the eighth month) the infant will visually follow a moving external object until it is out of sight. Active search for an object that has already gone out of sight heralds the fourth stage (roughly the eighth to the twelfth month), while recognition of the independent existence of an object (the twelfth to the sixteenth month) characterizes the fifth stage. When there is evidence for an ideational representation of the object that is independent of the organism's action orientation in relation to it, the sixth stage of sensorimotor development has been reached (sixteenth to eighteenth month) (Piaget, 1937; Wolff 1960; Décarie, 1965). The developing notions of space, object, and causality are traced in detail and reflect the general manner in which the individual's conceptions of external reality evolve.

Décarie (1965) attempted to compare the attainment of the object concept in Piaget's sense with the development of the libidinal object. To index the latter, she evolved empirical criteria ranging from indicators that the infant recognized the feeding situation through differential smiling, ability to delay crying when the mother disappeared, signs of affection such as returning a kiss or hug initiated by the mother, compliance with requests and prohibitions, and the ability to discriminate communicative signs intended to surprise from signs of disapproval. To assess the stages of object-concept development described by Piaget, she adapted techniques for evaluating the kinds of active search carried out by her young subjects for a vanished object. The criterion Décarie used to indicate that the object concept has been attained (and thus maintains its existence for the child when it is no longer perceptually present) is when the subject searches for a vanished object behind several screens even when he did not see the last placement of the object. This accomplishment ordinarily occurs at about 18 months and heralds the end of the development of sensorimotor intelligence, which, Piaget has pointed out, allows the utilization of deduction. The descriptions of the attainment of object constancy in the psychoanalytic sense (Hartmann, 1952, p. 173) appear roughly to coincide with Piaget's stage of object attainment. Décarie found (from her 90 subjects, aged 3 to 20 months, living in institutions, with adopted parents, or with real parents) that mental age was the most important factor underlying the attainment of the object concept in Piaget's sense, after which came the child's environment (i.e., whether raised in an orphanage or by real parents). The next most important factor was the level of libidinal-object attainment (as defined by the tasks summarized above). This reflects a substantial relationship between the conceptions of Piaget and of psychoanalytic investigators, but some disagreements remain as to the time when object permanence is assumed to occur.*

Accuracy of Perception

Accurate perception depends in part on the capacity to distinguish internal from external. Some universal sources of inaccurate perception are a replacement of reality by fantasy (Hartmann, 1939, p. 18); ideas that have strong value for the person (Hartmann, 1947, p. 48); prejudice, preconceived ideas (Waelder, 1949); apperceptive distortions, or the impingement of past images on current perception (Bellak, 1950b, pp. 11-12); and a combination of subjective emotional reactions, primitive affective identifications, and projections (Jacobson, 1964, p. 22). Hartmann's concepts of agglutination and irradiation of values (1947) cover two related ways in which reality testing is universally

---

*The disagreement over time of appearance may be clarified by a distinction between the relatively enduring mental representation (Piaget) and the less stable mental image that perhaps characterizes early libidinal-object constancy (Sandler & Rosenblatt, 1962).

impaired. Regarding the first notion, Hartmann writes that when a particular behavioral item is positively (or negatively) valued, there is a tendency to associate other positively (or negatively) valued items with it. This results in an interference with insight into the "structure of reality," because the common factor underlying their connection will be the person's positive (or negative) regard rather than the "real" connections (p. 47).* The irradiation notion reflects a converse connection between facts and values. Here, when an element is positively valued, other elements connected with it (in whatever way) are likely to become positively valued also. The term "halo effect" is frequently applied to such phenomena.

Weiss (1950) points out that in the early years it is normal for a child to take over many ideas about reality from his parents. Some early-acquired notions, because they become associated with feelings of security, are not changed or corrected by later-developed reality testing. He also noted that the more complicated or indirect the reality verification of a particular notion, the more likely it is that emotional factors will interfere with reality testing.

Prejudice is an ubiquitous phenomenon and sets a universal ceiling on the accuracy of reality testing. Waelder (1949) includes in the meaning of this term both unprovoked antagonism against groups and the presence of preconceived opinions. Among the contributory causes of group antagonism that may be considered universal, Waelder cites fear of strangers, competition (for any goal that all cannot equally attain), envy, and cultural difference, such as religious or political beliefs and moral-ethical values. He believes that tolerance (which would mean the absence of a distortion in reality testing vis-à-vis other people) is possible only when differences of attitudes do not entail issues fundamental for a given person or where the person does not hold a strong conviction. To quote Waelder, "If we hold any fundamental values dear, we will not countenance what would spell their undoing." Even when basic value differences are not present, antagonisms between individuals frequently develop over small differences, and distortions of some aspects of the other person follow. With regard to preconceived ideas as a basis for prejudice (and, for our focus, distortions in reality testing), Waelder cites such mechanisms as failure to differentiate between frequently found characteristics of a group (or even attributes of some in the group) and those of any particular group member. Another factor, found to some extent in everyone, is "the will to believe" — that is, the tendency for emotional factors such as love and hate to interfere with judgment.

Nunberg (1951) points out how in transference phenomena during psychoanalysis, as well as in everyday life, current situations serve as the stimulus for the revival of repressed ideas or emotions, which then result in inaccurate

---

*Rapaport made a comparable point and illustrated it in great detail in *Emotions and Memory* (1942).

perception of the current situation and engender attempts to mold the current situation to fit the earlier one (p. 3).

Now we turn to a consideration of what Hartmann has termed inner reality testing.

Inner Reality Testing

Hartmann discussed this notion a number of times (1947, pp. 64-66; 1953, pp. 200-202; 1956, pp. 264-267). By inner reality he specified the awareness of inner conflicts (1947, p. 65), cognizance of the inner world, and awareness of instinctual demands (1953, p. 202). He refers to "the restriction of inner-reality testing" as "withdrawal from insight" (1956, p. 266). Hartmann refers to superego factors being involved here. Distortions of inner reality are referred to as "typical and individual self deception" (1956, p. 266). By inner reality, then, Hartmann seems to mean awareness of mental phenomena capable of becoming conscious, such as motivational aspects of one's momentary behavior; affective reactions to, and feeling about, his own behavior; his emotional reactions; the behavior and characteristics of other people; his picture of himself; and his conception of how others view him. It could perhaps be summarized as insight, psychological-mindedness, and awareness of inner states. Inner reality testing, then, would include awareness of these inner states, and an accurate appraisal of them.

Rapaport distinguished between the inner world and the internal world (1957, p. 696). The former he characterized as one's inner map of the external world, while the internal world is composed of the major structures of the psychic apparatus: identifications, defense structures, ego, id, and so on.* Rapaport sees the relation between the two as perhaps being crucial for an understanding of the self (p. 697). Reflective awareness, which Rapaport repeatedly underscored as a central factor in that aspect of reality testing involving the distinction between perceptions and ideas (1951, p. 302, n. 56), may also be seen as a fruitful construct for unifying and clarifying the meaning of inner reality testing. The following passage provides a sample of the kinds of distinctions Rapaport included under the concept:

It seems to be a sub-species of the function that distinguishes imagery from hallucination and percept, thought from reality. The following are some form-variables of reflective awareness: ideation without specific awareness, ideation with awareness, awareness with awareness that one is aware, etc. Though the role in reality testing of some forms of reflective awareness is well

*The notion of a representational world as formulated by Sandler and Rosenblatt (1962), encompasses the person's schema of both the external and the internal environments, and is a valuable construct for a wide range of phenomena, including, central aspects of reality testing.

known, neither its phenomenology nor its dynamic role have so far been systematically studied. Ego-syntonic and ego-alien obsessional ideas provide an opportunity for such study. It seems probable that differences in the quality (and intensity?) of such reflective awareness will prove crucial in differentiating between various states of consciousness (1951, p. 302, n. 56).*

Frosch (1966) includes in inner reality memories, fantasies, impulses, desires, affects, thoughts, the body image, identity, self-representations, and somatic sensations (pain, heart rhythm).† Freud devoted a short section of *An Outline of Psycho-Analysis* (1940) to "The Inner World," where he discussed various implications of the superego and explained how, through identification with partly abandoned objects, some of what was previously in the external world becomes a part of the internal world (p. 205).

Yet another aspect of inner reality has been designated by Hartmann as value testing, by which he means the assessment of the authenticity of one's moral values in relation to "the psychological background of his acts of moral valuation" (1960). He also pointed out how moral value judgments, an aspect of superego functioning, may lead to reality distortions (p. 50). Jacobson (1964) noted that the overidealism and illusions of children and adolescents gradually give way to more reasonable goals, increased moral tolerance, and more mature moral judgment as a result of the evolving capacity to test inner and outer reality more accurately (p. 130).

Significant aspects of inner reality testing involve self-observation and self-evaluation, the latter especially being associated with superego functioning. Freud (1933) listed self-observation as one function of the superego (p. 66). Defects in self-observation are held to result in impaired reality testing (Waelder, 1936; Stein, 1966), and both ego and superego components are operative in self-observation. An example of how superego factors can interfere with reality testing is Freud's own momentary incredulity when first in Athens over the reality of the Acropolis, which he attributed to the sense of guilt related to excelling his father (1936).

EXTERNAL REALITY

Questions about the nature of external reality and how man can apprehend it have occupied philosophers for centuries. One version of the issue is the mind-body-problem, and thinkers have often been classified according to their

*Rapaport credits Schilder with refining the concept of reality testing by his knowledge of varieties of conscious experience as a result of his applications of Brentano's "act psychology" concepts to psychiatric conditions (Rapaport, in Schilder, 1953, p. 352).
†Mason (1961) gives detailed consideration to noncognitive aspects of internal perception or inner experience.

preferred solution: for example, monism, dualism, psychophysical parallelism, and so on. We summarize here some ideas about reality held by psychoanalysts to emphasize that the concept of reality testing depends in part on developing conceptions of external reality that are more detailed and sophisticated.

The importance of the reality concept in psychoanalysis can be gauged from a look at what Rapport judged to be the main contributions of progressive phases of psychoanalytic egopsychology. In the first phase (which he dated from Freud's earliest writings through 1897) the role assigned to external reality is seen as second in importance only to the concept of defense. In the next phase (1897-1923) Rapaport lists the reality principle along with the conceptions of secondary process and the analysis of repression as Freud's leading additions to egopsychology. The third phase (1923-1937) sees the reintroduction of external reality as a central concern, while the crucial role of instinctual drives remains. The fourth phase (1937 to the present) includes for the first time, in the work of Hartmann, the outline of a "generalized theory of reality relations." Regarding the psychoanalytic conception of external reality, Rapaport (1959) paraphrased Freud's 1915 position: "Reality in psychoanalytic theory designates the external source of stimuli, including the subject's body, but excepting the somatic sources of drives and affects . . ."

A rather extreme position regarding reality was spelled out by Dorsey (1943). He stated that psychic reality is the only reality we can know, and that "all observation is self-observation, all consciousness is self-consciousness" (p. 148). Zilboorg (1941) also stressed that reality is an unknowable, that human beings always function somewhere between animism and realism, and that one's sense (view) of reality is a combination of veridical perceptions, nihilistic and animistic qualities, plus fantasy projections into the image of reality (p. 197).

Hartmann accorded an important place to external reality in his writings. Numerous discussions of the external environment are included in his 1939 monograph, which played a central role in changing the focus of psychoanalytic theorizing from psychic reality to the reciprocal relationship between organism and environment via ego functioning and adaptation (i.e., reality mastery). He held that the adaptiveness of the organism could be evaluated only in relation to environmental conditions ("average expectable" or atypical, p. 23) and that the structure of society is a co-determiner of the adaptive potential of given behavioral forms (p. 31). In his later paper on "Psychoanalysis and Sociology" (1944), Hartmann discussed the importance of cultural factors in the development of central, as well as superficial, personality characteristics (p. 25 f.n.). He noted that the relation between an individual and his society can be discussed in terms of what effects the system exerts on a given structure of society and what social functions the system requires of the person. Hartmann stressed that psychoanalysis had always been centrally concerned with interpersonal relations and, in that respect, with an important aspect of the external environment.

Discussions involving reality are found in most of Hartmann's papers, although the characteristics of "external reality" are nowhere spelled out.

Loewald (1951) developed the position that reality has been conceptualized in psychoanalytic theory primarily as hostile and threatening to the organism. He holds that a second view of reality to be found in Freud's writings, but never integrated with the above, issues from the developmental conception of the ego, in which, during early stages, ego and external reality are not yet differentiated by the organism. Rather than conceiving of reality as a static entity "out there," Loewald sees the development of ego-reality relationships as a dynamic, interactive process in which a stable external reality is possible for a given individual only in conjunction with the achievement of a given level of ego development.* Indeed, when defensive processes result in a regression of psychic processes, reality also regresses, in the sense that it becomes less objective for the individual.

Erikson expressed the opinion that psychoanalytic conceptions of reality have been "often half-hearted and ambiguous" (1962, p. 452) and have failed to take account of important aspects of ego strength. He chooses to focus on what he considers to be one of the more obscure implications of the psychoanalytic concept of reality. This he calls actuality, "the world verified only in the ego's immersion in action" (p. 453). By this he means that the subjective reality of a given person depends on a number of factors, such as his developmental level and various cultural considerations. His distinction between reality and actuality is expressed as follows: "Reality, then. . .is the world of phenomenal experience, perceived with a minimum of idiosyncratic distortion and with a maximum of joint validation, while actuality is the world of participation, shared with a minimum of defensive maneuvers and a maximum of mutual activation."

The degree of structure of a stimulus situation (external environment) has long been found to influence the level of reality testing. Mayman (1964), for example, points out how the Rorschach ink blots invite a relaxation of reality-testing standards, which some people purposely accept, others are unable to resist, and some rigid individuals strongly reject (p. 4). Many psychological laboratory experiments have demonstrated that perceptual accuracy varies in part as a function of stimulus clarity. Macalpine (1950) has observed that the particular characteristics of the psychoanalytic situation tend to enhance the development of regressive functioning and transference reactions.

R.W. White (1963) emphasized the centrality of the consequences of one's actions in the process of reality testing and adaptation. In his words, "Knowledge of the environment is a consequence of action. It is a knowledge of the effects that can be produced by action" (p. 46-47). One implication of this emphasis on the action dimension is that participation in a wide range of

*A similar view has been expressed by Fenichel (1937, p. 29).

experiences provides the basis for a more differentiated and accurate reality-testing function (in the absence of pathological mitigating factors). It also tacitly points to the importance of the external environment, the knowledge about which may increase the adaptiveness of reality testing. In their discussion of accurate form perceptions on the Rorschach ink blots, Rapaport, Gill, and Schafer (1946) refer to the importance of (native) endowment, wealth of past experience, and the rapid availability of appropriate associative material (p. 193).

Holzman and Klein (1956) have expressed the issue of reality testing and the external environment in this way: "An adequate theory of reality testing must be based on a conception of what an object is, how it is registered as a percept, and how more general aspects of personality, such as motives, enter into this process of registration" (p. 183).

Sociologists have had much to say about the nature of reality, one aspect of which we consider here. It is the tendency of various kinds of groups (political, social, economic, and religious) to uphold the validity and "reality" of particular ideas and values which on close examination turn out to favor the political, social, economic, or other interests of the group members. The writings of Marx and Nietzsche especially include examples of this notion. It is in the work of Karl Mannheim (1936) that the most comprehensive treatment is given to what is called the sociology of knowledge, that is, how human thought and conceptions of reality are influenced by the social context in which these arise. Mannheim focused particularly on ideologies, that is, the dominant systems of ideas that are consistent with various dominant group structures and interests in given historical periods:

"Whereas the assertion (to cite the simplest case) that twice two equals four gives no clue as to when, where, and by whom it was formulated, it is always possible in the case of a work in the social sciences to say whether it was inspired by the "historical school," or "positivism" or "Marxism," and from what stage in the development of each of these it dates. In assertions of this sort, we may speak of an "infiltration of the social position" of the investigator into the results of his study and of the "situational-relativity" or the relationship of these assertions to the underlying reality (1936, p. 272).

Mannheim went beyond pointing out that an individual's personal interests are reflected in his thoughts, values, and ideologies, by finding specific connections between particular interest groups in society, and both the ideas and the ways of thinking found in those groups:

In analysing the mentality of a period of a given stratum in society, the sociology of knowledge concerns itself not merely with the ideas and modes of thinking that happen to flourish, but with the whole social setting in which this occurs. This must necessarily take account of the factors that are responsible for the acceptance or the rejection of certain ideas by certain groups in society, and of the motives and interests, that prompt these ideas and to disseminate them among wider sections (Worth, in Mannheim, vol. XXVIII, 1936).

In his study of *The True Believer*, Hoffer (1951) shows the common elements in all mass movements and how they engender fanaticism, which, we may add, always entails a decrease in aspects of reality testing.

Mannheim's emphasis was on ideas (i.e., the theoretical formulations of reality). Later workers have broadened the scope of the sociology of knowledge to include "commonsense knowledge" (Berger and Luckman, 1966). Berger and Luckman emphasize that one of the most important "realities" for human beings is the socially shared network of temporal and spatial events of "everyday life." They go on to analyze the institutions of a given society, which although constructed by men, tend to be experienced as an objective reality. They point out, as did Mannheim, how various social definitions of reality serve the function of maintaining the status quo and, we may add, will influence an individual's knowledge of reality and his reality testing in any society.

That an evaluation of reality testing must take into account the cultural and scientific context in which the person lives is demonstrated in Wulf Sach's (1937) account of the life of John Chavafambira, whom Sachs, an analyst trained in Europe, considered to be normal. Yet, he was described by Sachs as having a primitive notion of cause and effect, believed that most diseases (and insanity) were caused by poisoning from afar, and held many other ideas based on witchcraft.

Thus, knowledge about reality testing is enhanced when more is known about the external situation. In addition, understanding of reality testing can be increased through further study of the processes and functions on which reality testing is based, especially attention. For example, it has been found that schizophrenics whose symptoms prominently include delusions (and thus poor reality testing) differ in the amount of scanning behavior characterizing their attention response patterns from schizophrenics in whom delusions are not prominent. It has also been found that schizophrenic patients who appear to be withdrawn from their surroundings and apparently directing attention away from the environment are actually engaged in minimal scanning (i.e., anchoring attention on dominant objects in the stimulus field) and/or in a global or poorly articulated attending to sensory input (Silverman, 1964).

Finally, individual differences in attention deployment underscore the more general finding that consistencies for a given person obtain across perceptual, memorial, and conceptual spheres (Gardner, et al., 1959) and that it is possible to study reality testing in a given person in terms of his particular reality-contact style (Holzman and Klein, 1956).

CHAPTER 7

Judgment

"During World War II, at the beginning of the AAF Aviation Psychology Research Program, pilot instructors were consulted as to what they thought were the reasons why 1,000 students failed in learning to fly. The most frequent reason given was 'poor judgment,' When further enlightenment was sought as to what the instructors meant by poor judgment, however, it was found that they might be referring to anything from errors in judging distances to errors in choice of flight pattern. This should have been a hint of the fact that judgment is not any one thing. As so often happens, it is a term that covers a variety of things" (J. P. Guilford, 1967, p. 185).

Judging, in the sense of discriminating, is a central aspect of all secondary-process thinking. Judgment, as the term is used clinically, depends not only upon the ability to discriminate but also on anticipation and appropriateness. Good judgment is, therefore, not guaranteed by generally adequate thought functioning, and similarly, poor judgment can be found in the absence of a classical thought disorder, where neither dissociation, deviant verbalization, nor arbitrary or circumstantial reasoning are present (Weiner, 1966, p. 116).

In this chapter we shall review Freud's and other thinkers' statements about judgment, compare judgment and reality testing, and review some ways in which the term has been employed in philosophy, psychiatry, and psychology. Finally, we shall discuss anticipation, appropriateness, and disturbances in good judgment.

Judgment was discussed by Freud a number of times in his early systematizing effort, *Project for a Scientific Psychology* (1895). Strachey points out (S.E. I, p. 327) that in this work Freud used "judgment" and "cognition" virtually interchangeably, distinguishing between these, on the one side, and "reproductive thought" (which includes remembering, wishing, desiring and expecting), on the other. Freud defines "judgment" (1895, p. 328) as a process involving inhibition of the ego when wishful cathexis of a memory is compared with the related perceptual cathexis. He repeated this formulation in his 1925 paper on "Negation" in terms of a "refinding" through perception of an object corresponding to the given memory image, underscoring the relationship between judgment and reality testing. Freud also discussed sources of error in judgment: mistakes in one's premises, errors resulting from perception of a situation having been incomplete because aspects of the situation were unavailable to perception, and finally, errors due to insufficient or deflected attention during perception (p. 384).

Freud (1900) held that the function of judgment does not operate in dreams. Apparent judgmental activity in dreams does not result from the dreamwork he said, but rather has been taken from predream thoughts (p. 445). Various kinds of judgments (criticism, ridicule, or derision) are represented in dreams by absurd elements or situations in the manifest content.

In *Jokes and Their Relation to the Unconscious* (1905), Freud stated that there is probably no process resembling judgment in unconscious thinking. Rather than being rejected on the basis of judgment, something is repressed. Repression is characterized here as an intermediate step between a defensive reflex and a negative judgment.

In "Formulations on the Two Principles of Mental Functioning" (1911), Freud discussed how in mental development an impartial passing of judgment as to whether an idea is true or false (i.e., in agreement with reality) replaces the repression of those ideas that produce pain (anxiety). This judgmental decision is made, Freud said, by comparing the ideas with memory traces of reality. A few years later (1915), he again described rejection of an impulse based on judgment as a more advanced mechanism for dealing with instinctual impulses than flight or repression.

In "Negation" (1925), Freud discussed the meaning and origin of judgment, repeating the idea that a negative judgment is an intellectual substitute for repression. Judgment involves two kinds of decisions: one is affirming or denying that something has a particular property; the other is deciding whether a particular image exists in reality.

As to the psychological origins of the first mentioned aspect of judgment, Freud described the most primitive stage as the assessing of objects by putting them into one's mouth. The judgment was whether to eat it or to spit it out, take it inside or put it outside oneself. He had earlier in his papers on metapsychology (1915) described the stage of development in which the organism attempts to take inside itself everything that is good and to keep out whatever is bad. This then results in the equation of what is bad with what is outside the organism.

The second aspect of judgment — deciding whether a given image exists in reality—involves not whether to take in an external object but whether a referent for an image can be located (rediscovered) in the external world. This is the reality-testing function and requires a concern with reality as well as with pleasure considerations.

Freud thus had relatively little to say about judgment directly. Rapaport stated (Schilder, 1953, p. 351) that although Freud made judgment a central aspect of reality testing, he did not specify the formal characteristics of what he meant by the term.

Schilder (1931) held that judgment is the basic form of thinking, a conception which is similar to Freud's in the "Project." Schilder went on to say that judgment has to do with cognition of relationships between events, the goal being to attain "knowledge of a state of affairs." He pointed out the importance of affective and motivational factors in judgment: for example, one must be interested in objects for judgments to take place. He explained clinical manifestations of poor judgment of a kind found especially in paresis and senile psychoses as resulting from a failure to apply corrections (self-criticisms) to registrations and reproductions which normal persons apply. "All thought-processes end with awareness of the truth or falseness of the thought" (p. 560): Here Schilder is underscoring reflective awareness, which plays an important role in judgment and in reality testing. This brings us to the question of the relationships between judgment and reality testing.

JUDGMENT AND REALITY TESTING

As already mentioned, Freud considered an impartial passing of judgment to be an aspect of reality testing. Perhaps because of this many psychoanalysts have subsumed judgment under reality testing. Relationships between the two can certainly be found. In practice, the behavior of persons with organic brain syndromes is often described as reflecting "poor judgment," while similar behavior in persons suffering from functional psychoses and neuroses is described in terms of "poor reality testing" (Rapaport, Gill, and Schafer, 1946).

Rapaport hypothesized a close connection between, and overlapping of, reality testing, judgment, and reflective awareness, as we mentioned in the previous chapter. As part of his discussion of judgment in his notes to Freud's paper on "Negation," Rapaport (1951, p. 344) pointed out that while the original function of judgment concerned the differentiation between "me" and "not me" (which centrally relates to reality testing), the function of judgment can also differentiate varieties of conscious experience, such as the experiencing of ideas as dreams, percepts, memories, possibilities, or assumptions; as true or false; or as certain or uncertain. The latter are characteristics Rapaport attributed to reflective awareness (p. 702).

Reality testing and judgment are also related in that good judgment depends upon good reality testing. If any of the major components of reality testing is not functioning adaptively, judgment is likely to be secondarily affected. In a later section, we shall discuss a range of factors associated with poor judgment.

Despite these relationships and the fact that some aspects of judging (in the sense of deciding and discriminating) are often used in testing reality, we believe it is useful to evaluate judgment separately from reality testing. This is because anticipation and appropriateness play central roles in judgment as used clinically and in relation to psychopathology. While anticipation and appropriateness are also relevant to reality testing, they do go beyond distinguishing inner from outer, and beyond determining the accuracy of external and internal perception. Both anticipation and appropriateness will be discussed further on.

SOME USAGES OF THE CONCEPT OF JUDGMENT IN PHILOSOPHY, PSYCHIATRY, AND PSYCHOLOGY

In classical philosophy, judgment referred to (1) a quality of mind, (2) a faculty of mind, and (3) an act of mind. The last of these was discussed primarily in terms of propositions and logic; the notion of judgment as a quality of mind has been relevant to what we ordinarily mean when we say that a person shows sound (or poor) judgment.

Aristotle and Aquinas both held that practical wisdom or prudence was based on the mental qualities of deliberateness, judgment, and decisiveness. While these could occur separately, a prudent man was seen as possessing all three. Kant believed judgment to be one of the three faculties of cognition, along with understanding and reason, and thought that judgment is a bridge between the other two. Of the three primary faculties of mind, knowledge, pleasure-pain, and desire, Kant believed judgment functioned primarily with respect to the latter two.

Good judgment has also been frequently discussed as an aspect of prudence. Neither education nor learning is central but rather what the person has learned from experience. Aristotle distinguished between practical and scientific knowledge and stated that the former takes longer to acquire, because it depends upon experience with many particulars. But practical wisdom is difficult to communicate by precept or rule. Some noteworthy attempts are the Book of Ecclesiastes, many proverbs, and the advice given by Polonius to Laertes in *Hamlet*. Aristotle also concluded that prudence involves deliberation, a kind of thinking about variable and contingent factors that belongs to the realm of opinion.

In psychiatry, judgment has been assessed in the usual mental-status examination by an appraisal of a patient's awareness of his difficulties (and especially his "insight" into the reasons for his being in the hospital), indications of how well he plans things, and his "common sense."

Bleuler (1924) defined judgment in terms of associations acquired through experience. He distinguished between judgment in the logical sense—"the form in which cognitions are thought and expressed"—and the capacity to judge as it is used in psychiatry and jurisprudence, where the focus is on the ability to draw correct conclusions from the data of experience. The importance of emotional factors in the impairment of judgment is emphasized by Henderson and Gillespie in their widely used *Textbook of Psychiatry* (1950). While they hold that any interference with the associative processes can impair judgment, they put more emphasis on affective sources, distinguishing these from other kinds of interference, such as toxins, organic lesions, and congentially defective organization. We may add that of the physiological factors capable of affecting judgment, alcoholic toxicosis and drug-induced effects are the most common.

The concept of judgment is also important to forensic psychiatry and is implied in many legal definitions of insanity. For example, the McNaughton rule holds that it must be shown that at the time of the criminal act the accused did not know the nature and quality of the act; or, if he knew it, he was not cognizant that it was wrong. And the Vermont rule is concerned with whether the person lacks the capacity to appreciate the criminality of his conduct or to conduct himself in conformity with the requirements of the law (Roche, 1965).

In experimental psychology, judgment of weight, length, brightness, loudness, and others was early studied. The goal was to assess relationships between external stimuli and mental processes and to quantify psychological attributes or dimensions. This kind of endeavor was named psychophysics by Fechner, and various methods were worked out for studying and measuring the results. In all these procedures, judgments (of magnitudes and of just noticeable differences, etc.) were central. Judgment in this sense has to do with comparisons and discriminations between sensory stimuli. Various kinds of common errors of judgment were found, such as the time error (tendency to judge the first of two equal stimuli as greater because it was presented first), space errors (such as those commonly known as optical illusions), and these errors were studied in great detail. Aesthetic judgments were also studied and attempts were made to distinguish between those percepts that involve judgments and those that do not.

Judgment has also been used to designate the ability to assess what other people are like. Allport devoted a chapter to this topic in his classic work, *Personality* (1937). Clinical judgment, both as a process per se and as an aspect of human assessment, has also received considerable attention, including works focused on judgment of characteristics of good psychologists (Kelly and Fiske, 1951) and psychiatrists (Holt and Luborsky, 1958), referred to earlier.

An example of a study that assays clinical and social judgment from different points of view is that of Bieri and his associates (1966). These authors employ and explore the relevance of information theory, anchoring effects, the person's cognitive organization, and situational, structural, and affective factors. Their focus is on the problem of discriminability.

They distinguish the categorical viewpoint which requires the matching of discrete aspects of a stimulus within an ideal stimulus from the dimensional approach (in which judgments of stimulus magnitude on a continuum of intensity are made). Both processes are said to occur in clinical and social judgment. With regard to information theory, they focus on those aspects of input (stimulus) and output (response) systems that affect the judge's ability to discriminate among the stimuli available to him. Individual differences in the complexity of cognitive structures were found to be associated with individual differences in judgment.

The authors note that situational factors have usually been neglected in the psychological literature on judgment and that the nature of the situation in which judgments are made should be included in conceptualizations of processes of judgment.

Guilford (1967), in his comprehensive book *The Nature of Human Intelligence,* lists evaluative abilities as aspects of intelligence that have been neglected in the literature on intelligence functioning, despite Binet's belief that critical judgment was an important ability and despite the inclusion of a component labeled "Common Sense" in the carefully constructed and widely employed World War I Army Alpha Examination.

From factor analytic statistical studies of judgment (evaluation), Guilford defines "evaluation" as "a process of comparing a product of information according to logical criteria, making a decision concerning criterion satisfaction" (p. 185). The term "logical criteria" was included because tests were more likely to be valid measures of evaluative abilities when they emphasized identity, similarity, and consistency as criteria. While aesthetic and ethical criteria may also be important in judgment, factor analytic studies are not available to verify this possibility. As with the other major operations in his model of intelligence, Guilford analyzes evaluation in terms of units, classes, relations, systems, transformations, and implications.

We next consider the function of anticipation, which plays an important role in judgment.

ANTICIPATION

Philosophers have long identified the man of good judgment and prudence as one who has a high degree of foresight, a characteristic less dependent upon rational power than on memory and imagination, the ability to project past experience into the future. In experimental psychology, such concepts as mental set, determining tendencies, and *Einstellung* are all closely related to anticipation. These concepts provided a basis for understanding the continuity of ordered thinking being based on selective anticipation rather than on association of ideas based upon previous spatial or temporal contiguity (Rapaport, 1942).

Vigilance is another related concept that has been used in biology and comparative psychology. Animals respond to slight changes in their immediate environment with a vigilant attitude, which has the adaptive significance of allowing the organism to be ready for fight or flight.

The notion of anticipation in Freud's writings will be found primarily in his second theory of anxiety (1926), in which it is a central mechanism.* But the idea of a signal function of the ego, which is a kind of anticipation mechanism, can be found in earlier works of Freud. In the "Project for a Scientific Psychology" (1895), Freud spoke of a signal to the ego to set defenses in operation to restrict the generation of painful experiences (sec. 6, pt. II). The restriction of affect in thought activity to an amount sufficient for a signal is mentioned in *The Interpretation of Dreams* (1900, p. 602), and the signal function is applied to anxiety in Freud's paper on "The Unconscious" (1915, p. 183) and in *Introductory Lectures* (1916). (See also Strachey, Editor's Introduction to Freud, 1926.)**

The centrality of anticipation for anxiety is stated in "Inhibitions, Symptoms and Anxiety." (Supplementary remarks on anxiety." "Anxiety has an unmistakable relation to *expectation;* it is anxiety *about* something" (1926, pp. 164-165).

Anxiety is related to an anticipation of danger, and when it functions as a signal, the organism is usually able to avoid a traumatic situation—that is, one in which it feels helpless to deal with the danger, either external (physical danger) or internal (from instinctual drive sources). As Freud put it:

The signal announced: "I am expecting a situation of helplessness to set in," or: "The present situation reminds me of one of the traumatic experiences I have had before. Therefore I will anticipate the trauma and behave as though it had already come, while there is yet time to set it aside." Anxiety is therefore on the one hand an expectation of a trauma, and on the other, a repetition of it in mitigated form. (p. 166).

Concerning internal (instinctual drive) sources of danger, Freud formulated (1932) that when the ego becomes aware that the satisfaction of a drive would evoke a situation of danger (such as potential loss of the love object, loss of love, threat of castration), the ego anticipates satisfaction of the impulse, which produces some anxiety, activating repression.

These formulations of anticipatory functioning are applicable as well to situations in which danger is not central but anticipation of potential outcomes provides a major basis for good judgment.

*For a comparison of Freud's two anxiety theories, see Schur (1953).

**Eissler (1953) has discussed the signal function of affects in general and has suggested that an inability to experience affects as signals may be a basic defect in the ego functioning of some schizophrenics.

In the 1930's, Schilder emphasized the importance of anticipation or expectancy in the psychological processes underlying judgment. Rapaport summarized Schilder's formulation (Schilder, 1953) as follows:

Judgment, when functioning in relation to action, consists of a matching of the percept of the object to be acted on and the result of the action, with the anticipation and the concept of the object to which the motivation was directed. He also demonstrated that judgment, when functioning in relation to thought, consists in a matching of the anticipation pattern accompanying the motivation, with the memory-association of the sphere through which the thought-development had passed. In other words, passing through the various associations of the sphere, judgment matches the various associations met with by the anticipation patterns implicit to the motivation (p. 351).

Hartmann (1939) held that anticipation is an ego function of great importance in adaptation, that the reality principle implies the function of anticipating the future, and that we direct our actions by anticipating sequences of events, although in important areas it is rare that we can anticipate with scientific certainty. He included under the anticipatory function both knowledge of the external environment and of the inner life. Developmentally, indicators of rudimentary anticipation are seen to play a role in enabling the infant to gain some control over his body and over inanimate objects in the external world (Hartmann, Kris, and Loewenstein, 1946).

In their analysis of psychological test findings, Rapaport, Gill, and Schafer (1946) stated that judgment is probably implied when someone acts on an anticipation. They made the connection between anticipation and planning ability (which often involves judgment) and demonstrated how disturbances in anticipation can interfere with planning, where either a failure of anticipation or a false anticipation resulting from overvalent ideas could be involved.

Anticipation is generally regarded as an ego function. Spiegel (1966), however, holds that superego factors play an important role in internal anticipation, operating as an internal stimulus barrier against too great a quantity of drive energy. He underscores the place of superego functions in anticipation by citing obsessive rituals as an example of attempts to ward off feared future consequences. He also points out that major determinants of a concern for future consequences are parental injunctions and warnings: "If you do [don't do] this, such-and-such will happen to you." Spiegel holds that the parental concern is what becomes internalized; initially, the child carries out the activity not because of the reality consequences but because of the now-internalized parental commands. When the person responds to an "if...then" anticipation on the basis of reality considerations, the anticipation of consequences in this case will have become an ego function.

Spiegel views the function of anticipation as developing through stages, with the shift from anticipation based on the pleasure principle to the reality principle being facilitated by the attainment of object constancy. He reasons that an enduring mental image of the mother enables the infant to tolerate the discomfort of her disappearance and to correctly anticipate her return. He goes on to say, "A complete psychoanalytic theory of anticipation in the service of reality would attempt to trace the development of the function of anticipation from this point on to its widening and sophisticated use in the external world of real danger where specific object loss is not obviously involved" (p. 325-326).

Freud stated in the 1926 paper on anxiety that fear of the superego can constitute a danger situation. This implies anticipation of consequences from superego sources, which Beres (1966) formulated in terms of the superego increasing the ego's capacity to recognize danger situations through anticipatory pangs of conscience. Judgment can be adversely affected when this superego signal does not work (Loewenstein, 1972).

Spiegel's formulations highlight the problem of distinguishing ego and superego functions in this area. We encountered a similar problem concerning ego and superego components in self-observation in the previous chapter. Distinguishing ego from superego identifications is still another area of difficulty. The invocation of systematic criteria may be helpful: for example, that superego functions operate only according to the pleasure principle, whereas ego functions operate according to the reality principle (Beres, 1966).

Still, some overlap and ambiguity inevitably remain because of multiple function (Waelder, 1936) and because of the gap between concepts and the phenomena subsumed under them. Nevertheless, Speigel has underscored the concern for consequences in the judgmental function and pointed up the possible role of superego factors in these.

In summary, anticipation has been seen as an important function of the human and the subhuman organism. When anticipation goes awry, judgment is often centrally and crucially affected.

APPROPRIATENESS

The ability to apprehend what is appropriate to given situations is one aspect of good judgment. While knowledge and accurate thinking are both required, the more crucial ingredient is an emotional orientation that brings to mind the relevant possibilities from which an appropriate selection and emphasis must be made. As Rapaport, Gill, and Schafer (1946) put it:

"Judgment" appears to refer to the emotionally relevant use of one's assets in regard to the reality situation, where though intellectual and logical correctness are implied, they play a rather subordinate role. The terms "proper" and "appropriate" are other terms commonly used to indicate actions brought about by good judgment . . . a proper emotional orientation brings to consciousness and to execution, out of the multiplicity of logical possibilities that action which is labeled as one of "good judgment" (vol. I, p. 111)

It is the underlying emotional orientation that allows the person to act quickly in a way that reflects good judgment. A delaying of an initial impulse is often necessary, as is also an enumeration of various possibilities. Something additional, however, is required, an appropriate selection from among the various possibilities. While information can be taught, appropriate selection and emphasis can be learned only from example and experience.

Defensive constellations and cognitive styles can interfere with appropriateness. For example, in obsessive-compulsive conditions, observation and logical analysis substitute for the affective and ideational signals that usually regulate judgment and decision-making (Rapaport, Gill, and Schafer, 1946). The most typical kinds of inappropriate behaviors following loss of impulse control are acting out and psychotic manifestations.

Appropriateness is often a matter of social definition, social convention, and social consensus. Thus, rebelliousness or other factors that result in failure to accept a given social reality can result in socially inappropriate behavior, as well as social withdrawal and interference with awareness of social reality (Holt, in Rapaport, Gill, and Schafer, rev. ed. 1968). Sometimes, the issue of appropriate and inappropriate behavior in a social setting (such as in Nazi Germany, an extreme example) raises profound ethical and political considerations.

DISTURBANCES IN GOOD JUDGMENT

Within a psychoanalytic frame of reference, good judgment can be conceptualized as being vulnerable to interferences from id, superego, reality, physiological factors, or other ego sources. We will discuss each of these in turn. Because behavior is multiply determined, a given example of poor judgment will include most of the above aspects. For purposes of exposition we shall focus on these sources separately.

Interferences with judgment from drive sources are legion. Both sexual and aggressive drive derivatives may be involved, and in a variety of specific forms. Good judgment is perennially vulnerable to desires, wishes, and impulses. And the awareness of potential consequences can vary from none to full. At one extreme, the anticipatory function just does not operate, as in organic brain damage, toxic states, mental deficiency, and deteriorated psychotic conditions. With anticipatory functioning generally intact, but in circumstances where strong impulses have been stimulated, anticipations may be warded off, and rationalizations (or other defenses) may be evoked to justify behavior or to blur awareness of the probable consequences. For example, a patient who drove her hand through a glass window told one of the authors that just before the act she had been aware only of the desire to see what would happen. Neither her anger nor the probability of injury to her hand reached awareness. In other cases of strikingly poor judgment, major responsibilities are neglected, life savings are squandered on very unlikely schemes, and so on. Anticipations may be inaccurate or interfered with by drive derivatives within a delusional context or as a result of peremptory wishes more generally.

In cases where there is some anticipatory awareness of potential consequences, the urge may nevertheless be so compelling or the desire for gratification so strong that the behavior is carried out with the self-deception that the potential negative consequences will be something one can be concerned about later. When the anticipatory awareness is less interfered with or when a firmer sense of reality is present, the person may say to himself, "I know I'll be sorry afterwards, but I'm going to do it anyway."

Poor judgment may be found in many areas, or may be limited to situations in which particular drives or unconscious fantasies are activated. One person tends to show poor judgment in certain sexually-arousing situations, another when his anger is stimulated, a third when issues involving giving and getting are at the fore, still another when competitiveness and jealousy are mobilized, and someone else when a situation touches on narcissistic, self-aggrandizing possibilities.

Interferences with judgment from supergo sources include the unconscious needs for punishment, failure, and abuse (trends associated with moral masochism), which influence anticipation of consequences in a manner similar to that described for the id drives. In addition, some anticipations are influenced by supergo factors. These can be quite inaccurate, such as a sense of impending disaster or the phobic expectation of dire consequences (Spiegel, 1966). As already pointed out, anticipatory feelings of guilt constitute a superego signal that aids judgment. Thus, the warding off or defense against anticipatory guilt feelings may contribute to poor judgment, since these guilt feelings may inappropriately warn the person that the intended behavior can result in punishment or self-censure. Intended behaviors that include sexual, aggressive, narcissistic, or other drive aspects are a major basis for triggering the guilt signal.

Now we are ready to focus on ego factors associated with poor judgment. As already mentioned, intact reality testing is necessary for good judgment, as is the ability to anticipate. The ability to delay or postpone responses is another ego function required for good judgment, involving the function we have called regulation and control of drives, affects, and impulses. However strong or weak the drive or superego push for expression, the possibility of good judgment depends upon the delay of discharge to allow time for the processes underlying judgment to be exercised, for the anticipations to select from among the relevant possibilities brought to bear by memory. Immediate discharge is usually not compatible with good judgment (Fenichel, 1945, p. 39).

The strength and stability of the reality principle is also important in good judgment. One must be able to prevent the biasing of one's anticipations by what one wants to happen or what one fears will happen. And reality factors such as surprising events and catastrophes also affect judgment.

Defensive operations can result in a regressive alteration of ego functions. When reality testing, thinking, or synthesis undergo such changes, judgment may be secondarily affected. Thus, poor reality testing results in an inaccurate picture of the situation. Regarding aspects of thinking, memory loss can result in unavailability of relevant information on which sound judgments must be based. Errors in one's premises and insufficient or deflected attention also adversely affect judgment, as Freud pointed out (1895). And defensive alterations of synthetic functioning could result in relevant experience not being brought to bear on the problems at hand.

CHAPTER 8

Sense of Reality of the World and of the Self

This ego function is central to the experiencing of oneself and the world. It is related to reality testing but can be distinguished from the latter as we will demonstrate. An attempt to describe the sense of reality requires a consideration of body image, ego boundaries, the concept of self, and identity, as well as a review of some of its major disruptions, such as depersonalization and derealization.

A systematic investigation of the theoretical and metapsychological aspects of the concept of self has only been in progress since the 1950's, although important earlier contributions, such as Freud's formulations on narcissism and the ego ideal, as well as Federn's and those of a few others had been made. Hartmann's clarification of narcissism as the libidinal cathexis of the self rather than the ego (1950), Sterba's similar earlier clarification (1942), Erikson's elaboration of the identity concept (1950, 1956), Jacobson's paper (1954) and later monograph on *The Self and the Object World* (1964), work on narcissism (Kohut, 1966) and narcissistic conditions (Kernberg, 1970), all have contributed to a clearer conception of the self in psychoanalytic theory. Kohut's recent monograph on *The Self* (1971) is the most comprehensive set of formulations on this topic to date. The self is conceptualized as both a content of the mental apparatus and as a mental structure, the latter because it is enduring and is assumed to be cathected with instinctual energy.

Aspects of self-image and more enduring self-representations are seen to play an important role in the sense of reality, as this review will document. We have not attempted in this chapter, however, to integrate the most recent work on the self with the sense of reality.

Disturbances in the sense of reality are often clinically found to be associated with disruptions in object relations and in synthetic-integrative functioning, where body image, self-representations, and identity may be disturbed to varying degrees. The relative difference in adaptive adequacy between sense of reality and reality testing can be helpful, as we point out, in distinguishing between a psychosis and a psychotic character (Frosch, 1964).

Ego states (Federn, 1949) or states of consciousness (Rapaport, 1951) are quite relevant to the sense of reality. Federn believed ego states to be correlated with particular ego boundaries, the "contents" included within a given ego boundary at any point in time determining the particular ego state. The concept of ego feeling, which is close to what we are calling the sense of reality, is at the core of Federn's entire egopsychology, according to Bergmann (1963). For Rapaport (1951), awareness, or consciousness, is strongly related to the effectiveness of controls over impulses. Hypnagogic and hypnopompic experiences and fugue states and amnesias as altered states of consciousness were also discussed by Rapaport in the above mentioned paper.

Changes in the quality of self-awareness (and thus in the sense of reality) can be demonstrated in hypnotic induction (Gill and Brenman, 1959), in such altered-body ego experiences as dizziness, changes in experienced body size, weight, size of body parts, and loss of awareness of the body, or of some body parts, and in falling asleep and waking up.

Regarding other altered states of consciousness, Bellak (1958a) lists among others the following disturbances: depersonalization (a grossly altered state) and the feelings of unreality that accompany it; hypnagogic phenomena; "lightheadedness" in severe fatigue or hyperventilation; stage fright, oneirophrenia (a dreamlike feeling about the world); and cosmic delusions. The altered ego states listed by Woodbury (1966) include Isakower's hypnagogic phenomena; autoscopy; feelings of depersonalization (including micropsia and macropsia) and estrangement; synesthesias, hyperesthesias, and anesthesias; the psychosomatic components of anxiety; and psychotic experiences such as panic and hallucinations. The psychoanalytic patient on the couch also experiences an altered ego state when he cannot see the analyst.

FREUD'S CONTRIBUTIONS: A BRIEF CHRONOLOGY

Freud obliquely refers to a disturbance in the sense of reality in *The Interpretation of Dreams* (1900) in a discussion of the *déjà vu* phenomenon and other defects in judging whether or not things are real. He believed that the phenomena under consideration are produced by unconscious fantasies that cause a person to have an immediate feeling that he has "been there before" when, in fact, that may not have been the case. *Fausse reconnaissance* refers to the erroneous feeling of having seen exactly the same thing once before; *déjà raconté* refers to the illusion of having already reported something. Quoting a letter from Ferenczi, Freud stated: "I have convinced myself that the unaccountable feeling of familiarity is to be traced to unconscious phantasies of which one is unconsciously reminded in a situation of the present time" (1901, pp. 267-268).

Freud's next concern with sense of reality was within the more general context of his formulation of the reality and pleasure principles (1911). He observed that many patients told their analysts, "But I told you that already," when in fact they really had not. They did, however, intend to say what they falsely recalled. In "On Narcissism" (1914), Freud explicitly mentioned a loss of a sense of reality in schizophrenia due to shifts of cathexis from objects to the ego, resulting in feelings of unreality. He touched on two ego functions, reality testing and sense of reality, in speaking of both physical and psychic reality (1915) and in discussing the difference between the role of reality in the dream world and in schizophrenia. He discussed *fausse reconnaissance* in the setting of psychoanalytic treatment (1914) and some of his ideas on derealization in *The Future of an Illusion* (1927). Speaking of the feelings he had while on the Acropolis, he stated the crucial distinction between knowing about a thing and experiencing it:

"So it really *is* true, just as we learnt at school!" How shallow and weak must have been the belief I then acquired in the real truth of what I heard, if I could be so astonished now!. . .we are satisfied with letting what is taught at school be taken on trust; but we know that the path to acquiring a personal conviction remains open (1936, pp. 25-26).

Ego boundaries and the sense of self were included in *Civilization and Its Discontents* (1930). Reference was made here to an "oceanic feeling where immediate sensory experience suggests connection with the entire world." Although Freud allowed that being in love is only a nonpathological state in which the boundaries between ego and the object melt away, he mainly stressed pathological forms of such blurring:

Pathology has made us acquainted with a great number of states in which the boundary lines between the ego and the external world become uncertain . . . . There are cases in which parts of a person's own body, even portions of his own mental life—his perceptions, thoughts and feelings—appear alien to him and as not belonging to his ego; there are other cases in which he ascribes to the external world things that clearly originate in his own ego and that ought to be acknowledged by it. Thus even the feeling of our own ego is subject to disturbances and the boundaries of the ego are not constant. . . . originally the ego includes everything, later it separates off an external world from itself. Our present ego-feeling is, therefore, only a shrunken residue of a much more inclusive—indeed, an all-embracing—feeling which corresponded to a more intimate bond between the ego and the world about it (1930, p. 66). . . . there are many people in whose mental life this primary ego-feeling has persisted to a greater or lesser degree . . . side by side with the narrower and more sharply demarcated ego-feeling of maturity, like a kind of counterpoint to it (p. 68).

Finally, Freud's open letter to Romain Rolland on the occasion of his seventieth birthday, again describing his disturbance of memory on the Acropolis (1936) is pertinent: Freud's experience occurred in 1904, when he was 48. He connected it with a depression he had experienced while visiting Trieste; the feeling was one of incredulity and a subsequent attempt to repudiate a piece of reality. He felt he personally could not expect fate to grant anything so good; thus the momentary feeling, "What I see here is not real." Freud elaborated on this feeling saying, "I made an attempt to ward that feeling off, and I succeeded, at the cost of making a false pronouncement about the past." Freud offered the explanation that his experience was the result of oedipal guilt: he had surpassed his father, especially in this instance, by having gone further and having seen and achieved more. Freud distinguished derealization and depersonalization as follows:

These phenomena are to be observed in two forms: the subject feels either that a piece of reality or that a piece of his own self is strange to him. In the latter case we speak of "depersonalization"; derealizations and depersonalizations are intimately connected. There is another set of phenomena which may be regarded as their positive counterparts—what are known as *"fausse reconnaissance,"* *"déjà vu,"* *"déjà raconte,"* etc., illusions in which we seek to accept something as belonging to our ego. . .just as in the derealizations we are anxious to keep something out of us (1936, p. 245).

SENSE OF REALITY AND REALITY TESTING

Ferenczi (1913) started from Freud's description of the development of the reality principle and detailed stages in the development of the sense of reality: the period of unconditional omnipotence (intrauterine), in which all needs are automatically satisfied; the period of magical-hallucinatory omnipotence, the conviction that any wish or need can be satisfied by imagining its fulfillment, which as a result of insufficient reinforcement, evolves into the period of omnipotence by the help of magic gestures, in which the infant appears to assume that every wish can be satisfied if he performs given gestures (sucking movements, stretching out his hand toward objects he wants, etc.). Again as a result of inadequate reinforcement, the child now begins to distinguish between his own organism and the external environment, the latter comprising instances that do not obey his will consistently. There follows the animistic period, in which the child's own perceived characteristics and life qualities are attributed to both animate and inanimate objects. When language and verbal thinking have developed, the child goes through the period of magic thoughts and magic words, retaining some vestiges of the earlier omnipotence in the conviction that thoughts and some verbal formulas have the power of deeds. In a later paper (1926), Ferenczi again dealt with the problem of the acceptance of reality. Beginning with Freud's explanation of negation as a transition between denial of unpleasant realities and their acceptance, he hypothesized that unpleasant aspects of reality are accepted only when there is some compensation or when to do so avoids an even greater discomfort to the organism. Freud had made a related point earlier: "What appears to be a renunciation is really the formation of a substitute or surrogate" (1908, p. 145).

Glover (1933) found Ferenczi's hypothesized stages to provide no precise specification of the "wish-systems" involved (except for the stage of unconditional omnipotence, germane to the oral phase) nor of the nature of the relevant instinctual objects. He proposed (in part on the basis of the work of Melanie Klein) that beyond this, stages in the development of reality sense need to be considered not only with regard to impulse or object but also in terms of the stage of anxiety mastery, where both libidinal and destructive impulse are involved. Because one way of dealing with a reactivation of infantile anxiety in adult life is the development of perversions, Glover suggested that a study of the latter, especially fetishism in adult patients, could provide more accurate and detailed knowledge about the stages in the development of the sense of reality.

Federn (1952) differentiated the sense of reality from reality testing and gave the former a central place in his conception of the ego. He held that the human organism's knowledge of what is felt as belonging to the ego as opposed to the non-ego is based on a sensation, which he termed the sense of reality, rather than on a reality-testing function or mechanism (pp. 6-7). His concept of the ego was couched in terms of experience, although bodily and mental functions are included. Federn agreed with Freud's notion that the original distinction between internal and external was a result of bodily movements but went on to assume that through this primitive reality testing, dynamic "ego boundaries" are established that are tantamount to a sense organ at the flexible periphery of the ego. Once ego boundaries have been established, data impinging on the outer layers of the boundary are sensed as emanating from the external world, while phenomena approaching the inner boundary are automatically sensed as arising from within the organism and as not being real. Federn stated that the motoric basis for differentiating inner and outer is replaced relatively early by the ego boundaries and that subsequently no reality-testing function is needed or even effective in making the distinction. It is the sense of reality arising from the sensation of the ego boundary that is responsible for the crucial distinction, not a searching and comparing reality-testing function (1927, p. 43). He included under reality testing the obtaining of knowledge of realities and the subfunctions of memory and learning (p. 14). He used his notions of ego boundary and sense of reality in explaining such phenomena as estrangement (1927), delusions, hallucinations, and depersonalization (1948) and in the psychotherapy of psychoses (1943, 1947, 1948). It may be said that the capacity for reality testing depends in part on intact ego boundaries (Kernberg, 1967, p. 666).

Frosch points out interrelationships of reality testing, sense of reality, and relation to reality and underscores clinically useful distinctions between them (1964). "Reality testing" is defined as "the ability to arrive at a logical conclusion from a series of observable phenomena," and "sense of reality" as "the sense that phenomena going on around and within are real." It is the relative degree of disturbance of reality testing, on the one hand, and sense of reality and relationship with reality, on the other, Frosch contends, that differentiates a psychosis from a psychotic character. For example, if a patient feels that the floor is trembling or the walls are moving in on him (disturbances in the sense of reality), a crucial differential diagnostic factor is whether the patient can label the experience as based on internal, rather than on external, changes.

In comparing reality testing and sense of reality, Weisman (1958) says the following:*

Reality tests are intellectual, rational, and conceptual, while reality sense is emotional, intuitive and perceptual. For reality sense, objects are complete events in themselves, absolute and unequivocal. For reality testing, objects are part of a wider context, whose relations must be determined. Its results are only approximate and conditional. Reality testing finds its material in the conditions of experience, while reality sense functions with respect to the experience itself. Reality testing deals with shared experience through the common meaning of various propositions about it. Reality sense is essentially unshared, private, and complete in itself; it has no need for confirmation, since its criterion is the intensity, rather than the invariants of experience (p. 246).

And as Novey (1966) stated it:

In reality testing the ego calls upon its perceptual ability continuously to probe the environment by means of sensory modalities and to collate this information with its stored memories as a means of preparation for dealing with the environment. The "sense of reality," on the other hand, has to do with the inner experience of the self and the world as a cohesive unit having existence (p. 492-501).

In the chapter on reality testing we spoke of inner reality testing as involving an awareness of inner states and the accurate appraisal of them. In comparing reality testing and sense of reality, we can say that the awareness of inner states is most relevant to the sense of reality, while the accurate appraisal of these is most relevant to reality testing.

Body image, self-representations, and identity formation, as basic processes, are also related to the sense of reality. Each of these topics will be dealt with briefly. Some of the complex issues concerning their status and interrelationships cannot be discussed here. This is expecially true with regard to the self construct, as we pointed out above.

---

*Weisman (1965) provides an extensive consideration of reality testing and sense of reality.

BODY IMAGE

An important aspect of the sense of self is the image one has of one's body. Freud had characterized the ego as "first and foremost a body ego" (1923), that is, that bodily sensations influence the development of what is included in the ego construct. Fisher and Cleveland (1958) maintain that Freud's conception of the libido theory can be seen as a body-image-oriented theory. Thus, the dominance of the oral, anal, and phallic areas of the body during the evolving stages of psychosexual development implies that each of these areas in turn is dominant in the body scheme. Freud was also dealing with aspects of body image when he noted that various openings of the body tend to be equated, that parts of the body that protrude may be equated, and that sensations relevant to the genital region may be displaced upward. All of these result in what are now called body-image distortions.

Schilder (1935), following the work of Freud and Head, explored and clarified many aspects of the images, representations, and mental pictures people have of their interior and exterior bodies. He included the physiological bases for the body image (such as postural and tactile impressions), libidinal contributions (narcissistic factors and erogenic zones), and social aspects (spatial nearness to others, for example). He concluded that interactions with others have an important effect on the person's body image, with sadomasochistic relations often being deleterious. Schilder also studied body-image distortions in schizophrenics and brain-damaged individuals, as well as body-image perceptions of psychologically well-functioning people. He felt the distortions of schizophrenics and the brain-injured could not be clearly differentiated but were rather on a continuum. In schizophrenics, some body-image distortions were seen to result from poor object relations, while self-directed hostility can be reflected in feelings of disintegration of the body. Many other investigators have studied the body image, and much of this work has been reviewed by Fisher and Cleveland (1968).

The body image forms an important part of the self-image and self-representation.

SELF REPRESENTATIONS, SENSE OF SELF, AND IDENTITY

Freud sometimes used the terms "self" and "ego" interchangeably before he conceptualized the structural theory with the major components of id, ego, and superego. For example, Freud had formulated narcissism as the libidinal cathexis of the ego in 1914. As we already mentioned, Sterba (1942) and Hartmann (1950, p. 127) pointed out that narcissism is most accurately characterized as a libidinal cathexis of the self. It was in his 1950 paper "Comments on the

Psychoanalytic Theory of the Ego" that Hartmann suggested the term "self-representation" to oppose "object representation," the latter term having long been used in psychoanalysis to depict the mental representation of external objects, especially other people.

Jacobson (1964) describes the emergence of self-representations and their differentiation from object representations as follows:

From the ever-increasing memory traces of pleasurable and unpleasurable instinctual, emotional, ideational, and functional experiences and of perceptions with which they become associated, images of the love objects as well as those of the bodily and psychic self emerge. Vague and variable at first, they gradually expand and develop into consistent and more or less realistic endopsychic representations of the object world and of the self (p. 19).

As we pointed out in the chapter on reality testing, realistic self- and object-representations depend upon the use of reality testing rather than projective and introjective processes, since the latter two mechanisms result in self-images taking on the characteristics of object images, and vice versa (Jacobson, 1964, p. 47). Fenichel (1945) pointed out two sources of the self-image: direct awareness of inner experience and indirect self-perception and introspection where the person perceives his body and mental self as an object.

Self-representation has been defined as being

constructed by the ego out of a multitude of realistic and distorted self images which the individual has had at different times. It represents the person as he consciously and unconsciously perceives himself. It includes enduring representations of all the experienced body states, and all the experienced *drives* and *affects* which the individual has consciously or unconsciously perceived in himself at different times in reaction to himself and to the outer world . . . (Moore and Fine, 1968).

Self-representations are related to one's identity, and it may be said that one's perception of self-image (or self-representations) defines one's sense of identity (Moore and Fine, 1968, p. 50). Erikson's work on the topic of identity is the most widely known (1950, 1956, 1959), but other analysts have devoted considerable attention to the development of identity and its relations to self-representations and processes of identification (Jacobson, 1964). A self concept has been central to the work of Sullivan and Rogers, among others.

Erikson (1956) formulated ego-identity formation as a lifelong developmental process that is largely unconscious, begins in infancy, and continues throughout childhood as the youngster alternately feels he knows who he is and feels unsure, falling prey to the discontinuities of psychosocial development. As Erikson put it:

From a genetic point of view, then, the process of identity formation emerges as an *evolving configuration*—a configuration which is gradually established by successive ego syntheses and resyntheses throughout childhood; it is a configuration gradually integrating *constitutional givens, idiosyncratic libidinal needs, favored capacities, significant identifications, effective defenses, successful sublimations, and consistent roles* (p. 71).

Each psychosocial stage delineated by Erikson involves phase specific psychosocial crises (trust versus mistrust, autonomy versus shame and doubt, etc.) The psychosocial crisis of adolescence is identity versus identity diffusion. At the end of adolescence the various discordant and converging elements must be integrated into a unique and persistent sameness within the person, coupled with a persistent sharing of essential character aspects with others.

Failure to achieve a successful identity integration results in identity diffusion, which may be characterized by avoidance of choices, difficulties with intimacy, diffusion of industry, and the choice of a negative identity, that is, one other than what would be considered desirable by one's family or immediate community.

Since identity involves one's self-definition, it is an aspect of the sense of self and sense of reality. An extreme example of identity disturbance and disturbance in the sense of reality is the "as if" personality, described originally by Helene Deutsch (1942) as a person who has no stable identity and takes on attributes of those around him in chameleon fashion.

Jacobson (1964) believes that Erikson's term "ego identity" has been used too broadly. At the same time, she prefers not to limit identity formation to the ego and its synthetic forces but to understand identity formation as "a process that builds up the ability to preserve the whole psychic organization—despite its growing structuralization, differentiation, and complexity—as a highly individualized but coherent entity which has direction and continuity at any stage of human development" (p. 27).

Jacobson holds that serious identity problems are found in neurotic individuals with particular narcissistic conflicts and in borderline and psychotic people. We add that anyone with serious identity problems will show serious disruptions in the sense of reality.

Relationships between the concepts of body image, self, and identity have been pointed out, as well as attempts to differentiate these. Thus, Greenacre (1958) said that the body image is of permanent importance to the sense of identity. And Jacobson (1964) states that a solid identity depends upon firm boundaries between self- and object representations. A self-conscious sense of identity depends to a varying extent upon the persistence of unconscious fusion with objects, reflecting the hazy boundaries between self- and object identifications.

A distinction between the sense of self and the sense of identity is made by Levita (1966):

I believe that the concept of identity can enrich our terminology only when we can verbalize and clarify the difference between "sense of self" and "sense of identity." For that purpose, I shall define the self as the sum total of one's reflections upon oneself and identity as the cluster of roles one is enacting, i.e., the psychological representatives of these roles. Thus the self is a collective name for self-concept, self-perception, self-esteem, etc. Identity is a collective name as well, namely for different kinds of roles (p. 301).

Research on cognitive style, especially on field dependence-independence, shows relationships between modes of cognition and perception, on the one hand, and the sense of reality, on the other. Witkin (1965) believes that the degree of psychological differentiation is the cognitive component of field-dependent or field-independent perception. He has postulated an articulated versus global dimension of cognitive functioning. He believes that there is now considerable evidence that a tendency toward one or the other way of perceiving is a constant, pervasive characteristic of a person's perception. The rod-and-frame test and the tilted-room experiments were the major means used for evaluating people along this dimension, and from these techniques, field dependence was defined as a fusion in experience of the body and the field. Field independence is that condition in which subjects are able to bring their bodies close to the upright, indicating an immediate sense of the separateness of their bodies from the surrounding world. Thus defined, field independence is closely related to a good sense of reality. In the rod-and-frame test, for example, field-dependent perception is global: the subjects cannot differentiate the various elements of the field. Field-independent people are very analytical: the subjects can perceive a part of the field as discrete from the rest. Subjects who have an articulated cognitive style also have an articulated body concept. They experience their bodies as having definite limits or boundaries and the parts within as discrete yet interrelated and formed into a definite structure. In speaking of a sense of separate identity, Witkin says:

Persons with an articulated cognitive style give evidence of a developed sense of separate identity—that is to say, they have an awareness of needs, feelings, attributes which they recognize as their own and which they identify as distinct from those of others. Sense of separate identity implies experience of the self as segregated. It also implies experience of the self as structured: internal frames of reference have been formed and are available as guides for definition of the self. The less developed sense of separate identity of persons with a global cognitive style manifests itself in reliance on external sentiments and the view of themselves. . . (1965, p. 320).

DEPERSONALIZATION: A DISTURBANCE OF THE SENSE OF REALITY

Depersonalization involves feelings of strangeness and unfamiliarity with one's body or parts of it. Stamm (1962) defined it as follows:

I am including under the term depersonalization all those states in which the individual becomes aware of changes in himself, bodily or mental, or both, that lead to feelings of strangeness in himself. In such cases there is an alteration in the ego with a split into a part which feels estranged and one which carries on the observer's role (p. 762).

Arlow holds (1966) that depersonalization represents a dissociation of the function of immediate experiencing from that of self-observation. The patient reports feeling split or perhaps as having two selves at the same time. One self appears to be standing off at a distance in a detached and relatively objective manner, observing another representation of the self in action.

Bellak (1964) wrote the following:

Depersonalization is a state of *heightened and changed* awareness of the self and/or the body [in relation to the world], it is usually accompanied by an unpleasant feeling of unrealness sometimes with anxiety; it may involve the whole or only parts of the body; and in varying degrees it is accompanied by a feeling that the environment, and one's relationship to it, are strange. There is a feeling of loss of frame of reference in time, in place, in person, or perhaps in all three (p. 215).

Galdston (1947) presents a comprehensive review to that date of work on depersonalization, unearthing the first known description of the phenomenon by Krishaber in 1872; it was named, as such, 15 years later by Dugas (1887). An aspect of alteration in the sense of reality was discussed by Tausk (1933) in his classic work on the "influencing machine." He referred to certain patients' paranoid delusions of being controlled by machines that contain elements of their own body images. This externalized representation of the body image becomes a central reference point in the person's life. A great deal of interest has been aroused by an altered sense of self in the hypnagogic state discussed by Isakower (1938), generally referred to as Isakower's phenomenon, in which organs of the body are experienced as ego alien.

Most authors hold that depersonalization phenomena span the range from normality to psychosis. Federn (1949) regarded depersonalization as an ego disturbance that may be found in certain ego states that are in the normal range as well as in psychotic conditions. Schilder (1935) held that most neuroses include depersonalization phenomena in some phases of their development. But as late as 1958, Fisher and Cleveland stated that no systematic investigation of the frequency of depersonalization phenomena in various clinical groups had been published.

The occurrence of depersonalization phenomena in normal people has repeatedly been observed. Peto (1955) says that normal, but transitory, episodes of depersonalization sometimes occur in adolescents when they look in the mirror. Morgenstern had previously (1931) said that the depersonalized person may still be able to distinguish between his morbid sensations and reality itself. Jacobson (1959) described depersonalization phenomena in political prisoners in concentration camps that should not be considered pathological because they had been exposed to unusually strong, real, external dangers. To show one way in which depersonalization could aid adaptation, she describes the conditions under which prisoners handled their interrogators most adaptively, that is, when they felt detached or unreal. Along similar lines Bellak (1969) and Stewart (1964) say that many feelings of unreality involving the self, the world, the body, and the passage of time are nondelusional. They can result from participating in sensory-deprivation experiments, from experiences of loneliness and hardship, from drug intoxication and alterations in physiology (such as hyperventilation), and from hormonal changes. Depersonalization has normal prototypes in reactions to sudden shocks or extreme pain, hypnotic experiences, dreaming, and hypnopompic and hypnagogic experiences.

Explanations of depersonalization have included the concept of shifts in libidinal cathexis, of disturbances of ego boundaries, of defensive maneuvers, and also as reflecting conflicting identities within the personality. All of these explanations are pertinent and need to be included in a comprehensive metapsychological formulation.

As to the defensive nature of depersonalization, Rosenfeld (1947) sees it as a defense against guilt, as part of a schizoid process related to destructive impulses within the ego that are felt to be alien and "split off" and are ascribed to outsiders. According to Bergler (1950), defenses warding off exhibitionistic wishes account for depersonalization. The defensive use of depersonalization against a threatened eruption of id derivatives is described by Blank (1954), while Bird (1957) believes it is a defense against perception. Arlow states, "Depersonalization and derealization are examples of altered ego states instigated by defenses and dominated by regressive distortion of certain ego functions" (1966, p. 477). Sarlin (1962) describes depersonalization as a symptomatic defensive disturbance in ego function, manifested by an uncomfortable awareness of a pathological objectivity and estrangement from the self, which may affect the body and the mind. Bellak relates depersonalization to defenses as follows: "Repression and isolation are usually attempted first. Denial of one part of the self, or of reality, follows, and is accompanied by an overawareness of other parts of the self (or rather, of other ego functions, specifically the self-observing ones) which leads to the feeling of depersonalization" (1964, p. 225). Finally, Grinberg (1966) views depersonalization as a reaction to the loss of obsessive control.

To turn to explanations in terms of shifts in libidinal cathexis, Fenichel (1945) stated that depersonalization involves massive shifts of cathexis from objects to the ego. Nunberg (1955) expanded the idea of such shifts:

The perception of the loss of a love object or the lowering of libido quantities is accompanied by the feeling that the reality of the perceptions and sensations of the ego has been lost . . . the feelings of estrangement are the direct result of the *sudden* transposition of the libido from the object to the ego (p. 134).

The third category of explanation, ego boundaries, is found especially in Federn's work (1952).

My view of the cause of depersonalization is . . . as follows: when external objects are perceived by means of organs, all or part of which have not yet been included in the body ego, such objects are regarded as strange. This is not because the object is recognized with more difficulty, but because the object has impinged on a part of the ego boundary which has not been invested with narcissistic libido (pp. 35-36).

Depersonalization was considered as a consequence of conflicting identities by Oberndorf (1939, 1950), who stated that depersonalization can occur when there are inharmonious relationships between major identifications in the superego and the actual body ego. With a sexual identity conflict, too, one aspect of the self has to be repudiated. Analyzing depersonalization from the point of view of conflicting identities, Jacobson (1959) believed that it originates in the ego itself. One identity may be unacceptable to the other and repudiation of one of them may lead to depersonalization.

Disturbances in the development and maintenance of ego boundaries have been regarded by some as the central feature of the schizophrenic process. This position is summarized by Freeman, Cameron, and McGhie:

It is this factor of "ego feeling," or the ability to differentiate the self from the environment, that we regard as being damaged in chronic schizophrenia, thus leading to the patient experiencing internal and external sensations as a continuum. We believe that, once this basic disturbance is appreciated, all other schizophrenic manifestations can be viewed as necessary elaborations of it (1958, p. 51).

Another aspect of depersonalization is micropsia-macropsia, the tendency to perceive objects as much smaller or much larger than they really are. In his paper on "Gulliver Fantasies," Ferenczi (1926) emphasized the defensive aspect of perceiving as small an otherwise large and terrifying object. Greenacre (1955), also writing about Gulliver and the Lilliputians and about Alice in Wonderland, was particularly interested in certain biographical facts about the authors, Jonathan Swift and Lewis Carroll. She discussed the relationship between the body-size changes described in the writings of these two authors and their own personality patterns and early developmental experiences. At least one of these authors suffered from a disturbance of body image (Menière's disease) that produced dizziness and migraine. Micropsia was described by Bartemeir (1941) and by Lewy (1954) as being related to depersonalization. It is an expression of imminent ego disintegration and constitutes a projection of perception into the outer world. Micropsia occurs at a time when the ego is getting weaker and eventually disappears as the capacity for inner psychic perception further decreases.

OTHER DISTURBANCES RELATED TO THE SENSE OF REALITY

After depersonalization, derealization is perhaps the most frequently mentioned altered ego state. Freud (1936) treated it extensively, defining it as the momentary feeling. "What I see here is not real." Derealization is usually differentiated from depersonalization by its involvement of feelings of estrangement directed toward an external object, whereas in depersonalization the feeling of estrangement is directed toward the self. Arlow (1966) believes that derealization, like depersonalization, is instigated by defenses and dominated by the regressive distortion of certain ego functions.

Another category of altered ego states includes *déjà vu*, *fausse reconaissance*, and *déja raconté*. The major references to these phenomena are by Freud (1900, 1901, 1909, 1914) and have already been discussed in this chapter. Bellak (1958a) believes that *déjà vu* experiences may actually produce panicky awareness of a lack of definition of ego boundaries.

Pacella (1971) presents clinical material to illustrate how the *déjà vu* is structurally similar to, and probably the core of, most or all *déjà* experiences. He hypothesizes that it results from a sudden decathexis of the reality situation along with a recathexis of old fantasies and that the feeling of familiarity symbolically represents traces of visual and other sensations experienced in the mother-child dyad during the first year of life, expecially the mother's facial gestalt.

Still another altered ego state mentioned by Freud (1930) is the "oceanic feeling"—a feeling of an indissoluable bond with, of being one with, the external world as a whole or the sensation of limitless eternity. Fenichel (1945) believed that seeking oceanic reunion is a search for a feeling of "oneness" with the universe, found mainly in schizophrenics. Arieti (1967) uses Freud's oceanic feeling to exemplify an "endocept," or a primitive organization of perceptions and memory traces frequently found in schizophrenics.

There are scattered references to other altered ego states, including certain sexual feelings, autoscopic phenomena, and the "as if" personality. Keiser (1952) speaks of changes in the body ego during orgasm, noting that the body changes during sexual intercourse and especially during orgasm, in which there is intense local excitation, may cause the person to experience his body as altered, strange, and out of control. During orgasm there is a blurring of body boundaries that may be interpreted by some people as a disintegration or falling apart. The autoscopic phenomenon (Ostow, 1960) is the subjective experience of encountering an image of oneself in the form of hallucination, illusion, or fantasy. It occurs in melancholia, schizophrenia, and neurotic depression and represents an attempt to separate from the suffering ego the fragment that is felt to be the source of pain. Ross (1967) sees the "as if" personality in the same way as depersonalization, that is, as involving a feeling of unreality about the self.

Fugue states also represent a disturbance in the sense of reality and have been understood as an ego defense against derivatives of aggressive and erotic drives that are potentially dangerous. (Fisher and Joseph, 1949)

From the beginning of research interest in sensory deprivation, investigators have found that one of its consequences is an alteration in ego state and the sense of reality. Early reports by Bexton, Heron, and Scott (1954) indicate that subjects deprived of ordinary channels of stimulation report changes in their body awareness. In Lilly's sensory-deprivation experiments (1956), in which subjects were suspended in a tank of water, they reported a great deal of projection of visual imagery. Zuckerman and his associates (1962) offer as an explanation for altered body ego during sensory deprivation that external stimuli do not compete for attention, and internal stimuli therefore seem more than usually intense. Murphy and Spohn (1968) also feel that lack of knowledge about what constitutes the internal world and what constitutes the external world can produce cognitive confusion. For example, sensory deprivation sometimes results in hallucinations. Variations in ego feelings similar to those resulting from sensory deprivation have also been induced by LSD-25 (Savage, 1955). With LSD intake an increase in body awareness was pleasurable to normals but painful to anxious subjects. All subjects experienced a sense of timelessness. Savage concluded that in altered states such as those induced by LSD, ego boundaries may lose ego feeling and thus be dissolved altogether.

The psychology of falling asleep and its associated phenomena has been treated extensively in the literature on hypnagogic phenomena. Federn (1926) noted that in falling asleep, body boundaries become less definite. The body loses some of its three-dimensional quality; parts of the body feel vague and others seem to disappear, and a sort of depersonalization occurs. In Isakower's studies of the hypnagogic phenomenon, he reported how organs of the body are experienced as ego alien (1938). He explained that in the process of going to sleep there is a regression to earlier ego states, involving a hypercathexis of the mouth, the disintegration of parts and functions of the ego, and the diminution of ego differentiation. Typical would be the feeling upon falling asleep that a large object is approaching, which causes these oral sensations; this object image represents the early visual-tactile impression of the breast. Some support for this hypothesis comes from Hoffer's observations on hand-mouth coordination and ego integration (1949, 1950). He pointed out the intimate relationship between the hand, the mouth, and the eyes in the development of the body ego. Spitz

(1955, 1959) added that the hand, the labyrinth and skin-surface experiences are all woven into the oral phase and constitute an altered-body-ego experience.

In his work on sleep, the mouth and the "dream screen," Lewin (1946, 1948) related aspects of altered-body experience to the dream screen, or a "blank" dream of a white, contentless image based upon early experience of the mother's breast. In *The Psychoanalysis of Elation* (1950) he had introduced these ideas and formulated that the elated and manic patient has marked feelings of reality about such experiences. Somewhat related to elation is Milner's work *On Not Being Able to Paint* (1957). The author learned from her own experience that the astounding feeling of how good it is to be alive is necessary to that sense of self that in turn is necessary to create in an artistic medium. Stewart (1964) describes hypnagogic or hypnopompic experiences before or after dreaming, respectively, as normal prototypes of depersonalization.

SELF-ESTEEM

Self-esteem is related to the sense of reality and is also strongly influenced by superego factors, as we pointed out in Chapter 3. Ferenczi (1913), in an early reference to self-esteem, stated that the feeling of esteem expressed the infantile feeling of narcissistic omnipotence. And Bibring (1953) introduced the concept of lowered self-esteem as central to depressions. Epstein (1955) concluded that since there was some evidence that some schizophrenics narcissistically evaluate themselves more highly than do normals, they possess an inflated, omnipotent sense of self-esteem. Greenacre (1958) believes that normal self-esteem is dependent upon optimal feedback of a sense of worth. Even a mature person needs at least one other person similar to himself to reinforce his sense of self. In the same positive vein, Jacobson (1964) believes that self-esteem is the expression of harmony between self-representations and the wishful concept of the self. She puts it as follows:

Self-esteem is the ideational, especially the emotional, expression of self-evaluation and of the corresponding more or less neutralized libidinal and aggressive cathexis of the self-representations . . . Broadly defined, the level of self-esteem is expressive of the harmony or discrepancy between the self-representations and the wishful concept of the self, which is by no means always identical with the unconscious and conscious ego ideal. Hence, disturbances of self-esteem may originate from many sources and represent a very complex pathology: on the one hand, a pathology of the ego ideal or of the achievement standards and goals of the ego and, hence, of the self-critical ego and superego functions, and, on the other hand, a pathology of the ego functions and of the self-representations (pp. 130-131).

Annie Reich, in her paper on pathological forms of self-esteem regulation

(1960), describes narcissistic patients who have an exaggerated self-awareness and a high degree of body narcissism. These patients have suffered marked oscillations in their self-esteem, that is, in their positive and negative evaluations of the self. Sufficiently living up to the demands of the superego is a mature form of self-esteem regulation, whereas compensatory narcissistic self-inflation is among the most conspicuous forms of pathological self-esteem regulation. Such narcissistic individuals may show repetitive, violent oscillations of self-esteem, as their infantile value system includes only absolute perfection and complete imperfection.

J. de Saussure (1972) published a far-ranging paper on self-esteem regulation. She reports on a group of patients who experience pain as a loss of self-esteem and try to eliminate pain of any kind by narcissistic gratification. These patients usually show a high degree of actual accomplishment. Their self-esteem is controlled not by reality but by magical beliefs and regressed self-images. These images are related to a self capable of experiencing primary narcissism, which interferes with the ability to create and value adult self-images. Clinically, she suggests an examination of the representation of the idealized state and deduction (from it) to the characteristics of the primitive self implied. She reports on one patient who dreamed of himself as a cello from which unending bliss emanated. Descriptions of sensations predominated over structure of the body. Another patient used the self-imagery of being like a balloon. In this latter case, the lack of inner structure and the lack of boundaries between balloon and atmosphere (if there is an opening in the balloon) is significant. She relates the role of the primitive self-image to these patients' inability to regulate self-esteem within the normal fluctuations common to most other people. As a result of the archaic image of the self as measuring rod for the value of the self, these patients suffer from severe castration fears and concern with eruption of their own aggressive drives. The magical means of self-esteem regulation in turn becomes an important part of an obsessive defense against these fears. As real strengths are ignored and minor faults can threaten to burst the whole balloon, self-esteem fluctuates wildly, controlled mostly by attempts to give others the illusion of a perfect image of themselves.

CHAPTER 9

Regulation and Control of Drives, Affects, and Impulses

This ego function concerns the person's ability to tolerate anxiety, depression, disappointment, frustration, and the necessity of postponing expected satisfactions. It involves the expression of inner wishes, emotional strivings and urges in an harmonious and modulated manner. Included also is the ability to delay responses to inner promptings for tension discharge or for gratification (Moore and Fine, 1968). It is an expansion and refinement of that characteristic of the ego that involves deciding when instincts are to be allowed satisfaction by taking external circumstances into account. Anxiety tolerance is mentioned by Hartmann in 1939, and frustration tolerance was included among the ego functions by Bellak in 1949. The terms "regulation and control" of instinctual drives were used by Beres (1956) in his paper on "Ego Deviation and the Concept of Schizophrenia". About this function he says:

This is often described as the inhibitory apparatus serving postponement of discharge. It is manifested in the increasing capacity of the maturing ego to postpone gratification. It is part of the adaption to reality and brings into play progression from the pleasure principle to the reality principle, and from the primary process to the secondary process. It must be distinguished from the delay of gratification that can be induced as a conditioned response in animals or infants, as, for example, in housebreaking a puppy or in premature toilet training of the infant (p. 183).

The characteristics and development of instinctual drives are relevant to this chapter but are mostly dealt with in the chapter on the id. Superego aspects are similarly relevant but, again, are covered in the chapter on that topic. Ego defenses regulate and control drive, affect, and impulse expression, so that this ego function overlaps that of regulation and control. There is, however, a difference in focus and emphasis in our consideration of defensive functioning and regulation and control: in the latter, we are mostly concerned with impulsiveness; poor delay; and acting out, at one extreme, and inhibition and overcontrol, at the other. In defining and dimensionalizing defensive functioning, our focus is on the primitivity-maturity of defenses and their success in terms of the presence of anxiety, depression, and other dysphoric affects.

In his already-mentioned account of regulation and control, Beres (1956) pointed out that children with poor control of instinctual drives tend to manifest aggressive outbursts and also to have difficulty with pregenital and genital sexual impulses expressed in unusual eating habits, poorly controlled bowel function, and excessive masturbation. Superego defects are frequently found, and children who have central difficulties in tolerating frustration and delaying gratification often develop clinical pictures that prominently include antisocial and psychopathic aspects.

The meaning of instinctual drive in psychoanalysis is discussed in the chapter on the id. Instinctual drives have been assumed to have an ideational and an affect component, and it is through wishes, fantasies, images, and ideas, on the one hand, and affective states or feelings, on the other, that instinctual drives are known to us. Jacobson (1953) holds that some affects may correspond to instinctual drive processes and others to ego responses. She classifies affects as follows:

1. Simple and compound affects that arise from intrasystemic tensions (i.e., within one of the three psychic agencies: id, ego, or superego):
   A. Affects that represent instinctual drive proper or that rise directly from the id, such as sexual excitement and rage.
   B. Affects that develop directly from tensions in the ego, such as fear of reality and physical pain as well as components of the more enduring feelings such as object love and hate or interest in things.
2. Simple and compound affects induced by intersystemic tension (i.e., between any of the three psychic agencies):
   A. Affects influenced by tensions between the ego and the id, such as fear of the id components of disgust, shame, and pity.
   B. Affects induced by tensions between the ego and superego, such as guilt feelings and components of depressions.

We will not discuss the psychoanalytic view of affects further (see Rapaport, 1953), noting only that affects or feelings can be very strong and poorly regulated and controlled; may be inhibited or overcontrolled; are subject to defensive operations; and, when optimally regulated, serve an important adaptive function as signals (such as the anxiety signal discussed in the chapter on judgment) and as an aspect of reality testing.

Impulses are usually understood as urges that are difficult to resist, and in psychoanalysis they are assumed to be based on sexual and/or aggressive instinctual drives or on guilt. Impulsive disorders will be discussed further on. But we will first consider the issue of delay as an important aspect of regulation and control.

THE CONCEPT OF DELAY

In the "Project for a Scientific Psychology" (1895) Freud hypothesized that the primary function of the nervous system is to keep itself free from "stimulus" through discharge. He also discussed a secondary nervous-system function as opposing discharge by contact barriers (p. 298).

Freud elaborated this division between a primary and a secondary function in *The Interpretation of Dreams* (1900, Chap. 7) but in relation to the mental apparatus, not the nervous system. The first "structure" followed a reflex pattern attempting to free itself of sensory stimulation by motor discharge. Freud formulated this as follows: In early infancy, somatic needs, such as hunger, produce stimulation, and as hunger increases, the stimulation mounts. Attempts at discharge take the form of crying and thrashing about but fail to alleviate the hunger tension. In the absence of the need-satisfying object (breast), the infant is assumed to hallucinate satisfaction of the hunger by reevoking a memory of the original gratification when the hunger was actually gratified. But this "perceptual identity" also fails to quiet the need. So another approach to need satisfaction is required. As Freud put it:

In order to arrive at a more efficient expenditure of psychical force, it is necessary to bring the regression to a halt before it becomes complete, so that it does not proceed beyond the mnemic image, and is able to seek out other paths which lead eventually to the desired perceptual identity being established from the direction of the external world. *This inhibition of the regression and the subsequent diversion of the excitation become the business of a second system, which is in control of voluntary movement* — which for the first time, that is, makes use of movement for purposes remembered in advance (1900, p. 566; italics added).

Rapaport (1950) pointed out from this passage that the ability to delay, an internal control, evolves from an external circumstance, namely, the initial absence of the drive object.

Freud again discussed delay of gratification in his paper "Formulations on the Two Principles of Mental Functioning" (1911). The two principles are the pleasure and reality principles, which are central to the primary and secondary processes just referred to in the more primitive formulation beginning with the "Project for a Scientific Psychology" of 1895. Pressure for immediate discharge is central to the primary process. Delay of discharge, on the other hand, is a crucial characteristic of secondary process functioning:

Thus, while motor discharge under sway of the pleasure principle had served to unburden the mental apparatus of accumulated stimulation, it was now to be employed to alter reality, and this required a restraint on action. The postponement of discharge was accomplished by the process of thinking, which allowed the mental apparatus to tolerate additional tension during the delay (p. 221).

Also, delay of gratification was seen by Freud as a necessary condition for moving from autoerotic fantasy to real gratification in relation to the sexual object (p. 223).

Rapaport (1951) considered delay of gratification through motor discharge to be "the cradle of 'conscious experience'" (p. 690) and central to the psychoanalytic theory of thinking (p. 693). He also made Freud's formulation of delay of discharge due to the absence of the drive object a major aspect of his conceptual model of psychoanalysis (1951).

Frosch (1967) presented an evolutionary scheme for the development of the delay function, going from hallucination to motor delay, fantasy formation, thought, and successful action. Later difficulties in the ability to delay, together with problems in impulse control, result from disturbance during the development of the delay progression, with the form of the disturbance and its degree of primitivity (including the relative balance of primary- and secondary-process aspects) being related to the stage of ego development at the time.

IMPULSIVE BEHAVIOR

Everyone responds impulsively at one time or another. But people vary considerably in the frequency of impulsive behavior and in their ability to delay impulses and reflect on the wisdom of carrying them out. Indeed, there are considerable individual differences in the extent and kind of impulse awareness. At one extreme, there is a clear conscious registration of the impulsive tendency together with anticipatory anxiety, guilt, and other affect signals, as well as the ability to delay the impulse or deny it motoric or behavioral expression. At the other extreme is almost immediate motor response to a vaguely perceived internal prompting, with little awareness of signals, potential consequences, or ability to delay or prevent the response.

A number of psychiatric diagnoses centrally involve impulsiveness. For example, both the inadequate personality and the emotionally unstable personality display an inability to postpone immediate pleasure and develop self-control. Sociopathic (previously called psychopathic) personalities, ranging from impulsive and emotionally shallow to antisocial, are all characterized by impulsive actions and poor ability to delay. The experience of an irresistible impulse is common in the various sexual perversions, such as exhibitionism, voyeurism, fetishism, and transvestism. That is, a male exhibitionist feels an uncontrollable desire to display his genitals when he finds a solitary female in a somewhat secluded place. And the strength of the urge in addicted individuals to imbibe or indulge in their "habit" is most well known. Other impulsive disorders, such as kleptomania, pyromania, gambling, and impulsive running away, have periodically been the subject of popular concern. While an inability to delay and a response on the basis of the pleasure principle and the primary process are centrally involved in impulsive reactions, other considerations are also relevant: "For one thing, the tension resulting from a delay of discharge is responded to by the impulsive individual as dangerous, the prototype being hunger pangs in infancy. Thus, trauma resulting from excessive hunger tension built up during the early months after birth predispose a person to be intolerant of tension" (Fenichel, 1945).

Savitt (1963) has underscored how heroin addicts have little ability to bind tension or tolerate delay. As a result, they bypass oral incorporation for the more primitive intravenous route, thereby avoiding tension buildup, which they regard as dangerously traumatic. The tension reduction restores some archaic ego integrity but decreases perception and aids defensive denial.

Fenichel also pointed out that impulsive actions often involve an attempt to escape from, deny, or reassure oneself against a danger, including the danger of depression. In habitually impulsive individuals an oral regulation of self esteem is frequently found; there is overstrong dependence on getting things and on being loved and a tendency to become depressed when these things are not sufficiently forthcoming. Another aspect of early oral fixation is the tendency to respond to frustration with violent anger. A basic conflict in such individuals is between the tendency to express the frustration-anger and the fear that expressing it will result in loss of love. An additional conflict in the impulsive neuroses is between the longing for instinctual gratification and the experience of this longing as a dangerous instinctual tension. The impulse is experienced as ego syntonic (something the person wants to do to get pleasure) at the time even though guilt may be experienced later.

Reich, who introduced the concept of the impulsive character into the psychoanalytic literature in 1925, stated (1949) that such an individual experienced, as a child, a sudden and unexpected frustration of a fully developed libidinal drive, one that had not been substantially frustrated or repressed at the earliest stages of its development.

Frosch and Wortis (1954) divide disorders of impulse control into two main groups: symptom impulse disorders and character impulse disorders. Impulsive disturbances are caused by an inadequacy of relevant control apparatuses, which results either from direct deterioration of the control apparatus or from an increase in the strength of the impulse. Impulse disorders include isolated, but usually repetitive, impulses; a personality characterized by impulsiveness; pleasure derived from the impulsive act; ego syntonicity; and only minor distortion of the original impulse as it was expressed in the act. Further distinctions are made between symptom impulse disorders, which include impulsion neuroses, perversions, and catathymic crises, on the one hand, and character impulse disorders, which include impulse disturbances characterizing the whole personality, on the other.

Michaels (1959) has divided impulse disorders into two types: the impulsive psychopathic character and the impulsive neurotic character. In the former, along with general impulsiveness there is great hateful aggressiveness. The latter is seen as a more autoplastic disorder, involving neurotic mechanisms of the compulsive form. In the impulsive neurotic character, dormant psychopathic tendencies are held in check by the compulsive neurotic components of his character.

Low frustration tolerance is an important aspect of impulsiveness and poor regulation and control. Redl and Wineman (1951) found that frustration tolerance difficulties take two main forms in their poorly controlled patients: in one, the person refuses to be frustrated, and insists on impulse gratification; in the other, the child permits himself to be exposed to a degree of frustration but then is unable to control the aggression, anxiety, or panic that results. The authors point out ways in which delinquent children, as compared with more normal children, showed a paucity of techniques for reducing fear and anxiety while maintaining other ego functions intact. Mild fear or anxiety often resulted in a total breakdown of controls. These children responded to fear and anxiety with total flight and avoidance, or ferocious attack and diffuse destructiveness, while the fear or anxiety either did not register consciously or was repressed following the behavior. A less extreme reaction of these children is to tear around, bite, and threaten other children, actions that make them feel less vulnerable. A more normal child of this age would only fantasize being powerful or doing powerful things.

Another aspect of frustration tolerance is what Redl and Wineman call temptation resistance. A well-functioning ego responds to dangerous or guilt-producing temptations with danger signals. Impulsive children have a low resistance to temptation. When potentially gratifying objects are visually present, these children are powerfully drawn to them, irrespective of external prohibitions or danger. Their behavior is also strongly influenced by what they see other children doing. Thus, when they see other children throwing things around, a kind of contagion occurs, and urges that were dormant are too readily activated.

While more normal youngsters tend to use materials in ways that are consistent with their inherent potential to offer gratifications, impulsive children showed a kind of "sublimation deafness," tending to use objects and materials to gratify basic urges directly.

ACTING OUT

Acting out involves impulsive behavior but is considered to be on higher levels of organization. Formulations related to what later became the concept of acting out were introduced by Freud in *The Psychopathology of Everyday Life* (1901). In the sections on "Erroneously Carried-Out Actions" and "Symptomatic and Chance Actions," he gave many examples—from his own behavior and that of his friends and patients—of impulsive actions being carried out either contrary to conscious intentions or without a conscious intention and showed the unconscious intentions at work.

The concept of acting out is clearly described by Freud in a postscript to his case history of Dora (1905), who left analysis prematurely:

> In this way the transference took me unawares, and, because of the unknown quantity in me which reminded Dora of Herr K., she took her revenge on me as she wanted to take her revenge on him, and deserted me as she believed herself to have been deceived and deserted by him. Thus she *acted out* an essential part of her recollections and phantasies instead of reproducing it in the treatment (p. 119).

In "Remembering, Repeating and Working-Through" (1914), Freud reported how certain repressed and forgotten events were sometimes reproduced during psychoanalysis as actions (without realization) rather than as memories. As Freud put it: "For instance, the patient does not say that he remembers that he used to be defiant and critical towards his parents' authority; instead, he behaves in that way to the doctor" (p. 150). Freud also stated here that transference is a repetition of the forgotten past, and as will be seen, later authors have underscored the close relationship between transference manifestations and acting out.

Anna Freud (1936) discussed "acting in the transference" as an important source of information about patients in psychoanalytic therapy. In this formulation she emphasizes that when the transference is intensified, the patient "begins to act out in the behavior of his daily life both the instinctual impulses and the defensive reactions which are embodied in his transferred affects" (p. 24). Thus she describes a variation of acting out in which it occurs in daily life rather than in relation to the analyst.

Fenichel (1945) discussed neurotic acting out in relation to general impulsiveness, addictions, traumatic neuroses, and transference in the psycho-analytic situation. He found acting out to be closely related to all of these, a pattern of action that unconsciously relieves inner tension through a partial discharge of warded-off impulses, and in which energies from repressed memories are displaced onto a current situation. Acting out shares with neurotic symptoms an insufficient differentiation between past and present but differs from a symptom in that it is ego syntonic, whereas a neurotic symptom is ego alien. Acting out is most frequently found in people with impulse neuroses. Such persons may be restless or hyperactive, or their activity may be hidden and their life histories give the impression that they are toys of fate, the repetitions being experienced passively and rationalized as occurring against the person's will.

Intolerance of tension or an inability to perform the step from acting to thinking results in the immediate yielding of reasonable judgment to all impulses. A major aim of acting out is the avoidance of unpleasure rather than the attainment of pleasure. The irresistible character of addictions and some perversions is also found in acting out, and some forms of the latter are related to traumatic neuroses in the belated attempt at mastery by repetition of earlier situations that had been overwhelming. Preconditions for acting out listed by Fenichel are an alloplastic readiness (i.e., a tendency to change the environment rather than themselves), oral fixations, high narcissistic needs, an intolerance of tension, as just mentioned, and early traumata.

Greenacre (1950) defined acting out as

a special form of remembering in which the old memory is reenacted in a more or less organized and often only slightly disguised form. It is not a clearly conscious visual or verbal recollection, nor is there any awareness that the special activity is motivated by memory. His behavior seems to the subject to be plausible and appropriate, although to the analyst and to the patient's friends his actions appear to be singularly disappropriate and inappropriate (p. 225).

She distinguished acting out as a specific symptom from an habitual pattern, holding that difficulties in accepting and understanding current reality are found in people who habitually act out, together with low frustration tolerance, disturbance in self criticism, and a tendency toward marked motility or activity, frequently of a dramatic kind. To the factors mentioned by Fenichel as predisposing to habitual acting out, Greenacre adds two more: a special emphasis on visual sensitization (a derivative of exhibitionism and voyeurism that results in a tendency to dramatization) and a belief (largely unconscious) in the magic of action. She speculates that these factors may be related to a disturbance in speech during the second year in which its communicative function is compromised by its use for exhibitionist purposes or as a result of speech inhibition. In either case, there is a greater reliance on action than on speech and an increase in rapport by looking. The tendency to act out is increased when the young child repeatedly observes the parents in sexual intercourse (primal-scene experiences), when the sense of reality is incompletely developed, when narcissism is high, and when the ego is otherwise weak.

In a series of papers on motility and psychodynamics Mittelman (1954) noted that the control of motility gradually becomes an important aspect of impulse mastery. He discussed the motor function in relation to normal development and to psychogenic disturbances (1958). In the second year of life and for some years afterwards, motility provides a significant means of mastery, integration, and reality testing. A few of the characteristic features of the motor function during this period are rapid translation of impulses into action and increase in motor aggression. Regression to the motor level of development is apparent in several syndromes: the psychopath translates impulse into action too readily, and the schizophrenic frequently communicates motorically when the effective use of thought and language is difficult.

Adaptive aspects of acting out have also been considered. For example, Blos (1962) believes that in the adolescent acting out can be a phase-specific mechanism operating in the service of ego synthesis. For the adolescent, action assumes the quality of a magic gesture: it averts evil, it denies passive wishes, and it affirms a delusional control over reality. The processes that occur in normal adolescence can be accomplished only through synthesizing the past with both the present and the anticipated future, and one way of remembering the past is through acting out. And Ekstein and Friedman (1957) have maintained that acting out in adolescents may be seen as an attempt to resolve conflicts.

Bellak (1963) described clinical varieties of acting out and provided a metapsychological analysis of the concept, including dynamic, adaptive, structural, economic, topographical, and sociological aspects. Regarding the various clinical manifestations, he said, "Acting out involves phenomena of somewhat different complexity, different clinical syndromes, and may have episodic or more diffuse temporal characteristics." There is tremendous variation in the extent to which it dominates a personality. He listed seven clinical varieties: (1) episodic behavior that makes a simple unconscious statement; (2) psychotic acting out based on unrealistic perceptions and impulses; (3) hysterical acting out, in which mood swings and actions change rapidly in a rather short time; (4) behavior in certain dissociated states, in which a split-off part of the personality is permitted to act out ordinarily unacceptable impulses; (5) psychopathic, alloplastic (i.e., environment-changing) reactions, in which conflicts and drives are translated into behavior rather than into symptoms; (6) character disorders in individuals who tend to react to certain situations in a stereotyped way and in which activity is less episodic and more diffused through an entire "life style"; (7) excitability in people who constantly blow off one kind of affect or another. In his metapsychological treatment of acting out, Bellak starts with genetic aspects, stressing low frustration tolerance due to developmental interference. With respect to the dynamic point of view, acting out may have defensive elements as a cathartic and abreactive experience: when a person blows off steam, he may reduce tension. In its adaptive aspects, acting out may have certain social advantages, as in the active embracing of causes. Narcissistic overinvestment of certain ego functions, including those of action, motility, and the self, characterizes the economic aspects of acting out. As for topographical aspects, complex acting out is largely unconscious.

While Greenacre stressed the importance of visual sensitization, according to Bellak, people who habitually act out have often been subjected to overstimulation in general, beginning with nursing and rocking: "Such a person then has a lifelong excessive stimulus hunger, matched only by the inability for containment and the constant need for discharge" (p. 68). Deficiencies in synthetic functioning, inability to achieve object constancy, and failures in neutralization also are bases for habitual acting out that may or may not be associated with early overstimulation. Other related factors mentioned by Bellak are congenital differences in activity level (Fries and Woolf, 1953) and a low stimulus barrier. Bellak also underscores how the manifest form of acting out is often strongly influenced by the cultural milieu, social factors, and other contemporary determinants.

Some points from a panel discussion on the relationship of acting out to impulsive disorders (Kanzer, 1957) will round out our consideration of this topic.* While impulsive disorders contribute to acting out, they are not the same; rather, the two are on a continuum. Frosch called "acting on impulse" primary acting out, whereas "acting out" related to neurotic conflicts is at a higher level of organization and is more specific and localized. He specified stages in the evolution of delay mechanisms, from hallucination to motor delay, to fantasy formation, to thought, and then to successful action. Either insufficient frustration or too much frustration during early development can lead to problems in delay of impulses. Features common to the various impulse disorders are that the impulsive behavior is ego syntonic, that the behavior is pleasurable, that there is minimal distortion of the original impulse, and that the person experiences the impulse expression as irresistible.

Both Greenson and Hanna Fenichel underscored problems in identification among acting out individuals. Greenson emphasized that these people confuse identification with object relationships and have fragmented, multiple, or screen identities. H. Fenichel pointed out that identifications in acting out individuals are primitive, impulse controls sometimes being based on the fantasy of being part of another person's body.

Ekstein compared acting out to a "motoric form of screen memory used to deny the frustrations of the past, especially separation anxiety." He gave an account of the development of acting out: the first stage is the impulsiveness of the infant; later it evolves into play and then into fantasy without motor action. During adolescence, playacting appears, which is a way of rehearsing future real-life roles. In maturity, delay, and direction of action for adaptive purposes predominate.

---

*A later symposium on acting out was held at the 25th International Psychoanalytic Congress in 1967 and is published in the *International Journal of Psycho-Analysis 49*, 165 (1968).

Delinquency is an area related to impulse disorders, psychopathy, and acting out. Aichhorn (1935), who pioneered in the application of psychoanalytic knowledge to the treatment and reeducation of delinquent youth, discussed delinquency in terms of a disturbance in the ego-ideal. In regard to ego development, one type of delinquent shows generally poor drive and impulse control because during the earlier years the child's instinctual strivings were not sufficiently restricted, and in these children the pleasure principle was not sufficiently supplanted by the reality principle. This poor drive and impulse control is accompanied by inability to give up immediate pleasures, continual outbreaks of jealousy and quarreling, short interest span, and poor judgment. But in aspects of ego development that involve conforming to reality in the struggle for existence, these same delinquent youths are often quite well developed. Another basis for delinquency is the too-severe punishment of instinctual strivings in relation to the amount of love given by the parents. Here, there is insufficient incentive for the child to accept the reality principle, and rebellion against the parents and against society may occur.

In their definition of delinquency, Redl and Wineman (1951) refer to a delinquent ego as one that defends impulse gratification at any cost. Thus, rather than functioning to reconcile desires, reality demands, and social values, the individual throws his resources (at the moment) into impulse gratification. The ego of such a person may be overwhelmed by impulse at any time. (For a major source on delinquency from a psychoanalytic point of view, the reader is referred to the collection of papers in honor of Aichhorn edited by Eissler [1949].)

REGULATION AND CONTROL AND SUPEREGO CONSIDERATIONS

Freud early assumed that repression was a result of the unacceptability of the impulse or instinctual drive to the person's moral values. In this respect, the sense of guilt and what later more generally came to be called the superego were seen as having an important role in man's control of his instinctual drives and impulses. Freud (1916) also mentioned another and opposite effect of guilt, namely, the commission of a crime or misdeed in order to provoke punishment and thereby alleviate an underlying sense of guilt.

Aichhorn (1935) emphasized identification with the parents, especially the father, and the resultant ego-ideal of the person in the genesis of delinquency. If the child identifies with asocial or criminal parents, the ego-ideal he develops will not be acceptable to society. Or, identifications with parental figures may be weak because the father is unavailable, brutal, or weak and unstable or because there is too much conflict between the parents. Aichhorn conceded that hereditary factors may play a role in some cases and may influence the capacity for identification and for investment in other people.

On the basis of psychotherapy with children and their parents, Szurek (1942) concluded that when the parents of delinquent children were themselves neither delinquent nor notably actor-outers, they were nevertheless encouraging the child's delinquent behavior, through which they were vicariously gratifying some unintegrated and unacceptable needs of their own.

Johnson (1949), who was involved in the work with Szurek, enlarged and refined the above formulations. She pointed out that often the parents, after unconsciously encouraging the child's delinquent behavior, would then react punitively, thus having not only the vicarious gratification but an opportunity to express hostility toward their child. The parents increase the likelihood that their children will develop superego defects in given areas (superego lacunae) by an inordinate amount of checking to see if the child has carried out their directives or by insinuating that the child will probably not do what he is supposed to do, thus demonstrating a lack of trust in the child's integrity.

The family background, psychodynamics, and conscience development of some psychopathic personalities seen in psychoanalytic treatment have been described by Greenacre (1945). Consonant with the findings of others, she pinpointed deprivation of love in the psychopathic patients, reflected in a poor relationship with the parents from early infancy, although there may have been indulgence. The father of such a patient often is, in addition to being socially or otherwise prominent, a remote, stern, preoccupied, and fear-inspiring figure, while the mother is often indulgent and frivolous and implicitly contemptuous of her husband's importance. Pride and shame are very important in these families, and the external appearance of things is emphasized. Because the mother often views the child narcissistically as an extension of herself, this arouses undue aggression in the child and tends to both retard and impair processes of internalization. The child's inadequate internalizations contribute to an ambivalent attitude toward his parents and toward all authority, together with a fear of the father and a feeling that he (the son) is exempt from the consequences of his behavior because his father is so important. Because of the emphasis on the appearance of things, the implication that the child must not fail at anything and the denial of failure by the family, the child emphasizes facade rather than substance and has a weakened sense of reality testing, despite charm and skill in dealing with others.

In the genesis of the preoedipal roots of conscience, Greenacre, like Melanie Klein, stresses infantile aggression, which (as Freud originally pointed out) gets projected onto parental figures, who are consequently seen as terrifying, and then is introjected to become the basis for fear of punishment and of authority. When the quantity of this aggression is increased by illness, discomfort, frustration, restraint, or delay in the development of a sense of separateness, then the conscience will be more severe. While Melanie Klein pointed out the importance of this excess of preoedipal aggression for the development of schizophrenia, Greenacre believes it is also a contributing factor in some psychopaths if it combines with later characteristics that are central to psychopathic personality development.

Redl and Wineman (1951), who worked with delinquent boys in an institutional setting, did not find any of these youngsters to be without a conscience or free from guilt feelings. But they did find that these delinquent boys used a number of techniques to ward off guilt feelings and superego demands, such as "He did it first"; "Everybody else does such things anyway"; "We were all in on it"; "He had it coming to him"; "I didn't use the proceeds anyway"; "They are all against me, they are always picking on me"; and "I couldn't have gotten it any other way" (pp. 145-156).

These authors ascribe all power functions to the ego system and define the superego in terms of identification with value contents and the generating of danger signals when values are involved, specifically when there is a conflict between values and drive-related temptations or when there has been a violation of values. They ascribe to the ego system the task of deciding whether to heed or oppose a danger signal that concerns a value.

Some deficiencies in the superegos of the delinquent children described by Redl and Wineman are as follows: There are peculiarities in value content, such as a delinquent value code, often derived from their family or neighborhood. Even in those with a delinquent code, the authors found what they called "value islands," "value sensitivity," and "value respect," meaning that the delinquent values did not always hold sway. Another superego deficiency was the weakness of the signal function. Thus, the anticipatory pangs of conscience before a delinquent or destructive action were so weak that they were often ignored by the ego system. A variation of this was what the authors labeled a "post-action conscience," in which guilt feelings are not anticipated but are experienced only after the deed is done.

While the superego defects in these youths had a lot to do with their problems of regulating and controlling drives, affects, and impulses, Redl and Wineman hold that the presence of serious ego defects, such as low frustration tolerance, greatly complicate and compound the superego weakness.

Impulsiveness, acting out, and delinquency reflect one side of the regulation and control continuum. We will now consider the other side: inhibition and overcontrol.

INHIBITION-OVERCONTROL

Freud discussed inhibition in his important 1926 paper, and defined it as an ego function that uses energies available to the ego (p. 89). An inhibition may involve only a normal restriction of function but it may also take part in pathological symptom formation. Functions subject to inhibition that Freud discussed are sexual, eating, locomotion, and work. One important basis for an inhibition is an increase in the sexual significance of an activity, resulting in an ego renunciation of the activity to avoid conflict with the id. This formulation is one basis for Hartmann's later conception of deneutralization, which we discuss in the chapter on autonomous functioning.

Inhibitions can also be based on self-punishment, where success or gain are renounced so as to avoid a conflict with superego components. A more general basis for inhibition was Freud's idea that the energy available to the ego may become overdeployed. The implied notion of a given quantity of psychic energy has been very useful heuristically but has caused some theoretical difficulties.

Anna Freud (1936) compared and contrasted ego restriction and inhibition. In ego restriction, a child withdraws from activities because he feels that others do the task better than he. Such activities can be games of skill and school subjects, as well as tasks. In her analyses of children with such ego restrictions, Anna Freud found that the child was attempting to avoid the repetition of a painful competitive failure experienced earlier, usually in relation to one or the other parent. This method of avoiding pain is considered a normal aspect of ego maturation, but if it becomes extreme, it can result in impaired development. From one point of view, it can be seen as a kind of overcontrol of drives, affects, and impulses.

An ego inhibition, on the other hand, occurs when an activity has taken on the significance and meaning of a forbidden impulse, which Freud discussed in his 1926 paper summarized above. Here, the person avoids an activity because it would mean carrying out something forbidden. What is avoided stands either for a temptation of a warded-off instinctual drive, a feared punishment, or both (Fenichel, 1945, p. 169). A wide range of activities may be involved. As Freud (1926) pointed out, writing may be inhibited because letting the liquid out of a tube acquires the meaning of intercourse, or walking takes on the significance of stamping on Mother Earth. Social inhibitions, such as shyness, have been found to be based (in part) on a fear-wish that masturbation may be discovered. And intellectual inhibitions are often related to a repression of sexual curiosity or are based on sadistic meanings of thought functioning. Since all forbidden instinctual drives are continually pressing for expression in action, any one of them may lead to a general inhibition of motor activity (Fenichel, 1945, p. 184).

Direct inhibition of sexual functions is represented in impotence and frigidity. Partial sexual instincts also are subject to inhibition—for instance, eating difficulties, constipation, inability to look at certain kinds of things, and shyness in exhibiting oneself. And inhibition of aggression and hostility is related to a wide range of activities that may take on a destructive meaning and succumb to inhibition for that reason.

These different inhibitions influence the regulation and control of drives, affects, and impulses to varying degrees.

Inhibition may also be more general, that is, of virtually all instinctual drive manifestations and all affects and emotional stirrings. Reich (1935) maintains that someone with a generally inhibited character structure has been subjected to continual frustration of his instinctual drives throughout their development in childhood. The intimate relation between inhibition and defensive functioning is summarized by Fenichel as follows: "The inhibited states are clinical symptoms of the effectiveness of repression or other pathogenic defenses" (1945, p. 184).

We will close this chapter with a brief consideration of one aspect of frustration tolerance—the capacity to tolerate anxiety and depression.

THE ABILITY TO TOLERATE ANXIETY AND DEPRESSION

Anxiety and depression are two of the most important affects. Zetzel (1949, 1965) has focused on the capacity to bear them and has shown that such a capacity is necessary for successful ego development and that its failure predisposes to ego defects and vulnerability to psychopathology. Following the order of her papers, we will consider anxiety first and then depression.

Zetzel utilizes Freud's distinction (1926) between two kinds of anxiety: in one, the person feels helpless to deal with an overwhelming situation or stimulation, either external or internal and in the other, smaller quantities of anxiety serve as a signal for defensive efforts to prevent the development of a traumatic situation such as occurs in the first type of anxiety reaction. The latter is thus a purposive reaction to an internal danger situation, and the capacity to endure this secondary anxiety, Zetzel says, allows the development of adequate defenses against all danger situations, internal or external. To endure the anxiety related to an external situation means to avoid being overwhelmed, to avoid incapacitating physical symptoms or other reactions (phobias, blocking) that decrease the opportunity to deal adaptively with what is triggering the anxiety. Regarding internal sources, enduring the anxiety involves recognizing the danger situation as arising from within, without developing phobias, bodily symptoms, or denial of the danger situation.

In a group of men who neither developed nor tolerated anxiety under war conditions, Zetzel found that after a traumatic incident involving physical threat, they became resentful and depressed, somewhat paranoid, and quite hypochondriacal. In addition, full recovery could not be brought about. Those men who had a history of experiencing signal-type anxiety in previous stress situations showed a greater tendency toward full recovery. Zetzel found the inability to develop secondary anxiety in men who showed irreversible changes after a traumatic experience of physical threat to be associated with fear of castration. Thus, their denial of external danger was associated with their relative inability to endure the instinctual conflicts related to oedipal problems.

Zetzel proposes a three-point continuum in the ability to tolerate anxiety. First, there is the ability to experience purposive anxiety until positive defenses are operative. Second, where anxiety is pathological, by virtue of its intensity or the way it is defensively dealt with (resulting in phobic or psychosomatic symptoms), the person is not overwhelmed. Finally the anxiety increases to such an extent that the defenses break down, and the person feels helpless and overwhelmed by excitation; a traumatic situation has developed. The regressive aftereffects of this development are the presence and persistence of depression, hypochondriasis, and mild paranoid tendencies.

In her consideration of the ability to tolerate depression, Zetzel (1965) hypothesizes that such a capacity is necessary for optimal maturation, parallel to her conception of the necessity to tolerate anxiety. What is requisite here is, first, during development, the learning to tolerate and passively endure the pain of separation, loss, and frustration in relation to the mother (and father), probably between the end of the first year and the beginning of the genital-oedipal period. Melanie Klein has called this the depressive position (1935), and Mahler has written about problems of separation-individuation (1968). Zetzel maintains that in adults who have not successfully worked through the separation there may occur a loss of control, an impairment of reality testing, or a greater susceptibility to psychosis, suicide, or murder. Experiences of separation and frustration are what may bring on these manifestations, for the latter tend to be experienced as abandonment or rejection.

A second developmental task necessary to tolerate and master depression is the ability to actively seek gratification and achievement, rather than be involved with an exaggerated passivity and sense of helplessness.

Aichhorn (1935) hypothesized an involvement of hereditary, biological, and congenital factors in regulation and control, which suggested the likelihood of hereditary factors in some cases of delinquency, affecting the capacity for identification and for emotional investment in others. Schmideberg (1938) expressed the opinion that people who act out their conflicts have a constitutionally lower tolerance for frustration than have more inhibited individuals. Congenital activity types have been postulated by Fries and Woolf (1953), who believe that the active type is more prone to develop alloplastic than autoplastic defenses. And Sheldon Glueck and Eleanor Glueck (1956), using William Sheldon's system of body typing, reported a high incidence of mesomorphic body structure among persistent delinquents and chronically acting out males. Michaels, in his consideration of character structure (1959), regards the latter as a biosocial phenomenon. Specific organic states that influence regulation and control are brain defects, fatigue, endocrine disorders, and physiological reactions to drugs.

CHAPTER 10

Object Relations

Two major aspects of object relations are the ability to form friendly and loving bonds with others with a minimum of inappropriate hostility and the ability to sustain relationships over a period of time with little mutual exchange of hostility. Disturbances in object relations are reflected in emotional coldness and detachment, inability to fall in love or sustain love, self-centeredness, helpless dependency on others, need to dominate others, and perversions (Moore and Fine, 1968).

The development of object relations is central to psychoanalytic formulations of ego development. As Hartmann, Kris, and Loewenstein state (1949): "Every step in the formation of the object corresponds to a phase in psychic differentiation" (p. 21). And Kris said: "There seems little doubt that the intactness of ego functions is to a higher degree than ever before anticipated, determined by the nature of the child's earliest object relations" (1951, p. 166).

But psychoanalysts also recognize that later ego development can sometimes compensate for poor early object relations and that good early object relationships do not always lead to ego strengthening (Hartmann, 1952).

From the formidable amount of literature on object relations, we will review only a portion of the important articles and books, beginning with some writings by Freud relevant to the topic.

In the "Project for a Scientific Psychology" (1895), Freud formulated the contribution of object relations to the evolving of the pleasure and reality principles. He pointed out that the cooperation of a more mature person was necessary for the gratification of an instinctual impulse and that thus the initial helplessness of human beings is the primal source of all moral motives (p. 318).

Freud's first major focus on the object notion was, as already stated, on the sexual object as one aspect of instinctual drives, the others being source, aim, and impetus. "Let us call the person from whom sexual attraction proceeds the sexual object" (1905). He discussed the sexual object in homosexuals, children, and animals as sexual objects, and a fetish as an unsuitable sexual object. He was demonstrating how the libido theory could accommodate these disparate sexual choices. He also stated that the sucking in of nourishment forms the prototype for all later love relationships.

Freud's major interest during the development of libido theory was on the aim of the instinctual drive, rather than on its object. The object was seen primarily as the instrument by which an instinct may attain its aim (1915). But the aims of the component sexual instincts clearly reflected levels and aspects of object relations — devouring, biting, and ambivalence in the oral phase and pleasurable aggression during the anal phase. The libidinal aims of the genital phase, the giving and receiving of love, involve a sharing of satisfaction with another person.

Freud used aspects of object relations in conceptualizing serious psychopathology. He hypothesized in his paper on the Schreber case (1911) that the withdrawal of libidinal cathexis from other people and from the external world* was the basis for Schreber's world-catastrophe fears: "The end of the world is a projection of this internal catastrophe; his subjective world has come to an end since his withdrawal of his love from it" (p. 70).

In his paper "On Narcissism" (1914), Freud distinguished between self-love and love of others in the form of ego libido and object libido. He also conceptualized two kinds of object choice: narcissistic and anaclitic. In narcissistic object choice, the person tends to love someone who is like what he is, was, and would like to be, or was once part of himself. Object choice according to the anaclitic, or attachment, type involves being attracted to someone like the woman who fed him or the man who protected him, and/or the substitutes who took their places. Anaclitic referred to the sexual instincts being attached to the self-preservative (ego) instincts initially, since the first attachments of infants to others appear to be based upon experiences of satisfaction, such as nourishment, which involves a helping person. Anaclitic object choice has come to have the meaning of a dependent relationship.

The distinction between ego and object libido is used to shed light on schizophrenic withdrawal and megalomania, here attributed to the withdrawal of libidinal cathexis from people and things onto the ego (the self).

Freud considered the instinctual object in some detail in *Instincts and Their Vicissitudes* (1915). In his discussion of sadism and masochism, scopophilia and exhibitionism, love and hate, and their transformations (vicissitudes), he made a number of observations relevant to the importance of the other person as the various component instincts develop. At first autoerotic, the ego becomes interested in, and deals initially with, external objects in terms of the pleasure principle. He said:

Under the dominance of the pleasure principle, a further development now takes place in the ego. Insofar as the objects which are presented to it are sources of pleasure, it takes them into itself, introjects them (to use Ferenczi's 1909

---

*Jacobson (1953) has pointed out that it is the mental representation of the object that is cathected or decathected, not the object itself.

term); and on the other hand, it expels whatever with itself becomes a cause of unpleasure (pp. 135-136).

This use of the concept of introjection and a similar use of incorporation (p. 137) will later be supplemented by the concept of identification. All three constructs are important for object relations and have been more carefully differentiated in later psychoanalytic writings (Greenson, 1954; Schafer, 1968; Meissner, 1972).

In "Mourning and Melancholia" (1917), identification is described as a preliminary stage of object choice, the first way the ego picks out an object, where the ego incorporates the object into itself, as he had described in *Instincts and Their Vicissitudes,* with the oral incorporative aspects playing an important role. Freud's understanding of mourning and melancholia (depression) centers on object loss and, in melancholia, on what happens as a result of an object cathexis being regressively replaced by an identification.

In *Group Psychology and the Analysis of the Ego* (1921), identification is described as the "earliest expression of an emotional tie with another person" (p. 105), which precedes a true object cathexis. Identification is also described as a regressive substitute for a libidinal object tie. Freud distinguished between an identification and an object tie as follows:

It is easy to state in a formula the distinction between an identification with the father and the choice of the father as an object. In the first case one's father is what one would like to *be,* and in the second, he is what one would like to *have.* The distinction, that is, depends upon whether the tie attaches to the subject or to the object of the ego (p. 106).

A third way in which identification is important for object relations is when someone perceives an important common quality shared with another person who is not a sexual object. This may become the basis for a new object relationship.

In *The Ego and the Id* (1923), Freud describes the process of object ties regressively being replaced by an identification when the object is lost (as in melancholia):

We succeeded in explaining the painful disorder of melancholia by supposing that (in those suffering from it) an object which was lost has been set up again inside the ego — that is, that an object cathexis has been replaced by an identification . . . Since then we have come to understand that this kind of substitution has a great share in determining the form taken by the ego and that it makes an essential contribution toward building up what is called its "character" (p. 28).

It was also in *The Ego and the Id* that Freud stated that the character of the ego is a precipitate of abandoned object-cathexes and that it contains the history of those object choices. (p. 29)

Much of what Freud had to say about object relations during the years prior to 1923 had to do with object cathexis, object choice, and kinds of consideration for the object. He showed in many ways how the kind of object relationship was different at each stage of libidinal development. Thus, an anaclitic relationship predominates during the oral phase, and consideration for the external object appears during the anal phase (1933, p. 99). In the phallic phase, the oedipal concerns imply further development of object-relationship capacity. Sexual curiosity of children during this period also would have an impact on their object relations with other children. Freud treated the various possibilities for object choice that resulted from the Oedipus complex in detail in his papers "The Psychogenesis of a Case of Female Homosexuality" (1920), in which he discussed the relationship between object choice and the sexual characteristics and attitudes of an individual; the "Infantile Genital Organization of the Libido" (1923), discussing how maleness and femaleness are related to object choice; the "Dissolution of the Oedipus Complex," on the implications for object relations of alignments with mother or father; and "Some Psychological Consequences of the Anatomical Distinction Between the Sexes" (1925).

Two of the four basic anxiety situations formulated by Freud in 1926 have to do with object relations: fear of loss of the object and fear of loss of the object's love. While the first of these may developmentally precede the attainment of object love, it nevertheless plays an important role in the later object relations of many individuals.

Separation anxiety is called the prototype of all later anxiety: anxiety "can be reduced to a single condition, namely, that of missing someone who is loved and longed for . . . anxiety appears as a reaction to the felt loss of the object" (1926, p. 136).

In his last works, Freud showed a growing recognition of the importance of the early mother-child bond for the development of ego structures and for optimal later object relations, but he did not explore this aspect of the family ties as closely as he studied the later-developed oedipal relationships. In 1931, he pointed out that where a woman's attachment to her father was found in analysis, an earlier intense relationship to the mother was subsequently uncovered. In 1938, he described the child's attachment to its mother as "unique, without parallel, established unalterably for a whole lifetime as the first and strongest love-object and as the prototype of all later love-relations — for both sexes" (p. 188).

Stanton (1959) has pointed out that object choice in later life (after the oedipal period) is complicated by defenses, ego factors, ego interests, educational and cultural experiences, aspirations, and group identifications. In addition to the narcissistic and anaclitic bases for object choice, additional reality factors include availability, appropriateness, shared expectations or values, complementary views about sex roles, social skills, accepted times, ages, and places of courtship. All these latter imply social structure. As Stanton mentions, the study by Anna Freud and Sophie Dann (1951) on a group of six motherless concentration-camp children (aged 3-4), who cared about each other but no one else, demonstrates the dependence of object choice on group structure.

STAGES IN THE DEVELOPMENT OF OBJECT RELATIONS

Abraham (1924) presented a set of stages in the development of object love to parallel the stages of libidinal organization.

Table 10.1.   Abraham's Parallel Stages.

Stages of Libidinal Organization	Stages of Object-love	
Earlier oral stage (sucking)	Auto-erotism (without object):	pre-ambivalent
Later oral stage (cannibalistic)	Narcissism (total incorporation of object):	
Earlier anal-sadistic stage	Partial love with incorporation:	ambivalent
Later anal-sadistic stage	Partial love:	
Earlier genital stage (phallic)	Object-love with exclusion of genitals:	
Final genital stage	Object-love:	post-ambivalent

The table thus shows the movement of libido in terms of sexual aim and sexual object.

The development of object relations can be divided into phases in terms of various criteria, including the formation of object representations, the mode of libidinal and aggressive cathexes, or the development of psychic structure (Décarie, 1965, p. 74).

It was in the context of libidinal development that object relations were formulated and understood by Freud. Oral, anal, and phallic features were shown to dominate the object relations of individuals fixated on, or regressed to, these stages.

More recently, in line with the emphasis on ego aspects of development and functioning, a number of theorists have conceptualized the development of object relations in three stages. Hartmann called these primary narcissism, need gratification, and object constancy.

These stages can be examined from a number of vantage points, including the degree of development of psychic structures, and the distribution and mode of libidinal and aggressive cathexes. Here we will focus on the development of the object and rely substantially on the review by Décarie (1965).

During the narcissistic period (first three months of life, roughly) the infant is assumed to be dominated by needs, and objects are perceived only in relation to the satisfaction of those needs. The breast is the first object (or part-object), and the relationship an anaclitic one. As Anna Freud put it: "What is cathected with libidinal interest at that stage is the moment of blissful satisfaction, not the object which enables satisfaction to be attained" (1954, p. 58). Thus the mother "merely plays the role of a signal announcing the drive gratification through kinesthetic and cutaneous cues (Décarie, 1965, p. 93).

M. Balint (1937), as well as I. Hermann, Melanie Klein, and A. Balint, held that the first stage after birth is not objectless but rather involves a primary love relation between infant and mother: "In my opinion a very early, most likely the earliest, phase of the extra-uterine mental life is not narcissistic; it is directed towards objects, but this early object-relation is a passive one. Its aim is briefly this: *I shall be loved and satisfied, without being under any obligation to give anything in return*" (p. 82).

Mahler (1968) includes normal autism and then symbiosis in the period of primary narcissism. During normal autism (about the first month of life), the infant's attempts to achieve homeostasis are its main waking preoccupation. Beginning around the second month, the phase of normal symbiosis is reached, during which the infant presumably gains a dim awareness of the need-satisfying mother and "behaves and functions as though he and his mother were an omnipotent system – a dual unity within one common boundary" (p. 8).

The second intermediate period in the development of objects includes the emergence of the smiling response (Spitz), the ability to wait (Anna Freud, 1954), and the voluntary use of one part of the body to decrease tension in another part, as in thumb-sucking (Hoffer, 1955). It also corresponds to the period of need satisfaction (Hartmann, 1952). What had been an experience of need satisfaction becomes more personalized as the mother is seen more and more as the source of the satisfaction. But the other person is still a preobject and only a precursor of the true libidinal object. The smiling response occurs at this time, not only in reaction to visual presentation of the mother's face but also in reaction to another human face or even to a mask if each of these is moving slowly. Spitz says that in responding to the gestalt of the forehead, eyes, and nose, the infant recognizes the superficial attributes and not yet the essential qualities of the object that allow it to provide protection and satisfaction.

The symbiotic phase, which Mahler has divided into subphases, reaches its height at around four to five months, with the infant directing more attention to the outside world, checking back, however, to the mother's face; a kind of hatching process begins. The more optimal the symbiosis has been, the readier the youngster for hatching, that is, differentiating himself (his self-representations) out from the symbiotic unity.

A second subphase of the symbiotic phase occurs at the height of the hatching process when an increase in active locomotion spurs the child into greater and more frequent physical separations from the mother. This occurs beginning at about the ninth month.

The period of the development of the libidinal object or of true object relations takes place between 6 and 15 months and can be divided into two steps (Décarie, 1965). The wish for approval from the mother has become stronger than the wish for material gratification from her. Hartmann (1952) termed this situation object constancy, the infant being interested in the other person independently of the pressure of his needs. It also involves the presence of an object representation of the mother, which allows the child to tolerate the mother's absence. Object constancy is dated but unstable at about the end of the first year; it gradually becomes more stable during the second year.

If the mother, because of absence or other reasons, no longer satisfies the child's needs or if too many frustrations are associated with her, libidinal cathexis is withdrawn from her and the child finds another love object, which may be himself, his ego, or part of his body. These later cases are traumatic and usually lead to psychopathology.

Klein and Fairbairn have somewhat different conceptualizations of early development of object relations. In addition to their own writings (Klein, 1932, 1948, 1955; Fairbairn, 1952), a detailed summary of their theories has been provided by Guntrip (1964).

Melanie Klein expanded Freud's idea of psychic reality in emphasizing that there are two different realms of object relations: relations with real people in the external world and relations with internal objects. Internal objects, or imagos, result from the introjection or fantasied mental incorporation of the parents or parts of them. As Guntrip summed it up (1964):

> The figures with whom we have relationships in our phantasies are called appropriately, by Mrs. Klein, "internal objects" because we behave with respect to them, emotionally and impulsively, in the same ways as we do towards externally real persons, though in more violent degrees of intensity than would be socially permissible. The formation of this inner world of internal objects and situations proceeds from the very beginnings of life. Its basic figures or "inhabitants" date from so early a time as before the baby could grasp in perception the wholeness of its parents as persons. We must presume that at first all the baby knows or experiences is a breast (a "part object"), and that it takes time and development for the baby to become aware of the mother in her completeness (a "whole object") (p. 226).

The first object, the mother's breast, is assumed to be split into two separate imagos: the good (gratifying) breast and the bad (frustrating) breast, which corresponds to a split between love and hate. Klein assumes that the infant's aggressive trends (generated from oral frustration and from other sources) result in anxiety of annihilation. He fears being destroyed by his own aggressive impulses, which, according to Klein, are projected onto the mother's breast, and then he fears retaliation from the object. When the breast is then reintrojected, the bad breast and the fear of its retaliation become aspects of inner object relations. Fantasies of eating and destroying the mother's breast, of robbing the mother's body of its contents, of destroying her with urine and feces play an important role in early object relations. This fear of an attack on oneself, which Klein believes is dominant during the first three months after birth, when objects are still split into good and bad part objects, is an aspect of the paranoid-schizoid position; and if too much sadism and aggression are generated during this time because of (in part) unsatisfactory mothering, the conditions have been set for the likelihood of later serious psychopathology, with emphasis upon the danger from bad objects. When the mother begins to be experienced as a whole person because of the good and bad aspects being brought together, the depressive position has been reached, according to Klein, and anxiety is now experienced concerning the possible loss of love objects (separation anxiety). So, for Klein, early psychic development is dominated by persecutory and depressive anxiety, and both are seen as caused primarily by the infant's own aggression.

We cannot here recap the details of Klein's views on the development of object relations, nor can we enter upon a critical assessment of these. Her emphases on inner object relations, on the importance of aggression in the genesis and functioning of these, and on the mechanism of splitting are among her contributions. She has been most frequently criticized for her assumptions about the kind of mental activity that presumably takes place during the first months of life, the idea that object relations begin at birth and that the Oedipus complex, guilt, and the superego begin during the oral-sadistic phase.

Fairbairn used Klein's general idea of inner objects in developing his own object relations theory. He held (1941) that libido is essentially object seeking, that is, it is the relationship with the object and not impulse gratification that is the basic libidinal aim and that the phases of libidinal development (with the exception of the oral) are techniques used by the ego to regulate relationships with objects, especially internalized objects. Object relations provide the basis for Fairbairn's theory of ego development, which has three stages: infantile dependence, a transitional stage, and mature dependence.

Based on his study of schizoid individuals, Fairbairn decided that the major problems of these people involved the need for good object relationships, and he hypothesized the schizoid position as the basic one in mental development. The basic factor that underlies all psychopathology for Fairbairn is the inability of the mother to convey to the child that she loves him as a person in his own right. Guntrip (1961) sums this up as follows:

Limitations in the mother's personality and her emotional conflicts, amounting in some cases to open rejection and hate of the baby, though more often to unconscious and over-compensated rejection, influence her handling of it to all degrees of traumatic seriousness. The tone of voice, the kind of touch, the quality of attention and interest, the amount of notice, and the total emotional as well as physical adequacy of breast feeding, are all expressions of the genuineness or otherwise of the mother's personal relationship to the infant. From the moment of birth Fairbairn regards the mother-infant relationship as potentially fully personal on both sides, in however primitive and under-developed a way this is as yet felt by the baby. It is the breakdown of genuinely personal relations between the mother and the infant that is the basic cause of trouble. That is the factor that dominates all other and more detailed, particular issues such as oral deprivation, anal frustration, genital disapproval, negative and over-critical discipline and so on (p. 284).

Comparisons between the egopsychology of Hartmann, Kris, and Loewenstein and Rapaport, on the one hand, and Klein and Fairbairn, on the other, have been made by Guntrip (1969, chap. 15) and by Sutherland (1963). In his paper "Structural Derivatives of Object Relations" (1966), Kernberg integrates some of Klein's ideas about early object relations with autonomous-ego-development constructs of Hartmann.

THE EARLY MOTHER–CHILD RELATIONSHIP

Although Freud pioneered in stressing the importance of early childhood for later development and psychopathology and emphasized the centrality of relationships with the parents during formative years, the need of infants for a continuous and emotionally satisfying relationship to one person has only been explicitly recognized, as Brody (1956) points out, since World War II, when large numbers of children were separated from their parents in Great Britain (A. Freud and D. Burlingham, 1943). Also important here is the work of Spitz on hospitalism and anaclitic depression (1945, 1946, 1950). Spitz showed that deprivation of usual contact with the mother has disasterous effects not only on the development of object relations but on the development of all ego functions. He observed that the earliest age at which anaclitic depression, due to an interruption in the baby's dependent relationship with the mother, could occur was six months. Therefore, he concluded that at this age an object concept had already developed, and this extreme disorder was the reaction to the loss of that established love object. In 1965, Spitz summarized and brought new observations and theory to bear on these earlier discoveries by stating that object formation begins in the nursing situation when the infant looks at the mother while sucking the nipple. Institutionalized infants, separated from their mothers or from a consistent mothering person, were also studied by Provence and Ritvo

(1961) and Provence and Lipton (1962). Such infants showed, as we pointed out in the chapter on reality testing, less interest in exploring toys, failure to develop an attachment to a specific toy, and failure to search for a toy when it was moved out of sight.

ATTACHMENT, LOSS, AND DEPENDENCE

Bowlby has given detailed consideration to attachment behavior, which includes clinging, sucking, following, crying, and smiling. He does not use the term "dependency" because he believes, along with a number of ethologists, that the tie between infant and mother is primary, and not secondary, to the infant's needs for the mother as a source of tension reduction. Primary object love was put forth by Balint (1937) and others, as already mentioned. Bowlby (1958) holds that the infant's tie is based upon a constellation of instinctual responses or behavior patterns, mentioned above, that have survival value. He cites (1964) Harlow's observations on monkeys that attachment behavior is prominent even when the mothers are inadequate, rejecting, or cruel.

Pertinent here by contrast is Winnicott's paper (1956) on primary maternal preoccupation, a kind of withdrawn state that involves a heightened sensitivity of the mother to the infant, based upon an identification of the mother with the infant which begins toward the end of pregnancy and continues for a few weeks after delivery.

Bowlby also maintains that behavior patterns following separation and loss are essentially the same in adults as in children (1960). He states that the prototype of all anxiety is a reaction to the danger of losing the love object; the pain of mourning is a retreat from the actually lost object. Defense is a way of dealing with separation anxiety and mourning, protecting the ego against instinctual demands that threaten to overwhelm it in the absence of the object. The connection of grief and mourning with separation anxiety is the topic of a subsequent paper (1963), where Bowlby states that the rupture of the mother-child tie in the middle of the first year of life "leads to separation anxiety and grief and sets in train processes of mourning" that frequently lead to unfavorable personality development and predispose to psychiatric illness (p. 500). A. Freud, Schur, and Spitz all offered similar opinions on Bowlby's paper on grief and mourning in infancy and early childhood (1960). Anna Freud's major point (1960) is that in an ego theory of object relationships it is not possible to maintain that separation anxiety in the child and the adult are identical. She feels that the time needed to adjust to a substitute object is related to ego maturity and the degree of object constancy that develops before separation. Bowlby, she says, expounds a physiological theory as opposed to an egopsychology. Along these same lines Schur (1960) held that Bowlby and the ethologists, in seeing the child's and adult's reaction to separation as identical, are endowing instinct with qualities we usually attribute to the considerably developed ego. The capacity to delay gratification as the ego matures would be crucial in distinguishing the adult's from the child's response. According to Spitz (1960), the trauma of separation is greater the more inadequate the personality organization in terms of defense and mastery ability. He thus also rejects Bowlby's position that toddlers and grown-ups have similar reactions to separation. The urge to master real or potential object loss is believed to underlie the universal "peek-a-boo" game (summarized by Kleeman, 1967). This controversy continued into 1964 when Lois Murphy discussed the limitations of applying ethological concepts to human infants. She feels that Bowlby's approach is one-sided, that his list of instincts mediating the child's tie to the mother all reflect the infant's need for mere attachment to an object, and that he neglects the baby's need for active maternal support for its developing ego. The sucking, clinging, following, and similar behavior that Bowlby calls instincts are, she believes, precursors of, or even actual, autonomous ego processes and functions. "The fact that the mother not only meets nutritional and other body needs and gives and evokes love, but also supports the development of specific ego functions and the integrative functions of the ego is important for understanding the seriousness of separation problems of the second year of life before the child has achieved stable autonomy" (L. Murphy, 1964, p. 38).

Finally, Bowlby's (1969) most recent work on attachment and loss has been criticized by Engel (1971) because Bowlby does not clarify important differences between assumptions underlying object relations theories and those concerned with attachment behavior.

It is generally believed that before object loss can be recognized and tolerated, self-object differentiation and some ego identification must have occurred. In adults with good ego strength, object loss through death can be a maturing experience, increasing the capacity for instinctual renunciation.

A concept related to attachment is dependence, and the latter is a central aspect of object relations. It dominates the relationships of young children to others and, under favorable circumstances, decreases as self-reliance increases during development. Overly strong dependence in adults is associated with maladaptiveness in object relations. Parens and Saul (1971) review Freud's writings and some more recent psychoanalytic works relevant to dependence and trace the development and manifestations of the latter throughout the life cycle.

These authors find many formulations of Freud's that are concerned with dependence. Dependence in relation to helplessness and anxiety is traced through Freud's discussion of the basic danger situations, such as the fear of loss of the object and of the object's love. Freud's views of the psychological needs for religion were based upon the young child's helplessness and his longing for his father. Parens and Saul also point out that it is the libidinization of the dependency upon his parents that induces the child to place restrictions upon his impulse gratification and identify with his parents and that these latter developments contribute to psychic-structure formation.

Parens and Saul also describe what they call inner sustainment: "The degree to which one is libidinally sustained from within is reflected by the degree to which one is free from the need for sustainment from without" (p. 123). Thus, in the person's movement from the initial dependency of childhood to increasing self-reliance, the quality of the representations of object relations that are internalized are of central importance for a number of structural and dynamic factors related to inner sustainment and the decreased need for external sources of emotional and dependent support.

SOME DIMENSIONS FOR EVALUATING OBJECT RELATIONS

An assessment of the level of object relations can be made by evaluating where an individual stands on the following four dimensions: (1) symbiosis-separation-individuation; (2) primary narcissism, need-gratification, object constancy; (3) stability, quality, and differentiation of self-representations from object representations. (4) degree of separation or fusion of good and bad object representations. We will consider each of these briefly and illustratively.

The basic work on separation and individuation has been done by Mahler, and her descriptions of the autistic psychotic syndrome and the symbiotic psychotic syndrome in children (1952, 1968) are examples of extreme disturbances in object relations that are most fruitfully characterized along the separation-individuation continuum.

Withdrawal and schizoid trends in later life can also be understood in terms of the autistic-symbiotic-separation dimension. Both Klein and Fairbairn have focused on schizoid phenomena, both as normal developmental occurrences and as psychopathology but have stressed the mechanism of splitting and frustration.

Examples of how problems in the individuation process can adversely affect marital relations are provided by Rubin and Gertrude Blanck (1968). Thus, a spouse who has failed to successfully work through the symbiotic phase resents her husband paying attention to others: friends, colleagues, relatives, and even their own children. She also may expect that he not initiate independent activities, because she unconsciously experiences him as part of herself. Similarly, a husband who unconsciously maintains a symbiotic tie with his wife may feel abandoned and incomplete when the wife turns her attention to their newborn child.

Object relations can also be described in terms of whether they are predominantly on the level of primary narcissism, need-gratification, or object constancy. Individuals who have regressed to, or mostly function at, the level of primary narcissism have not developed meaningful object representations or clear self-representations and thus will be withdrawn or show very primitive modes of relating to others. Individuals at the need-gratification level respond to others as though the latter exist primarily to gratify their own needs. As Blanck and Blanck (1968) point out, the level of object relations usually fluctuates, so that a person may operate at the level of object constancy part of the time and regress to the need-gratifying level under stress or under the pressure of an unconscious wish. They suggest that an elaboration of the sublevels of primary narcissism, need-gratification, and object constancy would constitute a refinement of theory analogous to Mahler's delineation of the subphases of separation-individuation.

Searles (1961) described the psychotherapy of chronic schizophrenics in terms of the phases of the relationship with the therapist. These are out-of-contact phase, ambivalent symbiosis, preambivalent (full) symbiosis, resolution of the symbiosis, and, finally, the establishment of a new individuation through repudiation of outmoded identifications and development of new ones. The first three of these phases are seen by Searles as retracing in reverse the phases in the development of schizophrenia. His conceptualization is that "the etiological roots of schizophrenia are found when the mother-infant symbiosis fails to resolve into individuation of mother and infant – or, still more harmfully, fails even to become at all firmly established – because of deep ambivalence on the part of the mother which hinders the integration and differentiation of the infant's and the young child's ego" (p. 524).

Bak (1971) maintains that object constancy implies, in addition to the ability to sustain love for another person, a realistic perception and representation of the other person with a minimum of distortion. Beres and Joseph (1971) state that object constancy implies that the mental representation of the external object has a stable cathexis.   Since object relations are developmentally dependent upon, and related to, the development of both libidinal and aggressive drives, the attainment of object constancy may be delayed by the increased ambivalence in the anal sadistic stage, which may be seen as resulting from the increased aggression which is a maturational factor added at this time (Mahler, 1968).

We have discussed self and object-representation concepts in several previous chapters. In reality testing, the focus was on distinguishing between self and nonself, and how the fusion and refusion of self- and object images occurs in early childhood, with a gradual strengthening of boundaries between self- and object representations as both become progressively more based on perceptual and self-perceptual data (i.e., on reality testing). In the chapter on sense of reality, we discussed additional aspects of the emergence and differentiation of self-and object representatives and especially the self-image and factors contributing to self-representations. Various processes of internalization (incorporation, introjection, and identification) play an important role in the development of self-representations.

Examples of disturbed object relations based on a struggle against identification with a hated parental figure were described by Greenson (1954). The four patients under study both introjected and identified with the hated parent, but their entire life style was strongly influenced by an attempt to contradict this. They attempted to take on characteristics and behave in ways that were directly opposite to those of the hated parent, while at the same time manifesting strong tendencies to identify with new objects, but these attempts were unstable, transitory, and superficial. All the patients studied had large fluctuations in their self-concept, body-image disturbances, and defects in reality testing. They were also subject to impulsive acting-out episodes that resembled behavior of the consciously hated parent. Greenson's formulation is that these patients had regressed to a level where the ego is not able to maintain a separation between the introject and self-representations, and they thus have to deny the hated introject in order to avoid feeling devoured or feeling they were losing their identity.

More serious disturbances in self-and object representations are detailed by Jacobson in her paper on the metapsychology of psychotic identifications (1954). Here, she differentiates between identification mechanisms in manic-depressives as compared with schizophrenics and between normal ego and superego identifications, on the one hand, and psychotic identification mechanisms, on the other. In manic-depressives there may be a fusion of bad or good love-object images with the self-image and with the superego. This may lead to either a severe pathological conflict or a harmony between self-representations and the superego. In schizophrenics, the regressive processes may result in a total fusion between self-and object images, where the conflict between self-image and superego may be

retransformed into struggles between the image of the self and magic, sadistic, threatening love object figures. The pathological identifications are the expression of alternating introjective and projective processes that lead to a more or less total merging between these self and object images within the deteriorating ego-id. Insofar as powerful, lasting object images are reconstituted and reattached to the outside world, the ego-superego conflict may change into homosexual paranoid conflicts, with impulses to kill and fears of being persecuted and destroyed by outside representatives of these terrifying figures (p. 262).

In her recent book, *Depression* (1971), which has not as yet been entirely digested, Jacobson describes pathological aspects of object relations in depressive, schizophrenic, paranoid, sadomasochistic, and narcissistic individuals.

Bak has attempted to explain many pathological phenomena found in schizophrenics as a result of the vicissitudes of object relations. He hypothesized (1954) that withdrawal, projection, and ego regression (sometimes back to the undifferentiated phase) found in schizophrenics may be defensive attempts to deal with the disturbance in the capacity to neutralize aggression. He also posits (1971) a connection between the extent of withdrawal from objects and ego regression. It will be recalled that Freud had formulated that a loss of reality followed the withdrawal of libidinal cathexes from objects but stressed libidinal regression rather than the ego in the development of a psychosis. Bak sees disorders of thinking to be a direct result of cathectic changes that follow the early stages of object relationship regression. In those schizophrenics in whom the object representations have been destroyed or have regressed to their physiological forerunners, "the relation to objects takes place on the symbiotic level of self-and non-self undifferentiation. The inner experience of the threatened undifferentiation is felt by the schizophrenic as the oncoming loss of individuality. This is one of the major sources of the schizophrenic anxiety, together with the sense of failing ego functions and loss of contact with the world. The bizarre mannerisms of speech, language and conduct are attempts at demaracation, delineation of the self to prevent its merging into the collective or into the animal, or even into the inanimate world" (p. 237).

Two interesting research studies will illustrate some experimental work being done on aspects of object relations from a psychoanalytic point of view.

Grand, Freedman, and Steingart (1972) studied object representation in two groups of chronic schizophrenics, one characterized by relative solitariness or isolation and another by their assertiveness or belligerence in interpersonal behavior. The authors assessed the relative capacity to represent objects by evaluating speech-related movements in relation to the relative simplicity or complexity of language constructions in a clinical interview, and a test situation; and they also evaluated cognitive performance on the Stroop color-word test, which provides a measure of the ability to encode visually presented colored material and a measure of interference between incongruous object and word presentations. Results showed that the overtly belligerent chronic schizophrenics maintained a relative intactness of the ego's representational function in comparison with the withdrawn chronic schizophrenics. Thus, the isolated patients showed a deficit in using words to represent their experience, which resulted in greater difficulty in integrating thought and action. The difference between groups was discussed in terms of the relatively more impaired ability to deneutralize aggression in the withdrawn group and the concomitant loss of object representations.

Steingart and Freedman (1972) have examined self- and object representations in different clinical states by assessing language usage in clinical interviews with three language-construction measures. They analyzed eight therapy sessions of four different patients. The authors assessed language construction of a single patient who underwent a number of cyclical changes in her clinical state, and they also compared the language construction of this patient in her initial paranoid state with three other patients who showed mixtures of delusional-paranoid, schizophrenic, and psychotic-depressive features. They found that in the depressive state the cyclical patient showed relatively limited distinction between self and objects, in comparison with the verbalizations of the same patient when she was in a paranoid state. They also found that, when they compared the cyclical patient with the other three patients, a paranoid state involved more distinction between self and objects than did a depressive state and that a depressive state in turn showed more self-object differentiation than a schizophrenic state.

GOOD– AND BAD–OBJECT REPRESENTATIONS

The issue of fusion or integration of good and bad-object representations is related to object constancy. But we discuss the former separately here to highlight the importance of split-off, bad-object representations for object relations. We also briefly consider here the issue of hostility, which is central both to bad-object representations and many maladaptive forms of object relationships.

Melanie Klein has written extensively about good and bad objects and about the importance of aggression and hatred in object relations and psychopathology. We have already mentioned her formulation of a paranoid-schizoid position where fear of aggression and the projection of aggression onto the object plays an important role as a result of the object (breast or mother) being introjected and split off from other internalizations of the breast or mother and thereby later causing the person to distort the motives and actions of other people in relation to himself. Both excessive aggression (due to constitutionally high oral sadism) and excessive frustration of early nourishment intake and sucking are assumed to lead to the internalization of a bad-object representation and to excessive splitting, which interferes with or prevents the integration of bad (frustrating) and good (gratifying) aspects of the breast or the mother. The attainment of the libidinal object, referred to earlier, involves the integration of good and bad aspects.

Klein and her followers have emphasized the place of aggressive and hostile derivatives in object relations, such as hate, contempt, envy, jealousy, depreciation, rejection, rivalry, treachery, and hypocrisy (Riviere, 1937) and have related these to bad internal objects.

Bychowski (1966) has pointed out that individuals with strong aggressive or narcissistic endowment are more likely to develop violent hostility because these trends will probably be more strongly curbed by the parents. This hostility and the frustration-rage generated by pain and discomfort experienced in the presence of the caretaking adults results in the rage being part of the archaic bad-object images that are internalized and split off. They are later externalized and projected onto love-hate objects and their substitutes.

Events that have the symbolic meaning of separation, rejection, or lack of love may provoke the angry reactions associated with bad-object representations. While Bychowski emphasized that archaic bad-object representations that have remained intact are characteristic of seriously disturbed individuals, Sutherland (1963) describes a common pattern found in marital conflicts. After some period of a satisfactory marital relationship,

> there then begins an insidious process, frequently starting with more initiative from one partner, but sooner or later colluded in by both, through which the repressed relationships with the original significant parent figures are brought in . . . With these cases there are many complications, but the common characteristic keeps reappearing, namely, of the bringing into the good relationship the repressed bad aspects of the relationships with the parents. In marriage, processes of this kind are universal, but they are ordinarily contained by the balance in favor of the good relationship and its enrichment.

In addition to the original hostility, pathological splitting is a mechanism that plays a central role in the development of nonintegrated good- and bad-object representations. Kernberg (1966) has emphasized the presence in some borderline individuals of contradictory behaviors and attitudes that are alternatively activated but not seen in relationship to each other. A particular manifestation of pathological splitting is when objects are seen as all good or all bad. Such an individual will tend to turn away from a member of the opposite sex when frustrated or disappointed by the other person who has become a bad object thereby. He then begins searching for a new, good (perfect) object but will leave the new relationship when any disappointment occurs (Blanck and Blanck, 1968). Less extreme examples of partial integration or fusion of good- and bad-object representations are found in nonborderline individuals.

The problem of hostility, hatred, and aggression in object relations cannot be overestimated, and the space devoted to it here in no way reflects the importance we attach to these issues. While we have stressed the negative aspects of aggression in object relations, there is another important consideration. Aggression, as well as libidinal drives, is important in the formation of object relations. Hitting, biting, scratching, pulling, and kicking are ways for an infant to relate to another person and will usually be responded to by the other person. This kind of behavior, which may be assumed to reflect aggressive drive discharge, takes place in relation to the mother and has been hypothesized to aid perceptual orientation and to increase manipulative mastery. When the mother is not available for the infant to bite or hit, Spitz (1953) states that aggression tends to be turned inward, and the infant is more likely to become self-destructive.

Maladaptive factors in the four areas or dimensions just illustrated each and together will be associated with disturbed object relations of various kinds and will also interfere with the attainment of a mature love relationship. Some additional complexities in characterizing the positive ingredients of a mature (genital) love relationship have been considered by Balint (1948). More recently, Kernberg has discussed "Barriers to Being in Love" (1971) from the standpoint of narcissistic personality features.

We end this somewhat cursory account of object relations with the reflection that much has been learned about object relations through psychoanalytic observations and hypotheses but that much yet remains to be understood and integrated.

CHAPTER 11
Thought Processes

FREUD'S EARLY ADAPTIVE VIEW OF THINKING

Thinking, according to Freud (1896), is a form of trial action. The adaptive egopsychological aspect of thinking stated in this early formulation is dramatically exemplified in the problem-solving activity of Köhler's apes on Tenerife (1925). The apes were placed in a cage and given several sticks, each of which was too short to enable them to reach a banana lying outside the cage. As adherents of the Gestalt school of thought would have it, one of the apes suddenly had a configurational insight: he stuck two sticks together, retrieved the banana, and ate it in triumph.

Life is not as simple as laboratory situations, nor are people as simple as apes. Linguistic or other symbols are the usual vehicles of human thought. Beginning with Aristotle and his laws of association, thinking was the domain of logicians and other philosophers. Later, as an aspect of psychological behavior, it occupied not only Freud but child psychologists, experimental psychologists, and, of course, psychopathologists. Neurologists, too, studied thought by way of aphasia and other language disturbances (e.g., *salade de mots*). Investigations of concrete thinking resulting from brain injuries form a bridge to the study of thought disorders in schizophrenia and other psychoses.

Freud's work itself is one of the important transitional contributions from neuro anatomy to psychopathology. In his monograph on aphasia, translated by Stengel (1953), he was concerned not only with speech but also with thought. He was interested there in the arrangement of associations, in fact relying heavily on Hughlings Jackson's doctrine of evolution and dissolution of function. He used the concept of retrogression, which, in *The Interpretation of Dreams* (1900) nine years later, became regression. As Stengel points out in his introduction: "What Freud said about paraphasia, i.e., the mistaken use of words, reads like a prelude to the chapter on errors and slips of the tongue in *Psychopathology of Everyday Life.*"

It was in connection with *The Interpretation of Dreams* that Freud turned his interest to thinking most conspicuously.

There, dreamwork as a distorting mechanism of logical thinking is differentiated as primary-process thinking. Secondary-process thinking was regarded as characteristic of waking life. The ego in its early form as censor protects the sleeper from disruptive thoughts and affects by defensively employing distorting processes such as condensation, symbolization, and displacement. The censor, therefore, serves as an early version of an adaptive ego mechanism, standing guard between the conscious and the unconscious mind. While there is excellent supporting evidence for this view of the manifest dream content as serving a defensive function, much can also be said for the developmental view that primary-process thinking in the dream is actually "primary" — that is, it occurs without the benefit of learned hierarchical and complexly abstract relationships typical of adaptive adult thinking. In other words, primary-process thinking is not necessarily a result of defense (as in the dream) or of defense breakdown (as in psychosis) but is often simply a representation of earlier forms of thinking that take place without the benefit of a well-functioning adult ego, with its trial action, its semantic vehicles (other than simple pictorial ones), and the hierarchy of relationships that a child gradually becomes aware of and able to use (as demonstrated particularly well by Piaget and Werner).

A BRIEF REVIEW OF RECENT PSYCHOANALYTIC LITERATURE

An updated exploration of the psychoanalytic theory of thinking was undertaken in 1963 at a panel of the American Psychoanalytic Association. Guttman and Sloane discussed Freud's theory of thinking, which was based on the postulated tendency of the organism to maintain a low level of excitation. At the earliest developmental stage, when gratification of a need is not possible, the memory of previous fulfillment is revived and an hallucination of gratification occurs. This hallucinatory image is the forerunner of thought. When the reality principle is established, a delay of drive discharge is imperative. It is then that the thinking function of the ego increases in significance; since thought provides a limited discharge of tension, it also makes the delay more possible. The functions of memory, attention, and judgment were initially presumed to develop from this conflict between the desire for immediate drive gratification and the frustrations imposed by the environment. Hartmann (1939) reasoned that these functions developed independently of drive, conflict, and environmental frustration and were thus part of the conflict-free ego sphere. The secondary process is firmly established when repression is able to prevent drive impulses from reaching consciousness. Thus, a further basis for the sound evaluation of reality is made possible.

Charles Fisher, in his turn on this panel, suggested that the concept of the primary process itself be revised. He felt that ideational components of repressed material are within the ego and that primary-process thoughts derive from the ego organization and not primarily from the id. Arlow replied that thinking per se is an ego function and is probably autonomous in origin. Yet, it may temporarily become a means of drive discharge. At such times, it is characterized by primary-process modes of action. These primary-process tendencies themselves serve, however, as adaptive functions in many situations and therefore can no longer be considered universally pathological and in opposition to the secondary process.

In a paper on the psychoanalytic study of thinking, de Monchaux (1962) considers both negative and positive hallucinations as important forerunners of the thought process, the negative ones being forerunners of primal forms of denial. De Monchaux cites Bion's assumption of a primary cognitive experience of frustration tolerance and states that the capacity to think "no breast" is the prototype of the secondary process and depends on mutual inhibition of positive and negative hallucinatory functions. In a later paper (1965), de Monchaux stresses that there are two kinds of thinking: one controlled by inner needs and expressed in fantasy, the other dominated by attempts to control external reality. Psychoanalysis, she says, assumes that all thinking involves both types and that the extreme forms are at the ends of a hypothetical continuum. With maturity, the psychic organization becomes more adapted to obtaining gratification via real objects (i.e., external ones). De Monchaux considers dreams an example of how primitive thought forms are related to later adaptive ones. Thought, both in the waking and sleeping states, uses symbolization. During the waking period, symbolization leads to concept formation, whereas in a dream the same processes of condensation and displacement are used for the purpose of wish fulfillment. The final stage in the prototype occurs in old age, when thinking again becomes dominated by wish fulfillment and remembrances of the past.

Szekely (1962) comments that thinking is now, as it was not in the early days of psychoanalysis, considered an ego function. He too reviews Freud's formulations, namely, that in the absence of a satisfying object, an hallucinatory idea of previous satisfaction emerges. In the model of secondary-process thought, when instinct reaches threshold intensity, structuralized postponement and trial action with minimal energy expenditure come about. The first model is characterized by primary process and is regulated by the pleasure principle; the second is characterized by secondary process and the reality principle. Szekely describes two instruments of thought: (1) the temporary regression that is still accompanied by reality testing and the synthetic function of the ego and (2) the selective style of thought that is often used in mathematical thinking. He also comments on the fact that some psychoanalysts in the same symposium (e.g., Bion), feel that the decisive factor in bringing about secondary-process thinking is the degree of tolerance for frustration. If frustration is not adequately tolerated, in extreme cases adaptive thought does not develop at all. Abstract types of thinking are notably absent, whereas the apparatus of projective identification does develop.

Hacker (1957) refers specifically to the importance of symbols in thinking, as did M. Klein 15 years earlier. He says that symbols are used to manipulate inner and outer reality and that they make it possible to deal with objects in ways not necessarily inherent in actual experience. The capacity for symbolization arises in two ways: from conflict between id and reality and from a preformed rudiment in the ego. After development to a specific stage, thinking is structurally part of the unconscious, as well as of the conscious, ego.

Schilder (1953) studied many manifestations of thought disorder, among them aphasia and those found in schizophrenia and neuroses. He generalized that every thought undergoes a development before it becomes conscious in its final form. This development proceeds from indefinite to definite forms. Primary-process mechanisms play a greater role in the early phases than in the later phases of development, which are increasingly object- and reality-oriented. He considers the pathological forms of thought a result of premature closure of the processes of thought development. Schilder implied that even when thought developments reach completion, imagelike and affect-distorted preliminary developmental forms may come into consciousness alongside the completed thought.

The psychoanalytic theory of thinking is delineated differently by Rapaport (1950). He considers thinking an outgrowth of the earliest phases of ego development, when the primary process is operative. In a case of externally imposed delay of discharge, a major event in thought development is the emergence of an hallucinatory image of the object that is capable of satisfying the need. Rapaport considers this hallucinatory image the archetype of thought. The major difference between the primary and secondary processes lies in the change that occurs in the nature of the delay. Originally, in primary-process thought, the delay is caused by external circumstances, whereas in the secondary process the delay is produced by internal controls. Comparing primary- and secondary-process thinking, he points out that in the primary process, discharge of tension is striven for directly and that the process operates with mobile cathexes. In contrast, the secondary process permits no discharge until experimental action makes it likely that tension will be discharged. This latter process takes place with bound cathexes. Topographically, Rapaport sees thought processes as either unconscious or preconscious and conscious.

In his source book, *Organization and Pathology of Thought* (1951), Rapaport collected 27 selections from the fields of psychology, psychiatry, and psycho-analysis, many of which had not previously been available in English. A number of methods for investigating thought processes are illustrated in these papers. The material is organized into five sections: directed thinking, symbolism, motivation of thinking, fantasy thinking, and pathology of thinking. In addition to extensive clarifying notes on each paper, Rapaport contributed a concluding chapter entitled "Toward a Theory of Thinking." While he claims only to have extracted common theoretical implications of the various papers he selected, in fact he did much more. Beginning with a consideration of thought processes mainly from the standpoint of motivation, Rapaport develops the most comprehensive sketch of a psychoanalytic theory of thinking ever attempted. Some of his central concepts are delay of discharge, psychic structuring, drive organization, conceptual organization of memories, hierarchy of motivational factors, anticipations, and states of consciousness. The very scope of this effort has the drawback, as Rapaport himself recognized, of being so broad that thought processes are assumed to be an aspect of most psychological processes.

Kris (1950) distinguishes unconscious from preconscious processes on the basis that the former use mobile energy whereas the latter use bound energy. He considers variations in the mobility and energy cathexes of preconscious thought as determining whether it enters the preconscious or the unconscious. If more energy is removed from a preconscious thought, it is then drawn into the primary process and the id. In turn, an id derivative is cathected with ego energy. Unconscious mentation, when it receives extra ego energy, becomes preconscious mentation; and if it is invested with further cathexis, it becomes conscious mentation. This process can also be reversed. The problem is, how could this conceptualization be verified in any controlled way? To be sure, this energy "scale" is consonant with Ostow's conception of the psychotic process (1962). He feels that an ego depletion is crucial to the development of a psychosis and that energizers reverse the psychotic process. The difficulty is that there is no more verification of Ostow's particular hypothesis than there is of the original postulates concerning the relationship between increasing cathexis and ascendence of thought from the unconscious to the conscious mind.

Rosen (1953) examines the genetic development of abstract thinking in his discussion of mathematical illumination and mathematical thought processes. Usually, the concept of numbers develops concomitantly with the maturation of the perceptual apparatus during the oedipal period. Rosen believes that in mathematically gifted individuals, this maturation sequence occurs during an earlier stage of ego development. Thus, along with the preconscious concepts of numbers and quantity, certain archaic ego defense mechanisms remain, which are employed later, on a preconscious level, in the creative aspect of the mathematical process. Hypercathexis of preconscious mental activity and a capacity for decathexis of the conscious perceptual system are responsible for most of the achievements of mathematical thought. This is quite consistent with Kris's concept of regression in the service of the ego. As a matter of fact, Rosen sees the illumination experience in mathematical thought as a creative act, determined by a particular ego's capacity for controlled regression to infantile modes of perceiving space and number. He considers the illuminating experience to be a sublimatory process: mathematical thinking here is substituted for the release of aggression and libidinal drives, which are highly neutralized so as to ensure the sublimatory nature of the process. Rosen concludes that pure mathematical thought stands midway between scientific and artistic thought, whereas the secondary elaborative process is parallel to that of scientific thought.

Some of the basic psychoanalytic studies on the thinking of schizophrenics have been contributed by McGhie (1966). In one paper he points out that overinclusion,* referring to the characteristic phenomena of schizophrenic thought, describes the schizophrenic's inability to maintain conceptual boundaries. This leads to the diffusion of thought. He quotes Payne (1960) as suggesting that the thought disorder denoted by the concept of overinclusion may actually be a disorder in the process of selective attention. That is, the schizophrenic seems unable to select from the situation the material required for optimal response. McGhie notes that there is general agreement concerning the pathological distractibility of schizophrenics.

The defensive aspect of thinking in schizophrenics was specifically studied by Rycroft (1962). Genetically, he views the function of thinking as a mere defensive filling in of the psychic void that results from withdrawal from external objects and repression of instincts. Instead of relationships and activities, the patient cathects the process of thinking itself and derives pleasure from merely observing his own intellectual processes.† Because they are unrelated to reality objects, these intellectual processes can be bizarre. Rycroft sees these cursorily improvised thoughts as his patient's attempts to recreate a tolerable world (i.e., the world of his own thoughts). The second manifestation, genetically speaking, of the defensive function of thinking was that the patient's thinking was a form of masturbation. The third defensive aspect was the patient's attempt to find some significant conception of himself that would allay anxiety by making him not subject to love, hate, and fear — in other words, godlike.

One attempt at exploring thought processes experimentally and analytically was made by Corman, Escalona, and Reiser (1964). Eight psychotics and 12 neurotics were shown a subliminal stimulus by means of a tachistoscope. The experimenters then analytically investigated free and dream imagery obtained from the subjects. They wanted to appraise the ego processes involved in

---

*A term first used by Norman Cameron in 1939 (See Cameron, 1964).

† A patient may develop a thought disorder as a defense within the analytic session itself. One particular patient's thinking was perfectly good until she approached a conflict-arousing anxiety, namely, how her sister had pushed herself into a line in which others were waiting for a slice of birthday cake. Relating this episode was nearly impossible for her. Throughout several attempts to tell the story clearly, the patient reported that she felt herself getting fuzzy and that she wasn't sure if she could recount the incident. It became apparent that she could create what was almost a smokescreen by diffusing her thoughts and loosening her thought processes to avoid the conflict-arousing area.

microgenesis and imagery in this kind of experimental situation. Dream and imagery drawings produced by the subjects were analyzed in terms of form, content, and sequence. Results showed that the drawings varied greatly and did not all represent free imagery; most of the subjects' dreams included some elements referable to the experimental situation. It is concluded that areas of nuclear conflict are focused by the experimental situation itself and that adaptive techniques arise to cope with this situation. Many subjects showed evidence of the subliminal stimulus in imagery drawings and about 25 percent showed such evidence in the drawing of dreams. The patient's characteristic defense pattern apparently related to the way the subliminal stimulus was used. Corman, Escalona, and Reiser (1964) suggest that their method could be very useful for the psychoanalytic study of preconscious processes.

A REVIEW OF GENERAL PSYCHIATRIC LITERATURE ON THINKING

Much controversy concerning the concept and the "correct" diagnosis of schizophrenia has revolved around different opinions about the role of thought disturbances in various forms of that illness. Since Bleuler's discussion of thought in his 1911 volume on schizophrenia, disturbances of thinking have been considered either an important manifestation of, or in fact the primary symptom of, schizophrenia. By and large, we can probably say that those who consider schizophrenia a clearly circumscribed disease with one or another putative clear-cut organic basis — be it genogenic, chemogenic, or neurogenic — have tended to make the presence of a thought disorder their diagnostic touchstone. This group includes a majority of European, especially German, psychiatrists but also a substantial number of biologically oriented American psychiatrists.

A good number of clinicians, however, who consider psychogenic factors to contribute critically to the symptomatology of the schizophrenic syndrome, may also ascribe a crucial role to thought disorders that came into being by various developmental and interpersonal pathways (Arieti, 1965; Mednick, 1958; Wynne and Singer, 1963). Freeman, Cameron, and McGhie (1958) see thought disorders as resulting from the disruption of the boundary between the self and the non-self. They discuss primarily chronic schizophrenics, many of whom suffer thought disorders. Because of that limitation in scope, they do not deal with the general question of whether thought disorders are in addition necessarily a part of acute schizophrenic syndromes.

So crucial has been the attribution of thought disturbances to schizophrenia that a large number of investigators have attempted to subclassify schizophrenics by types of thought disorders (e.g., Payne, 1960).

As is well known, E. Bleuler, who originated the term "schizophrenia," claimed that the fundamental symptom of schizophrenic thought processes was that associations lose their continuity. Single associative threads or clusters are disrupted so that thinking becomes illogical and sometimes bizarre. In conjunction with this disruptive process, associations come to be determined in new ways: two ideas, only incidentally related, are selected and combined into one thought. Clang associations and indirect associations predominate. Bleuler also stresses the tendency to stereotype, which results in the patient's clinging to one idea. (The patient commonly manifests an extreme dearth of ideas.) Sometimes, the schizophrenic patient appears to be totally dependent upon, and distracted by, external stimuli, whereas at other times distractibility is nil, and no stimuli appear to influence his thoughts.

Bleuler notes two temporal disturbances in association: pressure of thoughts, or a pathologically increased stream of ideas, and blocking. In schizophrenics, what is normally the most important determinant of associations is lacking — the element of purpose. Their thoughts are subordinated to a general, often highly personalized idea, but they are not directed by any purpose or goal. In acute states, the disconnecting of associative threads is combined with other disturbances and a sequence of thoughts traceable by the observer is an exceptional event. This disconnectedness is termed dissociated thinking and reflects thought disturbances ranging from a maximum of total confusion to a minimum that is not easily detected. Even in cases where only a part of the associative thread is disturbed, influences other than logical directives are prominent. These influences are the same as those noted before that operate in the new ideational connections that develop after a total break in thought, such as condensations and stereotypes. Bleuler notes that these kinds of thought connections occur in normal psychological states also, but only occasionally, whereas in schizophrenia they often dominate thought processes.

In cases where all associative threads fail to function, blocking occurs and the thought chain is completely interrupted. The concept of blocking derives from Kraepelin, and Bleuler considers it to be fundamental in the symptomatology and diagnosis of schizophrenia. The cause of blocking generally lies in the symbolic or other significance of the blocked chain of thought for the patient. The confusion characteristic of schizophrenia may thus be the result of some or any combination of the following factors: (1) a dissolution of ideas; (2) a blocking by currently emerging ideas; (3) the suppression of single associative links concurrent with emergence of secondary associations; (4) a pressure of thoughts; and (5) hallucinations. Bleuler considers the disturbance of associations to be a primary symptom insofar as it involves a diminution or leveling of the number of affinities. Blocking and systematic splitting are regarded as secondary manifestations. The origin of secondary symptoms is explained by the weakening of logical functions, which results in the relative predominance of affects. Whatever is in conflict with the affects is split off. This leads to blocking, in which unpleasantly toned associations are immediately repressed. This mechanism leads to delusions and, even more significant, to the splitting of the psyche in accordance with emotionally charged complexes. The association-splitting can also result in pathological ambivalence such that contradictory thoughts or feelings coexist without influencing each other.

In schizophrenia the innumerable actual and latent ideas that determine associations in normal trains of thought may be rendered ineffective, singly or in any combination. Conversely, ideas that have little or no connection to the main idea and that should have been excluded from the train of thought may come into play, rendering thinking incoherent, bizarre, incorrect, and abrupt. After such blocking Bleuler held that ideas lacking any recognizable connection to previous ones may emerge.

Following the work of Bleuler, one of the early systematic studies of schizophrenic thinking was undertaken by Cameron (1938). His main thesis was that organized language and thinking in the adult are the result of repeated social communication, which in turn is based on the development of the ability to assume the role of the other person. He believes that disorganized schizophrenics have never developed adequate role-taking abilities and have therefore not been able to establish themselves firmly in the cultural communication pattern. When such people are confronted with conflict, they suffer a social disarticulation that results in a progressive loss of organized thinking. Cameron conducted a large experimental study of thinking, involving analysis of problems requiring the use of logic and those requiring manipulative sorting. The outstanding characteristics of schizophrenic thinking that he discovered and described are overinclusion and a variety of other peculiarities of schizophrenic thought: (1) asyndetic thinking, which consists of a lack of genuinely causal sequences and reflects the schizophrenic's inability to focus on the immediate task; (2) the use of metonyms, or imprecise approximations; that is, the use of vaguely related substitute words instead of the correct ones; (3) incongruity between acts and words, reflecting the schizophrenic's ability to withstand the coexistence of incongruous responses; and (4) demands to change the experimental conditions, which reflect both the patient's inability to handle difficult situations and his tendency to rely on a substitute (e.g., fantasy).

Another classic study is Kurt Goldstein's (1939). He stressed that psychopathology must relate symptoms and syndromes to the individual as a whole; the symptom is regarded as the organism's attempt to deal with its environment in the best way it can. Goldstein distinguished two types of thinking, abstract and concrete, and stated that a very high degree of concreteness is characteristic of the thinking of schizophrenics. In the concrete attitude, thinking is governed by external stimuli, which the patient experiences to an unusually high degree, and also by his own images, ideas, and thoughts. Symptoms arising from this attitude include illusions and autistic thought and action.

Goldstein points out that another characteristic of schizophrenia is the loss of constancy in the conception of the structure of objects, caused by the impairment of the abstract attitude. This impairment results in disturbance of visual discrimination, for example, an inability to distinguish between figure and ground. Goldstein concludes by stating that although brain-damaged patients suffer from some of the same impairments, schizophrenia cannot be considered simply an organic disease. The main difference between the schizophrenic's thinking and that of an organically disturbed person is that in the schizophrenic, in addition to extreme concreteness, idiosyncratic, peculiar, or autistic ideas appear in speech and behavior.

Kasanin's classic paper (1939) delineates three stages of development of thought in the child: (1) physiognomic thinking, in which the child "animates" objects and projects his own ego (self) into them; (2) the phase of concrete, literal, and overrealistic thinking; and (3) abstract or categorical thinking, which usually emerges after adolescence and signifies the ability to use language to form generalizations. Hanfmann and Kasanin (1942) used a sorting test that taps the capacity to form and test theories or concepts and that indicates whether the subject has lost the capacity to think categorically. They applied the test to schizophrenics, normals, and patients with organic brain disease and found that in schizophrenics categorical thinking is usually significantly reduced. The schizophrenics thought in concrete terms, attributing to things a personal rather than a symbolic value. The schizophrenics also tended to classify things according to purely physiognomic principles, whereas the organic patients never produced the "artistic" or fantasy-based physiognomic groupings that were frequently found among the schizophrenics.

Goldstein also observed similar differences between schizophrenics and organic patients. He says that even though both organic and schizophrenic patients tend to think concretely, the schizophrenic differs from the organic in that he projects himself into his verbalizations (what Kasanin calls physiognomic thinking). Kasanin cautions that although it is correct to postulate a reduction of abstract thinking in schizophrenics, the precise capacity of these patients to handle abstractions is still not definitely known. He offers the possibility that schizophrenics may have attained the level of abstract thinking and regressed, rather than never having attained it.

Angyal (1938) attempts to explain various aspects of schizophrenic thought disturbance by one hypothesis: the schizophrenic's thinking is impaired not because he does not understand relationships but rather because he is inept at solving intellectual problems. Thinking is thereby impaired in the apprehension of "system-connections." He feels that there is a basic and primary personality disorder in schizophrenics and that the disturbance of thought and language is but a secondary effect.

John D. Benjamin (1939)[1] reports a longterm study of schizophrenia in which the Rorschach Test and clinical investigations of patients were used to study thought disorders. The results of his study showed that in their Rorschach responses not all schizophrenics showed signs of intellectual malfunctioning that would correspond to a clinical thought disorder. Consistent with our own finding in the present study, Benjamin found that thought disorder is not a *necessary* criterion of schizophrenia. He also found that some of the signs seem to be independent of the stage of illness and not part of the clinical condition of the patient. He feels that this finding is significant since other methods had indicated that certain thought disorders in schizophrenia were not manifested in earlier recovered cases. He attributes prognostic significance to these signs. Clinical observation showed that only those persons with a formal thought disorder tend to deteriorate, and the more severe the disorder, the greater the likelihood of, and the quicker the course of, deterioration. Thus, he felt that the presence or absence of a formal thought disorder could provide the best criterion for differentiating between the process and reactive types of schizophrenics and possibly have etiologic implications.

The findings reported seem not at all compelling beyond the fact that apparently some diagnosed schizophrenics have thought disorders and some do not. The fact that those with thought disorders deteriorate more may imply no more than that the more seriously disturbed schizophrenics tend to show thought disorders. This may mean either that because they are more seriously disturbed, they may be predisposed to use thought disorder as a defense, or that a thought disorder has evolved as part of the effects of the schizophrenic process. It may also mean that those who display aspects of a thought disorder, such as overinclusion as a defense, are in fact poorly defended. They tend to become sicker than those who respond catatonically or with a paranoid disorder, including hallucinations and delusions as a form of defense. Benjamin incidentally reports that thought disorder had no definite relationship to degree of intelligence.

The notion that thought disorders are not specific to schizophrenia but are found to some degree in all psychiatric disorders (meaning by "thought disorder" simply one aspect of a regression and disturbance of other ego functions), which would tend to support a nonspecific defensive interpretation of thought disorder, is supported by Salzman, Goldstein, Atkins, and Babigian (1966). They conclude that cognitive impairment is not specifically attributable to schizophrenics, as it is also found in psychotic and nonpsychotic depressives, neurotics, and patients with character disorders.

Somewhat along these lines, Glasner (1966) speaks of benign paralogical thinking. He states that thought disorders range in degree from the most benign to the most malignant and that the existence of loose association in paralogical thinking unaccompanied by other symptoms does not justify the diagnosis of schizophrenia. Glasner describes a nonpsychotic thought disorder in terms of benign paralogical thinking and notes that it is common in both the clinical and nonclinical population. He emphasizes that schizophrenia should not be diagnosed merely because some thought disorder is present if there are no bizarre ideation, delusions, hallucinations, regressive behavior, tendency to deteriorate, or fragmentation of the personality and if reality relationships are intact. His work, in contradistinction to that of Benjamin, suggests that a thought disorder is not a *sufficient* criterion for the diagnosis of schizophrenia.

Von Domarus's ideas (1946) about thought have been embraced by the William Alanson White Institute of Psychoanalysis, and especially by Arieti (1963). According to the Domarus principle (as Domarus's ideas are often called), in normal logical thinking the conclusion is justified only if the major premise implicitly contains the minor premise. In what he calls paralogical thinking, as seen in schizophrenics, the patient's inferences about what follows logically are based on what he views as an identity of two premises concluded on the basis of the similar nature of adjectives. In Vigotsky's (1939) terms, the logician's conclusion of identity is based on identical subjects, whereas the paralogician's identity is based on identical predicates. For example, a schizophrenic may think, according to paralogic: "The Virgin Mary was a virgin. I am a virgin. Therefore, I am the Virgin Mary."

In the same paper Arieti emphasized that the type of thinking that von Domarus describes for schizophrenics can be found in normal children between the ages of one and three and one-half years, but only as a transient phenomenon. Arieti links this form of thinking to the fact that phylogenetically part-perception precedes whole perception. When a person reacts to a part of a given object in a certain way, he tends to respond in the same way to different objects that also have that part. Arieti stresses the close relation between thought disorders and psychodynamic factors. He criticizes Rapaport's treatment of thought processes, believing that Rapaport neglected to observe that cognitive processes themselves create emotional situations, and vice versa, thereby becoming significant dynamic forces. Arieti believes psychodynamically that thinking is explained by the interconnection between the affective and cognitive spheres. In some cases the patient regresses to lower levels of cognition in order to escape a negatively charged emotion or to increase his self-esteem. Finally, Arieti notes that thought disorders can be reversed, as indicated also by the fact that normal people regress to different forms of thinking when they dream and reinstitute normal thinking procedures when they awaken.

Bannister and Salmon (1966) apply personal-construct theory (PCT) to the problem of schizophrenic thought disorder. The proposition underlying PCT is that any person's total construct system is composed of several subsystems characterized by strong relationships between the constructs within each subsystem and comparatively weak relationships between constructs from different subsystems. The question raised is whether schizophrenic thought processes are generally disordered across all subsystems or whether they are more specifically disordered in certain areas than in others. Psychologists have traditionally accepted the view that a schizophrenic thought disorder is a defect of style or method, unrelated to content. Bannister and Salmon conducted a study and predicted that thought-disordered schizophrenics would not differ significantly from normals in their use of constructs about objects but would show significantly less stability in their use of constructs about people. Only the latter part of the hypothesis was supported. It was found, however, that the hypothesis was validated in relative terms; that is, schizophrenics lost much more stability in "construing" when they changed from objects to people than did the normals. These findings support the view that the area of maximal damage for thought-disordered schizophrenics with respect to object- and people-construing (i.e., making correct perceptions) is in fact, people-construing. These findings imply that in studying schizophrenic thought disorders, tests should be used that investigate both interpersonal and inanimate constructs and that explanations of schizophrenic thought disorder, whether or not they are organically based, need to account for different degrees of disorder in different construct subsystems.

In a series of four papers, Wynne and Singer examined "Thought Disorder and Family Relations of Schizophrenics" (1963a, 1963b, 1965a, 1965b). They reported on the use of projective techniques for "blind" prediction of links between schizophrenic subjects and their families. Predictions about which schizophrenic offspring would manifest thought disorders were based on (1) familial patterns of dealing with attention and meaning; (2) erratic and appropriate kinds of interpersonal behavior (distance and closeness); (3) underlying feelings of pervasive meaninglessness, pointlessness, and emptiness; and (4) a psychologically encompassing family structure, which is confusingly organized around denial or reinterpretation of the reality of major, anxiety-provoking feelings and events. Wynne and Singer conceptualize thought disorders along a continuum of amorphousness to fragmentation in language and communication. According to their studies, families tend to produce amorphous schizophrenics when they have vaguely defined, poorly organized expectations so that the growing child has difficulty in becoming oriented with any particular set. In contrast, in families of fragmented schizophrenics, parents reassign meanings that are far from clear and definite but are capriciously and arbitrarily at variance with their rigidly avowed beliefs and expectations.

The Wynne-Singer approach has been criticized by Schopler and Loftin (1969), who found that when parents' test-taking set was associated with their normal offspring, they showed less thought or communication impairment than when they were tested in association with their psychotic child. Another criticism of learning about the family interaction approach from communication patterns derived from psychological test data has been that it is often difficult to distinguish parental "influence" on offspring from parental response to his schizophrenic child.

Mosher (1971) enumerates five aspects of schizophrenic thought disorder: (1) looseness of associations; (2) blocking; (3) neologisms; (4) the expression of odd, bizarre, or distorted thoughts or associations (clang associations) that may be unusual—especially in context—but not necessarily illogical; and (5) irrelevant response. He also discusses the two ends of the thought disorder continuum: fragmentation and amorphousness. When thinking is fragmented, he says, the person is unable to speak, think, and reason; has elaborate percepts; but can give reasons for beliefs. He also makes illogical leaps between ideas, and there is marked variability in his cognitive organization over time, as well as great discontinuities between various life experiences. People with such thought disorders appear to have islands of relatively coherent cognitive functioning. Amorphous thought disorders, on the other hand, are characterized by perserveration, inability to elaborate ideas into more complex concepts, rambling, utter vagueness, the unsystematic interpenetration of ideas, and a drifting off, blocking, and drifting back. A pervasive lack of consensually valid ideas and a diffuseness and fogginess of cognitive organization are present, which may convey the impression of a total lack of cognitive structure.

Evidence from data on schizophrenic thought disorder suggests unequivocally that "whatever else, schizophrenics are an extremely heterogeneous group of patients" (Payne, 1960). Payne attempts to delineate three possible schizophrenic syndromes on the basis of objective studies of thought disorders: process schizophrenia, psychotic anxiety-reaction, and overinclusive psychosis. He says that we need to try to cluster the presence of thought disorder with other behavioral variables and presumed genogenic, chemogenic, neurogenic, and psychogenic factors, in order to see if interrelations of thought disorder and some other factors might lead to etiologically and pathologically definable subgroups of schizophrenics. Process schizophrenia has been associated with a low level of autonomic reactiveness (i.e., low level of "drive"). The basis for delineating a psychotic anxiety-reaction-type disorder, on the other hand, is a very high level of anxiety or a high degree of autonomic reactiveness. Not enough studies have been carried out on overinclusive psychosis to substantiate the explanatory hypothesis put forward concerning this third type of schizophrenic thought disorder.

The most extensive and careful review of the whole topic of schizophrenic thought disorder was done by Reed (1970). In discussing various papers on this topic, he often manages to state the main points more clearly than did the original authors. Among specific points of his own, he gives impressive evidence of "abnormalities" of everyday speech often considered typical of schizophrenics and suggests that schizophrenic thought disorders are quantitatively, rather than qualitatively, distinguishable. He considers underselectiveness (postulated by McGhie and by Payne) as resulting in overinclusion, typical of acute schizophrenics. He believes that in chronic schizophrenics overselectiveness of the "filter" leads in turn to underinclusion and concreteness. Reed considers the effect of filtering of both internal and external stimuli in these two directions as the most useful explanatory hypothesis concerning all reported observations in all schools of thought that discuss the nature of schizophrenia.

THE ROLE OF THOUGHT DISORDERS IN PSYCHIATRIC CLASSIFICATION

The most pressing question we face in defining thought disturbances in schizophrenia can be stated as follows: Is the presence of a thought disorder a necessary and sufficient criterion for a diagnosis of schizophrenia? What are the causes and what, if any, are the implications for understanding the etiology and pathogenesis of schizophrenia in either case?

First of all, it is entirely possible that thought disorders in schizophrenia are caused by structural or metabolic defects. It is well known that thought disorders occur in conditions other than those diagnosed as schizophrenic—for example, organic brain conditions as discussed by, among others, Cameron (1938), Vigotsky (1939), and Kasanin (1939).

There is also increasing interest in organic disorders with only "soft" neurological signs, that is, where the EEG and other aspects of the classical neurological examination reveal no pathology. Despite findings of mild disorders of coordination of equivocal status, such as the frequent presence of left-handedness, some tendency to reverse letters, and an assortment of other subtle features, there is little agreement in the literature on the presence and/or relevance of these possible symptoms of organic disorders. The most frequently present finding is a marked discrepancy between verbal and performance tests of intellectual functioning. On the Wechsler-Bellevue intelligence test, its subtests, and other standard batteries, performance of the eye-hand coordination tests and perceptual-patterns tests is usually significantly poorer than that on other tests; sometimes there is a difference of as much as 50 I.Q. points in otherwise highly competent children and successful adults. Among some children diagnosed as dyslexic or afflicted with minimal brain syndrome, there seems little doubt on clinical grounds that perceptual and organizational difficulties accompanied by late and deficient language development can lead to marked difficulties in thought processes (due to unavailability of the linguistic vehicle, and difficulty in perceiving and expressing various hierarchical relationships) and considerable emotional problems secondary to the aphasia-like bewilderment and the scholastic (mainly reading ability) and social difficulties.

A variety of toxic conditions, from ordinary alcoholic intoxication to the fascinating phenomena of Korsakoff's psychosis (especially symbolization and confabulation), suggest that toxic metabolic factors could be a causal factor in thought disorder in the schizophrenic syndrome.

A second factor causing thought disorders is probably best described in the "double bind" hypothesis of child-rearing (Bateson and Jackson, 1956), according to which there may be a "crossed signal" system: the parent says one thing while meaning another. Thus, many communications lose meaning. Or the parent may reward behavior he condemns and punish behavior he condones. The double bind may thus affect the adaptive aspect of thinking.

A third avenue leading to thought disorders might be a dynamic one. This idea is derived from two quite different sources. The first is the conception of Freeman, Cameron, and McGhie, who speak of the schizophrenic's tendency toward overinclusion and the inappropriate generalizations that occur because of the overinclusiveness of several logical categories (based in the long run on poor boundaries between the self and the outside world). In Chapman and McGhie we find the following examples (1961):

Patient 9: My thoughts get all jumbled up. I start thinking or talking about something but I never get there. Instead I wander off in the wrong direction and get caught up with all sorts of different things that may be connected with the things I want to say but in a way I can't explain. People listening to me get more lost than I do (p. 59).

Patient 20: My trouble is that I've got too many thoughts. You might think about something—let's say that ashtray—and just think, oh yes, that's for putting my cigarette in, but I would think of it and then I would think of a dozen different things connected with it at the same time (pp. 59-60).

Sarnoff Mednick (1958) expresses the opinion that schizophrenics tend to engage in this sort of overinclusion or in behaviorist terminology, generalizing, because it decreases their anxiety. To quote:

Meanwhile, what is happening to his (schizophrenic) thinking behavior? As the spiral of anxiety and generalization mounts, his drive level may increase to an almost insupportable degree. As this is taking place, his ability to discriminate is almost totally eclipsed by his generalization tendencies. Any unit of a thought sequence might call up still another remote associate (p. 86). . . .eventually (perhaps after several acute breaks), his thinking will present a varied though disorganized picture. At this point, if the patient perceiving the disorganization responds with the anxiety-provoking thought, "I am going crazy," he can defend against it by making an immediate associative transition to an irrelevant, tangential thought or by making use of a well-learned rationale such as "the radiators are broadcasting to me." This disorganized thinking will be continually self-reinforcing since it will enable him to evade anxiety-provoking stimuli (p. 90).

The degree of thought disorder in schizophrenics, most authorities agree, is by no means fixed; it varies along a continuum.

While thought disorders may result from an attempt to avoid anxiety in a defensive manner, this need not be the only psychogenic process that leads to thought disorders. On the contrary, it is entirely possible for the synthetic function to be severely afflicted (by a tremendous affective burden) or for a severe disorder of object relations to precede a breakthrough of the primary-process type of thinking (i.e., a thought disorder). Thus, the thought disorder may be a secondary effect of some other ego-function disturbance and is not necessarily an initially defensive function. Therefore, psychogenically speaking, thought disorders may be the result of various phenomena, including excessive defenses.

Extensive use of denial, for instance, leads to defective thought processes because some disturbing aspects of thought have to be blocked out. Defective thought processes in turn tend to impair other ego functions as well. Judgment in particular is affected by denial. Denial per se, however, is the classic defense mechanism of affective disorders; manics typically engage in the most extreme forms of this defense. Bertram Lewin, in his book on elation (1950), says that in denial we find centrifugal thought processes: a patient "goes away from" troublesome thought instead of talking about it. By inferring from the centrifugal direction the thoughts a patient is avoiding, one can interpret this denial and often dramatically transform an elation into a depression.

Schizophrenics, however, engage in something other than mere denial, and at this point we may be approaching one aspect of the necessary and sufficient factors for distinguishing the schizophrenic syndrome from the manic syndrome. That is, either denial is not enough to deal with anxiety (although a person may at first show an affective disorder with denial and then go on to a schizophrenic disorder with another type of thought disorder) or some people, by reason of a history of "double bind" or for somatic or strictly psychodynamic reasons, do not have a well-established system of secondary-process thinking. As a result, under a great amount of affective strain, the secondary process is easily disrupted. This weakness may well lead to intrusions of primary-process thinking and thus be termed a thought disorder. Regulation and control of drives may be poorly established; object relations might be poor because of an individual's particular psychological development, and under such circumstances the individual would be more susceptible to either the secondary affliction of thought processes by some traumatic situation or employing thought disorder as his form of defense. Of course, the choice of a particular symptom—not only a particular defense—is one of the issues in psychoanalysis that needs more precise understanding and conceptualization.

Some schizophrenics may be predisposed to choose a thought disorder as a means of defense and others not. For instance, a patient who had not acquired very firm secondary-process thinking might become hebephrenic. Another, with fairly solid secondary-thought processes, might "choose" a paranoid or other overideational solution in which thinking, except for the encapsulated areas involved in the paranoid ideation, remains relatively intact. Supporting such a notion is the fairly well established fact that paranoids as a group tend to have higher intelligence than other schizophrenics or other psychotics. In World War I, for example, when the Army Alpha Test was used for a survey of intelligence, it was found that officers had more paranoid tendencies and that enlisted men tended toward some other type of disorder. We can hypothesize that the more complex a person, the more intelligent he is even in a schizophrenic state; or perhaps the longer he is disturbed, the more disordered are the thoughts he permits to emerge and the more difficult it is to infer what he is talking about. The less intelligent the patient, the relatively less abstruse his disturbed thoughts may be; and the relatively more acute the disorder, the easier it will be to infer the undistorted meanings. The relatively more disturbed (if thought disturbance is used as a defense), the more disturbed the thinking in various forms of disturbance.

Should we therefore call all psychotics who are not demonstrably organically disturbed (with the possible exception of manic-depressives) schizophrenic? Perhaps the schizophrenic syndrome, in contradistinction to organic psychosis, is characterized by a low level of most ego functions but shows within that broad general grouping highly individual or specific profiles that become meaningful for subgrouping particular patterns of ego disturbances. Eventually we need to narrow down all the factors of schizophrenia into necessary or sufficient ones, or those that are necessary *and* sufficient, including all kinds of variables that will help us not only to postdict but also to predict who will become what kind of schizophrenic. Only if we can carefully define all the necessary and sufficient reasons for developing a specific condition will we be able to engage in rational prevention and more carefully reasoned treatment.

THINKING SPECIFICALLY AS AN EGO FUNCTION

As shown in the preceding discussion, thinking can be viewed in many different ways. One can study it from the formal standpoint—the way a semanticist might—and arrive at various subgroups of formal disturbances in schizophrenics. One can also study thinking from the genetic point of view, seeing adult thought processes and disturbances as the result of a developmental process. Piaget and Heinz Werner are the main original contributors to this genetic facet. Freud falls into this group to the extent that the change from the primary to the secondary process is viewed as a developmental process.

Psychoanalysis views thinking mostly from a dynamic standpoint, that is, in terms of defensive use and abuse, as in denial, rationalization, and projection. Cognitive psychology and psychiatry subsume thinking under the broad umbrella of the total organization of the cognitive field. This conception is relatively close to the egopsychological approach. The latter sees thinking and its disturbances from the adaptive point of view, that is, a person's adaptation to reality, the demands of his drives and of his superego in relation to various structural characteristics. These structural characteristics can be neurological, as in dyslexia, but also include such ego functions as regulation and control of drives and the synthetic-integrative function.

In studying the schizophrenic syndrome as an egopsychological disorder, we positioned our work in the last-mentioned conceptual framework (i.e., adaptation). We attempted to position the adaptiveness of thinking on a 13-point scale exactly as we did 11 other ego functions and similarly attempted the positioning of id and superego factors. The two component factors of thought processes — the ability to conceptualize and the extent to which language reflects primary- or secondary-process thinking—have been defined for each of the modal stops in our Manual for Rating Ego Functions from a Clinical Interview.

Our data, fully reported in Chapter 20, tend to support the proposition that in the absence of organic factors, severe thought disorder may be a sufficient sign for the diagnosis of schizophrenia but not a necessary one. Thought processes in acute schizophrenics may be relatively intact. Schizophrenia may be diagnosed when a majority of other ego functions are severely disturbed. On the other hand, an ego function or two may be intact even in schizophrenics whose thought processes are severely disturbed. A small drug study of the effects of valium (1972) also yielded evidence, supported by clinical findings in psychotherapy, that any therapeutic intervention (drug or psychotherapy) that lowers the level of anxiety generally also improves all ego functions, specifically thought processes.

Thinking and the disorders of thinking have in psychiatry been too long under the specific influence of Bleuler's concepts. He in turn was basically a product of the associationist school of thought, which flourished at the beginning of the twentieth century and also left its deep imprint on Freud and psychoanalysis.

Throughout the preceding discussion of general psychiatric literature, the specific psychoanalytic literature, and problems of diagnosis, we have cited many examples of the broader egopsychological conception of thinking as one of the adaptive functions.

Thinking, it was seen, can be taught and learned maladaptively, whether one follows Bateson and Jackson or Singer and Wynne. It interacts with the sense of self, as discussed by Cameron and associates. It is influenced by defenses, whether seen in the behavioristic terms of Mednick (as simple anxiety avoidance) or in the more complex terms of projection and the ensuing effect upon reality testing and judgment. Without appropriate drive control, thought and language have a poor chance to develop, and instead physical acting out may take the place of thought and language (Bellak, 1963). Greenacre (1950) has specifically suggested that lack of drive integration at age two and one-half may interfere with this development of thought into language and, one might add, of the use of language for the furtherance of thinking.

Thought develops in relation to objects. Without object relations, we observe autistic thinking in all its maladaptive ways. Defects of the primary autonomous functions—memory, attention—lead to disturbances of thinking and, in turn, to impaired secondary autonomous factors.

In adaptive regression in the service of the ego the oscillating role of thinking is at the very core of this creative form of adaptation. Concrete thinking is an almost definitive barrier to creativity in any form.

The synthetic function has a strong positive correlation to the adaptive task of thinking. The ability to bind, to organize and integrate, is vastly dependent upon thinking. And mastery and competence and a sense of competence without adaptation by thought is well-nigh inconceivable.

Indeed, Freud did summarize it all when he said that thinking is trial action: without adaptation to reality by trial and error in thought, man could not adapt to the world around him.

NOTE

1. In the article by Benjamin (1939) proverbs are also used to assist in the diagnosis of schizophrenic thought disorder. Those proverbs included in this article are the ones we used in the psychological laboratory assessment, which are referred to there as the Benjamin Proverb Test.

CHAPTER 12

Adaptive Regression in the Service of the Ego

Regression in the service of the ego (and the creative process it implies) is not generally included in lists of ego functions. We include it in our frame of reference because we believe that it does indeed play an important role in daily adaptation. In the broadest sense, creativity—the ability to meet life's demands with other than previously learned solutions—is the essence of adaptation. It is not a quality or a process relevant only to the arts and sciences, in which the end product is a cultural or technical success; it can be observed in more diverse and private sectors of living as well.

The term "regression in the service of the ego" was introduced by Ernst Kris in "The Psychology of Caricature" (1936):

... in dreams the ego abandons its supremacy and the primary process appears in control, whereas in wit and in caricature, this process *remains in the service of the ego*. This formulation alone suffices to show that the problem involved is a more general one: the contrast between an ego overwhelmed by regression and "regression in the service of the ego"—*si licet venia verbo*—covers a vast and imposing range of mental experience (1952, p. 177; italics added).

Thus the term "regression in the service of the ego" was created with a modest apology by Kris. Concepts, however, rarely spring into existence fully grown as did Athene from the head of Zeus. Kris himself relates his concept to Freud's formulations concerning wit and the comic.

Another early version of a concept similar to Kris's can be found in Varendonck's remarkable little volume on preconscious fantasizing and thinking, *The Psychology of Daydreams* (1921). Largely conceived during Varendonck's World War I service, this book presents systematically and with astounding clarity some of the author's own preconscious fantasies. He also describes what are now called primary- and secondary- process types of thinking, and he discusses the participation of preconscious processes in creative thinking:

It is in the act of conceiving* that the difference between voluntary and

---

*Anna Freud translates "act of conceiving" *as schopferisches Denken*. This is justified by Varendonck's later equation (p. 358) of the operation of conceiving with that of creating. Varendonck who wrote in English is sometimes obscure since English was not his mother tongue.

affective thinking is carried farthest; the conscious condemns proposed solutions which the foreconscious would admit because its discriminating power is smaller; it does not so easily lead to absurdity . . .(p. 357).

Thinking which aims at individual adaptation, at whatever level it takes place, is a process through which the ego comes into contact with the outer world; it is therefore necessarily egocentric. All authors agree that phantastic thinking also places the ego in the centre of the preoccupations; still, we have come across a certain number of musings . . . so that the rule is not absolute. *But this speculative thinking differs from the corresponding conscious process in more than one aspect; it is well known that the advantages of voluntary thinking have to be paid for by the sacrifice of a certain portion of the power of regression in the memory-system, which is a very serious sacrifice, as it constitutes the very basis of intellection.* Another comparative inferiority of voluntary thinking is caused by the circumstances that *the spontaneity of some of the processes constituting the operation of conceiving or creating is abandoned for a deliberate application of mental energy, which is less effective and more exhausting, as we have seen because the available amount of energy has to be distributed at the same time over protective functions and functions that are directly productive.*

However, these disadvantages may disappear when the two ways of thinking collaborate and unite, in a single mental operation, the superiorities proper to each form of ideation separately, while avoiding the defects of both. *When invention and inspiration take place in the fore-conscious state, the advantages of both directed and affective thinking are united for the fulfillment of the wish.* In the inventive chain the end-representation is well kept in view; although the association progresses behind the threshold we think in words, which renders us, as in the conscious state, independent of facts and allows of abstraction. These are usually two great privileges of voluntary conscious thinking. But as it is a wish that directs the concatenation, it disposes of the whole store of memory without apparent effort, and the strength of the affect not only detaches the mind from the outer world, but also preserves it from the disturbing perception of inner excitations, which are advantages proper to fore-consciousness.

What we should mark here is that speculative thinking in which the ego is left out of consideration is not a privilege of consciousness only, but is occasionally observable in the fore-consciousness state as well. Only in the waking state this tendency seems to have been developed systematically, so as to become independent of chance. However, *abstract thinking is most unsuccessful when it reverts to the fore-conscious level and borrows the primitive affective mechanisms. (p. 358; italics added).*

With these words Varendonck basically discusses what only later was called regression in the service of the ego. In a paragraph written subsequently, he also relates these phenomena to wit and other such processes, just as Kris did years later; Varendonck concludes his monograph as follows:

Finally, this investigation tends to establish that the unconscious, fore-conscious, and conscious thought-processes are three manifestations, varying only in degree, of the same function. This function originally regulating the relations of the individual with the outer world, constitutes a manifestation of universal energy, and is as eternal and unceasing as the other organic activities *in the service of adaptation* (p. 360; italics added).

In emphasizing adaptation, Varendonck also anticipated Bellak's much later (1958) suggestion that Kris's "regression in the service of the ego" be further specified as "adaptive" regression in the service of the ego, which we have designated by the acronym ARISE.

When Kris elaborated the concept of regression in the service of the ego in his paper "On Preconscious Mental Processes" (1950), he discussed Varendonck somewhat critically, agreeing with Freud's introduction to *The Psychology of Daydreams* (1921) that Varendonck did not differentiate clearly enough between the preconscious and the unconscious. In referring to his own earlier paper (1936), Kris mentions that his idea of regression of the ego

was rooted in Freud's explanation of wit (1905) according to which a preconscious thought is "entrusted for a moment to unconscious elaboration" and seemed to account for a variety of creative or other inventive processes . . . The general assumption is that under certain conditions, the ego regulates regression and that the integrative functions of the ego include voluntary and temporary withdrawal of cathexis, from one area or another to regain improved control (Kris, 1952, p. 312).

Further on, Kris notes that "alternation between the two phases may be rapid, oscillating, or distributed between long stretches of time" (p. 313). He was very much concerned with problems of cathexes and saw regression in the service of the ego as the ego's ability to control shifts in the cathexis of ego functions. He specified that this regression is a topographical one, involving primitivization of ego functions.

Bellak first expressed interest in the interaction of adaptive, projective, and expressive processes in creative responses to the T.A.T. in a paper on "The Concept of Projection" (1944). He was especially interested in the responses to the T.A.T. and Rorschach as they constitute creative tasks and pointed out that "creativity has to adapt itself to certain external conditions." Several years later Bellak (1949) suggested that in certain circumstances barbiturates or alcohol can be used to increase the ability to regress in the service of the ego, perhaps thus increasing creativity.

In a 1950 paper, "Thematic Apperception: Failures and the Defenses." Bellak pursued the topic of adaptiveness in relation to the creative task by stating that

the response to a test situation constitutes a problem which the patient has to solve . . . the situation demands an ego that can perform a specific task and yet allow some relaxation of its grip on the id impulses. It must be borne in mind in this context that it is a normal function of the ego to *exclude itself*. If this function of self-exclusion of the ego is disturbed we see such disorders as insomnia, inability to rest, and inability to perform creative tasks (p. 124).

In his volume on the T.A.T. and C.A.T. (1954), he focused on still another fact of creativity or productivity, suggesting that increasing the ambiguity of T.A.T. and Rorschach stimuli or increasing the pressure to respond by decreasing the amount of time the subject is exposed to the test stimuli would increase the response yield.

In 1954, Bellak's interest turned to Kris's concept of the ego's oscillating function, from self-exclusion to control. He conceptualized the degree of ego participation on a continuum from daydreams, fantasies, hypnagogic phenomena, preconscious fantasies, free association, and projective techniques. Later (1958) elaborating on this concept, Bellak stated that "under the adaptive components of the product we would subsume what was contributed by the autonomous ego functions..." In that same paper he alerts us to the relationship between vigilance, adaptation, and creativity: In a rapid oscillation, as Kris has pointed out, between regression and full vigilance, adaptive and emergent qualities of the creative product become integrated" (p. 367). It was here that Bellak reformulated and developed the concept of regression in the service of the ego:

... as a brief, oscillating, relative reduction of certain adaptive functions of the ego in the service of (i.e. for the facilitation of) other, specifically the "synthetic" ego functions. What happens is that cognitive, selective, adaptive functions are decreased; this weakens the sharply defined boundaries of figure and ground, of logical, temporal, spatial, and other relations, and permits them to reorder themselves into new configurations with new boundaries, under the scrutiny of the again sharply functioning adaptive forces.... Our main concern above was to stop speaking of "the ego" as an entity and to speak of different ego functions interacting at different levels of efficiency at the same time.

Second, some elaboration on the concept of "regression": some thought has been given to whether this involves primarily a topographical regression or a temporal (ego) regression (to earlier points of libidinal organization). In the first case we are concerned with a change from the conscious to the preconscious or unconscious. In the second instance we are concerned with a regression to earlier, childhood levels of functioning. The distinction cannot be made quite definite since, by definition, nonconscious thinking involves primary-process thinking of infancy and childhood.

It will be more precise to say that a *topographical regression of the cognitive processes* (as one ego function) takes place which involves simultaneously a temporal regression to primary-process levels; *the synthetic function does not regress at all but remains, or rises in fact, to optimal levels* (1958b, p. 367; italics added).

Finally, he says that "the relationship between regression and adaptation should be a good measure of a potentially creative, inventive, flexible mind" (p. 368).

In a paper on free association (1961), Bellak noted how specific ego functions bore upon the relationship between regression and adaptation. The concept of regression in the service of the ego, he said, involves a *relative* reduction of *certain* adaptive functions, including a reduction in the level of certain secondary-process qualities of thought:

. . . thus, the ability to perceive sharply the boundaries of figure and ground, and to see things in hierarchical, spatial and temporal relationship is reduced. The length of time for which this relative reduction takes place varies from occasion to occasion and certainly from patient to patient.

This first phase is succeeded, or sometimes accompanied in individually differing ways, by an *increase* in adaptive and synthetic ego functioning. As in the artistically creative process, so in associating, the temporarily decreased boundaries permit fusions of new *Gestalten,* new emergences of different temporal, logical, and other orders; *insight* emerges, partly as spontaneous new wholes, partly by trial and error, as a result of oscillation from regression of certain ego functions to an increase in others. The regression facilitates the new synthesis: it is in this sense that we understand it to be "in the service of the ego."

The regressive process itself involves at least two aspects which are difficult to separate: one is the regression of ego functions temporarily, to levels characteristic of earlier ages—to childhood years when the secondary process was weak and when only little order could be made out of the primary data of perception.* The second aspect is that we deal with a topographical regression, from primarily conscious functioning to functioning at the preconscious and unconscious level: the topographical regression of certain ego functions is not only accompanied by a temporal regression of these same ego functions, but also involves a regression in the libidinal zones and modes; this, we have stressed above, is alternated with (and possibly accompanied by) an increase in synthetic and some cognitive ego functioning.

To make sure that this is more than playing with words, let us attempt to illustrate its clinical usefulness. The patient who associates well is able to oscillate between reduction and increased adaptive functions while exercising the synthetic functioning, and thereby producing new insights, working through and reintegrating previous apperceptive distortions. In certain types of associative disturbances, those found in obsessives for example, the patient presents the analyst with "travelogue," a faithful account of realistic events; he does not focus upon internal observation, nor does he regress topographically to preconscious levels or give up his cognitive vigilance. On the contrary, he often increases it, much like the sexually disturbed person who becomes excessively

---

*Children cannot "free associate" in the psychoanalytic sense because of a lack of development of self-observation and other aspects of the oscillating function.

aware of every thought, every feeling, and every action during intercourse—even the ticking of a clock.

In other patients, notably hysterics and borderline psychotics, the regression of ego functioning to preconscious levels and early libidinal stages takes place easily and the material out of which case histories are made pours forth. Often this regression is neither accompanied nor followed by increased perceptual acuity, and the synthetic functioning which leads to the awareness of new configurations, to insight, is lacking. The observations are faithfully reported but no active second phase of the oscillation takes place.

In fact, for some patients, as we know, the absence in the analytic situation of the customarily structuring stimuli of the social situation seems to make it impossible for the patient to maintain the secondary processes; the adaptive and cognitive ego functions are so reduced that the patient fails to distinguish the boundaries of the self, and tends towards hallucinatory, delusional experiences (1961, pp. 14-15).

Generally in the psychoanalytic literature, ARISE has been used to develop an understanding of wit and humor, artistic creativity, productive fantasy and imaginative processes, problem-solving, the capacity for orgiastic experience, ego-building identifications, motherliness, empathic writing, love, and the therapeutic process.*

Roy Schafer (in Lindzey, 1958), examined the concept of regression in the service of the ego. He too sees it as a partial, temporary, and controlled decrease in the level of psychic functioning to improve adaptation "by maintaining, restoring, or improving inner balance and organization, interpersonal relations, and work." Thus, he views regression in a very broad, adaptive sense. In the process of regression in the service of the ego, the primary and secondary autonomy of highly developed ego functions is not disrupted; the primary process is given more than usual freedom to act in order that ego interests (for example, creativity and empathy) be promoted.

Schafer enumerates six conditions in the personality that favor regression in the service of the ego. First, a well-developed set of affect signals is required so that when the regressive process threatens to reach certain drives or affects not suitable for consciousness, an appropriate signal can set off a reversal of the process. Second, a secure sense of self and/or a well-defined ego identity is necessary, enabling tolerance of a temporary blurring of the boundaries between ego and id. Third, a relative mastery of early traumata should have been accomplished, such that the individual can now safely have subjective experiences that are related to the once-threatening feelings he had as a child. Fourth, superego pressures should be mild rather than severe, just as defenses should be flexible rather than rigid. A fifth factor is a history of sufficient trust and

---

*Schachtel (1959) puts forth the view that the creative process involves an openness to the characteristics of the object of the creative endeavor, and does not depend on regression to primary process thought functioning.

mutuality in interpersonal relations, especially in the early mother-child relationship. Such a history will promote tolerant, accepting feelings, rather than negative ones, toward regressive experiences. The final condition listed by Schafer is that cultural meaningfulness accrues from the results of the process: self-awareness and communication with others are improved. He notes that regressive adaptations such as empathy and intimacy, which are related to direct interpersonal relations, may also be dependent on these facilitating factors, possibly even more than are artistic, scientific, and comic creativity.

Schafer returned to the topic of regression in the service of the ego again in his 1968 book on internalization. Among his interests here are the relations between daydreaming, reality testing, and regression in the service of the ego. In ordinary reality testing, the thinker's self-representation is one of the thinker of the thought, and he is reflectively aware of himself as such. In ordinary daydreaming the reflective self-representation that one is the thinker is suspended, and a temporary oscillation permits a reemergence of the awareness that one is the thinker. Thus, the person's orientation to reality testing remains strong, and the regression's duration and intensity are limited. The daydream is a preconscious and possibly conscious commitment to reality, the daydreamer can have controllable daydreams that produce pleasure. In pathological conditions, objectivity about the real world is vulnerable, and even temporary regressions may be threatening. Schafer quotes Kris as saying that "such phenomena as the fear of sleeping and dreaming indicate an inability to attain or tolerate regression in the service of the ego." Schafer concludes that an important prerequisite to regression in the service of the ego is temporary suspension of the reflective awareness of the self-representation.

Pine and Holt (1960) studied the amount of expression and *effective control* of primary-process thinking as an operational measure of adaptive regression, using the T.A.T. and a variety of other tests. They concluded that both expression and control of primary process are relevant to promoting the creative process. Most significant, they firmly conclude that Kris's concept of regression in the service of the ego can be operationally defined and that predictions derived from it can be studied with quantitative scoring techniques.

Wild (1965) also performed an experimental study, "Creativity and Adaptive Regression." She compared the performance of 30 art students with that of 26 teachers and 26 schizophrenics on the Word Association and Object Sorting Tests. The tests were given first with instructions to be spontaneous and then with instructions geared to induce either regulated or unregulated thought. Art students reacted more favorably to the unregulated-thought instructions than did teachers or schizophrenics. Wild felt that her findings demonstrating the artist's ability to shift from more to less regulated thinking in the creative process support the concept of regression in the service of the ego.

While Kris equates creativity with health, Weisman relates it to pathology. According to Weisman (1969), the fantasies of creative people are modified so that they are more hallucinatory or delusional than the typical fantasies of noncreative people. This unique alteration in fantasies is caused by phenomena that Weisman designates as "beyond the reality principle." This phrase implies an aspect of mental functioning characterized by fusion of the reality principle and the pleasure principle in the creative process. He emphasizes functioning in the service of the ego-ideal, rather than the ego, in that an adaptation in the service of the ego-ideal is applied to an unreal fantasy world. He presents some clinical material to support his belief that the fantasies of creative people are characterized by features of an hallucinatory residue of their original wishes for unreal objects. The artist may retain early hallucinatory perceptions of the world side by side with a highly developed sense of reality, using what Weisman calls desynthesizing and synthesizing ego functions to transform his fantasies into new perspectives of the real world. He believes that the creative person is unique because in early life he had the ability to hypercathect imaginary objects and as an adult he remains indifferent to real objects. In that sense, Weisman defines the creative process as a transient hallucinatory residue of their psychosis,* without ego regression, but reinforced and maintained by the coordinated activities of the disassociative and integrative functions of the ego.

It is interesting to find that in an earlier paper on ego functioning in creativity (1968) Weisman insists that more than controlled regression in the service of the ego is necessary. The creative process required a dissociative or desynthesizing function. He also believes that the character traits of eccentricity and rebelliousness in the creative personality develop early in life and continue to develop under the direction of archaic desynthesizing functions. He believes that the desynthesizing function allows a malleability of the ego that induces creativity. He stresses, therefore, the role of sublimation and neutralization in creativity.

In another paper (1961) Weisman had specifically discussed developmental creativity in the actor and playwright, a topic on which he has published widely. He believes that regression in the service of the ego is operative only in the case of the dramatist and is accompanied by simultaneous intensification of defenses against direct instinctual gratification.

In a paper on the scope of the contribution of psychoanalysis to the biography of the artist, Wangh (1957) postulates that a particular condition is required for the occurrence of controlled regression. The ego must be secure in a position outside the creative one, as well as within it, if temporary regression is to be achieved. For example, in sleep, the inhibition of motion establishes a

*It seems unfortunate to us to use a term like "psychosis" for the creative processes of normal people.

pivot of stability of the ego. In the creative situation the pivot is very probably provided by the artist's identification with the anticipated audience.

Waelder (1960) emphasized that joking involves a regression in the service of the ego, helping to decrease temporarily the control of the ego, similar to what happens for humor generally. Thus, Freud's discussion of the relationship of wit, humor, and the comic is brought up to date in relation to the concept of regression in the service of the ego.

Kubie (1958) contrasted the creative process with the neurotic process, stressing the important role of the preconscious system in creativity and the predominantly unconscious processes in the neuroses: the preconscious processes are in constant conflict with, and may be obstructed by, both the conscious and unconscious systems. A creative process of finding new connections between, and configurations of, elements and new meanings depends upon one's not being tied either to the conscious symbolic process or to unconscious processes. In a paper on the psychology of adaptation and creative problem-solving, Joffe and Sandler (1968) add the concept of autonomy from superego introjects to Rapaport's concept of autonomy from the drives and from the environment: a high degree of autonomy from drives, environment, and the superego results in greater ranges of adaptive responses in problem-solving. Joffe and Sandler conceive of adaptation not only in relation to the external world but also in relation to inner states, as would the thinkers concerned with relative autonomy from environment and drives as a condition for adaptation.

Geleerd (1964) discusses adaptive regression in relation to adolescence. She says that in order to attain adulthood the adolescent goes through states of partial regression, alternatively or simultaneously with processes of progression. Gill and Brenman in their volume on hypnosis and related states (1959), postulate that all regression could be considered to be in the service of adaptation, since even psychotic regression is a form of adaptation.

Schneir (1951) agrees with Melanie Klein's interpretation of creativity as stemming from the child's attempt to master his destructive impulses by repairing the "destroyed objects." According to the restitution theory, the artist employs symbolic means to perform an act of restitution, while the spectator similarly experiences such restitution on an unconscious level.

Bush (1969) feels that excessive emphasis, at least with respect to scientific creativity, has been placed on the role of regression in the service of the ego in creativity. He enumerates a number of processes involved but stresses a special secondary process: cognitive facility. He discusses the importance to the creative process of cognitive styles such as leveling-sharpening, tolerance for unrealistic experiences, scanning, constriction-flexibility, and field dependence-independence. He mentions as positively related to creativity, the capacity to sustain such ambiguity, the ability to resist premature closure, and the ability to tolerate percepts and thoughts that do not conform to familar schematizations. He also suggests that certain primary-process characteristics, such as habitually thinking in concrete visual rather than verbal forms, are not per se regressive modes but may be a person's characteristic modes of functioning. Such scientists have never progressed fully to verbal secondary-process functioning. They think in ways that represent earlier developmental modes, so that technically one cannot call the modes regressive.*

Bush concludes that "regression, be it in the service of the ego or otherwise, is not a necessary or sufficient condition for scientific creation. It is often over-emphasized and ambiguously employed while the creative use of secondary process functioning may be relatively neglected (1969, p. 187).† Giovacchini (1960) also discussed the relevance of regression in the service of the ego to the creative thought processes of scientists. He says that in the group that he studied he did not find a suspension of the organizing function; the ego maintained high integrative and adaptational levels simultaneously with primitive mechanisms such as fantasy.

An empirical approach to creativity is adapted by Rothenberg (1969) in a study specifically concerned with O'Neill's *The Iceman Cometh*. He suggests that the most fruitful research focus is on the creative process: attempting to study what goes on in an artist's head when he is in the process of creating. He examines different stages of O'Neill's play and correlates his findings with life-history material. His observations suggest that the artist separates himself from his creation by a process of deleting material that is closest to his own immediate preconscious wishes and motivations. Rothenberg suggests that the development of ideas in creation proceeds in part by a process of oppositional thinking: a notion and its opposite are conceptualized simultaneously. This may give the appearance of primary-process thinking but actually belongs mostly to the secondary-process thought level. In choosing to integrate these oppositional ideas the artist is influenced by his knowledge of reality demands as well as by his own emotional values.

THE BROAD BASIS OF ARISE

The concept of creativity is culturally so closely affiliated with artistic or scientific endeavors that most of the time we may not be aware of its manifestations in other areas. It is probably for this reason that ARISE has not previously been considered the valuable variable of general personality assessment that we now believe it to be. There may be a number of reasons for this

*Kris and Bellak, however, make clear that in their use of the concept of ARISE, topographic regression from the conscious to the preconscious, and sometimes to the unconscious, is also involved even where there may be no developmental or temporal regression.

†We are not entirely convinced by his argument that it is not a necessary condition for creativity.

delayed recognition. In ordinary circumstances one probably has less reason to appraise a person's ARISE than other personality characteristics. Job interviewing exemplifies a nonordinary circumstance in which its assessment is quite relevant. Second, in many life situations the chance for exercising ARISE does not readily occur. Many people may possess a high ARISE factor without usually having occasion to display it; many rise to higher levels of functioning when an occasion demands it.

It has often been remarked that children seem more spontaneously creative than adults, artistically, conceptually, and most obviously in play. If any of this creative potential is lost in the process of maturation, it may be because the boundary between primary and secondary processes becomes firmer. In terms of pathological development it is unfortunately true that in many people creativity—the ability to regress adaptively in the service of the ego—becomes narrowed by a large variety of defenses and character structures. The requirement for ARISE, after all, is only that two or more gestalten be so perceived as to lead to a new (and adaptively useful) configuration of figure and ground.

Presidents of the United States often "rise to the occasion" and respond creatively and adaptively to the demands of the job; their opportunities to use ARISE are many. For the most part, however, many social and work settings discourage ARISE, such as large organizations, the army, civil service. They tend to discourage independent thinking and creative problem-solving and to stifle ARISE in the individual. The matter of social setting and ARISE is, however, a very general one. Some cultures undoubtedly place a higher value on it than others, and it would have to take different forms in different cultural settings. As with all ego functions, we are discussing this one with regard to one particular culture: our American, largely middle-class society. Cultural differences are, however, as we point out elsewhere, not at all a limitation on the value of our appraisal of ego functions. On the contrary, for diagnostic comparisons it is useful to define each person within his particular cultural or subcultural context: then one has the advantage of being able to compare the relative presence of ARISE from one culture to another or to compare impulse control in people belonging to varying cultures, with each person defined within his own culture.

This brings us also to the problem of ARISE distribution in the general population. Unlike the bell-shaped curve basic to intelligence measurement, the curve we have assumed is a rather skewed one for all our ego functions with five constituting the mode on a seven-point scale, if not the mean. The curve of ARISE appears, at first glance, to be bimodal rather than normal or even somewhat skewed. That is, some people have a great deal of creativity, or ARISE, and others very little. We believe that this assumption probably contains a bias, induced by the social definition of creativity in terms of arts and science. If one looked for ARISE in everyday life, one might be impressed by the ability of a housekeeper, for example, to arrive at creative new solutions to the small problems that normally confront her.

A matter not unrelated to the problem of distribution is the relationship between ARISE and intelligence. Since intelligence has a normal distribution by definition, we have two choices with respect to postulating the ARISE distribution. One possibility is that, as some claim, intelligence and ARISE are so highly correlated that we may not be able to rate ARISE validly. There is, however, good reason to doubt that ARISE shows a high correlation with the intelligence quotient. It is highly likely that ARISE is related to some parts of the Wechsler Adult Intelligence Scale (WAIS) and not to others. By and large, those aspects of intelligence that have to do with insightful experience are either closely related or identical to ARISE. Getzels and Jackson (1962) have shown in detail that creative ability and high I.Q. do not always go together. Highly creative adolescents were shown to differ from highly intelligent adolescents with regard to imaginative productions, personal values, family background, and career goals.

When Köhler's apes finally put the sticks together in a way that enabled them to reach the banana, they arrived at an adaptive solution (1925). While this act may not have necessitated a regression to a primary process type of thinking, analogous human acts do necessitate a topographical regression to preconscious thinking, as well as sufficient blurring of the field to permit a restructuring of it. On the other hand, scores on parts of intelligence tests that involve good memory or information may not correlate with ARISE at all. It might, indeed, be a good idea to include an ARISE scale in future intelligence tests, since the score on such a scale would relate to actual functioning in ways that existing tests do not.

Experience suggests that some people with high ARISE do not necessarily have a high level of general intelligence. The Seabees, which reputedly contained a high percentage of people who could fix anything with anything in any circumstances, demonstrated a basically high ARISE. Many professors of engineering and of physics, have been amazed and embarrassed by the ease with which some handyman or mechanic could solve a problem over which they could do nothing but shake their heads. Aside from cases of special ability, these manifestations of ARISE probably have more to do with neutralization and sublimation of libidinal and aggressive drives than with I.Q. Only if a firm structure is established can one permit oneself the regression in the service of the ego necessary for adaptive creative acts. It is in this context that we have examined ARISE in our study. In studying ARISE, we evaluated the two component factors—the oscillating phase and the synthetic phase—separately. Detailed descriptions of both are found in the Interview Rating Manual for each of the modal stops. As with all other ego functions, ARISE was studied through interviews, psychological tests, and experimental techniques.

CHAPTER 13

Defensive Functioning

Freud stated in "The History of the Psychoanalytic Movement" (1914) that repression (defense) was the most essential part of psychoanalysis, and the foundation stone on which it rested. He had used the defense mechanism as a crucial aspect of neurotic symptom formation since the 1890's. Defense was defined by Freud in 1926 in *Inhibitions, Symptoms, and Anxiety* as "a general designation for all the techniques which the ego makes use of in conflicts which may lead to a neurosis."

More attention has been devoted to defenses than any other ego function, with the possible exception of object relations. There are many complex issues related to defensive functioning. In this chapter we will review some of the relevant important papers and indicate some of the issues involved.

The term "repression" first occurs in the preliminary communication of the *Studies on Hysteria* by Breuer and Freud (1893). With regard to patients who had not reacted to traumatic situations as might have been expected, the authors formulated that there were things the person "wished to forget, and therefore intentionally repressed from his conscious thought and inhibited and suppressed" (1893, p. 10). The word "defense" occurs for the first time in "The Neuropsychoses of Defense" (1894), where Freud illustrated how unpleasant or unbearable ideas were defended against in certain cases of hysteria, phobias, obsessions, and hallucinatory psychoses. In "Obsessions and Phobias" (1895), Freud said that in the defense of the ego against the incompatible idea, the expulsion from consciousness sometimes results from a deliberate effort, but in other cases it "is brought about in an unconscious manner which has left no trace in the patient's memory" (p. 80). Thus, the earliest notions of repression and defense were seen as sometimes conscious and sometimes unconscious processes.

In 1896, he described the nature and mechanism of obsessional neurosis and first used the phrase "return of the repressed" to characterize the failure of defense against unpleasant ideas that are manifest as obsessional thoughts and affects. Thus, symptoms were seen as a compromise between repressed and repressing ideas and indicated a failure of the defense. The term "projection" is also used here to describe how, in paranoia, self-reproaches are repressed and return in delusional ideas (p. 184).

Freud's discussion of censorship and the censor in *The Interpretation of Dreams* (1900) is closely related to the ideas of defense and repression, since it was the function of censorship to prevent certain mental events from becoming conscious. A more detailed discussion of projection as a central aspect of symptom formation in paranoia is discussed by Freud in his "Psychoanalytic Notes on an Autobiographical Account of a Case of Paranoia" (1911).

Freud used the terms defense and repression somewhat interchangeably in his early writings, though Strachey (S.E., XX, appendix A, pp. 173-174) points out that in *"Studies on Hysteria"* (1895), Freud employed "repression" to the process and "defense" to signify the motive for it. After Freud's collaboration with Breuer ended (1897), the term "defense" was used only occasionally, while "repression" was used more frequently to refer to processes of defense. But by the time of the metapsychological papers (1915), Freud was again using defense as the more inclusive term. It was only in *"Inhibitions, Symptoms, and Anxiety"* (1926) that Freud explicitly introduced the concept of defense as the means by which the ego protects against instinctual demands and repression as one special case of this (p. 164).

In *Three Essays on the Theory of Sexuality* (1905), Freud added sublimation to characterize the diversion of sexual impulses from their original aims to ones involving cultural achievement (p. 178). The development of the reaction formations of disgust, shame, and morality was discussed as a means of avoiding unpleasurable feelings triggered by childhood sexual impulses. In his case presentation of the "Rat-man" (1909), Freud illustrated how an obsession may involve a reaction formation against a contrary, hostile impulse. He also discussed isolation and undoing as defense mechanisms employed by obsessional neurotics. He described the process as follows: "The trauma, instead of being forgotten, is deprived of its affective cathexis; so that what remains in consciousness is nothing but its ideational content, which is perfectly colourless and is judged to be unimportant" (p. 196).

In "Instincts and Their Vicissitudes" (1915), Freud stated that instincts are subject to reversal into the opposite, turning round upon the self, repression, and sublimation. Because these vicissitudes are based on forces working against the unmodified expression of the instinct, Freud also saw the vicissitudes as modes of defense against the instincts. He also discussed introjection, a term coined and previously used by Ferenczi, as a process whereby objects that represent sources of pleasure are absorbed by the ego.

Freud's papers on "Repression" and "The Unconscious," both published in 1915, include his most detailed accounts of repression. He is using the concept in the broad sense of defense here, in showing how repression uses reaction formation, for example, in obsessional neurosis. Repression was described in the first of the two papers as being something between flight and condemnation, the motive of which is the avoidance of unpleasure. Its essence is in turning something away and keeping it at a distance from consciousness. The mechanism is divided into primal repression and repression proper. The former was assumed to prevent instinctual derivatives from reaching consciousness, the latter as removing from consciousness instinct derivatives and trains of thought that have come in contact with them.

In his paper on "The Unconscious" (1915), in a section on the topography and dynamics of repression, Freud formulated how repression works: first by a withdrawal of cathexis by the preconscious system, which establishes repression, and then by a second process, an anticathexis, which maintains the repression. The withdrawal of cathexis only occurs in repression proper, while the anticathexis (which has since been referred to as countercathexis) is hypothesized to occur in both primal repression and in repression proper.

Regression as a defense is a return to an earlier stage of development in which conflict was less is implied in Freud's discussion of the concept in *Introductory Lectures.* The concepts of fixation and regression were the major mechanisms in Freud's formulation of symptom formation. Later (1926), Freud conceptualized regression as a defense in the following way: "Further investigations have shown that in obsessional neurosis a regression of the instinctual impulses to an earlier libidinal stage is brought about through the opposition of the ego, and that this regression, although it does not make repression unnecessary, clearly works in the same sense as repression" (p. 164).

Also in *Introductory Lectures,* which can be seen as a stock-taking of Freud's views at the time of World War I, Freud stated (Lecture 19) that the pathogenic process demonstrated by resistance is called repression and that this is a precondition for symptom formation.

The change from the topographic to the structural model (1923) was based substantially, as we have already pointed out, on Freud's realization that both repressed and repressing forces were unconscious. Thus, a need to clarify the functioning of defenses played an important role in the development of the structural theory.

In *Inhibitions, Symptoms, and Anxiety* (1926), Freud explicitly defined "defenses" as the general term for all the techniques used by the ego in dealing with conflicts that may lead to a neurosis and includes all processes that protect the ego against instinctual demands. Repression is now to be clearly seen as one particular method of defense. Freud also discussed reaction formation, undoing, regression, and isolation in obsessional neuroses.

His conceptualization of defense at this time included the idea that a symptom is the result of the failure of a defense against an instinctual drive derivative, eventuating in signal anxiety and subsequent defensive efforts to ward off the unpleasant affects. He specified the main danger situations leading to anxiety to be fear of loss of the object, fear of loss of love, fear of castration, and fear of the superego.

In "Analysis Terminable and Interminable" (1937), Freud discussed how defense mechanisms that had earlier been directed against danger situations are found in the psychoanalytic treatment situation as resistances against recovery.

Wilhelm Reich, in his work on character analysis (1933), underscored the distinction between the content and the form of the resistances and demonstrated the defensive aspect of character structure. As he put it, "The character consists in a *chronic* alteration of the ego which one might describe as rigidity. It is the basis of the becoming chronic of a person's characteristic mode of reaction. *Its meaning is the protection of the ego against external and internal dangers*" (1949, p. 145; italics added). He also saw that a given individual will use the same form of defense, whatever the id impulse, while the same id impulse is warded off in different ways by different individuals (pp. 65-66).

Anna Freud's book *The Ego and the Mechanisms of Defense* (1936) was important both for psychoanalytic technique and for the theory of the defenses of the ego. She pointed out some of the shortcomings of focusing exclusively on the instinctual drive derivation in analysis and that the analyst needs to analyze unconscious aspects of all three psychic institutions, ego and superego, as well as id.

While Freud had suggested that a connection exists between certain defenses and particular neuroses, Anna Freud showed this connection to be more general and to link the kind of symptom formation, the kind of defense used against instinctual drive derivatives and affects, and the kind of ego resistance found in analysis. She pointed out that each person chooses a limited number of these mechanisms in defensive activity.

Anna Freud underscored that to understand the transformations undergone by instinctual drives and the ways these have influenced the personality structure it is necessary to analyze the ego's unconscious defensive operations. In clinical psychoanalysis, it is in the patient's resistance to the analysis of his instinctual drives that these defensive operations can be understood. But she also reminds the reader that there are forms of resistance that derive from sources other than defenses.

Anna Freud listed 10 different defense mechanisms: regression, repression, reaction formation, isolation, undoing, projection, introjection, turning against the self, reversal, and sublimation. These are described as 10 different methods at the disposal of the ego in its conflicts with instinctual drive derivatives and affects. In practice, repression is frequently used in conjunction with other mechanisms. It is the most efficient defense mechanism because it only need occur once (although continual countercathexis is required), while the others have to be repeated each time to control the instinctual drive manifestations. It is also the most dangerous because when aspects of the instinctual and affective life are removed from consciousness, the integrity of the personality is affected, more than with other mechanisms. We will qualify this notion later on.

She made some attempts at a chronological classification of defense. One was that each defense arose at a particular phase of infantile development and in the attempt to master a specific instinctual urge (suggested by Helene Deutsch). And, she expanded Freud's suggestion from his 1926 paper on anxiety that different methods of defense may well be used before the clear differentiation of ego and id and before superego formation. Thus, she pointed out that repression can only occur after the ego and id have differentiated. Anna Freud suggested that regression, reversal, and turning round on the self are probably the oldest defense mechanisms and are independent of the stage of psychic development.

She pointed out reasons why some of these chronological suggestions did not jibe with clinical experience and also analyzed the motives for defense in relation to the sources of anxiety in adult neurosis with regard to objective anxiety in infantile neurosis (dread of punishment from adults) and from the standpoint of instinctual anxiety (fear of the strength of instincts). In her discussion of denial and ego restriction as preliminary stages of defense, she was expanding the concept beyond protection of the ego against instinctual demands, to include protection against external reality and danger.

Hartmann (1939) suggested the value of studying conflicts and defenses in relation to the conflict-free ego sphere or the autonomous functions of the ego. He also pointed out that defenses, in addition to operating against instinctual drives, can be seen to have an adaptive aspect. He said,"We are interested in what manner and to what extent is defense directly regulated by those functions which are not currently involved in the conflict" (p. 15).

Hartmann's stress on the adaptive point of view, the change of function, and primary and secondary autonomy (which we discuss in other chapters), all have central importance for defensive functioning. The adaptive aspect of defensive functioning we just mentioned. Change of function frequently involves a behavior or trend that begins as primarily defensive taking on other functions and meanings and vice versa. The idea of ego apparatuses and functions that do not grow out of a conflict between instinctual drive derivatives and defensive measures helped to clarify and delimit the place of defensive functioning in the ego organization.

While Anna Freud had referred to defenses against affects, Fenichel (1945) went into greater detail here and discussed blocking or repression, postponement, displacement of affects, and affect equivalents (i.e., through physical expression such as blushing, habitual throat clearing, and the various psychosomatic expressions). He also discussed defenses against guilt feelings, which include repression, projection, reaction formation, isolation, and regression.

Fenichel clearly distinguished between the motives of defense and defense mechanisms. The motives for defense in a neurotic conflict situation are anxiety, guilt feelings, and shame or disgust, which are activated when an ego-alien instinctual drive derivative threatens to break into awareness or behavior. Fenichel also classified defenses into successful and unsuccessful. The former "bring about a cessation of that which is warded off," and the latter require a repeating of the warding-off process in order to prevent the ego-alien impulse derivatives from erupting into awareness.

Having reviewed these basic writings on defensive functioning, we will now consider some relevant topics that have been discussed in the literature.

DEFENSE MECHANISM, DEFENSE FUNCTIONING, AND DEFENSE ORGANIZATION

The defense mechanisms delineated by Anna Freud are complex, overlap, and work together (Gero, 1951). Waelder (1951) pointed out that they range from elementary responses to highly complex composites, and he argued for an alphabet of defense mechanisms, "a catalog of elementary response." He suggested arranging the elementary defense mechanisms that deal with instinctual drives in terms of the extent to which they impose a change in these drives.

In a danger situation, typically a number of defense mechanisms are called forth by the ego. This observation was consistent with the position put forth by Hoffer (1954) that defense mechanisms and processes operate within a defensive organization and that this is one aspect of the ego organization. Hartmann had emphasized the value and importance of assessing the interrelationships among defenses and autonomous and synthetic functions of the ego (1950, pp. 139-140).*

The relationship of the defense organization to all the major aspects of mental functioning was emphasized in the Symposium on Mechanisms of Defense and Their Place in Psychoanalytic Technique at the Eighteenth International Psychoanalytical Congress in 1953, of which the paper by Hoffer was a part. As Loewenstein put it: "Essentially, the task of the psychoanalytic treatment has been defined as enabling the patient to find a new solution to the pathogenic conflicts which formerly had led to neurotic symptoms. This is achieved by submitting the patient's conflict between his drives and defenses to the scrutinizing of his autonomous ego" (p. 189).

He also stated that little was known at that time about what happened to defenses during analysis, although it was known that they did not disappear and that regression was partly replaced by suppression or sublimation.

*This point is discussed in Chapter 18.

S. Sperling (1957) proposed four categories of defensive functioning to help clarify what he believed had become a confusing situation because of the great diversity of phenomena attributed to defense mechanisms. He would confine the term "defense mechanism" to elementary, pathological, countercathectic activity, which prevents instinctual strivings or superego demands from gaining access to consciousness and discharge. This would include the mechanisms of repression, denial, isolation, reaction formation, projection, introjection, undoing, and simple unconscious forms of inhibition and avoidance.

Sperling would confine the term "defense" to the "not too complex," pathological, countercathectic activity employed mostly by the unconscious ego in inhibiting perceptual stimuli, instinctual drive derivatives, and superego demands from access to awareness and discharge. It is assumed here that some direct cathectic discharge occurs in such processes as identification and rationalization.

By "used for defense" or "in its defensive aspect," Sperling means to characterize processes that allow considerable direct discharge in comparison with their countercathectic function. And the fourth category, which involves secondary defensive aspects, would subsume processes that involve only a minor countercathectic function. These would include memories, affects, and symptom complexes. Mental mechanisms such as displacement, substitution, reversal, and turning round on the self are not seen by Sperling as defensive mechanisms but as elementary ingredients from which more organized defenses are built.

Rather than conceptualizing defense mechanisms as pathological per se, the general trend is to examine both their pathological and their adaptive aspects. We will discuss this issue further on. Lampl de Groot (1957) underscored the place of the defense organization in the adaptation and regulation of all processes dealing with mental conflicts. And Mahler and McDevitt (1968) explored the origins of some defensive and adaptive processes and their interrelationships. Anna Freud summed up the issue as follows:

All defense mechanisms serve simultaneously internal drive restriction and external adaptation, which are merely two sides of the same picture. There is no antithesis between development and defense, since the strengthening of the ego and its defense organization is itself an essential part of the child's growth and comparable in importance to the unfolding and maturing of the drives (1965, p. 177).

A recent differentiation between defense mechanism and defense is given by Siegel (1969):

A defense mechanism is a construct that denotes a mode of functioning of the mind. It describes how behaviors, affects, and ideas serve to inhibit, avert, or modulate unwanted impulse discharges. Defenses, in contrast to defense mechanisms, are behaviors, affects, or ideas which serve defensive purposes. Their functioning is explained in terms of the operation of the defense mechanisms. Defenses range from discrete attributes explicable by reference to complex behavioral and characterologic constellations that are likewise specific, recurrent, and serve defensive purposes. These more complex configurations are variously called the defensive operations, defensive patterns, maneuvers, etc. They are made up of various combinations and sequences of behaviors, affects, and ideas, the operations of which are explicable by reference to a variety of "classical" defense mechanisms, admixed with other ego activities (pp. 791-792).

Hoffer in 1968 said about the defense organization that it includes all aspects of defensive activity, both adaptive and pathological; it is one more component of ego organization, and its function is the regulation of anxiety. The defense organization must be viewed in interaction with id and superego factors and other aspects of the ego organization, especially the autonomous ego functions.

Anna Freud (1965) provided some criteria by which to evaluate the status of the defense organization in children. She specified a consideration of whether defense was being employed against specific instinctual drives or against drive activity and instinctual pleasure per se, whether defenses are age adequate (too primitive or too precocious), and whether they are balanced (where a number of important mechanisms are available or where there is an overuse of particular ones). She includes in addition the question of how effective the defenses are in dealing with anxiety and the extent of secondary interference of defensive functioning on ego achievements.

An answer to the problem of what happens to defenses during analysis was provided by Weiss (1967), who held that the defense organization becomes more integrated during successful analysis and that there is a change from being segregated and beyond the control of the conscious ego, toward being integrated with ego-syntonic control mechanisms. There are two kinds of intrapsychic conflicts affected by this greater integration. The first aspect is related to the unconscious defense warding off instinctual drive derivatives, and the other is the defensive functioning resulting in an interference with other ego functions or processes. Both kinds of conflicts are alleviated when the defensive integration increases.

The defensive organization seen as a general regulatory principle (Lichtenberg and Slap, 1971) provides the basis for raising such questions as what the developmental stages of the defense organization are and how the latter relates to maturation and environmental stimuli.

The purpose of defense has most frequently been assumed to be the preventing of potentially threatening or painful conscious experience. Gardner and Moriarty (1968) hold that a more general purpose of defense is the preservation of effective order in consciousness, with regard to both the kinds of ideas, memories, and percepts and the quality of consciousness characteristic for the given person.

Ego organization can be seen also from a psychocultural perspective. Schupper and Calogeras (1971) have pointed out and illustrated how regression is replacing repression as a central defense mechanism in the youth of the 1970's in Western societies and that there is a concomitant withdrawal of cultural institutional support for repression and repression-type defenses in the sanctioning of hippie behavior, institutional changes in attitudes toward homosexual behavior, drug use, and pornography.

PRECURSORS AND PRESTAGES OF DEFENSE

Freud (1915) saw, as precursors of repression, those action patterns that prevent continual stimulation to the sensory organs and thus hide from the mental apparatus awareness of this stimulation. Some of these action patterns are covering the eyes or closing the eyelids, shifting the eyes, or not focusing optically; turning away from sounds or not listening; and withdrawal from contact. Anna Freud discussed the avoidance of external pain and objective danger as preliminary stages of defense. And S. Sperling (1957) listed displacement, substitution, and turning round upon the self as elementary ingredients from which the more organized defense mechanisms are constructed.

Hartmann (1950) hypothesized that a correlation exists between observable individual differences in stimulus barrier and in the inhibition and postponement of discharge and between later developed defense mechanisms. Such early autonomous ego processes as these and such responses as closing the eyelids to light and flight reactions seem to be the models for later defenses (1950). Provence (1966) offers data to support Hartmann's notion of a genetic correlation between an infant's way of handling stimuli and subsequent defense mechanisms (p. 108). It has been proposed in addition that cognitive control principles (discussed further below), which represent basic organizational schemata in adaptive behavior, "may thus be preconditions for the emergence of defensive structures" (Gardner et al., 1959, p. 128).

Hartmann has also pointed out that drive patterns provide a partial basis on which some defenses are modeled, such as identification and projection (1939). He expressed the opinion (1952) that both the choice and chronology of defense mechanisms would likely be clarified by greater knowledge of the development of their precursors.

Mahler and McDevitt (1968), in discussing the common roots of defense and adaptation, say that some behavioral sequences may appear from birth on to serve adaptation, while others serve a primary defensive function. Some behavioral sequences may initially be adaptive and later, through a change of function, become true defense mechanisms of the ego and vice versa.

Greenacre (1958) holds that physiological processes already serve defensive functions in the neonate, and Lewis (1963) describes a number of primitive defense precursors (blushing, crying, pilomotor erection), which he calls mantle defenses. Another approach to defensive origins is revealed in a report by Despert (1949) on the manifest content of dreams of two- to five-year-old normal preschool children. The author identified manifestations of repression, projection, identification, displacement, and denial.

Precursors and prototypes of defenses have been hypothesized by Spitz (1961, 1965), whose aim has been to identify defense analogues (i.e., phenomena similar in function but different in structure and origin). His general position (1961) is based in part on observations of infants during which he saw the neonatal organism manifesting a capacity for learning, variable modes of adaptation, and the potential for employing neurophysiological and morphological components in dealing with environmental conditions. These innate givens are available to the organism, and some will serve as prototypes for what will become ego defenses. The choice, emphasis, and patterning of defenses and defensive functioning in each child will be decisively influenced by the nature of the unfolding relationship between the child and the particular mothering person. The details of how this epigenetic process takes place is in need of further study. Prototypes of ego defenses discussed by Spitz are the stimulus barrier (for repression), closing the eyelids (for denial), regurgitation (for projection), and sleep (for regression and possibly denial and undoing).

Benjamin (1965) has questioned the value of an analogical approach in understanding defenses, while other workers (Beres and Arlow, 1966) have expressed concern over the danger of reductionism. The value of the Spitz type of hypothesis is in organizing observations of infant behavior and in extending the theory of defensive functioning.

Siegel (1969) summed up the issue of relating precursors to later defenses: "The problem of relating so-called 'precursors' to defense processes which have their origins in a time when ego development is diffuse, undifferentiated, and in flux, to functioning defense mechanisms in the adult, is a difficult and unsolved one" (p. 797).

HIERARCHICAL LAYERING OF DEFENSES

While Freud's discussions of defenses were mostly focused upon the relationship of particular mechanisms to particular forms of psychopathology, what he said about censorship and resistance included the notion of a defense hierarchy. Thus, he said in 1915 that "to every transition from one system to that immediately above it there corresponds a new censorship" (p. 192). Glover said about this (1948) that "Freud was prepared to postulate the existence of a series of censorships lying between the repression barrier and perceptual-consciousness, that is to say, operating at different levels of the preconscious system up to and including the margins of consciousness" (pp. 340-341). Gero (1951) emphasized this same point in terms of the stratification of defenses in relation to their closeness to consciousness.

Glover himself rather early (1936) pointed out that defense mechanisms have a progressive development, constituting an hierarchy where a combination of mechanisms is characteristic for given developmental phases in particular danger situations. And even earlier Jones, in his discussion of "Fear, Guilt, and Hate" (1929), showed how these can be hierarchically layered in the service of defense. Thus, conscious fear or hate may cover and defend against unconscious guilt. The unconscious guilt, in turn, defends against a still deeper layer of hate (p. 305).

As we discuss in the chapter on synthetic-integrative functioning, the idea of an hierarchical series of synthetic functions layered one over the other was spelled out by Schilder in 1930 (in Rapaport, 1951, pp. 579-580). And in his discussion of character analysis (1933), Reich underscored a layering of defensive processes.

Fenichel (1940) pointed out how one instinctual derivative may be used as a defense against another, the one "nearer to the ego" serving as a defense. As he put it:

It is therefore, although an instinct, one of the relatively *defensive* kind, in comparison with the deeper repressed instincts. . . . Nearly always the rejected impulses break through the defense, and there is further repression of the instinct-laden defense as well. There are reaction-formations against reaction-formations. We see not only the three-layer arrangement of instinct-defense-instinct breaking through again, but also instinct-defense-repression of the defense (p. 188).

Rapaport discussed the concept of hierarchical layering in a number of his writings. He saw the layering of drive and defense as a method of personality-structure formation and as the way in which instinctual drives are tamed into adult motives (1951). The more richly developed the hierarchical countercathectic energy distributions, the greater the modulation of affects and the less the likelihood of massive affect outbursts (1953).

Hartmann's hypothesis that countercathexes operate with different degrees of neutralization (1950, 1955) implies that a hierarchy of defenses can be considered from the economic point of view (Gill, 1963). Gill discusses the hierarchy of defenses from this economic point of view and proposes that "defensive functioning takes place on a hierarchy from primary to secondary process and that it regulates the discharge of more or less nonneutralized cathexes" (p. 119). Regarding the levels of defense, he said the following:

We cannot draw a hard-and-fast line between the various levels of defense. If the defenses exist in a hierarchy, the lower levels must be unconscious and automatic, and may be pathogenic. The defenses high in the hierarchy must be conscious and voluntary, and may be adaptive. And, of course, specific defensive behaviors may include both kinds of characteristics (p. 123).

It has already been stated that a manifestation may be an instinctual derivative but serve as a defense against manifestations lower on the hierarchy. This idea can be taken one step further: namely, behaviors may simultaneously be seen to have an impulse and a defense aspect. Anna Freud (1936) had pointed out that defenses are based both on the ego and on the "essential nature of the instinctual processes" (p. 192). Fenichel (1941) had said that some discharge of what is being defended against is afforded by defensive behavior, and Freud, in his discussion of isolation and undoing (1926), implies that these defense mechanisms simultaneously involve an instinctual act and the defense against it (Schafer, 1968).

Gill (1963) showed how defenses use primary process and pointed out that primitive defenses rather closely resemble the impulse being defended against. Schafer (1968) deals with this issue by proposing that defenses be conceptualized as motives or wishes (i.e., dynamic tendencies with mental content). As we have seen, the usual way that conflicts are conceptualized from the dynamic point of view is that there is an id wish or cathexis and an ego countercathexis opposing it. As an alternative formulation, Schafer holds that defensive processes either provide discharge or lead to it and that defense mechanisms not only imply negative assertions ("It never happened;" "There's no connection;" I can't feel it;") but also positive assertions ("I do have a penis;" "I am fully fed;" "I kill him"). As he summed it up:

I submit that the study of defense mechanisms will remain incomplete so long as they are regarded chiefly as wardings off, renunciations, and negative assertions; their study will have to be rounded out with an account of defenses as implementations, gratifications, and positive assertions. In other words, they must be viewed as expressing the unity of the ego and the id and not just the division and enmity of the two (p. 58).

Thus, the overlapping of manifestations relevant to id and ego constructs is particularly relevant to defensive functioning but is also relevant to all functions attributed to the ego.

We turn now to a consideration of defense and adaptation.

ADAPTIVE AND MALADAPTIVE ASPECTS OF DEFENSES

The idea of a continuum between pathology and normality in defensive functioning was first implied by Freud when he said the defenses become pathological only when used in exaggeration (1895). This idea was later developed (1937) when he stated that while the defenses are indispensable for satisfactory development, they may become dangerous as a result of the amount of energy necessary to maintain them and because of the ego deformations that may result from their overuse. He also wrote about the splitting of the ego in the process of defense (1940). The maladaptive aspects of defensive functioning were integral to most of Freud's descriptions and discussions of defense mechanisms.

The adaptive aspects of defensive functioning were reflected in Freud's formulation of signal anxiety (1926) as an anticipatory mechanism that mobilizes defensive activity against potential danger situations, both from within and from without. Anna Freud (1936) distinguished pathological from adaptive defensive functioning in terms of whether defense leads to symptom formation or to healthy social adaptation. She stressed the quantitative factor in pointing out that the overdoing of drive restraint, irrespective of the mechanism employed, would lead to a neurotic outcome. And Hartmann (1939) has illustrated the adaptive aspect of defenses.

Hoffer (1954) refers to various normal or adaptive aspects of defenses to which Anna Freud had pointed: namely, that introjection helps construct the ego, projection protects against ego destruction, reaction-formation is ego stabilizing, and sublimation is ego enriching.

Fenichel (1945) classified defenses as successful (i.e., bring about the cessation of what is warded off) and unsuccessful (i.e., necessitate a repetition or perpetuation of the warding-off process to prevent the eruption of the warded-off impulses). Nunberg (1932) said that drives and defenses are part of the normal human mind as well as playing a role in pathogenic processes. Hendrick also took exception to the innate pathological character of defenses (1938). S. Sperling (1957), as already discussed, emphasized that defenses always result in a pathological impairment of the integrative function, and he concluded that they are thus always pathological.

Loewenstein (1967) says that in regard to their pathogenicity, some defense mechanisms may be either too weak in relation to some drives or too strong in relation to some other types of drives. He thinks, however, it would seem preferable to speak of effectiveness or ineffectiveness of defenses rather than of strength or weakness. Some defense mechanisms are inappropriate in respect to the ego and to the reality situation of a given individual. Their rigidity at various developmental stages and in the light of changing reality situations can make them pathogenic. Pathology also occurs when defense mechanisms are overgeneralized: that is when the behavior they elicit is not limited to a specific person but appears in stereotyped form and is directed at people at large. Loewenstein adds that even a neurotic symptom resulting from an interaction between drive derivatives and defensive processes can on occasion be viewed as reflecting the ego's function of adaptation. One can thus state that certain processes that result in a neurosis are guided by the function of adaptation, although they did not end up being adaptive in the usual sense of the term.

Cognitive controls (Klein and Schlessinger, 1949; Gardner et al., 1959) serve functions similar to defenses with emphasis on the degree of congruence with reality factors (i.e., with adaptation). They resemble character defenses in that they are "ways of contacting reality, whereby one's intentions are coordinated with the properties, relations, and limitations of events and objects" (Klein, 1968, p. 88). Defenses have an adaptive aspect, as noted earlier. But while defenses are by definition involved with internal conflict, cognitive controls need not be. General relationships between defenses and cognitive control principles can be summarized as follows: both are mental structures; both provide an instrumental means for drive discharge; and both "modulate drive discharge processes to accord with established modes of confronting the reality context in which consummation is sought" (Gardner et al., 1959, p. 12). Gardner, Klein, and their colleagues demonstrated various relationships between defense and cognitive style. For example, they showed that males who relied heavily on defense of repression tended to be levelers (i.e., manifested relatively undifferentiated memory patterns for temporal series of stimuli). Males who relied heavily on the defense of isolation tended to be sharpeners (i.e. manifested well-differentiated memories for successive stimuli). A relationship is thus shown to hold between certain defenses and the cognitive control principle of leveling and sharpening.

Defense mechanisms can be characterized according to their degree of pathology. Relatively pathological defenses are denial, regression, projection, and introjection. Kernberg (1966) has emphasized that the defense mechanism of splitting is primitive and is especially characteristic of adults who show an alternating activation of contradictory ego states. But the mechanisms can vary considerably in their pathology and adaptiveness, depending upon when they are employed, against what they are directed, and the status of the various ego functions. Thus, while denial may result in ego arrest when employed against recognizing the meaningfulness of the death of a parent during childhood, it can reflect a psychotic level of functioning if the loss itself is denied (Altschul, 1968). Denial has also been described as necessary for normal functioning: a denial in the service of the need to survive, which wards off anxiety over aspects of painful external reality, which are inevitable (Geleerd, 1965).

Regression is also frequently pathological and may result in a neurotic or in a psychotic level of functioning, depending upon what undergoes regression and to what extent. Regression may occur on the instinctual-drive level, ego-function level, or superego-function level. The extent to which defensive functioning has adversely affected other ego functions defines a major basis for evaluating the adaptiveness of defensive functioning.

Arlow and Brenner (1964) have discussed various psychotic manifestations and symptoms in terms of a regression of particular ego functions as a defensive attempt to avoid anxiety.* Especially essential for psychosis are regressions that result in a disintegration of repression and countercathexes. It is held that psychotic reactions can be classified in relation to the intactness of repression (Freeman, Cameron, and McGhie, 1966). But regressions that do not include marked ego function disturbance do not lead to a psychotic outcome. Still there are times when regressions can be in the service of the ego and aid adaptation (Kris, 1936), as we described in detail in Chapter 12.

Projection and introjection can be used by relatively normal individuals but also as an important defensive aspect of psychotic delusion. Frosch points out (1970), as we described in Chapter 4, that in psychosis the basic danger situations specified by Freud (1926) were fear of object loss, loss of object's love, castration fear, and superego fear. Regressive dedifferentiation, introjection, projection, projective identification, fragmentation, massive denial, splitting, and somatization are some of the defenses used by seriously disturbed individuals. These defenses may themselves increase the likelihood of loss of self, such as in the use of dedifferentiation, and thus potentially bring about the very situation they were instituted to defend against (Frosch, 1967).

Freud had suggested (1926), and Anna Freud had expanded, the idea that particular forms of psychopathology are associated with particular defenses. Frosch broadens this by assuming a close relationship between the nature of the basic conflict, the defensive operations, altered ego states, and defects in various ego functions (1970). Defenses are also more likely to be maladaptive if they are used in a steroty ped way, regardless of external circumstances (Valenstein, 1972).

Many of the bases for classifying defenses have implications for pathology versus adaptation. Thus, defenses have been classified as follows:

(1) According to their relative success in warding off anxiety-arousing stimuli (Fenichel, 1945). Weak defenses are implied when an anxiety signal is followed by anxiety attacks, panic reactions, or other dysphoric affects.

(2) According to the degree to which they change the instinctual drive (Waelder, 1951).

(3) According to the degree of primary- versus secondary-process characteristics (Hartmann, 1950, 1955; Gill, 1963).

(4) According to their degree of structure (Witkin, 1962).

(5) According to the degree to which a given defense can undergo a change of function (Lustman, 1966).

Defenses most frequently characterized as best suiting reality requirements because of their stability and lack of interference with other ego functions are repression and isolation (Beres, 1956), secondary identification (the selective taking on of attitudes, behaviors, and values of an admired person, the defensive aspect being the denial of separateness from the person), and reaction-formation

*We reviewed various aspects of regression in Chapter 4.

(Freeman, Cameron, and McGhie, 1966). But even with well-functioning repression, memory has been interfered with to some extent and so has synthetic-integrative functioning. It also leads back to fixation and impoverishment of both instinctual drive functioning and object relations (Altschul, 1968).

Defensive functioning can thus interfere with adaptation in three main ways. Early overuse of various defenses can lead to ego distortion, deviation, or defect. Defenses can also interfere with other ego functions because of the processes involved. And regressive alterations of ego functions in the service of defense can decrease overall adaptive functioning.

In this chapter we have discussed only some of the important issues and papers relevant to defensive functioning. While this is true for all the chapters on individual ego functions, it is especially here that we have not reviewed all relevant work because of the large number of books and papers devoted to defensive functioning.

CHAPTER 14

Stimulus Barrier*

"New York City...The humidity is wetter, the heat hotter, the fun more intense, the buildings gaudier...than the humidity, heat, fun and buildings of any other time or place...Such cacophonies as the dismantling of sky-scrapers, the screech of subway wheels, the curses of cab drivers, the maniacal rumble of unleashed automobilies hurtling down the avenues in search of some hapless pedestrian – all these fall on deadened eardrums while visitors from outside are breaking out in hives,...ulcers,...and mental illness... (Some New Yorkers,) self-protective deafness may explain why New York is the world capital of overstatement. To penetrate minds coated in thick layers of protective insulation against unnatural environment, men are compelled to seek extremes. The insulation is not limited to aural defenses against the din, but extends through a wide range of defenses against all the threats to privacy that result from the city's overcrowding...The defensive mechanisms of survival may be outstripping the offensive machinery of overstatement. New Yorkers can no longer hear their own noises."[†]

Baker's statement implies so much of what Freud was saying when he developed his idea of the stimulus barrier (*Reizschutz*, or "protective shield").The above quote dramatizes the "what" of it – that is, the phenomenon of stimulus barrier. This chapter will attempt to delineate the "hows" and the "whys" of it – historically, conceptually, and clinically.

Stimulus barrier as an important personality factor has attracted too little attention. Yet, in the development of children it may play a crucial role. In some adults a particularly high or low stimulus barrier may be an outstanding characteristic. It may also be true that in the functioning of a large number of adults, stimulus barrier does not play a marked role. In distinction to its role in children, it may have something of an all-or-none quality in some adults.

This chapter will be clearly divided into three sections: (1) a general review of the concept; (2) a review of the literature implying that stimulus barrier may be usefully classified as an ego function; and (3) a specific reformulation of stimulus barrier as an ego function originally proposed by Bellak and that has

[†]Russell Baker, in *The New York Times,* Sunday, June 25, 1967: "The Earplug Defenses of New York."

*A version of this chapter, written by Helen K. Gediman, Ph.D., appeared in *The International Journal of Psycho-analysis,* 1971, Vol. 52, pp. 243-257.

emerged from our ongoing research on 11 other ego functions as well. The specific idea proposed here is that stimulus barrier is a complex ego function, rather than a simple sensory or perceptual threshold, composed of a number of component factors observable and measurable along a continuum of maladapt-iveness-adaptiveness.

GENERAL REVIEW OF THE CONCEPT

Although it was in *Beyond the Pleasure Principle* (1920) that Freud most fully elaborated his ideas on stimulus barrier, early harbingers of his interest are found in the *Fliess Papers* (1892) and "Project" (1895). In the latter, he introduced the notion that the *Reizschutz* (stimulus barrier) was a necessity for the organism's survival in a stimulus-charged world. The most intensive presentation of his ideas occurred after World War I, when he had occasion to observe many men suffering from the trauma of shellshock. Thus, the concept of stimulus barrier arose in the context of the traumatic neuroses. It was a way of explaining how a person managed to survive in an environment bombarding him with too much stimulation or excitation (1920). The traumatic neuroses were assumed to result from a breach in the stimulus barrier.

Freud felt that any experience is traumatic when a stimulus is too powerful to be dealt with in the usual way and that a traumatic neurosis represents a breach or extensive rupture in the stimulus barrier caused by powerful excitation exerted from the external world. The mental apparatus becomes flooded by large amounts of stimulation (1920). Fenichel elaborates the relation of traumatic neurosis to *Reizschutz*: The excitation already at hand has to be mastered before new stimuli can be accepted. The organism develops different ways of protecting itself against too great a quantity of stimulation (*Reizschutz*). Refusing to accept new stimulation is a primitive means of establishing such protection after it has been broken down by the trauma (1945, p. 118).

Furst, as editor of a recent book, *Psychic Trauma* (1967), compiled a series of contributions expanding on the trauma concept. He feels there has been a blurring of the stimulus barrier concept recently because of a broadening of the trauma concept. Trauma, as now conceived, does not always imply a one-shot manifest breakthrough of the stimulus barrier and an ensuing state of helplessness. It could also involve a rent or crack in the barrier instead of a breakthrough or else a slow breaking through rather than a piercing trauma (M. Kris, 1964). Such phenomena have been variously called strain trauma (Kris, 1956) or cumulative trauma (Khan, 1963). Properly functioning, the stimulus barrier scales down the intensity of external stimuli to a level that the organism can manage. Although described by Freud mainly in the context of trauma, the stimulus barrier concept was clearly applied by him to all pathological states as well as to normalcy. Later (1940) it was seen as a constitutional precursor of the ego, serving a primitive defense function that foretells the ego's more elaborate and highly developed protective mechanisms. Freud described the workings of the stimulus barrier in *Beyond the Pleasure Principle* (1920): the external covering of the apparatus to manage excess stimulation is directed against incoming stimuli, while the next layer is differentiated into an organ for the perception of stimuli. Even this second layer only processes minimum quantities, or samples, of incoming stimuli.

Now let us look further into what Freud said about this mechanism to which he attributed the dual function of protection against, and reception of, stimuli:

Let us picture a living organism in its most simplified possible form as an undifferentiated vesicle of a substance that is susceptible to stimulation . . . It would be easy to suppose, then, that as a result of the ceaseless impact of external stimuli on the surface of the vesicle, its substance to a certain depth may have become permanently modified so that . . . . it would present the most favorable conditions for the reception of stimuli . . . This little fragment of living substance is suspended in the middle of an *external* world charged with the most powerful energies and it would be killed by the stimulation emanating from these if it were not provided with a protective shield against stimuli . . . its outermost surface . . . becomes to some degree inorganic and . . . resistant to stimuli . . . *Protection* against stimuli is an almost more important function for the living organism than reception of stimuli . . . The main purpose of the reception of stimuli is to discover the direction and nature of the external stimuli; and for that it is enough to take small specimens of the external world. In highly developed organisms the receptive *cortical layer* has long been withdrawn into the depths of the interior of the body, though portions of it have been left behind on the surface immediately beneath the general shield against stimuli. These are the sense organs, which consist essentially of apparatuses for the reception of certain specific effects of stimulation, but which also include special arrangements for further protection against excessive amounts of stimulation and for excluding unsuitable kinds of stimuli . . . they deal only with very *small quantities* of external stimulation and only take in samples of the external world. They may perhaps be compared with feelers which are all the time making tentative advances towards the external world and then drawing back from it (1920, pp. 26-29; italics added).

Under the influence of the external world, a portion of the id has undergone special development—what was originally a cortical layer equipped with organs for receiving stimuli and with arrangements for acting as a protective shield against stimuli . . . [from this] a special organization called the *ego* has arisen (1940, p. 145; italics added).

These quotations present concisely a number of thought-provoking issues: the subsequently much-questioned (even by Freud) notion that the stimulus barrier functions only to regulate the impact of external (as opposed to internal, or drive) stimuli; the recently disputed neurological assumptions underlying Freud's conceptual model of stimulus barrier, in which levels of abstraction shift and in which the boundaries between a purely neurological model and a psychological one seem hazy; the relation of stimulus hunger to the protection against stimuli; elaborations of the relation of psychic trauma to stimulus barrier. The issues foreshadow current lines of thought and research which treat stimulus barrier not only as a threshold mechanism, but also as the precursor of an ego function, and an ego function as such. Let us deal with each of these issues in turn.

Protection Against Inner or Outer Stimuli?

One question (which we shall see is now moot) is whether the stimulus barrier is erected against outer reality alone or against both inner and outer reality. What makes the question now moot are the expanded notions of reality, both inner and outer. Freud repeatedly stated that there was no *Reizschutz* protecting the psychic apparatus from the *drives* but only from external environmental reality or from injurious effects from without. His early position was that "the organism cannot withdraw itself from [endogenous stimuli] as it does from external stimuli" (1895, p. 297). Still later, he made the following distinction:

Let us imagine ourselves in the situation of an almost entirely helpless living organism . . . which is receiving stimuli in its nervous substance. . . . On the one hand, it will be aware of stimuli which can be avoided by muscular action [flight] ; these it ascribes to an external world. On the other hand, it will also be aware of stimuli against which such action is of no avail . . . instinctual needs (1915, p. 119).

In his late writings Freud somewhat obscures the functional differences between protection against outer and inner stimuli: "An excessive strength of instinct can damage the ego in a similar way to an excessive stimulus from the external world" (1940, p. 199). Anna Freud (1967) speaks for those who interpret Freud's distinction as implying two stimulus barriers: one against inner and one against outer stimuli.

In later elaborations of Freud's stimulus barrier concept, a number of writers independently came to the conclusion that the inner-outer distinctions do not hold, either conceptually or experientially. Clinical data abound with evidence of the organism treating disturbing internal stimuli as though they were external and attempting to deploy the same protective measures against both. Experimental evidence points to the same conclusion, reversing the emphasis. Eagle, summarizing the evidence on subliminal sensitivity, concludes that the residue of external input acts exactly like internal intuition or "hunch." When information was presented without any indication of where it came from, subjects reacted to it as if it were a drive derivative: the ways they tended to deal with drives predicted sensitivity to subliminal stimuli (1962). In keeping with these findings, Benjamin (1965) broadens the concept of stimulus barrier, stating that projection makes use of stimulus barrier; that the infant often treats internal stimuli as external and does so also at a later date; and that the assumption that the shield is effective only against external stimulation implies the development of an outside-inside differentiation, which is in fact difficult to determine.

Early on (1939), Hartmann believed there was no barrier against instinctual drives, but later he appears to have revised this view: "The ego . . . serves as a protective barrier against excessive external and, in a somewhat different sense, internal stimuli" (1950, pp. 114-115). Later on (1958), we find Winnicott stating that impingements on the organism indicate a failure to regulate stimuli, both internal and external. If inner stimuli can be conceived of as other than drive or instinct in the classical sense, it becomes easier to view the stimulus barrier as protecting against both inner and outer stimuli. It is not difficult to see the pseudo nature of the inner-outer dispute. We can assuredly say that the stimulus barrier concept, when introduced, did not deal with drive states (in the psychoanalytic sense); it would be too limiting to ban the concept from application to many other inner states. We would summarize this issue, agreeing with Holt's discussion of Freud's comparison of stimulus barrier with cell-membrane: "It seems to me therefore useful to conceive of the ego membrane as protecting the conscious ego . . . from inner emotional impressions as well as from outer ones" (1948, p. 9).

Biological and Neurological Assumptions

The chief biological assumption that Freud used to account for the workings of the stimulus barrier was that of the constancy, stability, or Nirvana principle: "The nervous system is an apparatus which has the function of getting rid of the stimuli that breach it, or of reducing them to the lowest possible level; or which, if it were feasible, would maintain itself in an altogether unstimulated condition" (1915, p. 120). Thus, Freud said, the stimulus barrier, following the laws of the Nirvana principle, strives to keep stimulation at a minimum. Now, this tension-reduction theory has been the subject of much controversy. There is certainly some very convincing evidence to show that at times people indeed do whatever they can to keep themselves in a relatively tensionless state. But we also are confronted at the other extreme with unequivocal observational data of people whose life appears dedicated to the pursuit of stimuli, as in the sensory-happy seekers of psychedelic experiences or among the "hippies" of today. Do these data invalidate the Nirvana principle, or can that tenet be modified to include the seemingly contradictory clinical observations? We must also consider here the plethora of biological and neurological writings appearing these days, both as evidence confirming or refuting Freud's biological assumptions and as analogues to illustrate them.

Among the first to consider the issue of stimulus hunger in relation to tension-reduction theory was Fenichel, whose ideas were elaborations of the simple observation that the life of the infant alternates between states of hunger and other disturbing stimuli and the state of sleep. He described a basic contradiction in human life: the longing for complete relaxation (constancy or Nirvana principle) and a longing for objects (stimulus hunger). Wolff, too, borrowing Piaget's concept of nutriment or aliment, feels that both increase and decrease of tension are essential for structure formation. The point being made has to do with "optimal" stimulation rather than with overstimulation. Amacher (1965) feels there were flaws in Freud's neurological education that greatly influenced psychoanalytic theory. Mainly, he feels that included in the erroneous set of assumptions Freud inherited from his teachers was the view that there is no protective shield against drives. Therefore, Freud saw reality as composed of isolated, momentary stimuli, whereas he regarded drives as continuous. The nervous system was regarded by Freud as passive, with the primary function of ridding itself of stimulation in such a way that external stimulus energies entering directly into the nervous system needed to be scaled down by the stimulus barrier.

Much criticism of the Nirvana principle is summarized in Greenfield and Lewis's compendium, *Psychoanalysis and Current Biological Thought* (1965). This book contains contributions by people whose ideas have evolved from Freud's major concepts. It attempts to update the biological assumptions in psychoanalytic theory in order to bring them in line with present-day knowledge, yet without at the same time discarding Freud's major concepts and clinical observations, especially those regarding the stimulus barrier. According to Benjamin, Freud's attribution of major importance to the concept of protective shield was a logical consequence of his views of the essential noxiousness of stimulation. While the Nirvana or constancy principle played a major role in Freud's metapsychology, most of the findings of neuroanatomy speak against any general validity for this thesis of Freud's. Says Benjamin:

There is spontaneous activity not only in the brain, but also in the sense organs, themselves, the discovery of positive reinforcement as well as aversive centers in the limbic system . . . and, following Hebb's original work, the results of many behavioral studies of the effects of partial afferent isolation are sufficient evidence . . . that the concept that the organism strives to keep stimulation at a minimum, or if possible at a zero level, is without biological foundation (p. 61).

Pertinent here are Magoun's conclusions about the function of the ascending reticular system (1958) and also the work of others questioning Freud's biology in the light of current knowledge: (Bexton et al., 1954; Delgado et al., 1954; Lilly, 1956; Olds and Milner, 1954; Pribram, 1965; and Solomon et al., 1961). All this discussion leads naturally into some more intensive consideration of stimulus hunger in general and its relation to stimulus barrier in particular.

Stimulus Hunger

Regarding stimulus barrier, Bellak has made frequent reference to the concept of stimulus hunger. An early reference to stimulus hunger following sensory deprivation is found in the work of Buerger-Prinz and Kaila (1930), who note that in some cases of brain pathology there are no satiation experiences with respect to various stimuli. They feel this is a most impressive example of a lack of stimulus barrier and not that this hunger reflects a too high or strong stimulus barrier. More recently, Rapaport (1957 and 1967), Wolff (1960), Rubinfine (1962), Wallerstein (1966), and Engel (1962) have used the concept of stimulus aliment or nutriment (as coined by Piaget) to explain certain relationships between the seeking of sensory stimulation, on the one hand, and stimulus barrier, on the other. Wallerstein cites the conclusions of a panel that agrees that the stimulus barrier itself guarantees an appropriate intake of *optimal* level stimulation in addition to protecting against too much. Spitz, in his work on hospitalism and anaclitic depression in infants, presents convincing evidence of the need for optimal stimulation to insure survival in infants (1945, 1946). Bellak (1963), offering some conceptual considerations of diffuse acting out, says such behavior is caused by "a general overstimulation and sensitization for all stimuli. . . . An infant needs a certain amount of sensory input for development. . . . It also seems that a 'system' may get a permanent overload; such a person then has a lifelong experience of excessive stimulus hunger, matched only by the inability for containment and the constant need for discharge" (p. 381). We often deal with the apparent paradox of a person attempting to reduce the impact of a stimulus upon himself through stimulus-seeking behavior. Sometimes we have to recognize defensive raising and lowering of thresholds through such behavior. Perhaps the quest for excitement serves to reduce the effectivenss of other potentially more threatening stimuli, such as those resulting from closeness in object relations. Attention is thus deflected from the relatively more conflictual to a less conflictual source of stimulation.

There are other ways as well to understand the apparent paradox of people seeking overstimulation, who by all other indications have a very *low* stimulus barrier. Many a frenetic seeker of stimuli suffered greatly as a child from exposure to frequent rantings and ravings of a psychotic mother who provided a maternal, household setting of chronic overexcitement. We might assume that such a person was left helpless and undefended, with no provisions for effectively warding off massive stimulus assaults. The quest in adolescence and young adulthood for similar stimulation might represent an attempt to master the early trauma through repetition. It seems likely that this stimulus hunger results not from stimulus deprivation and/or a weak stimulus barrier but from a chronic overstimulation in infancy and childhood and/or a weak stimulus barrier—despite their apparent ability to tolerate high levels of sensory input.

Cumulative Trauma, Object Relations, and Mothering

The term "cumulative trauma," introduced by Khan (1963), can replace "traumatic neurosis" to bring fresh perspective to the developmental and ego aspects of stimulus barrier. Khan contrasts the nature of cumulative trauma with what has been called traumatic neurosis:

My argument is that cumulative trauma is the result of breaches in the mother's role as a protective shield over the whole course of the child's development, from infancy to adolescence—that is to say, in all those areas of experience where the child continues to need the mother as an auxiliary ego to support his immature and unstable ego function. . . . Cumulative trauma thus derives from the strains and context of his ego dependence on the mother as his protective shield and auxiliary ego (p. 288).

Singly, these breaches need not be traumatic but may achieve the effect of trauma, affecting the stimulus barrier as they accumulate silently over the course of time. Anna Freud also refers to cumulative trauma as successive failures of the mother to act as the child's protective shield, but she feels this trauma occurs only during infancy, when the child is most vulnerable to stresses and strain. Like Khan, Rangell (1967) sees cumulative and retrospective trauma as resulting from events not traumatic at any one point in life but which become traumatic when their magnitude has accumulated sufficiently so that they would have such effects on anyone when the sensitization or reaction point of the particular host has been reached.

Rubinfine (1962) notes how attempts at relative autonomy from thralldom to painful stimuli are originally directed to percepts threatening object loss and thus have a special role in conserving object relations. Engel (1962) indicates that when there is loss of supplies needed to retain an object (and thus to enhance self-esteem) and all solutions to regain the object fail, there may be a giving up of the object and a raising of the barrier against stimuli from outside. Infants experiencing unusual stress, say Brody and Axelrad (1966), may have a reduced readiness to perceive external stimuli and to organize perception. We should then find an inverse relationship between cumulative physiological stress and the capacity for object perception that leads to object cathexis.

The relationship between stimulus barrier and mothering could hardly be called new, considering that Freud, in 1895, in "The Project for a Scientific Psychology," had this to say: "When the helpful person had performed the work of the specific action in the external world for the helpless one [child], the latter is in a position . . . to carry out in the interior of his body the activity necessary for removing the endogenous stimulus" (p. 318). Khan elaborates on Freud's ideas: "If we replace in Freud's model 'the undifferentiated vesicle of a substance that is susceptible to stimulation' by a live human infant, then we get what Winnicott (1963) has described as 'an infant in care.' The infant in care has for his protective shield the caretaking mother" (p. 290). He adds that the mother's role as a protective shield constitutes the average expectable environment for the anaclitic needs of the infant. By making herself available as a protective shield, she enables growth of autonomous ego functions and instinctual processes and allows herself to become maximally receptive to the infant's needs. She also facilitates the synthetic functioning of the ego, and helps to build up primary narcissism by lending the infant her own ego functions through her role as a protective shield. Khan's reference to Winnicott's notion that "an infant in care has for his protective shield the caretaking mother" (1965) is expanded here by quoting from Winnicott:

The mother who is able to give herself over, for a limited spell, to . . . her natural task, is able to protect her infant's going-on-being. If reacting to impingements is the pattern of an infant's life, then there is a serious interference with the natural tendency that exists in the infant to become an integrated unit, able to have a self with a past, present, and future (1963, p. 86).

Parallel lines of thought have been expressed by Jacobson (1964), who says that maternal stimulation of motor, proprioceptive, kinesthetic, tactile, temperature, visual, and acoustic pleasure experience promotes ego growth; by Rubinfine (1962), who says that maternal care can serve as an adequate buffer against too intense stimulation; and by L. Murphy (1962), who concludes that a child's thresholds for tension are dependent upon the total dynamic setting, especially the mother-child relation. Benjamin, too, stresses that the mother-figure must intervene to help in tension-reduction or else the infant will be overwhelmed by stimuli and become prone to outbursts of undifferentiated negative affect expression (1961). Elsewhere he states that the enhanced vulnerability of the infant during that time when the passive stimulus barrier is no longer effective and the active one has not developed makes greater demands on the mother or mother-substitute. During this critical period, the infant's "protective function must . . . be taken over by the mother, undoubtedly the best of all potential 'stimulus barriers' for the young infant, though by no means always a successful one in practice" (Benjamin, 1965, p. 61). Winnicott goes so far as to define inadequate mothering as identical with her failure as a stimulus barrier or as her allowing too many impingements to reach the child during its infancy so that it cannot achieve a real ego or "true self." Because impingements are so disruptive to true ego integration, they lead to premature or disruptive defensive integration and functioning (1958, 1960, 1963). Following Winnicott's observations, Guntrip (1964) defines bad mothering as the permitting of impingements on the infant or the forcing of the infant to be aware of pressures of external and interfering reality when he is not feeling such needs. Impingement is thus an intrusion on the infant at times when he is not reaching out actively into the outer world for stimulation, and it results in forms of withdrawal from the unwanted impact. Khan (1963) sees three types of failure of the mother as a protective shield: (1) excessive intrusion of the mother's pathology; (2) loss of, or separation from, the mother; and (3) constitutional sensitivity of the child imposing handicaps on the mother. The effects of strain and impingements in the mother's role as a protective shield may lead to any or all of the following conditions: premature ego development; special responsiveness to the mother's mood; precocious functioning without a "coherent ego;" excessive concern for the mother; and precocious organization of inner and outer reality and disruption of the synthetic function. Finally, we quote Rubinfine's statement of the mother's function as stimulus barrier:

Maternal care serves as an adequate buffer against too intense external or internal stimulation. However, if the maternal partner adds to the excessive external stimulation, or if internal stimuli are too intense or prolonged, the result is that aggression differentiates first . . . it seems to me that such a failure of mothering is responsible for the reduction in the effectiveness of the stimulus barrier (1962, p. 269).

SOME CRITICISMS OF THE STIMULUS BARRIER CONCEPT

One of the major difficulties in the early literature on stimulus barrier was the failure to differentiate clearly between a biological-neurological model of the psychic apparatus—in particular stimulus barrier—and a psychological one. The notion that appears most questionable from a conceptual point of view is Freud's description of the perceptive apparatus as having two layers: an external protective barrier against stimuli whose task it is to diminish stimulation, and a surface behind it that receives the stimuli, namely, the system Pcpt-Cs. Thus, Freud said, stimulus barrier is one of two layers of a purely psychological structural concept, "the perceptive apparatus of the mind" (1925). At another time, in the "Project," Freud considered the *Reizschutz* in more neurophysiolog-ical terms, in which sources of excitation come up against nerve endings and are broken up into quotients by "contact barriers," summation and resistance in the paths of conduction in neurons (1895, p. 315). Bergman and Escalona (1949) feel these switches in conceptual level make stimulus barrier a baffling and provocative concept applied by Freud to a variety of related, but not identical, phenomena. Wallerstein (1966), summarizing a panel report, emphasized the conceptual problems in making the transition from biological to psychological consideration yet concluded that in the long run, neurophysiology and psychoanalysis complement each other. This way of putting the matter in a sense begs the question, or at least diverts us with a ready-made reconciliation without going into careful theory-building analysis. In our opinion the most thoughtful critical discussion of Freud's model-building with respect to stimulus barrier is offered by Holt. He notes that Freud sometimes thinks of the shield as anatomical (sense organs arranged for the reception of, and protection against, stimuli), while later he makes it one of two layers of a purely psychological structural concept. In a review of Freud's biological assumptions, Holt (1965) elaborates this issue:

> The central concept of protective shield is tantalizingly elusive. . . . When he first introduces it, by his first fanciful genetic hypothesis of a one-celled organism, the protective crust baked on by environmental energies is clearly physical in nature. Then . . . he switches to the realm of metaphor: The barrier is no longer physical, since "preparedness of anxiety and the hypercathexis of the receptive system constitute the last line of defense of the shield against stimuli" *(Beyond the Pleasure Principle.* p. 31). On the one hand, it sounds continually as if the protective shield is some sort of physical barrier since it guards against the inflow of physical energies which have to be mastered lest they overwhelm the organism; yet the rupture of the barrier in traumatic neurosis does not mean that the skin is broken, for we are told that a "gross physical injury caused simultaneously by the trauma *diminishes* the chances that a neurosis will develop" *(Beyond the Pleasure Principle,* p. 33). If Freud had kept to an anatomical-physiological model, he would never have been able to make his concept perform such gymnastics and would not have approached an explanation in this way at all (p. 117; italics added).

Most recently, Holt has summarized this point by saying that Freud relied too much on metaphor instead of serious model-building: "The basic trouble is that this metaphorical way of thinking makes too many easy equations and generalizations about matters that are determined by more or less independent structures (specific sensory thresholds, absolute and differential; thresholds of emotional arousal; empathy; capacity to concentrate and isolate, etc.)" (personal communication, 1967). Now that these internal inconsistencies have been noted, we would like to further develop the clinical usefulness of this concept. Perhaps our final model of stimulus barrier as an adaptive ego function will not depart too much from Freud's original concept, even if the latter stands only as an analogue to the phenomena we have been studying.

REVIEW OF STIMULUS BARRIER CONCEPT AS EGO FUNCTION

The position taken here is that stimulus barrier can best be conceptualized as a complex ego function having multiple component factors, rather than as a simple threshold measure or concretized "membrane." A review of pertinent literature will lead to a specific reformulation of stimulus barrier as used in our current work on ego functions.

In this connection Freud (1892) described the first threshold, representing the stimulus barrier as that quantity of excitation from the outside, coming against nerve endings and broken up into quotients, below which no quotient at all comes into being. The effectivenss of stimuli is thus restricted more or less to medium quantitites. Germane to the threshold discussions were Freud's considerations of "contact barriers" and "cortical layers," related to the receptive and protective functions of the stimulus barrier (1895; 1920). Recently the threshold notion has been elaborated by Bellak, for one, who in a clinical context describes certain forms of acting out as resulting from "a general overstimulation and sensitization for all stimuli—in the sense of a much lowered threshold for both input and output" (1963). Engel (1962) views stimulus barrier as a threshold apparatus of the autonomous ego that includes systems of perception. Shevrin and Toussieng functionally define threshold as a protective measure controlling cognition of cravings (1965).

Hints that thresholds are not such a simple matter when considered in relation to *Reizschutz* come from a good deal of speculation and empirical data that they may be either raised or lowered when excitations increase. One consequence of a raised threshold representing a lowered stimulus barrier is the defense of withdrawal (Rubinfine, 1962). Allied to this is Anna Freud's observation (1967) that children react with either sensitization (lowering of thresholds) or adaptation (raising of thresholds) when there is a traumatic onslaught of stimuli. Similarly, Bridger (1962) notes the apparent paradox that a strong stimulus produces sleep in the neonate, but when the stimulus intensity increases, a point is reached where the baby wakens. The same phenomena are described by Cameron (1963), who says that a low or weak stimulus barrier accounts for such behavior as being engrossed in activity or falling asleep. The issue of raising and lowering of thresholds is discussed most extensively by Shevrin and Toussieng (1962, 1965). In the context of tactile stimuli especially, they state: "The main ways . . . these children cope with tactile conflicts is either by a defensive raising of thresholds . . . or through protective fluctuations in the physical distance between themselves and other people" (1965, p. 311). Elaborating on defensive withdrawal as a means of coping with excessive stimulation, they state that when thresholds are excessively raised and the child is spending considerable time sleeping, impoverishment of inner stimulation gets matched by withdrawal from external stimuli, as more and more potential satisfactions become a threat and require compensatory thresholds.

Engel (1962), too, sees a defensive or paradoxical behavioral raising of the stimulus barrier among people for whom it is constitutionally low, as leading to defensive withdrawal following attempts to reduce incoming stimuli. Schizophrenic children especially would appear to show a hypersensitivity to strong sensory stimulation. Goldfarb summarizes these observations: "The term, hypersensitivity, may be confusing since sometimes it signifies sensory threshold and at other times signifies manifestations of distress and defensive avoidance" (1961, p. 96). He goes on to say that hypersensitivity is not the consequence only of lowered sensory thresholds (acuity) but also of the *integration* of sensory experience.

Perhaps the best known work on thresholds in the newborn is that of Bergman and Escalona (1949), who also refer to protection against stimuli by thresholds. Although they would probably see stimulus barrier purely as a threshold measure, they do state its relation to ego functioning by saying that when the stimulus barrier is too low or too high, ego development is interfered with. Escalona has written that she prefers to limit the term "stimulus barrier" to perceptual sensitivity, since it is descriptive and "has the advantage that one is not committed to a host of theoretical implications" (personal communication, April 1967). Thus, she opts to steer clear of conceptualizing stimulus barrier as a complex, adaptive ego function.

Apparently all people are congenitally endowed with threshold potentials for stimuli in all sensory modalities and thus bring to bear in their total response repertoire something called "state" of the organism. But the ego, in its totality of developmental vicissitudes and multiple functions, is responsible for the eventuation of congenitally determined sensory thresholds in each person's unique mode of responding to stimuli by *organizing and integrating* his sensory experience. So, there are ego-response measures other than absolute or differential thresholds for stimuli, which determine the status of stimulus barrier as an ego function. The literature has often focused on either the threshold aspect or the integrative aspect of sensory experience.

A focus on the congenital component alone might be inferred from Anna Freud, who stated (1967) that there is a constitutional tolerance underlying individual differences in the degree of stimuli with which one can cope. A view that holds the stimulus barrier as congenitally determined but that defines "congenital" in terms broader than purely genetic is presented by Greenacre. She feels that an overload of potential in the prenatal, neonatal, and immediate postnatal experience leads to a "genuine physiological sensitivity, a kind of increased indelibility of reaction to experience" (1941, p. 50). Then there are numerous references that focus on environmental impact as most crucial for the stimulus barrier: Benjamin's *overstimulation* during critical periods" (1965); Bellak's concern that "a 'system' may get a permanent *overload*" (1963); Winnicott's treatment of *impingements* (1963); Kris's discussion of "a specific kind of overstimulation which was bound to produce mounting tension in the child" (1962); Wallerstein's panel discussion of *surplus excitation* in the postnatal period (1967); and Furst's description of the mental apparatus being *flooded* (1967). We have italicized certain key terms that, together with other such frequently found words as "overwhelming," "bombarding," "disorganizing," could form a lexicon of terms found in the psychoanalytic literature alerting us to what happens when there is a breach in the stimulus barrier. According to Freud, a breach in the stimulus barrier is a function of the strength and intensity and the degree of preparedness of the barrier.

Brody and Axelrad (1966) review literature on interrelationships of congenital "states" and other activities of the organism (Brazelton, 1962; Brown, 1964; Escalona, 1962; and Paine, 1965). They conclude that differences in states affect the neonate's freedom to distinguish and adapt to external stimuli. Of course when we speak of organism-environment interactions directed toward adaptation, we are considering the ego, or at least a potential ego. It should be noted that other ego functions, particularly the autonomous and synthetic, traditionally have been regarded as having both congenital and other elements.

Freud made an explicit statement of the stimulus barrier as a "potential ego," ego root, or nucleus. Benjamin's summary of Freud's position states that the stimulus barrier is a true *precursor* of various aspects of defensive and adaptive ego functioning:

> This concept of the *Reizschutz* as a prototypic homologue of some defensive and adaptive functions of the ego, or perhaps even a true precursor in the sense of a co-determinant of one important but limited ego function, seems entirely plausible. . . . Specifically, individual variability in the degree with which the young infant masters external stimulation by this means may turn out to have some demonstrable predictive value as a co-determinant . . . of defensive and adaptive ego functioning as a whole" (1965, p. 63).

Using a variety of behavioral indices, Benjamin developed a scale to measure how infants protect themselves from excessive stimulation by actively exerting effort (1959, 1963). These indices have, he claims, proved to be one of the more accurate predictors of later ego development. Freud's other followers also have emphasized that the mastery aspect may be regarded as a prototype or precursor of later ego functioning (Hartmann, 1933). Expanding on Hartmann's work about the conflict-free sphere of ego function, Rapaport comments in a note to Bergman and Escalona's major paper (1949) that unusual endowments in children with special sensitivity to stimuli facilitate conflict-free solutions of problems and are related to innate differences in stimulus barrier. There will be fragmentary development of ego functions, particularly those related to intellect. The need to erect a secondary protective barrier against external stimuli, say Bergman and Escalona, produces the capacity for certain ego functions that ordinarily would mature at a later date.

Integration of sensory experience is the focus of Goldfarb's work with schizophrenic children (1961). He became convinced that hypersensitivity to stimuli is not a simple consequence of sensory acuity or lowered sensory thresholds but also of the integration of sensory experience by an active, volitional effort of the ego. A most compelling presentation of the relation of mastery of stimuli to ego development is offered by Lois Murphy: "The average expectable amount of stimulation is more than some infants and children can handle, while it is insufficient for others. Thus, the area of management of stimulation, whether eliciting more of it or selecting and reducing it is *not only a basic coping task related to sensory thresholds. . . but is central for shaping coping style*" (1962, p. 339). Holt (1948) states that sensitivity, receptivity, and perceptivity are not related merely to threshold or a constitutional barrier against stimuli. He feels these observable events are involved with a whole set of ego functions which grow to take over and extend the job originally performed by the neonatal stimulus barrier. The ego functions then operate in a unitary fashion and could be generalized to a *higher level of abstraction as the ego equivalent of the functional stimulus barrier of infancy*. Holt's position seems consistent with ours and more or less summarizes the major concept of stimulus barrier as an ego function.

STIMULUS BARRIER: ACTIVE OR PASSIVE MECHANISM?

Any consideration of mastery must imply active, if not "volitional," efforts on the part of the ego. Therefore, Freud's original notes on mastery of excessive stimulation in the repetition compulsion (1920) might be regarded as a good foundation for conceptualizing an active stimulus barrier in addition to regarding it as merely a congenital threshold. The latter was the focus of considerations regarding *Reizschutz* as essentially passive and a developmental consequence of certain neonatal neurological maturation. It would seem as though passive aspects of the stimulus barrier refer to a certain neurological state of affairs in the neonate. Spitz has dwelled at length (1950) on the neonatal stimulus barrier as a manifestation of neural immaturity that recedes after several months. Emphasis on the passive aspects, even of so-called active mastery, comes from Pumpian-Mindlin's review (1966) of some aspects of the repetition compulsion that are now questionable—for example, the presentation of the repetition compulsion and death instinct as primitive, stereotyped, passive defensive behavior, exemplified in traumatic dreams, traumatic neuroses, and fate neuroses. For example, in considering stimulus barrier as arising not from the id but as an autonomous ego function, Hartmann says: "It might be that the ways in which infants deal with stimuli . . . are later used by the ego in an active way. We consider this active use for its own purposes of primordial forms of reaction a rather general characteristic of the developed ego" (1950, p. 125). Holt feels it is difficult to account for ego autonomy as long as the assumption of a basically passive psychic apparatus is retained. He concludes that Freud's model of the protective shield in *Beyond the Pleasure Principle* pictures the organism as passive and helplessly at the mercy of dangerous energies penetrating the presumably passive screening effects of the *Reizschutz* (1965). Holt invokes

Murray's concept of "press" (1938) as one way of describing how active coping is involved in escaping from stimuli. He feels that input from the environment is relevant to behavior not only as it provokes passive reactivity to stimuli but also as it supplies information and tonic support (1965). A major contribution to the active-integrative aspects of stimulus barrier comes from Brody and Axelrad:

The essential nature of the protective shield with which we are dealing is not whether the shield can be pierced by stimuli of a certain intensity – that is a matter of neurophysiological responsiveness. We are concerned rather with the psychological organization of manifold stimuli which impinge upon the organism – an active integrative process, rather than a mechanical registration: a process advanced by both the protective *and* the receptive functions of the protective shield (1966, p. 224).

The concern here is with both passive and active elements of the stimulus barrier, where the passive aspects relate to the receptive function (threshold) and the active aspects are based on the protective function (active accommodation to stimuli). Hartmann (1953) also feels there is both an active and a passive stimulus barrier that can be broken through, an idea on which Holt elaborates by saying that autonomy from the environment may involve freedom from distracting stimuli by either of two strategies that cut down afferent inputs to the cortex: sensory deprivation or concentration on something else. The former is a passive function; the latter, active.

We come now to the most recent and, to us, the most original and persuasive presentation of stimulus barrier as an active, adaptive ego function. This is Benjamin's approach, which does not disregard the clinically valid observations of its passive aspects. His article is a major contribution to the book on *Psychoanalysis and Current Biological Thought* (Greenfield and Lewis, 1965). He bases his conclusions on the observation that infants display increased sensitivity to stimulation at age three to four weeks and have EEG's that shift from being relatively flat and undifferentiated to distinctly periodic. Benjamin assumes that this sudden appearance of behavioral change is a function of neuroanatomical and physiological maturation at this particular time, and he states his position:

We consider our findings point rather strongly to the conclusion that the so-called stimulus barrier or protective shield against stimulation of the very young infant (which is, of course, only a relative and in no sense an absolute "barrier") is . . . a purely passive mechanism, due to relative lack of functioning connections. In contrast, we see later how the older infant and young child (as well as the adult) often exerts efforts to protect himself from excessive stimulation (p. 60).

He believes that the capacity to actively shut out stimuli starts to develop at approximately 8 to 10 weeks and matures rapidly. The stimulus barrier is important in that the mature organism has developed a variety of ways of receiving, processing, and warding off stimulation. He thus postulates two barriers against external stimulation in infancy: the passive barrier, which is a function of a lack of neural maturation and the active barrier, which might be a precursor or prototype of defense yet is in itself a more advanced stage of neural maturation:

This concept of the *Reizschutz* as a prototypic homologue of some defensive and *adaptive functions of the ego,* or perhaps even a true precursor in the sense of a co-determinant of one important but limited ego function, seems entirely plausible or even probable with respect to our "active stimulus barrier," but much less so with respect to "passive neonatal behavior." In the latter case, one is at best dealing with an analogy without genetic continuity; in the former, with a phenomenon that, in one respect at least, is a true precursor, and beyond that may conceivably have value as an indicator of other defensive and adaptive aspects of ego functioning (p. 63; italics added).

Benjamin interprets recent neurological findings to mean that between 4 weeks (the disappearance of the passive stimulus barrier) and 8 weeks (the appearance of the active stimulus barrier), there is no mechanism at all for warding off stimuli, and the infant is so vulnerable that all protection must come from the mother. A good deal of Benjamin's paper is devoted to citing the pertinent neurological evidence for those physiological mechanisms that are central influences on afferent transmission.

The studies that involve the question of central influences on afferent transmission, or the physiological mechanisms pertinent to an active stimulus barrier, are available to the interested reader (Dawson, 1958, French, 1960; Galambos, 1955; Granit and Kadda, 1952; Hogbarth and Kerr, 1954, Livingston, 1958; Magni et al., 1959; Magoun, 1958; Perl et al., 1962; Satterfield, 1962; Scherrer and Hernandez-Peon, 1955).

A number of works adopt a point of view that comes close to our position: that stimulus barrier is an adaptive ego function, locatable somewhere in the hierarchy of other ego functions and comprised of various component factors. One such study is presented by Lois Murphy (1962). She provides some specific information gleaned from a small sample of children, about the interrelationships of constitutional strength of the barrier and some other activities (in this case, strength of drive) that it affects. The children with average drive and marked sensitivity did not show the good capacity to struggle with deprivations, as did those with marked sensitivity and high drive. Without high drive, high sensitivity tended to produce withdrawing tendencies and little effort to develop active, direct methods of dealing with the environment. With respect to devices used for the active management of stimulation, it is well to note Murphy's conclusion:

Shutting out stimuli that come at an unwanted time by turning away so as not to see, covering up ears, protesting, rejecting habitually stimuli that cannot be handled successfully, diminishing or terminating stimulation that is too much for pleasure; or after satiation; or in greater extremity, destroying or attacking painful stimuli. On the positive side of stimulus management, we see the beginnings not only of choice and selection, approach, and seeking, but of techniques for evoking response, getting more of interpersonal stimulation as well as impersonal stimuli; restructuring or merely organizing stimuli to enhance the satisfaction from exchanges with the environment (1962, p. 339).

For "successful and unsuccessful management," we need only substitute the terms "adaptive" and "maladaptive" to see how closely Murphy's ideas parallel our own with respect to stimulus barrier as an adaptive ego function.

Waelder (1967) sees the stimulus barrier as an "active regulator," also implying an adaptive function. Implicit in the idea of traumatic excitations powerful enough to break through the shield are assumptions that the organism can deal with an onslaught of stimuli by either autoplastic adjustment (making an internal change so as to live with the external conditions without unbearable suffering) or by alloplastic adjustment (bringing about changes in the outer world to eliminate the source of tension). Both methods are used in the sense that the organism tries to eliminate as much of the outer disturbance as possible and to "accept and learn to live with the remainder." Only when the stimulus barrier is taxed by too much stimulation and the person cannot handle the tidal wave by the usual processes (autoplastic and alloplastic adjustment) will there be a breakdown of the personality, analogous to physical diseases in which a massive virulent invasion can break down even an otherwise immune organism. One more quotation documenting the basis for the present position comes from Goldfarb's discussion of the adaptive, integrating efforts of the ego in its attempt to master stimuli:

The term, hypersensitivity, may be confusing since sometimes it signifies lowered sensory threshold, and at other times it signifies manifestations of distress and defensive avoidance. These *two facets of ego responses* ought to be differentiated for: (1) threshold of sensory acuity, and (2) the child's integration of the sensory experience in terms of acceptance or exclusion, pleasure or distress, comfort or discomfort, and its meaning in terms of object relations (1961, p. 96, italics added).

These "two facets of ego responses" are essentially the two component factors of stimulus barrier that will be described in the final section of this chapter.

STIMULUS BARRIER AS A REFORMULATION: AN ADAPTIVE EGO FUNCTION

The complex and often contradictory ideas presented thus far require some new organization and context in which to understand stimulus barrier as not only a sensory or perceptual threshold measure but one involving ego responses as well, with greater or lesser integrational-organizational aspects.

Let us now turn to some of these additional specific functions of the ego pertinent to *Reizschutz*: specific motor and sensori motor responses other than direct sensory threshold indicators, defensive functioning, active ego efforts, and those aspects of the ego that reflect on object relations and stimulus barrier.

While measures of sensory threshold from which we may make inferences about the nature of the stimulus barrier are not always easy to obtain outside the laboratory, it is nevertheless often possible to make inferences about stimulus barrier from direct observations of such responses as motor discharge patterns. Holt (1956) and Rapaport (1951), for example, claim that stimulus barrier is related to motor thresholds as well as receptivity to stimuli. Agitated or chaotic motor behavior and sleep disturbances are among the most reliable indicators that the stimulus barrier tends toward the maladaptive; they have been extensively considered in the literature. Among many who have been concerned with specific aspects of motor discharge and stimulus barrier is Bellak, who describes some children who have been exposed to tremendous overstimulation of nearly all sense modalities (1963). He feels that the person's system then gets a permanent overload, leading to a lifelong inability for containment and the constant need for discharge. Benjamin (1965) notes how the overstimulated infant becomes prone to outbursts of undifferentiated affect expression. He also says that the mechanism for dealing with excessive stimulation through more directed motor action does not develop until much later than early infancy. Here, he obviously is referring to the *adaptive, coping function of motor activity* in containing motor stimulation, rather than to diffuse motor discharge as an expressive indicator of a maladaptive stimulus barrier.

Recent research on sleep in general has illuminated some aspects of sleep and the stimulus barrier. Cameron (1963) has observed that some adults fall asleep in the midst of excessive sensory bombardment. In referring to impingements produced by stimulus deprivations, Provence and Lipton (1962) found that infants in institutions slept longer than noninstitutionalized babies. Discussing how falling asleep may be used defensively early in life, Wallerstein (1966) sees sleep as an *Anlage* of defense and stimulus barrier.

Both thresholds and responses to stimuli contribute to adaptation by the organism's potential for responding to high, average, or low sensory input, so that optimal homeostasis (as well as adaptation) is maintained. Stimulus barrier determines, in part, how resilient a person is or how he readapts after the stress and impingements are no longer present.

CHAPTER 15

Autonomous Functioning

Many of the ego functions discussed in this book (reality testing, thinking, synthesis) are "autonomous" ego functions in the sense that they are based on primary and secondary autonomy as these concepts will be described in the present chapter. Areas of functioning relevant to ego autonomy but not central to the other ego functions on our list can also be assessed, such as habit patterns, skills, routines, hobbies, interests, learning, intentionality, and motility. Intentionality is partly covered in the chapter on judgment, in the section devoted to anticipation. Motility is dealt with to a lesser degree in the chapter on regulation and control of drives, affects, and impulses. In this chapter, we will discuss the concept of ego autonomy put forth by Hartmann and the amplifications of Rapaport and later workers. After a brief consideration of autonomous ego development, we then review automatization and ego interests. Next we take up some assessments and implications of ego autonomy, the concept of neutralization and, finally, disturbances in autonomous functioning in the narrower sense employed in our assessment scale.

One way to evaluate ego autonomy in Freud's work is in terms of how strong he viewed the ego to be in relation to other aspects of mental functioning. We have discussed this issue earlier. As we have shown, he emphasized the strength of the drives and the relative weakness of the ego in some passages and the strength of the ego in relation to the drives in others, depending upon the context and upon the stage of his writings. We know that Freud's conception of the ego became progressively more systematic in later works.

Another basis on which to evaluate ego autonomy is in terms of the ego's origin. As we have shown, Freud's most frequent assumption was that the ego developed out of the id. But he also suggested (1937) that the ego has biological roots of its own. Hartmann (1956) argued that Freud was emphasizing the biological function of the ego in his structural model, especially in the functions of adaptation, control, and integration.

Still another basis for assessing ego autonomy is in terms of its source of energy, and this issue we shall discuss below. The ego was sometimes seen as using its own energy; at other times, it was seen as relying upon energy borrowed from instinctual drives.

Freud thus emphasized both ego strength and ego weakness. At various times he attributed to the ego considerable autonomy, including its own energy source and independent roots. But in a number of places he also put forth the assumption that the ego arises from the id and that its autonomy from the id drives is tenuous.

THE CONCEPT OF EGO AUTONOMY

Hartmann introduces his ideas about ego autonomy in *Ego Psychology and the Problem of Adaptation* (1939) and discussed them further in many of his writings, especially in "Comments on the Psychoanalytic Theory of the Ego" (1950), "The Mutual Influences in the Development of Ego and Id" (1952), and "Notes on the Theory of Sublimation" (1955). Two groups of hypotheses or propositions are involved and can be discussed separately. These are called primary and secondary autonomy. By primary autonomy Hartmann meant that in addition to the instinctual drives and the impact of external reality circumstances, ego development has a third basis, which can be referred to as inborn. Specifically, he held that such processes as perception, intention, object comprehension, thinking, and language do not depend upon conflict for their genesis or development. Hartmann referred to these aspects of "ego constitution" as ego apparatuses or inherited ego characteristics, and they constitute (along with characteristics that attain secondary autonomy) what he called the conflict-free ego sphere. Consistent with these notions is Hartmann's related assumption that id and ego develop from a common undifferentiated matrix or phase. He held that both maturation and learning (experience) influence the form of various autonomous processes. He further assumed that some early autonomous processes, such as delay of discharge and stimulus barrier, are precursors of, and prototypes for, defense mechanisms. Hartmann emphasized the importance of studying how mental conflict and autonomous functions and structures aid and hamper one another. For example, he pointed out that in assessing the success of a defensive operation, notice should be taken of the effect on ego functions not involved in the conflict, in addition to what happens to the instinctual drive and what protection is provided the ego.

Secondary autonomy was adumbrated in the 1939 monograph in the notion of change of function, a concept similar to G. Allport's functional autonomy of motives (1938). As Hartmann put it, "A behavior-form which originated in a certain realm of life may, in the course of development, appear in an entirely different realm and role" (1939, pp. 25-26). He cited an example: "An attitude which arose originally in the service of defense against an instinctual drive, may . . . become an independent structure, in which case the instinctual drive merely triggers [it] , but . . . does not determine the details of its action" (p. 26).

In this way, conflict-related manifestations may eventually become largely independent of their roots.

Secondary autonomy was seen as on a continuum with the degree of autonomy defined by the extent to which the activity in question is removed from id-ego conflicts, from regressive pressures exerted by id determinants, and from sexualization and aggressivization. In short, the extent to which the manifestation is refractory to regression and instinctualization determines the degree of secondary autonomy. Hartmann is stressing relative functional independence together with genetic continuity. Secondarily autonomous structures are sometimes irreversible, sometimes not. Hartmann's concept of neutralization, which he says is related to secondary autonomy, is a central hypothesized process by which secondary autonomy occurs.

In his 1951 paper on "The Autonomy of the Ego," Rapaport makes the formulation that the inborn ego apparatuses have structural characteristics (i.e., thresholds) that limit drive discharge even in the undifferentiated phase and thereby probably precipitate the differentiation between ego and id. He goes on to say that "the developing ego then integrates these structural apparatuses and re-represents their discharge-limiting and -regulating function in forms usually described as defenses. These are the foundations of the primary autonomy of the ego" (p. 363). Rapaport underscored the stability of secondarily autonomous manifestations as well as the primary ones but pointed out, as had Hartmann, that both autonomies are relative and can become involved in conflict. The motoric disorders of hysterics and the motor mannerisms of schizophrenics are examples he gives of an apparatus of primary autonomy becoming involved in conflict.

In his second paper on ego autonomy, Rapaport (1958) brought into focus the relative autonomy of the ego from the environment. He then discussed the bases for ego autonomy from the id and from the environment and the relationship of the two autonomies to each other. He concluded that autonomy from the id is guaranteed by the apparatuses of primary autonomy (i.e., the constitutionally given apparatuses of reality relatedness). Autonomy from the environment, said Rapaport, is ultimately guaranteed by the drives. Both autonomies are secondarily guaranteed by cognitive organizations, including ego interests, values, ideals, ego identity, and superego influences.

Rapaport concluded that the relationship between the two autonomies (i.e., from the id and from the environment) is a reciprocal one; that is, when the ego's autonomy from the environment is maximized, a reduction in autonomy from the id results, as in sensory deprivation. When ego autonomy from the id is maximized, autonomy from the environment is decreased, and the result is slavery to external stimuli. Likewise, a decrease in either of the ego autonomies results in an increase in the ego's autonomy for the other. A further implication of this reciprocity is that there is an optimal range of ego autonomy from both

230 The 12 Ego Functions of Our Study

id and environment: "Since reality relations guarantee autonomy from the id, excessive autonomy from the environment must impair autonomy from the id; and since drives are the ultimate guarantees of the autonomy from the environment, an excessive autonomy from the id must impair the autonomy from the environment" (p. 733).

Rapaport also applied Piaget's concept of nutriment to ego autonomy and demonstrated how both the autonomies depend for their maintenance on stimulation, either from the external environment or from internal sources, including the drives. The more autonomous the ego, the more nutriment is supplied from internal sources, such as ego structures and motivations arising from them.

Gill and Brenman (1959) give detailed consideration to ego autonomy in their study of hypnosis. They point out that autonomy may be intrasystemic, in which an ego activity may be relatively independent of other ego activities, or intersystemic, in which an ego activity may be relatively autonomous from id and superego domination or any psychic institution may be relatively independent from the external environment. Relative autonomy from the environment does not mean lessened information about, or disregard for, the environment but rather that the environment does not determine in detail perception of or action upon it. Similarly, autonomy from the id does not mean unawareness of motivational promptings but rather the ability to evaluate them and then either respond or not.

The external environment can usefully be divided into the space-time environment and the social environment. The social environment is much more subject to distortion by drive than is the space-time environment. A decrease in relative autonomy may result from limitation of environmental or drive input or from either strong environmental pressure or strong inner urges. The limitation of environmental input could range from almost total sensory deprivation to merely monotonous stimulus conditions, while an increase could be caused by social pressure or pressure to attend very carefully to a stimulus. A decrease in drive input is due to some kind of repression, or more generally to countercathexis, while an increase could be maturational (as in puberty) or caused by a particular external stimulus (usually a person).

Gill and Brenman see the two autonomies as asymmetrical rather than as parallel and reciprocal and spell out a number of different relationships between the two depending on particular conditions. In addition, they point out that an interpersonal relationship is both an environmental force and the expression of a drive urge, and in this respect a surrender to the environment may be consonant with an id urge.

Hartmann devoted a chapter of his 1939 monograph to the issue of autonomous ego development. The apparatuses of primary autonomy (perception, motility,

AUTONOMOUS EGO DEVELOPMENT

thinking) constitute the ego constitution. Other ego mechanisms and functions appear to be patterned on instinctual drives (e.g., projection and introjection). It will be remembered that earlier psychoanalytic theorists had attempted to understand all mental mechanisms and processes as resulting from the impact of experience on instinctual drives.

Hartmann put forth the important notion that ego mechanisms and instinctual-drive processes have a common origin and grow out of an undifferentiated phase of development. Those mechanisms that are "unequivocally" in the service of the ego after differentiation from the common matrix are what Hartmann termed the inborn ego apparatuses. Once they have been structuralized out of this phase, however, ego mechanisms and instinctual-drive factors interrelate in many ways.

Both maturation and learning are important aspects of autonomous ego development. Differences in the rate of maturation of various ego functions in relation to drives tend to result in conflicts. A universal conflict results from the fact that drives are experienced as dangerous, partly because immature ego mechanisms are unable to gratify them.

Hartmann, Kris, and Loewenstein (1946) incorporated the implications of autonomous ego development in their paper on the formation of psychic structure. They hold that aspects of what will be the apparatuses of primary autonomy (perception, motility, and some thought processes) undergo some maturation during the undifferentiated phase. These apparatuses become fully developed and integrated only after the undifferentiated phase is past. In their summary of some steps in mental development, they include the contribution of developing ego capacities to the understanding of the overall picture. Thus, while pointing out the importance of sufficient gratification and optimal deprivation and the relationship with the mother in the ability to distinguish self from the environment, the development of this capacity also depends on the maturation of the perceptual apparatus. They also point out how the shift from the pleasure principle to the reality principle depends on the function of anticipation, which is an aspect of ego development. They illustrate how ego development proceeds along with the development of object relations. In general, what the authors do in this paper is to show how ego development enters the process of mental development as an independent variable.

Zetzel (1969) presents a developmental model in which the beginnings of major ego functions are seen in relation to the early mother-child relationship. She contends that if the mother responds to her infant intuitively and without undue ambivalence during the earliest period, before the self-object differentiation, a basically positive ego identification will be internalized, which provides the nucleus for the development of those ego capacities of secondary autonomy. She also believes that secondary autonomy includes the ability to recognize and tolerate affect (especially anxiety and depression) and the ability to permit some regression without impairment of autonomous ego functions.

AUTOMATIZATION

How is the concept of automatization related to ego autonomy? Hartmann devoted a chapter of his 1939 monograph to a discussion of automatisms. He pointed out that motor behavior, perception, and thinking all show some automatization. By "automatism" he means the somatic and preconscious ego apparatuses that are adaptive or are used by adaptive processes. These he distinguishes from habits, although the two are related. He differentiates normal automatisms from pathological ones (such as compulsions, tics, and catatonia), by saying that the former may serve as the starting point for the latter but are not to be equated with them. Automatisms — as Hartmann uses the term — are also distinguished from the repetition compulsion, which is seen as an older form of regulation and a characteristic of instinctual drives. He believes the repetition compulsion may be one of the roots of automatisms and that under certain conditions the ego can put the repetition compulsion to its own use.*

A major implication of how automatization is related to the autonomy of the ego is found in the following passage:

It is obvious that automatization may have economic advantages, in saving attention cathexes in particular and simple cathexes of consciousness in general. In using automatisms we apply means which already exist, which we need not create anew at every occasion, and consequently the means-end relations in some areas are, so to speak "not subject to argument." In the case of physiological automatisms, it is known that increased practice decreases their metabolic requirements. These apparatuses achieve what we expect of any apparatus: they facilitate the transformation and saving of energy (Hartmann, 1939, p. 91).

Hartmann is thus assuming a relationship between automatization and neutralization (transformation of energy). In addition, Rapaport (1967, 1956) understood this passage to mean that Hartmann was proposing automatization as the process by which secondary autonomy is accomplished via a change of function and that automatization is a mental structure-building process.

---

*A recent paper by Malev (1969) offers a persuasive formulation along these lines, illustrated with case material.

Gill and Brenman (1959) hold that deautomatization can result in either an increase or a decrease of autonomy. Deautomatization may be brought about by a change in the distribution of attention aimed at the functioning of an apparatus. But neither decreased input (from environment or drives) nor increased urge or environmental pressure necessarily leads to the changes in attention necessary for deautomatization.

Simon (1967) showed that conscious effort can have a paradoxical effect on automatized functions. Before Hartmann's proposal of the concept of autonomous ego aspects, psychoanalytic theory had assumed that the decrease in efficiency following extra effort was caused by a conflict between drive and defense, and that regression — instituted to protect the ego against being overwhelmed — would result in a reduced level of ego functioning. Basing his formulation on the autonomy of the ego and the conflict-free sphere, Simon assumes that once a function has become automatized, the effect of effort is to focus attention on the automatic aspects of performance, which leads to deautomatization and performance decrement. But deautomatization may make more adaptive automatizations possible. As we shall see, there are formulations regarding the loss of automatization that do include hypotheses of drive intrusion.

Glauber (1968) illustrates the notion of dysautomatization in relation to a group of functions that are optimal only when they are preconscious (i.e., not in the center of awareness; for example, speech). His prototype of dysautomatization is stuttering. It is a pathological condition that emerges while speech in its automatic form is still being mastered and that is the result of the repetitive intrusion of attempts at conscious attention in a process that is persisting in automatic functioning (preconscious). Glauber hypothesized that such repetitive intrusion is caused by trauma, specifically by the child's feeling of separation from the mother. The sense of ego weakness engendered by trauma results in lack of confidence in preconscious functioning and in overemphasis on *conscious ego control*. The consequence for the individual is a feeling of *depersonalization*. As a result of trauma, the speech function is learned incorrectly and the stuttering itself becomes an aspect of adaptive functioning owing to the important adaptive purpose that speech serves; the stuttering becomes secondarily automatized. The stutter is now ego syntonic, and therefore difficult to treat. If a new learning situation can be created that approximates the original speech-learning situation, a preconscious automatism can evolve. Glauber underscores the difference between a disturbance of an automatism and a classical neurosis in terms of the relative separateness from the associated characterological disorder of the automatism disturbance, unlike the fusion of the two in the classical neuroses.

EGO INTERESTS

The term "ego interest" was first used by Freud in describing how libidinal interest may be withdrawn from objects and returned to the ego (1914). In *Introductory Lectures on Psycho-Analysis* Freud said: "We termed the cathexes of energy which the ego directs towards the objects of its sexual desires 'libido'; all others, which are sent out by the self-preservative instincts, we termed 'interest'" (1917, p. 414). Ego interests were thus aspects and derivatives of the self-preservative instincts.

Ego interests are considered by Hartmann to consist of a set of ego functions that mostly entail secondary autonomy. They include what Freud had called the ego instincts, which concern self-preservation and egoism and to which narcissism is the libidinal complement. Hartmann suggests that in addition to these interests, which center on the self, ego interests include aims that involve other persons, things, values, aspects of one's own mental functioning (such as intellectual activity), and aims originally relevant to the superego that have been taken over by the ego. Some of the most common ego interests in our culture are the striving for wealth, power, and prestige.

Ego interests are usually preconscious, use neutralized energy, and may oppose instinctual drives. But most of them have been partly determined by drive factors (i.e., oral, anal, urethral, exhibitionist, and aggressive tendencies). They also include either direct drive influences or the earmarks of defenses against them. In addition, these ego interests are codetermined by superego factors, other ego interests of the person, and the status of other ego functions (such as synthetic capacities, relation to reality). We can assume that different ego interests would be seen by Hartmann as using energy of varying degrees of neutralization. Ego interests are also considered subject to reinstinctualization.

Rapaport and Gill, in their paper "The Points of View and Assumptions of Metapsychology" (1959), include ego interests under the rubric "psychological forces," along with drives and conflicts. In his paper on motivation (1960), Rapaport states that when the instinctual drives are ego syntonic, they coincide with ego interests.

Ego interests also have been viewed as one basis for personal identity. Being the result of striving for what a person considers useful, they represent choices that center on, and help define, the self (Tabachnick, 1965).

ASSESSMENTS AND IMPLICATIONS OF AUTONOMY

Grauer (1958) believed that the concept of secondary autonomy is unnecessary. He reasoned that if we accept Hartmann's assumption of an undifferentiated phase of development out of which both id and ego arise, it is reasonable to assume further that the ego energy derives from this source. It becomes superfluous to assume that the undifferentiated energy is first transmuted into drive energy and must then be neutralized for use by the ego. He proposes that the term "autonomous ego functions" be applied to ego manifestations that use the ego's own energy. He posits a continuum at one end of which are ego activities that are dominated by the ego and use ego energy and at the other of which are activities that are primarily influenced by the drives; in between are ego activities that are energized by neutralized or sublimated drives.

Some studies have appeared in the literature that were interpreted in terms of the autonomy formulations of Hartmann and Rapaport. For example, Boorstein (1959) developed a milieu therapeutic approach based on Rapaport's ideas that there is a reciprocal relationship between autonomy from the drives, on the one hand, and autonomy from the environment, on the other; that there is an optimal range of distance from both; and that ego structures require stimulation for their maintenance. We believe that all contemporary psychiatric therapeutic measures can be conceived of as either increasing or decreasing the ego's successful interaction with the id or the environment. Boorstein used industrial, social, and game therapy programs to promote greater ego autonomy from drives and to decrease primary-process thinking.

Voth and Mayman (1962) carried out a study in which they attempted to evaluate several propositions related to ego autonomy. They defined the dimension ego-close — ego-distant in terms of the degree of dependence-independence on the external environment. Using reactions to the autokinetic phenomenon as a measure, they hypothesized that persons in the mid-range of the ego-close — ego-distant continuum (moderate autokinetic movement) will recover from mental illness more rapidly than patients at either end; that ego-distant subjects (reporting varying degrees of autokinetic movement), whose autokinetic movement is decreased after somatotherapy, would show more clinical improvement than those who do not undergo such a reduction; and that decrease of ego closeness should be positively correlated with recovery from psychosis. The first two hypotheses were statistically confirmed; the third was supported by clinical observation.

The results of the study support two general propositions related to the autonomy concept. The first is that one aspect of ego organization relates to closeness to external reality, some persons being close and others distant. The second is Rapaport's notions that maximum autonomy can be preserved only when the ego has certain relationships to reality and to the drives and that too much or too little contact with either drives or reality decreases ego autonomy. Two deductions from the first proposition are that persons may change their position on the ego closeness-distance continuum and that the ease with which they change ego position is positively correlated with recovery from psychosis and with the establishment of ego autonomy. Results of the study support this deduction. A third deduction based on the first hypothesis is that a "home base" position, in which the ego is not too close to or distant from reality, favors the preservation of ego autonomy, which is consistent with Rapaport's notion that autonomy is diminished when the ego's relationship to external reality and the id becomes less than optimal.

Rapaport saw an important relationship between the issues of ego autonomy and activity-passivity. In regard to these, Ekstein and Caruth (1968) pointed out that motoric activity can reflect ego autonomy, as in goal-directed behavior, or may reflect ego passivity, as in automatic behavior (e.g., echopraxia and echolalia). Similarly, motoric passivity may reflect ego autonomy, as in potent, yet motorically passive, "acts" of civil disobedience (e.g., those of Martin Luther King, Jr., and Gandhi), or may reflect ego passivity. An ego-paralyzed obsessive, who vacillates and cannot act (for instance, Buridan's ass who starved between equidistant bales of hay and pails of water), reflects this ego passivity.

The healthy autonomous ego is capable of a greater or lesser degree of motoric activity in relation to objects, to reality orientation, and to instinctual expression. It is capable of establishing an optimal balance between active and passive modes of behavior and inner degree of ego autonomy. A normal child's behavior tends to show relative consistency between the inner and outer states. When psychologically helpless or intimidated by either inner or outer stimuli, the child tends to be motorically inactive; when psychologically active, he tends to be more physically active or engaged in future-oriented behavior.

In an application of ego autonomy to severe psychopathology, St. John (1966) points out that the defenses of chronic schizophrenics do not show a substantial degree of secondary autonomy but instead are focused on id strivings and external stimuli. When id strivings threaten to overwhelm the ego (partly, Hartmann assumed, because the person's ability to neutralize aggression is defective), id strivings are blocked off in the attempt to maintain the ego's integrity. This hinders the ego's differentiation from the environment. Similarly, avoidance of interpersonal relations can be understood as an attempt to protect against the id strivings that tend to be stirred up by contact with other people.

Miller (1962) examines the implications for ego autonomy of experiments in sensory deprivation, accounts of explorers and prisoners who experienced isolation, observations from clinical medicine, and aspects of psychoanalytic theory. Rapaport had assumed that either modification or delay of response to environmental stimulation is more likely than usual to occur when there is little environmental stimulation (as in sensory isolation experiments) and, thus, that sensory deprivation maximizes the ego's autonomy from the environment. Miller cites experimental evidence to show that the opposite effect occurs, and he concurs with Gill and Brenman that decreased information from the environment is not a definition of autonomy from the environment.

Miller holds that autonomy from the id and from the environment are symmetrical rather than reciprocal, coming close to the Gill and Brenman position. He disagrees with Rapaport's notion that the drives are the ultimate guarantee of the ego's autonomy from the environment, on the grounds that there is no justification for describing an ego that does the bidding of the id as autonomous. In place of Rapaport's idea that autonomy has to do with the ability to modify or postpone response and Gill and Brenman's formulation in terms of the ability to pit forces against drives or external stimuli, Miller offers a version of his own. This is that ego autonomy is the "capacity for self government in relation to both the demanding and nondemanding aspects of the id and of the environment" (p. 15). This formulation is based on the attempt to deal with the problems related to the Rapaport and Gill and Brenman positions discussed above. It also involves making central Gill and Brenman's distinction between press and information. Miller holds that there are aspects of the external environment and the id that provide (rather than prompt). From the environment there are the sounds and sights of everyday life, and from intrapsychic sources, affective and ideational signals.

Miller mentions that two aspects of autonomy that have not been sufficiently thought through are the autonomy of the superego and the autonomy of various ego functions in relation to each other. We have discussed the latter issue in Chapter 18.

Holt finds the concept of ego autonomy the utopian ideal of ego psychology and a balance to the earlier overemphasis on drive and then on defense in psychoanalytic theory. He believes that in the future the focus will not be on the issue of autonomy but rather on describing "the relative roles of drive, external stimuli and press, and various inner structures in determining behavior, and the complex interactions between them" (1965, p. 157).

In discussing many of the issues related to ego autonomy, Holt points out that Rapaport did not distinguish clearly between structure-building and structure maintenance in the notion that mental structures require nutriment for their maintenance. While he grants that stimulation is necessary for structure-building, Holt presents a number of considerations that contradict the assumption that all structures break down when deprived of environmental stimulation. He also offers evidence to support Rapaport's notion of the maintenance need for stimulus nutriment in visual perceptual structures.

Holt takes issue with Miller's formulation of the sensory-deprivation experiments, according to which, when environmental information and press are withheld, the drives are released and become the major basis for reconstituting the external environment. He maintains that a decrease in external input interferes with drive processes and suggests that the psychoanalytic concept of drive needs to be reformulated as an interactive concept that gives as much weight to environmental factors as to intrapsychic ones.

Finally, Holt sees drive and affect discharge thresholds as an innate guarantee of ego autonomy from the drives and underscores Rapaport's inclusion of them among the major apparatuses of primary autonomy: "These drive-thresholds are the nuclei around which defenses and controls accrue and build up a steadily growing conflict-free sphere of the ego or area of autonomous functioning, in which it is possible to tolerate a widening range of inner urge-states" (1965, p. 166).

NEUTRALIZATION

Hartmann, Kris, and Loewenstein (1949) agreed with Freud's general notion of desexualization of libidinal drive energy and added that aggressive drive energy can be deaggressivized and can also be used by the ego (and the superego). The change of both libidinal and aggressive energy "away from the instinctual and toward a non-instinctual mode" (p. 277) is termed neutralization and is intended by these authors to be an expansion of the concept of sublimation. Thus, Hartmann, Kris, and Loewenstein expanded the concept of sublimation, called it neutralization, and made this hypothetical process the energic basis for the secondary autonomy of the ego. Hartmann (1955) assumed that neutralization starts early in life and is a continuous process, that there are degrees of neutralization, and that the ego's ability to neutralize instinctual energy is probably correlated with ego strength and is reflected in breadth of interests and richness of affects. He proposed that different degrees of neutralization are required for optimal ego functioning in different activities, and that it plays an important role in reality mastery, object constancy, thinking, action, and intentionality.

Neutralization is the concept Hartmann uses to explain how secondary autonomy of ego interests, habits, and skills can come about. Consistent with this is the formulation that while the ego can use libidinal and aggressive energy, there is the consequent risk of a disturbance of function. The same issue would be formulated from the structural and dynamic points of view in terms of ego functions, such as perception, being susceptible to interference from instinctual drive factors. Freud (1926) discussed this very issue in regard to inhibitions. One basis for the latter was when the sexual significance of an activity increased, resulting in the renunciation of the activity by the ego to avoid conflict with the id (p. 90). A more detailed formulation following Hartmann would be that ego functions are cathected with libidinal and aggressive energies, which become more neutralized as development proceeds, but that when an autonomous ego function becomes involved in conflict, either it becomes "suffused" with less neutralized energy or there is an "influx" of unneutralized energy followed by a regression of ego functioning in the given area. Hartmann (1952) applied the concepts of neutralization and deneutralization widely to psychopathology and to mental health and assumed with regard to the former that a defect in the capacity for neutralization of aggressive energy results in the unstable defenses seen in different forms of child psychopathology and in schizophrenia. In addition to neutralization, Hartmann believed that a primary neutral energy is available to the ego (1955), a notion consonant with his earlier idea of primary ego autonomy (1939) and with Freud's suggestion of an hereditary ego core (1937). While he discussed neutralization in a number of papers, Hartmann did not elaborate on the concept of neutral energy.

For many psychoanalysts, cathexis, neutralization, and deneutralization are very useful concepts. Many papers in the literature include formulations employing these concepts. Some workers, however, have questioned the validity of energy transformation, which is part of the neutralization-deneutralization hypothesis. In addition, the more general issue has been raised of the value and scientific status of energic formulations in psychoanalysis altogether.

White (1963), Apfelbaum (1965), Rubinstein (1965, 1967), and Holt (1967) have offered critiques of the notion that mental energy can be transformed from one mode to another. White concluded that the concept of neutralization should be abandoned, and the concept of independent ego energies (i.e., neutral energy) substituted, since he believes the latter can accommodate everything that has been attributed to the former and does not require the added and dubious assumption of transformability. Another formulation that accounts for some of the same phenomena for which Hartmann hypothesized neutralization but does not employ the notion of energy transformation is that of Sandler and Joffe (1966). They assume that desexualization or sublimation results from the freeing or separating from particular forms of discharge that component of the drive that does not have quality (i.e., pleasure-pain aspects). On the basis of developmental findings, they assume that an increasing distance is gradually established between various skills and adaptive behaviors and the pleasure-pain feelings that originally accompanied stimulation and discharge from somatic sources. Tasks and behaviors can be described in terms of the directness or indirectness of drive discharge.

Apfelbaum (1966) points out that a conception of drive maturation is an alternative to that of neutralization. As an example, he cites Kris's formulation (1956) that various interfering motives must be detached or neutralized to allow the possibility of genuine insight in psychoanalytic therapy. Apfelbaum proposes the alternative explanation that these very motives (along with the desire for growth) at a higher level of development and integration provide the basis for the genuine analytic insight. The question of drive maturation, which will not be discussed here, is considered in the Apfelbaum paper and in our chapter on the id.

The value of energic hypotheses in psychoanalysis has been questioned by some for a long time (Kubie, 1947; Pumpian-Mindlin, 1959; Apfelbaum, 1962-1965). In the American Psychoanalytic Association 1962 panel on the concept of psychic energy (Modell, 1963), opinions were divided on whether the psychic energy notion should be retained. While the difficulties and shortcomings of the psychic energy conception were pointed out by a number of contributors, some felt that the conception was still useful at this stage of psychoanalytic development. Since then, others (Rubinstein, 1967; Holt, 1967; Rosenblatt and Thicksteen, 1970) have pointed out a number of reasons why energic concepts should be dropped. An example of how a psychoanalytically relevant issue (powerfully motivated ideations) can be formulated without recourse to energic considerations has been provided by G. Klein (1967).

On the other hand, cathexis, neutralization, and deneutralization have been used in many theoretical formulations and seem to be useful concepts to many psychoanalysts. In his remarks about Arlow and Brenner's proposed revision of the psychoanalytic theory of the psychopathology of psychoses, one of Freeman's (1969) main points was his belief that they did not sufficiently emphasize energic or economic factors, specifically, the strength and cathexis of instinctual drive energies in relation to object representations. Schafer, while accepting aspects of the psychic energy conception, has expressed the opinion that "clinical interpretation has never really depended on complex psychoeconomic theorizing" (1970, p. 438).

In the Kris Study Group monograph on transient ego regressions described in an earlier chapter, a relationship between drive energy, neutralization, and the regression of ego functions is hypothesized. The evidence for ego-function regression is adequate. The problem is how to demonstrate the reinstinctualization (which is assumed to initiate or to accompany ego regression) independent of the regression. This difficulty does not appear to have been solved.

DISTURBANCES IN AUTONOMOUS FUNCTIONING

We shall focus first on primary autonomy. All the apparatuses, functions, and manifestations of primary autonomy are subject to disturbances in functioning. Visual, auditory, motor, and tactile disturbances without organic cause were frequently seen in the late nineteenth century and were usually classified as manifestations of hysteria. Malfunctioning in these areas is also found in psychoses, especially as motor disturbances (mannerisms, catatonic rigidity and excitement, etc.). Attention and concentration are interfered with in many acutely disturbed patients and, to a milder degree, in individuals who are not seen for evaluation or treatment. Intentionality is most clearly disturbed in catatonic and deeply depressed individuals but also in many less disturbed individuals with a variety of character structures.

Memory difficulties of various kinds and degrees are found in a wide range of psychopathological conditions and range from amnesia to memory distortions to hyperamnesias. Joseph (1966) states that memory is always involved in conflict situations, no matter what other ego functions are implicated.

Learning difficulties without known organic pathology are frequently reported in the psychiatric and psychological literature, and some important psychoanalytic studies on this topic have been carried out by child analysts.

Language and speech disturbances are frequently found in individuals who show serious psychopathology and have been found in psychopathology generally.

Intentionality is most seriously disturbed in patients with catatonic and severe depressive symptoms but is also prominent in some obsessive-compulsive conditions and in passive-dependent individuals. Either cognitive or motoric aspects may be conflicted or interfered with.

As already mentioned, the major ego functions discussed in this book (reality testing, thinking, synthesis, etc.) are autonomous ego functions that are based on both primary and secondary autonomy. Since the characteristics of, and disturbances in, these ego functions are discussed in other chapters, here we will mention some autonomous functions not central to the main ego functions referred to above. These are habit patterns, skills, routines, hobbies and interests, learning, intentionality, and motility.

When such autonomous functions are impaired, there may be difficulty in carrying out one's usual job or difficulty and interference with dressing, grooming, household chores, playing golf, or baseball. Impairment can vary from complete inability to the need for extra effort in an activity that usually does not require it.

One basis that Hartmann proposed for disturbance in either primary or secondary autonomy is the sexualization or aggressivization of the activity; that is, when the energy involved comes too close to the instinctual mode. Another way to formulate this that does not include any energic assumptions is to say that the given activity has taken on a predominantly sexual or aggressive meaning. Yet another formulation, which does not exclude any of the above, is that the activity is interfered with in a defensive attempt to protect the organism from an anxiety experience or from a threat of ego dissolution. Here, habit patterns, skills, or hobbies may be interfered with not because the specific relevant activities have become sexualized or aggressivized but because of massive defensive efforts that interfere with performance secondarily or as a result of a general regression in the level of functioning.

While Hartmann's conception of secondary autonomy and its loss depended on a change of energy (i.e., neutralization), we believe that autonomous functioning can be assessed without necessarily assuming that either neutralization or deneutralization of mental energy has taken place. We favor an explanation for interference with the functioning of skills in terms of the activity acquiring a sexual or an aggressive meaning. And we also underscore the importance of secondary interference with autonomous activities as a result of defensive activity or serious regression.

CHAPTER 16

Synthetic-Integrative Functioning

Hartmann (1939) assumed that the synthetic function of the ego is superordinate to all the other ego functions (see also Hacker, 1962). This judgment appears to be supported by Freud's definition of a major task of the ego as being to reconcile the often conflicting demands of the id, superego, and outside world, since reconciling conflicting trends is a central aspect of the synthetic function. Synthesis or integration is also a pivotal concept for other personality theorists (Lecky, 1945; Rogers, 1942; Angyal, 1965; and Goldstein, 1939).

SUMMARY OF FREUD'S FORMULATIONS

The notion of a synthetic tendency was implicit in Freud's writings from the 1890's on. Thus, Strachey understands the term "incompatible ideas" (Freud, 1894) to mean "that which could not be synthesized by the ego" (S.E. XXII, p. 76). In his discussion of secondary revision as an aspect of the dream work, Freud (1900) identified the processes as similar to the activity of waking thought in that there is a tendency to "establish order in material of that kind, to set up relations in it, and to make it conform to our expectations of an intelligible whole" (p. 499). These characteristics are similar to what he later referred to as the synthetic function.

Freud again discussed secondary revision in *Totem and Taboo* (1913), this time as a manifestation of a property of the mind: "There is an intellectual function in us which demands unity, connection, and intelligibility from any material, whether of perception or thought, that comes within its grasp." He goes on to say that the unifying tendency operates to make correct connections but also incorrect ones; for "if, as a result of special circumstances, it is unable to establish a true connection, it does not hesitate to fabricate a false one" (p. 95). Freud applied the idea of a natural tendency toward unification to his therapeutic technique in stating that when barriers are removed by analysis, previously split-off instinctual impulses automatically fit themselves in with other mental phenomena and do not require any efforts at psychosynthesis by the analyst.

In *Inhibitions, Symptoms and Anxiety* (1926), one basis on which Freud distinguished between the ego and the id was that the ego is an organization, whereas the id is not. This point was reiterated in *The Question of Lay Analysis* (1926, p. 196) and in *New Introductory Lectures* (1932, p. 76), where Freud described how the synthetic function operates in symptom formation and how the symptom is a result of attempts to synthesize conflicting needs for satisfaction, on the one hand, and punishment, on the other.

Regarding the relationship between the synthetic function and neurosis, Freud stated in *Dostoevsky and Parricide* (1928) that neurosis is an indication that the ego has given up its unity in an unsuccessful attempt at synthesis. In later formulations relevant to synthetic functioning, Freud also emphasized the interferences with this tendency, namely, splitting of the ego. Thus, Freud explained the perversion of fetishism in terms of an ego split (1927). In using the fetish as a substitute for the woman's fantasied penis, the fetishist is both disavowing castration and affirming the absence of a penis. It is the indications of both disavowal and affirmation that reflect a split in the ego. Freud showed parallels to this disavowal-affirmation in a case of obsessional neurosis, where one attitude consistent with a wish and another, contrary one consistent with reality were both found.

The idea that a splitting of the ego occurs in psychoses, neuroses, and some perversions is more generally discussed in *An Outline of Psycho-Analysis* (1938); the hallmark of this split being that two contradictory attitudes are present "side by side," without influencing one another. The same topic is given its last treatment by Freud in the unfinished paper "Splitting of the Ego in the Process of Defense" (1938). Here Freud posed a hypothetical situation in which a child is faced with a conflict between continuing an instinctual satisfaction and thereby being subject to danger, and renouncing the satisfaction to avoid the danger. Rather than choosing between the two courses of action, the child takes both. This is accomplished by continuing the instinctual gratification (and thereby rejecting the reality danger), while also developing a pathological symptom, which includes a fear of the danger, and then attempting to overcome the fear. Such a solution to the conflict results in a rift in the ego "which never heals, but which increases as time goes on" (p. 276). Freud added that the synthetic function is subject to a number of disturbances.

The main features of Freud's conception of synthesis, then, are that there is a tendency of the mental apparatus to make connections and establish intelligibility from perceptual data and thought products but that the connections may be incorrect as well as correct. It is involved in the process of secondary revision in dreams and operates in symptom formation to establish the compromise between the conflicting trends.

SYNTHETIC FUNCTIONING AS DESCRIBED BY LATER WORKERS

Nunberg's paper on the synthetic function (delivered in 1929 and published in

1930) was the most detailed statement on the subject up to that time. It illustrated the manifestations of the ego's synthetic capacity in the assimilation of alien elements, both from within and from without, in the mediating between opposing elements, in reconciling opposites, and in setting "mental productivity in train" (p. 122). Such characteristics of mental functioning as the search for causality, the finding of connections, and the tendencies to simplify and to generalize are also attributed to the synthetic function. The functioning of the ego is made more economical by resolving contradictions in thought, feeling, and action. Such contradictions or inconsistencies are found especially in the functioning of children and primitives, because their mental development is incomplete. They also accompany mental disintegration, as in confusional states and catatonic stupors. An indiscriminate increase in synthetic functioning can also occur, and mental events or contents may be combined or fused in ways that lead to bizarre outcomes. Nunberg argued that a failure in synthetic functioning is discernible in all mental symptom formation. In the initial stage of events leading to symptom formation, there is a failure to reconcile the claims of conflicting forces. The ensuing symptom, which is a compromise between the conflicting claims (and includes some degree of gratification of each of them), is then experienced as alien to the ego (in neurotic conditions). But the synthetic function operates to reintegrate the alien neurotic symptom, a process that is enhanced through the development of secondary gains. In the development of paranoid delusional systems, Nunberg sees the synthetic function as responsible for the relating together of ideas and events that are irrelevant to one another in order to support a previously generated idea. He attributes the origin of the synthetic function to Eros, the ultimate source of binding and productive power.

French has long emphasized the organization of goal-directed behavior. He applied some concepts of Kurt Lewin, Edward Tolman, and Henry Murray relevant to what psychoanalysts refer to as synthetic functioning. In his 1941 paper, French introduced and defined integrative capacity of the cognitive field. It is the amount of tension, and therefore conflict, that can be withstood in a goal-directed striving without disintegration (such as diffuse motor discharge). Confidence in one's ability to achieve one's goal (and thus to satisfy the underlying wish) increases the integrative capacity, while the strength of the wish, beyond a certain point, increases the likelihood of diffuse discharge.

In a later paper (1945) French developed his idea of integrative capacity in the area of social integration. He discussed dependency and the responsibility for others as mechanisms of social integration. In dependency, the person is attempting to decrease his integrative load by shifting part of his integrative task onto someone else. Taking responsibility for others requires an integrative capacity in excess of what is required to satisfy one's own needs. French (1952, 1953, 1958) further developed the concepts of integrative task, integrative field, and integrative capacity in his multivolume work, *The Integration of Behavior.*

MULTIPLE SYNTHETIC FUNCTIONS AND HIERARCHICAL LAYERING

While Nunberg spelled out a number of manifestations of the synthetic function, he seemed to be assuming that one process is operative and lies behind the phenomena described. Freud's discussions of secondary revision (1913) in the dream; paranoia; phobias; animism; religion; and science imply a number of synthetic functions, according to Rapaport (1960). He claims independent support for this notion in his own experiments described in his paper "Cognitive Structures" (1957).

In his monograph, *Ego Psychology and the Problem of Adaptation*, Hartmann (1939) entitled one chapter "Some Integrative Functions of the Ego," and it is clear that complex and multidimensional processes are assumed: "The full range of synthetic factors is not yet known: some of them belong to the superego, most of them to the ego, and some of these belong partly to the conflict-free regulative functions of the ego. We understand some of the unconscious synthetic factors, but we know very little of the preconscious and conscious ones" (1939, p. 75). More generally, Hartmann referred to the synthetic function as the psychological manifestation of the broader biological concept of fitting together. He held that different aspects of synthetic functioning have varying degrees of biological importance, and he contrasted the primitive synthetic mechanisms involved in superego formation with the kinds of synthetic achievements that are the goals of psychoanalytic treatment.

Along these very lines, Kris (1956) suggested that the degree of neutralization or instinctualization can provide the basis for distinguishing between the terms "synthesis," "organization," and "integration." Synthesis would involve the lowest degree of neutralization, as when it contributes to symptom formation as a compromise between drive and defense. By integrative functions he means organizing functions that are autonomous, that is, that use neutralized energy and are therefore largely free from libidinal and aggressive aims. With regard to insight in psychoanalysis this would mean that integrative insight is largely free from the wish to win the analyst's praise, to merge with him, or to be competitive with him, for example.

Miller, Isaacs, and Haggard (1965) elaborate on Kris's distinctions between the ego's synthesizing and integrative functions. Synthesizing and integrative functions differ with regard to the kinds of elements involved, the degree of conflict or harmony between them, the flexibility of their organization, and the extent to which the material in question is in harmony with other personality aspects. These authors see the synthetic function as synthesizing elements into relatively enduring substructures that are sometimes bound together rather rigidly. Some of the elements may be in conflict, and the substructure may be isolated from the major psychic structures, as happens in symptom formation and in paranoid systematization. Structures that function integratively, on the other hand, harmonize elements flexibly and bring them into relation with the major psychic structures.

The idea that the synthetic function is subject to hierarchical layering was expressed in 1930 by Schilder:

> The raw material of perception is integrated by an unconscious synthetic function. . . . In the next phase of thought development the raw material of perception and imagery is integrated on a higher level, and implicit object-relationships are apperceived. . . . In the subsequent phase of thought development, perceptions and presentations are integrated into higher units corresponding to objects, and are then conceptually evaluated. Finally, in the completing phase of thought development all this perceptual raw material and organized perceptual material is put into relationship with the personality, with the personal wish directing the experience, with the attitudes of the person, that is to say, with the central drive-layer of the psyche. . . . In all these layers, disorders lead to the same basic difficulties: the whole cannot be differentiated into its parts, the parts cannot be integrated into a whole (in Rapaport, 1951, pp. 579-580).

Schilder provided examples of specific kinds of disorders that occur at each of the above integrative levels. His formulation implies that there are a number of synthetic functions layered over one another in a hierarchic series.

The idea of layering in the personality was developed considerably by Wilhelm Reich in his *Character Analysis* (1933) and by Fenichel (1938), who pointed out that what is defense in relation to one layer is what is warded off in relation to another layer. Rapaport, too, stressed the importance of hierarchical layering in a number of his writings: "Much about personality-organization in general, and thought organization in particular, cannot be understood unless we assume that the process here described repeats itself in a hierarchic series, controlling organizations thus being layered over each other" (1951, p. 701).

Lustman (1966) holds that the hierarchical structure of the ego is responsible for much of the power of synthesis or the synthetic function:

> By functional differentiation, the synthetic aspects of this laminate structure (with its built-in relationships) may modify its own activity, so that further structure building has a cohesiveness and synthetic quality imposed by the nature of the already existing structure. This hierarchy is further implied in the relationship-preserving aspects of the primary and secondary processes, in which one does not *replace* the other, but *overlays* it (p. 204).

DEVELOPMENTAL CONSIDERATIONS

Glover (1930) held that the primitive ego is a composite of unrelated, unsynthesized elements, and that perhaps "there are as many primary egos as there are combinations of erotogenic zones with reactive discharge systems" (p. 120). In his paper on the classification of mental disorders (1932), the theory of ego nuclei is developed as an outgrowth of the above assumption. He summarizes the essence of this theory as follows:

Any psychic system which a) represents a positive libidinal relation to objects or part-objects; b) can discharge reactive tension (i.e., aggression and hate against objects); and c) in one or other of these ways reduces anxiety, is entitled to be called an ego system or ego-nucleus. Thus an oral system gratifies instinct on a part-object (mother's nipple); it can exert aggression toward the nipple (sucking, pulling, biting), and it is able to prevent some degree of anxiety. This is the model or prototype of an independent, autonomic, primitive ego nucleus (p. 169).

Gradually, these various ego nuclei merge and integrate. Glover places the first signs of effective synthesis at the time of the second anal-sadistic phase (the phase of controlling and retaining): "However fragmented the early ego, there is from the first a synthetic function of the psyche, which operates with gradually increasing strength. As development proceeds, the nuclei merge more or less (it is always a case of more or less with ego-synthesis)" (1943, p. 318).

Spitz (1965) agrees with Glover that a synthetic tendency is present from the beginning and becomes increasingly powerful. But Spitz believes that effective synthesis occurs first at about three months of age with the establishment of the libidinal object, as documented in the baby's smiling response to a human face. He had earlier (1959) conceptualized the first year of ego development in terms of organizing factors ("organizers of the psyche"), which usher in progressive stages or periods. Spitz holds that these factors (smiling response, eight-month anxiety, and the development of speech) result in organizing and differentiating the ego functions.

Federn (1947) believed the crystallization of ego nuclei theory to be in error. He held that the ego develops not through crystallization but through organization, reacting as a whole in the beginning and able to react in part after some maturation.

Federn's position seems consistent with Coghill's conclusion derived from observation of the salamander, namely, that development proceeds from primitive mass action to more coordinated reaction. Glover's formulation also seems supportable. We can thus speculate that there is some discrete and some global ego functioning very early in life and that with maturation results of some previously discrete processes are integrated, and some previously global responses are differentiated.

Hartmann (1947) stated that synthetic functioning develops gradually, parallel to ego development, and that it also contributes to the development of psychic structure (and thus to ego development). He also said that synthetic functioning is clearly discernible in superego development.

Erikson (1956) holds that an aspect of the synthetic function of the ego is the integration of psychosexual and psychosocial features at each developmental level and the integration of new identity elements with those already present. His conception of identity formation depends centrally upon synthetic-integrative functioning:

From a genetic point of view, then, the process of identity formation emerges as an evolving configuration — a configuration which is gradually established by successive ego syntheses and resyntheses throughout childhood, it is a configuration gradually integrating *constitutional givens, idiosyncratic libidinal needs, favored capacities, significant identifications, effective defenses, successful sublimations, and consistent roles* (p. 116).

To continue with developmental aspects of synthetic functioning, Kardos and Peto (1956) discuss play as a disintegrative-integrative process in which split-off parts of the ego are reintegrated. They assume that the infantile ego is constantly affected by traumata from internal and external sources and that impulses and images may be repressed and become split off from the conscious ego. Play enables the split-off parts of the ego to be projected outside and then resynthesized into the ego.

Rosen (1955) sees imagination as a synthetic process of the ego that develops from early experiences with the disappearance and reappearance of objects, especially the mother.

The value of a developmental approach to synthetic-integrative functioning is underscored by Frankl (1961), who also acknowledges the difficult methodological problems involved. She proposes to compare observations of children who show early developmental imbalances with psychoanalytic case material derived from the treatment of neurotic children who manifest ego regressions (to provide a view of early integrative efforts) and with material from the analyses of children who manifest an exaggerated use of defensive splitting. Frankl points out that the aims of various integrative efforts may be viewed as forming a developmental hierarchy; the focus is successively on the body ego, the self, mental representation of important human relationships, the outside world, and ego identity. In the cases discussed, Frankl found one example of developmental imbalance in which the relative contribution of external factors versus internal factors was unclear. In another case, integration difficulties were attributed to an internal defect in synthetic functioning. In still another, disturbances in body-ego integration were described as the basis for disturbances in the self, in mental representations of important objects, and in the outside world. The author stressed the importance of distinguishing between integration disturbances resulting from arrested development, developmental imbalance, regression to earlier developmental levels, and ego splitting.

Khan (1962) states that a basic function of mothering is to enhance the integration of libidinal and ego development in the child. He describes a group of patients whose symptoms involve intense emotionality expressed through polymorphous-perverse body experiences and attempts to establish a certain kind of coercive intimacy in their affective relationships. These symptoms reflect a failure at synthesis resulting in a form of developmental arrest even though neither the libidinal nor the ego development separately had failed to progress adequately. Indeed, a premature ego development, which leads to early attempts at mastery of all conflict-producing experiences and premature identification with the mother's role (with a consequent disturbance in pregenital sexuality), is what Khan sees as creating a basic split in the ego.

Kernberg (1966) presents a model of ego development in which splitting and synthesis are central mechanisms. He holds that early positive and negative introjections are originally separate because the primitive affects related to each (positive libidinal in the former, negative aggressive in the latter) are associated with disparate perceptual constellations that the ego at that very early stage is unable to integrate. An active keeping-apart of these positive and negative introjections is later instituted as a defensive measure to prevent a generalization of anxiety from negative to positive introjections. Excessive splitting at this stage interferes with the integration of affects, of self, and of object images and with the organization and integration of the ego. Insufficient anxiety tolerance will interfere with this synthesis, as will an excess of aggression. As maturation of the autonomous ego apparatuses and other structures continues, relevant positive and negative introjections synthesize, and this development brings on guilt reactions, ideal-self and ideal-object images. Synthesis of introjections and identifications alternates with regressive splitting, as self-images, object images, and ideal-self and ideal-object images become further delineated. Synthetic processes consolidate introjections and identifications into an ego identity; the fusion and synthesis of prohibitive parent images and ideal-object images become superego precursors.

SPLITTING AND FRAGMENTATION

The idea that autonomous, split-off fragments of the personality are related to the pathogenesis of nervous illness is found in late nineteenth-century psychiatry, especially in the work of Janet, who stressed the splitting-off of personality fragments in his theories of hysteria and mental disease (Ellenberger, 1970). Breuer's concept of hypnoid states, spelled out in *Studies on Hysteria*

(1893-1895), involved a splitting mechanism. Freud disagreed with Breuer's conception of the hypnoid state, preferring an emphasis on defense rather than on splitting. He said; "I looked upon psychical splitting itself as an effect of a process of repelling which at that time I called a 'defense,' and later 'repression'" (1914, p. 11).   Freud himself referred to splits of various kinds in his writings, however. He discusses a split between tender and sensual feelings in some men who cannot experience both feelings toward the same woman (1912). A split in the ego in perversions (1927) and splitting as a defense mechanism (1940) have already been mentioned.

Ferenczi (1930) stated that living organisms react to unpleasant stimuli with fragmentation. He saw primal repression as the original splitting of the personality and concluded that in this sense all adults are split (i.e., are not one psychic unit).

Namnum (1963), in another context, points out that the idea of a split or division in the psychic apparatus was seen by Sachs (1925) as between ego and id, by Rado (1925) and Alexander (1923) as between ego and superego, and by Sterba (1934) and Fenichel (1941) as a split within the ego itself.

The kind of split in the ego described by Sterba (1934) occurs during psychoanalytic psychotherapy. This is the dissociation between the patient's experiencing and observing aspects. As Sterba put it: "The subject's consciousness shifts from the centre of affective experience to that of intellectual contemplation" (p. 121). Such a state of affairs, which Sterba calls the fate of the ego in analytic therapy, together with the function of synthesis, is what he believes makes psychoanalytic psychotherapy possible. Freud in his *New Introductory Lectures* (1932), makes the similar point that the ego can take itself as an object, observe itself, and criticize itself and that the ego becomes dissociated or split during many of its functions.

Bleuler's preference for the term "schizophrenia" (1911) over "dementia praecox" underscores the importance he placed on splitting of mental functions in these most severe mental conditions. Formulations about the process of splitting and the keeping apart of good and bad objects were published by M. Klein as early as 1930; the hypothesis of a paranoid position (which she later changed to the paranoid-schizoid position on the basis of a suggestion by Fairbairn) appeared in 1935. In her paper on schizoid phenomena (1946), Klein discussed splitting as a process that occurs virtually from the beginning of life. She considers the mother's breast to be the infant's first object and assumes that there is a split between its gratifying and frustrating aspects, resulting in a split between love and hate. The mechanism of splitting was seen as one of the typical defenses of the early ego and provided the basis for the later-adopted paranoid phase or position. Klein hypothesized that internalizing the experience of gratifying breast-suckling increased ego cohesiveness and integration and counteracted ego splitting. The latter was especially likely to occur in response to aggressive forces. She discussed splitting of internal and external objects and of affects and aspects of the ego, assuming a close connection between splitting, omnipotence, and denial. Klein saw these mechanisms as serving the same functions as repression (i.e., as a defense against anxiety) but at an earlier level of ego development and splitting of parts of the self and projecting them onto other people as necessary for normal development. Klein believed that excessive splitting in infancy (occurring too frequently or continuing too long) provides the basis for childhood or adult schizophrenia.

Fairbairn's (1946) theory of personality was based upon the idea of splitting of the ego. Some degree of ego splitting is found in everyone, and he thus agrees with M. Klein that the schizoid position is the basic one in the psyche. The crucial issue for a given individual is the level at which the splitting occurs. Fairbairn sees splitting of the ego as the most fundamental factor in schizoid conditions, a conclusion similar to Bleuler's.

Erikson's concept of identity diffusion is closely related to the splitting of the ego: "In identity diffusion, a split of self images is suggested, a loss of centrality, a sense of dispersion and confusion and a fear of dissolution" (1956, pp. 122-123). For most adolescents this state of affairs tends to come to the fore when they are simultaneously faced with situations involving and requiring physical intimacy, occupational choice, competition, and psychosocial self-definition.

A balance between synthesis and fragmentation (splitting) is necessary for normal functioning. Silberman (1961) posits that prolonged imbalance results in psychological malfunctioning. He agrees with the idea that the energy for synthesis derives from the libido and the energy for fragmentation from the aggressive drives. Both fragmentation and synthesis can be observed in the id, ego, and superego, and both processes accompany ego maturation. Silberman says that harmonious interplay between fragmentation and synthesis results in differentiation and is based upon a proper degree of neutralization of libido and aggression.

One function of defensive splitting is to keep positive introjections and identifications apart from negative introjections and identifications (Kernberg, 1967). Clinical indications of the process can be alternating manifestations of one side of a conflict and then the other without reconciliation of the contradiction between the two. Splitting is also operative in periodic break-throughs of primitive impulses that are ego syntonic at the time (reflecting a selective lowering of the impulse control level) or in the apprehension of other people as all good or all bad accompanied by a periodic shifting of a given person from one category to the other. Finally, Kernberg mentions the repetitive switching from given self-characterizations to contradictory ones.

Schafer (1968) conceptualizes the idea of a split in the ego in terms of the antagonistic or difficult-to-integrate suborganizations of motives, mental processes, and representations within the ego system. But id and superego aspects are also involved, so that he sees the problem as an intersystemic one involving relationships between id, ego, and superego systems.

IS SYNTHESIS A FUNCTION OF THE EGO OR OF THE TOTAL PSYCHE?

Rapaport contended (1955) that the synthetic function would best be defined as pertaining to the ego only and not to the whole personality. He suggested that the major mechanism involved is the elimination of contradictions in the ego. In the id, contradictions result from the process of fusion of libidinal and aggressive drive energies.

Apfelbaum (1966), on the other hand, has maintained that synthesis is perhaps better characterized as a function of the total psyche than as only an ego function. Prelinger (1958) reasons that if the basic definition of synthetic functioning revolves around the elimination of contradictions within the ego, synthetic functioning must operate according to secondary-process characteristics because in the primary process, contradictions may exist side by side. Other mental processes that relate psychic components, but without regard to contradictions and logical requirements, are fusion and condensation — primary-process mechanisms. Prelinger points out that different kinds of organizing components usually contribute to a given behavioral event, ranging from condensation and fusion through integration of conflicting trends. The degree to which primary—or secondary—process characteristics predominate varies with the level of ego development, specifically, to the extent to which the reality principle is adhered to. When ego regression occurs and the reality principle is less decisive in the impulse-defense-adaptation balance, then organizing activity will also tend to shift toward the primary-process mechanisms of fusion and condensation.

Consistent with Rapaport's suggestion to limit consideration of synthetic functioning to the ego, Schafer (1968) talks about establishing order among competing ideas and the tendencies they represent. He stresses that the range of phenomena that can be synthesized (or remain unsynthesized) can vary from contradictory or uncoordinated superficial ideas to contradictory major personality suborganizations: "Thus, the scope, mass, and content of the unsynthesized fragments can vary greatly. Also, according to this view, some syntheses are more urgent, more important, and more difficult than others" (p. 98).

Schafer describes several processes by which synthesizing takes place: exclusion (the use of logic and judgment to reject ideas inconsistent with existing organizations); inclusion or coordination, whereby ideas initially thought to be either contradictory or unrelated are subsequently found to be consistent with, and related to, existing organizations of ideas and are then included in the latter;

transformation, that is, the assimilation of unintegrated elements into the major organizations by "defining their nature more precisely and objectively, decreasing emphasis on keeping them apart, evolving more neutralized and assimilable versions of them, and changing actions in certain ways, all with the aim of rendering these elements compatible, mutually supportive, or even synergistic" (p. 98).

To the integration of contradictory trends in the ego, Prelinger adds another aspect of the synthetic function: the relating of ego aspects that are not necessarily contradictory. Nunberg (1930) had alluded to this important facet, and Schilder (1930) gave it detailed consideration. Prelinger hypothesized that, from the economic point of view, synthetic functioning, by establishing new integrations, can be seen to follow a principle of minimal cathectic expenditure, as do automatizations (Hartmann, 1939). This is similar to Rapaport's hypothesis about what happens in concept formation (1951), according to which the grouping of a number of individual items under one category allows a decrease in the cathexis of the many particular items in favor of one encompassing concept.

These considerations support the value of viewing synthesis as a function of the ego. But they do not rule out the likelihood that synthetic processes are relevant to other aspects of mental functioning. Most especially, there is the question of how integrated or unintegrated is superego functioning.

SYNTHESIS AND DIFFERENTIATION-DISCRIMINATION

Hartmann (1947) felt that synthesis and differentiation are both aspects of the organizing function of the ego. Searles (1959) holds that differentiation and integration are opposite sides of a single growth process. Psychic contents must be partially differentiated from each other in order to become integrated. And, he says, functions or contents must be integrated to some extent before any differentiation can take place. The author finds that both integration and differentiation are impaired in schizophrenia but not to the same extent at any particular time and that the balance of relative impairment shifts from time to time.

Prelinger (1958), on the other hand, points out that the synthetic and differentiating functions are opposites. By definition, differentiation involves a separating and dividing of what had been together and, thus, is the opposite of synthesis. It can lead to fragmentation and concreteness when not balanced by synthetic functioning.

Hacker (1962) sees the discriminatory functions as "the exact dialectic correlate and opposite of the synthetic functions." The interplay and integration of these processes make the ego more than the total of its various functions;

they make it an active structure. Discriminatory processes, by disturbing existing equilibria, facilitate new integrations at higher levels. All hierarchical ordering and increased structural complexity is accompanied by discriminatory functioning.

CHAPTER 17

Mastery-Competence

Mastery-competence has not usually been considered as a separate ego function. We include it to differentiate between individuals with regard to their degree of active striving to deal with situations, overcome obstacles, and actualize their potentials. It takes account of "ego passivity," which is frequently a factor in the relative success of psychotherapy, personality change, and growth. The most extensive treatment of mastery-competence has been provided by White (1963). While this work has received a mixed reaction among psychoanalysts, there is general agreement that mastery and competence are important. Cameron (1963) has said the following about mastery:

> We see mastery develop even in the nursing situation; we see it in the continual perceptual-motor explorations of early infancy; we see it in the mastery of space and locomotion that comes as soon as a child can get to his feet alone. Ego adaptation, maturation and mastery together form rising spirals. As a child matures, he increases the effectiveness of his ego adaptation; as he adapts and masters more and more, he matures faster; and as he matures further, his ego adaptations and mastery take on new dimensions and new complexities. The gratifications that once came only with direct discharge now come from the performance of complex maneuvers itself. The end may become less important than the way in which it is achieved. This is obvious in children's play and in many adult rituals (p. 178).

SOME VIEWS OF MASTERY, BEGINNING WITH FREUD

The urge to master the external world was attributed by Freud rather early to the ego or self-preservative instincts, as we discussed in the chapter on the id. In 1905, he attributed the "instinct for knowledge" in part to sexual curiosity and in part to "a sublimated manner of obtaining mastery" (p. 194). While he acknowledged that many children report a feeling of excitement in their genitals while romping, he left open the question of the relation between strong need for active muscular exercise in children and sexuality (p. 202).

The reality principle (1911) includes an increased concern with external reality, as well as implying the dealing-with and mastering situations emanating from it. Freud's focus was on the curbing, and thereby mastering, of internal needs in the wake of reality demands, but his descriptions of attention, reality testing, and thinking are all necessary for, and relevant to, mastery experiences.

In his writings devoted to the development of the libidinal drives, Freud discussed the instinct to mastery as sometimes being related to activity and to sadism: "Activity is supplied by the common instinct to mastery, which we call sadism when we find it in the service of the sexual function" (1913, p. 322).*

Freud also saw the feeling of self-regard and competence being generated at least in part by one's achievements:

In the first place self regard appears to us to be an expression of the size of the ego; what the various elements are which go to determine that size is irrelevant. Everything a person possesses or achieves, every remnant of the primitive feeling of omnipotence which his experience has confirmed, helps to increase his self regard (1914, p. 98).

The notion of a compulsion to repeat experiences, especially traumatic ones, was discussed most fully by Freud in *Beyond the Pleasure Principle* (1920). He attributed the repetition compulsion to the death instinct, the tendency of organic matter to return to an inorganic state. But his descriptions of the repeating of traumatic events, and even of children's repetitive play, suggested that the activity was based on an attempt to master a situation by actively carrying out (even if symbolically) something that had been passively experienced.

He described a little boy who had a habit of playing "gone" with his toys, and then he expressed satisfaction when he would find or retrieve them. Freud interpreted this game as a cultural achievement for the child: it symbolically represented the ability to let his mother go without his protesting. The child turned his separation-anxiety experience into a game in which he was initially passive and overpowered:

but by repeating it, unpleasurable though it was, as a game, he took an active part. These efforts might be put down to an instinct for mastery that was acting independently of whether the memory was in itself pleasurable or not (p. 16).

It is clear that in their play children repeat everything that has made a great impression on them in real life, and that in doing so they abreact the strength of the impression and, as one might put it, make themselves master of the situation. But on the other hand, it is obvious that all their play is influenced by a wish that dominates them the whole time − the wish to be grown up and to be able to do what grown-up people do (pp.16-17).

In *An Outline of Psycho-analysis* (1938), Freud lists as one of the principal characteristics of the ego, the "learning to bring about expedient changes in the external world to its own advantage (through activity)" (p. 145).

Thus, Freud had very little to say directly about what is here called

*Efforts to achieve mastery over the body, and over external obstacles, are central to the anal-sadistic phase.

mastery-competence, although a concern with adaptation and mastery of the environment is implied in many of his writings.

Alfred Adler treated mastery extensively in his writings. Because of the helplessness and dependence of childhood, feelings of inferiority are universal and may be increased by body or organ defects (real or imagined), parental neglect, rejection, older siblings, and other factors. Compensatory strivings for power, personal achievement, and mastery over the external environment follow.

Hendrick discussed a concept of mastery in a number of papers as "an inborn drive to do and to learn how to do" (1942, p. 40). He saw it as an ego instinct, the others being the needs for self-preservation and for nourishment (1943). He argued that psychoanalysts tended to regard the executant functions of the ego as defensive, rather than being exercised to achieve or to master. He also emphasized that ego-function defects must be taken into account in understanding serious mental disturbances in addition to conflict, repression, and defenses against castration anxiety and loss of love (1943). He was thus stressing structural egopsychological factors at a time when most other psychoanalysts were still defining the ego primarily in terms of defense. A major exception to this trend of course was Hartmann's 1939 monograph *Ego Psychology and the Problem of Adaptation*. Hendrick believed that evidence for the infant's need to master its environment by practicing sensory, motor, and intellectual activities had been neglected by psychoanalysts up to that time, although Freud had referred to these as early as 1905, as we have already pointed out.

The mastery instinct was defined as follows:

I refer to the development of ability to master a segment of the environment. The primary need to perform those functions which serve this purpose I shall refer to as an "instinct to master." By this I mean an inborn drive to do and to learn how to do. This instinct appears to determine more of the behavior of the child during the first two years than even the need for sensual pleasure (1942, p. 40).

Hendrick (1943) concluded that the pleasure and reality principles were not sufficient to account for the psychosocial activities of the total organism. He said:

I shall suggest that work is not primarily motivated by sexual need or associated aggressions, but by the need for efficient use of the muscular and intellectual tools, regardless of what secondary needs — self preservative, aggressive or sexual — a work performance may also satisfy. I shall call this thesis the *work principle*, the principle that primary pleasure is sought by efficient use of the central nervous system for the performance of well-integrated ego functions which enable the individual to control or alter his environment (p. 311).

Contrasting the instinct to master with the sexual instincts, Hendrick stated that while the aim of the latter is sensual pleasure, the aim of the mastery instinct is the pleasure in executing a function successfully, irrespective of its sensual pleasure. The manifestations of the mastery instinct are the rudiments of the various ego functions, and their purpose is the "adjusting the environment to oneself" (p. 41). While Freud assumed that the need to repeat is beyond the pleasure principle, Hendrick assumed that the need to repeat is an expression of the instinct to master and can serve the pleasure principle.

and E. Bibring were summarized by Hendrick (1943) along the following lines:

(1) It is simpler to regard the ego as an organization distinguished from the id and providing forms of pleasure that are not themselves instinctual gratifications.

(2) The mastery instinct is unnecessary, since the phenomena discussed by Hendrick, it was claimed, could be adequately dealt with in terms of the then-existing instinct classifications.

(3) It adds confusion to the already difficult psychoanalytic theory of the instincts.

As to (1), Hendrick rebutted that his dynamic concept provided an exploration for what made the ego function. As to (2), he believed that since instincts were classified according to their goals, ego goals were not adequately defined by libido theory. He further felt that mastery could be distinguished from aggression (the goal of which is destruction) and from sadism (aggression toward a sexually cathected object).

For Hendrick, the mastery instinct provided a force and a dynamic explanation for the development and exercise of ego functions and a concept to account for adaptive strivings. Hartmann's concept of autonomous ego functions and neutralization of sexual and aggressive energies and an emphasis on adaptation can be seen as related, but alternative, formulations; they have been widely utilized, while Hendrick's concepts have not generally found a positive response among psychoanalysts.

WHITE'S CONTRIBUTIONS

White introduced a conception of an *active* ego striving for mastery that is seen to serve the biological purpose of competence. His ideas are put forth in a number of papers and in his monograph *Ego and Reality in Psychoanalytic Theory: A Proposal Regarding Independent Ego Energies* (1963). In his paper "Motivation Reconsidered: The Concept of Competence" (1959), White proposed the concept of an "effectance" motivation to account for competence in relation to reality; the "capacity to interact effectively with [the] environment and for the slow attainment of this capacity through 'learning' " (1959, p. 297). Observations of spontaneous activity, exploratory behavior, and curiosity were the bases for his reconsideration of motivation. He introduced and defined competence as follows:

As used here, competence will refer to an organism's capacity to interact effectively with its environment. . . . fitness to interact with the environment is slowly attained through prolonged feats of learning. In view of the directedness and persistence of the behavior that leads to these feats of learning, I consider it necessary to treat competence as having a motivational aspect and my central argument will be that the motivation needed to attain competence cannot be wholly derived from sources of energy currently conceptualized as drives or instincts (1959, p. 297).

White further developed his ideas about independent ego energies in the 1963 monograph. He holds that exploration, manipulation, locomotion, language, the practicing of motor skills, growth of cognition, development of plans and intentional actions, and the emergence of higher thought processes are not satisfactorily accounted for in psychoanalytic theory. Acknowledging Hendrick's proposal of an instinct to master, White states that his theory "corresponds roughly with the idea mentioned by Freud, but never more than casually, that the ego apparatus might have intrinsic energies of its own and that there might be a natural satisfaction in the exercises of ego functions" (1963, p. 184). While the satisfaction derived from the exercise of a function itself had been discussed earlier, White presents this point as follows: "The playful exploratory and manipulative activities of children provide the basis for a theory of independent ego energies . . . attention is given longer to objects upon which it is possible to have large effects" (1963, p. 185). White elects to call the energy behind such behavior *effectance,* and the affect attending a *feeling of efficacy*: "Effectance thus refers to the active tendency to put forth effort to influence the environment, while feeling of efficacy refers to the satisfaction that comes with producing efforts" (p. 185). The biological significance of effectance is described as follows: "Competence is the cumulative result of the history of interactions with the environment. Sense of competence is suggested as a suitable term for the subjective side of this, signifying one's consciously or unconsciously felt competence — one's confidence — in dealing with aspects of the environment" (p. 186). White repeatedly stressed the importance of supplementing psychoanalytic theory with concepts of action and efficacy.

In linking his own view of energy theory with his concepts of effectance and competence, White believes that independent ego energies supplant the psychoanalytic concept of neutralization. He acknowledges that the following three urges may be available from the start: effectance (an urge toward sensory and motor activity); aggression (an urge toward forceful destructiveness); and eroticism (an urge toward pleasurable stimulation of sensitive zones). As we pointed out in the chapter on autonomous functioning, White believes that independent ego energies can account for anything neutralized energies can account for and do not require the assumption of energy transformation. "Effectance" implies a primary positive interest in the world apart from its drive-reducing properties; "competence" describes a person's existing capacity to interact effectively with his environment and is a cumulative result of the whole history of transactions with the environment, no matter how they were motivated. "Sense of competence" describes the subjective side of one's actual experience. The feeling of efficacy is what is experienced in each individual transaction, while "sense of competence" refers to accumulated and organized consequences in later stages of ego development.

While he stressed the independent ego energies in his 1963 monograph, White later pointed out that he believes the main value of his effectance concept to be an explanation for the "cumulative structuring of the personality that results from taking action and learning about the consequences of action." Thus, in his 1967 paper he said, "Sense of competence signifies the degree to which a person feels able to produce desired effects upon his environment, human and inanimate – how able he feels to secure the goals that are important to him and to elicit from others the behavior he desires" (1967, p. 44).

Self-confidence is a manifestation of the sense of competence: trusting one's own judgment, accepting difficult undertakings. Motor manifestations are one's posture and movement, a firm tread, a sure grasp of tools. Lack of self-confidence and anxiety at having to make decisions are characteristic of many patients in psychotherapy. White ventures the idea that a strong sense of competence may be one of the most important bases for differentiating psychological health from neurosis. (1967, p. 44)

White has also attempted to delimit his concept of competence. As he said (1960):

As a simple and sovereign concept it will never do. A person developed wholly along lines of competence, with no dimensions of passion, love, or friendliness, would never qualify for maturity. Competence is not intended to describe such experiences as enjoying food, immersing oneself in a sexual relation, loving children, cherishing friends, being moved by natural beauty or great works of art; nor is it designed to swallow up the problems created by aggression or anxiety (p. 136).

But with regard to anxiety, White does state that when a sense of competence has been established in an area as a result of successful dealings, anxiety is less likely to disrupt activity in this given area. Conversely, when anxiety has developed in relation to particular actions or areas, the growth of competence in these areas is likely to be inhibited (1967).

In emphasizing his contention that competence, sense of competence, effectance, and feeling of efficacy cannot be reduced to derivatives of sexual and aggressive drives, White reexamines Freud's stages of psychosexual development from the standpoint of the competence model (1960). He acknowledges the importance of the psychosexual factors at each stage of development but argues that there is an important additional competence aspect: in the oral period it is the infant's exploratory play and active interaction with the environment. He believes that weaning, while strongly influenced by the affectionate bond between mother and child, also involves an inherent satisfaction to the child in bringing a part of the environment (cup and spoon) under his own control.

The urge to master the environment and experience success in dealing with it are stressed by White in the anal phase. He sees the prominent oppositional behavior found at this time to be in the service of allowing the child to increase inner control by resisting external influence. Again, he acknowledges the importance of anal eroticism (i.e., the libidinal aspect) but holds that the competence aspect goes beyond the libidinal and cannot be derived from it, although at some junctures the libidinal aspect can mask the competence aspect.

In their formulation of development, a number of psychoanalytic theorists, including Spitz, Mahler, and Erikson, have pointed out and included mastery factors, and Hartmann's primary autonomy and conflict-free sphere also provide a theoretical framework for integrating active attempts at adaptation. White should nevertheless be credited with the most thorough, careful, and useful consideration of the importance of feelings of competence and for his development of the rationale for an original neutral ego energy source. Finally, while much has been written about the sources of self-esteem, White has most clearly emphasized that while self-esteem depends in part upon feeling that one is loved, another important part depends upon being effective in dealing with environmental demands, challenges, and requirements.

COPING

E. and W. Menaker, in their book *Ego in Evolution*, (1965) agree with White about the need for the conception of "an active ego serving the biological purpose of competence." Another kind of active mastery that has been extensively treated is often designated "coping." Visotsky and his associates (1961) were concerned with active mastery as shown in coping behavior under extreme stress. They used polio as an example of a severe disability that occurs suddenly and as posing an extreme test of coping resources, and they discuss factors that favor the resolution of psychosocial problems that are concurrent with, and persist after, the disease. They discovered, first, that many patients show an especially good ability to work out new life patterns. Second, for each stage of disability a number of specific strategies are used to come to terms with the threatening aspects of the situation. Third, the following adaptive responses are observed in most patients: they make efforts to minimize the impact of the illness; they deny the seriousness of the illness; they recognize the reality to some extent; they employ strategies that aid in coping with the problem; meaningful group membership is an important factor aiding resolution of difficulties; mastery of difficult problems in the past may help in dealing with the current situation.

A comprehensive work on active mastery and coping has been done by Lois Murphy and her associates (1962). She defines the process of mastery as involving the simultaneous and successive use of various devices and resources in response to new challenges. The child's perceptions of his capacities change as he masters a new task. In mastering a motor task, for example, the child must first estimate his own readiness for the task and then make the decision to attempt it, moving through the sequence of limited goal, more ambitious goal, and then to final autonomous accomplishment of the task. Coping capacity derives from native equipment for the ability to use integrative capacities flexibly and from environmental support.

The concept of mastery is certainly related to such ideas as volition, will, and conscious active efforts. Wheelis, in a paper on will and psychoanalysis (1956), says of psychoanalysis' past neglect of these phenomena that in our understanding of human nature we have "gained determinism, but lost determination." He says, furthermore, that therapists rarely include in their public reports the interventions they make toward the end of an analysis: for example, "Nothing is achieved without effort" or "You have to try." He feels that analysts feel uncomfortable about making appeals to volition, as though they might be using something they did not believe in, and might also think such interventions would be unnecessary if they had analyzed their patients more skillfully.

ORIGINS OF MASTERY IN INFANCY AND EARLY CHILDHOOD

Some of the earliest work on the origins of mastery were considerations of the pleasure inherent in the function or exercise of an activity, as opposed to the pleasure contingent on drive or tension reduction. A very early reference comes from Groos (1901) in his book *The Play of Man*, which discusses the pleasure derived from functioning and from the effect of an activity. This idea may be more familiar to most readers from the work originally developed by K. Buhler (1930) on *Funktionslust*: the pleasure derived from the effect of an activity and from the functioning itself, what we might now call the "I can do it!" phenomenon. Most recently, L. Murphy (1962) found that the enjoyment of novelty is associated with the capacity to struggle and the drive to mastery. Characteristics found to correlate most highly with capacity to cope with the environment were the child's general resources for gratification; his capacity for pleasure; and interest in, and enjoyment of, his activities. Motor skill and agility similarly seem to have a relation to effective coping, since they in part determine a child's ability to gain gratification from the environment.

Besides the work on function pleasure, much has now been written on factors in childhood and on the child's relation to his mother, which contributes significantly to the development of mastery. Waelder (1932) said that Freud's theory of play emphasized the repetition compulsion and the mastery of painful situations by a shift from passivity to activity. Early activity was also emphasized by Benedek (1938), who said that learning is acquired through an ability to tolerate delay and to endure postponement of gratification. Tolerance for delay is acquired when fairly prompt gratification can be anticipated, and this in turn depends upon the infant's gaining some experience of the consequences of his own actions. While most of the writers reviewed see play in the context of ego functioning and mastery, some still focus primarily on id aspects. Kardos and Peto (1956) believe that play is primarily an expression of infantile sexuality, and they do not consider the autonomous aspects of mastery and gratifications in the function of play.

Finally, there has been a considerable amount of observation and theory about the mother's role in promoting the child's ability to exercise his own mastery and to achieve competence. Belmont (1955) discusses factors responsible for severe ego difficulties in children, emphasizing the interaction of constitutional and environmental influences in the causation of these disturbances. Each child handles life situations differently, depending upon his constitutional endowment. The mother either hampers or helps the child in mastering such situations, but the child has a role in this too. Mahler (1958), for example, says that locomotion enables the child to separate from the mother and to enjoy independence and mastery. Mahler (1963) has also pointed out how the child makes active efforts to get the attention and help of adults when it is needed. Spitz (1958) has stated that the young child's identificatory imitations have the quality of mastery and that such actions originate from the child's insurgence against his infantile helplessness.

MASTERY AND ADAPTATION

The "adaptational school" of psychoanalysis, represented by Rado and his colleagues, has been concerned with mastery and adaptation to the environment. Hartmann (1939), as we reviewed earlier, spoke of adaptation in terms of reality mastery: one's productivity, ability to enjoy life, and mental equilibrium. He referred then to three forms of adaptation: alloplastic action, in which adaptation comes about by changes that the individual imposes on his environment; autoplastic action, in which changes are made in the individual's psychophysical system; and a third form that consists of choosing a new environment advantageous for the functioning of the individual. In summary,

Hartmann states that development of the individual's inner world and its functions permits an adaptation process that consists of withdrawal from the external world and return to it with increased mastery.

Like Hartmann, Rado (1956) specifies alloplastic and autoplastic adaptations as improving the organism's pattern of interaction with the environment. Rado's treatment procedures are focused on creating for the patient opportunities to practice self-reliance. He interprets to the patient his life performance in an adaptational framework, with the goal of increasing adaptive potential. Rado and Daniels (Kardiner, 1961) feel that the organization of any specific culture results from the way in which its people solve the problem of adaptation.

Rapaport (1959) stated that curiosity motives, motives for novelty, and all others contributing to what White called competence motivation are all — like attention cathexis — nonparoxysmal and newly triggered into action by the appearance of objects. He argued that White's "effectance motivation" is not motivation in the psychoanalytic sense and thus requires an explanation other than that which may be provided by the drive concept. He also held that Freud provided an adequate means of accounting for the roles of external stimulation in instinctual discharge without introducing, as White did, a special motive. Effectance would not be seen as motivated because it is voluntary, and motivated behaviors are those we cannot help doing: "In labeling effectance a motive, we explain nothing unless we can demonstrate that it, like drives, is purposive, expends energy, aims at consummation, and is to some degree peremptory" (1960, p. 895). While Rapaport criticized the effectance concept as not qualifying as a motive, his line of reasoning certainly does not rule out its being a function. However, he felt that the main issues were to clarify whether the role of external stimulation involves a special kind of motivation, as White believes, or only nonmotivational causation. Rapaport says, in agreement with White, that the potentiality for acquiring competence is present from the beginning; but he is doubtful if an effectance motivation or any other motivation is the basis of this potentiality, and it is possible that its basis is an apparatus of consciousness of the sort Rapaport had described, requiring a theory of relations to the environment and of learning other than the more prevalent drive reinforcement theory.

As we have already stated, White did not assume that effectance motivation is the same as instinctual drive motivation and specifically emphasized that it was not derivable from either libidinal or aggressive sources.

Another point of view attributes no particular merit to distinguishing between libidinal energies on the one hand and independent ego energies on the other. L. Murphy (1962), for example, feels that the process of mastery involves the simultaneous and successive use of various drives and resources in response to new challenges, whatever the source of these coping mechanisms may be. E. and W. Menaker (1965) agree with White in regard to an active principle in the ego but see no need for assuming independent ego energies:

The energy for ego functioning then derives from the energy available to the central nervous system, which in turn taps the resources of total life energy within the organism (p. 85).

While it is convincing that ego energies are mobilized in the name of feelings of efficacy and competence, as White persuasively argues, such energies are postulated from a concept too limited in scope to fully explain the "biological purpose" of an action ego (pp. 85-86).

Thus opinions differ as to the conceptual status of mastery-competence. We include it as an ego function because we believe it taps an aspect of behavior and mental functioning that is not directly covered by any of the other ego functions and is important for adaptation.

CHAPTER 18

Interrelationships Among Ego Functions

SOME THEORETICAL CONSIDERATIONS

Hartmann discussed aspects of the problem of the interrelation of ego functions many times. In addition to the general issues of interference, mutual enhancement, and hierarchy, he underscored an evaluation of the relationships among three main areas: autonomous functions, defenses, and synthetic functions (1950). He stated in his 1939 monograph that all reality relations and probably many other ego functions depend upon autonomous ego development.* An important aspect of ego strength is the structural hierarchy of the autonomous functions and the extent to which they can withstand impairment as a result of defensive operations (1950). Hartmann did much to focus psychoanalytic interest on the interrelationship among ego functions, and his comments on this topic arise from a broad and informed view of the way to move psychoanalysis toward being a general psychology.

One basic issue central to the question of interrelationship is that of discreteness. Hartmann stated (1950) that ego function deficits are discrete rather than global. Beres (1956) and Arlow and Brenner (1964) make this same point. But the ego functions are generally recognized to be interrelated and interdependent, and in the report of the Kris Study Group summarized above, the authors felt their case material suggested that ego's capacity to deal with all conflict situations was involved in any particular autonomous-ego-function regression and that when a disturbance obtains in one ego function, other functions are also disturbed. The issue is, then, how much discreteness or possibility of independent variation there is among ego functions and under what conditions.

One important factor is the level of personality differentiation (Witkin et al., 1962). The less differentiated the personality, the greater the tendency for a number of ego functions to show maladaptive features at the same time. Many kinds of difficulties and traumata that result in developmental arrest increase the

---

*Hartmann and others often use the term "autonomous function" in a broader sense than the one we have specifically defined as autonomous functioning, one of the 12 ego functions in this volume.

intercorrelation among ego functions at a low level of adaptive adequacy. For example, when the mechanism of splitting is relied upon excessively for defensive reasons early in life, the resulting split between various aspects of the person's self-representations and object representations will influence and retard the development of object constancy, the level of object relations, the scope of synthetic functioning, the development of the sense of self, and the strength of repression and other high-level defenses (Kernberg, 1966). Defective sensory and neurological equipment can result in lack of discreteness in the adaptive level of many ego functions, as can a range of early disturbances in the mother-infant relationship (Spitz, 1951; Provence and Lipton, 1962; Mahler with Furer, 1969).

It is not surprising that the more serious the psychopathology, the more disturbance in related ego functions. By definition ego functions have to do with adaptation, and serious psychopathological symptoms and signs always include or imply ego function deficits or malfunctioning. In our study, in which interview material of schizophrenics, neurotics, and normals was rated on 12 ego functions, we would expect the adaptive adequacy of the schizophrenics to be lowest, neurotics next, and normals highest. This was indeed the case in preliminary studies (Hurvich and Bellak, 1968; Bellak and Hurvich, 1969). In the 1969 study, variability in the level of adaptive adequacy of the ego functions for each subject showed that the schizophrenics were the most variable, the neurotics next, with normals showing the least variability among the functions. Thus, subjects selected for the absence of significant psychopathology showed both a high and a uniform level of adaptiveness (and an absence of serious regression) of their ego functions. There is reason to believe that a person who has attained a high level of psychological development or who characteristically shows little psychopathology, will tend to show less ego function regression under stress. He would also show maximum discreteness in ego function regression if the latter occurs. That is, selected functions will show regression, others will not. This expectation is consistent with Hartmann's formulation cited earlier, that a central aspect of ego strength is the capacity to withstand the regressive alteration of autonomous ego functions by defensive operations. In this case, then, a uniform level of adaptive adequacy is associated with a high likelihood of discreteness in the regression of particular ego functions. Indeed, it is likely that more uniformity in the adaptive level of functions of the schizophrenics in our study would have been found had chronic schizophrenics been included rather than acutely disturbed ones.

Although a number of ego functions tend to be disturbed in psychotics, reports in the literature show that deficits are uneven to varying degrees. In one case described by Wallerstein (1967), reality testing was widely interfered with, although the patient did not manifest a classical thought disorder. We can surmise from the presented material that Wallerstein's patient was also showing a marked decrease in the adaptive level of impulse control and in synthetic-integrative functioning.

As another example, there is evidence that attention and concentration can function adequately even when thinking and perception are in some ways disturbed, as in cases of paranoid schizophrenia. On the other hand, some defects in conceptual thinking and perception are accompanied by the inability to attend and to concentrate. And, in a case described by Freeman, Cameron, and McGhie (1966), despite the instability of the identity aspects of the self-representations, the patient was still able to discriminate between subject and object (p. 86). So the degree of discreteness of ego functions depends in part on the extent of psychological development, on the level of psychopathology, and on the individual's unique characteristics. We now turn to a discussion of related aspects of ego function interrelationships.

First, we will consider the question of interference. Waelder (1930) proposed the principle of multiple function as an improvement on Freud's concept of overdetermination and related it to the synthetic function of the ego (p. 54, n.1). Waelder meant by this principle that each psychic act must be conceptualized as a simultaneous attempted solution to eight different groups of problems: four imposed on the ego from without (by the external world, the id, the superego, and compulsion to repeat) and four that the ego imposes on itself (in relation to these same factors: external world, id, etc.). Since these problems are frequently at variance with each other (such as the demand for instinct gratification, which is inconsistent with the demand for instinct control), they cannot all be solved to the same degree, and frequently the solution of one interferes with that of another. Each psychic act that serves these multiple functions must also have multiple meanings — that is, an impulse aspect, a superego aspect, and so on.

Hartmann later applied the interference notion to the various ego functions; he often emphasized the importance of determining the ways in which various ego functions interfere with each other in the process of adaptation. Interference with other ego functions by defensive operations are readily specifiable, for example, when repression decreases memory, when denial obstructs reality testing, and when isolation decreases synthesis. It appears likely that the interference of defensive processes with other areas of ego functioning provides the best example of interference as a way in which ego functions interrelate when there is an absence of severe ego regression. But when regression is severe, interference takes the form of secondary failure of one ego function because of the regression of another. For example, a patient unable to differentiate between himself and others is no longer able to maintain object relationships (Freeman, Cameron, and McGhie, 1966, p. 94). Cognitive functions may vary in the degree of regression when the quality of an important object relation changes (Rosenfeld, 1952). And when attention is interfered with, perception is affected. When thinking is defective, speech is influenced. Sandler and Joffe (1965) point out that changes resulting from functional ego regression (mentioned earlier in chapter 4) may secondarily interfere with other aspects of ego functioning.

Sometimes, the presence of multiple ego function deficits and regressions is noted, and it is difficult to determine which are secondary to others and which are more directly a result of defensively motivated regression in the conflicts over drive and/or superego factors. Even so, both for therapeutic and for theoretical reasons, it is important to index (in addition to what is being warded off, what constitutes the danger situation, etc.) which ego functions are disturbed, in what respects, and to what degree.

Hartmann talked about cooperation among ego functions as a major way in which they interrelate. Reality testing, for example, depends on at least the ego functions and processes of attention, perception, memory, secondary-process thinking, delay of discharge, judgment, and reflective awareness (Hurvich, 1970). Secondary-process thinking involves synthetic functioning (Rapaport, 1951), while inadequate impulse control is a factor in many examples of poor judgment. A focus on the general issue of cooperation brings the problem of overlap into focus. It is generally recognized that ego functions overlap (Beres, 1956) and that id, ego, and superego do also (Freud, 1923; Waelder, 1930). While nothing prevents us from naming different functions, the problem of how much they overlap is not thereby solved. Indeed, Freud's notion of overdetermination, Waelder's principle of multiple function, as well as Hartmann's and Rapaport's emphasis on the hierarchical organization of mental processes, all attest to the need for multifaceted and multilevel formulations in this field. Even so, attempts to state overlap explicitly increases the meaningfulness and precision of the intrasystemic approach emphasized by Hartmann and need not be antithetical to postulating a hierarchical organization. Clear distinctions among ego functions and their differential implications are more the exception than the rule. One such exception involves the distinctions made between (the related ego functions) reality testing and sense of reality (Weiss, 1950; Weisman, 1958; Frosch, 1964). Thus, Frosch hypothesizes that the relative degree of disturbance in reality testing over the sense of reality is a central factor in the differences between a psychosis and a psychotic character.

Clarity is increased when the level of focus for statements about ego functions and their interrelationships are specified. For example, a high relationship between impulse control and synthetic functioning may hold true for the schizophrenic group on the average but not hold true for a given individual. For a given subject's ego-function profile, the relationships among ego functions vary widely from the overall results.

Thus, depending on a number of factors, such as which drive derivatives are involved, what superego aspects become activated, the kind and degree of environmental press or stress, the person's adaptive level with regard to a given ego function can vary considerably. For example, a patient demonstrates good (i.e., highly adaptive) judgment in a variety of situations. But under certain rather specific circumstances, he tends to engage in sexual behavior that, among other things, is markedly inconsistent with good judgment. The implications are that the term "good judgment" often needs to be qualified by additional statements. The same is true for good reality testing, sense of reality, impulse control, and so on. All the major ego functions are multidimensional and complex, rather than unitary and simple. For example, in evaluating reality testing in an individual with constricted, compulsive personality features, the ability to distinguish internal from external may be quite good, and accuracy of perception may also be high, while inner reality testing is poor, the latter because this individual tends not to be aware of inner psychological events and reactions. With regard to synthetic-integrative functioning, an individual may show poor synthesis of certain conflicting trends but may, nevertheless, manifest an unusually high capacity to synthesize and integrate areas of experience not in conflict, to an extent greater than an individual who shows more overall personality integration and synthesis. In these examples, different component aspects of reality testing and synthetic-integrative functioning are demonstrated to be predominantely independent of each other, although examples could be provided in which all major components of reality testing or synthesis show regression. On the basis of the extent to which component aspects of the ego functions could vary independently, we have prepared a revision of our ego function rating manual that allows each component factor to be rated separately.

INTERRELATIONS AMONG EGO FUNCTIONS AND THE CONCEPT OF INTELLIGENCE

We believe the problem of the interrelationship of ego functions can be advantageously examined in the light of the history of the concept of intelligence (Bellak, 1958a). As with intelligence, the total adaptive ability, ego strength, often tends to be thought of as a unitary phenomenon, while workers dealing with schizophrenics and with others suffering from extremes of ego disturbance have been struck by the variant afflictions of different ego functions. M. Katan (1953) has spoken of an "intact residue" of ego functions, with the implication that different residues will be found in the treatment of different schizophrenic individuals. Eissler, Bellak, and others have similarly spoken of the variable strengths and weaknesses of ego functions within the same patient.

In the history of intelligence testing, there were those like Binet and the early Spearman, who felt that intelligence was a general phenomenon. There were others like Thurstone (1938) who held that intelligence was the manifestation of several different "primary" abilities or specific factors, i.e., numerical, verbal, spatial, fluency, and others. Then there was the British school (later Spearman,

Burt, Vernon), which suggested that intelligence could best be understood as the manifestation of a general factor and some less general "group" factors ($g + s_1 + s_2 - [s = \text{Factor}]$).

It is the general-plus-group conception more than any other that underlies the internationally most widely used intelligence test, the Wechsler-Bellevue Intelligence scales. The current edition of the adult scales consists of 11 subtests whose pattern of correlations with each other define two groups (verbal and performance) and one general (full scale) I.Q. Our conception of ego functions follows the Spearman model. We found it useful to define 12 ego functions that overlap in varying ways with each other and that are related to total ego strength. On the one hand, if the intercorrelation among the functions is too high, there is no basis to speak of different ego functions, only overall ego strength. On the other hand, if the functions showed only minimal intercorrelation, then there would be no basis to speak of ego strength. We earlier pointed out that some circularity is involved in defining the ego by its functions and that use of the term "the ego" is subject to this circularity problem. It is also clear from the data analysis that in assessing the various ego functions either from clinical interviews or from psychological tests, some raters show more intercorrelation among their ratings than do others. Thus, the issue of intercorrelation among ego functions involves their correlation in the subject and their correlation in the rater.

The average degree of intercorrelation of the ego function scales turns out to be rather close to the average intercorrelation of the WAIS scales. Intercorrelations among the 11 subscales were published in the manual (Wechsler, 1955) at three levels. We have determined the medians and ranges for the three groups, which are found in Table 18.1.

Table 18.1.   Medians and Range of WAIS

	Ages 18-19 (100 males, 100 females)	Ages 25-34 (150 males, 150 females)	Ages 45-54 (150 males, 150 females)
Median	.52	.52	.52
Range	.39-.81	.30-.81	.42-.85

These median correlations are similar to those found for the intercorrelation among ego function scales for each of the groups we evaluated, which are found in Table 18.2.

Table 18.2.   Medians and Range of Ego Function Scales

	Schizophrenics (N=50)	Neurotics (N=25)	Normals (N=25)
Median	.49	.57	.52
Range	.001-.74	.14-.84	.04-.79

The difference between the two is found in the range, with the ego function ratings showing by far the greater.

Bellak had proposed in 1952 that ego strength be appraised with a scale that resembled the ones for intelligence testing. Most of the conception underlying the development of our scale is predicated on this proposition.

SOME SPECIFIC INTERRELATIONSHIPS SUGGESTED IN THE LITERATURE

The following material on interrelationships is not exhaustive of the literature but rather demonstrates some representative formulations concerning the variations of ego functions with each other. This section also does not illuminate the relatively greater importance of some ego function interrelationships as compared to some others. These facts are discussed in the chapter on results of the clinical interview ratings.

Reality Testing and Sense of Reality

Some relationships between reality testing and sense of reality have been discussed in the chapter on reality testing. A particular component factor of our definition of reality testing — reflective awareness — is seen by Arlow (1966) as related to the sense of self: the immediate participation and awareness of observing one's self in action (i.e., self-observation). Piaget (1937) equated the sense of reality of the world with testing of reality through motor activity. He stated that whatever is capable of alteration in the external world by motor activity is real. Roland (1967) offers a distinction between the two by contrasting the transference phenomena in psychotherapy with realities of the analytic relationship; such a contrast represents the function of reality testing. According to Ross (1967), in the as-if personality, which is indicative of disturbance in the sense of reality, reality testing shows no significant deficits.

A few references have been found, linking the sense of reality with regulation and control of drives. Greenacre (1950) says a "jaded" sense of reality characterizes people who act out. Depersonalization has been regarded as a means for preserving control of drives (Grinberg, 1966). Grinberg also believes that the phenomena of ego disintegration and restitution that take place during sleep are connected with some aspect of depersonalization and loss of obsessive control. Novey (1966) holds that integrating various aspects of the self into a coherent self-concept parallels an ability to cope with conflicting drives within one's self. Objectivity toward one's self implies the ability to interact with others and to tolerate the inevitable frustrations between persons.

Possibly the most overlap in conceptualization occurs between sense of reality and object relations, for a major component of each is "the distinction between self and object representations," or the extent of maintaining ego boundaries. Self-esteem, the development of which depends partly on adequate object relationships, has also been the concern of E. Menaker (1942). She feels that a new object relationship develops in the psychoanalytic relationship alongside the neurotic transference responses, and the former helps to develop a sense of reality about the analyst and, thus, all people. Balint (1963) also talks of a proper sense of feedback from the mother or analyst, essential to the development of object relations and the sense of reality. Along the same lines, Novey (1966) feels the analyst needs an accurate sense of reality to do his job. His objectivity implies a capacity to see the patient for what he really is and to sort out a reality picture from conflicting reports about himself or others. The analyst "must have lived" to have a well-developed sense of reality — the ability to empathically experience with another.

As for self-representations and object representations bridging both object relations and the sense of reality, Hartmann (1950) speaks of fusion and refusion of self and object images and representations. The idea is expanded by Bellak (1958a), who says, "The sense of reality is closely interrelated with the development of object relations. The sense of self results from the differentiation of the self and other objects." Jacobson (1964) speaks of introjective and projective mechanisms whereby the self-images take on attributes of object images and vice versa, making for shaky boundaries. Weedbury (1966) states that altered body experiences — the sensations of change in organization and sense of unity of the body ego — have effects upon object representations and self-representations and the relationship between the two.

One way in which the sense of reality has been related to thought processes is in the relation of perception and cognition to field dependence-independence. Roshco (1967) more specifically relates denial and depersonalization to alterations in perception and cognition and, thus, to an altered sense of reality concerning the self.

A number of sources relate sense of reality to ARISE. Milner (1957) found that in studying the artistic medium (free drawing) she learned of her sense of self through a blanking out of consciousness, which led to new forms of art integration. Beres (1960) said that "without imagination, reality is only sensed and experienced; with imagination, reality becomes an object of awareness. With his imagination, man participates in reality, alters it, and even to some extent controls it" (p. 334). A more direct statement of the relationship is made by Kafka (1964): "A solid anchor in one reality co-existing with an ability to encompass many realities, even paradoxical patterns of subjective equivalences, could be described in terms of ability to 'regress in the service of the ego'" (p. 577). Further along these lines, Rose (1964) says: "The effect of a creative imagination is to achieve a deepening awareness of oneself in respect to an expanding perspective of the world. There is a change in the relationship of the ego to the inner (bodily) and outer worlds" (p. 75). Later (1966), he states that the body ego participates through creative imagination in the task of reality construction.

Relating sense of reality to defenses, the formulation that depersonalization may represent a defense against intrapsychic conflict (Arlow, 1966) has already been reviewed. In addition, the relation of reality sense to specific defenses has been discussed by various authors. Glover (1955) believes that strengthening the patient's sense of reality gives him more freedom to analyze projections. Angel (1965) feels the defense of acting out may be a defense against the danger of loss of identity, as often seen in borderline cases. As already reported, Grinberg (1966) believes depersonalization to involve a loss of obsessive defense mechanisms. Roshco (1967) states that an altered sense of reality concerning the self may be an effect of denial of actual perception or a denial in fantasy. Schimek (1968) relates field dependence to a failure in ability to use the defense of intellectualization.

Only one reference was found connecting sense of reality with stimulus barrier. Federn (1949) believed that the depersonalized person was irritable and sensitive, almost like the allergic person, to the slightest emotional or external stimuli.

According to Beres (1956), man may participate in, and alter, reality and his sense of it through active efforts to control it. The relation of sense of reality to mastery-competence has been treated in greatest detail by White (1963), who holds that with respect to the ego and reality, there are independent ego energies that he calls effectance and that the ability to make changes in the surrounding reality involved is called "efficacy." Competence in coping with the environment is the biological reward for these activities.

Regulation and Control

Touching on the relation of regulation and control to reality testing, Hartmann (1956) says that the ego yields more readily to the influence of the reality principle, whereas sexual drives remain longer under the control of the pleasure principle. The ego also becomes a source of pleasure by providing ways of achieving instinctual gratification and through sublimation. Relating acting out to defects in reality testing, Caroll (1954) says that people who started acting out as children did so because real facts seemed to them to differ from what their parents said; therefore their orientation to reality developed in an idiosyncratic manner. According to Greenacre (1950), in psychotic acting out there is a complete takeover of the current situation by early unconscious memories, which severely affect reality perception.

Although there are very few references to the relationship between regulation (and control) and judgment in the literature, the correlation between those two functions would appear to be quite strong. The pressure, or urgency, of drives would be a major factor in impulsive behavior, which by its very definition would reflect poor judgment. Stated another way, under extreme drive pressure, perceptions and judgments of reality would be expected to suffer (see chapter on judgment).

Greenacre (1950) states that in acting out, there may be problems in accepting and understanding current reality and also a disturbance in the sense of reality. Also related to sense of reality is the work on impulse expression reported by Sanford and his associates (1957), who discovered that people who were rated high on impulsivity were found to have relatively unstable ego identities.

Thought processes relate to regulation and control in a special way, first discussed by Freud (1895), who said that thought provides for a limited discharge of tension. He added that the secondary process is firmly established when repression is able to prevent drive impulses from reaching consciousness. In the person who acts out, failure to assimilate language as a concise method of conceptualization and communication is associated with a tendency to act out complete dramatic sequences rather than to select some detail for symbolic representation (Greenacre, 1953; Caroll, 1954). Rapaport (1951) summarizes the relationship between drive control and thinking (earlier spelled out by Freud) by saying that inhibition and the use of delay in psychic functioning are important factors in the development of thought. Thought develops out of the inhibition of primary drives: inhibition causes a delay in motor behavior, and out of this conflict comes symbolic representation and thought. Michaels (1959) says that individuals who act on impulse have a primary orientation to senses and things, so that perception and concreteness take precedence over conception and abstraction. Other relationships between regulation and control and thought processes are mentioned by Bak (1954), who says that the basic anxiety in schizophrenia is related to an increased sense of losing control over thought processes. Another aspect of the relationship is treated by Kupper (1950), who says that the intellectual's pursuit of truth and knowledge is in part a search for instinctual gratification as well as representing the activity of a mature ego. He demonstrates that children who later become intellectuals are frequently subjected to a repressive environment, which drives the individual to give up sexual activities in favor of indulgence in sexualized intellectual activity.

ARISE has been linked to regulation and control in a number of instances. Harper (1955) mentions that artistic creativity — a form of sublimation — serves the integrative function, biologically and psychologically, by, among other things, reducing tension. Berezin (1958) also feels that central to the artistic process is the effort by the ego to master various tension-producing stimuli. The artist must arouse only optimal doses of tension in the audience, similar in concept to the optimum doses of anxiety and displeasure necessary for adequate psychic functioning and development. An artistic endeavor must, he says, be aesthetic, utilizing sublimation and other mature ego functions rather than merely discharging affect. From the ego's standpoint, the id content is secondary to ego functions.

Regulation and control overlaps a good deal with defensive functioning. Freud originally characterized neurosis as an excessive repression of libidinal impulses. Repression was viewed as leading not only to prevention of drive derivatives from entering consciousness but also to prevention of affect and voluntary motor activity. Here there seems to be great overlap of the two functions in Freud's early thinking. Brenner (1957) summarizes this line of thought by stating that failures of repression, whether temporary or permanent, are caused by weakening of ego defenses, strengthening of drives, or similarity of current experiences to the content of repressed drives. Michaels (1959) states that the egos of persons who act upon impulse are not equipped to bind anxieties. A specific relation of acting out to defenses is noted by Spiegel (1954) who states that some acting out derives from pregenital impulses, the gratification of which serves as a defense against the recognition of infantile genital impulses.

It is not surprising at all to imagine how difficulty in control of impulse, affect, and drive could affect one's relationships to other people (i.e., object relations). Freud noted the connection (1915) by stating that the object of an instinct is that in diffuse acting out there is a general overstimulation and sensitization for all stimuli, in the sense of a much lowered threshold for both input and output. It is likely that Bergman and Escalona's stimulus-barrier observations (1949) are relevant to congenital differences in acting out.

A relationship to autonomous functioning is noted by Bak (1954), who feels that the schizophrenic's loss of impulse control affects both primary and secondary autonomous functions of the ego. Michaels (1959) feels that the constitutional determination of impulse strength and vicissitudes would also have to affect the unlearned, primary autonomous functions.

Finally, with respect to the synthetic-integrative function, Blos (1962) states that acting out in the adolescent can operate in the service of ego synthesis as a phase-specific mechanism. Bellak (1963), in a metapsychological consideration of acting out, states that people who act out have multiple diverse identifications with a lack of synthesis of ego nuclei. This lack of fusion of ego nuclei would naturally manifest itself in a deficiency in the synthetic function of the ego.

Object Relations

Relating object relations to reality testing, Fenichel (1945) believes that schizophrenic attempts at restitution with lost objects are sometimes based on ideas of saving mankind, where patients actually project their own need for salvation from their loss of objects. Disturbances in reality testing among neurotics are seen when objects are transference representations of real objects and do not correspond to the reality of the person being responded to. Consideration of the object as a real person, said Ferenczi (1926), is a condition of full development of object relations; he called this the erotic sense of reality. A full appreciation of reality is lacking in persons who remain fixated at the precursor stages of love. According to Spitz (1965), the shift from contact to distance perception promotes better reality testing.

The relationship between object relations and sense of reality is touched upon by Fenichel (1945) in his discussion of love "addicts" who use objects to regulate their own self-esteem. Their dependent and narcissistic type of object choice reflects a defect in the sense of reality of the self.

Impulsive neurotics, with difficulties in regulation and control of drives, do not see persons as real objects in their own right (Fenichel, 1945) but only as deliverers of supplies and as interchangeable, one with another. Among such people, object relationships are not personal, but are used for the purpose of relieving inner tensions. Speaking of more adaptive aspects of regulation and control, Décarie (1965) says that when the child understands the communicative signs of the object, he can remain attached to it even if it is the source of severe frustration of instinctual need. This is a description of object constancy. The ability to wait for any gratification is an indication of ego formation and a turning point in object development.

Since there appears to be a relationship between the stage of concept formation and phase of object development (Decarie, 1965, we might expect on this basis that object relations correlate highly with thought processes. Freeman, Cameron, and McGhie (1966) provide evidence for this same notion.

References to defensive functioning are also to be found in Fenichel's discussion of the adaptive, restitutional purposes of schizophrenic disorders of object relations. The specific defense of deanimation of people helps the psychotic child to cope with change and unfamiliarity (Mahler and Furer, 1968).

An interesting note on ARISE comes from Dubos and Kessler, who feel that there may be a creative manifestation of symbiosis, where the symbiotic systems may result in structures or products that neither of the two participants could create alone. Nacht (1960) states that regressive states during psychoanalytic treatment can be used in the service of adaptation in the following way: the analyst introduces the reality principle by offering himself as a real person — not as a transference object — to bring the patient out of regressions that might otherwise be nonproductive.

Stimulus barrier relates to object relations mainly in considerations of the mother acting as a protective shield (Khan, 1963) and in observing the maladaptive effects on stimulus barrier where there is excessive maternal intrusiveness (Coppolilillo, 1967) in the earliest years of infancy. The first relation to the mother deals nearly exclusively with the formation of stimulus barrier through well-geared maternal ministrations and sensitivity to her child (Murphy, 1964). Shields (1964) refers to a process of "ego swamping" by the too good, overaccommodating mother. Mahler (1968), in the same vein, feels that maternal overstimulation is more detrimental to ego function than inanimate overstimulation (e.g., noise, temperature, light).

Autonomous functioning, especially in relation to drive neutralization, has been considered fairly extensively in an object-relations context. Kris (1950) states the more completely that aggressive and libidinal energies are fused in the cathexis of the object, the higher the chances of successful neutralization. During the separation-individuation process, disturbances in object relations may result in impoverishment of neutralized energy available to the ego (Mahler, 1968). The mother's emotional availability is essential if the child's autonomous ego is to attain functional capacity. Specific ego processes and functions that begin in the earliest weeks with the infant's contact with the mother, are an expression of the activity of the developing innate structures — looking, listening, touching, and so on — and are autonomous ego functions but are dependent on the external support of the mother (Murphy, 1964).

Décarie (1965) states that with the onset of true object relations, drive fusion and the development of the synthetic function may also be observed. Schafer (1968) refers to the relatively advanced stage of object relations in which there is no longer a splitting of the ego. Instead, the synthetic function develops to establish order among the competing tendencies and ideas of the ego.

Defensive Functioning

As already noted, Hartmann contrasted defensive, autonomous, and synthetic ego functions. In 1950 he also stressed the importance of the autonomous ego's ability to create stable and effective defenses. Specifically, Hartmann stated that autonomous functions can be involved in the ego's defense against reality and against the superego. A year later he said that inhibitory actions are "actions against the outside world which in part probably belong to the ego's primary autonomy and only later, in situations of psychic conflicts, do they develop into what we specifically call mechanisms of defense."

In discussing change of function (1939) and reactive character formation (1952), he shows how a function that originally served a defensive purpose could later serve an autonomous one. Reactive character formation, originating in defense against drives, may gradually take over a great many other ego functions and continue to exist long after its function as a defense mechanism has receded (secondary autonomy of the ego; see chapter on autonomous functioning). Hoffer (1967) elaborated on this point, stating that because defenses interact with the autonomous functions, the defensive organization must be credited with positive achievements and often positively creative activities of the ego.

Freud (1925) stated that the fundamental nature of defenses may be understood by reviewing the reality-testing function of the psychic apparatus. A more specific statement on the relation of defenses to reality testing is made by S. Sperling (1958). He says that defenses are dynamisms acquired by the ego in relating instinctual strivings to the demands of reality. Freud postulated stimulus barrier as the chief inborn defense. This idea was later adopted by Spitz (1961), who viewed stimulus barrier as a precursor of defense or the prototype for repression. Spitz (1961) related defense to object relations by stating that the prototypes of ego defenses are processed through the mother-child relationship throughout the course of development. A specific example of this relationship is offered by Mahler and McDevitt (1968), who believe that certain infant behavior such as stiffening of the body and pushing away from the lap suggests a defensive warding-off of symbiotic closeness to the mother.

The sense of reality has been regarded by some as related to defensive functioning in that depersonalization (i.e., a disturbance in the sense of reality) has at times been considered one way of defending one's self against the awareness of aggression.

When defenses interact with autonomous functions of the ego, the defensive organization must often be credited with sublimated and creative activities (Hoffer, 1967). Thus, they could also relate to adaptive regression.

When defensive functioning is maladaptive, the synthetic function may be impaired. This relationship was considered by Sperling (1958), who maintained that resorting to a defense mechanism always entails impairment of the ego's integrative function. Such a relationship obtains, of course, only if defense mechanisms are regarded solely as maladaptive.

Mastery-Competence

Mastery-competence might be defined as depending somewhat upon the degree of adaptation expressed in all other functions, even if we hold to the narrow view of adaptation. It is related to reality testing, according to Murphy (1962), in that the development of a picture of reality is implicit in the concept of coping. White (1963) says that the sense of competence is derived in part from knowledge that something efficacious can be done to alleviate needs, alter the environment, and so on and that this knowledge is built up by experience in testing reality.

The sense of reality may be defined as completely encompassing the *sense* of competence, for sense of competence is part of self-regard or self-esteem. It is in fact a component factor of the sense of reality as we define it. White (1963) says that self-esteem is related to the sense of competence and, ultimately, to the experience of efficacy. He feels also that Freud was headed in the opposite direction from him regarding mastery because of his particular concept of self-esteem. For Freud self-esteem was dependent on narcissistic libido rather than on sense of competence resulting from effective action. According to

Mahler (1958), the sense of individual identity is mediated by bodily sensations arising from body image and coming directly from locomotion activities involved in mastery behavior.

A statement from White illustrates the relation between mastery-competence and regulation and control of drives: "Tolerance of delay depends on a confidence, born of experience, that something efficacious can be done if need waxes painful" (1963). Murphy (1962) says that a characteristic of coping sequences is delay, which can be used variously to size up a situation in which the resultant cognitive mastery may either facilitate well-directed control or lead to freer use of available materials.

Relating mastery to object relations, Mahler (1958) says that locomotion enables the child to separate from the mother and to enjoy independence and mastery. Mastery and the child's relation to the mother is also discussed by Murphy (1962), who says that the enjoyment of novelty is associated with the capacity to struggle and the drive to mastery. Anxiety experienced by children in novel situations is correlated with separation problems and with disorganization in family life. The child whose ego development is handicapped by motor limitations, sensitivity, or inner stress is more apt to be anxious in novel situations, to be realistically more dependent upon the mother, and, thus, to have a greater separation problem as a result of this real need for maternal support. She notes also that children who have developed a healthy sense of mastery are more likely to respond to offers of help from others.

Defenses and mastery are also discussed by Murphy. She states that coping includes all the complex ways in which the child interacts with his reality. Evading or erecting barriers against reality are part of coping when direct ways of handling reality are not available. The ego is the center of the impulse toward mastery, a process that can involve defense mechanisms also.

Brief reference is made to adaptive regression by Hartmann in a discussion of mastery and adaptation (1939). From the standpoint of adaptation, an increased mastery of reality is often achieved by withdrawal from it temporarily in some fashion (e.g., regression). The fruits of this regressive withdrawal are then put to creative-adaptive use through mastery.

Mastery and stimulus barrier are discussed by Murphy (1962) in her description of three coping styles. She reported that children of average drive and marked sensitivity did not have the capacity to struggle against deprivation and that without high drive, high sensitivity led to withdrawal; under such circumstances, little active effort was directed toward the environment.

Mastery-competence would reasonably be expected to relate most often to autonomous function, and it would apparently be hard to distinguish the two under many circumstances. Again Murphy specifically states some of the interrelations: the child's perception of his capacities changes as he gains mastery in a new task, and he develops increasing autonomy. In mastering a motor task, for example, the child must first estimate his readiness for the task and then make the decision to attempt it, moving through the sequence of having a limited goal, a more ambitious goal, and then to final accomplishment of the task — autonomously. An aspect of autonomy is the capacity to set limits to demands and pressures from the environment. This allows for familiarization and also permits the child to master one task at a time. In general, motor skill and agility — both subsuming primary and secondary autonomy — seem to bear a relation to coping ability, since they partly determine ability to gain gratification from the environment.

As for synthetic function and mastery-competence, Hartmann (1939) felt that synthesis of regressive and mastery responses is a prerequisite of adaptation. Murphy (1962) states that since coping is an integrative concept, the specific methods and resources of coping are not the only valuable behaviors; the way in which these resources are organized is equally important.

SOME CLINICAL HUNCHES REGARDING INTERRELATIONSHIPS AMONG EGO FUNCTIONS

To start with, we engaged in an armchair analysis of our hypothesis of the likely degrees of independent variation of 11 different ego functions. We drew up a schematic diagram of the list of the ego functions in relation to each other (See Table 18.3, which shows one person's armchair analysis for two functions). We asked ourselves on the basis of our clinical experience just how high all other ego functions could theoretically be if the ones under consideration were optimal (a rating of 7) and minimal (a rating of 1).

The 10 people who thus speculated were also given four options (see a, b, c, d of Table 18.3), including an hypothesized range from 1 to 7 for all functions if the one under consideration was either optimal or minimal. Table 18.4 summarizes the group consensus on ranges for all functions when reality testing and judgment were the target ego functions and Table 18.5 when sense of reality and regulation and control were target functions.

This armchair analysis alerted us to many of the issues underlying the problem of overlap. We knew, however, that our own empirical statistical findings concerning the variance and interrelationships of these 11 ego functions would have to provide the more definitive answers. The armchair analysis as a thought experiment assisted us in selecting ego functions for empirical trial and error. Actual analysis of interviews, ratings, and rater conferences provided the next step. Once we established ego functions that seemed both necessary and sufficient, we could assess ego functions in different groups and individuals.

The conceptual model of ego-function interrelationships would then also

Table 18.3   Armchair Analysis: Examples of Possible Interrelationships Among Ego Functions

(a) Could vary from 1 to 7	(c) Would be no lower than ____
(b) Would be a specific score (e.g., 1 or 2)	(d) Would be no higher than ____ and no lower than ____

	If reality testing is: optimal (7)-minimal (1)				If judgment is: optimal (7)-minimal (1)			
Then it could be that								
Reality testing is:					(d)	6	(c)	2
Judgment is:	(d)	6	(c)	3				
Sense of reality is:	(d)	6	(c)	4	(d)	6	(c)	3
Regulation and control is:	(d)	6	(c)	4	(d)	6	(c)	3
Object relations is:	(d)	5	(c)	2	(d)	6	(c)	3
Thought processes is:	(d)	6	(c)	1	(d)	6	(c)	2
ARISE is:	(d)	7	(c)	2	(d)	7	(c)	2
Defensive functioning is:	(d)	6	(c)	2	(d)	6	(c)	2
Stimulus barrier is:	(a)		(c)	5	(a)		(c)	6
Autonomous functioning is:	(d)	6	(c)	3	(d)	6	(c)	5
Synthetic functioning is:	(d)	6	(c)	2	(d)	6	(c)	3

Table 18.4.   Armchair Analysis: Consensus on Armchair Analysis of Ego Functions

	If reality testing is: optimal (7)-minimal (1)		If judgment is: optimal (7)-minimal (1)	
Then it could be that				
Reality testing is:			7	1-3
Judgment is:	4-7	1		
Sense of reality is:	4-7	no more than 3	4-7	1-3
Regulation and control is:	4-7	1-3	4-7	1-4
Object relations is:	4-7	1-2	4-7	1-4
Thought processes is:	4-7	1-3	4-7	1-4
ARISE is:	1-7	1-3	1-7	1-3
Defensive functioning is:	4-7	1-3	4-7	1-3
Stimulus Barrier is:	4-7	1-4	1-7	1-7
Autonomous functioning is:	4-7	1-3	4-7	1-4
Synthetic functioning is:	4-7	1-3	4-7	1-3

permit one to deal, among other things, with some heretofore unexplored issues — for example, the case of the egopsychological equivalent of an idiot savant (as in the classic case of someone with excellent memory who is an idiot otherwise). Similarly, there are probably quite a few people who excel in one ego function while functioning in an average way, or even poorly, on all others (e.g., various forms of the "mad genius," such as van Gogh).

Table 18.5.   Armchair Analysis

(a) Could vary from 1-7   (c) Would be no higher than _____
(b) Would be a specific score   (d) Would be no lower than _____
   (e.g., 1 or 2 or 3)

	If sense of reality is: optimal (7)-minimal (1)			If regulation and control is: optimal (7)-minimal (1)
Then it could be that				
Reality testing is:	(d)	7	(c) 1	6-1
Judgment is:	(d)	7	(c) 1	6-2
Sense of reality is:				
Regulation and control is:	(d)	6	(c) 1	6-3
Object relations is:	(d)	7	(c) 1	6-3
Thought processes is:	(d)	6	(c) 1	6-2
ARISE	(d)	7	(c) 2	5-2
Defensive functioning is:	(d)	6	(c) 1	6-1
Stimulus barrier is:	(a)		(c) 1	6-1
Autonomous functioning is:	(d)	6	(c) 5	6-3
Synthetic functioning is:	(d)	7	(c) 1	6-1

Part 3

THE RESEARCH PROJECT

CHAPTER 19

Ego Functions in Schizophrenics, Neurotics, and Normals

The aims of this part of the study were (1) to select a list of major ego functions and specify their major dimensions or component factors; (2) to develop procedures for assessing these in schizophrenic, neurotic, and well-functioning individuals, from interview material, psychological-test responses, and psychological-laboratory techniques; and (3) to look for different patterns of ego function weaknesses and strengths within a group of individuals diagnosed as schizophrenic. As already stated, we could only do a study involving a relatively small sample of subjects and realized that work on reliability, validity, and possible subpatterns of functions would have to be supplemented and complemented by additional subsequent studies.

We first selected and defined the ego functions and then proceeded to develop the interview and clinical psychological and laboratory procedures. Small groups of project participants worked in each of the three assessment areas, while some of us worked in all three and coordinated developments. We assumed that interviews, psychological tests, and laboratory procedures would tap different facets or levels of ego functioning, with some degree of interrelation.

As it turned out, we focused most of our attention and energy on the interview measures and results because of the greater methodological and practical difficulties encountered in the other two areas. Thus, while the results in the interview area are at best tentative, they are even more tentative in the other two areas. Methodological issues are discussed in relation to each of the procedures.

SUBJECTS

We decided to include 50 schizophrenic, 25 neurotic, and 25 normal subjects in the study. We were aware that this relatively small sampling could only provide a preliminary basis for the reliability and validity of the ego function scales; but it would allow an initial assessment, and this was consistent with the resources available and the goal we set for ourselves.

286

To control for background factors of the three groups, subjects were matched as closely as possible on the variables of age, education, I.Q., and socioeconomic status, the last measured by the Hollingshead Index. The background characteristics of the three groups are listed here, and their relationship to ego function ratings are discussed in the next chapter.

Table 19.1.   Backgrounds of Subject Groups

	Schizophrenic	Neurotic	Normal
	N=50	N=25	N=25
Mean age	30.3	27.4	26.4
Sex male	50%	25%	25%
Sex female	50%	75%	75%
Mean education	1 yr. college	1 yr. college	1 yr. college
I.Q.	107	118	116
Social class index (Hollingshead)	III (37)	III (37.1)	III (34.6)

The effects of these background variables have been reported by many. Mednick (1967) emphasized that in many studies, control subjects have not usually shared the same life conditions as the schizophrenics with whom they were compared. Thus, differences between schizophrenics and controls in a given variable were often attributable to one of the background factors, such as education or social class and not to the schizophrenic condition as such. Issues related to the selection of subjects in each group will be discussed separately.

Schizophrenic Subjects

For the schizophrenic sample, we wanted individuals between the ages of 20 and 45 who were diagnosed schizophrenic by two different hospital staff psychiatrists not connected with our project. Since indications of disturbed ego functions are frequently used as a basis for the clinical diagnosis of schizophrenia, some unavoidable contamination of the criterion may have occurred here. The best we could do was to make sure that the examining psychiatrists were not familiar with our ego function scales. Beyond this was the problem of unreliability of psychiatric diagnosis generally. In addition to unreliability among diagnosticians because of their different degrees of training and experience, poorly defined and overlapping categories, and variation in the quantity and quality of information available (Beck, 1962), there are individual differences between psychiatrists in reliance on the history, the symptom pattern, and the quality of the patients' behavior (Katz, Cole, and Lowery, 1969). Finally, psychiatrists differ in their theoretical orientations, and one authority has concluded that, with regard to schizophrenia, the particular psychiatrist's conception of the illness provides the basis for the diagnosis (Freeman, 1969).

We specifically ruled out potential subjects who gave evidence of brain syndrome, alcoholism, or the use of hard drugs. In addition, we wanted to exclude subjects who had been hospitalized for a long time, because they might have undergone deteriorative changes as a result of the regimentation and impoverishment of a total institution (Goffman, 1957). We thus included only subjects who had not been hospitalized for a total of more than one year. As a result, a number of our subjects were first admissions.

Hospital charts were scrutinized by our project administrative personnel; and when a schizophrenic patient meeting our criteria was found, the psychiatrist in charge of the patient was sent a note asking him to request the patient to volunteer to participate in the research project and explain to the patient what would be involved. The treating psychiatrist was asked to say the following to the patient:

I would like you to see another doctor here at the hospital for an interview. He will be talking with you in order to learn more about you, and gain more knowledge for the entire field, which may be of benefit also to other patients. Then on another day, you will spend several hours looking at pictures, following moving lights, and doing similar tasks, none of which is in any way painful or dangerous.

I will have a chance to see the findings of these procedures and can use this information in helping me to work with you. And you will receive $25 for your cooperation, if you do participate.

O.K.?...Would you sign this authorization form?

You'll notice that the doctor will be tape-recording the interview, but I don't believe that will be any problem for you.

Table 19.2 is a diagnostic breakdown of the 50 subjects included in the schizophrenic sample.

Several further comments are relevant. There are no schizophrenics diagnosed hebephrenic or catatonic. Neither hebephrenics nor classical catatonics (mute, rigid) could be expected to provide the verbal information required by our interview, psychological test, and laboratory approach, in which cooperation of the patient is necessary.

A total of 20 percent of the cases are not definitely diagnosed as schizophrenic (10 percent borderline and 10 percent probably schizophrenic). While these subjects were included at the time because we had no other patients to test that particular week and could not afford to fall too far behind, other aspects seem relevant to us. For one thing, such cases tend to decrease differences between schizophrenic and neurotic groups; group differences had to occur in spite of the probably better ego functioning of these subjects. It can

Table 19.2.   Diagnostic Breakdown of 50 Schizophrenics Included in the Factor Analysis

	Percentage of Cases
Schizophrenic reaction (paranoid type)	36%
Acute 20%	
Chronic 12%	
Unspecified 4%	
Schizophrenic reaction (undifferentiated type)	22%
Acute 16%	
Chronic 6%	
Schizophrenic reaction (type unspecified)	16%
Borderline schizophrenic	10%
Possibly schizophrenic	10%
Schizophrenic-affective psychosis	4%
Incipient schizophrenia	2%

also be said that since we wanted a goodly number of acute, recent-onset cases and had to exclude any of those who were too upset or uncooperative to be tested diagnostic unsureness on some of the remaining potential cases was almost inevitable.

Neurotic Subjects

The 25 subjects for the neurotic sample were drawn from patients at a large outpatient psychotherapy clinic (the Lincoln Institute for Psychotherapy, New York) and were chosen to match schizophrenic subjects on background variables. Subjects were asked (through a memorandum posted near the clinic entrance and similar to the one for normal subjects reproduced below) to volunteer for the study. Lists were compiled of all volunteers, and their psychotherapists were interviewed to determine which patients met the criteria for the neurotic sample and which provided the best match with the schizophrenic sample on background variables. The absence of psychotic and borderline features and the predominance of neurotic manifestations (anxiety, phobias, obsessions) over signs of character disorder were the major diagnostic considerations.

Normal Subjects

The 25 normal, or well-functioning, subjects were selected from hospital administrative personnel. Volunteers responded to the following memorandum, sent to all hospital employees other than M.D.'s and Ph.D.'s:

Roosevelt Hospital [or Gracie Square Hospital] is currently cooperating with research being conducted by Doctor Leopold Bellak. This research project is seeking volunteers from hospital personnel for use as a normal control group. If you would like to cooperate with this endeavor, you will be asked to undertake about four interviews and testing sessions at the hospital, arranged at your convenience (not during hospital working hours). The total time involved would be approximately 12 hours. All participants will be awarded a $25 honorarium for their cooperation in this project. A short description of the procedures involved follows.

Interview: About a two-hour interview will be conducted in a private office by a psychiatrist. Questions will be asked about your past and present life situation, involving family, friends, work, leisure time activities, etc. (Your name will not be used in order to insure your anonymity.)

Standard Clinical Tests: These will be administered over about a three-hour session and are meant to elicit your responses to a series of pictures, designs, and short objective questions.

Experimental Tasks: These will probably last approximately two sessions. They consist of a number of different procedures involving reading and writing, and visual and auditory tasks.

Those interested in participating were asked to contact a project staff member who would interview them to determine their suitability for the study. The criteria for selection were: no record of psychiatric hospitalization or outpatient psychotherapy, no admission of the presence of neurotic symptoms and manifestations in response to the Screening Inventory (see below), evidence of satisfactory adjustment in personal relationships and professional activities, and no apparent significant disturbances during the interview. The screening inventory for normal subjects ran as follows:

(Instructions to administering personnel: reword and/or reorder specific questions in order to decrease the social desirability/undesirability aspect.)

I. *Symptoms*
   a. How often do you feel "blue" or depressed?
   b. Do you have any special fear, such as heights, closed places, traveling, etc.?
   c. How often do you feel anxious?
   d. Do you have any trouble sleeping? Any nightmares?
   e. Do you ever have any ideas running through your mind that you can't get rid of?
   f. Are there any behaviors that you have to engage in, over and over, such as washing your hands, keeping everything exactly neat and in its place, etc.
   g. Have you had any trouble with stomach aches, headaches, asthma, constipation, or diarrhea?

II. *Work and Personal Adjustment*
   a. Are you satisfied with your work?
   b. Do you consider your relationships with your family satisfactory?

III. *General Satisfaction with Life*
   a. Are you generally satisfied with your life situation? (Don't take a simple yes or no for an answer.)

IV. *Behavior During the Interview*
   a. Look for the presence of tics, mannerisms, tension and anxiety (posturing, sweating, voice modulation, hypermotility).

While 100 subjects are reported in this study, 130 were seen. A total of 10 subjects (from all groups) had to be dropped because the electromagnetic tapes on which their interviews had been recorded were found to be inaudible, and no amount of sound engineering could salvage them. Of the schizophrenic sample 5 subjects left the hospital before completing the interview, 2 refused to complete the interview having once begun it, and 3 had to be dropped because information available only after they had begun the procedures indicated their length of previous hospitalization was too great to meet our criteria. Finally, screening volunteers for the normal sample resulted in a rejection of 10 out of 35 because maladjustment was evident.

CLINICAL INTERVIEW

Constructing the Interview

The major purpose of the clinical interview was to provide information on each of the 12 ego functions, as well as on relevant id and superego manifestations, which would be ratable according to each of the corresponding rating scales. While ratable information could be obtained from any intake interview, the latter is not specifically geared to assessing ego functions and would probably not provide sufficient information to rate all functions. Indeed, we pondered the question of whether any one interview could elicit sufficient data for reliable and valid ratings based on our standard interview with therapists' ratings based on material derived from psychotherapy sessions. This will be reported in a later chapter.

The interview is structured to the extent that it contains sets of specific questions, each set keyed to its corresponding ego functions as put forth in the Rating Manual. It is unstructured in the sense that flexibility and ingenuity are also required of the interviewer, who must be able to recognize and follow up a patient's responses in order to maximize ratable material. The interviewer's discretion dictates what questions will best elicit information about current, characteristic, highest, and lowest levels of functioning. Interviewers also need to obtain information to help determine the status of ego function deficits and strengths at critical phases in the life cycle and in response to stress or trauma. The interview may thus be considered as semistructured.

We found that sometimes it was important to make questions very direct, except in the case of certain paranoid patients who were guarded and resistant in the interview setting. Directness helped especially when psychological-mindedness was poor—for example, "Give me an example of when you show bad judgment." At best, it was difficult to get reliable and valid responses from some subjects. Questions and suggestions were not intended to inhibit interviewers from using their own clinical styles. Interviewers were encouraged to adapt questions to a subject's intellectual level and to depart from the order of questions if this made it easier for the subject to respond. For example, the interviewer often found it profitable to pursue a patient's presenting complaint in rather great detail. Keeping the necessary ego function in mind, he could, at his discretion, interject relevant questions, which would elicit ratable information. In sum, the interview while structured to yield information on ego functions, could be adapted to any interviewer's or subject's style and to the nature of the material available.*

The scales were constructed in the following way: Component factors that we thought would include the major dimensions of the given ego function were first worked out. We then proceeded to specify examples of these component factors at the most regressed levels. We thought of patients we had observed who manifested extreme deficit in each of the areas included under the given ego function. Using a combination of clinical experience and developmental guidelines, we dimensionalized seven levels of adequacy for each ego function, with an undefined intermediate stop. For the highest level on the scale, we included relevant behavior that reflects unusually adaptive functioning. At the lower levels, then, the ego function descriptions include many symptom items because symptoms, by definition, centrally involve regression and maladaptive aspects. Scale descriptions at higher levels include more behavior facets and reactions that characterize nonsymptom functioning.† Some important sources of unreliability that we were not able to overcome completely in using a clinical interview came to our attention during the tooling-up phase. We found that conscious attempts to distort information tended to occur when the subject was a hospitalized patient who had assumed that the interviewer would influence his

---

*The interview guide included in Appendix A is a revised version of the one used in the study reported herein. Changes from the original guide to the revised version are attempts to improve the guide based on our experience with it over the course of the study. The two versions bear a substantial resemblance. A copy of the version used in the study may be obtained for a fee from Microfiche Publications. "See NAPS document #02099 for 120 pages of supplementary material. Order from ASIS/NAPS c/o Microfiche Publications, 305 E. 46th St., New York, N. Y. 10017. Remit in advance for each NAPS accession number $1.50 for microfiche or $5.00 for photocopies up to 30 pages, 15¢ for each additional page. Make checks payble to Microfiche Publications."

†The interview scoring manual included in Appendix B is a revised version of the one used in this study. The changes made from the original were what we felt were improvements based on our experience during the study. The major difference between the two versions is that in the revised version entries in the manual are organized separately under the various component factors, while in the earlier version they are not. A copy of the earlier version may be purchased from Microfiche Publications, as above.

being released from the hospital. Even when this source of distortion was not present, aspects of character style can influence the quantity and quality of ratable verbal material. For example, patients with paranoid trends will usually not respond to questions as candidly and fully as other patients. Those who rely heavily on denial will not admit to experiences or behavior that are actually part of their history or experience.

A still more general problem with the interview follows from the fact that the subject's introspective report is the basis for much of the data. A subject may be asked to recount particular historical events. The accuracy of his responses will depend on the adequacy of his memory, the quality of his judgment, the intactness of his reflective awareness, and the degree and kind of perceptual distortion at the time of the events and subsequent apperceptive distortions. The subject is also asked to evaluate a wide range of his behavior and reactions. He may be asked to reflect on his experience (e.g., "Do you ever get confused about where you are or what day it is?"). Or he may be asked to make a judgment about himself in relation to others (e.g., "Do you have any special capacity that makes you different from other people?"). He may be asked whether he has had experiences or manifested behavior whose social desirability is low or negative. Thus, the ability for accurate introspective reporting is central to the validity of the interview data.

After some time, another source of potential unreliability in rating ego functions from the clinical interview emerged. Raters agreed that it was difficult to characterize subjects with respect to adaptiveness of ego functions when only one rating, based solely on functioning at any given point in time, was called for. Some patients were interviewed following an acute break with dramatic symptomatology, but their characteristic functioning was rather good. Others had responded well to hospitalization and treatment, so that at the time they were interviewed, ego functions were rated higher than they would have been a month earlier. These examples underscored the influence of acuteness of psychopathological manifestations on the reliability and validity of ego function ratings. If a subject is suffering an acute psychotic episode, with hallucinations, delusions, disorientation, or panic-level anxiety, an accurate assessment of the lowest level and, of course, his current level of functioning can be made for a number of ego functions. Characteristic level of functioning and highest level of functioning, however, cannot be accurately rated during such an acute episode but can only be estimated by extrapolation from responses to the questions and from the history. After we realized the importance of these considerations, we asked raters to assess highest, lowest, characteristic, and current levels of functioning.

The current level has been found useful in evaluating ego function status over a period of time and in discovering how relatively stable an aspect of personality any given ego function may be. Our study of the effect of Valium on ego functions of patients in psychotherapy, as reported here in the chapter on treatment, uses current-level ratings. Current level of functioning would also be useful in developing behavioral rating scales and in comparing interview data with data obtained from experimental techniques, since the latter deal essentially with current behavior.

Our six interviewers were all psychoanalysts or psychoanalytically oriented psychotherapists. We also trained several graduate-student interviewers. Interviewer training consisted of thorough familiarization with all ego function definitions and all scales in the Rating Manual, so that the interviewer would know what questions in the guide were most relevant to what ego function and just how much information was required to rate a function adequately. Interviewers were asked to listen to taped prototypical interviews. After their first interviews were taped, their technique was evaluated by other interviewers. Feedback enabled the interviewer to improve his technique. Admittedly, the various interviewers differed in skill and motivation, but most of the taped interviews yielded ratable information on all ego functions.

The four interview raters were all interviewers, but their ratings were always from tapes of an interviewer other than themselves. During the tooling phase prior to the study proper, raters independently scored practice protocols, correlations were computed, and discrepancies were discussed.

Raters were supplied with rating forms (See Appendix C) for making their global ratings of each ego function. Space is provided for recording evidence from the tape. As a rater is listening to a recorded tape, he writes down the primary data, and secondary inferences he might make about it, in the space representing the component factor of the particular ego function that he judges best categorizes that primary data. The rating forms provide an opportunity to rate each component factor on characteristic and current levels of functioning, and each ego function, globally, on characteristic, current, highest, and lowest levels. It was discovered that frequency, intensity, pervasiveness, extent, and acuteness-chronicity of any phenomenon being rated cannot be accounted for adequately in any one given rating.

Although the assessment procedure provides for four separate ratings of each component factor, the number of levels actually needed varies with the strategy and aims of the particular research. To arrive at the characteristic-level rating, we must obtain an assessment of the subject's current functioning at the time of the interview (this may or may not represent an acute episode of illness); of the subject's lowest level of functioning (usually an acute episode lasting some time or a series of chronic episode failures in adaptation); and of his highest level of functioning (often highly inferential when we are dealing with hospitalized patients). Since all of these ratings are usually based on one interview, varying degrees of inference from the obtained data are required for the ratings. Thus, we must often estimate the highest level of functioning from what the subject tells us about himself while he may be functioning below his characteristic level.

Once a subject had been selected, an interview was scheduled. Neither the interviewer nor the raters took part in the selection of subjects or interview assignments. Still, a double-blind procedure was not guaranteed, particularly for a subject in the schizophrenic sample. While all subjects were wearing street clothes when they were brought to the interview room, there are numerous ways in which a subject from the schizophrenic sample could have been so recognized by the interviewer, such as if the subject made a remark about conditions on the ward or references to a psychotic episode. This potential source of confounding could not be avoided, although we did conduct a double-blind check study (discussed in the next chapter) to control for hospitalization. The possibility of an interviewer being able to distinguish whether a subject was in the neurotic or in the normal group was less but not impossible. Raters did not see the subjects but also would have a basis to guess the group affiliation of some subjects from material in the taped interview. While acknowledging that we did not have a double-blind procedure for the study proper, we do not believe the obtained results are explainable on this basis, and the check study mentioned above supports this belief.

PSYCHOLOGICAL TESTS

Hundreds of studies aimed at validation of the Rorschach, T.A.T., Bender Gestalt, and Figure Drawing tests have appeared in the psychological literature; scores of reviews of these studies are also available. The problems of validity are complex. Among them are too many inadequate criterion measures against which to evaluate the procedures. At least one study demonstrates a relationship between research bias and outcome, suggesting that investigators with positive attitude toward projective tests more often tend to find positive results than investigators who do not like these procedures (Levy and Orr, 1959). This finding is reminiscent of the tendency of rats in Hull's laboratories to learn by reinforcement, thus "verifying" the reinforcement theory, while rats in Tolmanian laboratories learned according to insight, "verifying" a theory that contradicted Hull's. It is nevertheless true that none of the psychological tests mentioned above can be said to have attained satisfactory reliability and validity as psychometric devices (Zubin, Eron, and Schumer, 1965). We are not attempting to employ these procedures as psychometric devices but rather as a source of data from which to rate ego functions.

To evaluate ego functions from clinical psychological tests, we chose the standard battery, which includes the Bender Visual-Motor Gestalt, Figure Drawing, Wechsler Adult Intelligence Scale, Rorschach, and Thematic Appercep-tion tests. We believed that the responses to these procedures could be scored for adaptive level of ego functioning according to criteria we would develop. While we were constructing a scoring manual to assess the same ego functions for which the interview scoring manual was developed, no attempt was made to gear each of the psychological-test score-level criteria descriptions to those in the interview manual. Rather, criteria for each ego function were spelled out and then roughly dimensionalized in terms of various degrees of adaptiveness-maladaptiveness of those particular indicators. We did not try to produce completely objective rating procedures, nor were the raters instructed to rely totally on the clinical "feel" of the material. Our approach involved reliance on specific criteria modified by more general impressions from the test. Clinical examples drawn from protocols were added to the Manual; negative illustrations were included when positive examples did not appear sufficient. Raters scored each function of the six psychological tests in the battery on a seven-point scale and then came up with an overall rating for each ego function based on all the tests. As a result of this approach, it was possible to determine the contribution of each specific test to the assessment of the different ego functions. We assumed that the various test procedures differed in their contribution to assessing the various ego functions.

Test raters were all Ph.D. psychologists with some postdoctoral experience. None of them was an interviewer or an interview rater. They met at regular intervals to confer about disagreements, first on practice test batteries, and then on the protocols included in the study. At the end of the study, the Scoring Manual was revised to include more and better criteria at each level, based on experience during the study.*

Since most of the schizophrenic subjects came from a hospital where psychological tests were administered as part of the routine hospital workups, we decided to use the available tests, which were administered by preinternship-level graduate students in psychology. Even though the psychological test raters were all Ph.D. psychologists with some postdoctoral experience, some unknown degree of reliability and validity may have been sacrificed in order to conserve project time and money. Subjects in the neurotic and normal samples were tested by graduate students with the same level of experience as those who tested the schizophrenic subjects. Copies of the psychological test protocols were distributed, together with rating forms, to two of four raters. As in the case of the interview procedures, cases to rater pairs were stratified by subject group so that any variance attributable to rater style in relation to patient status would be equalized as much as possible. Raters scored each function on every one of the six psychological tests in the battery and then came up with an overall rating for each ego function based on all the tests. As a result of this approach, it

*Because of space considerations, neither the psychological test manual used in the study nor the revised manual is included in the Appendix. Both can be obtained from Microfiche Publications, as previously mentioned.

would be possible to determine the contribution of each specific test (Rorschach, T.A.T., etc.) to the assessment of the different ego functions. This issue is discussed in the chapter on psychological test results.

EXPERIMENTAL LABORATORY PROCEDURES

The third way in which ego functions were studied was the use of laboratory techniques derived from experimental psychology. In some respects, these are easier to administer than is the usual projective test. They require less sophistication on the part of the test administrator and are generally easier to interpret. Because they are easier to administer, laboratory tests are particularly useful in studying large numbers of subjects. On a more theoretical level, it is important to measure the reliability and validity of clinical findings by the utilization of more objective behavioral measures. The use of laboratory tests and the objective behavior patterns associated with them provides an opportunity to make such measurements. The critical question, of course, concerns the problem of validity. Is it possible to develop laboratory tests that are in fact valid with respect to the assessment of ego functions as defined in this study? A proper laboratory approach to an ego function assessment scheme such as that proposed here requires the use of more than one test. The totality of ego functions to be studied encompasses many different kinds of behavior patterns. Therefore, it was necessary to develop a battery of tests.

It was necessary to establish some kind of face validity, that is, rational correspondence between the ego function and test content, between the test under consideration and the ego function we wished to test with it. For instance, not all laboratory tests or instruments are equally useful in the assessment of reality testing, although it could be argued on theoretical grounds that for any laboratory test some aspects of reality testing are involved in a subject's behavior. Tests were selected, then, which had an apparent, direct, and immediate relevance to the ego function they purported to measure. Among the prime difficulties in selecting appropriate laboratory procedures is their relevance to ego functioning in real-life situations. Ego functions, as understood by the clinician, concern processes occuring over time in a normal ecological environment.

Ease of administration was the second criterion. Here the problem was a practical one. With 11 ego functions to consider and a number of tasks being presented for each of them, it was clear that any single test in the battery could not be too time-consuming or cumbersome.

Availability of equipment and facilities was a final consideration in selecting tests for the battery. Certain tests that might have been quite useful simply could not be performed because we did not have adequate facilities. For example, studies in signal-detection might have been very useful in measuring stimulus-barrier characteristics, but we did not have the necessary tools with which to carry out such studies.

The initial battery is listed below, by ego function.

Ego Function	Procedures
(1) Reality testing	Perky Phenomena Cattell tape-auditory halluci- nations Ames distorted room
(2) Judgment	Level of aspirations Time-estimation tasks Social intelligence test
(3) Sense of reality	Rod and Frame Test Somatic Apperception Test Delayed Auditory Feedback with Draw-A-Person Finger Apposition Test
(4) Regulation and control of drives	Cognitive Inhibition Task Delayed Writing Task
(5) Object relations	Tomkins Faces-Recognition & Response to Affect Embedded Faces Cattell Friends and Acquain- tances Test
(6) Thought processes	Pattern Perception Benjamin Proverbs Object Sorting Test Cattell Test of Psychotic Skidding
(7) ARISE	"What if" questions Object Sorting under Regu- lated and Unregulated Conditions
(8) Defensive functioning	Stroop Color Word with Drive-Related Material Tachistoscopic Presentation of Neutral and Drive- Related Words

Ego Function	Procedures
(9) Stimulus barrier	Reaction Time Study with Interfering Stimuli
(10) Autonomous functioning	Pursuit Rotor with Neutral and Drive-Related Conditions Hurvich Sorting Test
(11) Synthetic-integrative functioning	Mooney Closure Figures Witkin Embedded Figures "Blind" Jig-Saw Puzzle Assembly Cattell Test of Time Estimation

DISCUSSION

Sources of Noncorrelated Variance Between Interview, Psychological Tests, and Laboratory Procedures

The interview was designed to elicit instances of adequate and inadequate ego functioning in the context of particular periods and events in subjects' lives, thus permitting rating the lowest, highest, characteristic, and current levels of functioning. However, only the characteristic level had been rated from the very beginning of the research and is the one that is reported in the analyses of the interview data. Both the psychological- and experimental-test data, on the other hand, are most indicative of current functioning only.

In the laboratory procedures, primarily, a further basis for disagreement grows out of a discrepancy between personally relevant and personally irrelevant sources of "stress." Had a systematic introduction of universal sources of stress (loss, attack, restraint, and threats of these, as pointed out by Levin, 1966) been defined in relation to each ego function or a select number of them, a current measure of the subject's functioning under stress would be available to compare with previous life stresses.

Because of ethical and other considerations, such stresses could not be included in experimental procedures. The method adopted by us involved the presentation of interfering stimuli during the procedures chosen to assess particular ego functions. Such interferences included time pressure, sexual and aggressive stimuli, and ambiguous stimulus conditions.

A further reason for a less than perfect correlation stems from the issue of specific stress vulnerabilities and their relation to the characteristic level of the various ego functions. For example, under the threat of object loss or disruption of an important object relationship (or under threats to self-esteem or under frustration conditions of a specific and limited nature), individual A may function considerably below his characteristic level on regulation and control of drives, affects, and impulses. Individual B, on the other hand, may show a relatively low characteristic level of regulation and control. Virtually all the time, and in response to a very wide variety of mildly stressful stimuli, individual C may characteristically function at approximately the same characteristic level as individual A but with different specific vulnerabilities than A. It is unlikely that our laboratory battery and our interview data will correlate highly on the three hypothetical individuals for regulation and control. Similar examples can be provided relevant to the other ego functions.

CHAPTER 20

Results From the Clinical Interview

This chapter covers five topics. First, consideration is given to interrater reliability and other ways of evaluating agreement among judges in rating ego functions from interview material. Second, some variables related to differences between raters—such as social class, I.Q., and education level—are discussed. Third, ego function scores for schizophrenics, neurotics, and normals are discussed, with special emphasis upon average group scores, variabilities, and extent of overlap. Fourth, interrelationships among ego functions are explored through a preliminary factor analysis, and finally, some specific data on thought processes are discussed.

AGREEMENT AMONG RATERS

Two independent ratings of each interview were obtained by randomly assigning every protocol to two of the four interview raters. Agreement between each pair of raters is summarized by reliability coefficients for all 100 cases (50 schizophrenics, 25 neurotics, and 25 normals). These figures are based upon product-moment correlation coefficients of the two sets of ratings on each subject (Table 20.1.).

For the overall results from all groups, least agreement among raters was obtained on ARISE and stimulus barrier, the two functions we had greatest difficulty in dimensionalizing. Both these functions are easy to rate at their extremes, but for many subjects only a limited amount of relevant interview material was obtained. Interview questions included to elicit information about them were also not optimal. This illustrates the relationship between difficulty in dimensionalizing ego function concepts and reliability in rating them once they have been dimensionalized.

The level of the reliability coefficients in Table 20.1 is raised by the substantial mean differences between the schizophrenic, neurotic, and normal samples and is partly a function of these between-group differences. Table 20.2 presents the reliability coefficients within the schizophrenic, neurotic, and normal groups, as well as the mean reliability coefficient and its standard deviation.

Table 20.1.   Interrater Reliabilities for Ego Function Rating

(100 subjects; 2 judges)

Reality testing	.85	
Judgment	.71	
Sense of reality	.80	
Regulation and control	.73	
Object relations	.83	mean correlation = .77
Thought processes	.80	
ARISE	.68	range: .61—.88
Defensive functioning	.81	
Stimulus barrier	.61	
Autonomous functioning	.88	
Synthetic functioning	.80	

[a]Insufficient data on mastery-competence, the twelfth ego function, were available for inclusion in this analysis.

[b]These product-moment correlations are adjusted for two judges using the Spearman-Brown formula. This formula allows an approximation of the reliability of x number of raters when the reliability of one rater is known. According to Guilford (1954), the same principle applies here as in tests: namely, the greatest gain in reliability results from increasing the number of raters when the initial reliability is low. Also, as the number of raters is increased, the law of diminishing returns sets in rapidly, so that while reliability can be substantially increased by adding the first two or three raters, very little increase in reliability will result beyond a total of five raters.

Intraclass correlations are more accurate than product-moment correlations when ratings from a number of judges are used. Rater agreements were reported in terms of intraclass correlations in our earliest report (Hurvich and Bellak, 1968). In all later reports, based on progressively more cases rated by the same group of raters, product-moment correlations were used because of the greater ease in handling the data this way. On inspection, the means and standard deviations of the various raters looked similar enough to suggest that the product-moment correlations would approximate intraclass correlations.

Table 20.2.   Interrater Reliabilities by Group[a]

Group	N = 50 Schizophrenics	25 Neurotics	25 Normals
Reality testing	.84	.31	.28
Judgment	.40	.63	.58
Sense of reality	.55	.47	.04
Regulation and control	.64	.43	.26
Object relations	.58	.45	.76
Thought processes	.71	.53	.15
ARISE	.70	.11	.08
Defensive functioning	.33	.35	.41
Stimulus barrier	.45	.10	.53
Autonomous functioning	.73	.72	.21

Table 20.2.   (Cont.)

N =	50 Schizophrenics	25 Neurotics	25 Normals
Synthetic functioning	.63	.21	.32
Mean	.60	.39	.33
Range	.33-.84	.10-.72	.04-.58

[a]Spearman-Brown corrected.

Reliability coefficients can be expected to be lower when they are based on ratings from a limited range of the scale. While the mean reliability coefficient for the schizophrenic group is .60, that for the neurotic and normal groups is considerably lower. The latter two groups each consisted of 25 cases, and less of the scale range was used in rating these subjects than was used in rating the schizophrenics. In view of these facts, another method was used to shed light on the degree of agreement obtained in the three groups. This was to calculate the extent of disagreement among raters in scale points. That is, if rater 1 gave a subject a score of 6 on reality testing and rater 2 gave the same subject a score of 5, the degree of disagreement was 1 scale point. Average (mean) disagreements for each ego function for all three groups are presented in Table 20.3.

Table 20.3.   Mean Disagreements Among Raters for Each Ego Function by Group

	Schizophrenics	Neurotics	Normals
Reality testing	1.38	1.83	1.32
Judgment	1.48	1.67	1.54
Sense of reality	1.44	1.21	1.54
Regulation and control	1.22	1.39	1.32
Object relations	1.36	1.54	1.07
Thought processes	1.36	1.46	1.14
ARISE	1.56	1.88	1.39
Defensive functioning	1.13	1.42	1.14
Stimulus barrier	1.64	1.92	1.21
Autonomous functioning	1.47	1.38	1.04
Synthetic functioning	1.51	1.96	1.43
Mean	1.41	1.61	1.29

This analysis of the ratings shows that on no ego function was the average disagreement as much as 2 scale points and that it was less than 1.5 scale points for a majority of the ego functions (22 out of the 33).

When the extent of the agreement and disagreement is figured in percentages by group, the results presented in Table 20.4 are obtained.

Here the percentage agreement and disagreement is close at most levels for the three groups. For all groups combined, there was total agreement between

Table 20.4.   Extent of Disagreement Among Raters by Group (Percentages)

	Extent of Disagreement (in scale points)						
	0	1	2	3	4	5	6
Schizophrenics	24	36	23	11	4	1	1
Cumulative	24	60	83	94	98	99	100
Neurotics	21	30	31	11	5	1	
Cumulative	21	51	82	93	98	99	
Normals	27	39	21	8	4	1	
Cumulative	27	66	87	95	99	100	
Total	24	36	24	10	4	1	
Cumulative	24	60	84	94	98	99	

the two judges on 24 percent of the ratings, 60 percent were within 1 scale point, 84 percent within 2 scale points, and 94 percent within 3. These results reflect a substantial degree of agreement among the raters for all three groups, more than is suggested by the reliability coefficients.

We now turn to a consideration of some factors associated with differences between raters.

Background Factors, Halo Effects, and Response Sets

A rater's assessment of any attribute of a person, including ego functions, can be influenced by such characteristics as the person's social class, educational level, intelligence, and sex. Differences among raters are found in the degree of correlation between the subjects' background factors and their ratings of the subjects (see Table 20.5).

Table 20.5.   Mean Correlations of Background Factors with Interview Ratings by Rater

	N = 59 Rater 1	N = 51 Rater 2	N = 40 Rater 3	N = 48 Rater 4
Hollingshead	-.21	-.18	-.11	-.30
Education	-.21	-.26	-.16	-.35
I.Q.	+.21	+.18	-.05	+.35
Age	-.15	-.19	.12	-.27
Mean (ignoring signs)	.21	.20	.11	.32

Scores given by raters 1 and 2 show a similar average degree of correlation with the background factors. Scores from rater 3 show a considerably lower average correlation (for all four background factors), and scores from rater 4, a considerably higher one (for three of the four). In general, these findings show that there is a slight tendency for the ego function ratings assigned to the subjects to be positively correlated with their social class, education,* and I.Q., and negatively with their age.

Raters also differed in the degree to which their ratings for each subject were differentiated (e.g., for each rater, the closeness with which the score given a particular subject for reality testing matched the score assigned to him for judgment, object relations, etc.). While we expected the adaptive levels of the major ego functions in a given person to be substantially correlated, it is always possible that the degree of relationship found among ego functions is being augmented by halo effects and response sets (see Holt, 1965). An index of the extent to which each rating of a judge is similar to his other ratings of the same subject is obtained by calculating correlation coefficients for each judge's ratings. Average within-judge correlations for the total sample (ignoring sign) are presented in Table 20.6.

Table 20.6.   Average Within-Judge Correlations (Ignoring Sign)

Rater	Within-Rater Correlation
1	.20
2	.47
3	.61
4	.59

Noteworthy here is the substantially lower average intercorrelation of the ratings of rater 1, meaning that in his case any given rating is less similar to, and more differentiated from, his ratings of the other ego functions in the same subject.

Within-Group Rater Reliability

Because the intercorrelation of ratings was high for three of the four interview raters, presumably indicating considerable halo and/or response set, the within-group reliability check was carried out in the following way. Three new raters were trained, and they scored 25 of the schizophrenic cases already judged by rater 1. Two of these new raters (raters 5 and 6) rated a total of 25 cases (15 and 10, respectively), and the third (rater 7) rerated 10 of these 25. Reliability coefficients for these comparisons are presented in Table 20.7.

Focusing first on the 25-case comparison (the third column), the mean reliability coefficient, .64, is lower than the earlier mean correlation of .77 based on the neurotic and normal as well as schizophrenic subjects (see Table 20.1). As was pointed out, the level of these coefficients was increased by the mean differences in ego function scores between the three groups. Lower reliability

*Correlations on the Hollingshead Index and educational level are negative because in Hollingshead's scoring system lower scores are assigned to higher social class and educational levels. A negative sign, therefore, indicates a *positive* relationship between the ratings of adaptiveness of ego functioning, on the one hand, and social class and education level, on the other.

Table 20.7.   Reliability Coefficients on 25 Schizophrenic Cases By 3 Judges

Rater:	1&5	1&6	1 vs. 5&6	1&7	6&7	1 vs. 6&7
N =	15	10	25	10	10	10
Reality testing	.73	.93	.83	.92	.94	.95
Judgment	.43	.72	.54	.82	.65	.81
Sense of reality	−.47	.85	.02	.61	.77	.82
Regulation and control	.87	.40	.73	.44	.53	.56
Object relations	.74	.26	.54	.68	.55	.62
Thought processes	.88	.73	.82	.81	.97	.89
ARISE	.80	.96	.83	.97	.95	.97
Defensive functioning	.61	.77	.67	.71	.44	.84
Stimulus barrier	.81	.47	.65	.80	.63	.73
Autonomous functioning	.68	.87	.77	.67	.89	.88
Synthetic functioning	.68	.53	.67	.33	.53	.57
Mean	.61	.68	.64	.71	.71	.76

coefficients are therefore to be expected here, since this sample includes only schizophrenic subjects.

The negligible correlation between raters 1 versus 5 and 6 for sense of reality is the result of a large negative relationship between ratings on this function by raters 1 and 5. A recheck of the rater's comments about the clinical-interview material suggested that the two judges had different conceptions of this ego function, which influenced their respective interpretations of the rating-manual guidelines. That this result is atypical for the sense of reality ego function is suggested by the relatively high correlations between the other pairs of raters on this function. If we omit the .02 correlation for the moment as being atypical and probably idiosyncratic, the mean correlation for the other 10 scales rises to .70.

From these reliability coefficients, we conclude that raters trained in the use of the rating manual can substantially agree on the adaptive level of the various ego functions even when the subjects are from a relatively restricted group (hospitalized patients who have been diagnosed as schizophrenic).

Of the three newly trained raters, one was a clinical research psychologist (rater 6), and two were graduate students in psychology (raters 5 and 7); the latter two were unfamiliar with ego function constructs. This choice of new raters was partly based on our interest in exploring the relevance of clinical experience and knowledge of ego functions to the rating and training procedures.

In the comparisons between the least experienced and least knowledgeable judge (rater 7) with each of the two most experienced judges (raters 1 and 6), the mean reliability coefficients are the same (.71). They are also comparable to the level of agreement attained by the two most experienced raters with each other (.68). These findings suggest that graduate psychology students can use the ego function rating scales with schizophrenic subjects as well as can more experienced and knowledgeable psychologists.

In order to determine the degree of agreement among judges in ranking the relative levels of ego functioning for a given subject, within-subject reliabilities were computed. Agreements among raters in the analysis reported above underscore the average degree of agreement by two raters on each ego function summed for all ego functions for all subjects in the group. The within-subjects reliabilities to be reported now show how well two raters agree in judging the level of all ego functions within each subject.

For the 25 schizophrenic subjects included in the third column of Table 20.7 (judged by raters 1, 5, and 6), the mean two-rater reliability is .72 (Spearman-Brown corrected). This reflects considerable average agreement among judges in assessment of the subjects' relative strengths and weaknesses in the various ego functions.

Reliability coefficients on individual subjects ranged from .23 to .96. Raters thus varied considerably in their assessments of the relative strengths and weaknesses of the ego functions for a given subject in this sample. One consideration relevant to the degree of agreement here is the range of variation between the ego functions for a given subject. The likelihood of higher reliability coefficients is greater when there is greater variability between functions, and conversely, reliability coefficients will probably be lower when variability between the functions is lower.

Further work in the interrater agreement area is needed. Revisions of both the Rating Manual and the Interview Guide have been carried out (April, 1971) and have been used for ratings of only a few subjects not included in the analyses reported here.

Differences Between Groups

Table 20.8 provides, by group, the mean ego function ratings, the standard deviations, and the significance levels of differences between groups when calculated by analyses of variance. Scores for each ego function in this analysis were based on the mean or average rating of the two judges scoring the particular case protocol.[1] This procedure is intended to increase the validity of the ratings by splitting the difference of the disagreement between the two raters' scores.

The f ratios are all highly significant for the main effects, and all mean differences are in the predicted direction. With regard to the differences between schizophrenics and neurotics and between neurotics and normals, the Duncan Multiple Range Test (Edwards, 1960) showed that all the mean differences between the two pairs of groups were significant beyond the .001 level. Since schizophrenics would generally be expected to show less adaptive functioning

Table 20.8.   Ego Function Mean Scores, Standard Deviations, and Significance of Differences Between Groups Based on Analyses of Variance from Interview Material[a]

Ego Function	Schizophrenic (50)		Neurotic (25)		Normal (25)		F Ratio	P
	Mean	SD	Mean	SD	Mean	SD		
Reality testing	6.76	1.9	8.44	1.6	9.78	1.1	58.	<.0001
Judgment	6.30	1.7	7.44	2.1	9.12	1.7	35.	<.0001
Sense of reality	5.60	1.7	7.00	1.1	9.40	1.2	88.	<.0001
Regulation and control	5.72	1.4	6.68	1.3	8.30	1.3	47.	<.0001
Object relations	5.08	1.5	6.76	1.4	8.76	1.4	71.	<.0001
Thought Processes	6.20	2.0	8.26	1.7	9.78	0.9	41.	<.0001
ARISE	6.16	1.9	7.78	1.3	8.32	1.3	26.	<.0001
Defensive functioning	4.86	1.4	6.94	1.4	8.66	0.9	123.	<.0001
Stimulus barrier	6.70	1.9	7.82	1.5	9.12	1.4	28.	<.0001
Autonomous functioning	5.84	2.0	7.68	1.9	9.32	0.9	73.	<.0001
Synthetic functioning	5.22	1.9	6.84	1.6	9.28	1.3	76.	<.0001
Mean	5.86	1.7	7.42	1.5	9.08	1.2		

[a]Using 100 schizophrenic, neurotic, and normal subjects.

than neurotics and neurotics less than normals, these results add a measure of validity to the ego function rating procedure. That is, the results support the interpretation that the rating scales used in assessing interview material are measuring something related to the adaptive level of ego functioning in these groups of subjects under study.

All ratings in Table 20.8 are based on judgments of the subject's characteristic level of functioning. Mean scores for the schizophrenic subjects ranged from 4.86 to 6.76 (with standard deviations of 1.4 and 1.9); scores for the normal subjects ranged from 8.30 to 8.78 (with standard deviations of 1.3 and 1.1). There is thus room at the lower end of the scale for schizophrenics who function more poorly, and at the upper end of the scale for normals who function better than those we studied. Had we included more chronic and deteriorated cases (such as patients diagnosed as hebephrenic), greater variability within the schizophrenic group would probably have resulted. It is also likely that persons could be found with higher levels of ego functioning than the normals we included in the study.

A graphic illustration of the spread of the three group distributions is presented in Figure 20.1. This includes the mean of each group, with two standard deviations above and below the mean, thus encompassing 95 percent of the cases in all groups. The mean of the standard deviations for the schizophrenics is highest (1.71), that for the neurotics is next highest (1.51), and the mean standard deviation for the normals is lowest (1.21). These mean-standard-deviation differences are statistically significant beyond the .001 level ($f = 12.07$). The differences between the schizophrenic and neurotic groups and between the neurotic and normal groups are each significant beyond the .001 level (Duncan Multiple Range Test). With regard to the scores of schizophrenics compared with neurotics, the largest mean differences are found in defensive functioning (2.08) and thought processes (2.06). In the neurotic-normal comparison, the two largest differences occur in synthetic functioning (2.44) and sense of reality (2.40).

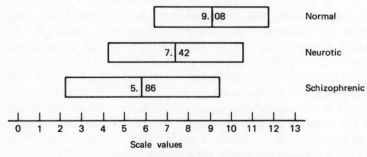

Figure 20.1.   Means, plus and minus two standard deviations.

That the ratings and their intercorrelations were influenced by halo effects and response sets has already been suggested in the section on reliability of ratings. We now turn to various possible sources of bias in the ratings and subject characteristics other than adaptive level of ego functioning that may have influenced the differences found between the groups.

BACKGROUND FACTORS

Such characteristics as education, I.Q., sex, and social class may influence, or be correlated with, the level of the various ego functions. Every attempt was made to select subjects for the schizophrenic, neurotic, and normal groups who were approximately equal on these background factors, but many considerations influenced group composition, a most important one being subject availability. Table 20.9 presents data on the background variables.

Table 20.9.   Mean Scores and Significance Levels of Background Variables by Group

	Schizophrenic	Neurotic	Normal	f Ratio	p Value
Social-class rating[a]	35.3	33.4	33.8	.33	.72
Education[a]	3.08	2.84	2.92	.56	.58
WAIS I.Q.	108.4	118.5	114.6	6.6	.002
Age	30.3	27.4	26.4	2.5	.09

[a]Lower numbers are assigned to higher social class and education (Hollingshead, 1957).

The groups did not differ significantly in social class or education. Age differences approach the 5 percent level of significance, and differences in I.Q. are clearly significant. With regard to age, the schizophrenics are oldest, the neurotics are next, and normals are the youngest. However, the mean difference in age between schizophrenics and normals is almost four years. Although this difference approaches statistical significance, it seems unlikely to us that the differences in ego function scores are attributable to age.

The slightly more than ten-point difference in mean I.Q. scores between neurotics and schizophrenics, which is statistically significant, merits some discussion. A number of studies report that the mean I.Q. of psychotics is lower than that of nonpsychotics (Rabin, 1965). With regard to schizophrenia, a large study of 1000 consecutive admissions to a state mental hospital showed that patients diagnosed as schizophrenic had a mean I.Q. 5.7 points lower than patients with a nonpsychotic diagnosis (Rabin, 1965). To the extent that the lower I.Q. scores of schizophrenics reflect an I.Q. decline related to schizophrenia, it could be argued that levels of ego function may be lowered as the result of similar processes or conditions in the organism.

In the current context, the major issue is whether the differences in ego function level found between the schizophrenics, neurotics, and normals can be shown not to be a function of I.Q. differences between the groups. Through an analysis of covariance, it is possible to test whether the group differences in ego function levels are attributable to the group I.Q. difference. This analysis, based on each subject's mean ego function score and his WAIS I.Q., produced an f value of 85.6 (which is significant beyond the .001 level) and t values of 6.2 between schizophrenics and neurotics and 6.4 between neurotics and normals, (both of which are significant beyond the .01 level). We can, therefore, state with confidence that the I.Q. differences between groups are not responsible for the ego function differences, which remain significantly different when the I.Q. factor is removed.

To assess the influence of sex differences, t tests were calculated to compare the scores of male versus those of female schizophrenic subjects on all ego functions. None of the differences based on the sex of the subject approach statistical significance. This means that there is no evidence that the male and female schizophrenic subjects included in this study differed in the degree of adaptiveness or maladaptiveness in the ego function scores assigned to them by random pairs of male and female raters.

Yet another important difference between the groups is that all subjects in the schizophrenic group were hospitalized, whereas none of the subjects in the neurotic and normal groups were. Hospitalization as such could influence a subject's reactions to the interview, and it could also subtly affect the interviewer's questions and the rater's judgments. Especially with regard to the latter, one could argue that clues to hospitalization — direct or inferable — could influence the rater to assign lower ratings on all ego functions to the hospitalized subjects. This would contaminate the ratings. To control for this possibility, hospitalized schizophrenics were compared with a group of psychiatrically hospitalized nonschizophrenics on all ego function measures. Neither the interviewers nor the raters were informed of this "check study," so that a double-blind approach could be maintained.

Table 20.10 presents the results from comparing ego function ratings for 15 hospitalized schizophrenics with 15 psychiatrically hospitalized nonschizophrenics. The two groups were matched for background variables.

Mean scores for schizophrenics are significantly lower on eight of the ego function categories at the .05 level or beyond, for two-tailed comparisons using the Mann-Whitney U Test. The groups did not differ significantly on the other three: regulation and control of drives, ARISE, and stimulus barrier. These results suggest that the earlier reported differences between schizophrenic, neurotic, and normal subjects cannot be attributed solely, or even primarily, to contamination resulting from possible knowledge of hospitalization.

Table 20.10. Comparison of Hospitalized Schizophrenics with Psychiatrically Hospitalized Nonschizophrenics on Ego Function Ratings From Clinical Interview Material

	Schizophrenic (N=15)	Nonschizophrenic (N=15)	Significant Level (2-tailed)
Reality testing	4.89	7.68	.002
Judgment	5.89	6.79	.05
Sense of reality	5.75	6.92	.05
Regulation and control	5.67	5.66	a
Object relations	5.00	6.46	.02
Thought processes	6.32	7.56	.02
ARISE	6.46	6.82	a
Defensive functioning	4.60	6.31	.002
Stimulus barrier	6.82	6.89	*a*
Autonomous functioning	5.64	7.61	.02
Synthetic functioning	4.79	6.94	.02

[a]Not significant.

INTERRELATIONSHIPS AMONG EGO FUNCTIONS

We will now briefly discuss the relationships among the ego function scales within the schizophrenic, neurotic, and normal groups, which are summarized in Table 20.11.

Table 20.11. Summary of Intercorrelations Among Ego Functions Based on Combined Ratings of Interview Material Within Schizophrenic, Neurotic, and Normal Groups

Group	N	Mean Correlation	Range
Schizophrenic	50	.46	.00-.74
Neurotic	25	.61	.14-.84
Normal	25	.52	.04-.78

This moderate degree of intercorrelation among the ego function scales within each of the three groups suggests the presence of a general characteristic or factor that can be labeled "ego strength." We expected to find a moderate degree of intercorrelation among the ego functions, analogous to that found among the various subscales of the WAIS. It turns out that the average degree of correlation among the ego function scales is close to that for the WAIS subtest scores based on intercorrelation figures among the 10 subscales included in Wechsler's Manual (1954) at three age levels. We determined the means and ranges from these, which are included in Table 20.12.

The difference between ego function and WAIS-subtest correlations is in the range, with the ego function ratings showing by far the greatest.

Table 20.12. Mean Correlations Among WAIS Subtest Scores (calculated from Wechsler, 1954)

	Ages 18-19 (100 males, 100 females)	Ages 25-34 (150 males, 150 females)	Ages 45-54 (150 males, 150 females)
Mean	.56	.53	.57
Range	.39-.61	.30-.81	.42-.85

Correlations between scores for pairs of ego functions by group, based on the combined ratings of two judges, are included in Tables 20.13-15, rank-ordered from highest to lowest.

Table 20.13. Correlation Between Ego Functions[a] Based on Combined Ratings: Schizophrenics

11 × 10 − .74	5 × 3 − .54	10 × 2 − .35
11 × 8 − .72	10 × 3 − .53	11 × 7 − .33
8 × 6 − .66	6 × 2 − .52	5 × 1 − .32
10 × 8 − .65	11 × 1 − .52	9 × 2 − .31
2 × 1 − .63	8 × 3 − .52	9 × 8 − .31
7 × 6 − .62	10 × 7 − .51	9 × 1 − .31
6 × 3 − .60	10 × 1 − .50	11 × 9 − .30
8 × 1 − .60	8 × 7 − .49	7 × 1 − .30
10 × 5 − .60	11 × 6 − .49	9 × 4 − .30
6 × 1 − .59	5 × 4 − .48	11 × 4 − .27
6 × 5 − .59	8 × 2 − .47	6 × 4 − .27
8 × 5 − .58	9 × 6 − .46	4 × 3 − .24
4 × 2 − .57	5 × 2 − .41	4 × 1 − .18
3 × 1 − .55	7 × 5 − .41	8 × 4 − .12
11 × 2 − .55	9 × 5 − .41	7 × 2 − .06
10 × 9 − .54	9 × 3 − .40	10 × 4 − .06
11 × 3 − .54	7 × 3 − .39	7 × 4 − .00
10 × 6 − .54	9 × 7 − .39	

Mean correlation: .46

[a](1) reality testing, (2) judgment, (3) sense of reality, (4) regulation and control, (5) object relations, (6) thought processes, (7) adaptive regression, (8) defensive functioning, (9) stimulus barrier, (10) autonomous functioning, (11) synthetic functioning.

In Table 20.16, the intercorrelations among ego functions are included for the combined ratings for all three groups and for rater 1 for the schizophrenic group.

The intercorrelations for rater 1 are much lower than for the combined data, and these findings are consistent with what was illustrated in Table 20.6. The two mean figures for rater 1 (.20 in Table 20.6 and .23 in Table 20.16) are

Table 20.14. Correlation Between Ego Functions[a] Based on Combined Ratings: Neurotics

2 × 1	− .84	3 × 1	− .62	9 × 6	− .53
11 × 8	− .83	7 × 6	− .61	5 × 4	− .53
8 × 7	− .78	10 × 2	− .61	11 × 9	− .52
8 × 3	− .77	4 × 2	− .61	10 × 3	− .52
11 × 10	− .77	8 × 5	− .61	6 × 2	− .51
11 × 5	− .76	6 × 3	− .60	5 × 2	− .51
10 × 9	− .75	7 × 3	− .58	10 × 7	− .50
11 × 6	− .74	11 × 2	− .57	7 × 2	− .46
10 × 9	− .71	8 × 2	− .57	11 × 4	− .45
11 × 7	− .71	5 × 3	− .56	7 × 4	− .44
8 × 6	− .71	11 × 1	− .56	8 × 4	− .40
9 × 8	− .70	5 × 6	− .55	9 × 5	− .40
11 × 3	− .69	5 × 1	− .55	9 × 3	− .39
10 × 6	− .67	10 × 3	− .55	4 × 3	− .38
6 × 1	− .66	10 × 1	− .55	9 × 2	− .37
7 × 5	− .65	9 × 7	− .54	9 × 1	− .34
7 × 1	− .63	3 × 2	− .53	10 × 4	− .33
8 × 1	− .62	4 × 1	− .53	6 × 4	− .23

Mean correlation: .61

[a]See note to Table 20.13.

Table 20.15. Correlations Between Ego Functions[a] Based on Combined Ratings: Normals

10 × 11	− .78	9 × 11	− .62	1 × 11	− .40
4 × 5	− .77	3 × 8	− .61	8 × 10	− .40
5 × 8	− .74	2 × 4	− .61	1 × 10	− .36
2 × 3	− .73	1 × 2	− .59	4 × 6	− .34
9 × 10	− .70	1 × 9	− .58	4 × 7	− .32
4 × 11	− .69	4 × 10	− .58	6 × 11	− .30
4 × 9	− .68	3 × 11	− .57	2 × 6	− .27
1 × 3	− .68	5 × 11	− .55	6 × 7	− .24
4 × 8	− .67	2 × 11	− .54	7 × 8	− .22
1 × 8	− .66	3 × 9	− .53	7 × 10	− .22
8 × 11	− .66	2 × 8	− .52	7 × 11	− .22
5 × 9	− .65	2 × 9	− .48	3 × 6	− .19
6 × 8	− .65	3 × 10	− .48	5 × 7	− .19
2 × 5	− .64	5 × 10	− .48	6 × 10	− .17
8 × 9	− .64	1 × 4	− .47	3 × 7	− .15
1 × 6	− .62	1 × 5	− .47	7 × 9	− .11
3 × 4	− .62	6 × 9	− .47	1 × 7	− .07
3 × 5	− .62	2 × 10	− .46	2 × 7	− .04
		5 × 6	− .41		

Mean correlation: .52

[a]See note to Table 20.13.

Table 20.16. Mean Correlation of Each Ego Function With All Others (Excluding That Function)

	Schizophrenic (N = 50)		Neurotic (N = 25)	Normal (N = 25)
	Combined Data	Rater 1 Alone		
Reality testing	.45	.24	.66	.44
Judgment	.44	.23	.59	.47
Sense of reality	.49	.22	.61	.47
Regulation and control	.25	.10	.44	.52
Object relations	.49	.23	.60	.50
Thought processes	.53	.29	.69	.33
ARISE	.35	.19	.67	.15
Defensive functioning	.51	.32	.74	.52
Stimulus barrier	.37	.18	.51	.49
Autonomous functioning	.50	.32	.66	.42
Synthetic functioning	.50	.25	.81	.41
Mean	.44	.23	.63	.43
Range	.25-.51	.10-.32	.44-.81	.15-.52

Table 20.17. Factor Analysis of Scores of 50 Schizophrenics

Factor	Factor Label	Factor Loading
I Synthetic functioning		.749
Autonomous functioning	Integrative capacity	.625
Defensive functioning		.431
II Judgment		.709
Sense of reality	Reality orientation	.582
Reality testing		
III Regulation and control	Socialization	.696
Object relations		.575
IV Thought processes	Adaptive thinking	.611
ARISE		.603
V Stimulus barrier	—	.457

different because the earlier table includes ratings from all subjects judged by rater 1, while the latter includes only schizophrenic subjects.

Also noteworthy is the higher degree of intercorrelation among scores for the neurotic subjects as compared with the other two groups.

A more refined indication of the interrelationships among the ego functions is provided by factor analysis. The ratings of the schizophrenic group were selected for factor analysis because it contained 50 subjects (there were only 25 in each of the other two groups) and because the schizophrenic subjects showed the most variability between functions. Rater 1's scores of schizophrenic subjects were chosen for this analysis because they showed the least intercorrelation and, presumably, the least halo and response-set effects. The scores of the 50 schizophrenic subjects on 11 ego functions were submitted to a principal-components factor analysis with varimax rotation. The factors, with their loadings and the labels assigned to them, are presented in Table 20.17.

Factor V is not a common factor but a specific one, and because factors III and IV each include only two scales, their interpretation must be tentative. Indeed a factor analysis based on 11 scores from 50 cases must be interpreted cautiously altogether. Other qualifications of these findings are that the 50 schizophrenic subjects cannot be assumed to constitute a random sample of all persons diagnosed as schizophrenic. One clear indication of this is that none of these subjects had been diagnosed as catatonic or hebephrenic.* Factor analyses of data from other samples of schizophrenic persons are needed to clarify the reliability of the factor groupings found in the current study. Finally, of the number of factors extracted in the present case, five (one of which is a specific rather than a common factor) involve a degree of judgment as to their interpretation.

Since the factor-analytic data were based on the ratings of only one judge, we tested the reliability of the factors obtained by calculating factor scores for each subject (based on the mean score for the scales each factor comprised) and converting these to z scores. The scores produced by raters 5 and 6 were then converted into factor scores (based on the factors obtained from rater 1's scores as described above), and these also were converted to z scores. Product-moment correlations were then calculated for the 25 schizophrenic cases listed in Table 20.7 (see Table 20.18).

Table 20.18.   Product-Moment Correlations for Schizophrenics

Factor	Correlation
I	.73
II	.68
III	.66
IV	.85
V	.68

[a]Spearman-Brown corrected.
*The difficulty of getting ratable verbal information from subjects with these diagnoses was the reason for their exclusion from this study, as previously stated.

These correlations add to the likelihood that the factors obtained are not peculiar to rater 1 for this sample of subjects. We would hope, however, that refinements of the scoring manual would yield still higher correlations.

These factor scores, which have been converted to z scores, can be grouped in various ways. A preliminary sorting is in terms of the degree of variation between them. Taking the group factor scores only (i.e., deleting stimulus barrier), we find 17 cases to have a total range (from highest to lowest) of .41 to .97, 16 cases ranging from .98 to 1.51, and 17 cases ranging from 1.54 to 3.00.

In analyzing some relationships between the factor scores, we removed from the schizophrenic sample those 10 cases that had been diagnosed "borderline" or "possibly schizophrenic." The remaining 40 cases were then cast into three approximately equal groups. Group A includes those 13 schizophrenic cases that showed the least variation between highest and lowest factor scores. The within-subjects differences range from .42 to 1.09. As noted earlier, all factor scores have been transformed into standard (z) scores. We have not included stimulus barrier results in this analysis, because it is not a group factor. Group B includes the next 13 cases in terms of variation by subject between highest and lowest factor scores (from 1.12 to 1.54). The 14 cases with the greatest variation between factor scores by subject (1.63 to 3.0) constitute group C. Mean or average ranks for the factor scores by group are found in Table 20.19. Since a rank of 1 is given to the highest score in each instance, the lowest mean rank will reflect the highest mean score.

Table 20.19.   Mean Within Subject Ranks for Factor Scores by Groups Based on Degree of Within-Subject Variation

	Reality Orientation	Socialization	Adaptive Thinking	Integrative Capacity
Group A (N=13)	1.77	2.85	2.69	2.69
Group B (N=13)	2.46	2.11	2.88	2.54
Group C (N=14)	2.5	2.64	2.36	2.5

For group A, reality orientation has the largest number of highest scores among the factors with a mean rank of 1.77. When the actual obtained scores for reality orientation are compared with the scores of each of the three other factors, reality orientation is found to be higher than each of these to a statistically significant degree ($p < .05$, Wilcoxin Matched-Pairs, Signed-Ranks Test). Thus, for the one-third of the schizophrenic sample under consideration that shows the least variation between highest and lowest scores within subjects, ego functioning in the area of reality orientation is superior to functioning on socialization, adaptive thinking, and integrative capacity.

For group B, socialization has the lowest mean rank and, thus, the highest scores on the average within subjects. The actual mean scores for subjects in group B are all minus, that is, fall below the average for the schizophrenic group as a whole.* For group A, all mean scores were positive, except for socialization. None of the differences between factor scores for group B are statistically significant.

Group C shows adaptive thinking to be the highest on the average with a mean rank of 2.36. All means for the factor scores in this group are plus, that is, above the average for the group as a whole.* Again, none of these differences in group C is statistically significant.

In summary of this section, reality orientation is significantly higher on the average for that one-third of the schizophrenic subjects who show the least variation within subjects between the four factor scores. Socialization is the highest for group B, and adaptive thinking is highest for group C; but the latter two are not large enough to be statistically significant. These results thus suggest that there may be a relationship between the degree of within-subject variation between ego function factors and the relative adequacy of particular ego function factors. This must be verified by replication with larger samples and with groups of subjects in which the preponderance and kind of schizophrenic subtype is different from those in the present study.

For the group of 10 "borderline" and "possibly schizophrenic" cases that were deleted from the above analysis, adaptive thinking is found to be the highest factor score on the average, with a mean rank of 2.0. Socialization is the next highest (mean rank of 2.6), while both reality orientation and integrative capacity receive mean ranks of 2.7. Factor-score differences between adaptive thinking and reality orientation are the largest, but this difference does not reach statistical significance.

We turn now to a consideration of some relationships between groups A, B, and C (as defined above) and diagnosis. The subtypes of schizophrenia for the 40 subjects are found in Table 20.20.

Table 20.20.   Subtypes of Schizophrenia in 40 Subjects

Type	Group A	Group B	Group C
Schizophrenic reaction-paranoid	4	7	7
Schizophrenic reaction-undifferentiated	6	2	2
Schizophrenic reaction-unspecified	2	3	4
Schizoaffective psychosis	1	1	—
Incipient schizophrenic	—	—	1

If the cases in the "unspecified" category are combined with those in the "undifferentiated" group, and the schizoaffective and incipient are deleted, we

*That average had been based on these 40 cases plus the 10 we have removed for the present analyses.

have a comparison between subjects diagnosed paranoid schizophrenic versus a group that roughly approximates undifferentiated and mixed, that is where (for the latter) the clinical psychiatric evaluation suggested none of the classical subgroupings of schizophrenia. A chi-square test of the distribution of frequencies for the paranoid-undifferentiated comparison across groups A, B, and C is just short of the .10 level of probability. This finding is not considered statistically significant but suggests a trend. Because the sample is small and the range of diagnoses within the schizophrenic syndrome is limited, this analysis is only illustrative. With a larger and broader sample of schizophrenic subjects, it will be possible to assess the extent to which the various clinically diagnosed subtypes of schizophrenics show particular relationships among various ego functions and groups of ego functions.

Another way to compare factor scores is to limit consideration to those scores that are as high as +1.0 and higher, and as low as -1.0 and lower. With these criteria for inclusion, the four factors for the 40 subjects from the schizophrenic sample distribute as shown in Table 20.21.

Table 20.21.   Distribution of Four Factors in Schizophrenic Sample

	Number of Cases 1.0 and Above	Number of Cases -1.0 and Below	Total
Reality orientation	9	9	18
Socialization	0	0	0
Adaptive thinking	5	9	14
Integrative capacity	7	6	13
Total	21	24	45

In Table 20.21 reality orientation is shown to have the largest number of extreme positive and negative standardized factor scores. Socialization is found to include no scores as high as 1.0 or as low as -1.0. This means that for the cases under consideration the socialization factor shows less discrimination between and among subjects than do the other factors. Said another way, subjects in the schizophrenic sample varied most between each other on reality orientation, least on socialization.

In terms of high and low scores, reality orientation shows an equal number of high and low values. The same is true for socialization. Integrative capacity is almost even (7 above, 6 below), while adaptive thinking shows a preponderance of lower scores over higher ones. The latter result is consistent with what we reported on adaptive thinking separately.

If we look at pairs of factor scores, reality orientation and integrative capacity together have a total of 16 scores above 1.0 (9 for the former and 7 for the latter). It is thus possible for these 16 scores to include a maximum of 8 pairs of scores for the same subjects on these two factors. As it turns out, 6 of the 16 scores above 1.0 for the two factors come from the same subjects and, thus, 3 pairs out of 8 or 35 percent. For these same two ego function factors, there are 7 possible pairs for the -1.0 group, and 3 pairs are again from the same subjects, or about 42 percent. For reality orientation and adaptive thinking, there is 1 common pair above out of a possible 7 or 14 percent and 4 pairs below out of 9, which is 44 percent. Adaptive thinking and integrative capacity show 4 out of 6 common pairs above (67 percent) and 3 out of 7 below (42 percent).

There is thus a variable tendency for high and low scores on one factor to be associated with high and low scores on another factor for individual subjects. A systematic analysis of these relationships, as well as other approaches to profile and pattern analysis, should suggest additional hypotheses about the interrelationships among ego functions within and between subgroups of schizophrenics, other patient groups, and nonpatient groups. All the data reported here were based on the characteristic level of functioning, as this is assessed by our procedures. The inclusion of data on highest, lowest, and current levels of ego functioning, in addition to characteristic level, will allow more differentiation in the assessment of ego function interrelationships.

SOME SPECIFIC DATA ON THOUGHT PROCESSES

Thought processes and their disturbances have played a central role in the concept of schizophrenia ever since Bleuler. Following Bleuler, many have held thought disturbances to be pathognomonic of schizophrenia, while only a few others dissented (see chapter on thought processes). We therefore felt it particularly interesting to study thought processes in our sample.

As described in detail in the Appendices, our scale of thought processes includes the following three component factors: (1) degree of adequacy of memory, concept formation, attention, and concentration; (2) the ability to conceptualize and the extent to which abstract and concrete modes of thinking are appropriate to the situation; and (3) the extent to which language and communication reflect primary or secondary-process thinking. Since subjects were judged on the degree of adequacy and adaptiveness of these, their score on thought processes provides an indication of the extent of thought disturbance. Because we rated 10 ego functions in addition to thought functioning, it is also possible to compare the degree of disturbance in thought with the degree of disturbance in other major ego functions. We hasten to point out, as we did earlier, that since our scales are ordinal rather than equal interval, the equivalence of differences between parallel scale points across functions can only be approximate.

For the schizophrenic group of 50 cases, the mean of thought is fourth highest out of 11 ego functions. When the 10 cases diagnosed as borderline or questionable are deleted, the 40 remaining cases show the following: for the combined ratings (i.e., the mean score from the two independent ratings on each case), thought functioning is higher than the mean of the other 10 ego functions 21 times and lower than the mean of all others 10 times. When the scores for all 11 ego functions are looked at subject by subject, thought is the highest score of all functions for 3 subjects, the lowest score of all functions for 7 subjects, and neither the highest nor the lowest for the remaining 30 subjects. These results thus do not show the degree of disturbance in thought functioning to be markedly lower than the extent of disturbance in other ego functions. Rather, for some subjects diagnosed as schizophrenic, thought functioning is lowest; for a lesser number of subjects it is the highest score; and for most subjects in the schizophrenic group, it falls neither highest nor lowest. (See Table 20.22.)

Factor-score results are quite similar. For the same 40 subjects, adaptive thinking is highest 9 times, lowest 13 times, and falls between 18 times in comparison with the other three group factors (reality orientation, socialization, and integrative capacity). When the four factor scores are ranked for each of the 40 schizophrenic subjects, the mean rank of adaptive thinking (2.41) is almost identical with the mean rank for the other three group factors combined (2.48).

An interesting contrast occurs for the 10 borderline and questionable schizophrenic cases. For the factor scores, adaptive thinking is highest six times, second highest twice, and lowest twice. The average rank is 1.8 for thought functioning, while that for the mean of the other three factors together is 2.73. Thus, for the borderline and questionable schizophrenics, adaptive thinking is the most intact ego function factor. But for the 40 subjects most confidently diagnosed as schizophrenic, thought functioning is not predominantly the most disturbed function, although for some subjects it is, while for others it is the least disturbed.

These findings must, or course, be qualified by the reliability and validity considerations already discussed and by the fact that the diagnosis of schizophrenia is heavily influenced by the examiner's notion of what schizophrenia is or involves. Any systematic bias with regard to thought processes and schizophrenia in the group of psychiatrists (two or more of whom had made the diagnosis independently), which was unrelated to the project, is extremely unlikely. Even when all reasonable qualifications are taken into account, the obtained results are more consistent with the idea that individuals diagnosed schizophrenic can show a variety of serious ego function disturbances than with the classical conception that a serious disturbance of thought processes is the hallmark of schizophrenia.

SUMMARY

Interrater reliabilities in judging ego functions from interview material were calculated in several ways. They show that judges agree on the average within

Table 20.22.   Scores on Thought Functioning Compared with the Mean of 10 Other Ego Functions Based on Mean of Combined Scores of Rater Pairs on 40 Schizophrenic Subjects

Thought Functioning	Mean of Other Ego Functions
9	7.8
3	4.6
5	5.5
5	4.8
6	4.9
7	6.8
10	6.0
4	5.4
4.5	4.8
4	4.7
3.5	4.8
5	5.6
6.5	5.4
4.5	5.4
5	6.0
9	6.6
6.5	5.1
5.5	5.8
6.5	5.3
5	5.6
3.5	4.2
8.5	6.9
5.5	5.0
7.5	4.9
3	3,9
8	7.2
6.5	5.6
6	6.6
3	2.9
9	7.0
7	5.8
4.5	4.6
6	5.0
7	6.3
9.5	6.9
6.5	6.6
5.5	7.4
8.5	6.4
5	5.4
6.25	6.3
Total 240.75	225.80
Mean 6.02	5.64

approximately 1.5 scale points considering all ego functions and all groups. There is a mild tendency for ego function ratings to be correlated with the subject's social class, education, I.Q., and age, and the four judges' ratings show different degrees of relationship with these background variables. Raters also differed in the degee of intercorrelation of their ratings. With comparable training on the Ego Function Rating Manual, graduate psychology students can attain a degree of agreement comparable to that of more experienced and knowledgeable psychologists.

Differences in ego function scores for 50 schizophrenics, 25 neurotics, and 25 normal subjects are in the predicted directions and are statistically significant for all 11 ego functions rated. These differences are not attributable to any of the background factors nor to the possible contaminative effects of the fact that all subjects in the schizophrenic group were hospitalized and all subjects in the other two groups were nonhospitalized.

In a principal-components factor analysis with varimax rotation of ratings from schizophrenic subjects, four common factors were tentatively identified: they were labeled reality orientation, socialization, adaptive thinking, and integrative capacity.

We have summarized some relationships between the factor scores and presented some data on thought processes in relation to the other ego functions.

NOTE

1. As was stated on p. 292, 7 levels were spelled out for every ego function, and, in addition, an undefined intermediate score was included between each of the defined levels. This gave raters a total of 13 possible scores. For statistical analyses, we therefore converted the obtained ratings to a 13-point scale (by multiplying each score by two and then subtracting one).

CHAPTER 21

Psychological Test Results

AGREEMENT AMONG RATERS

The degree of agreement among raters as reflected in reliability coefficients for 85 cases (35 schizophrenics, 25 neurotics, and 25 normals) is found in Table 21.1.

Table 21.1   Interrater Reliability for Ego Function Ratings of Psychological Tests
(N = 85; for two judges[a])

Function	Correlation		
Reality testing	.68		
Judgment	.71		
Sense of reality	.68		
Regulation and control	.57	Mean correlation:	.65
Object relations	.68		
ARISE	.73	Range:	.54 = .73
Defensive functioning	.54		
Stimulus barrier	.68		
Autonomous functioning	.64		
Synthetic functioning	.60		

[a] Spearman-Brown corrected.

The mean correlation of .65 is somewhat lower than the correlation found for the interview ratings (.77). Greatest agreement is obtained on ARISE, a function more readily measured by psychological tests than by clinical interviews. The test battery probably affords a better opportunity to evaluate creative functioning than does the interview, because it is more task-oriented, whereas in the interview we had to rely either on the subject's own judgment of his creativity or on quite limited task responses (e.g., response to "Describe one of the most creative ideas you've ever had").

Reliability coefficients for psychological-test ratings by group are found in Table 21.2.

As expected, these values are lower than those derived from all three groups combined, since the range of scores for each group is less than the range for all

Table 21.2.   Interrater Reliabilities for Psychological Tests by Group[a]

	Schizophrenics (N = 35)	Neurotics (N = 25)	Normals (N = 25)
Reality testing	.47	.69	.44
Judgment	.57	.58	.59
Sense of reality	.28	.49	.71
Regulation and control	.04	.77	.36
Object relations	.15	.71	.63
Thought processes	.47	.66	.38
ARISE	.56	.57	.36
Defensive functioning	.02	.45	.52
Stimulus barrier	.51	.56	.37
Autonomous functioning	.29	.57	.35
Synthetic functioning	.35	.59	.37
Mean	.34	.59	.49
Range	.02-.57	.45-.77	.35-.71

[a] Spearman-Brown corrected.

three. Agreement is lowest on ratings for the schizophrenic subjects, whereas for the interview ratings, agreement on schizophrenics was highest. The negligible agreement on regulation and control and on defensive functioning considerably lowered the mean reliability for the schizophrenics.

Scale-point discrepancies between pairs of raters are presented in Table 21.3.

Table 21.3   Mean Disagreement (Plus or Minus) Among Raters for Each Ego Function Group

	Schizophrenics (N = 35)	Neurotics (N = 25)	Normals (N = 25)
Reality testing	1.50	1.17	1.75
Judgment	1.42	1.56	1.50
Sense of reality	1.77	1.33	1.24
Regulation and control	1.96	1.22	1.40
Object relations	1.69	1.17	1.05
Thought processes	2.08	1.94	1.85
ARISE	1.85	1.39	1.60
Defensive functioning	2.23	1.50	1.50
Stimulus barrier	1.67	1.33	1.15
Autonomous functioning	2.08	1.62	1.55
Synthetic functioning	2.00	1.67	1.55
Mean	1.84	1.45	1.47
Range	1.42-2.23	1.17-1.94	1.05-1.85

Table 21.3 shows that on the average, raters agreed with each other within plus or minus 1-2 scale points for all ego functions, across all groups. The average degree of disagreement was 1.5 or less in close to half of the ego functions across the three groups (15 out of 33) and was 2 scale points or more for 4 of the 33 values, all of the latter occurring in the ratings for subjects in the schizophrenic group.

The extent of disagreement among raters for all groups in percentages is presented in Table 21.4.

Table 21.4.   Extent of Disagreement Among Raters by Group by Percent

	Scale Points of Disagreement						
	0	1	2	3	4	5	6
Schizophrenics	16	29	25	16	11	2	1
Cumulative	16	45	70	86	97	99	100
Neurotics	23	34	30	6	4	2	1
Cumulative	23	57	87	93	97	99	100
Normals	18	33	33	13	2	1	
Cumulative	18	51	84	97	99	100	
Mean	19	32	29	12	5	2	1
Cumulative	19	51	80	92	97	99	100

Thus, for all groups combined, perfect agreement was reached on approximately one-fifth of the cases (19%), agreement within one scale point (plus or minus) on half the cases (51%), and agreement within three scale stops on 92% of the cases. As indicated in previous tables, raters agree less about the schizophrenic subjects than about the other two groups.

Compared with the interview ratings, the psychological test ratings are less reliable in each of the above ways of assessing degree of agreement. A comparison of, and contrast between, the two ways of assessing ego functions show several things. Interview questions were constructed to elicit information relevant to each ego function under investigation. The interview was not a standard one (for level of psychopathology, family history, symptom review, etc.) but rather a special one. For the psychological test assessments, however, the standard battery was used, with responses cued to the scoring manual. The test stimuli were therefore not as specific to the various ego functions as were the interview questions. The task of writing a scoring manual was therefore more complex, and the probability of independent raters reaching agreement was less. Rater agreement was also decreased by the difficulty of assigning the correct weight to a pathological indicator when a number of other responses relevant to the same ego function showed considerable adaptive adequacy. A more detailed manual, based on responses to test stimuli included specifically to elicit material relevant to each of the various ego functions, would probably yield greater agreement among raters.

In addition, the data were gathered by second-year graduate students in routine clinical work-ups; data gathered by more experienced psychologists who expected the data to be used for scoring ego functions might have been better. Finally, test raters did not have the opportunity to hear the data-gathering session on tape (as had the interview raters) and received no information other than the test responses. Comments, reactions, and behavior of the subjects in relation to the test responses themselves were not reliably available to the raters from the protocol. For these reasons, we believe that the likelihood of obtaining agreement about adaptive levels of ego functioning was less for psychological tests than for interview material.

In this regard, it is interesting to note that Prelinger, Zimet, Schafer, and Levin (1964) found higher reliabilities for their psychological test ratings than for their interview ratings. They believed that was because they had conceptualized psychological testing in greater detail than the interview approach. In addition to the other considerations just enumerated, the greater reliability of the interview material in our study is the result, we believe, of our focus and the greater amount of time we spent on interview material. We do not believe that our study demonstrates that ego functions are necessarily more reliably rated by interview than by psychological tests. With equal attention to the development of scales for both, it is probable that some functions would be more reliably and validly rated by interview and others more reliably rated by psychological tests.

We next present average correlations between background factors and psychological test ratings.

BACKGROUND FACTORS, HALO EFFECTS, AND RESPONSE SETS

In Table 21.5 the mean correlation for the three raters with the background variables ranges from .20 to .27 and is thus rather similar. Raters do vary quite a bit, however, in the relative degree of correlation from background factor to background factor, and we do not find the consistently high or low correlations across background factors that we found for the interview raters.

Table 21.5. Mean Correlation of Background Factors with Psychological Test Ratings by Rater

	Rater 1	Rater 2	Rater 3
Hollingshead	−.21	−.30	−.25
Education	−.26	−.05	−.15
I.Q.	.47	.28	.39
Age	−.15	.19	−.18
Mean (ignoring sign)	.27	.20	.22

328   The Research Project

For the background variables, correlations with I.Q. scores are the highest. Since the psychological test raters used the I.Q.-test responses directly, they were more specifically aware of this dimension than were the interview raters and were therefore probably more influenced by I.Q. level.

As for halo effects, psychological test raters reported a tendency to see the test data as reflecting a general level of adaptive adequacy. Since the same tests were providing the basis for ratings of all ego functions, it was difficult to keep the ratings independent of one another, and substantial halo effects resulted. Test stimuli designed to elicit information more specific to each ego function, with a rating manual based on these stimuli, would tend to decrease such halo effects.

Response sets also were present in the form of how ego function deficits manifest themselves on psychological tests. A major difference between raters in the current study was in the tendency to rely on content versus a tendency to base judgments on formal aspects of responses. As Schafer has pointed out (1954), both content and form should be used in interpreting psychological tests.

DIFFERENCES BETWEEN GROUPS[1]

A comparison of mean ego function ratings, standard deviations, and significance levels for group differences based on analyses of variance is presented in Table

Table 21.6.   Ego Function Mean Scores, Standard Deviations, and Significance of Differences Between Groups, Based on Analyses of Variance from Psychological Test Material

Ego Function	Schizophrenics (N = 35)		Neurotics (N = 25)		Normals (N = 25)		f	p
	Mean	S.D.	Mean	S.D.	Mean	S.D.		
Reality testing	6.13	1.36	7.86	1.57	8.04	1.25	15.93	0.001
Judgment	6.23	1.39	7.80	1.53	8.26	1.30	16.07	0.001
Sense of reality	5.00	1.10	6.70	1.19	7.10	1.23	23.27	0.001
Regulation and control	5.86	1.22	6.98	1.54	7.26	1.07	12.05	0.001
Object relations	4.97	.96	6.40	1.27	6.76	1.07	20.83	0.001
Thought processes	5.79	1.38	7.62	1.68	7.88	1.23	16.51	0.001
ARISE	5.40	1.10	7.28	1.44	7.28	1.01	23.22	0.001
Defensive functioning	5.27	1.10	6.80	1.65	7.26	1.09	21.62	0.001
Stimulus barrier	5.50	1.21	6.88	1.37	7.30	1.13	15.27	0.001
Autonomous functioning	5.51	1.20	7.32	1.49	7.76	1.09	25.77	0.001
Synthetic functioning	5.89	1.39	7.62	1.52	7.74	1.22	16.95	0.001
Mean	5.60	1.22	7.21	1.48	7.51	1.15		

1. As was true for the inverview ratings, the psychological test ratings were based on 7 defined scale points and 6 intermediate undefined points. For statistical purposes these were converted to a 13 full-point scale by multiplying obtained ratings by two and then subtracting one.

21.6. These ego function scores are based on the average of two independent ratings.

All differences are in the predicted direction (except for one tie between neurotics and normals on ARISE), and all the main effects of the analyses of variance are statistically highly significant. In the two-group comparisons, the mean of the schizophrenics for all ego functions together is significantly lower than the mean of the neurotics (<.05, Duncan Multiple Range Test), while the mean of the neurotics is not significantly lower than the mean of normals.

With regard to individual ego function comparisons, all differences between schizophrenics and neurotics are significant beyond the .01 level, but none of the differences between neurotics and normals is significant. Psychological test raters were thus able to differentiate between schizophrenic and neurotic subjects but not between neurotics and normals. All three groups scored consistently high on judgment and reality testing and consistently low on object relations.

INDIVIDUAL TESTS

As mentioned earlier, psychological test judges rated scores for each test in the battery (Rorschach, WAIS, etc.) before making an overall rating for each ego function on the basis of all the psychological test material. It was expected that a given subject's rating on reality testing might be different when based on the Bender Gestalt from the rating based on the WAIS or the Rorschach, etc. Each test procedure presents different stimuli and different requirements, and the responses to each test differ in their degree of relevance to the various ego functions. Each rater had been instructed to arrive at the overall rating for each ego function by weighting the material from the individual tests globally, in whatever way he thought would give the most valid rating for the given ego function.

It may then be asked which test results were most relied upon in reaching the overall rating for each ego function. Some indications may be found by correlating the rater's overall score for the 11 ego functions with his score from each of the five psychological test procedures. This was done for three of the four original psychological test raters. We omitted the fourth rater and his replacement from this analysis because each had rated only half as many cases as the other three raters. Correlations for each of the three raters are found in Table 21.5. Since the statistical significance of the difference between any pair of correlations has not been calculated, these findings are to be viewed as illustrative.

For rater 1, correlations between overall score and T.A.T. were highest for 6 out of 11 functions; overall score and WAIS, for 3 out of 11; and overall score and Figure Drawings, for 2 out of 11. The Rorschach did not correlate most highly with overall score for any ego functions.

Table 21.7. Correlation of Raters' Overall Scores for 11 Ego Functions with Scales from Psychological Tests

	T.A.T.	Rorschach	WAIS	Fig.	Bender	Av.
Rater 1:						
Reality testing	.90	.77	.78	—	.72	3.17 .79
Judgment	.86	.85	.88	.78	.73	4.10 .82
Sense of reality	.88	.80	.79	.76	.70	3.93 .78
Regulation and control	.76	.70	.77	.63	.56	3.42 .68
Object relations	.83	.80	.68	.86	.63	3.8 .76
Thought processes	.89	.78	.84	.92	.76	4.19 .8.4
ARISE	.81	.78	.61	.66	—	2.86 .72
Defensive functioning	.77	.76	.60	.56	—	2.69 .67
Stimulus barrier	.87	.84	.82	—	—	2.53 .84
Autonomous functioning	.78	.69	.79	.64	.72	3.62 .72
Synthetic functioning	.84	.70	.75	—	.72	3.01 .75
Rater 2:						
Reality testing	.86	.89	.67	—	.56	2.98 .74
Judgment	.85	.91	.46	.61	.63	3.46 .69
Sense of reality	.89	.88	.66	.65	.66	3.74 .75
Regulation and control	.80	.83	.76	.47	.74	3.60 .72
Object relations	.92	.87	.77	.75	.50	3.81
Thought processes	.84	.93	.73	.80	.64	3.94
ARISE	.88	.86	.62	.63	—	2.99
Defensive functioning	.92	.94	.75	.61	—	3.22
Stimulus barrier	.79	.83	.82	—	—	2.44
Autonomous functioning	.90	.93	.75	.55	.68	3.81
Synthetic functioning	.83	.83	.65	—	.58	2.89
Rater 3:						
Reality testing	.76	.75	.72	.29	.05	2.57
Judgment	.77	.71	.80	.63	−.15	3.06
Sense of reality	.91	.84	.67	.77	−.10	3.29
Regulation and control	.81	.49	.60	.69	.03	2.60
Object relations	.91	.71	.79	.65	.84	3.9

Table 21.7. (Continued)

	T.A.T.	Rorschach	WAIS	Fig.	Bender	Av.
Thought processes	.75	.71	.81	.53	.33	3.13
ARISE	.82	.67	.66	.79	–	2.94
Defensive functioning	.75	.71	.66	.67	–	2.79
Stimulus barrier	.85	.65	.75	–	–	2.25
Autonomous functioning	.82	.80	.82	.67	.71	3.82
Synthetic functioning	.86	.79	.71	.44	.58	3.38

For rater 2, T.A.T. and overall score correlated the highest 8 out of 11 times; WAIS and overall score correlated highest twice; and there was one tie between the two.

Summing across judges, the correlation between the T.A.T. rating and the overall rating for the same ego function for all subjects seen by the rater was highest in 17 out of a possible 33 comparisons, or about half of the time. The Rorschach was highest 7 times, WAIS 5 times, and Figure Drawings twice. These findings suggest individual differences in the weighting of test materials for rating ego functions. Some workers will probably be surprised to see that the T.A.T. rating correlated the highest with overall rating more than twice as often as did the Rorschach rating.*

The revised Psychological Test Manual was constructed so as to include more scoring criteria at each level. Also, ratings were set up so that each ego function is scored in terms of frequency or the relative amount of time the subject could be expected to operate at a given adaptive level. For example, a subject can be rated for unusually good functioning (score value 13) on rare occasions (1-15 percent of the time); nondisturbed functioning (score value 11), every now and then; moderately disturbed behavior (score value 6), a substantial segment of the time (30-50 percent); and severely disturbed behavior (score value 4), most of the time. It was not possible within the time available for completing the current study to assess adequately the reliability and validity of this revision (worked out by Lloyd Silverman, Ph.D.).

*These raters had no prior relationships to—nor did they include—the senior author, who has worked primarily with the T.A.T. Nor were they selected with any knowledge of, or regard for, their own preferences for particular test procedures.
†The interview scoring manual included in Appendix B is a revised version of the one used in this study. The changes made from the original were what we felt were improvements based on our experience during the study. The major difference between the two versions is that in the revised version entries in the manual are organized separately under the various component factors, while in the earlier version they are not. A copy of the earlier version may be purchased from Microfiche Publications, as above.

Part 4

CLINICAL APPLICATION OF EGO FUNCTION PROFILES

CHAPTER 22

Diagnosis

A diagnostic concept is an heuristic hypothesis. It involves propositions concerning the etiology, treatment, and prognosis of the disease or syndrome under consideration. In that sense, the diagnostic hypothesis must be measured by the traditional scientific criteria of validity and reliability. In the broadest sense, the usefulness of a diagnostic hypothesis is indicated by its ability to help one understand, predict, and control: to understand means to see the particular set of conditions involved in the diagnosis in the matrix of a sequence of causal events. "Prediction" in the clinical sense means prognosis—long-range and short-range prognosis—if the statements are really to be useful. "Control" in a medical setting means therapeutic control, changing the sequence of events by clearly formulated steps of intervention.

Regrettably, clinicians are usually not explicitly aware of all the propositions involved in their work. The series of diagnostic procedures a clinician employs in the attempt to arrive at a diagnosis are informal attempts to insure the validity and coherence of the diagnostic hypothesis. In that sense, his initial diagnosis is a hypothesis of lower validity than his final diagnosis. In clinical medicine and surgery, the pathologist of a given hospital is often a much dreaded figure as the final judge of the validity of the diagnostic hypothesis. Psychiatric concepts have had a measure of difficulty because of the absence of that particular checking device.

An important aspect of the usefulness of a concept in a hypothesis is also the range of its applicability, the width of phenomena it encompasses. While much is to be said for the idiographic approach, for the progress of science, nomothetic statements, permitting a broad level of generalization, are necessary. This does not imply abdication to the computer: every nomothetic diagnosis has room for a specific, personalized idiographic statement, as we propose to show for the concept of schizophrenia.

The concept of schizophrenia has had some problems concerning validity and reliability. Diagnostic fashions vary from country to country, from state to state, from hospital to hospital, and from clinician to clinician. One might call this problem of diagnosis one of interrater reliability. Another problem, as Aaron Beck (1962) points out, is what one might call temporal reliability; that is, once several "judges" agree that a patient is to be considered schizophrenic, what are the chances that he will remain usefully described as schizophrenic, rather than as manic-depressive, sociopathic, neurotic, or normal? We shall return to both these problems, but we believe that they are more closely related to artifacts and misconceptions than to an intrinsic lack of validity of the concept.

Cancro and Pruyser (1969) have traced the history of the concept. Also, Karl Menninger, in *The Vital Balance* (1963), has eruditely discussed the history and fate of psychiatric nosology in general and of schizophrenia in particular. He points out that the diagnostic disease concept leads to a proliferation of diagnostic terms and eventual fragmentation. He seems to suggest a unitary disease concept but makes quite clear that he does not mean to discard terminology or syndrome applications, including the schizophrenic syndrome.

What he militates against, apparently, is a reification of a disease concept, "schizophrenia" or saying "a patient with a schizophrenia." Such a position is not only easy to agree with but is the only one that seems to make sense. Whether one refers to a patient as "being schizophrenic," however, is merely a semantic nicety to which one might or might not be able to pay consistent attention in the usual clinical shorthand. The important proof of one's broad conception lies in its implications for therapy and prognosis.

In the age of field theory and, specifically, Selye's stress and field theory, there is hardly any place anywhere in medicine for a reified concept, be it of kidney dysfunction or schizophrenia. The psychodynamic basis for our thinking, which must be part of the biosociopsychic dynamics, is the only one that makes sense. It permits us to see an interplay of forces on a continuum. It permits us to see a person suffering from the schizophrenic syndrome as possibly moving to a neurotic or depressed one. Bellak formulated these thoughts graphically as a diagnostic continuum with mobility in both directions (1958).

To what extent any dynamic constellation may become a structural one is a problem to return to later in this chapter. It relates, however, to a difference in viewpoint often raised. There are those who feel that there is only a quantitative difference between neurotic and schizophrenic syndromes and those who feel there are qualitative ones, that schizophrenics are "different." A continuum of ego functions obviously is one of quantitative difference, but there need not be any quarrel about it. From Hegel's concept of *"Umschlag von Quantität zu Qualität"* to Gestalt psychology and the processes in chemistry, it is quite clear that quantitative changes may result in newly emergent qualitative ones. Frequently, a quantitative change in the opposite direction may again reverse the qualitative changes.

With this understanding of diagnosis, one can reaffirm a belief in the usefulness of the concept of the schizophrenic syndrome. It is valid and useful both clinically and for research if one defines it appropriately. For over two decades, Bellak has spoken of the schizophrenic syndrome as the final common path of a number of etiologic and pathogenic factors. These are sometimes effective alone but most often, probably, in combination and are primarily genogenic, chemogenic, psychogenic, and neurogenic factors. This theory has been called the multiple-factor, psychosomatic, egopsychological theory, because of the belief that psychic and somatic factors play a role and that they all lead to a severe impairment of ego functions. For the sake of convenience, one can speak of the sum total of ego functions as "ego strength" with about as much, or as little, justification as one can subsume Wechsler's 11 subcategories on the WAIS under intelligence. There is as much need to pay heed to the pattern of subscores on ratings of ego functions as on intelligence tests. Schizophrenia is seen then as a *range* at one end of a continuum of ego strength, falling somewhere within the 23 percent that the Midtown Study found to be severely disturbed. On the other end of the range of the continuum would be the 18 percent that the Midtown Study found without significant emotional pathology. In between ranges the average "community representative," shading into more and more neurosis and eventually borderline states as the schizophrenic end is approached. We want to make quite clear that we are speaking of a *range* of ego disturbances on both ends of the continuum. For our purposes that means that there are clearly more ill and less ill schizophrenics and well-adjusted and less well-adjusted normals. In principle, every person can move in either direction over the whole continuum. Also, different nonschizophrenic people, as well as different schizophrenics, definitely have different ego function patterns; for example, some have poor object relations, and others have primarily poor thought processes. All these statements are meaningful only if they can be made operationally and be verified quantitatively by independent raters.

The diagnostic concept of schizophrenia can be valid and useful then (1) if this diagnosis is arrived at by an operational definition of ego functions that permit interrater reliability; (2) if this diagnosis allows for a sociophysiopsychodynamic conception of changes in the person over time; (3) if this diagnosis defines schizophrenia as pertaining to a range of ego functions generally below 7 on a scale on which 13 signifies the very best of functioning; (4) if this diagnosis allows for markedly individual patterns of ego functioning, primarily within the lower range of the scale; (5) if this diagnosis allows each ego function or its disturbance to be relative to the sociocultural setting of the person (i.e., the scheme should permit cross-cultural, international comparisons); (6) if it is understood that a specific ego function's strength and pattern is the result of quantitatively varying and dynamic forces and is therefore changeable to another pattern or on another part of the continuum with the same pattern (e.g., from schizophrenic to nonschizophrenic, from character disorder to character traits, from symptom to dream manifestation); and (7) if it is also understood that the dynamic constellation of forces represented in an ego function pattern tends to have a certain stability and even attains structural quality (e.g., a schizophrenic type of compromise solution or pattern of forces). More often than not the stability and permanence of such patterns—normal, neurotic, or psychotic, and schizophrenic specifically—is such as to make the concept of heuristic diagnostic and prognostic value. This last point holds less true in adolescents than in adults.

The diagnosis "schizophrenic syndrome" makes sense by the criteria stated if one subscribes for practical purposes to the concept of a panpsychosis, or "unitary disease concept," (Menninger, 1963). In the absence of organic findings, in the absence of obvious clinical criteria such as symptoms of involution (flushes, etc.), or symptoms of arteriosclerotic effects, any psychosis will be called schizophrenia. This makes sense since we do not even know whether involutional psychosis and arteriosclerotic psychosis are simply so labeled because they occur at a certain time, rather than because they are really distinguishable from schizophrenia on the basis of independent criteria.

A special exception, however, remains with regard to the diagnosis of manic-depressive disorder. Ego function differentiation of manic-depressive psychosis remains a task of the future. On face validity, one would assume that a manic-depressive profile will usually show less severe disturbances of reality testing and judgment (except in the area of self-blame) and reveal little impairment of thought processes but marked fluctuations between highest and lowest level on impulse control and possibly on object relations and defenses.

With all the above qualifications and reservations, the diagnosis of schizophrenia or schizophrenic syndrome makes sense if defined by ego functions as suggested here.

Specific data with regard to delimitation of normals, neurotics, and schizophrenics in our sample can be found in the chapter on results from the clinical interview (e.g., in Figure 20.1). In our sample, the mean for normals is 9.08; for neurotics, 7.42; and for schizophrenics, 5.86. As shown in the bar diagram, the value of each extending plus and minus two standard deviations has our schizophrenics ranging approximately from 2 to 9, the neurotics from 4 to 10, and the normals from 6 to 12. Aside from illustrating the here often-stated concept of the continuum and overlap of these labels, it also shows that in our sample we had neither exceptionally well-functioning normal nor exceptionally regressed people. Further data will be necessary to put a pragmatic, quantitative definition of the schizophrenic syndrome, for example, on a sound statistical basis. What is more, our data did not provide enough of a sample for statistics on borderline conditions. A more hypothetical distribution would have to allow for the fact that at least some psychotics would have some ego functions regressed down to 1 and therefore have the psychotic spread between 1 and 6, with the mean at about 3; a borderline area between 4 and 8, with the mean at about 6.5; a neurotic range from about 6 to 10, with a mean at about 8; and with normals ranging from 8 to 13, with a mean at about 11. What this hypothetical arrangement (see Figure 22.1) indicates is both the overlap of different diagnostic levels and a demonstration of the continuum. The net results of this is

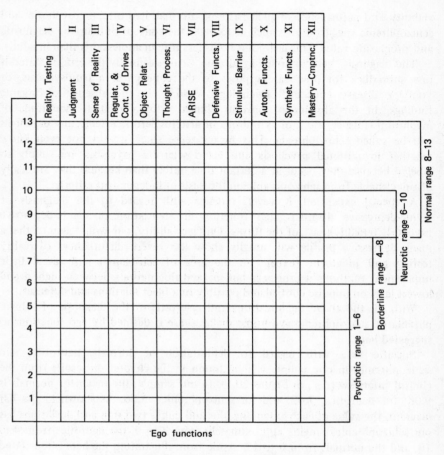

Figure 22.1. Schematic diagnostic ranges.

that we are allowing a rather broad range of 5 stops both for psychosis and normalcy with neurosis and borderline conditions overlapping in both directions.

Some profiles of schizophrenic ego function patterns follow to illustrate the usefulness of this concept. All profiles are based on ratings of interviews, except Profile 22.1A, which is based on ratings of psychological tests. (In this chapter only the assessment of ego functions is discussed. In fact, our assessment also includes a rating scale for superego and id factors.)

Profile 22.1 is that of a young man in his twenties whose functions nearly all fall around or below 5. His ratings on the psychological test performance (Profile

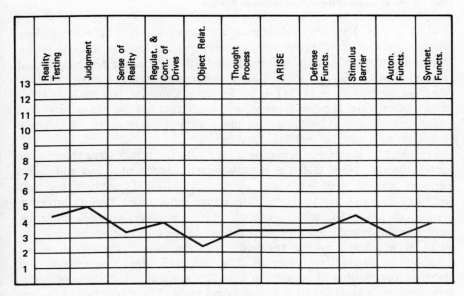

Profile 22.1

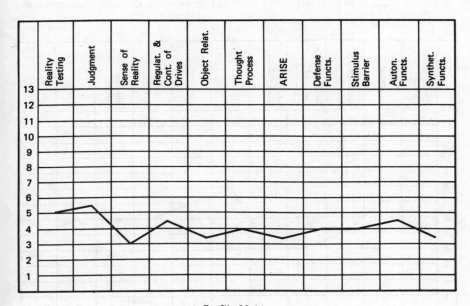

Profile 22.1A

22.1A) and on interview performance are almost identical. The most likely interpretation of the close similarity between the two levels in the case of this patient is that his clinical picture has leveled off at the lowest denominator and that chronicity has set in. Protracted therapeutic attention along the lines sketched by Sechehaye (1951) or by Freeman, Cameron, and McGhie (1958) might offer some hope after very long treatment; but he had a very poor short-range, as well as long-range, prognosis without this intensive and extensive treatment by a maximally skilled therapist.

Profile 22.2 shows a patient in remission with the help of drug therapy and psychotherapy. Note that the regulation and control of drives and object relations are still low. When she was acutely disturbed, reality testing and judgment were very low, as she was deluded and hallucinated. Thought processes were much lower. The still-low synthetic function shows that so far there has been a remission only from the acute process. If one were to diagnose her at the point at which this profile was made, borderline-condition diagnosis would probably be favored. (A paper by Fox and some other case material will illustrate the plotting of progress in clinical stauts.) The short-range prognosis continues to be good the thought processes improved considerably, but the low synthetic functioning suggests a fairly poor long-range prognosis.

Profile 22.3 is that of a patient who had fairly good thought processes and

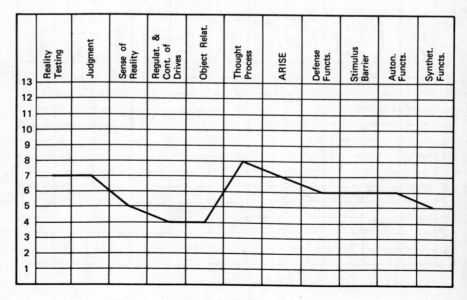

Profile 22.2

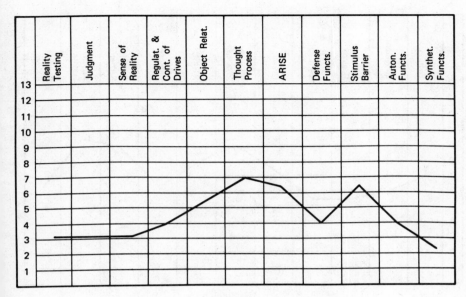

Profile 22.3

seemed a good prospect for psychotherapy, with a mixture of phenothiazine and amitryptiline providing control of drives and mood and a rehabilitation workshop providing the general setting for a building and rebuilding of a self-esteem that had been poorly compensated by grandiose goals. While the cluster of high ratings for object relations, thought processes, and ARISE constitutes a basis for therapeutic optimism, the poor ratings on regulation and control of drives and defensive functioning are liabilities. The low scores on autonomous and synthetic functions are reasons for concern with regard to long-range prognosis (i.e., the ultimate stability of the improvement). The low scores for reality testing and judgment reflect the acute disturbance in the form of hallucinations and delusions. This could be a central area for intervention— that is, for exploration of the dynamics of the apperceptive distortions. In this young man's prepsychotic state, his disturbance manifested itself primarily in unrealistic fantasies of achievement and in defensive denial, which were sometimes responsible for elation and sometimes helped increase his actual achievement, although only over the short run. This profile of ego functions leads to a prediction of successful psychotherapy and a good short-range prognosis, which has since been borne out.

Profile 22.4 is that of a severely neurotic 22-year-old female. The relatively low ratings on the triad of reality testing, judgment, and sense of reality are

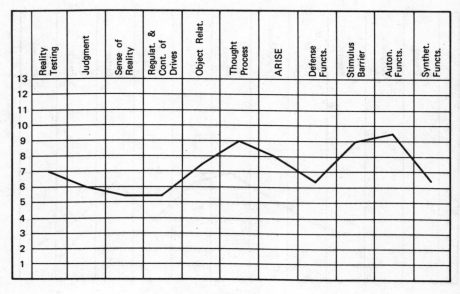

Profile 22.4

based on her lack of awareness of inner feelings secondary to her repressive style. Also, indications of inaccuracies in perception (occasional vagueness about what day of the week it is) and in judgment are caused by her problem of regulation and control of drives and defenses. Thought processes receive a very high profile score because thinking is succinct, relevant, and clear. Attention, concentration, memory, and other thought functions do not show interference. Synthetic functioning, on the other hand, is less adaptive, in that she tends not to use past experience well in dealing with present difficulties and holds out a fairly poor prognosis for utilization of psychotherapy.

Profile 22.5 is that of a playwright of some modest success who seems to have too poor thought processes to be very promising professionally, despite a rather good ARISE. He is an overideational and very anxious person who needs high doses of tranquilizers to be able to function at all. Extensive psychotherapeutic work on his apperceptive distortions (which are associated with overwhelming anxiety, apparently induced by an extremely anxious and probably psychotic mother) appears indicated and only moderately successful even over the short term. In his case, the fairly good ability for creativity (ARISE) is offset by his poor thought processes and defensive functioning. His success at writing is very much of the fringe variety, and chances are that he belongs to that group of artists who have access to the unconscious in the first phases of regression in the

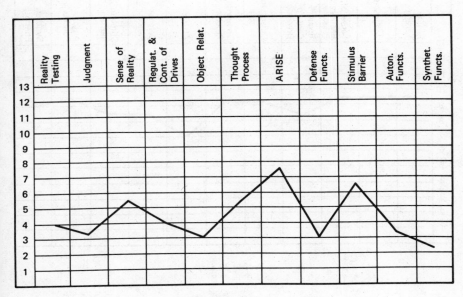

Profile 22.5

service of the ego but hardly any synthesizing-integrating ability in the second phase of the oscillation. His poor object relationships are a negative psychotherapeutic factor, and the low autonomous and synthetic functioning are poor long-range prognostic signs for this schizophrenic person.

Profile 22.6, for a cheerful comparison, is that of a normal person. It is a hospital worker who was interviewed and rated by people who did not know her previously. Several of us on the project knew her fairly well for a couple of years and suggested her for the normal sample. As can be seen, only her ARISE, her creativity potential, is fairly low, which is quite consistent with the social impression she makes of living happily without too great a spark of inspiration.

The rest of the profiles of ego function scores for some selected subjects in our sample are also presented along with descriptive material garnered from the ego function interview and some clinical hypotheses based on this material. These profiles again illustrate the usefulness of graphic presentation of the ego function scores.

A young woman (originally from our neurotic sample) with superior intelligence worked as a clerk and typist. Her lowest score, shown in Profile 22.7, is on object relations because of schizoid withdrawal, severe reactions to love-object loss, and predominantly sadomasochistic relationships. A low rating on regulation and control of drives is based primarily on overcontrol of both sexual and aggressive urges and on occasional undercontrol, reflected in physical

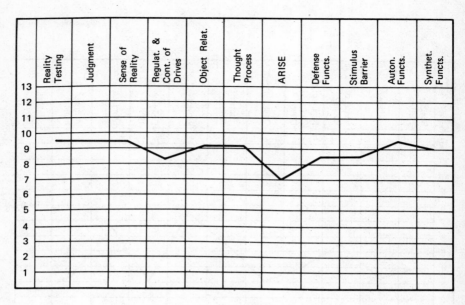

Profile 22.6

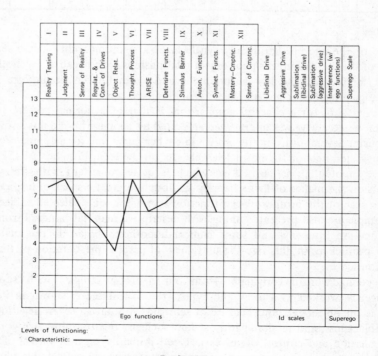

Levels of functioning:
Characteristic: ——————

Profile 22.7

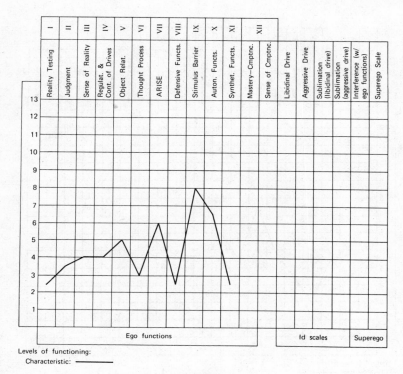

Profile 22.8

fights with her roommate and bouts of overeating. This behavior and her scores are consistent with a borderline condition and are offset only by relatively high scores on reality testing, judgment, thought processes, and autonomous functioning.

The 25-year-old woman in Profile 22.8 is a ballet dancer in New York City who was brought to the hospital by the police after she started to disrobe in Central Park. She believed that the police tried to arrest her because they wanted to see her undressed and she even heard voices that she took as unequivocal evidence for this belief. Thus, she scores very low on reality testing. In contrast, her autonomous functioning is relatively intact: she can hold a job dancing and complex skills are not interfered with. Synthetic functioning is ominously low (see chapter on prognosis).

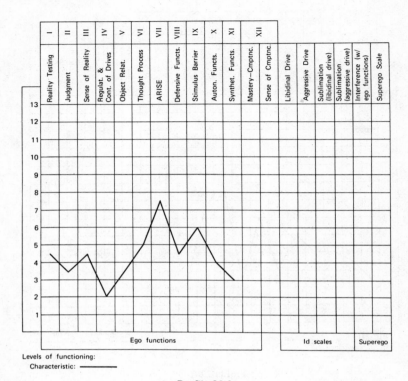

Profile 22.9

The subject in Profile 22.9 is an unusually attractive and talented woman, a successful published writer in her early thirties. Her sexual activities, however, were so imbued with conflict that on occasion she resorted to prostitution in the course of a generally promiscuous behavioral style. Her creative potential and her problem in impulse control are documented in the profile. Her lowest rating was obtained on regulation and control of drives; her highest on ARISE. Relatively low scores on autonomous and synthetic-integrative functioning in this context suggest a guarded long-range prognosis. The functions reality testing, judgment, and sense of reality may be areas for intervention: this patient professed on admission to be the first woman president of the United States.

During the course of rating ego functions, we realized that subjects showed unique individual differences in the extent to which adaptive adequacy for the various ego functions varied *over time.* For example, one subject whose characteristic level of reality testing is 6, gives evidence of never operating below

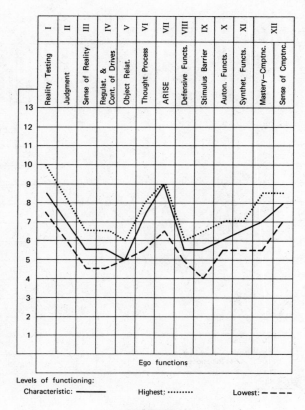

Profile 22.10

a 5 or above a 7 on this ego function, while another subject rated 6 for characteristic level had displayed behavior under certain circumstances that merited only a 2. Thus, in addition to characteristic level we began rating lowest and highest levels for each ego function. Profiles 22.10 and 22.11 illustrate this graphically. For some important assessments such as changes during the course of psychotherapy or as a result of psychotropic medication, the evaluation of current level of functioning would be the most relevant.

Variability may be observed by noting the degree of difference between ratings of highest, lowest, and characteristic levels of functioning. In Profile 22.10 there is a relatively small difference between lowest, highest, and characteristic levels for any and all ego functions. In Profile 22.11, on the other

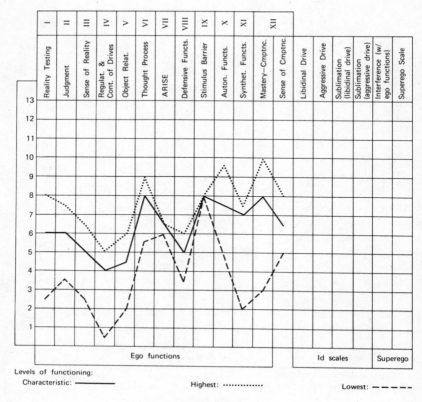

Profile 22.11

hand, there are large differences between characteristic and lowest level on a number of functions, especially on regulation and control of drives, synthetic functioning, and mastery-competence. In addition to underscoring the variability or consistency for a given function, these profiles highlight the areas of vulnerability for the individual: the likelihood is that the ego functions that have dropped most in the past during periods of stress — or where the discrepancy between lowest and characteristic levels are the greatest — will be the ones most vulnerable to possible future drops.

It has been demonstrated, we hope, that the diagnosis of schizophrenia can be made usefully and reliably. While the nomothetic use of the term seems justified by defining the schizophrenic syndrome as lying at the low end of a range of ego functions, the individual idiographic, highly personal constellation is emphasized. It may remain useful to add to the egopsychological statements and diagnostic formulations some descriptive terms such as "acute," "subacute," "chronic," as well as such terms as "catatonic symptomatology" and "paranoid ideation."

The egopsychological conception of the schizophrenic syndrome permits us to understand the coexistence of neurotic symptoms; also, as the system of forces affecting the ego function balance changes, the result may be an hysterical, obsessive, compulsive, or other syndrome. The forces involved may be a change in the neurogenic factors — for example, as modified by psychotropic drugs — or a change in the psychogenic factors brought about by a spontaneous or planned modification of the milieu or by insight psychotherapy.

The ego function approach to diagnosis has the further advantage that it is part of a larger dynamic conceptual scheme that permits us to understand not only movement from one diagnostic syndrome to another but also the coexistence of supposedly discrete phenomena, such as obsessions, phobias, and hysterical symptoms in someone primarily diagnosed as showing the schizophrenic syndrome. This approach allows us to understand that the various symptoms are merely different dynamic attempts at conflict resolutions.

The egopsychological definition of the schizophrenic syndrome, employing clearly stated, ratable criteria, should improve interrater reliability. An egopsychological diagnosis has an advantage over the traditional "mental status" diagnosis by signs and symptoms in that ego functions are continuous, unlike signs and symptoms. The stability of the diagnostic implications, as mentioned earlier in reference to Beck's paper (1962), has to be understood as possibly a pseudoproblem. The patient has no obligation to remain schizophrenic and this conceptualization helps us understand why he may move to other parts of the diagnostic continuum, including normality.

We certainly believe that some schizophrenics are curable, that is, reversible to where by any method the personality is not distinguishable from the relatively normal. In some schizophrenics this reversal may be of a reasonable stability, and one may expect as much stability from it as from any process, including the psychodynamic constellations in "normal" people. Many other schizophrenics reach either only a partial reversibility or a full reversibility of a less stable nature.

Nevertheless, the nomothetic connotation "schizophrenic syndrome" remains useful. There are enough *intragroup similarities among people at a point diagnosed as schizophrenic* to differentiate them, on the basis of intergroup differences, from other groups of people.

Having said earlier that we do not believe "once a schizophrenic, always a schizophrenic" and having given reasons for this view, we regretfully add that to overstate this position would be a mistake. The unfortunate reality at present is that the majority of people with schizophrenic personalities do not get into treatment anywhere. If they do get into a hospital, there is little chance for them to get the sort of treatment likely to reverse the process. Even more unfortunately, not all the schizophrenic people treated by the best available means and people become nonschizophrenic forever or even at all. Therefore, the diagnostic concept of the schizophrenic syndrome, realistically speaking (even allowing for some spontaneous cures), is still useful for conveying the information that once schizophrenic, one is extremely likely to retain – or regress again to – a schizophrenic or other severe psychopathology. To say anything else for the majority of the population involved would be a pipe dream. It will be our job to change this dream into reality by research and by community mental-health measures, which should go a long way toward prevention of at least manifestly severe disorders and/or their earlier treatment and greater reversibility.

So far we have spoken only of individual diagnoses and not mentioned two specific areas of interest to us. One is the fact, briefly referred to in the chapter on data, that it is our hope that ego function assessment of future larger samples will lead to subgroups of ego function patterns that will allow for diagnostic subcategories more useful than the customary ones of catatonic, hebephrenic, simple, and paranoid subtypes. What is more, we hope that eventually such subgroups characterized by clusters of ego functions will correspond to subgroups of etiologic and pathogenic nature, and, on that basis, lend themselves to specific and rational design of treatment and statements re prognosis.

The other fact was briefly mentioned above – that the ego function assessment as a form of diagnosis should make it possible to compare schizophrenic incidence (and other forms of pathology) cross-culturally. So far, differences in standards of emotionality, of criteria for "normal" reality testing, and so on have varied so much from culture to culture that accepted beliefs in one culture are considered psychotic in another. Some superstitions are just that but are widely accepted in some more primitive cultures, while appearing as delusional to the Western investigator.

If one establishes rating scales with rating stops defined for each given culture, it should be possible to compare cross-culturally. Although the standards of impulse control among Portuguese and Hawaiians, or Japanese and Italians, or Brazilians and Swiss, may vary a good deal, it is possible to establish the normal range within each culture and to define, say a schizophrenic, for that given culture within its own norms. If the prevalance of schizophrenia is then established within a culture by that criterion, it can be compared to the prevalence of schizophrenia by ratings established with regard to the norms of another culture.

Having such culture-related criteria should be useful for a wide range of problems.

1. A version of this paper has previously been published by Leopold Bellak, M.D., as the "Validity and Usefulness of the Concept of the Schizophrenic Syndrome" in R. Cancro, Ed. *The Schizophrenic Reactions,* Brunner/Mazel, New York, 1970.

CHAPTER 23

TREATMENT

INTRODUCTION

The treatment of any disorder is rational only if it is predicated on some clear conceptions about the etiology and pathogenesis of the disorder. Rational treatment must, then, be based on interlocking hypotheses concerning etiology and pathogenesis and on a persuasive rationale for the sequence of steps involved in the therapy itself. There cannot, of course, be any assumption that a given theory of etiology and pathogenesis from which we derive therapeutic formulations is the whole truth and nothing but the truth, since every theory needs verification, modification, or refutation with the passage of time. Indeed, hypotheses about the etiology, pathogenesis, diagnosis, and treatment of any disorder must be under constant examination for reliability and validity. It is with these qualifications in mind that the present scheme for the treatment of schizophrenia is offered.

There are therapists who consider only one form of therapy useful and effective for all forms of schizophrenia. They are found among the advocates of Electro Convulsive Therapy (ECT), lobotomy, and chemotherapy, as well as among those of psychotherapy or psychoanalysis.

Our research study, in contradistinction to the all-or-none approaches, is predicated upon the hypothesis that the schizophrenic syndrome is the final common outcome of etiologic and pathogenic variables affecting what, for the sake of semantic convenience, we speak of as the functions of the ego. As previously stated, it is our basic conception that chemogenic, genogenic, psychogenic, neurophysiological, and social factors (and possibly others), occasionally singly but usually in interaction with one another, can all produce the terminal result that we recognize as the schizophrenic syndrome.

Although differences between schizophrenics certainly exist, it is useful to classify persons with very severe ego function disturbances homogeneously as suffering from the schizophrenic syndrome, because their intragroup similarity is greater than any similarity to neurotics or normals (see chapter on diagnosis). It must therefore also be possible to formulate some very general principles of treatment for this general schizophrenic constellation that transcend any specific

351

measures of somatotherapy, environmental intervention, or other methods that may be useful.

To begin with, all patients generally need an understanding human relationship within which all other therapeutic measures can be effective. More specifically, a man suffering an aphasia because of traumatic destruction of some cortical tissue also suffers from perplexity and anxiety. He needs, and will benefit from, an understanding, supportive attitude in those who deal with his neurological dysfunction, regardless of what other specific treatment measures may be indicated. Thus, while general clinical training, sensitivity, knowledge, and understanding of the schizophrenic are necessary, so too are highly specialized skills in a variety of treatment forms. Compassion and warm support alone are not a sufficient treatment for people suffering from the schizophrenic syndrome in its general and specific varieties, except possibly in the rare instance of very acute symptoms where a benign, supportive setting promotes at least a temporary progression to better health.

One must also differentiate between the treatment of pronounced schizophrenic symptoms only and the treatment of the whole of the patient's personality. This distinction of goals will separate and subcategorize many of the therapies, including the psychoanalytic therapies, from more classical psychoanalytic approaches as practiced recently especially by Boyer and Giovacchini (1967) from those Kleinian ones described by Rosenfeld (1952) and other Kleinians, and from Arieti (1955) and other Sullivanians.

The whole large field of therapy of schizophrenia has recently been reviewed elsewhere (Bellak and Loeb, 1969). It is sufficient to say here that we are aware of a wide spectrum of approaches. In basing our treatment on an ego function approach, we do not ignore other dynamic considerations or any other considerations, including the option of an only slightly varied classical psychoanalytic approach for which the ego functions are merely a specific frame of reference.

Similarly, egopsychological diagnosis should also be useful for guiding treatment that is not primarily psychotherapeutic or psychotherapeutic in a dyadic sense. One may wish to make an egopsychological diagnosis for pharmacotherapy, for instance. Low impulse control combined with poor thought processes may be a good reason for prescribing phenothiazines, particularly if poor object relations hold little promise for establishing a transference relationship without the drugs or at all. An ego function profile that is relatively flat as well as low on the scale suggests a chronic process that is unlikely to respond to either psychotherapy or drug therapy. Grinspoon's study (1972) at the Massachusetts Mental Health Center suggests that patients who had been previously hospitalized in a state hospital for three years did not profit from two years of skilled psychotherapy and profited only slightly and symptomatically from prolonged drug therapy.

These considerations recommend the egopsychological approach for assessment of a broad range of care such as should be part of every community mental-health program (Bellak, 1972; see also chapter on prognosis). The "revolving-door" phenomenon is the main problem of community psychiatry at present: while fewer patients occupy beds and stay shorter periods of time than they used to if one looks over the figures of the last 15 years, they are also more frequently admitted and readmitted. One way of meeting this problem may well be in careful assessment not only of what therapy the patient might be suitable for, but also what the next step might be on the bridge across the gap from full hospital care to full functioning in the community. Placement in hotel wards (Zwerling, 1972), day hospitals, special apartments in the community, or the patients' own homes might be some of the decisions involved. Above all, some patients may not be able to return to full or even partial functioning in the community. The patient with a relatively flat and low profile but considerable fluctuation in impulse control between highest and lowest ratings is probably better provided with some continued custodial care. Returning him to the community will only make the door turn faster.

The egopsychological treatment of schizophrenia, then, is here closely tied to the egopsychological diagnosis of schizophrenia. Earlier (Chapter 20), we illustrated different patterns of ego function disturbance and arrived at a five-factor solution for our sample (representing five patterns of ego functions). Such subgrouping, however, is only an approximate classification of groups of subjects. For the individual, a specific constellation of ego functions — as well as id and superego factors — within a given cultural and subcultural setting at a given time, considered in relation to the patient's past, present, and presumable future, constitute the basis for an individually tailored treatment plan.

Let us anticipate some of the ramifications of this ego function approach. Therapeutic steps taken to improve ego functioning must be taken within the cultural framework of the patient. This obvious truth is less likely to be forgotten with people from really alien cultures than, for instance, with those of some subculture within the American community. Even if two patients have exactly the same type of profile of patterning of the 12 functions measured, an egopsychological diagnosis and treatment plan must take into account differences in sociocultural settings. One patient might have far greater family resources, financial and otherwise, to fall back on than the other, and a treatment plan sensible for one might be quite senseless for the other. Ideally, the ego function profile would permit as accurate an appraisal of a Fiji Islander's ego functions in his particular culture as of a Manhattan-dweller in his very different cultural setting.

Above all, the treatment approach takes into account each patient's specific defects in ego functioning. The most important consideration to keep in mind is that some patients show disturbances of ego functions because they never reached a higher level − that is, they suffer from a lack of progression − whereas others have regressed from higher levels previously reached (Bellak, 1958a). The therapeutic approach must take such facts into account; the task of building a function differs from that of resurrecting it. In this sense, a score of 5 on our ego function scale could imply different things for two different patients and needs some annotation to that effect.

In our attempts to scale adaptiveness-maladaptiveness, we drew on clinical experiences with extremes of maladaptiveness and adaptive functioning. To a certain extent, extremes of maladaptiveness correspond to earliest infantile functioning and the heights of adaptiveness to the highest levels of adult mature functioning. This correlation is very rough, however, and waits further information on steps of ego development for future refinement.

Another set of general rules must be mentioned here (see Bellak and Small, 1965, for an extensive discussion): the need for careful conceptualization of therapeutic interventions with regard to *area* of intervention, *method* of intervention, and the *sequence of methods* of intervention.

The therapist must decide which area of the patient's personality needs − and can tolerate − his immediate attention. In one patient, one may wish to strengthen superego aspects to increase control; in another, one may wish to interpret aggression cathartically as a form of intervention in the area of impulse control (Bellak and Small, 1965). In yet another, auxiliary reality testing may be the first concern of therapy.

The type of intervention chosen may also vary widely, depending upon the patient, the environmental circumstances, and the means available. Sometimes drug therapy is best, sometimes family therapy, sometimes ECT, or individual therapy.

In one patient, the sequence of interventions may be a reduction of the thought disorder with phenothiazines followed by psychotherapy. In another patient, removal from a sexually or aggressively overstimulating environment to a more quiet one may be required before other steps are possible or likely to be useful.

Such careful individual planning is essential; otherwise, the suggestions made below for the treatment of individual ego-function defects may be mechanically implemented and, thus, misunderstood.

TREATMENT OF SPECIFIC EGO FUNCTION DEFECTS

Earlier in this monograph we made clear that the ego functions are, to a considerable extent, interdependent. For that reason, specific suggestions for the treatment of one ego function defect frequently involve other ego functions as well. In what follows, we offer a schematic catalog of therapeutic techniques predicated upon various patterns of ego functions and their disturbances, based upon earlier formulations (Bellak, 1958a; Bellak and Loeb, 1969). We emphasize that any such schematic discussion is oversimplified and overgeneralized since it is sometimes necessary to consider single variables (i.e., to focus on a single ego function as though it could exist in isolation, when in fact ego functions are interdependent). Treatment of a particular syndrome must often address several ego functions simultaneously and/or alternately. On the one hand, even a single interpretive sentence will often affect more than one ego function; on the other hand, in psychotherapeutic intervention or psychotropic drug treatment some of the therapeutic steps recommended for one ego function will have to be repeated for another ego function.

Reality Testing

Major Components of Function	*Some Disturbances**
a. Distinction between inner and outer stimuli.	Hallucinations and delusions; disorientation as to time, place, or person; perceptual distortion; limited reflective awareness.
b. Accuracy of perception of external events.	
c. Accuracy of inner-reality testing.	

Treatment of Disturbances of Reality Testing
Whatever the severity of disturbance of reality testing, the therapist's role is to a certain extent that of an *auxiliary ego.*

If the disturbance of reality testing is severe (e.g., if the patient lives primarily in a world of delusions and hallucinations), a number of preliminary steps are necessary: entering into the patient's world, establishing understanding on a primary-process level, gaining the patient's confidence. Letting the patient know that he is being understood decreases his secondary terror (about his strange world) and makes possible some bridging of the gap between the psychotic world and reality.

Interpretation of some of the distortions is then possible. There may be cathartic interpretations of feared drive impulses (best exemplified by John Rosen's technique), of defenses, or of the superego factors, *judiciously paced.*

Therapy may have to include *sensitizing* the patient to the perception of *internal reality*: for example, getting him to recognize anger or anxiety before they are translated into major or minor projections. Prediction of possible distortion of emerging events will play a major role in the patient's avoiding the distortion and helping him recognize traumatic situations. This holds true particularly for defects in judgment, as seen in various degrees of acting out.

*See Manual for further details about the functions and their disturbances.

Education may play a role if some of the defects in reality testing are exacerbated by inadequate information (e.g., a fear of becoming pregnant from a kiss).

Drugs may play a major role in the control of excess drives responsible for the distortion of reality. Psychotropic drugs, for example, can improve reality testing indirectly, and the phenothiazines may have an effect on the synthetic function, thereby improving the quality of thinking and, in turn, reality testing.

Group psychotherapy, like a rehabilitation-workshop setting, may provide feedback for reality testing: if the patient behaves or talks unrealistically, the group or workshop personnel lets him know. Inasmuch as faulty reality testing in such settings leads not to dire consequences but to therapeutic intervention, they are "settings of self-correcting reality."

Id and superego are actively involved in reality testing: for instance, unrealistic guilt feelings may be at the root of self-harming, masochistic behavior. Excessive sexual push (e.g., in involutional disorders) may lead specifically to grossly sexual delusions and hallucinations. In such cases, the whole therapeutic armamentarium, from interpretations to achieve insight to drug therapy, is appropriate in the service of improved reality testing.

Judgment

Function	*Some Disturbances*
a. Anticipation of probable consequences of intended behavior.	Oblivion to severe dangers to life and limb; unrealistic appraisal of consequences of actions; failure to learn from experience; inappropriate behavior in relation to social definitions of situations.
b. Extent to which manifest behavior reflects an awareness of its probable consequences.	
c. Appropriateness of behavior.	

Treatment of Disturbances of Judgment

It is entirely possible to be able to test reality adequately and yet be insufficiently aware of the probable consequences of ill-considered action. A common example of such a situation is acting out, which spans normal, neurotic, and psychotic behavior. Persons given to acting out can, if queried about the details of reality, offer perfectly accurate accounts. Because of the impulses motivating their behavior, however, they engage in acts that obviously to everybody else, show poor judgment. Even eminent scientists and outstanding statesmen make such mistakes. A scientist of great repute, who certainly must ordinarily have excellent judgment, nearly came to grief when he and his son, neither of whom could swim, went sailing on the ocean. A highly placed government figure of ascetic personality, in accepting a relatively minor gift, ruined his career with a presumably single instance of poor judgment.

On the other hand, the superego, too, not infrequently interferes with good judgment, in neurotics and normals as well as in psychotics. There are those who feel, for instance, that John Foster Dulles's diplomacy was sometimes adversely affected by his evaluation of other nations according to his own moral standards.

Psychotic defects in judgment are most likely to be rooted in firm delusional systems, particularly of a paranoid nature; very intelligent patients are especially likely to use exquisite reality testing as a basis for acts showing poor judgment.

Defects in judgment may occur with some degree of independence from reality testing, since judgment involves a proper matching of perceived reality with memory material regarding social, physical, and other factors. Apparently, the process of matching may be interfered with in minor or major ways by fatigue, disruptive impulses, undue superego pressure, or failure either of superego functioning or of signal anxiety. A businessman who is perfectly capable of judging contemporary reality may permit himself undue optimism and buy a trainload of lumber when a small truckload would do. Conversely, depression may color judgment so as to cause unduly pessimistic anticipations from relatively correctly perceived reality. Anxiety may so affect one's anticipation of consequences from a relatively correctly perceived reality as to lead to disastrous and even psychotic decisions.

In the majority of psychotics (particularly in cases of affective disturbances and of the schizophrenic syndrome with affective features), defects in judgment occur relatively independent of reality testing.

Although defects in judgment may be relatively independent of reality testing, they are usually fused with defects in reality testing and are often combined with problems of impulse control and/or disturbances of defenses and other ego functions.

Treatment of poor judgment is largely treatment of the factors underlying it: that is of elation, depression, anxiety, or defective reality testing, poor impulse control, projection, and other disturbances of the defenses. Disruption of the stimulus barrier is sometimes serious enough to lead to poor judgment.

Patients who habitually use poor judgment need constant review of cause and effect. Sometimes prediction of poor judgment in specified circumstances will help to prevent it (Bellak, 1963). Another important strategy for preventing acts based upon poor judgment is to have the patient agree to a delay of the action — for instance, an ill-advised marriage or business deal. Homicidal, suicidal, or delusional acts may lose their motivation if the patient can be made to agree to postpone action. He will then retain his freedom of choice, except for a delay. Delay interferes with the pleasure of immediate impulse discharge, thus obviating the act.

Frequently, an outstanding part of the treatment is to increase the patient's "signal awareness" or anticipation of mental sets or reality circumstances that are particularly likely to trigger poor judgment.

Sense of Reality of the World and of the Self

Components of Function	*Some Disturbances*
a. The experience of external events as real and as embedded in a familiar context.	Alienation; hypnagogic and hypnopompic phenomena; stage fright; emotional isolation as a result of obsessive defenses; déjà vu; depersonalization; derealization; dreamlike states; trances; fugues, major dissociations; world destruction fantasies; identity diffusion.
b. The experience of one's body (or parts of it) and its functioning and one's behavior as familiar and unobstructive and as belonging to (or emanating from) oneself.	
c. The degree of development of individuality, uniqueness, and a sense of self and self-esteem.	
d. The degree of separation of one's self-representations from one's object representations.	

Treatment of Disturbances of Sense of Reality of the World and of the Self

Disturbances in the sense of self are closely allied to disturbances of the sense of identity. The concepts of identity crisis and loss of identity are at present in wide use (from Erikson, Edith Jacobson, and Rosenfeld, to Laing and Sartre). Freeman, Cameron, and McGhie (1958) have placed a disturbance in the sense of self at the center of the schizophrenic disorder. In this they closely follow Federn's (1952) conception of an underlying disorder of self-boundaries, which he described primarily in terms of shifts of cathexis depleting healthy ego cathexis. On the other hand, Freud spoke primarily of a libidinal withdrawal from object cathexis onto the self. Federn, and Freeman, Cameron, and McGhie, put the emphasis upon the loss of what are best called self-boundaries rather than ego boundaries. Varying degrees of disturbance in the sense of self may in fact be caused by a variety of factors, and therefore treatment also varies a great deal (Bellak, 1964).

In some persons, the sense of self may never have developed well because of autistic or symbiotic relations with the maternal figure by virtue of poor, inconsistent introjects. A crucial factor in a poor sense of self lies in a conflict between two parts of the self, which results in an increase in the self-observing function of the ego. Withdrawal of libidinal energy from outside subjects may also play a role in a poor sense of self. On quite a different level, hysterical focusing on the distance when looking at near objects may also produce depersonalization and so may hyperventilation, with subsequent dizziness and changes in proprioception. Perceptual isolation, fatigue, and drugs (a para-doxical, anxiety-arousing effect of sedatives, for instance) may cause it. More than ordinary awareness of usually automatic functions, such as walking (onto a stage, for instance), may lead to what Simon (1971) calls the deautomatizing effect of consciousness and of special effort.

Aside from interpretation of relevant dynamic aspects, depersonalization may be treated by drugs if it is caused by panic or if it is caused either by overbreathing or by nuchal rigidity.

In severe psychotic disturbances of the sense of self, the work of Federn and Sechehaye (1952) and Freeman and associates (1958) needs to be consulted. Sechehaye painstakingly restored a sense of self-boundaries in individual patients by body contact and interpretation. May and associates' (1963) Body Ego Technic (first developed by Salkan and Schoop) permits patients to relearn through rhythmical movements, proprioception, and so on. Gindler's technique of muscle reeducation is also very useful, especially for minor disturbances of body image, as described in Meyer (1961).

The more disturbed the patient, the more active the therapist has to be in helping him build (or rebuild) self-esteem and in helping him structure his life, at least temporarily, so as to avoid self-esteem-destroying experiences: do not let him take on a larger task than he is likely to be able to manage. Specific self-concepts need analyzing: concretization of the self as something dirty, dangerous, and loathsome is frequent and needs great attention.

A few joint consultations with the patient and the important figures in his life may be very helpful if there are specific disturbances of role perception, especially in relation to one or more of these significant people.

Mintz (1965) has suggested ways to strengthen the sense of self by helping the patient become more aware of aspects of his body image; she suggests improvement of reality testing in borderline patients by increasing their awareness of cause and effect and by strengthening the patient's time sense. She sees this therapeutic intervention as different from influencing the patient directly through guidance and encouragement. Bellak and Small (1965) offered a number of other techniques in their book on emergency psychotherapy.

Regulation and Control of Drive, Affect, and Impulse

Components of Function	Some Disturbances
a. The directedness of impulse expression. b. The effectiveness of delay and control and the degree of frustration tolerance.	Temper outbursts; habit and conduct disorders; low frustration tolerance; acting out; tendencies toward murder or suicide; impulsiveness; drive-dominated behavior; chronic irritability and rage; excessive control of impulse.

Treatment of Disturbances of Regulation and Control of Drive, Affect, and Impulse

Poor regulation and control of drives is probably the most frequent cause for hospitalization of psychotics. It causes more social disruption than most other ego function disturbances and is generally most easily perceived as a threat. Historically, unenlightened response to psychotic behavior primarily entailed an interference with freedom by chains and incarceration. When a person was said to be possessed by the devil, reference was almost always to his loss of regulation and control of drives and impulses.

The more recent traditional forms of dealing with severe disturbances of drive regulation and control were restraining sheets, wet packs, various other hydrotherapeutic procedures, camisoles, and locked doors. These means of dealing with psychotic disturbances of control have been almost entirely replaced by chemical restraints, psychotropic drugs, and reform of hospital wards into therapeutic communities with patient government, nurses out of uniform, and open doors. Among the latest psychotropic drugs, lithium carbonate as a specific treatment of manic excitement is particularly relevant to the control of excessive drive.

Drugs play a crucial role not only generally in the treatment of psychotics but also in psychotherapy and in the classical analysis of patients suffering extreme disturbances in drive regulation and control: in Ostow's (1962) hands, psychoanalysis of schizophrenics is made possible by a sort of "drug sandwich": drugs of the phenothiazine variety are used to put a ceiling on the patient's drives, and stimulants, energizers, and antidepressants are used to establish a bottom (something akin to titration establishes the most useful midpoint between excessive control and lack of control within which to carry on the analytic process).

The strictly psychotherapeutic treatment of a lack of drive regulation and control still has a large role to play. Cathartic interpretation, as practiced especially by John Rosen (1962), may be very useful for diminishing uncontrolled behavior or interfering with excessive control (catatonic or depressed). A strengthening of the superego, as well as a decrease of the drives, by interpretation, is often an important strategy (Bellak, 1963). Typically, the superego of the very disturbed person is inconsistent: in part too severe and in part too lenient. The appropriate psychotherapeutic operations strive toward greater consistency by strengthening some parts and weakening others. In all grades of severity of acting out, it is important to establish continuity for the patient in place of the discontinuity that exists through his use of denial, magical thinking, and other distortions. In addition, repeated prediction of the consequences of acting out is a useful therapeutic strategy (Bellak, 1963). Excessive aggressive behavior may, of course, be a denial of fear of passivity. Recent studies suggest that if delusions of grandeur used as a means of inflating self-esteem are interfered with, violent actions, including homicide, are easily precipitated.

Very often a lack of regulation and control in an adult is caused by a lack of education, as well as by early overstimulation of aggressive and sexual drives. In such cases, the building of controls and the decrease of stimulation necessitates a long, drawn-out therapeutic effort that strongly resembles education. Interpretation of apperceptive distortions (which incite excessive response from the patient) is a traditionally helpful intervention. If it is difficult to modify an inconsistent superego psychotherapeutically, it is even more difficult to bring about a progression of drive from pregenital to genital orientation, neutralization, and sublimation. Where strictly psychotherapeutic means do not suffice, active changes of the environment may be necessary: a patient whose sadism is excessively stimulated in a butcher shop or in whose homosexuality is excessively aroused a barber shop needs to be helped to change his occupation.

Above all, the patient needs to be helped to develop better signal functions of the ego, awareness of both a dangerous buildup of drive and the lack of an appropriate response before it becomes excessive.

Very general measures for tension reduction and drive reduction, such as vigorous exercise (especially in the presence of an excessive aggressive drive), may temporarily play a very useful role.

Object Relations

Components of Function

a. The degree and kind of relatedness to others.
b. The extent to which present relationships are adaptively or maladaptively influenced by, or patterned upon, older ones and serve present mature aims rather than past immature ones.

Some Disturbances

Defensive social overactivity; withdrawal; detachment; narcissistic overinvestment of self; symbiotic-dependent attachments; difficulty in perceiving others as separate.

Treatment of Disturbances of Object Relations

The readmission rate within five years for first-admission schizophrenics is 15-25 percent in the United States, but only 5 percent in Denmark and Finland (Schulsinger and Axe, 1971). This difference is ascribed to the attention that the Scandinavians pay to the psychosocial aspects in the overall treatment program. The disturbance of object relations is one that will probably remain in the area of psychodynamic treatment (via transference) regardless of what future developments there are in drugs or in the etiology and pathogenesis of severe disturbances of object relations. Drugs may help those for whom object relations are very conflict-ridden and tension-arousing, but they cannot help a person *develop* object relationships that are not there.

Sechehaye's (1951) accounts of the painstaking development of object relations via the transference relationship are especially dramatic. Both Rosenfeld (1965) and Searles (1965) are particularly concerned with the schizophrenic's fear of being destroyed or of destroying the object.

Group-therapy settings and rehabilitation workshops like Altro (Bellak and Black 1956) attempt to help the patient learn object relationships in group settings and permit corrections in object relationships without the great penalties, such as total rejection, which might occur elsewhere. The workshop may help the person to develop an optimal distance or closeness to other people, as well as to learn to tolerate what is for him an optimal number of object relationships. Except by the sociometrists, rather little attention has been paid so far to proximity and distance or to the different number of relationships and tolerance for them in different people called the Porcupine Index(Bellak, 1971).

Thought Processes

Components of Function	*Some Disturbances*
a. The adequacy of processes that adaptively guide and sustain thought (attention, concentration, anticipation, concept formation, memory, language).	Magical thinking; autistic logic; condensations; attention lapses; inability to concentrate; memory disturbances; concreteness; primary-process manifestations; and primitive thought functioning.
b. The relative primary- and secondary-process influences on thought (extent to which thinking is unrealistic, illogical, and/or loose).	

Treatment of Disturbances of Thought Processes

Disturbances of thought processes have played a major role in the conception of schizophrenia since Bleuler first described them as being primarily characterized by "loose associations." The specific types of thought disorders have been subjects of much controversy and experimentation. (See chapter on thought processes).

The close interconnection of thought processes with other ego functions has been emphasized by many. Cameron (1944), one of the earliest investigators, suggested the normal adult thinking is the result of repeated social communication and that disorganized schizophrenics have never developed adequate role-taking skill. Disturbances of communication patterns (Singer and Wynne, 1966) and the double-bind concept of Bateson and Jackson (1956) continue to play important roles. These conceptualizations all imply a close relationship between object relations and thought processes. It is evident that if schizophrenic thought disorder is caused by the failure of persons to develop, among other things, syllogistic thinking because of poor object relations or disturbed communication patterns with other people, particularly parents, with whom they grew up, the establishment of thought processes via good object relations is individual therapy, group therapy, or rehabilitation workshop plays a major role. Investigators as diverse as Mednick and Arieti agree that anxiety and other emotions may interfere with thought processes and lead to a regression, developmentally speaking, from secondary-process to primary-process thinking. Mednick (1958) sees thought disorder in terms of conditioned avoidance; Arieti (1963), from the psychoanalytic point of view, sees it as a defense. On either hypothesis, it is obvious that treatment of thought disorder must often address itself to anxiety and other disturbing affects. This may be done by drugs, by psychotherapy, or by a combination of the two. A study by Bellak and Chassan (1964) suggested that Librium and psychotherapy are able to reduce primary-process thinking; the phenothiazines are well known to be especially able to produce this change in the severely disturbed. Such changes can be attained relatively easily if good secondary-process thinking had ever been attained by the patient. Constant review of events for the patient may decrease dissociation and show him logical relationships between one mood and another.

Evidence of the Valium effect and clinical evidence from psychotherapy suggest that any therapeutic intervention—drug or psychotherapy—that reduces anxiety improves all ego functions and, specifically, thought processes. Patient 03 in the Valium study (see "Case Studies: A Study of Progress . . ." later in this chapter), clearly showed improvement. This patient's scattergram also shows that in almost every instance the drug was superior to the placebo in improving thought processes (as well as the other functions). Anyone who has ever witnessed the effect of cathartic interpretations on psychotic patients will have observed a similar improvement in thought processes almost instantly. What is more, intravenous sodium amytal or pentothal dramatically transformed catatonics into almost normally behaving people while the drug lasted. The drug also brought about dramatic, if temporary, improvement in the verbal productions and thought processes of a good many patients who had appeared hebephrenic. Nobody would claim that barbiturates have a specific antipsychotic affect. It is doubtful, therefore, that the phenothiazines have anything but a secondary effect on thinking, by virtue of improving drive control and decreasing anxiety. They are, however, as a class (including the many commerical variations), the most effective "antipsychotic" drugs.

If one becomes aware of actual gaps in the patient's thinking, it is important to illustrate them to him repeatedly—that is, sometimes thought processes are discontinuous because the patient is simply too narcissistic to engage in the role playing that Cameron considers essential to good thought processes and to pay enough attention to whether the thoughts expressed are intelligible to the listener. If the patient reveals overinclusive thinking, which so many consider the most frequent and basic disorder in schizophrenic thinking, again it is important to illustrate this to him and to interpret the reasons for his doing it.

In other instances, one has to enter the extremely disturbed schizophrenic's world by thinking in "schizophrenese." One woman, for instance, thought that she was able to understand and talk to the birds. It was necessary to understand the ellipses in her thinking to enter into meaningful communication with her. In principle, this is more difficult than to interpolate into the thoughts of the manic patient. As Lewin has pointed out, the manic patient's thinking is centrifugal (1950). His primary defense mechanism is denial; his thoughts rush away from what troubles him, but one can infer what it is from listening to the centrifugal trend.

Disturbed thinking is much more difficult to treat if the patient has never acquired very much secondary-process thinking. Then the patient must virtually be trained in syllogisms and in the logical hierarchy of socially acceptable thought. Concrete thinking is a particular problem, especially in patients suffering from somatic delusions. In others, cathartic interpretations, practiced especially by John Rosen (1962), may be necessary—for instance, "You are holding your hand in this particular way because you want to hit your father." One patient, a man who apparently complained only of constipation the way many people do, in fact had a thinly disguised somatic delusion that some living organism was interfering with the function of his intestines and needed to be taken out. His delusion that an embryo was in there had to be interpreted very directly to deal with the disorganization of thought processes that occurred whenever this conflictual topic came up. The use of syllogistic interpretations is almost entirely without effect in such patients until they have very much improved.

Paranoid delusions and thought disorders can be very tightly organized, as they represent attempts at solutions of extremely painful conflicts that may show great resistance to change. It is in such circumstances that the use of LSD to bring about a disorganization of a too-well-formed paranoid system may possibly be useful: after the disorganization, it may be possible to help the patient attain better compromise formations than the paranoid one.

ARISE

Components of Function	*Some Disturbances*
a. First phase of an oscillating process: relaxation of perceptual and conceptual acuity (and other ego controls), with a concomitant increase in awareness of previous preconscious and unconscious contents. b. Second phase of the oscillating process: the induction of new configurations that increase adaptive potential as a result of creative integrations.	Extreme rigidity in character structure and thinking where fantasy and play are difficult or impossible; regression of any ego function, produces anxiety and disruption of functioning; lack of creativity; stereotyped thinking; intolerance of ambiguity; prejudice and sterility; if the first phase predominates, overideational thinking, pseudointellectuality, pseudoartistic tendencies, eccentricity.

Treatment of Disturbances of ARISE

Unlike work with other ego functions, a relative *reduction* of creativity (ARISE) in the therapy of psychotics may play a desirable and important part in the increase of defenses against the emergence of primary-process material. Therefore, plans for improvement in that area in some patients should be very carefully weighed, since the price may be too high to pay. Sometimes, as a relatively desperate measure, a decrease of ARISE may be a therapeutic goal precisely in the attempt to stem an influx of overwhelming psychotic thought. If nothing else will help, some therapists have suggested not only no interference with, but the active encouragement of, fads, "obsessive" occupations, or interest in religious ritual, as forms of defense at the cost of ARISE. Parenthetically, it may be remarked that rather healthy siblings of psychotics often suffer from constriction and loss of ARISE because they are afraid "to be crazy" like their brother or sister, in essence, a phobic defense.

Dynamic psychotherapy may be affected by a disturbance of ARISE, because a lack of tolerance of ambiguity is involved. Syllogisms, which are the basis for all dynamic interpretation, are impossible for the patient to engage in. In the extreme, concrete thinking is present. Patients with disturbances of ARISE, even if not psychotic, cannot possibly tell a story about a T.A.T. card other than the merest description. In such patients it is the first phase of the oscillating process that is disturbed. No decrease in perceptual acuity is permitted. In the workaday world there are many borderline psychotics who function by virtue of doing the same thing in the same way every day of their lives, and those in contact with them soon discover the futility of any attempt to get them to react adaptively to a change in circumstances.

A psychotherapeutic attempt to change this rigidity can sometimes be predicated on illustrating to them that other people see things differently or see different things in the Rorschach and other tests or have different stories to tell for the T.A.T. pictures. Long ago Bellak suggested that barbiturates (sometimes mixed with stimulants) may help produce the first phase of ARISE in the psychotherapeutic session and provide an avenue for further work (Bellak, 1949). Interpretation of extremely rigid defenses may be helpful. In patients given to very concrete thinking, decreasing the equation of a thought with an act will also decrease anxiety and produce more adaptive ability.

Extreme disturbance of the first phase of the oscillating process necessary for ARISE is more often seen in people best diagnosed as psychotic characters than in obsessive characters.

An extreme ability to regress in the first phase combined with insufficient ability to return to adaptive structural functioning in the second phase characterizes psychotics in their artistic productions as well as in their other activities. Such people often appear to be gifted not only artistically but in many other ways. Structurally or educationally, however, they do not have enough adaptive potential for their efforts to lead to any fruition. Psychotherapy to strengthen reality testing and drive control is necessary. There are probably exceptional people in whom a disturbance in the second phase of ARISE coexists with congenital ability or acquired structural and adaptive characteristics of such strength that, although they are psychotic for all other purposes, their productions are still artistic in the sense of communicating powerfully (rather than having only private meaning). In such instances, strengthening of the adaptive functions by psychotherapy, training (for instance, learning the craft aspects of their art), and drugs are indicated.

Defensive Functioning

Major Components of Function	*Some Disturbances*
a. Degree to which defenses adaptively affect ideation and behavior. b. Extent to which defenses have symptomatically succeeded or failed (degree of emergence of anxiety, depression, and other dysphoric affects).	Emergence of unconscious contents triggering extreme anxiety and panic, which can affect concentration and memory functioning; pervasive feelings of vulnerability; fear of cracking up and falling apart; massive withdrawal in an attempt to prevent uncontrolled drive expression.

Treatment of Disturbances of Defensive Functioning

The treatment of the disturbance of the defensive functions preeminently involves, of course, insight psychotherapy of the primary impulses, the apperceptive distortions, and the inappropriate defenses. In part it parallels the treatment for loss of drive control – for example, manipulation of the environment to decrease stimulus, changes in vocation, living place, and habits. Drugs are useful. The therapist must assess dynamics quickly and, if the patient is psychotic, insist upon even drastic changes rather than stay aloof from decisions that involve reality.

In taking an ego function approach to therapy the importance of general dynamic understanding must be stressed. This includes the likelihood that the decreased effectiveness of ego functions is the result of a defensive attempt to avoid anxiety. Thus, in psychotherapy, attempts to improve the adaptiveness of a given ego function include interpreting to the patient the defensive aspect of his symptoms and interpreting what was being defended against.

Interference with ego functions as a result of defensive reactions must be distinguished from secondary interference resulting from regression of another ego function: for example, poor memory will secondarily affect problem-solving and other ego functions.

Stimulus Barrier

Components of Function	*Some Disturbances*
a. Sensitivity to external and internal stimuli and degree of adaptation. b. Organization and integration of responses to various levels of sensory stimulation.	Oversensitivity to bright lights, loud sounds, temperature extremes, pain, resulting in withdrawal, physical symptoms, or irritability; thresholds too high; oblivion to nuances, underresponsiveness to environmental stimuli, impoverishment of aesthetic sensibilities.

Treatment of Disturbances of Stimulus Barrier

The stimulus barrier has not usually been treated as an ego function. The argument against doing so has been based on the idea that the stimulus barrier is congenitally given, rather than a result of development or experience.

It is questionable whether stimulus barrier is more of a congenitally given factor than some other autonomous ego functions. Certainly, stimulus barrier may also be the result of early infantile, and even later, experiences. Excessive stimulation of infants and cramped, noisy quarters probably raise both the stimulus barrier and the arousal level: such people may be in a higher state of arousal and need more stimulation (stimulus hunger) (Bellak and Berneman, 1971) but at the same time have a higher barrier against input.

It is, however, likely that some children are born with a relatively low stimulus barrier and others with a relatively high one. If low stimulus barrier is diagnosed early enough, it would appear rational to try to decrease the amount of perceptual input for such children, as extreme overloading may be responsible for the development of some schizophrenic conditions. Such children are likely to overreact to physiological events, such as teething, fatigue, and the auditory, visual, and tactile stimulations of everyday life. On the other hand, some autistic-appearing children may be suffering primarily from a high stimulus barrier, and in such cases greater efforts to communicate with them must be made. Systematic attempts to stimulate their sensory capacities may be appropriate and necessary for optimal maturation (similar both to the Montessori methods and to those used in Luria's Institute of Defectology, in Moscow).

It is conceivable that a low stimulus barrier coexists with a disturbed electroencephalogram in *some* cases, for which drugs to correct the electrical functioning of the brain may be useful.

Some physiological states, such as premenstrual water retention and changes in the electrolyte balance, lower the stimulus barrier and are probably primarily responsible for many marital conflicts. Conversely, dehydrating drugs frequently upset the electrolyte balance, which may in turn seriously affect the normal stimulus barrier.

Certain social conditions, such as the sharing of one room day and night by a large number of impoverished people, may result in such tremendous aggressive, sexual, and other overstimulation as to cause a lack of, or loss of, control and certainly interfere with optimal development. Only socioeconomic changes are likely to solve those problems.

Therapeutically, one may have to take advantage of whatever environmental changes are possible. Changes in living conditions are sometimes possible. Changes in vocation or daily routine designed to avoid an "overload" may be essential for the prevention of further ego disorganization.

Tranquilizers may in part have their effect by increasing the stimulus barrier. The effect of lithium on manic states has been ascribed by some to its slowing down the processing of information. Lithium does not seem to have that effect on schizophrenics, but it suggests that a drug with such an effect on schizophrenics may be found. Overideational states, as well as catatonic excitement, might then be more amenable to a drug approach. There is some clinical evidence that catatonic stupor is, among other things, an attempt to decrease stimulus input (as well as to control affect); if so, such a drug would more specifically affect that condition than do the phenothiazines.

Autonomous Functioning

Components of Function	*Some Disturbances*
a. Degree of freedom from impairment of "apparatuses" of primary autonomy (e.g., sight, hearing, intention, language, memory, learning, motor function, intelligence).	Functional blindness or deafness; catatonic postures; inability to feed, dress, or care for one's self; disturbances of will, skills, habits; ready interference with automatized behavior by drive-related stimuli; expenditure of great effort to carry out routine tasks.
b. Degree of freedom from impairment of "apparatuses" of secondary autonomy (e.g., habit patterns, complex learned skills, work routines, hobbies, interests).	

Treatment of Disturbances of Autonomous Functioning

The need for relative intactness of autonomous functions for the work of classical psychoanalysis has been pointed out by Loewenstein (1954, 1967, 1972); his broad definition of autonomous functions includes reality testing, anticipation, and self-observation.

In psychotics, the primary autonomous functions, such as memory, intention, movement, and language, may be severely afflicted. Nevertheless, even within impaired areas some aspects of secondary autonomy may remain remarkably intact. A patient who stood around in a frozen catatonic stance could play rapid and brilliant ping-pong once he was positioned to receive the ball at the end of the table. A kind of automatized function seemed to take over. As soon as the ball dropped from the table, by his or his opponent's doing, he froze back into a catatonic stance. Continued attempts to play ping-pong with him led to an increasing continuity of movement within the table-tennis setting and later to an abandonment of catatonic rigidity in other situations.

Special skills other than motor ones often resist psychotic impairment. Many a person with severe defects in reality testing, judgment, and control of impulses remains a skilled worker and retains special information — even several foreign languages — or professional competence. In such cases the still-intact functions are most important, as they may be used in an attempt to improve the defective functions. In a rehabilitation workshop, a skilled mechanic may improve his object relations (Bellak and Black 1960) while engaged in productive work. Any situation that helps to neutralize and sublimate drives, such as occupational therapy, music therapy, or athletics, is likely to improve autonomous functions.

In certain circumstances, very specific drugs may ameliorate psychotic afflictions of primary autonomous functions. Estrogens may be useful in the treatment of paranoid conditions, such as may be present in a woman of involutional age where olfactory delusions are frequent. The primary disturbance in these cases is probably a change in the mucous membranes of the nose (and sometimes, when fear of being poisoned is a preoccupation, of the mouth), caused in turn by endocrine changes. The correctly perceived subjective changes in perception are then misinterpreted in the form of hallucinations and delusions (for instance, that enemies are producing evil smells by spreading manure).

Symptoms resembling tunnel vision and motor paralysis of a conversion nature are not rare concomitants of schizophrenic psychoses. Such symptoms, as well as catatonic rigidity, echopraxia, and "schizophrenese" language, lend themselves to both interpretation and treatment by barbiturates (sodium amytal or pentothal injections by vein had a particular vogue during, and right after, World War II) and psychotropic drugs such as the phenothiazines.

Synthetic-Integrative Functioning

Components of Function	Some Disturbances
a. Degree of reconciliation or integration of *discrepant* or potentially incongruent (contradictory) attitudes, values, affects, behavior, and self-representations (e.g., role conflicts).	Disorganized behavior, incongruity between thoughts, feelings, and actions; absence of consistent life goal; poor planning, little effort to relate different areas of experience; fluctuating emotional states without appropriate awareness of the change, as in hysterics; minor and major forms of dissociation, from parapraxes to amnesia, fugues, and multiple personalities; many other ego functions affected, sometimes very pathologically (as in psychotic defenses), because integrative function is such a basic one.
b. Degree of *active* relating together (i.e., integrating) of psychic and behavioral events, whether contradictory or not.	

Treatment of Disturbances of Synthetic-Integrative Functioning

The treatment of disturbed synthetic function may proceed by strengthening other ego functions and by dealing with drive disturbances impairing the synthetic function. Drugs may also be useful. It may be necessary to advise the patient to decrease his burdens, at least temporarily. In such a case the decrease in demands serves like the splinting of a broken limb and permits the synthetic function to improve again almost spontaneously. In patients who have particular difficulty in synthesizing affect and thought, it is essential to establish continuity where they experience discontinuity.

It is very likely that perceptual-motor disturbances, to which increasing attention is being paid in connection with dyslexia and other learning difficulties, are related to some problems of synthetic functioning in the young and that educational help is necessary. In some such children, because of a primary lack of synthesis or perhaps a secondary continued frustration over their inability to perform routine motor and perceptual tasks, emotional explosiveness may also be part of a failure of the synthetic function.

Inconsistent upbringing is certainly likely to impede the maturation of synthetic functioning, and prevention of disturbances will have to be the ultimate treatment.

Mastery—Competence

Major Components of Function	*Some Disturbances*
a. Competence: how well the person actually performs in relation to his existing capacity to interact with and *actively* master and affect his environment.	The person does almost nothing to alter, affect, or interact with his environment, because he is largely unable to use abilities and capacities in relation to reality. What he is able to do might be seen as merely a passive reaction rather than as an active coping. The sense of competence is almost nil, and in most ways the person feels powerless to act effectively, regardless of his actual performance.
b. The person's subjective feeling of competence with respect to mastering and affecting his environment; the person's expectations of success, or actual performance (how he feels about how he does and what he can do); sense of competence is scored *at face value* (e.g., higher than actual competence if there is an exaggerated sense of competence).	
c. The degree of discrepancy between component a and component b (i.e., between actual competence and sense of competence). It may be negative (−), in which case actual competence exceeds sense of competence. It may be equal (=), in which case actual competence and sense of competence are congruent. It	

Major Components of Function   *Some Disturbances*

may be positive (+), in which
case sense of competence exceeds actual competence.

Treatment of Disturbances of Mastery-Competence

A feeling of impotence toward the forces of life, of an inability to master or alter them, seems characteristic of modern man, particularly in the post-World War II period and the atomic age. Existentialism (philosophical and literary) concerns itself primarily with man's relation to powerful forces. Camus's literary characters are helpless, confused, and at the mercy of both their drives and fate. Laing (1960), who is probably the most widely known latter-day exponent of the existential viewpoint in psychiatry, deals specifically with the schizophrenic living in today's world.

An improvement of object relations or impulse control, of reality testing or judgment, is bound to have an indirect effect upon mastery and competence. Self-esteem is of course related to the *sense* of competence. Many outstanding psychotic delusions and hallucinations are the direct result of disturbances in self-esteem, in objective competence, and in the subjective feeling of competence. Classically, delusions of grandeur — frequently encountered in schizophrenic patients with paranoid and/or manic disturbances — both defend against, and are intricately interwoven with, a deep feeling of impotence. A schizophrenic, especially one with manic tendencies, may well imagine himself to be an exalted personage. This easily leads to paranoid delusions — for example, that because he is so important, not only are many people interested in him but many are also inimical to him and eager to put him out of the way. At the heart of these grandiose feelings and the paranoid ones are feelings of smallness and passivity. One could well say that the psychotic makes himself so big because he feels so small; he feels so powerful and conceives of such powerful enemies because he feels so weak and helpless when it comes to *affecting* himself and his world.

Central to the treatment of disturbances of mastery and competence, therefore, is the treatment of low self-esteem. Such therapy may involve interpreting the pathological means of inflating or otherwise regulating self-esteem and then dealing with whatever precipitated the particular instance of lowered self-esteem. For example a patient's delusion of being extremely wealthy may have started with a business failure of objectively rather small proportions but of great importance to him in terms of his actual and subjective sense of mastery-competence.

AN EGOPSYCHOLOGICAL APPROACH TO DIAGNOSIS AND THERAPY WITH BORDERLINE SCHIZOPHRENIC AND SCHIZOPHRENIC ADOLESCENTS – WRITTEN BY MURIEL FOX, Ph.D.

Bellak (1949a) defines schizophrenia and borderline schizophrenia in terms of patterns of ego-subfunction deficiencies. This case study demonstrates the value of applying this approach to the diagnosis, formulation of treatment plans, and actual treatment of borderline schizophrenic and schizophrenic adolescents. The turmoil characteristic of adolescence makes diagnosis difficult (Blos, 1962). Any procedure that increases the accuracy of assessment of adolescents would fill an important need.

The approach to ego function assessment reported in this book, although developed for adults, is useful for all diagnostic categories and ages because it demonstrates ego strengths and weaknesses and, therefore, adaptive potential. Because of the normally confusing behavior of adolescents, the approach may be very useful with them, whether they are disturbed or not. With adolescents as with schizophrenics, a comprehensive and sensitive assessment of areas, degrees, and patterns of ego strengths and weaknesses can cut through behavioral vicissitudes to the basic personality pattern. To the understanding of the sources of adolescents' stress (increased drive strength, superego vicissitudes, and environmental demands), one can, with the ego assessment procedure, add a more detailed picture of the impact of these pressures on the teenagers' adaptive apparatuses.

The usefulness of the Ego Function Scales in cutting through the manifest behavior of the teen-ager's underlying ego strengths and weaknesses can be seen by a comparison of two patients, Linda and Ginny. Linda came into therapy with almost classical psychotic symptoms. Tight, drab, squinty, and withdrawn, she seemed consumed in a struggle with introjected judges and afflicted with auditory hallucinations of long standing. Clinically, she showed few available strengths other than persistence and intelligence. Her prognosis seemed poor. Ginny, in contrast, came into therapy with complaints that seemed, at least initially, almost normal. She reported feeling left out, described a fear of failure, and talked of a compelling need for independence from her parents. Clinically, there were slight rumblings of some distant problems, but these were vague and, because of her acknowledged dramatization of events, of questionable significance. Her prognosis seemed good.

To assess ego functions in these two patients, the therapist rated the patients on the 12 functions as they are scaled in the Manual for Assessing Ego Functions from a Clinical Interview (see Profile 23.1). No structured ego function interview was administered. Rather, the therapist relied exclusively on material that had emerged during the treatment sessions themselves.

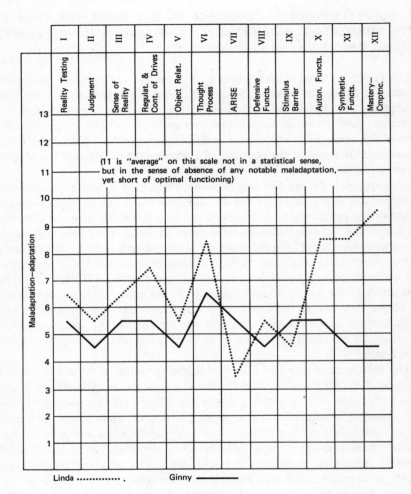

Profile 23.1

Ginny's ego profile showed a weakness in almost all the 12 ego functions. Linda, in contrast, proved deficient in only 7 functions: reality testing, judgment, sense of reality, object relations, ARISE, defensive functioning, and stimulus barrier. The girls had certain different ego weaknesses; the weaknesses they had in common were manifested in qualitatively different behavior. For example, while both girls showed poor defensive functioning, Linda's was manifested in unusually rigid behavior and Ginny's in depressions and dissociated ideas; Ginny flipped and slid from anxiety to depression, to feelings of depersonalization, to excited periods, and then back again. Linda had an enormous capacity for dissociation and intellectualization, whereas Ginny ran the gamut of defenses. While both girls were markedly dependent, Ginny expressed this need more openly and indiscriminately, often subordinating most of her work and social life to its fulfillment. Dependency was more ego alien to Linda and found expression only indirectly.

Critical differences lay in their strengths. Specifically, although both girls were deficient in many ego functions, Linda demonstrated a constant sense of self. She had a coherent, albeit rigid, "self" composed of firmly internalized and persistent defenses and standards originating in the environment but now quite independent of it. The very rigidity of these standards provided a core around which she could organize new experiences. Ginny's "self" was temporary. She ricocheted from one role to another, generally adrift and disconnected from yesterday's self and identity. Linda, unlike Ginny, had strong and generally intact thought processes and an outstanding capacity for integration. Linda also had an overactive drive for mastery and competence that enabled her to maximize learning. In contrast, Ginny's open dependence blocked her drive for mastery. She relied upon the strength and effectiveness of others.

These profiles led to personality pictures and prognoses quite different from those based on the original clinical impressions and several psychological tests. The profiles showed that Linda, however psychotic she appeared, had important ego strengths, whereas Ginny's seeming strengths were ephemeral, a thin imitative facade soon to be stripped away by the demands of adolescence. Ginny, in fact, turned out to be one of the increasingly numerous teen-agers who lacks clear psychotic personality structures but has latent ego defects that surface during adolescence and leave her at times functionally indistinguishable from a schizophrenic.

A profile of ego strengths and weaknesses also provides guidelines for appropriate treatment plans. Therapy with adolescents may be conceived of as an ever-changing balance of three different processes: (1) analyses of unconscious conflicts and attitudes, (2) specific interventions to restore or to develop deficient ego structures, and (3) a real relationship between a "transitional" authority figure and a young patient. The ego function profile helps in determining the desirable balance of these three therapeutic techniques in a treatment plan. The cases of Linda and Ginny are useful in demonstrating this point also. The ego function scales showed that Linda, despite her psychotic symptoms, had developed a psychic structure with enough strength for a modified standard psychotherapeutic approach, supplemented by selective ego-building procedures. In contrast, the treatment of choice for Ginny, at least initially, was a "real," long-term relationship intended to provide a matrix for the development of a stronger psychic structure preparatory to more standard psychotherapy.

In Linda's therapy, described below, a psychoanalytic approach, ego-development procedures, and the ongoing therapist-patient relationship — real and transference — were used. The first goal of Linda's therapy, accomplished largely by interpretation and role playing by the therapist, was a reorganization of psychic structures. To achieve this, the therapist participated in Linda's internalized struggle with a vivid introject, "Tiny Old Man" or "Tom."* By this controlled move into Linda's fantasy, the therapist tried to make herself useful to this very withdrawn and "internally persecuted" girl and, in the process, to weaken her reified conscience, to relate the internalized struggle to her family life, to reconstruct her stringent superego, and, thereby, to make her feelings, daydreams, and drives more available.

Tom was changed in a lengthy dialogue in which the therapist became an authoritative defender of teen-agers, persuading *him* that times have changed, new ways are possible, and so on. The therapist became a spokesman for Linda's hidden thoughts, an auxiliary ego, and at times a new model for Linda to introject or to graft onto herself piece by piece.

In the struggle with Tom, interpretations were made about the nature of Linda's defenses and needs, the underlying conflicts, and the source of the conflicts. There were, concurrent with these interpretations, ego-development procedures, direct attempts to strengthen ego functions shown to be deficient on the ego scale. For example, attempts were made to improve Linda's sense of reality and reality testing. Reality at times was reviewed and reconstructed sector by sector, while her sense of reality, another ego function, became sharper and stronger from interpretations of motives and behavior and from constant anamnestic reviews of her life. Her sense of self was also enlarged and reinforced by the therapist's mirroring of her behavior in the therapy sessions. The therapist pointed out repeatedly, for example, how Linda presented herself as a scholar whenever possible, both in her schoolmarmish dress and her manner. This posture was later discussed as a defense against emotion and, on a deeper level, as a magical protection against being swallowed up by the therapist. As the scholar role faded, the "new," more lively Linda was acknowledged and contrasted with her earlier behavior. Her undeveloped body image required special attention because of repression that left her almost anaesthetized from her neck down. This was handled by coupling interpretations of fear of loss of control and oedipal guilt with supplemental dance, drama, and gymnastic programs geared to sensitize her to body feelings.

*The "Tiny Old Man" was basically a reified conscience, a reinforced superego transformed into an imaginary demigod to strengthen her defenses against impulses, at the same time providing her with an ever-present sexualized male adult companion.

Feelings of any sort were difficult for Linda. Because of the ease with which her feelings dissolved and slipped away and because of her apparent unfamiliarity with feelings, the therapist often deliberately shared her own feelings or gently prodded Linda to reexperience emotional reactions that she would otherwise have tried to ignore or deny. At times Linda's capacity for feeling seemed almost atrophied and in need of active external stimulation of the sort one might institute in physiotherapy with atrophied muscles. This is perhaps an extreme example of the thesis that in addition to analyses — that is, in addition to discussions of the dynamics of life situations — therapy may actually have to provide, within its own limits or through supplemental activities, specific corrective experiences designed for specific ego deficiencies. For example, with Linda, in an effort to make feelings real and ego syntonic, the therapist (a) interpreted the transference relationship, (b) provoked and sanctioned feelings, and (c) fostered real relatedness in the therapeutic situation. Similarly, attempts were made to improve her object relationships directly and indirectly throughout therapy (a) by means of analyses of her responses in and out of therapy, (b) through the more specialized approaches to ego construction, and (c) through the real relationship in therapy, which was alternately supportive, specifically satisfying of one need or another, and deliberately corrective to corroborate and augment the verbal interpretations.

Therapy with Linda was productive because of her outstanding striving for mastery, which had a particularly catalytic effect upon the entire therapeutic procedure. Phenomenologically, this seemed like a strident "will" or élan, constantly maximizing learning opportunities and, in the last analysis, possibly the single most important factor accounting for a remarkable ability to change.

Now to turn to Ginny and the contrasting therapeutic plan suggested by her ego profile. Ginny's profile, in fact her whole personality, showed a kind of structural impoverishment that necessitated a different balance of therapeutic techniques than the one prescribed for Linda. Instead of the loosening of defenses and easing of the superego that were required for Linda, Ginny needed a strengthening of her defenses and consolidation and development of her rudimentary and fragmented superego. Instead of using an already advanced integrative function, an organizational ability had first to be developed. Instead of expanding an existing sense of self, a feeling of self had largely to be started from scratch, and feelings, labile and rampant, required integration in a stable pattern of relatedness. Ginny's deficiencies pointed to a "growing up baby" type of therapy, a long-term, "real," and broadly educational relationship, one that could primarily become the matrix for identification, incorporation of standards, and imitation of controls and coping behavior. With Linda the therapeutic emphasis was more on augmenting existing, although basic, functions. The emphasis with Ginny was more on "building in" structures.

In Ginny's therapy, the therapist seemed to be the major catalytic agent. A beacon solidly in the middle of Ginny's life, the therapist made herself useful, reliable, available, underscoring her presence as an examplar* who relates in a stubborn, organized, and consistent way to the inconsistent and regressive confusion of the patient. For example, Ginny regularly badgered the therapist to change interpretations. Ginny's parents had invariably reversed themselves and behaved inconsistently as a result of their alternately reacting to her as an object of envy, punishment, or education or as the vehicle through which they could act out their own unconscious and frustrated asocial needs. It seemed of prime importance for Ginny to have a definitively outlined and clearly consistent therapist. Unlike the situation with Linda, therefore, where the therapist tried to be loose and flexible to counteract Linda's frozen character, the therapist tried, with the fluid and fragmented Ginny, to remain firm, almost like a benign cigar-store Indian. The therapist at times came across as a friendly anchor or a firm magnet, especially in reaction to Ginny's ever changing plans and goals. Here the therapist became the nagging reminder of the past and, through a review of the past and reconstruction of sequences of motives, for example, encouraged Ginny to set limits herself and to value persistence and consistency more highly. Planted dead center in Ginny's life, the therapist became an object of identification and imitation, an interested and solid source of personality grafts that were more permanent than those from her alternately detached, overstimulating, and inconsistent parents.

From this central vantage point, the therapist functioned in the reciprocally enhancing roles of exemplar and educator—therapist. The therapist as exemplar was a partial source of superego functions. The therapist as trainer then reinforced this "graft" by mirroring superego functions, selectively rewarding certain behavior patterns and suggesting alternate drive outlets concordant with the developing superego. Ginny engaged in a lot of asocial behavior. For example, she regularly stole things. Stealing was interpreted as an expression of affect hunger and social alienation. Stealing was made more ego alien with the help of a strong positive transference and a real and clearly supportive relationship in which stealing was repudiated. Stealing was further blocked by redirecting Ginny to more socially acceptable forms of love and to more controlled outlets for attacks on society.

Within this broad plan other techniques for enhancing ego development were used, often similar to those employed with Linda, to build a clear, longitudinally continuous and three-dimensional identity, to couple that with a feeling self, to strengthen reality testing and judgment, and to improve object relationships. In addition to mirroring and reviews, constant discrimination was necessary to select one from among Ginny's multitude of roles, to make connections between

*Dr. Ruth-Jean Eisenbud contributed to this formulation in a personal communication.

the many roles, and to embed her feelings in an ongoing self and in real relationships. With Ginny, special attention was paid to reinforcing drive controls and a consistent and stable pattern of defenses and to strengthening autonomous structures. Equally important was the work done, first, to interest this highly dependent girl in personal mastery and organizational skills and, second, to develop these functions with the therapist both as exemplar and educator-therapist. Ginny was encouraged not only to imitate forms of integration but to branch out with her own forms, always under circumstances in which the therapist stressed what *Ginny could do,* thereby giving her license to be a distinct person, a role unknown in her family. The therapist also alerted Ginny to the strengths within her and to her own ego boundaries.

With Ginny, more than with Linda, the therapist functioned as a transitional authority figure between the parents and peers, whom Ginny could attach herself to and use as an auxiliary ego and a constant and consistent model until the time when she could learn, rediscover, or develop enough psychic structure to benefit from a more classical form of interpretive therapy.

The therapy processes were thus different for the two girls because of their varying patterns of ego strengths and weaknesses. With Linda, a modified psychoanalytically oriented approach was used because her profile showed the kinds of ego strengths required for the success of this type of therapy. Ginny's profile showed the need for a long-term supportive educational approach preparatory to more standard therapeutic interventions. The ego profiles led to different treatment plans and to plans that were at variance with those suggested by the initial clinical interviews and psychological tests.

In summary, therapy with two teen-agers was discussed to support the thesis that diagnosis and therapy with teen-agers should be particularly attentive to ego strengths and the correction of ego weaknesses. An egopsychological profile was used to show that ego assessments significantly increase the armamentarium of diagnostic tools and get beyond shifting and often confusing behavioral phenomena to psychic structures. Therapy with adolescents was described as an ever-changing balance of three processes: (1) interpretations of unconscious conflicts and attitudes, (2) specific interventions to restore or to develop deficient ego structures, and (3) a real relationship between a "transitional" authority figure and a young patient. An egopsychological approach is valuable in therapy because it helps identify the ego functions in need of development and thus sets broad outlines for the kinds of appropriate interventions.

CASE STUDIES: A STUDY OF PROGRESS IN PSYCHOTHERAPY AND DRUG THERAPY IN TERMS OF EGO FUNCTIONS

A large body of literature describes the attempts at, and problems of, evaluating therapy, in general, and psychotherapy, in particular. Ego functions may serve as a good means of studying progress during, or resulting from, therapeutic interventions. Ego function ratings, as described by us, provide a meaningful, valid, and reliable criterion of adaptive capacity. Their use in the study of drug effects has been suggested elsewhere (Bellak et al., 1968). Chassan (1967) has formulated a statistical method for the intensive design study of either a single patient or a few patients. His method of using each patient as his own control, with frequent sampling of the patient under specific conditions, offers a means of avoiding the nearly insoluble problem of properly matching control groups. Bellak and Chassan (1964) have used this method for the study of a patient in psychotherapy who was also on a carefully designed program of chlordiazepoxide (Librium). We shall now report another study using the intensive design technique, an evaluation of psychotherapy combined with diazepam administration.* Chassan designed the sequence in which placebos and diazepam were given to the patients in a double blind procedure (Figure 23.1).

The hypothesis underlying the expectation that diazepam might affect ego functions (in addition to the effects of psychotherapy) was that it might reduce anxiety. Reduced anxiety, in turn, would promote better ego functioning. That a disturbance in thought processes, even as severe as is found in schizophrenia, might be related to anxiety has been suggested by representatives of very different views. Mednick (1958), for instance, from a behaviorist viewpoint, has suggested that already present anxiety leads some people to avoid anxiety-arousing thoughts to such a degree as to produce overinclusion and other typical thought defects. Basic to psychoanalytic theory, on the other hand, is the assumption that anxiety may lead to primary-process thinking, as well as to a weakening of defenses, which in turn leads to a regression of object relations and of most other aspects of functioning.

A severely neurotic patient was included in this program. At the beginning of each week the patient was given a bottle of tablets and asked to take one three times a day. He was expected to stay on the drug during six months of psychotherapy. During and after each psychotherapeutic session, the therapist rated the patient on all ego functions, making illustrative and explanatory comments in addition to the ratings.

The study served several purposes: (1) to illustrate the use of ego function ratings in the course of therapy, (2) to evaluate the possible effect of Valium as seen through twice-a-week psychotherapy, and (3) to evaluate whether *clinical* ego ratings correlated highly enough with ratings on our specifically designed standard interview. In the present discussion we focus on the first point, the

*We are grateful to Hoffmann-La Roche, Inc. for providing both the diazepam and th carefully matched samples of placebo and for some financial aid for this part of ou research.

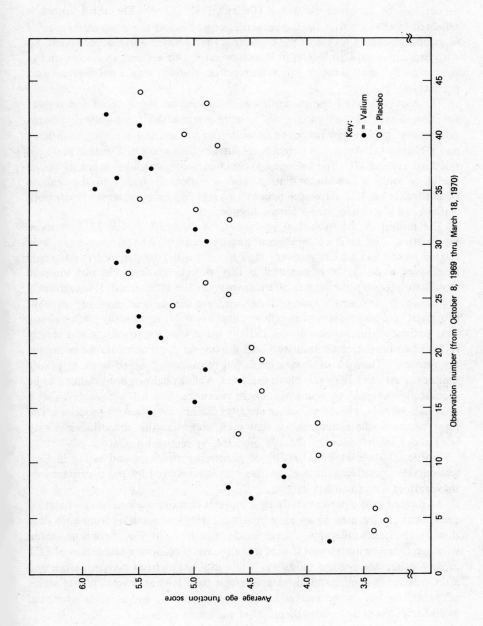

Figure 23.1

illustration of the use of ego functions for an evaluation of therapy. The second aspect will be reported elsewhere (Bellak et al., 1973). The third aspect is reflected in the fact that for the patient discussed below the mean of the ratings of two independent judges of the therapist's therapeutic interview correlated .80 with the structural Ego Function Interview ratings of a therapist session on the same day by the therapist (of a therapeutic session, significant beyond one percent level).

The therapist rated the patient's ego functions on the basis of the regular function scores of one patient on a seven-point scale, the highly significant differences for nine ego functions between the Valium and placebo conditions, and a change (although not a significant one) in the expected direction in object relations and ARISE. The average ego function score, or global score, although useful to only a certain extent, is also significantly higher in the Valium condition. Table 23.2 shows the patient's average ego function scores under both Valium and placebo in the 44 observation periods.

The ratings of the individual ego functions shown in Profile 23.2 are more informative. The lack of significant improvement in ARISE may have been related to the fact that it was very high to start with (the patient had had some success as a poet). It is regrettable that object relations did not improve significantly during the course of treatment. On the other hand, it is extremely important that reality testing, judgment, regulation and control, thought processes, and so on showed significant improvement, specifically with Valium. This patient's stimulus barrier was initially quite low; improvement was clearly reflected in his increased ability to bear the impact of stimuli without becoming disorganized. Thought processes improved remarkably, which is an especially significant result: unlike the phenothiazines, Valium has not been claimed to be specifically designed to improve thought processes. The findings suggest that a drug like Valium, which can reduce anxiety, can improve thought processes. The most parsimonious assumption is that even drugs like the phenothiazines may bring about improvement of thought processes by reducing anxiety.

Profile 23.2 shows initial rating of patient by therapist and rating in final session. The possibility of a subjective bias is countered by the consistency of these ratings with the other data.

As limited as the present study is, it suggests that our method of ego function assessment can be used to appraise progress during and resulting from both drug therapy and psychotherapy. If large studies confirm this one, there is no reason why ego function assessment should not also lend itself to the evaluation of ECT or any other therapeutic modality. While evaluation from ratings before and after treatment is economical, sampling ego functions at several points seems advisable. At least some ratings before, at the end of, and at some stipulated period after the end of active therapy are probably optimal.

Table 23-1. Average Ego Function Scores on Valium and Placebo

	Reality Testing	Judgment	Sense of Reality	Regula. & Control of Drives	Object Relat.	Thought Processes	ARISE	Defensive Functs.	Stimulus Barrier	Auton. Functs.	Synthet. Functs.	Global Score
Valium	5.52	5.41	5.26	5.00	4.93	5.35	5.57	4.87	4.02	5.09	4.89	5.09
Placebo	4.86	4.83	4.81	4.31	4.60	4.70	5.53	4.24	3.55	4.48	4.36	4.55
Difference	0.66	0.58	0.45	0.69	0.33	0.65	0.04	0.63	0.47	0.61	0.53	0.54
t	2.88	2.79	1.85	3.41	1.42	2.79	0.23	3.00	2.51	2.70	2.13	2.78
p<	.002	.003	.04[a]	.001	—	.003	—	.003	.01	.005	.02	.003

[a] Single-tailed.

383

Table 23.2.   Average Ego Function Scores Under Valium and Placebo

Observation Period	Valium	Placebo
1	4.5	
2	3.8	
3		3.4
4		3.3
5		3.4
6	4.5	
7	4.7	
8	4.2	
9	4.2	
10		3.9
11		3.8
12		4.6
13		3.9
14	5.4	
15	5.0	
16		4.4
17	4.6	
18	4.9	
19		4.4
20		4.5
21	5.3	
22	5.5	
23	5.5	
24		5.2
25		4.7
26		4.9
27		5.6
28	5.7	
29	5.6	
30	4.9	
31	5.0	
32		4.7
33		5.0
34		5.5
35	5.9	
36	5.7	
37	5.4	
38	5.5	
39		4.8
40		5.1
41	5.5	
42	5.8	
43		4.9
44		5.5

Leopold Bellak, M.D.,
Principal Investigator
PATTERNS OF EGO FUNCTIONS
RESEARCH PROJECT
N.I.M.H. Grant # ROI MH 14260

Subject # _____
Group # _Valium_
Rater(s) _____

Levels of functioning:
Therapist's rating ———— before   — — — — after

Profile 23.2

In the next section, the desirable assessment of ego functions a year after treatment ended and a comparison with the ratings before therapy are presented for another patient.

CASE STUDIES: A PROFILE COMPARISON BEFORE AND AFTER PSYCHOANALYTIC THERAPY

This 24-year-old man was part of the schizophrenic population of one study and was first seen in 1969. To preserve anonymity, only the aspects of the case history that are useful for illustrative purposes and pertain to the ego function profile will be mentioned. The patient was referred to the senior author by a clinician in the western United States. The young man had traveled there for a vacation and one evening became acutely disturbed. He ran through the streets of the town singing and shouting, eventually taking off his clothes and setting them on fire. The police subdued him with a toxic gas and hospitalized him.

In the initial clinical interview it was learned that the patient had gone to college in the Northeast. Although he did not do very well scholastically, he was active as a booking agent for musicians. Just before his departure for the West, he suffered both a major business reversal and a serious disappointment with a girlfriend. At some time between those events and his being picked up by the police, he apparently developed grandiose ideas, for example, expecting to be sent to Vietnam to end the war. At the same time, he was afraid that any number of people would interfere with the plan and felt spied upon by the FBI and the CIA. He thought that he was being observed on television and that people could read his mind. Being subdued by the police in the manner described above further confirmed his notions that people were out to do him harm.

After very brief hospitalization, his return to New York was arranged. He was admitted to a hospital for acute psychiatric disturbances where the initial interview and the initial psychodynamic studies were performed. By this time he was receiving very heavy medication, as much as 800 mg of Mellaril a day, which produced some Parkinsonism. In the hospital the dose was promptly reduced to a minimal maintenance level, and psychotherapy was begun. The psychotherapy centered on the patient's use of denial. His delusions of grandeur and his occasional high spirits were interpreted to him as a way of dealing with the two disappointments mentioned above. The patient had previously undergone some psychotherapy and was able to respond very promptly and with considerable insight. He also participated in group meetings and occasional therapy in the hospital clinic. He showed marked improvement within a couple of weeks. He was then introduced to a psychoanalyst who saw him twice in the hospital and then continued treatment for two years extramurally. A complete psychological test battery was administered by a member of our research team.

The psychological testing included the WAIS, Figure-Drawing, T.A.T., the Rorschach, and Projective Queries. The scores were as follows: comprehension was the highest score prorated to an I.Q. of 142; object assembly and picture arrangement were as low as 80. To the extent to which finger dexterity was involved in some of the subtests, such as object assembly, the medication may well have been responsible for his low scores. A thought disorder was suggested by some of his responses on the similarity subtest. The disturbance of his logic on the most difficult items of this particular scale constitutes an extreme that was not consistent with the patient's coherence and relevence in the clinical examination and as revealed in his responses during the standard interview. Projective tests suggested grandiosity of an effective nature rather than paranoid megalomania. Primary-process material was close to the surface and readily available. A great deal of guilt about sexuality was evident and some suicidal preoccupation. In view of the patient's outstanding use of denial, the psychologist's report suggests a diagnosis of schizoaffective psychosis as the most appropriate.

Our complete ego function assessment procedure was used before treatment and again one year after termination of psychotherapy.*

In the ego function profile based on the combined ratings of two significantly correlated raters (.71, significant at .05 percent level) on the initial research interview (see Profile 23.3), several functions were commented on at the time:

A patient with fairly good object relations and fairly good thought processes . . . seemed a good prospect for psychotherapy, with a mixture of phenothiazine and amitriptypine providng control of drives and mood, and a rehabilitation workshop providing the general setting for a building and rebuilding of self-esteem poorly compensated by grandiose goals. While the cluster of high ratings for object relations and thought processes constitutes a basis for therapeutic optimism, the poor ratings on regulation and control of drives and the poor defensive functioning are liabilities, and the low autonomous and synthetic functions are reasons for concern with regard to the ultimate stability of improvement. The low scores for reality testing and judgment reflect the acute disturbance, in the form of hallucinations and delusions. This could be a central *area* for intervention, i.e., for exploration of the dynamics of the apperceptive distortions. In this young man's prepsychotic state, his disturbance manifested itself primarily in unrealistic phantasies of achievement and in defensive denial, which were responsible sometimes for elation (and sometimes helped increase his actual achievement although only over a short run) Bellak, Hurvich and Crawford, (1970, p. 539).

Two years later, two independent raters rated him; the correlation of their scores is .67, significant at the 0.05 level, and their combined ratings are seen in Profile 23.4.

At the time of the second research interview (1971), the patient was also interviewed informally. He appeared to be free of manifest symptoms and said he felt generally well, was gainfully employed, and had a satisfying social life, including a girlfriend. He was not entirely confident as yet that his path would remain smooth. He had terminated treatment because of parental pressure rather than of his own accord.

The research evaluation, his progress in therapy, the clinical impression at the last interview, and the rating by his therapist essentially support the original contention, based on the ego function profile, that the prognosis was relatively good, that the patient was suited to dynamic psychoanalytic psychotherapy, and

*The patient's therapist had also rated the patient similarly, but as his second ratings were retrospective rather than done at the time we saw him last, they are not included here.

Leopold Bellak, M. D. Principal Investigator
MULTIDISCIPLINARY STUDY OF SCHIZOPHRENIA
RESEARCH PROJECT
N.I.M.H. Grant #18395

Subject # _093_
Group #
Rater(s)
Date

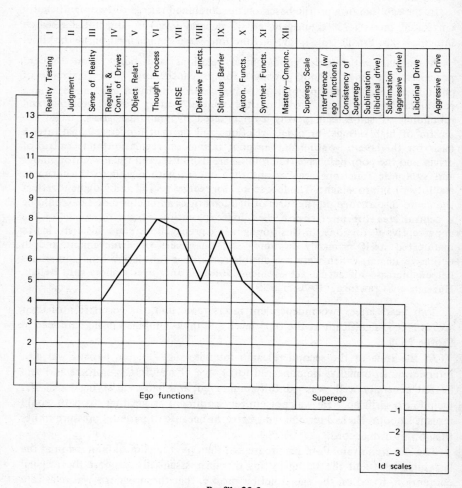

Profile 23.3

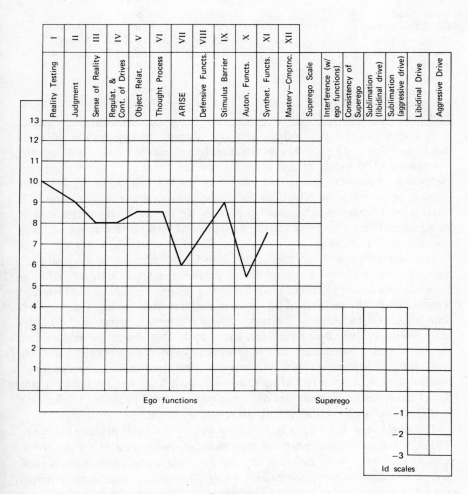

Profile 23.4

389

that thereby his ego functions would be particularly improved.

Table 23.3   Mean Ego Function Scores for Two Sets of Project Raters Before and After
Psychotherapy of Subject #093

	Before	After	Difference
Reality testing	4	10	6
Judgment	4	9	5
Sense of reality	4	8	4
Regulation control	5	8	3
Object relations	6.5	8.5	2
Thought Processes	8	8.5	.5
ARISE	7.5	6	-1.5
Defensive Functioning	5	7.5	2.5
Stimulus Barrier	7.5	9	1.5
Autonomous Functioning	5	5.5	.5
Synthetic Functioning	4	7.5	3.5

A comparison of the before- and after-therapy ratings of the different functions (Table 23.3) shows substantial improvement in the level of ego functioning. The higher ratings after therapy are consistent with the psychotherapist's impression that substantial improvement had occurred. It is not possible to separate the effects of psychotherapy, spontaneous remission, and improvement from other unspecified sources. We present these comparisons as an additional bit of evidence for the usefulness of ego function rating scales in the assessment of therapy.

The improvement from the acute disorder is reflected in the patient's markedly better scores on reality testing, judgment, sense of self, regulation of impulses, and object relations, *in that order*. A deeper, more basic improvement is suggested by the increase of 3.5 units in synthetic functioning. This person is now better able to reconcile the many divergent affects, impulses, and thoughts that previously had been markedly dissociated. This change promises some continued better functioning. The improvement in his defenses is also gratifying and nearly as promising. Thought processes show only minimal improvement because they were not badly affected to begin with. The one regrettable finding is that the autonomous functions did not improve more. The slight improvement in stimulus barrier is consistent with the rest of the results.

The single most interesting finding may well be the small negative change in ARISE. It suggests that adaptive regression, so highly related to creativity, actually decreased as the defenses and impulse control became stronger. A good deal of investigation would be necessary to judge whether the creative potential was actually decreased or whether a rather loose facility for slightly overinclusive thinking and playfulness was involved. We do know that the art of some schizophrenics is pseudocreative, having little communicative value and excessively subjective meaning.

This is not the place for a discussion of the nature of art, nor is it necessary: the therapeutic improvement was possibly, to a certain extent, attained at the price of creativity. It is a point frequently discussed in the literature. The present case bears out an expectation of Bellak's (1963), but the stipulation he mentions in the same paper must also be kept in mind: particularly in people less disturbed than the patient under discussion, analytic therapy is likely to increase ARISE by virtue of decreasing pathological defenses and increasing synthetic functioning. To test this contention, it will be necessary to rate creatively gifted neurotic persons before and after psychoanalysis.

CASE STUDIES: GEMINI

The following case is presented because there exists independently gathered, detailed clinical information about the patient against which to check the data obtained from the formal assessment of ego functions. One of the authors was in a position to assess the patient's ego functioning from the vantage point of individual psychotherapy. The formal interview was conducted and rated by one of the other authors, who at the time knew almost nothing about the patient. Areas of congruence of the therapists' judgments and the interviewers' and raters' judgments thus support a belief in the value of formal ego function assessment. There is, moreover, the exceptional opportunity of comparing the ego functions of an ill girl with those of her healthy twin.

Patient L.O., a 20-year-old female who has a fraternal twin sister, was seen after she had been treated elsewhere for two years for manifest schizophrenia. She had been under the care of several psychiatrists and had been carefully studied for any neurological illness or other physical disorder while hospitalized for two months. No organic pathology was found. L.O. had been on a heavy regimen of a variety of psychotropic drugs—especially Thioridazine (Mellaril) — that produced some rigidity of the face and failed to free her from her disturbing hallucinations and delusions. Immediately before referral to one of the authors, she had been under the treatment of a psychiatrist specializing in multivitamin therapy, therapy which had little apparent effect on her psychotic state.

The manifest problems had apparently started when the patient was 16 and found the demands of adolescent sexuality frightening. She became irritable, explosive, and complained of tubular vision. Sometimes she had only lateral vision and no central vision. Because of these symptoms she had been given a careful neurological examination. The patient also claimed at times to be almost totally blind and able to walk around only by virtue of certain signs, such as red arrows she saw on the floor. She was troubled by a variety of disturbing hallucinations and delusions, such as that somebody was trying to catch her in a net and choke her and that people were trying to "get her" by molesting her and by embarrassing her. She was in love with, and later harbored delusions about, a teacher whom she believed to have diabolical sexual powers over her. At night she was preoccupied with a 10-foot figure—an hallucinatory manifestation of God—that hovered over her and loved her but also scared her and about whom she had overt sexual fantasies.

At the time of this latest referral, she still had most of these symptoms, had some paranoid ideas, heard voices calling her, and had frightening visions of headless turkeys, blood, and so on. She also laughed inappropriately and engaged in clowning. She exhibited many mannerisms that were part of her hallucinatory interaction with the God-figure. She was unable to sleep without very heavy doses of phenothiazine. She daydreamed of being powerful and wanted to be Caesar, suggesting a fusion of her idealized self-representation with the hallucinated God-like object. She had become 30-35 pounds overweight and had no social life. Although she had graduated from high school and gone to secretarial school, she was unable to carry on from there and was generally unable to direct her life in any purposeful way.

Her father was a civil servant of rather strict mores and rigid character. Her mother was a tense, volatile woman who consciously tried to take as good care of the patient as she could. L.O. described her fraternal twin sister as always having been intelligent, always knowing right from wrong, having willpower so she could study and hold her own—all in contradistiction to herself. The patient's I.Q. at that time was 110 on the Bellevue-Wechsler. Psychological testing, which included projective tests, in addition to confirming the diagnosis of schizophrenia, revealed a specific disturbance of thought processes.

At the time of intake, informal clinical evaluation of the patient's current ego functions by the therapist yielded the following ratings (13-point scale):

Reality testing	4
Judgment (at its lowest)	4
Sense of reality	4
Regulation and control of drive and affect	5
Object relations	4
Thought processes	3
ARISE	4
Defensive functioning	3
Stimulus barrier	8
Autonomous functioning	4
Synthetic functioning	4

The patient spent much of her time in her room fantasizing or hallucinating. Her reality testing and judgment were not good enough for her to come to the doctor's office on her own. She might go off with any stranger or become panicky at any time. She had occasional tantrums directed against her mother and spent much of the night wandering around and eating. Her thought process strayed from any given topic, and she had to be brought back to it to maintain an even somewhat continuous discussion for any length of time. She painted pictures of her hallucinatory experiences that were rife with symbolism but nevertheless of some artistic merit. Projection mechanisms were prominent, and repression insufficient. She was not, however, especially easily distracted by noise or other interferences, nor was she subjectively troubled by distractions. She retained her ability to express herself in several languages, had available a considerable fund of information, and her memory was confused but not otherwise impaired. Affect and thought were often disparate: typically unhappy experiences were described with a grin. She felt unable to perform any work and unequal to any of the everyday tasks.

The history taken from both father and mother suggested that L.O. was "different" from her sister practically from birth (i.e., more sluggish, less responsive). Later on, in school, she was more sensitive than her twin and less able to concentrate. Compared with her twin, she had an intense emotional involvement with her father and a hostile relationship with her mother. This turmoil in object relations was both a further cause and a result of a weakened ego.

As the heavy doses of Mellaril had not produced satisfactory clinical results and had induced some slight Parkinsonism, the patient was switched to trifluoperazine (Stelazine) 5 mg, t.i.d. The patient was also given imipramine (Tofranil) 25 mg, morning and noon, to counteract lethargy. She was sent to a rehabilitation workshop, and psychotherapy was begun. It was soon apparent, however, that neither pharmacotherapy nor psychotherapy nor rehabilitation could produce more than very minor improvement as long as L.O. stayed at home in hostile interactions with her mother. A two-month removal from home to some distant relatives was therefore recommended and arranged. Care at the relatives' home with the possibility of rehabilitation in that environment was also discussed, and a psychiatrist in that city was advised of her status. During this time the patient was maintained on the drugs described above. At the end of the two-month period, the patient returned home very much improved, although still not in a condition to work or travel by herself. She was still occasionally troubled by nighttime hallucinations of God hovering over her. Now, however, she was in condition to bear and profit from more active psychotherapy. Since she felt more comfortable and spoke more openly about important matters in the company of her sister, joint psychotherapy with her twin was arranged. This arrangement made the transference situation less threatening to her. The three of us discussed the period of adolescence and the experiences that had been particularly upsetting to L. O. Her sister provided supplementary information about her twin's condition at the time. After about two months of such therapy it was possible to work through some of the patient's anxieties and misconceptions. With the aid of Stelazine, the patient was able to take jobs as a babysitter. A clinical evaluation of her ego functions at this point suggested that current regulation and control of drives were such that no potentially dangerous impulsive outbursts were to be expected. Defensive functioning had improved considerably, and her autonomous functioning was good enough for her to perform relatively simple tasks. As for thought processes, the patient at this point in treatment started planning for further education, but it was clear that her thinking was not yet good enough for that to be possible for perhaps another six months.

For the time being, future planning involved only modest goals. L.O. seemed to love children, probably by identification, and wanted to enter the field of baby-nursing. Whatever hostility she had seemed to be directed toward adults, not toward children. She did not, therefore, seem to be a danger to prospective charges. Some semiprofessional field with two years of training above the level of a practical nurse but below the level of a registered nurse was considered. It was also understood that such training and later occupation would provide her with an opportunity to sleep in dormitories and thus to live away from her parents.

About three months after *active* psychotherapy began, a formal ego-function-assessment interview was conducted and the functions rated by another member of the research team. The pattern of ego functions is presented in Profile 23.5. It can be seen that reality testing and judgment are within normal limits in ratings for the highest level of functioning and that they were assessed as dropping to psychotic levels for the lowest level of functioning. Much of L.O.'s current level of functioning had reached the characteristic level of functioning but not the highest levels. Currently, the low levels of adaptive regression and defensive functioning together may reflect rigidity and constriction because of the enormous defensive expenditure needed to help control the drives. Synthetic functioning is moderate. Normal intelligence and moderately good synthetic functioning suggest a fair to good long-range prognosis. One other aspect of the profile that has to make one cautious, however, is the considerable spread between highest and lowest levels on some of the functions, leaving open the possibility of future episodes of lability. However, the highest-level ratings for reality testing, autonomous functioning, and judgment are within normal limits. A therapeutic goal based in part on this information is to help this patient function within her intellectual, educational, and psychodynamic limitations in a relatively simple setting so that the four relatively normal functions may be permitted to develop to what the profile shows are the highest levels she is capable of achieving.

To attain these goals in treatment, the psychotherapist served as an "auxiliary

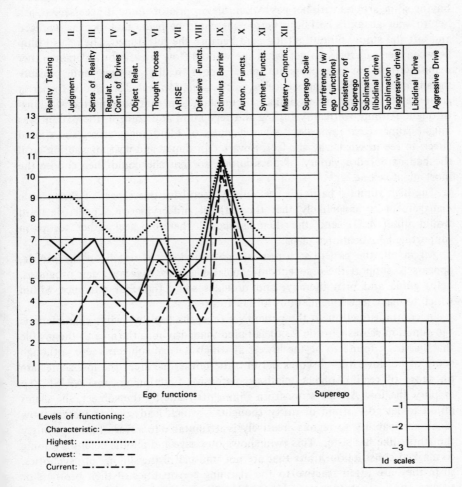

Leopold Bellak, M. D. Principal Investigator
MULTIDISCIPLINARY STUDY OF SCHIZOPHRENIA
RESEARCH PROJECT
N.I.M.H. Grant #18395

Subject #   *Gemini #1*
Group #
Rater(s)
Date

Levels of functioning:
Characteristic: ——————
Highest: ....
Lowest: — — — — —
Current: —·—·—·—·—

Profile 23.5

ego" with regard to the functions of reality testing and regulation and control, actively helping her to improve both. The impairment of these is often reflected, for L.O., in a paranoid feeling of being taken advantage of, which is probably related to some difficulty in comprehending issues and to a low frustration tolerance. For example, for a while the patient worked quite satisfactorily as a saleswoman in a shop, but she became incensed one Friday afternoon when her paycheck was delayed for a short while. She had especially looked forward to buying some articles with her pay. When the proprietor found it necessary to ask her to wait an extra half-hour before she could be paid, L.O. became enraged and left the store without getting paid because she felt duped. The relationship between her eagerness to get what she wanted (low frustration tolerance), her manifestations of inappropriate anger, poor reality testing, and possibly maladaptive, self-defeating solutions to the situation was discussed with her in great detail. Several other similar circumstances permitted repeated working-through. To improve reality testing and regulation and control, the patient was taught some *signal awareness*: when feelings of blind anger arose, she should check to see in what way she feels thwarted or duped and postpone action until she had explored a variety of possibilities, so that she could then choose the most adaptive one.

The high stimulus barrier is particularly useful for one aspect of therapeutic management: it is unlikely that the turmoil and crying on a pediatric ward would upset L.O., and the therapist could therefore feel rather secure in supporting her vocational plans.

All in all, the patient's pattern of ego functions, as noted on the profile, appears to support the independent clinical diagnosis, suggests a fair prognosis, helps guide and plan therapy, and provides some frame of reference within which to make recommendations for her future.

In contradistinction to the patient's scores, the healthy twin's characteristic ego function scores (Profile 23.6) fall predominantly into the area of the profile that has been found to be the lowest at which normal subjects score, although some of her lowest-level scores fall into the borderline area—the low scores are on sense of reality, object relations, defensive functioning, and ARISE. To amplify the low ARISE score from comments made by the subject, she seems afraid to let go—"afraid of nutty thoughts"—which leads one to wonder how much her inability to regress creatively is attributable to a fear of having "nutty thoughts" like her sister. This twin shows obsessive and phobic defenses leading to marked constriction, traits that are not unusual in the siblings of psychotics, since they are often reactive to the alarming personalities of their brothers or sisters. In the present case, Heston's notion that the healthy members of schizophrenic families tend to be especially creative is not born out. Neither the healthy twin, her parents, her older brother, nor anyone else in the family is notably creative. In fact, the low ARISE and defenses in the healthy twin

Leopold Bellak, M. D. Principal Investigator
MULTIDISCIPLINARY STUDY OF SCHIZOPHRENIA
RESEARCH PROJECT
N.I.M.H. Grant #18395

Subject # *Gemini #2*
Group # _____
Rater(s) ___ ___ ___
Date ___ ___ ___

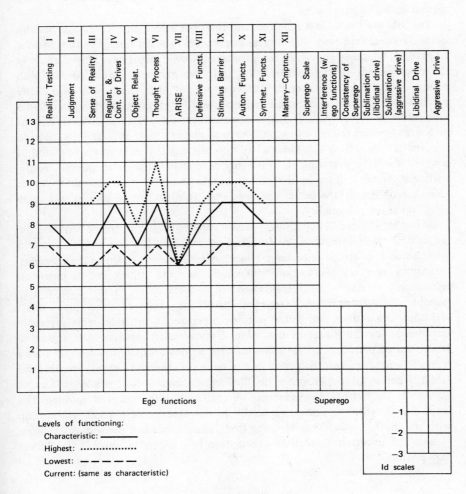

Profile 23.6

suggest that siblings of disturbed children need special care so as not to take refuge in excessively constrictive defenses.

The highest-level rating for thought is 11, impulse control is fair, and libidinal and aggressive drive strength are rather low. These strengths, together with adaptive levels of superego function, complete the picture of a well-adapted person whose ego functioning is not outstanding in any respect and is even quite poor in some. The overall picture is healthy enough for the possibility of future mental illness to be remote.

The low level of object relations and the poor sense of reality in this healthy twin are consistent with the clinical impression that the family setting was far from ideal. Whatever genetic or constitutional *Anlage* might have played a role in the development of the schizophrenic girl, two extremely tense parents with highly critical and even hostile attitudes suggest that there were also many precipitating factors in the social environment. If the healthy twin had had a high rating in object relations (the sense of reality may, to a considerable extent, be a derivative of these), one would have to assume that, at least in relation to her, the family setting was benign. As it is, the healthy twin serves as a kind of control: the family setting was probably pathogenic enough to interact badly with congenital factors in the schizophrenic twin but not enough to cause serious problems in the better endowed one, although, to be sure, it had some effect upon her personality.

A further circumstantial clinical factor appears to be that the patient was the father's favorite: she seems to have had an excessive libidinal pull to contend with. In each of six pairs of female monozygotic twins known to the therapist, one twin was markedly more disturbed than the other, and a disturbed relationship to one of the parents seemed an outstanding factor. It is entirely possible that, from infancy on, the "sick" one induced some unfavorable attitudes rather than that initial unfavorable parental attitudes were primarily responsible for the illness of that twin. Unsystematic impressions from such a small sample permit only tentative inferences; however, it may be said that a warm relationship with the parent of the same sex seemed to have a constructive effect, whereas an inappropriate libidinal involvement with the father or lack of warmth in the mother always seems to be paired with the sicker offerspring. The involvement with the father, especially in the absence of a good relationship with the mother, was felt as resulting from, and stimulating, dangerous impulses. Meager and uncertain as such an observation is, it seems consistent with clinical expectation.

CHAPTER 24

Prognosis and the Profile

If diagnosis must generate heuristic hypotheses that permit one to understand, predict, and control (see chapter on diagnosis), and if prediction in the clinical setting means prognosis, then careful diagnosis and useful prognosis are inseparably associated with each other. The problem of prognosis in the field of schizophrenia has subsumed a great many other problems of the field as well. Bellak (1958a) has previously pointed out the lack of control of variables implied in statements about therapy and prognosis that were made without any attempt at controlling or carefully defining the circumstances to which they referred. As a result of such laxity, insulin treatment, ECT psychotherapy, and many other forms of treatment were often pronounced successful without even such minimal considerations as a statement of the time limit within which the treatment was considered successful, to say nothing of attempts to grade success meaningfully. The minimal precaution of stating and checking on short- and long-range prognosis particularly bedevils the study of schizophrenia within psychiatry. In the *Special Report on Schizophrenia* of the National Institute of Mental Health (NIMH) (1971) reference is made to the fact that the number of beds occupied at one time by schizophrenics has decreased by 30 percent in the past 15 years, seemingly a tremendous achievement. Yet, the same survey also reports that over these same 15 years the rate of admission of schizophrenics has steadily increased. In brief, what these two figures add up to is generally known as the revolving-door phenomenon, as touched upon in the chapter on treatment. Patients have a much shorter hospital stay at any one given time but are much more frequently admitted — or rather readmitted. These figures have implications for short- and long-term prognosis. Short-term prognosis for schizophrenia has improved with the advent of psychotropic drugs, hospitalization in facilities close to the home of the patient, and, consequently, more-readily accomplished discharge into a community now more willing than before to tolerate schizophrenics (at present 2-3 million people are officially diagnosed as such). Long-term prognosis involving the illness itself does not appear to have altered much.

The complexities of diagnosis and prognosis are discussed in that same NIMH report. Although New York and California have about the same number of residents, New York has five times as many patients in treatment for functional psychosis (80 percent of whom are schizophrenic) than California. Moreover, the overall decline in the number of hospitalized patients started in California considerably before the introduction of psychotropic drugs. It appears that this decline is caused primarily by a decision by the California legislature, in the early 1950's, not to build any more state hospitals and to concentrate instead on active therapy and community-centered care. Again, statements about treatment understood in the context of expanded contexts—here to include possibly physical and social climates—become more easily interpretable than when they are limited to mere demography. California's general milieu may have encouraged its legislators to risk increased community treatment and decreased hospital treatment.

The very concept of schizophrenia is, of course, another factor affecting both diagnosis and prognosis. In Kraepelin's day the diagnosis of schizophrenia—then called dementia praecox—almost always implied the prognosis of a progressive deterioration. Diagnosticians had only to hear the word "schizophrenia" to advance a poor prognosis. The course of illness, the phase of illness, and other aspects of it were rarely accounted for. Bleuler's concept of schizophrenia held less automatically dire implications, since he regarded the absence of competent treatment, and not merely the presence of illness, as sufficient for a prediction of considerable liability toward repeated breakdown, even among persons who had shown some spontaneous improvement or recovery from a given episode of disturbance.

Clinical experience has demonstrated that some classically catatonic schizophrenic patients hospitalized in a state institution may have as many as a dozen episodes throughout their lives, returning after each to the same baseline of relative health and good social functioning. A small number of patients, once ill, remain ill and are described as "chronics." Many of these remain hospitalized, however, because of lack of appropriate treatment or an appropriate social setting into which they can be discharged.

As mentioned earlier, the overall figures for the United States show that there has been a steady decrease in the number of resident patients in state and county mental hospitals.

Nationwide, this trend is not only continuing but seems to be accelerating . . . During 1968, for example, [the number of] resident patients in state and county mental hospitals declined from 210,000 to 195,000. Despite these very hopeful statistics and the seeming acceleration in the rate of decline in chronicity, significant problems remain, . . . Admission rates have continued to rise. In 1968 alone, there were more than 320,000 episodes of illness diagnosed as schizophrenia in the United States. The cost of schizophrenia to our country is correspondingly great—estimated at 14 billion dollars annually. This figure represents the indirect as well as the direct costs being borne by society for the two to three million living Americans carrying this diagnosis. The rising admission rate seems to be, in part, a result of multiple hospital stays of individual patients. . . . The probability of readmission within two years of discharge from an initial episode of schizophrenia, for example, varies between 40 and 60 per cent, depending on the study. In the U.S., between 15 and 25 per cent of discharged schizophrenics will eventually be readmitted and receive continued care for a prolonged period of time (*Special Report on Schizophrenia,* 1971, p. 1).

Yolles and Kramer (Bellak and Loeb, 1969) reported a median duration of stay for resident schizophrenics as approximately 13 years. Interpreted by itself without ancillary information, this figure could be misleading, for it refers to median duration of stay of schizophrenics in the *resident* population of state hospitals. Only a small percentage of schizophrenic patients remains hospitalized for so many years. If one compares this figure with the one that shows that just over 70 percent of schizophrenic patients are released within the first year, one gets the impression of a vast spectrum of prognoses for the schizophrenic syndrome. The fact that in the United States some quickly discharged patients are soon readmitted (Schulsinger and Axe, in Cancro, 1971, report a much lower readmission rate for Denmark and Finland) only complicates the problem of rational prognosis. This holds true even if one keeps in mind the "background factors" — economic, social, educational, and intellectual differences, for instance — even though they may account for a good deal of variation in hospital stay independent of the clinical picture itself.

The lack of agreement about prognosis may go hand-in-hand with the fact that the condition of schizophrenia has very few accepted prognostic signs. Huston and associates (Bellak, 1958) review the literature on prognostic findings. L. Small, summarizing the criteria, described some relatively stable factors, such as premorbid level of adjustment, considered to be related to prognosis.

A breakdown of variables such as that in Table 24.1 is one approach to rational prognosis and, thereby, treatment. By and large, however, little of real value, clinically or statistically, has been contributed to improve prognosis for the schizophrenic syndrome (Kind, 1969).

The ego function profile is likely to be a helpful visual aid in offering a more specific prognosis based on *patterns* of ego functioning. It is particularly valuable in summarizing a person's potential for recovery. In practice, the prognosis will, of course, be influenced by the quality of treatment offered and the life circumstances of the patient, as well as by his high and low areas of ego functioning. Even after the best treatment, if a patient is discharged into a highly pathogenic environment (e.g., a very disturbed family) the chances for maintained health are very poor. We have only now developed a scale for rating the pathogenicity of the family environment that could be used systematically

Table 24.1.   Prognostic Indices[a]

Favorable	Unfavorable
Clinical Factors	
Acute onset[b]	Gradual onset[b]
External precipitant[b]	Long duration of illness prior to hospitalization[b]
Short duration of illness prior to hospitalization[b]	Flat affect[b]
Preservation of affect[b]	Inappropriate affect[b]
Tension and anxiety	Little overt hostility
Depression	Definitely paranoid
Manifest moderate hostility	
Self-reproaching delusions	
Compliantly paranoid	
Ability to rationalize reality lapses	
Social - and Personal-History Factors	
Upper socioeconomic group	Lowest socioeconomic group
Good educational history	Single, divorced, or separated
Good occupational history	Over 35
Steady church attendance	
Married	
Good marital adjustment	
Good recent sexual adjustment	
Relatively stable prior to onset	
Under 30	
Psychological-Test Factors	
High I.Q.[b]	Low I.Q. (under 90)[b]
Functioning at level lower than potential	Marked impairment of abstract thinking
Little impairment of abstract thinking	
Favorable Rorschach indices (M, C, total R, F)	
Constitutional Factors	
Ecto-mesomorphic	Endomorphic
Physiological Factors	
Chills after mecholyl	Increased blood pressure response to mecholyl
Anxiety precipitated only by mecholyl	
Small blood-pressure response (or decrease) to mecholyl	
Moderate blood-pressure response to epinephrine	

[a]This table was formulated by Dr. Leonard Small, in the chapter on "Prognosis in Schizophrenia" by Huston and Pepernick, in Bellak, *Schizophrenia: A Review of the Syndrome* (1958).

[b]These factors have a reliability that is *apparently* higher than the others.

to evaluate prognosis derived from the ego function profile in relation to the environment the patient has to live in and deal with. Furthermore, in every case it is very important to insist that a short-range and a long-range prognosis be formulated. Many a person may have a good short-range prognosis but a poor long-range one. Occasionally, chances for improvement in a short period of time are poor, while chances for continuing improvement with further maturation or change in life circumstances are good. Some generalizations have been suggested from the ego function profiles of patients for whom we have independent validating data from treatment. If autonomous and synthetic functions are good and if thought processes are relatively intact, the prognosis tends to be rather favorable. If functioning in these three areas is poor, then the long-range prognosis by and large tends to be poor.

We offer here tentative prognoses for some of our 50 schizophrenics, who were rated on three levels of functioning—characteristic, highest, and lowest. Because a study of prognosis was not part of the original research design, we can offer a discussion of these cases only speculatively. Regrettably, we were unable to arrange for a meaningful follow-up of these patients. Without knowing about, and allowing for, the pathogenicity of the social environment into which they were discharged, there may be a confusing difference between what we expect from them prognostically on the basis of ego functioning and the way they actually fare at some future time. A particular prognosis then might be correct within an "average expectable environment" but might well be counteracted by a very pathogenic environment. A prognosis might also be better than we thought if the patient were discharged into an unusually healthful environment.

In making short- and long-term prognoses, the following guidelines were heavily relied upon. First, there is a good a priori basis for expecting the synthetic function of the ego to correlate very highly with overall ego strength. The synthetic-integrative function, as defined, is hierarchically more complex and may reflect a higher level of functioning than any of the other functions. The triad of synthetic functioning, autonomous functioning, and thought processes is assumed to be most highly related to a good long-term prognosis, as subjects who rate high in those areas are believed to have better-integrated premorbid personalities. In the profiles, the lowest level of functioning is interpreted to reflect the acute stage of the illness, while the characteristic level reflects both the premorbid personality potential and what is to be expected upon recovery from acute episodes. *Discrepancies* between characteristic and lowest ratings for given functions or patterns of functions form a crucial basis for making inferences re a possible poor prognosis for a given patient based on ego function profiles. The functions showing the largest gap between lowest and characteristic levels are the functions that are lowered during an acute illness. Stated another way, when there is a large discrepancy between lowest and characteristic ratings, we are dealing with an acute illness. When there is a minimal distance between the lowest and characteristic level and where both are low, we are dealing with a chronic condition.

Here, then, are some tentative suggestions for making statements about long- and short-range prognoses: if autonomous and synthetic functioning and thought processes are characteristically low, then long-term prognosis is low. When these functions are high, long-term prognosis may be good if other functions are low only on the lowest level. For example, when defensive functioning and regulation and control are the only really low-rated functions on the lowest level and are rated high for characteristic level, we may make a good short-term prognosis—possibly from drug therapy based on these two lowered functions (representing treatable anxiety and tension)—and also a good long-term prognosis. Similarly, if reality testing, judgment, and sense of reality are low on the lowest level but higher on the characteristic level and if the three crucial functions are all high, prognosis may be good. When lowest- and characteristic-level ratings are not discrepant and are also fairly high, showing good levels of adaptation, the long- and short-term prognoses are both good.

Following are profiles of ego functions and brief prognostic hunches, ranging roughly from best to poorest prognosis.

Subject 132. Because of some very low scores (see Profile 24.1) on the lowest level of functioning, this patient might look clinically quite disturbed, and possibly violent, in the acute stage. Short-term prognosis may be good since any acutely ill patient with problems of control and defense may show immediate improvement with medication. Because thought processes, autonomous functioning, and synthetic functioning are relatively good, a good long-range prognosis is also possible.

A good prognosis is also made because on the highest level of functioning, no function was rated below 7: synthetic functioning was rated 12; autonomous functioning, 12; and mastery-competence, 12. On the lowest level, thought processes and autonomous functioning were rated 8. Breakdown occurs primarily in regulation and control of drives and object relations: both were rated only 5 on the characteristic level.

Subject 127. Good prognosis (see Profile 24.2). Judgment and thought processes are poorer than in subject 132, but autonomous functioning, synthetic functioning, and mastery-competence are nearly as good. Like subject 132, control and defenses are low, but reality testing is less affected. Thus, generally good long- and short-range prognoses can be made.

Subject 095. Fairly good prognosis (see Profile 24.3), although not quite as good as subject 127. The disturbance is more acute, with the first few variables rating low at the lowest level. On characteristic level, thought processes, autonomous functioning, and synthetic functioning are fairly good and should therefore be quite good at recovery.

Leopold Bellak, M. D. Principal Investigator
MULTIDISCIPLINARY STUDY OF SCHIZOPHRENIA
RESEARCH PROJECT
N.I.M.H. Grant #18395

Subject # _132_
Group #
Rater(s) _H. G._
Date _ _ _

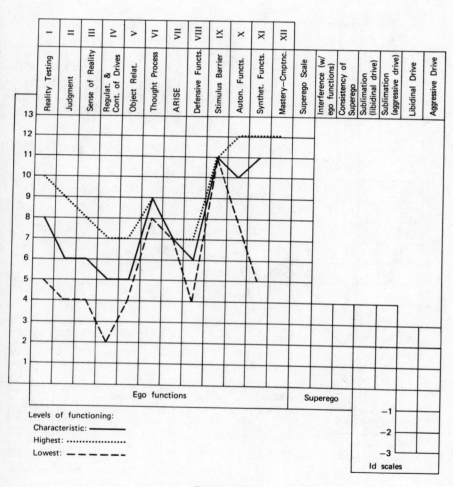

Profile 24.1

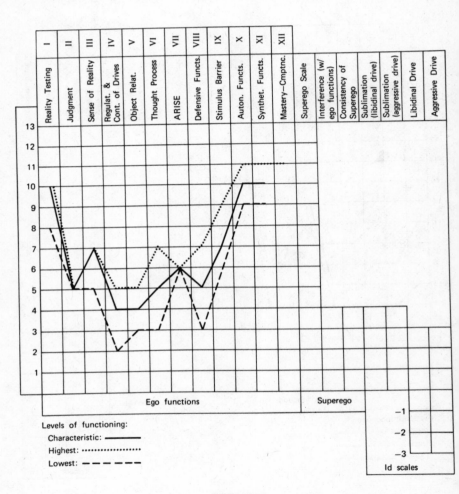

Leopold Bellak, M. D. Principal Investigator
MULTIDISCIPLINARY STUDY OF SCHIZOPHRENIA
RESEARCH PROJECT
N.I.M.H. Grant #18395

Subject # _127_
Group #
Rater(s) _H. G._
Date

Profile 24.2

Leopold Bellak, M. D. Principal Investigator
MULTIDISCIPLINARY STUDY OF SCHIZOPHRENIA
RESEARCH PROJECT
N.I.M.H. Grant #18395

Subject # __095__
Group # _____
Rater(s) __H. G.__
Date __ __ __

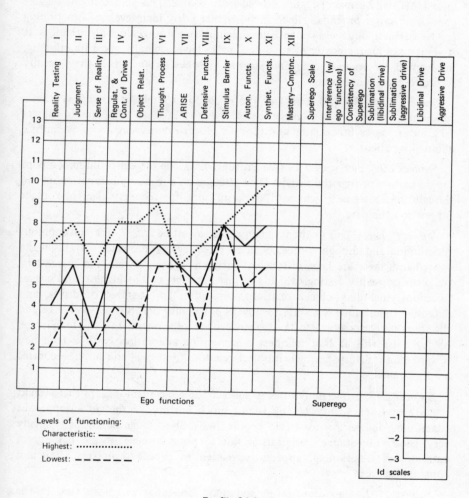

Profile 24.3

Subject 096. Good prognosis (see Profile 24.4). Most highest ratings were within the "normal" range (9-13), except for object relations, which did not, however, further diminish in the acute phase. Lowest (acute) rating is on sense of reality; the last few variables did not fall below 6. The poor sense of self is consistent with a tendency toward acute depersonalization and a general liability for acute disturbances, since reality testing ranged from a highest of 11 to a lowest of 3 and sense of reality ranged from 8 to 2. This spread might suggest good short-range prognosis, since it shows that fairly high levels of functioning can be attained, but there still remains a liability for future acute disturbances. It is sometimes characteristic of such persons to have generally good functioning, interrupted by several acute and stormy episodes, from which they usually return to good functioning.

Subject 155. Fair prognosis (see Profile 24.5). It could be good if synthetic functioning had not fallen on the lowest level to a 3. When compared to subject 132, autonomous functioning and thought processes make one more pessimistic about this patient.

Subject 092. Fair prognosis (see Profile 24.6). The subject could have a poor prognosis except that the highest level attained on autonomous functioning and thought processes is 9, which offers more hope for recovery than one might otherwise anticipate.

Subject 128. This patient maintained a rating of 7 for autonomous functioning and thought processes at all three levels (see Profile 24.7). On the other hand, there are large differences between highest, lowest, and characteristic levels on reality testing, which was rated as high as 9 at highest; and several functions, including object relations, regulation and control of drives, and defensive functioning were rated as low as 3. We infer that this person is likely in the short range to return to the higher level of adjustment. For the long range, however, he will at best manifest a borderline adaptation, with a tendency toward acute disturbances when object relations, defenses, and impulse control are threatened.

Subject 143. Some similarities to subject 128 are evident, except that even at the lowest level, reality testing is not much impaired, although autonomous functioning fell as low as 4 (see Profile 24.8). Short-range prognosis is largely very good. Long-range prognosis is fair to poor because of the liability in autonomous functioning, apparently related to problems in regulation and control of drives.

Subject 101. Fair short-range and poor long-range prognosis (see Profile 24.9). Some improvement is expected with the use of creative potential. A fair short-range prognosis is expected on the basis of a highest-level rating for reality testing of 9, while the spread of relatively low autonomous and synthetic

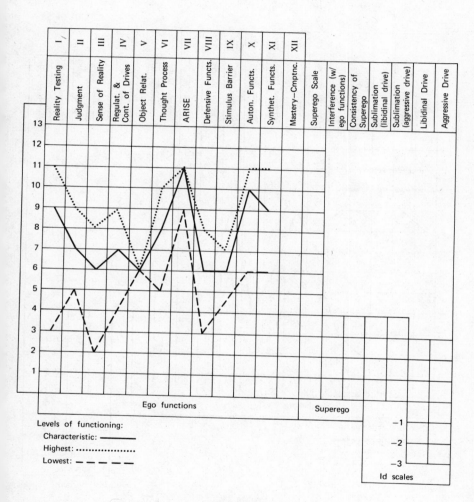

Leopold Bellak, M. D. Principal Investigator
MULTIDISCIPLINARY STUDY OF SCHIZOPHRENIA
RESEARCH PROJECT
N.I.M.H. Grant #18395

Subject # _096_
Group # _____
Rater(s) _H. G._
Date ___ ___ ___

Levels of functioning:
Characteristic: ——————
Highest: ••••••••••••••••••••
Lowest: — — — — —

Ego functions

Superego

Id scales

Profile 24.4

409

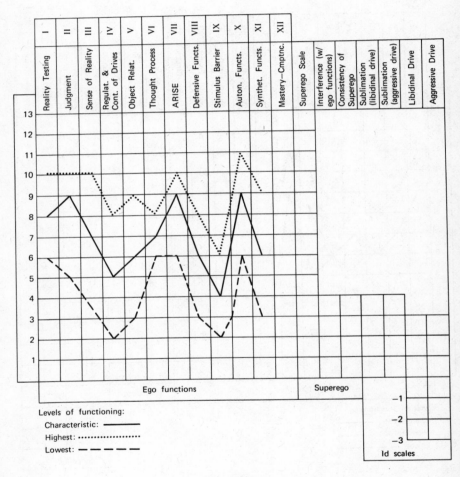

Leopold Bellak, M. D. Principal Investigator
MULTIDISCIPLINARY STUDY OF SCHIZOPHRENIA
RESEARCH PROJECT
N.I.M.H. Grant #18395

Subject # *155*
Group #
Rater(s) *H. G.*
Date

Profile 24.5

Leopold Bellak, M. D. Principal Investigator
MULTIDISCIPLINARY STUDY OF SCHIZOPHRENIA
RESEARCH PROJECT
N.I.M.H. Grant #18395

Subject # _092_
Group # _____
Rater(s) _H. G._
Date ___ ___ ___

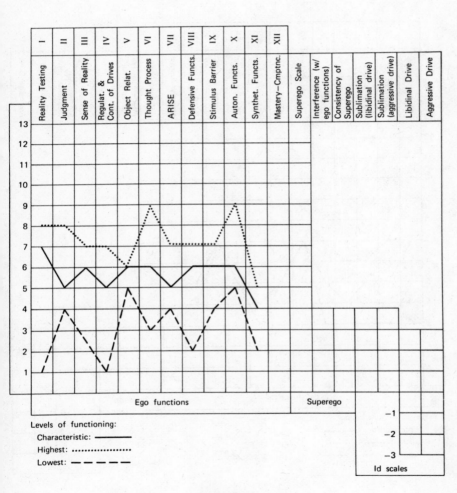

Profile 24.6

411

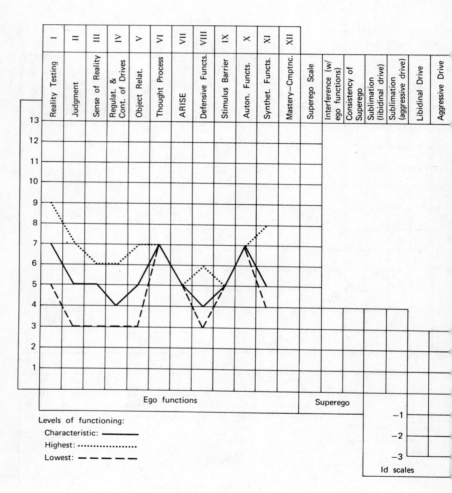

Leopold Bellak, M. D. Principal Investigator
MULTIDISCIPLINARY STUDY OF SCHIZOPHRENIA
RESEARCH PROJECT
N.I.M.H. Grant #18395

Subject # _128_
Group # _____
Rater(s) _H. G._
Date ___ ___ ___

Profile 24.7

412

Leopold Bellak, M. D. Principal Investigator
MULTIDISCIPLINARY STUDY OF SCHIZOPHRENIA
RESEARCH PROJECT
N.I.M.H. Grant #18395

Subject # _143_
Group # _____
Rater(s) _H. G._
Date ___ ___ ___

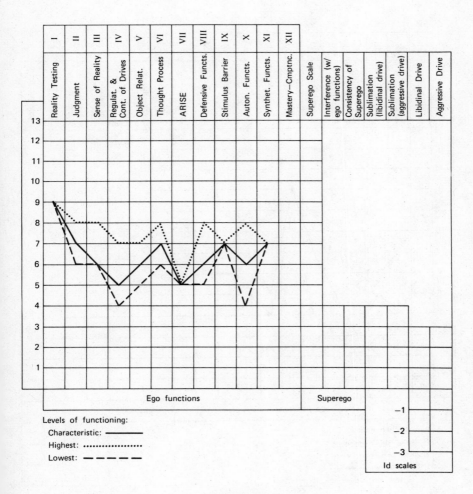

Profile 24.8

413

Leopold Bellak, M. D. Principal Investigator
MULTIDISCIPLINARY STUDY OF SCHIZOPHRENIA
RESEARCH PROJECT
N.I.M.H. Grant #18395

Subject # _101_
Group #
Rater(s) _H. G._
Date

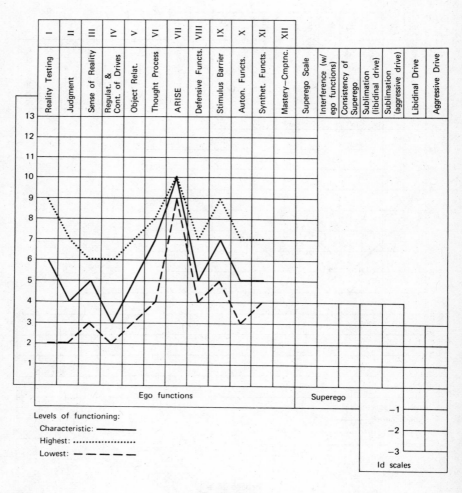

Profile 24.9

414

functioning at both lowest and characteristic levels presages a poor long-range prognosis.

To the extent to which we deal with *patterns* involving the 12 variables, the above predictions must be interpreted cautiously. Actually, the prognosis relies on fewer variables for long-range prognosis, as only autonomous, synthetic, and thought processes are taken as the crucial measures. In comparing these patients, it becomes clear that autonomous and synthetic functions held more weight for predicting long-range prognosis than thought processes, for example.

In this section we have attempted to present some systematic statements about prognosis. The ultimate test of their validity must lie in follow-up studies of the patients rated. Ideally, patients should be reinterviewed and rerated at regular intervals for a number of years so that we can see the extent to which statements about both short-term and long-term prognoses are validated.

CHAPTER 25

Early Ego Function Assessment and Prevention of Schizophrenic Development

Unfortunately, most attempts to deal with the schizophrenic syndrome may be of no avail unless and until we know how to prevent at least certain manifestations of its phenotypes. To achieve that aim, our efforts would best be directed next to assessing ego functions in very young children so that we may plan effectively to intervene in time to promote adaptive ego development before those critical periods when ego impairments become irreversible.

Our current data on ego functions and their various strengths and weaknesses are of very circumscribed value for any such endeavor, as they are derived exclusively from adults. They do, however, permit us some speculation on what one might pay attention to in children. Such speculation must eventually be put to test by exhaustive longitudinal studies of the development of ego functions in a normal population as well as in the various high-risk groups. By "high-risk," we mean the predisposition of some children to develop schizophrenia because they are genetically burdened—there is high familial incidence of schizophrenia— because they may have some ascertainable congenital, neurophysiological, or biochemical *Anlagen*, and, of course, because they may have been subjected to pathological "schizophrenographic" upbringing.

In speaking of prevention, it is customary to distinguish primary, secondary, and tertiary prevention. We will limit our discussion here to suggestions for primary prevention, as secondary and tertiary refer to arresting the further development of a schizophrenic process in people who are either acutely or chronically ill, respectively.

What can we possibly say about the schizophrenic syndrome if it is presumed to be the result of a variety of causal factors, more or less interacting, and none of them definitely established? How can we detect it in its incipient stages and then prevent its further development? And what may we venture to say about how our knowledge of ego functions may contribute to prevention of the schizophrenic syndrome?

We have a few fairly good hunches about *some* factors that play *some* significant role in the etiology and pathogenesis of the schizophrenic syndrome. Goldfarb's (1971) findings are very persuasive and consistent with findings from
416

many other sources: he found that among schizophrenic children, one group showed marked neurological symptomatology and another group did not. The family atmosphere in the latter group was characterized by significantly higher psychopathology than was the group with neurological involvement.

These data suggest that in some young children neurological abnormalities may be sufficient to produce a schizophrenic outcome; in other children, emotional experiences in the family milieu may be sufficient. Neither factor seems necessary, but each appears at least contributory in a major way.

The data by Rosenthal (1963), by Rosenthal and associates (1968), and by Pollin, Stabenau, and associates (1968) suggest that genetic factors play *some* role in *some* schizophrenics—not a necessary or sufficient role in all schizophrenics but maybe the necessary role in some or possibly the sufficient one in others.

Summarizing these major research efforts, at least three sources of increased risk seem likely candidates for schizophrenogenesis and target areas for prevention: neurological problems—especially diffuse, minimal brain damage—severe emotional family pathology, and high familial incidence of schizophrenia, especially in twins or parents. It is very likely that certain studies on high-risk populations, such as the ones being conducted by Mednick and Schulsinger (1968), will provide further tentative leads.

Speaking generally now, if any of the above hypotheses about high risk pans out empirically, then screening of children with these backgrounds or problems should be a first step toward prevention of at least *manifest* schizophrenic problems. An ego function assessment holds promise as a systematic way of assessing liabilities and assets in such children and adolescents. We must now encourage the development of research programs based upon a rapprochement of high-risk studies and ego function assessment. Such broadly based strategies would constitute a rational approach to attempts to lower morbidity rates.

If, for example, one determined that a baby had a low stimulus barrier, one could safely infer that other ego functions as well would be vulnerable to impairment, as the stimulus barrier is regarded as a precursor of ego development generally. A stimulus overload in infancy thus could interfere with integration, synthesis, and the development or utilization of defensive and autonomous functions. It seems advisable then to avoid overstimulation where feasible, first of all, through the critical process of "good enough" mothering, but also with such simple measures as protecting infants with poor stimulus barrier from any excessive pain during teething (by analgesics) and avoiding exposure to average—but for these hypersensitive babies, excessive—sound, light, and other stimuli. These precautions may well also include less "noxious" human input (e.g., less rough and more soothing handling, avoidance of overstimulation by horseplay or of excessively seductive contacts), which could be more than this particular kind of child can bear. A much more carefully guided than average adolescence, when sexual impacts can be overwhelming, would also be advisable.

A stimulus overload can make it especially difficult to accomplish a synthesis of drive and affect with the rest of the personality; it also interferes with functions of primary and secondary autonomy. Such overstimulation may, for instance, lead to difficulties in language development and a liability toward acting out behavior when linguistic expression would be more adaptively appropriate. Impingement of too intense stimuli is also likely to express itself in such well-known infantile disturbances as headbanging, knee-elbow rocking, and other overactivity, all reflecting maladaptive attempts to discharge surplus excitation brought about by stimulus overload.

To a certain extent, the manifestations of a low stimulus barrier are likely to reflect aspects of what Mednick and Schulsinger (1968) describe as physiological and psychological overreactivity in the so-called high-risk group of children of schizophrenic parents. The hypothesis of low stimulus barrier predisposing to psychosis is also consistent with the findings of Anthony (1971) that offspring of reactive psychotics with very dramatic symptomatology fare worse than those of parents with endogenous, insidious, quiet, psychotic manifestations: the "noisy" input by the ill parent is particularly disruptive.

If Mednick's, Anthony's, and our ideas should be confirmed, one form of primary prevention of schizophrenia or other psychopathology might possibly be obtained by careful restriction of input in infants and children with a low stimulus barrier. They merit protection against exorbitant learning burdens, intrusive grandmothers, and grandfathers who mindlessly puff cigar smoke into their faces. Hopefully, their mothering will be guided so as to minimize such commonplace hazards to the optimal development of such hypersensitive children.

Adding our knowledge of ego functions to what is known about family interaction patterns, it is not difficult to understand that any tendency toward "double bind" in the family is bound to lead to problems in reality testing, judgment, and object relations, at the very least. If we could develop procedures for ego function assessment and screening of all children at school entry (Bellak, 1971b), prevention of later serious psychiatric disturbance might be feasible, so that we could maximize our chances to identify target groups for preventive intervention very early in life.

Neurophysiological disturbances, as in the dyslexias or in some hyperkinetic children, are likely to lead to disturbances in most ego functions, particularly to conceptual confusion and disturbances of impulse control and the concomitant disturbances in object relations. Early detection of general neurophysiological and specific ego function impairments could then permit primary prevention of a psychiatric disorder that might only later be clearly manifest. We know that if signs of dyslexia are prominent, acquisition of language in written and verbal form may be impaired. A dyslexic child with such academic handicaps often feels stupid, is ridiculed, and then experiences emotional burdens, adding to whatever neurological liabilities he was originally saddled with. The large extent to which right-left conflicts are part of that clinical picture determines a faulty development of self boundaries and spatial orientation. Unless these ego deficits are remedied by skilled training in such orientation, in eye-hand coordination and other functions relating to the sense of reality of the self and the world, there could be additional difficulties in the child's development leading to secondary, as well as primary, emotional burdens.

Ego function assessment in young children could point to any number of other possible trouble areas, be they object relations, impulse control, or thought disorder. If troubled areas are discovered early enough, remedial steps requiring manpower and equipment would not have to be forbiddingly expensive. Some relatively simple changes in the school curriculum for high-risk (or perhaps all) children might go a long way toward minimizing the probability of manifest disturbances of a schizophrenic nature in later life. One could generalize and say that early discovery of any ego-function disturbance could in principle lead to useful measures of primary prevention.

Much that has already been said about treatment is applicable to secondary prevention, which involves treatment of relatively acute disorders, and to tertiary prevention, which seeks to ameliorate chronic disorders (see chapter on treatment). In all these instances, the ego function profile serves as a guide to diagnosis and treatment. It holds promise for casefinding at any stage of pathology, which is the backbone of public-health intervention. One specific, dramatic example of the possibility of early casefinding is exemplified in the instance of an 8-year-old boy described in the first edition of *The T.A.T. and C.A.T. in Clinical Use* (Bellak, 1954). A follow-up 17 years later (1971) saw the grim success of the dire predictions, which were based on the subject's lack of impulse control inferred from his C.A.T. productions. The fate of the early signs of violence was dramatically borne out by his having committed a series of asocial acts, culminating eventually in a murder. The case also serves to illustrate the serious limitations of existing social legislation in carrying out what we, as responsible professionals, *might* be able to recommend on the basis of our appraisals, in the event that parents would not be willing to cooperate with early recommendations. Regrettably, preventive community mental-health measures as a part of general public-health policy (Bellak, 1971b), are still in their infancy when it comes to social endorsement and technical implementation.

As it seems inevitable that psychiatry increasingly becomes a branch of preventive medicine and community mental health a part of public health (Bellak, 1970, 1971), the use of ego function assessments, among other tools, for preventive purposes seems appropriate.

APPENDICES

APPENDIX A

An Interview Guide for the Clinical Assessment of Ego Functions

INTERVIEW GUIDE

CONTENTS

GENERAL ORIENTATION FOR INTERVIEWS

Questions Coordinated to Rating Scales

This guide contains 12 sets of specific questions, each set keyed to its corresponding ego function scale as specified in the Manual for Rating Ego

422

Functions from a Clinical Interview. Wherever possible, the specific component factors will be designated in the margin. Where the interview questions could not be specifically tailored to the rating-scale format, the interviewer is expected to do this job by himself, by his clinical skills, judgment, *thorough knowledge of the Rating Manual and its relation to the Interview Guide*, and the aims of the raters. The major purpose of the clinical interview is to provide data on the 12 ego functions and their components such that they can be reliably rated.

Rigor and Flexibility

These suggestions are not intended to inhibit the interviewer in using his own clinical style, but rather to help him in furthering the major purposes of the interview.

Ingenuity (which at times may have to include direct departures from the suggested questions) will be required, especially when a subject dodges the questions being asked. Some firmness and control will also be necessary to limit the extent of digressions. At other times, the interviewer may devise shortcuts to condense areas of questioning. Parsimony is always desirable.

Ingenuity and flexibility will also be required in probing for specific details whenever a subject reveals any information crucial to rating any aspect or component of any of the ego functions, no matter what function is being formally pursued at the time. At some places in the Interview Guide there are parenthetical remarks directed to the interviewers to do specific probing. Such standard interviewing directions as "Tell me more," "When did it start," "Give a specific example," "Do you still feel that way," will not be included. Interviewers will be presumed to be experienced and skilled enough to probe at their own discretion.

By and large it is best to follow the guide, function by function, but occasional patients with communication difficulties might best be interviewed in a more flexible way, following their own leads as to what function gets covered at what point.

Present and Past Status of Ego Functioning

While we want to know the current (often acute) status of any ego function being rated, we are equally interested in what a person's *characteristic level* of adaptation-maladaptation with respect to each function has been, as well as his highest and lowest level. When the Interview Guide does not explicitly direct the interviewer to obtain such information, the interviewer should nevertheless attempt to discover (a) when the person began to have trouble with respect to the function and what level of development was reached prior to illness; (b) to what extent the difficulties interfered with adaptation; (c) how long the interference lasted; (d) how often it tended to recur; and (e) how easily the person recovered after a disturbance. We are also interested in determining the status of ego deficits at critical phases in the life cycle – infancy, childhood, adolescence, adulthood, old age – as well as in response to specific stress or trauma. Although the questions are not always specifically geared to tap these areas, the interviewer is advised to obtain the information whenever it is appropriate during the interview: in the initial section dealing with presenting complaints and history of illness or during the questioning about specific ego functioning. Obtaining a clinical history should thus be limited to relevant ratable yield of information about ego functions, especially with the aim of rating current characteristic, highest, and lowest levels of functioning.

Miscellaneous Issues

If, while obtaining information about a specific ego function, you discover that the subject offers information on other ego functions, do not hesitate to follow up on the other functions at that time, as well as when the guide explicitly directs you to do so. Remember also that from the rater's point of view, any responses may be pertinent to one or more ego functions.

Although the guide offers specific questions worded in a particular way, you need not desert your usual attempt to gear your verbalization of the questions to the particular subject's background and intelligence. If you judge something in the guide to be worded in a way that is either too sophisticated or might sound too patronizingly naive for the subject you happen to be interviewing, feel free to substitute a more appropriate terminology.

INITIAL RAPPORT

What is your full name, please?
Your age?
And your address? How long have you been living there? Who else lives in your current household? Where are you originally from?
What kind of work do you do? And your education? (If any degree or school not completed, ask why.) (If any discrepancy between education level and nature of job, inquire about it.)
What brought you to the hospital (treatment)? (Pursue presenting complaint, focussing especially on all information about ego function strength and deficiency.)

I. REALITY TESTING

a   1.   Do you ever have trouble deciding whether something really happened or if it was a dream?

a   2. Have you ever wondered if a thing only happened in your mind?

a,b 3. Have you ever been surprised to find that what you thought was going on really wasn't?

b   4. Do you sometimes feel that you see what you want to see rather than what's really there? Like an ostrich burying his head in the sand?

b   5. Do you ever read into other people's behavior things that really aren't there? Has anyone ever told you that you do this?

b   6. Do you have the feeling that you're out of touch? Is it important for you to be in touch with everything about you? (Or: Does it upset you when you don't know what's going on?)

b   7. Have you ever been confused about things? Have people ever told you you're confused about things? Do you get confused easily? Disoriented? (Time, place, people)

a,b 8. Have others ever told you that you're not with it? Out of step with the
c   rest of the world? Do you think they're right?

b   9. Do people often misunderstand what you are trying to tell them?

a,b 10. Have you ever been told by people that what you say doesn't make sense? That your ideas are way off?

a   11. Have you ever been convinced of the reality of something even though everyone around you disagreed? Has this been about things you saw? heard? thought?

c   12. When you distort and misinterpret things, are you able to correct those notions?

a,c 13. Have you ever heard strange sounds in your ears that you couldn't account for on a physiological basis? Ever heard voices? What about visual experiences? In such cases, have you known that the voice (or whatever) couldn't be real even though it seemed real at the time?

a   14. Have you ever hallucinated?

c   15. How did you eventually find out that you had been hallucinating?

c   16. Do you pay attention to what goes on inside of you, like emotions, aches and pains? Possibly too much attention?

II. JUDGMENT

c   1. What are some of the things you've done which have shown poor judgment?

c   2. Do you care what other people think of you?

c   3. Have you ever felt awkward socially? Have you ever put your foot in your mouth or offended someone without intending to?

a,c 4. Are you good at sizing people up? At anticipating their responses to you?

c   5. Have you had the experience of being shocked or surprised that something you did had rubbed people the wrong way? Or when you thought you were being pleasant, you had actually annoyed someone or made him angry?

c,a 6. Do you ever find that you misjudge people?

a,b 7. Are you ever too trusting of people?

a   8. How do you go about making decisions? (Like taking a new job, quitting school, breaking up with a girlfriend/boyfriend, getting married?) Do you consider all the angles or do you act without thinking too long about things?

a   9. Are you a planner in that you think a lot about the consequences of what you might do? Do you have trouble estimating how long it would take or how much work is required in getting something done?

a,b 10. Are you an impulsive person? Are you careless with yourself or your health?

b   11. Are you a daredevil? Do you like to take chances? What if other people are involved?

a,b 12. Have you ever felt that you could get away with things that the average person couldn't? Like doing something risky that could get you into trouble? Like applying for a job for which you had no proper skills or training? Like speeding or driving without a license? If you get away with it, is it luck or something else?

b   13. Do you ever do dangerous things, like walking around the city at night (unaccompanied)? Opening your door to strangers before you know what they want? Riding in a car with defective brakes?

III. SENSE OF REALITY

a   1. Most people sometimes have the experience that things are happening that have happened before, like a déjà vu. Have you ever had this experience? Like you had been to a certain place before, or heard, thought, or said something, even though you knew it couldn't possibly be so? Did you wonder if it really happened or was just your imagination?

a   2. Do people and things around you sometimes feel unreal to you? As though they really weren't there, or couldn't have happened?

a   3. Do people and things sometimes look foggy or as though seen through a haze, or perhaps as though there were a glass wall between you and the rest of the world?

a   4. Have people and things ever looked closer or further away, larger or smaller than you know them actually to be?

b   5. Have you ever felt as though you were walking around in a trance?

b   6. Have you ever felt that you were not real?

b   7. Have you ever had strange feelings in various parts of your body that there was no physical explanation for? (As if electricity was going through you; as if your head, tongue, or some other part of your body was feeling much bigger or smaller than usual; as if some part of your body is changing shape; or as if you were literally physically empty or had a hole in your stomach?)

a   8. Have you ever had a physical subjective feeling or sensation as though the world were going to collapse or fall apart? As though you could cause it, for example, by some act, thought, dream?

c   9. Do you spend much time thinking about the question "Who am I?"

d   10. Have you ever had trouble feeling yourself to be a person separate and independent from other people?

c,d 11. Describe yourself.

c   12. Do you have special ways to make yourself feel good about yourself?

c   13. What kinds of things make you feel humiliated?

c,d 14. Are you more affected in your opinions about yourself if someone says you're great or if someone says you're doing terribly?

c,d 15. Can you tell me of any times when you feel important or good living through someone else's accomplishment? Because they are perhaps intelligent, good-looking, popular, or very successful? When they're not around, do you get depressed or feel generally bad?

d   16. Is it very important for you to feel as though you were in special communication with someone else? Feeling merged or fused together? Do you feel you can read someone's mind, or they yours? Have you ever believed you possessed a capacity for ESP?

a,b, 17. Do you smoke pot or take other drugs? What kinds of feelings does
c,d   this give you? Do they effect any of the things we've just discussed? Even after the effect of the drug has worn off?

IV. REGULATION AND CONTROL OF DRIVE, AFFECT, AND IMPULSE

a   1. Do you have a lot of drive to be physically active? Do you have to be on the go all the time? Or do you ever find it hard to get going?

a,b 2. Do you tend to be emotional and excitable about things, or are you relatively calm and detached? Do you consider yourself to be an undercontrolled or an overcontrolled person? What do other people think about you?

b   3. Do you ever have rapid changes in your mood — going from high to low rather quickly?

b   4. Have other people ever told you that you were overdramatizing or overreacting to something?

a,b   5. Are you a defiant or rebellious person? Are you spiteful? Do you tend to be well behaved? Polite?

b   6. Are you a patient or impatient person?

b   7. If you don't get your way or what you want immediately, how do you react? Are you easily frustrated? Can you stand frustration for any length of time?

b   8. How well do you think you tolerate feelings of anxiety when there is no immediate way of getting rid of them? How do you get relief from anxiety?

a,b   9. Do you feel much inner pressure to act? Pressure to talk?

a   10. Do you find it hard to be frank and direct about the way you feel? About something you want?

a   11. Do you spend much time daydreaming about things you want or about things you'd like to be? Do you find daydreaming more pleasant or satisfying than reality?

a,b 12. What sort of things make you angry? How angry do you get?
      A. How are these feelings expressed? Do they come out directly or do you do something else with them? Think? Dream? Daydream?
      B. Do you argue? Throw things? Hit people? Ever wanted to kill someone?
      C. Do you think you control these feelings too well or not enough?

a,b 13. What sort of things make you sad, blue, depressed? Are you sad a lot or a little?
      A. What do you do when you are feeling depressed?
      B. Do you cry a lot? Ever wish you would die? Did you ever think about committing suicide? Ever actually try it?
      C. How well or poorly do you think you control emotions like these?

a,b 14. A. What are the usual outlets for your sexual feelings? How frequently does this occur?
      B. How often do you masturbate? Under what circumstances? Any fantasies?
      C. In general, do you think a lot or a little about sex? Do you dream or daydream about sex? Do these thoughts or feelings ever worry you?
      D. Under what circumstances have your sexual urges been stronger than is usual for you? Weaker?
      E. Have you ever had the urge to do certain things sexually that you've thought it would be better not to do? Or that you wouldn't dare do?

F. Do your sexual feelings ever get out of control? Or do you feel that you control them too much?

V. OBJECT RELATIONS

a,b c,d   **1.** What was your father like? Your mother? How was your home life? Your current home life?

a,b c,d   **2.** How do you get along with your girlfriend/spouse/boss/parent?

b   **3.** Have you discovered that no matter how hard you try to avoid them, the same difficulties crop up in most important relationships?

b   **4.** Do you keep getting involved with the same kind of person? Like even when you thought he/she was going to be different?

a,d   **5.** Do you generally prefer to be close to people or keep your distance? How do you feel most comfortable, with intense relationships or cool ones? Which kinds for which sorts of things?

a,d   **6.** Is it hard to get close? To stay close? What are the kinds of things that make you want to retain distance? In close relationships do you often reach a point where things are getting too intimate? So that you've wanted to or actually have broken it up?

a,d   **7.** Have you ever run away from or broken up a relationship for fear of getting hurt if you got too close? Or do you find it hard to let go even when things are going bad?

d   **8.** Did you ever feel that someone rejected you or a friend abandoned you?

d   **9.** How easily are your feelings hurt? Are you sensitive to criticism? To being left out of things? Do you often feel you've been rejected or abandoned?

a,d   **10.** Have you been hurt a lot in your life? Have you felt it's your fate to always be on the losing end? When you are hurt, do you have ways of trying or wishing to get back?

a,d   **11.** Have there ever been times in your life when you had to live alone? Or wanted very much to live alone? How do feel when "X" (whomever patient lives with) is away for the weekend? Or longer?

a,d   **12.** Have you ever gone to a restaurant or movie alone?

c   **13.** How well do you understand other people? How well do they understand you?

c   **14.** Have you felt that things would be all right if only he/she/they would change?

c   **15.** Do you try to change the way people are and how they act so that they'd be the way you'd like them?

c 16. How do you get what you want from other people?

c 17. What kinds of things do you do to make people pay attention to you? (Life of the party, crying, temper, dressing well, etc.)

c 18. Do you enjoy exercising power over other people? Is that a secret pleasure?

a 19. Who handles what in your household? Like making major decisions. (Who's responsible for the caring of children? Who handles finances?) Who *really* runs things?

a 20. Who usually makes the initial approaches for sex, you or your girlfriend/boyfriend/spouse? Immediately after sex, what do you like to do?

a 21. Have you ever been involved in love affairs or involved sexually with more than one person at a time? Is this (or would this be) difficult for you to sustain emotionally, or do you (or do you think you would) prefer it that way?

22. Do you play games like "cat and mouse" with people close to you?

VI. THOUGHT PROCESSES

a 1. Do you have trouble keeping your mind on what you're doing? For example, when reading a book or newspaper, do you find yourself being distracted by noises or find your attention wandering?

a 2. How well do you concentrate? Is it ever difficult for you? When? Do you ever find that you have so many thoughts racing through your mind that you can't concentrate on any particular thing?

a 3. Do you ever think of yourself as a forgetful person?

a 4. If you think as far back as you can, what's the earliest thing you remember? What are the most significant things you remember about your early years?

a,b 5. Are you ever troubled by thoughts that seem to stick in your mind so that you can't get rid of them? Do they ever seem to run on by themselves without your control? Tell me about them. What ideas do you have about how they got there?

b 6. Do you ever have thoughts that you think others would not understand? Tell me about them.

b 7. What's foolish, or does not make good sense, about these:
    A. They put a cake of ice on the stove to keep it from melting.
    B. As he crossed the finish-line ahead of his rivals, he saw them still running in front of him.

a,b 8. What are these sayings supposed to mean?
    A. You catch more flies with honey than with vinegar.

       B. Strike while the iron is hot.
9. In what way are an orange and a banana alike? A coat and a dress? An axe and a saw? A dog and a lion? North and West? Eye and Ear? Air and Water? A table and a chair? An egg and a seed? A poem and statue? Wood and alcohol? Praise and punishment? A fly and a tree?

VII. ARISE

a,b 1. What do you do when you're alone and have nothing to do?

a,b 2. Do you daydream? What about? Are they more like fantasies, or do they involve thoughts and plans about actual things you may be doing?

a,b 3. Describe one of the most creative ideas you've ever had.

a   4. Are you ever able to let go and think strange and "nutty" thoughts without being upset or frightened? Describe one of the wildest, most fantastic ideas you've ever had. Do you ever get so carried away by your own ideas that it's hard to come back "down to earth"?

a,b 5. What is one of the most creative things you've ever done? What is the most spontaneous thing you've ever done? Are you generally spontaneous?

a,b 6. When you listen to the kind of music you enjoy, what's it like? What about art? Poetry? Literature? Making things? Inventing things?

      7. Do you like to cook? Do you usually follow recipes or do you prefer making things up as you go along?

VIII. DEFENSIVE FUNCTIONING

b 1. Do things easily upset you? Which things? Do you ever feel restless or jumpy and not know why? How long do these feelings last? Do you have any special ways of getting rid of such feelings?

b 2. Are you an anxious person? Describe your feelings.

b 3. Do you feel you have ways to protect yourself from too many worries and anxieties?

b 4. Have you ever felt that you were falling apart? Rocky? Cracking up?

a 5. When things throw you, how well are you able to pull yourself together afterwards?

a 6. Do you ever find that you don't catch on to jokes that everyone around you is laughing at? Or that you miss the point of things?

b 7. Do you ever have strange or frightening thoughts? Nightmares? Tell me about them.

a   8. Do you have any special fears? Like claustrophobia, fear of travel, fear of crowds?

a   9. Have you ever been concerned about what other people are saying about you?

IX. STIMULUS BARRIER

a   1. Are you especially sensitive to anything like light, sound, or temperature?

b   2. Have you ever been irritable or jumpy when there's too much noise around you?

b   3. What do you do if you are bothered (by the above)? Accept it? Grin and bear it? React in some way to show how uncomfortable you are? Tune it out yet still not leave the scene?

b   4. Do you ever seek solitude when outside irritants get to be too much?

b   5. Do you ever feel like "jumping out of your skin" if things get too much for you?

a   6. Do you have particularly sensitive skin? Any itching that nobody found a satisfactory explanation for?

a,b 7. How long does it usually take you to fall asleep? What seems to keep you up? Anything like light or sound or things outside of yourself?

a,b 8. Are you easily awakened by traffic noises? Lights if the shades aren't down all the way? Any other sleep problems?

a,b 9. (For women) Just before your menstrual periods, do you ever feel particularly bad? (Tense, depressed, irritable?) What do you do about it? (Go about your business? Stay in bed? Keep away from people as much as possible?)

a,b 10. Are you sick often? Can you feel an illness coming on, or does it usually get pretty advanced before you realize that you are sick?

a,b 11. Do you get headaches often? What brings them on?

a   12. Have you ever been regarded as the "Princess on the Pea" (or male equivalent) — extremely sensitive, fragile, delicate, to be treated with kid gloves?

a   13. Do you get bored when things aren't exciting enough? Does excitement rattle you?

a,b 14. After being in some peaceful state (like being away in a quiet place, a for a weekend or a vacation) how do you feel getting back to the pace din, noise of everyday life?

X. AUTONOMOUS FUNCTIONING

a   1. Does reading ever make you tense? Have you ever had trouble with hearing or vision that you know is not caused by any physical illness or defect? When you are upset or excited, do you forget things that are ordinarily easy to remember?

a   2. Do you ever get tongue-tied? Does your speech ever get garbled when you are self-conscious or embarrassed?

a   3. Are you physically awkward? Is this generally true or only in special situations?

a,b   4. Have you ever had trouble with routine things, like getting dressed, walking down steps, or carrying on with your usual work routine?

a   5. Do you ever get lost in the middle of what you're doing so that you have to stop and think about what the next step is?

a,b   6. How is your energy or drive level? Have you ever felt so lacking in energy that you couldn't carry through with things that you ordinarily do? Have you ever had any work blocks?

b   7. Is it hard to get going on something that you want to do? Are you at all lazy? About what sort of things?

b   8. When you get some free or leisure time, do you get to carry out the things you had just thought about when you were too busy or do you procrastinate?

XI. SYNTHETIC-INTEGRATIVE FUNCTIONING

b   1. Can you adapt easily to change or does it throw you out of gear? Like changes in your usual routine, or where you suddenly have to change plans?

a,b   2. When you're busy doing one thing and then something else comes up that needs to be done, can you continue doing what you were originally doing? Can you do both at once?

a   3. Do you think it's only possible to do one major thing well? For instance, can a person be both a leader and a follower? A student and a teacher? Can you imagine being both a leader and a follower yourself?

a   4. (For women) Can you imagine (How do you find) being a mother and holding down some job? How might you accomplish this?

a   5. (For men) Can you imagine being in charge of things at home but mostly following instructions at work? Can a man really be both ways? How might you accomplish this?

a   6. Can you imagine a serious job being fun, or do you think that work is work and play is play?

a   7. Do you often find yourself doing or saying things that seem very unlike you? When you don't really feel or act like yourself? Do you feel surprised?

b   8. How well organized are you in your daily life? What sorts of things disorganize you?

b   9. Do you like to live from day to day or do you prefer planning for the future? To what extent?

b   10. Are you bothered by having bits and pieces or loose ends around? To what extent do you need to tie things together and how well are you able to do this? How well can you stand things being left undone and up in the air?

XII. MASTERY AND COMPETENCE

a   1. Do you function as well as you believe you are capable of functioning? If not, what do you think gets in the way?

a   2. Do you feel that you generally stay on top of things? Do you like to be in charge of things?

a,b 3. Do you live up to your own expectations of yourself? Have you ever felt that you could make more of yourself and your life than you have thus far?

b   4. Do you ever feel that you are missing out on life? Why do you think this is so?

b   5. Do you feel very much at the mercy of events, or do you feel that you are master of your own fate? Do you feel that you could effectively alter your life or influence the people around you to get what you want and need?

SUPEREGO QUESTIONS

1. Does your conscience bother you a lot or a little? Are you strict with yourself or lenient?

2. Do you feel guilty a lot or a little? Do you sometimes feel guilty about things that you know aren't your fault?

3. Do you often stew over something you have said or done and wished you had not said or done it?

4. How often do you get feelings of unworthiness or of being just no good?

5. What are your expectations of how you ought to be? Are you a person who expects too much of yourself? Too little? Do you live up to the expectations of your parents?

6. Are you particularly concerned about the meaning of right and wrong? Whether a thing is moral, ethical, proper?

7. Do you think people are generally responsible?

8. Do you believe our society permits too much or too little sexual expression? What about expression of angry feelings?

9. To what extent would you be willing to step on others' toes to achieve something really important?

APPENDIX B

Manual for Rating Ego Functions From a Clinical Interview

CONTENTS

GENERAL GUIDE FOR USE OF THE MANUAL

The Manual consists of scales for rating each ego function, id, and superego. "Instructions to Raters" precede each scale. They explain each particular ego function in terms of the component factors and suggest ways to interpret and apply each scale.

Ordinal Scales

Each of the 12 ego function scales is an ordinal scale. The variables are dimensionalized on a seven-point continuum and are numbered 1 to 7. Raters

436

are encouraged to score a subject 1.5, 2.5, and so on when the relevant data seem to fall between any two defined scale points, here called modal stops. Modal stop 1 represents the most maladaptive manifestation of the function being rated, and modal stop 7 represents the most adaptive.[1] Each ego function scale is also broken down into separate scales representing the "component factors" of the function being rated.

Although the scales are ordinal and not equal-interval, an attempt has been made to peg all stops across scales so that they reflect about the same degree of adaptation at any given stop. That is, stop 3 on any given scale is *approximately* equal in maladaptiveness to stop 3 on other scales, but this can only be approximate. While stops 1 and 7 serve primarily as anchor points to orient the rater with respect to the two extremes of the dimension(s) he is rating for each function, they may infrequently apply literally to a subject, such as a "back-ward" patient of many years standing or an unusually well-functioning individual.

A final point about the rank ordering of modal stops involves the scale placement of "average" functioning. It was decided to consider stop 6 as average. Thus, the meaning of "average" as used here has less to do with the statistical norm of functioning of some known population group and more with a meaning denoting the sense of absence of any notable maladaptation or pathology, yet short of optimal.

Global Ratings

The rater's major task is to make a global rating on a 13-point scale (1 through 7 with "half" points) for each of the 12 ego functions. The global rating will be influenced by his separate ratings of each component factor for each ego function.

In the absence of statistical weighting of the contribution of each component factor to the overall ego function score, the latter must be obtained from a global clinical estimate of the overall adaptive level of that function.

An attempt has been made to describe the function each scale represents, both abstractly (as in accordance with the component-factor definitions) and concretely (with illustrative descriptive material for each stop).

Concerning characteristic, current, highest, and lowest ratings, the frequency, intensity, and pervasiveness of any phenomenon being rated cannot be accounted for adequately in any one given rating. Thus, we need four separate ratings for each component factor and for each ego function. All of the qualities listed above would constitute the characteristic rating for a given subject(S). We must also obtain assessment of S's current level of functioning at the time of the interview, an assessment of S's lowest level of functioning, and his highest level of functioning (often highly inferential if we are dealing with hospitalized patients).

For any scale it is important to note whether the evidence for some given item of pathology is observed only currently or whether it has been noted throughout the life history. That is, the distinctions between acute, in remission, and chronic should influence the rating assigned. That is, one episode would be distinguished from episodic occurrences. The latter would score lower on characteristic level, whereas the former might conceivably rate lower on current level. Adaptive resilience and rate of recovery after temporary lapses in functioning should also be considered. For lowest level, we would not usually score a one-time lapse or regression. "Lowest" ordinarily applies to functioning during a reasonable time period, but there are exceptions here.

With respect to the type of data gleaned from interviews, some scales lend themselves best to global ratings from the subject's responses to the questions *designed specifically* to tap information pertinent to the function being rated (e.g., stimulus barrier). Other scales are applied most effectively to the person's *general style* of answering all *interview questions* (e.g., defensive functioning).

Another factor for the rater to keep in mind in making his final assessment is the congruence between degree of actual disruption in behavior at any level of ego functioning and the degree of disturbance reported as such. Thus, a person may report no difficulty in certain areas, but the interviewer can infer from other interview data that there is a greater disturbance in functioning that the subject either does not experience or does not report. Such a disturbance would be rated lower than a mere acceptance of the person's self-report would superficially suggest.

Rating Procedure

The following sequential approach has been found useful by our raters:

(1) The rater should familiarize himself with all scales, the component factors and the implied psychological dimensions upon which the modal stops of each have been ordered.

(2) The rater should be familiar with the interview questions. This will be of great help in identifying the function about which any particular interview segment provides information. In the Interview Guide, questions are organized according to function, and component factors are designated in the margin.

(3) The rater should read through, or listen to, the complete interview, making *notes* as he goes along, indicating on his rating sheet what ego function and what component factor of that function (not necessarily what stop) is reflected whenever such a judgment is possible from the material.

(4) The *rating sheets* provide sections for recording evidence for each component factor of each ego function. The rater enters on the rating sheets each bit of evidence that represents the function being rated. If he is listening to a tape, he can insert the pertinent evidence in its proper place as he goes along.

For each function, the component factors are designated on the rating sheet so the rater can immediately record his data under the component factor to which it pertains. The rater then picks the scale point that most closely reflects the subject's characteristic and current levels for the given component factor, basing the rating on the specific data he has recorded on the rating sheet, qualified by his overall impression from the entire interview. When the subject falls between two defined (modal) scale points, then the rating should be made at the nondefined stop falling between the two (i.e., 1.5, 2.5, 3.5, etc.). Finally, he makes four overall global ratings (highest, lowest, characteristic, and current) for the ego function as a whole. In the absence of statistical weighting of the contribution of each component factor to the overall ego function score, the latter must be arrived at from a global clinical estimate of the adaptive capacity of that function and not from an arithmetic mean of the component scores.

1. The defined scale points plus the undefined stops add up to 13. If the user of this scale desires to work with whole numbers, any score on the above scale can be converted to a 13 full-point scale by multiplying by two and then subtracting one.

I. REALITY TESTING

Instructions to Raters. The ability to differentiate between *inner and outer stimuli* involves continuous selective scanning and matching contemporary percepts against past percepts and ideas. Reality testing here also involves checking data from one sense against data from other senses. Social contexts and norms will always be relevant in assessing reality testing.

Inner-reality testing is included in this scale insofar as it refers to a person's subjective sense of the accuracy of his perceptions. Another way of stating this is the relation between the observing and participating aspects of ego functioning or the extent to which the ego is free to perceive itself. Inner-reality testing is also reflected here in the degree to which the person is in touch with his inner self. Stated another way, this implies "psychological-mindedness" or "reflective awareness."

The most maladaptive end of the scale includes those disturbances of reality testing involving delusions and hallucinations, severe disturbances in orientation with regard to time, place, and person, in general, the encroachment of drives and regressive ego states upon perceptual functioning. These disturbances become less severe, less pervasive, and less frequent at stops 2 and 3, which represent transitional states between hallucinations and optimal perception. At stops 4 and 5 perceptual vigilance is included, as well as less pathological forms of the sorts of inadequate reality testing described in stops 1 and 3. Optimal reality testing is defined along these dimensions as sharp, automatic, and flexible, including some lowering of vigilance in the service of overall adaptation.

**Reality Testing
(a, b, c-components**

Stop	a	b	c
	Distinction between inner and outer stimuli	Accuracy of perception of external events including orientation to time and place.	Accuracy of perception of internal events. Includes reflective awareness or extent to which person is aware of accuracy/distortions of inner reality.
1	Hallucinations and delusions pervade. Minimal ability to distinguish events occurring in dreams from those occurring in waking life; and between idea, image and hallucinations. Perceptual experience, especially, is grossly disturbed (e.g., moving things look still and vice versa).	Extreme disorientation or confusion with respect to time, place and person (e.g., inability to identify current year, month, or day). Interpretations of the meaning of events are extremely inaccurate and subject to severe distortion. This may accompany either poor attention to internal and external stimulation or hypervigilance, which could cause "overinterpretation." Thus, often highly inaccurate interpretations of perceptions. General failure to recognize familiar people, objects, and places. Frequent attribution of familiarity to strange (unfamiliar) objects, people, and places.	Minimal reflective awareness. Virtual inability to provide reasons to explain feelings and behavior. Almost no psychological mindedness (e.g., when S is sad, he may have little awareness of it).
2	Hallucinations and delusions are severe but limited to one or more content areas. May show considerable doubt about distinguishing whether an event really happened or happened in his mind or a dream.	A high degree of disorientation to time, place and person. Feels confused. A goodly amount of distortion in perceptions and in interpretation of	Subjective awareness of inaccuracies of perception is largely absent. Even long after the fact S may not realize that hallucination was a hallucination.

Reality Testing (Continued)

Stop	a	b	c
2 (cont)		their meanings. Distortions are limited to selected areas and thus do not pervade in all areas of functioning.	
3	Illusions are more likely to be found than hallucinations. S may be aware that he sees and hears things that are not there, but he knows that others don't see or hear them.	Distortions and misinterpretations of reality are likely, but occur mostly under provoking circumstances like the influence of drugs, alcohol and fatigue, or charged emotional situations. Failures in orientation are also sporadic here and only moderately pronounced.	Beginning emergence of some subjective sense of one's misperceptions, but usually after the fact, (e.g., "I realize now that I wasn't understanding things correctly last year when I was so upset". S may know that he feels bad but cannot say why, in terms of his own inner states.
4	Projection of inner states onto external reality is more likely than frank hallucinations or delusions. A "stimulus-bound" reality testing may occur at the cost of libidinal investments and gratifications.	Reality is distorted to conform to strong need states. When the latter are absent, perceptions are reasonably accurate, despite occasional cases of misinterpretations. There might also be perceptual vigilance that interferes moderately with adaptation. May be very upset when not in touch with everything.	Can usually recover from distortions when not in the situation that precipitated them. Moderate degree of awareness of feelings as emanating from self; occasionally may be a hypervigilance toward inner states, interfering some with adaptation.
5	Confusion about inner and outer states occurs mainly upon awakening or going to sleep.	Relatively minor perceptual inaccuracies. Minor, sporadic difficulties with orientation. Selective perception notable.	Resiliency is noted in ability to recover to a state of objectivity after certain perceptual inaccuracies. Can correct distortions fairly easily. With most inaccuracies, S is aware of his deviant perceptions at the time they occur. Mostly aware of inner states or overly

Reality Testing (Continued)

Stop	a	b	c
5 (cont)			attuned to own feelings and their possible meanings.
6	Inner and outer stimuli are well distinguished. Occasional denial of external reality in the service of adaptation.	Accurate perception of external events prevails.	Has good subjective awareness of accuracies and inaccuracies. Can correct distortions easily. Well in tune with inner states.
7	Clear awareness of whether events occurred in dreams or waking life. Correct identification of the source of cognitive and/or perceptual content as being idea or image and accurate identification of its source as internal or external. Distinction between outer and inner percepts holds up even under extreme stress. Checking one's perceptions against reality occurs with a very high degree of automaticity.	Sharp and flexible, thus extremely accurate attributions of meaning to reality, even in stressful and emotionally burdensome circumstances. Interpretive distortions are minimal. Orientation is excellent, with virtually no social contagion when there might be attempts to influence orientation or perception.	Reflective awareness and psychological-mindedness are optimal. Subjective sense of accuracy of his own perceptions is great, and corresponds to inner and outer reality. This is often gleaned from excellent use of consensual validation: checking one's own perceptions against those of others. Highly in touch with own feelings.

II. JUDGMENT

Instructions to Raters. Ratings for judgment are based on interview data indicating comprehension and appraisals of hypothetical and real situations, and S's evaluations of the consequences of action or other behavior related to these situations. Contemplated future judgmental activity and answers to questions about hypothetical "what would you do if" type situations should be taken into account, noting especially any discrepancies between what S says he will do in the future (or in a hypothetical situation) and what he in fact is doing or has done.

A guideline to rating here is that *activity* based on poor judgment will get a more maladaptive rating than either poor evaluations made *short* of action or poorly contemplated future activity. For example, the college student who actually cheats on an exam in full view of the proctor and is convinced that he will not be caught would be rated lower than the student who either merely announces that he plans to cheat in the future or one who makes the statement that if he were to cheat in this situation, he would not be caught.

An expansion and guide for use of two of the component factors follows:

(a) At the maladaptive end of the scale, there is no cognizance of actual dangers inherent in dangerous situations, and poor anticipation of garden-variety threats. Toward the middle of the scale, S may be aware of consequences of extreme dangers but not of more moderate ones. Overestimation as well as underestimation of real dangers must be evaluated.

(b) Here we have to consider how *behavior* is related to the anticipation of consequences of dangers. Ratings would tend toward the maladaptive end when behavior is congruent with extremely poor anticipations of its consequences and would tend toward the somewhat more adaptive if behavior were appropriate despite poor anticipations. Degree of repetition of behavior involving defective judgment must also be assessed.

This scale differs in one crucial respect from reality testing: anticipation of the consequences is the central dimension for judgment, together with a sense of appropriateness, whereas degree of distortion in perceptions and so on is crucial for reality testing. It differs from regulation and control in that judgment must be independently assessed, although drives and urges are the predominant basis for inappropriateness of behavior.

Judgment

Stop	a	b	c
	Anticipation of likely consequences of intended behavior (e.g., anticipating probable dangers, legal culpabilities, social censure, disapproval or inappropriateness, and physical harm).	Extent to which manifest behavior reflects the awareness of its likely consequences and the extent to which behavior expressing maladaptive judgment is repeated.	Appropriateness of behavior, extent to which person is able to attune himself emotionally to relevant aspects of external reality.
1	S minimally aware of consequences of his behavior. S may believe he is invulnerable or supervulnerable to anticipated dangers. Little awareness of severe dangers (e.g., consequences of jumping from 20-story building; (S may think he is	S acts in accordance with his faulty anticipations so that there is real danger to life and limb. Such behavior tends to be repeated with no regard for the reality of the situation. May act on belief	Behavior may be extremely inappropriate, socially and otherwise, and remains uncorrected. May disrobe in public, dance at a funeral, come to church clad in a bathing suit.

Judgment (Continued)

Stop	a1	b	c
1 (Cont)	too well padded to get hurt). Also, the most benign situations may seem extremely dangerous (e.g., a threat to life). Extreme "infantile omnipotence" may be a prominent feature. Among the situations highly misjudged are other people's intentions and behaviors.	that he is invulnerable (e.g., attempting to jump from 20-story building; giving himself the protection of an amulet or of his belief in his exceptional powers). May show no effective learning from past, identical errors in judgment.	
2	A history of inappropriate judgments involving moderate danger to life and limb. Awareness of consequences is quite defective. S may not anticipate, for example, that a prolonged starvation diet will affect his health; or that disrobing in park will lead to arrest; or that driving with very defective brakes could lead to an accident.	S actually does take unnecessary risks; has a history of behavior showing poor judgment. (e.g., will actually drive with defective brakes; is very negligent with respect to his health; socially may be quite bizarre, unwittingly provoking others to do him harm, or jail him).	May have strong conviction that cracking jokes out loud during funeral services will ease people's grief, and act accordingly. Soldier sticking tongue out at a general.
3	Anticipation of consequences of behavior is faulty (e.g., in an advance course requiring very technical and specialized knowledge, S may believe he could get an A without ever studying because his I.Q. is high). May often misjudge other people's intentions.	Behavioral consequences of defective judgment are present but not so severe as to cause serious danger to life, but could endanger health, work, and interpersonal relationships. Might repeatedly take exams without studying despite history of failure.	Inappropriate social-emotional responses might include repeated errors in appraising how a relationship might work out (e.g., after strong relationships with an alcoholic mate, S still chooses alcoholics, "feeling" it will work out O.K. this time).
4	Awareness of consequences fluctuates from one situation to another. Fairly encapsulated areas of faulty anticipation overestimation of dangers is limited to specific phobiclike reactions (e.g., person who has been a relative	Moderate behavioral manifestations of moderately poor judgment are observable mainly in relation to specific types of situations (e.g., although a person may continue to look for	General attempts to be friendly may alienate people. Inappropriateness may take the form of chronic intrusions on others privacy with belief that this is just being friendly.

Judgment (Continued)

Stop	a	b	c
4 (Cont)	failure in his chosen field of work believes that it is all caused by fate and he hasn't received enough lucky breaks). In overestimating, S may feel a symptom is inevitably a dangerous sign, despite reassurance to the contrary (moderate hypochondriasis). Lacunae in judgment (e.g., may be excellent in professional sphere but relatively poor in others).	jobs in a field where he has attained only marginal success and does not prepare to work in a more suitable area, he still responds with relatively good judgment in other areas of life. Misjudging people's ability to handle jobs.	Or having frequent contacts with people making sexual advances, yet feeling outraged when a "pass" is made.
5	Occasional errors in appraising his own and others' intended behavior. Trouble in estimating time and work to be done in meeting a deadline.	Behavior related to the more garden variety of situations may be inappropriate, reflecting minor, circumscribed errors in judgment (e.g., S puts off medical checkup for one inconsequential reason or another). May walk through dangerous areas of the city at night unaccompanied or may be overcautious in day-to-day routine behavior.	Social-emotional judgment approaches appropriate levels with lacunae limited to a few areas where inappropriateness may be moderate to pronounced (e.g., presumptuousness in calling a very formal person by his first name; being overly ebullient to a reserved person).
6	Average. Very few errors in anticipation of consequences. Appraisals of his own and others' intended behavior are pretty accurate and anticipated in advance. Estimation of time and resources required to complete tasks is good.	Behavior shows quite good judgment in all spheres. Past errors in judgment are only occasionally repeated. Pretty good ability to apply past learning to current behavior involving judgment.	Mostly in tune emotionally so that virtually no inappropriateness results. Emotionally out of tune only in alien situations and initially, before there is time for good judgmental appraisals to occur.
7	S shows sound awareness of the consequences of his behavior. Very fine appraisals of his own and others' intended behavior. Consequences of planned behavior	Behavior shows extremely sound judgment in all spheres: social physical, work, etc. This results from careful planning and decision-making and	Outstanding emotional intuneness to reality. Affective responses and appropriate behavior occur automatically and flexibly even in new

Judgment (Continued)

Stop	a	b	c
7 (Cont)	are very well thought out and anticipated in advance. Consequences of more immediate, spontaneous behavior are grasped with a very high degree of automaticity, with conscious awareness not necessarily intervening.	more rapid, automatic decisions about sound, appropriate actions. Past errors in judgment are almost never repeated, because of excellent ability to apply past learning to current decisions involving judgments about reality.	situations and alien surroundings.

III. SENSE OF REALITY OF THE WORLD AND OF THE SELF

Instructions to Raters. This scale assesses disturbances in the sense of one's self, as it relates to the outside world. It refers, on the optimally adaptive end, to a subjective experience, usually preconscious, of one's unique, dynamic wholeness, mentally and physically, as defined by clearly delimited self boundaries from other people and the general physical and social environment.

IV. REGULATION AND CONTROL OF DRIVES, AFFECTS, AND IMPULSES

Instructions to Raters. This function refers to the extent to which delaying and controlling mechanisms allow drive derivatives to be expressed in a modulated and adaptive way, characterized, optimally, by neither under- nor overcontrol.

Evidence here is from overt behavior, associated or indirect behavioral manifestations, fantasies and other ideation, dreams, and inferences made from symptoms, defenses, and controls. (For drive strength per se, we use ratings from the id scales.)

Regulation and control might very well be regarded as one aspect of defensive functioning, but since our concerns here are limited to behavioral and ideational indices of impulse expression and since drives and impulses may be controlled and channeled by ego structures other than defenses, regulation and control would appear to merit a scale of its own. Defensive functioning also relates in its own way to dealing with anxiety and intrapsychic conflict, thus differing from regulation and control.

Among the drives under consideration are the libidinal and aggressive, in both their developmentally earlier and more advanced forms. Included also are

Sense of Reality of the World and of the Self

Stop	a	b	c	d
	The extent to which external events are experienced as real and as being embedded in a familiar context.	The extent to which the body (or parts of it) and its functioning and one's behavior are experienced as familiar and unobtrusive and as belonging to (or emanating from) S.	The degree to which S has developed individuality, uniqueness, a sense of self, a stable body image, and self-esteem.	The extent to which the ego boundaries are clearly demarcated between the self and the outside world.
1	Extreme derealization. Feels the world as being a completely strange place. Otherwise familiar objects and events appear alien. Extreme déjà vu experiences. Surrounding people and things feel unreal, changed in appearance, as though they weren't there or couldn't have happened. All of the above are experienced as subjective sensations. May feel the world is in chaos or disintegrating (very prominent "world-destruction" fantasies). Very slight environmental changes may produce strange sensations.	Extreme depersonalization. May be oceanic feeling of nothingness, feeling dead, inanimate, selfless. Parts of body may feel unreal, extremely strange, or disconnected from the rest of the body (e.g., head or tongue or other part feels very much bigger or smaller than usual; the shape of some part feels changing). Feeling literally or physically empty inside. Feeling literally like two or more different people.	Identity grossly distorted and unstable: esteem is so low that S may feel extremely worthless. Or extreme grandiosity may be apparent. Unsuccessful and pathological means of regulating self-esteem are repeated ineffectually. Continuous feedback from external sources is ineffectual in helping the individual to establish a stable sense of self. There is virtually no continuity in self-feeling from past to present, moment-to-moment. Self-evaluations practically never correspond to realistic aspects of the self. Indications of excessive departures of body image from actual bodily configurations. Enormous discrepancy between sense of self and ego-ideal.	May experience states of extreme fusion or merging with others, suggesting near-total loss of boundaries between the self and the outside world. Opinions about self may be affected in a chameleonlike fashion, depending on what S knows others feel about him. S may believe he possesses mystical powers of communication with others, such as exceptional talent for ESP. At this stop, body boundaries may be extremely fluid and permeable, or else S erects firm or hard, nonpenetrable, exaggerated barriers.

Sense of Reality of the World and of the Self (Continued)

Stop	a	b	c	d
2	Somewhat less than extreme derealization. Trances, fugues, and other dreamlike states. Outer reality often seems unfamiliar and produces feelings of confusion and estrangement. May feel as though a glass boundary separates him from his surroundings.	Strong feelings of depersonalization. Some major disassociations. Body and its functioning are often experienced as strange, peculiar, and unfamiliar. Things may seem to be happening to "someone else" rather than to own self. Many strange and peculiar feelings, like hole in stomach, electricity sensations.	Strong, unrealistic feelings of unworthiness. Or strong feelings of grandiosity. Marked use of pathological self-esteem regulators. Feedback from external sources is rarely effectual in establishing stable sense of self. Large discrepancy between self-image and ego-ideal.	Fusion phenomena are prominent, without total loss of distinction between self and outer reality. May also be overreaction to fusion needs by exaggerating separateness: as in severely overprotesting one's integrity as a person.
3	Marked but partial derealization likely to be less pronounced than depersonalization.	Marked but partial depersonalization. Parts of body may seem somewhat bigger or smaller than usual.	Self-esteem is quite poor. Identity is fragmented, unintegrated, and not very stable. Insatiable quests for money, status, assurance of sexual attractiveness. May often ruminate, "Who am I."	Self-image usually dependent on external feedback. Where feedback is negative or absent, sense of self as a separate entity falters. Often feels in "special communication" with others.
4	Very occasional signs of derealization, such as being in a fog or at sea. Seeing people through a haze. May sometimes feel on the outside looking in.	Occasional signs of depersonalization, usually under stressful circumstances. Some moderately unrealistic feelings about the body (e.g., becoming too bloated, fat, or thin when actual changes are in fact minimal).	May be "as-if" personality, or other manifestations of role-playing at identity rather than experiencing it from within. Often feels humiliated.	Sometimes dependent on external feedback to maintain identity. Under relatively stable conditions he is not dependent on outside support and can maintain a feeling of separateness.

Sense of Reality of the World and of the Self (Continued)

Stop	a	b	c	d
	Altered views of external reality are the exception rather than the rule, occuring primarily with radical environmental changes.	Depersonalization phenomena are fairly rare and limited to unusual conditions: falling asleep; waking up; drugs producing altered ego states.	More or less stable identity, self-image and self-esteem noted here. Identity sense may falter when external circumstances and people are unfamiliar or novel. Often feels important through significant others' accomplishments.	There are signs here of an independent sense of self, with a moderately good sense of inner reality, continuity, and internalized self-representations. Only sometimes does S depend on external cues for his full sense of individuality.
6	Derealization occurs only under conditions of extreme environmental alteration. It disappears with restoration of average expectable conditions.	Depersonalization occurs only under conditions of extreme environmental alterations. It disappears with restoration of average expectable conditions.	Stable identity, a distinct sense of self, and self-esteem are well internalized.	Requires only occasional feedback to maintain a sense of one's self as solidly separate from others.
7	Under average expectable environmental conditions or under conditions of extreme change and stress, experience of the world remains stable.	No disturbances in the sense of reality of the self, the body, or the body image.	Stable identity, distinct sense of self, and self-esteem are so well established and solid that they remain intact even under conditions of unusual stress or of minimal external cues ordinarily required for self-anchorage points.	S is exceptionally well able to differentiate between his own feelings, thoughts, and motives, those of others. Minimal feedback from external sources is required for him to delineate his own self-boundaries. While S may enjoy temporary regressed states of fusion, merging, and unusual communication with others, he does not require them for the maintenance of his own sense of separate identity. Virtually no

Sense of Reality of the World and of the Self (Continued)

Stop	a	b	c	d
7 (Cont)				confusion between experiences emanating from within one's self and phenomena with points of origin outside the self.

impulse expressions deriving from superego pressures such as guilt and self-destructive urges, ranging from suicidal tendencies to less extreme manifestations of depression, then moral and instinctual masochism. Where relevant, we would also include pressures from the ego-ideal, such as "driving ambition," which, when it regulates self-esteem, may reflect varying degrees of impulse control.

It is important for the rater to distinguish between what the regulation-and-control scale measures and what the id scales of libidinal- and aggressive-drive components measure. The former concerns itself with the ego aspects pertaining to adaptation — the way that drive, affect, and impulse are controlled relevant to environmental context. The latter focuses on *strength* of drive, rather than the fate of the drive with respect to behavioral and ideational adaptation.

The rater will find it useful to think of degree of directness or sublimation as a relevant dimension for scaling regulation and control but not for scaling id scales of drive strength. For example, a person can have a high drive strength whether or not that drive is culturally adaptive.

Regulation and Control of Drive, Affect and Impulse

Stop	a	b
	The directness of impulse expression (ranging from primitive and psychopathic acting out, through activity of the impulse-ridden character, through neurotic acting out, to relatively indirect forms of behavioral expression). Maladaptiveness would be a function of the extent to which awareness of drive, affect, and impulse is experienced and expressed disruptively.	The effectiveness of delay and control mechanisms (including both under- and over-control); the degree of frustration-tolerance and the extent to which drive-derivatives are channeled through ideation, affective expression, and manifest behavior.
1	Aggression, and/or depression and/or sexual manifestations at their most disruptive extreme. Persons may have committed or attempted murder, suicide, or rape. Indirect or associated drive behavior is not observed at this stop, as impulses achieve full discharge through direct expression. Polymorphous perverse behavior in the extreme and in many areas (e.g., feces-smearing).	Extreme lack of control. Minimal frustration-tolerance inferable from inability to restrain impulse-dominated behavior. When thinking is at all rational, there is no evidence to show that this rationality exercises any delay or control over impulse expression. Weak controls in relation to the experience of extreme drive pressure leave physical or externally imposed constraints as about the only effective way to curb most urges. At times, no matter how hard the person tries to control urges, he cannot.
2	Aggression, depression, and sexual manifestations are quite disruptive. May be impulse-ridden personality.	S has great difficulty holding back sexual, aggressive, or other urges because of weak controls in relation to the experience of

Regulation and Control of Drive, Affect and Impulse (Continued)

Stop	a	b
2	Psychopathic behavior may be quite pronounced. Assaultive-type acts short of homicide. Sadistic superego pressure against the self could include serious self-inflicted injury short of suicide. Fantasy content would vary only a little from actual sexual or aggressive behavior, hardly ever as substitute formations at this level. May be rapid mood changes from one extreme to the other.	drive pressure. Physical constraints are the most effective way of curbing most urges. Frustration tolerance is almost always poor. Very little tolerance for anxiety or depression.
3	Strong urges are usually acted upon. Sometimes, although present, they are not experienced at all, and knowledge of them can only be deduced from behavior. There may be sporadic rages, tantrums or binges, as with alcohol, food, or sex. Affects and moods may be very labile, crying one moment, laughing the next. May be psychopathic personality. May be hyperkinetic, or need to be physically on the go all the time.	Urges are controlled either very poorly or excessively (overcontrol is first scored here). Excessive controls would be of the extremely rigid or brittle sort so that periods of overcontrol alternate with flurries of impulsive breakthroughs or psychosomatic spill-over. Where urges are extremely low (as in prolonged depressive states), few overt outlets are available. In cases of overcontrol of strong urges, sexual and aggressive preoccupations receive outlets in areas other than overt behavior. With strong urges and undercontrol, outlets might be voyeurism, promiscuity, "addiction" to pornographic material.
4	Drive-dominated behavior shows a few signs of adaptive directedness here. Aggressive behavior is more often verbal than physical, sometimes quite disguised and indirect, as in occupational choice of correction officer, butcher, photographer's model. May be overeating or have excessive interest in collecting and neatness. Acting out of unconscious wishes and fantasies may be quite prominent. May be general rebelliousness. Moderately high general excitability.	Controls may appear reasonably good but are of the "grit-your-teeth" or "count-to-ten" variety rather than of the smooth, automatic sort. Attempts to keep a rein on drive expression may also lead to a somewhat rigid picture. May involve overreacting, overdramatizing.
5	Drives, etc., are experienced and expressed either somewhat more	Controls are somewhat less than automatic but may be automatic in conflict-free areas.

Regulation and Control of Drives, Affects and Impulses (Continued)

Stop	a	b
5 (Cont)	or somewhat less than average. Irritability, arousability, or impulsivity in behavior tend to be responses to specific or conflict-ridden areas or to situational stress and external provocations. Associated, indirect behavior and interests may include mild teasing, sparring repartee, mildly inappropriate flirting or secualization of work. Some symptomatic acting out of unconscious conflicts. Moderate depressions (disappointments).	When not automatic, they can be mustered on the spot with moderate effort. Occasional work or social inhibitions.
6	When general behavior and interests are aggressively and sexually oriented, it is with effective sublimnation and neutralization (e.g., physical assaultiveness occurs only in the interest of survival of self and others when there is no other alternative). Intercourse is preferred outlet for sexual urges. Unusual sexual or aggressive behavior is seen only under extreme provocation or prolonged stress.	Reasonably smooth expression of urges, behaviorally, with the aid of fairly flexible controls. Degree of tightening or relaxing of controls is appropriate to the situation and is generally volitional and/or fairly automatic.
7	Overly aggressive behavior or its derivatives are seen only when there is no alternative, as in the interest of survival and the regulation of self-esteem along effective, adaptive lines. Effective action, whether automatic or by conscious choice in mastering tasks and achieving life goals, makes unnecessary any sort of aggressive behavior short of that mentioned above. Preferred sexual behavior is sexual intercourse. Depression and related states are limited to sadness, grief, and mourning in response to expectably provocative losses.	Control of urges to motility, etc., comes fairly quickly, calmly, and automatically. Flexibility of delay and control mechanisms allows S to respond according to his own choice rather than to pressures beyond his control. A minimum of subjective and automatic difficulties with automatic regulation and control of drive expression, such that the person functions extremely smoothly in work, sex, play, and object relations generally.

V. OBJECT RELATIONS

Instructions to Raters. Optimal relationships are relatively free of maladaptive elements suggesting patterns of interaction that were more appropriate to old situations than to the present ones. The most pathological extreme would be essentially an absence of relationships with any people; next would be present relations based on early fixations, unresolved conflicts, and very hostile, sadomasochistic relationships. Optimal relations would be the most mature, relatively free of distortions, and gratifying to adult libidinal, aggressive, and ego needs.

Intensity, diversity, and pervasiveness are not always essential components to span the entire scale, but to make global ratings, the rater is instructed to keep in mind the *quality* of the person's relationships to central and peripheral people. For more pathological adaptations the disturbances in object relations will be assumed to extend to a broader range of contacts than they would in the moderately maladaptive categories, where pathology might be limited to one or two significant relationships.

VI. THOUGHT PROCESSES

Instructions to Raters. Ratings will be based to a great extent on formal questioning, but person's overall style of language and other communications to interviewer in general will also be determining factors in evaluating this function.

VII. ARISE

Instructions to Raters. Adaptive regression in the service of the ego (ARISE) refers to the ability of the ego to initiate a partial, temporary, and controlled lowering of its own functions (keep in mind here the component factors of the other 11 ego functions) in the furtherance of its interests (i.e., promoting adaptation). Such regressions result in a relatively free, but controlled, play of the primary process.

The two components together make up what is known as the "oscillating function" – or the alterations between regressions – on the one hand, and integration into new configurations, on the other.

It will be important to assess manifestations of ARISE in the middle ranges of the population, that is, nonartists who make up the bulk of any sample to be studied. ARISE may be difficult to rate accurately in many people.

In this scale, the oscillating function can be reflected in the global ratings of the function as a whole. The general rationale for the ARISE scale is as follows:

Object Relations

Stop	a	b	c	d
	The degree and kind of relatedness to others (taking account of narcissism, symbiosis, separation-individuation, withdrawal trends, egocentricity, narcissistic object choice, or extent of mutuality, reciprocity, empathy, ease of communication). Degree of closeness-distance and degree of flexibility and choice in maintaining object relations.	The primitivity-maturity of object relations. Includes the extent to which present relationships are adaptively or maladaptively influenced by, or patterned upon, older ones.	The extent to which the person perceives and responds to others as independent entities rather than as extensions of himself.	The extent to which he can maintain object constancy, i.e., can sustain both the physical absence of the object and the presence of frustration or anxiety related to the object. Degree and kind of internalization (the way S perceives and responds to people who aren't physically present).
1	Essential lack of any object relatedness. Withdrawal, as into stupor or muteness; or living like a hermit or recluse. "Relationships: are presymbiotic, mostly autistic. When rudiments of relationships are present, they are fraught with turmoil, struggle, and other near total disruptive elements, deteriorating quite rapidly. "Distance regulators" are poor. S can tolerate little stimulation from other people.	Because of impoverishment and essential lack of relatedness, only the most primitive early elements characterize "relationships."	Minimal ability to perceive people in their own right. Extreme "parasitism," or narcissism.	Not developed enough even for separation anxiety. Bland withdrawal in response to "object loss." People do not "exist" when not present.

455

Object Relations (Continued)

Stop	a	b	c	d
2	Considerable withdrawal-schizoid detachment rather than total withdrawal. Severely narcissistic, parasitic, or symbiotic relationships; folie à deux, vicarious objects, intensely sadomasochistic binds. Either overattachment or underattachment of an infantile nature.	Present relationships characterized by transference based on very early fixations and may reflect disturbances in early mother-child relationships. Recurrent difficulties are the rule rather than the exception.	People's feelings, motives and beliefs are rarely understood from the other's point of view, but mostly in terms of the direct impact they have upon S. Exceedingly difficult for S to ignore his own needs as he responds to others primarily from an egocentric frame of reference. Derives pleasure from exercising "power" over others.	Separation anxiety may be prominent and may be maladaptive reaction to object loss, loss of love, or narcissistic injury. Reactions to loss still tend to be fairly catastrophic.
3	Relationships may be characterized by detachment or else by some overdependence and clinging. Considerable difficulty striking a comfortable balance between distance and closeness. Prefers either very intense or very cool relationships. May be distant for fear of a close relationship breaking up.	Present relationships are quite childlike and bear marks of earlier, similar ones. Expects to be "fed" emotionally. May wait for things to get better.	Other people only very occasionally are perceived and responded to as existing in their own right. Many "self-references" in responding to others. Own identity overly dependent on perception of others. Inordinate attempts to "change" others with belief that this will crystallize self-identity. May use and exploit people to satisfy own ambitions, oblivious to how others feel about this.	Inordinate strivings for either dependence on, or independence from, significant others, exaggerated attempts to prove one's self sufficiency. Or S may feel quite easily hurt or rejected. Representations of significant people still not too well internalized—over reactions to loss and separations. Virtually unable to live alone; or else distinctly prefers isolation from people in living arrangement.

456

Object Relations (Continued)

Stop	a	b	c	d
4	Relations with significant others are characterized by neurotic-type interactions. Can be of withdrawn, narcissistic, or symbiotic types, but such manifestations are more complex than primitive. Examples would be Don Juanism, more "advanced" forms of sado-masochism, where usually just significant relationships are of this sort. Also includes the fringe, hanger-on person, most of whose relationships are superficial. "Game-playing."	Contains elements of conflicts characterizing early childhood, including relationships with both parents. In this sense they are a step more mature than relationships reflecting only the earliest ties to the mother, alone.	Other people can be responded to in their own right in situations that are not too emotionally charged or are neutral or nonstressful. Under more difficult circumstances, emphasis may be on trying to get other people to change in order to promote a stable self-feeling.	Sensitive to potential rejections and abandonments when not being clearly focused in others' attention. Loneliness, living alone are not tolerated very well.
5	Disturbed interactions with only a few people, and sporadically rather than chronically. Object choice and behavior with significant people shows some important degree of flexibility, but under stress becomes more compulsive or less free.	Transference and repetitions of early patterns of relating are the exception rather than the rule in everyday encounters, but may persist under very charged conditions. Some recurrent difficulties in important relationships.	Others are perceived as separate and well differentiated from the self, except under rather stressful or charged circumstances. E.g., S may recognize the other person's feelings, understand them, and respond appropriately, but when threatened, may have unreasonable expectation of what others urge and can do.	Internalization of objects is evident, but under severe or prolonged stress, absences and losses are overreacted to. May have some difficulty living alone, but finds ways to compensate for loneliness.
6	Flexibility of choice and mode in most relationships,	Tending toward mature object relations with goals that	S is usually responsive to other people as separate individuals	Object constancy is well developed, as important people are internalized.

Object Relations (Continued)

Stop	a	b	c	d
6 (Cont)	with conscious and automatic maintenance of optimal distance.	are mutually satisfying to self and significant others.	in their own rights. A reasonably good degree of empathy, but not so much as to get "lost" in the other person's feelings or point of view.	Losses, separations, and other such potential traumas are weathered without undue strain. Thoughts about, reactions to, and respect for others continue whether or not the others are physically present.
7	Relationships are characterized by mutuality, reciprocity, depth, and extensivity. They maintain smoothness and stability despite stresses that might otherwise threaten them. They are flexibly maintained out of choice, as opposed to compulsion. "Distance regulators" are optimal. S functions adaptively even with maximal stimulation and excitement generated by other people.	No substantial evidence of fixations or distortions from early relationships. Maturity nearly completely replaces primitivity. Gratifications in relationships are in response to current adult needs. Flexibility and choice characterize object relationships.	Person responds to others as people in their own right, empathetic to their needs as separate people. Understands people for what they are and not from an egocentric frame of reference. Person can temporarily ignore his own needs in an effort to respond primarily to the other person. High degree of "field independence."	Object constancy excellent as judged by easy adaptations to separations, adaptive resiliency following loss of important objects. Relationships to significant others are highly viable, even when those people are not physically present.

Thought Processes

Stop	a	b	c
	Degree of adaptiveness in memory, concentration, and attention.	The ability to conceptualize. The extent to which abstract and concrete modes of thinking are appropriate to the situation.	The extent to which language and communication reflect primary- or secondary-process thinking.
1	Memory, concentration and attention are grossly disturbed.	Person rarely, if ever, can conceptualize, generalize, or use abstract thinking in problem-solving or other tasks. Either the extremely concrete or the extremely syncretistic (overinclusive) modes of categorizing objects and experiences predominates. Person cannot understand metaphors or similes, is unable to grasp the general meaning of proverbs, and may show excessive literalness. No distinction is made between the object and the sign or symbol that represents the object. Capacity for syllogistic reasoning is nil.	Minimal ability to communicate verbally, owing to either mutism, extreme autism, word salad, flood of loosely or barely associated sounds, words, and phrases. Neologisms and clang associations. Practically no ability to comprehend the meaning of what other people are saying. Verbalizations contain fragmentation, primary-process influenced condensations, and contradictions. Extremely queer and peculiar expressions prevent meaningful verbal exchange.
2	Memory for only stereotyped content such as name, colors. Attention and concentration poor — very easily distractible. Foggy "sensorium."	Prominent failures of abstract reasoning. Overly concrete or overly general, with little ability to see relationships between discrete events.	Some autistic and many peculiar ideas. Thinking may sometimes be fragmented. Rigid or loose thinking often prevents adequate communication. Blocking and peculiarities in verbal expression. Thinking frequently illogical.
3	Large gaps in memory. Easily sidetracked by own thoughts and external distractions	Episodic failures of abstract reasoning and conceptualization.	At times, thoughts are organized and difficult to follow. Some

Thought Processes (Continued)

Stop	a	b	c
3 (Cont)	when attempting to concentrate. Attention and concentration remain unimpaired only if there are no competing distractions. Some trouble with remote and current memory.	Relies heavily on concrete or overideational or overinclusive modes of thought. Some little ability to see relationships and differences between events. Sometimes, difficulty in making distinctions between gradations and subtleties leads to "all-or-none" type thinking. When rigidity of thinking is present, it is difficult to entertain more than one possibility.	peculiar and queer ideas. Frequent but circumscribed disruptions in communication, possibly caused by intrusions of fantasy and drive-related thoughts that impede the flow of thought through language. Questionable logic.
4	Memory, attention, and concentration show periodic lapses, as in emotionally charged situations and with mildly compelling competing distractions. Great effort often required to exercise these functions effectively.	Occasional manifestations of flexibility in conceptualization, but under stress concrete or syncretistic modes of thought emerge. Thinking may be disordered or illogical while under stress.	Some rigid or meticulous modes of communication or else moderate degrees of looseness and disorganization. Some doubting and blocking. Occasional peculiar ideas. Mildly imprecise substitutions, expressions, or malapropisms. Some distractibility of intruding thoughts resulting in disruptive communication, particularly under stress. Some rigidity or looseness may interfere with free exchange and exploration.
5	Moderately strong competing stimuli cause lapses in memory, concentration, and attention, but mild distractions generally do not affect these functions. Moderate effort generally required to mobilize these functions.	Minor failures of conceptualization. Under stress there may be a tendency toward concreteness or overgenerality, but S can correct these lapses when asked to expand or delimit concepts.	Occasional vagueness, unclarity, or obsessionally overprecise thinking under stress. Occasional inability to stick to trend of thought because of pressure from intruding associations. Few peculiarities,

Thought Processes (Continued)

Stop	a	b	c
5 (Cont)			personalized associations, rigidity, looseness, or inability to go beyond the objective facts.
6	May forget names or be distracted from attending and concentrating when bored, sick, or upset, but otherwise, no substantial lapses in memory, concentration, or attention.	Satisfactory use of conceptualization. Evidence of flexibility in willingness to entertain and explore new ideas and in shifting back and forth between abstract and concrete modes.	More often than not, communication is clear, precise, and flexible. Possible egocentric modes of expressions, but no serious peculiarities in language. Thinking is for the most part logical and ordered.
7	Can concentrate exceptionally well even with strong distractions. Recent and remote memory is excellent for all kinds of events. These functions and attention are automatic and resistant to intrusions.	Conceptual thinking developed to its highest degree. Person shifts appropriately from abstract to concrete modes, and vice versa, when necessary.	Associations are meaningfully integrated into precise, but not overprecise, communications. No significant peculiarities of expression. Excellent ability to shift levels of discourse. Communications are unambiguous and reflect shared meanings of words and idea.

at the most maladaptive end, one sees only a primarily primitive or uncontrolled regression. In the "middle," one sees the oscillating function only with great difficulty or else a general absence of regression in the context of overcontrolled defensiveness. At the most adaptive end of the scale, one finds smoothly oscillating and flexibly controlled regressions in the service of new awareness and new integrations.

The rater is instructed to consider the final product (e.g., the work of art, the solved problem, the creative act) only insofar as it reflects the *process* of regression in the service of the ego. It is conceivable that a lesser work of art could involve more adaptive use of controlled regressions than a greater work of art. Raters should also keep in mind creative problem-solving in nonartistic areas: scientific and everyday resourcefulness.

ARISE

Stop	a	b
	First phase of an oscillating process: degree of relaxation of perceptual and conceptual acuity with corresponding increase in awareness of previously preconscious and unconscious contents and the extent to which these "regressions" disrupt adaptation or are uncontrolled.	Extent of controlled use of primary-process thinking in the induction of new configurations. Extent of increase in adaptive potential as a result of creative integrations produced by ultimately controlled and secondary-process use of regressions.
1	Regressions are extremely prominent and primitively disrupt adaptive behavior (e.g., "wild" fantasies intrude willy-nilly and may either be distressing or disabling, creating confusion and chaos).	New configurations are largely absent, or when they do occur, they are not a product of controlled regressions but may be a result of "rote" learning or other very simplified, uncreative processes. No oscillating function is observed. Artistic productions might be aimless smearing or "tracing" with a stencil.
2	Regression phenomena are still fairly primitive and do not afford pleasure and enjoyment. Disruptions in adaptation may be seen in being "carried away" by one's own fantasies; highly regressed use of artistic materials (e.g., clay used only for kneading or throwing).	Occasionally, elements from dreams, fantasies, or other regressed states may be discovered in planned activities. Their effect, however, is not very marked, and thus their influence on new or creative ways of looking at things to promote adaptation is nil. Unimaginative approach to problem-solving leads to sterility and stereotype.
3	Regressive phenomena may be observed here, but so, too, may be a virtual absence of regressive phenomena. Specifically, there might be a relative inability to loosen or relinquish the more constricted types of control that one sees in unimaginative or obsessional people, who find it difficult to engage in playful fantasy or humor. Regressions of all ego functions in that instance are experienced as ego-alien threats. Or, regressive behavior is enjoyable but may be overly prolonged and resistant to recovery.	The transition from regression to adaptation is hampered by difficulties in smoothly emerging from the regressed state. Regressions and controls work separately, not together, so that creative efforts are still not aided by controlled regressions (e.g., humor may be silly, products may be sloppy or uninspired because of lack of coordination between the two phases of the oscillating function).
4	S may be able to enjoy primitive thoughts, feelings, fantasies, and regressed ego states generally. The regressions are only somewhat controlled. Or, S may be quite controlled,	S has some difficulty in adaptively channeling the outcomes of regressively based enjoyments (e.g., fantasies or daydreams may be reasonably rich but not often carried over

ARISE (Continued)

Stop	a	b
4 (Cont)	so that playful regressions and their enjoyment are somewhat difficult to achieve.	into productive activity). May never deviate from recipe when cooking.
5	Enjoyment of regressions may be fairly high, possibly owing to an acceptance of temporary passivity. S demonstrates a fair amount of control in initiating and in emerging from regressed states. Can be somewhat playful in attempting to solve a problem, but may feel compelled to return to a serious stance a bit prematurely.	Regressions are employed fairly adaptively. The oscillating function, however, lacks the sustaining power and smooth operation that would ensure truly creative-adaptive uses of regression in the service of the ego. Can be playful one moment, serious the next, without the smooth transition needed for optimal productivity.
6	Regressions to primary-process thinking and activities are well controlled and pleasurable. S may be silly, humorous, playful, fantasy-ridden — but can usually engage in and suspend these activities at will.	The adaptive-creative uses of regressive content are quite highly developed. Achievement of new integrations is often arrived at by regressive detours (e.g., controlled use of regressive humor or self-analysis may be put to use in a well-constructed story or autobiography).
7	Regressions are "controlled" and promote maximal enjoyment of and/or active participation in art, humor, play, sexuality, imagination, and creativity. The regressions "oscillate" with component b. S enjoys the absurd, and is spontaneous in producing and/or enjoying jokes.	Achievement of adaptive, integrative, creative ego function is arrived at by a regressive detour. The role of the oscillating function in this achievement is maximally observable. The adaptive-creative uses of regressive content are maximally developed, and the oscillation leading to the creative channeling of regressions is flexible and automatically controlled.

VIII. DEFENSIVE FUNCTIONING

Instructions to Raters. Defenses protect preconscious and conscious organizations from the intrusions of id derivatives, unconscious ego, and superego tendencies. They aid adaptation by controlling the emergence of anxiety-arousing or other dysphoric psychic content, such as ego-alien instinctual wishes and affects (including depression), which conflict with reality demands. Any function may at specifiable times be erected defensively against any other ego function, and a drive derivative (e.g., aggression) may defend against another (e.g., passivity).

This scale differs from the regulation-and-control-of-drives scale in that the latter measures the degree of impulse expression and motor discharge in behavior. Defensive functioning is not a scale of impulsivity but of measures employed to deal with disturbing elements of mental content, anxiety, and intrapsychic conflict.

Formation of a hierarchical ordering of the specific, classic 10 or 12 defenses with respect to pathology is an issue that has yet to be resolved in psychoanalytic theory, so the basis for ordering the scale will mainly be a dimensionalization of the efficacy of defensive functioning rather than an attempt to order specific mechanisms along an adaptive continuum. While certain stops explicitly list certain defenses and not others, the rater is to rate according to the overall rationale of the scale.

Excessive use of defenses is added at stop 3 in addition to relative failure of defenses. Stops 4 and 5 illustrate defenses as they are used in symptoms or compromises; stops 6 and 7 delineate circumstances where the defenses operate optimally to accomplish the most adaptive aims of the ego, and not as intrusions.

In making his ratings, the rater is instructed to rely not only on the specific questions designed to tap defensive functioning but on the person's *style* of responding to all questions throughout the interview. For example, pedantry in verbal behavior generally might tell more about how excessive the person's defensive functioning is than would a direct answer to a specific question about defenses.

Defensive Functioning

Stop	a	b
	Extent to which defense mechanisms, character defenses, and other defensive functioning have maladaptively affected ideation, behavior, and the adaptive level of other ego functions.	Extent to which defenses have succeeded or failed (e.g., degree of emergence of anxiety, depression, and/or other dysphoric affects).
1	Defense mechanisms and elements are among those in the general hierarchy of defense mechanisms that reflect least adaptation or are most pathological. Might be projection at its most extreme, manifest in broad delusional systems. Massive repression and denial might rule out any reflective thinking. Splitting mechanisms are prominent.	Massive failure and/or pathological misuse of defensive functioning, so that there is emergence of id derivatives and unconscious contents producing extreme anxiety, depression, or other dysphoric affect. Degree of anxiety and panic is extreme.
2	Rather extensive and inflexible use of primitive defenses (denial, splitting)	Considerable failure of defenses. Anxiety likely to be free-floating and unbound thus interferes with adaptive functioning to a

Defensive Functioning (Continued)

Stop	a	b

2 (Cont) are generalized in character and behavior. Affect storms usually defend against reflective thinking since thoughts may be potentially disturbing. Extreme uses of projection. Socially pathological forms of identification with the aggressor. Functioning has a highly defensive quality which interferes considerably with general adaptation.

significant degree. May be chronic depressive states. Feels as though he is falling apart.

3 Defenses analogous to "overcontrol" score here. May be extreme over-ideational defenses, such as isolation and intellectualization, where thought predominates over affect. May also be fairly pervasive projections, quasi delusions, perceptual vigilance, avoidance, evasions, severe inhibitions and ego restriction. Whatever the defenses, their effect is more maladaptive than adaptive.

Frequent breakthroughs of anxiety, depression, drive-related material, ego-alien thoughts, parapraxes. Free-floating anxiety of the sort seen in agoraphobia or claustrophobia. A pervasive feeling of vulnerability.

4 S may show evidence of rationalization, reaction-formation, transient projections, occasional parapraxes, and malapropisms. Also, symptomatic acting out (where action is a substitute for a repressed thought). Generally defensive behavior is fairly prominent.

Anxiety more likely to be bound in symptoms than free-floating. Tolerance for anxiety and other dysphoric states is not very good. When jumpy, upset, or anxious, means of protection and recovery do not come easily.

5 Some ability to adaptively relinquish or adaptively employ defensive operations, whatever they may be, except in situations that are characteristically conflictual for the individual.

Anxiety is present to a moderate degree; there is some tolerance for it, so that while it sometimes interferes with functioning, it need not do so markedly. May feel temporarily thrown but shows some adaptive resilience in recovery.

6 Defensive functioning, or the lack of it, is employed primarily in the service of adaptation with good resilience and recovery to nondefensive modes. An absence of excessive or insufficient use of defenses.

Anxiety present only when appropriate to situational stress and is well tolerated.

Defensive Functioning (Continued)

Stop	a	b
7	Only the most adaptive defensive elements are present (e.g., denial when in the service of adaptation to reality). The warding off of painful or dysphoric material is accomplished by recognizing, considering, making judgments and taking appropriate action about it. Defensive functions observable at this stop are in the service of adaptation to external events as well as involved in the resolution of intrapsychic conflict. Under conditions of stress, there is minimal disruption of other ego functions by defensive functioning.	Access to unconscious contents and id derivatives does not produce disruption and/or anxiety.

IX. STIMULUS BARRIER

Instructions to Raters. Both thresholds and responses to stimuli contribute to adaptation by the organism's potential for responding to high, average, or low sensory input, so that optimal homeostasis (as well as adaptation) is maintained. Stimulus barrier determines, in part, how resilient a person is or how he readapts after the stress and impingements are no longer present.

Thresholds, as described in component a, refer not only to reaction to external stimuli but also to internal stimuli that provide proprioceptive cues or those originating within the body but eventually impinging on sensory organs. Light, sound, temperature, pain, pressure, drugs, and intoxicants are the stimuli to be considered relevant to assessing thresholds. Responses to varying degrees of stimulation from people are assessed in the object-relations scale. Stimulus barrier focuses on inanimate stimuli.

Responses other than sensory threshold (component a) include motor responses, coping mechanisms, effects on sleep, and mood (component b).

Stimulus Barrier

Stop	a	b
	Threshold for, sensitivity to, or registration of external and internal stimuli impinging upon various sensory modalities (corresponds to "receptive function").	Degree of adaptation, organization, and integration of responses to various levels of sensory stimulation. The effectiveness of "coping mechanisms" in relation to degree of sensory stimulation—whether observed in

Stimulus Barrier (Continued)

Stop	a	b
		motor behavior, affective response, or cognition.

1	Extremely low thresholds to most or all sensory stimuli. Awareness of sensory impingements may be hyperacute. Sensitivity to subliminal incidental or peripheral stimulation is also extremely acute. Or thresholds may be exceedingly low with no awareness (i.e., S is hypersensitive, but doesn't know to what, such as noise, that he doesn't hear").	Coping modes reflect vulnerability and lack of ego integration through hyperkinetic or chaotic type of motor discharge patterns. May be aimless flailing about under conditions of even mild sensory stimulation. Sensory stimulation may lead to sleep disturbances, "psychosomatic spill-over" or possibly migraine headaches. Excessive response to drugs and intoxicants. Noise, light, crowds, multiple stimuli produce disorganized reactions.
2	Very low thresholds to most sensory stimuli. Quite aware of minor bodily changes. High, low, and relatively small changes in temperature produce considerable discomfort. Noise may produce a diffuse excitability, and too much light may cause agitation. May or may not know source of discomfort.	S often feels like "jumping out of his skin." Adaptive efforts at keeping stimulation low or minimizing one's reactions to it are very poor. Severe insomnia may reflect poor response to high sensory stimulation. Women may experience high degree of premenstrual tension and agitation. Adaptive behavior is largely immobilized because attention and efforts are riveted on the experience of overstimulation. The fabled "princess and the pea."
3	Thresholds to most sensory stimuli are quite low. About average sensitivity to "irrelevant," peripheral, or incidental stimuli. Cold, heat, noise, bright lights are very bothersome. May hear, see, and smell things that the average person would not be aware of. There may be a stimulus-seeking or stimulus-hunger. Paradoxically, S may enjoy being "turned on" despite his hypersensitivity and excitability.	Less chaotic motor discharge and more general irritability. Adaptive efforts at "filtering" stimulation are relatively ineffective. Disorganization or withdrawal may follow upon exposure to strong stimuli. Can stick with adaptive tasks for only a short time with sensory overload. Sleep patterns are irregular. May react with headaches in response to stimuli. Adaptive efforts while "turned on" are not very effective. In women, premenstrual tension may take the form of extreme irritability
4	Thresholds to sensory stimuli from fairly low to average and a bit above. S may be sensitive to specific noises but not to others or to light. Or flashing lights would be bothersome but steady daylight quite tolerable. Specific stimulus hungers	While occasionally irritable, grumpy, or annoyed by the circumscribed range of distressing stimuli, S is able to contain his responses to stimulation fairly adaptively. He may grin and bear it despite inner irritability, although the effort thus expended may lead to fatigue and/or relatively poor recovery and

Stimulus Barrier (Continued)

Stop	a	b
4 (Cont)	may be noted. May or may not be aware of source of stimulation.	adaptive resilience. Adaptive behavior is only moderately disrupted by peripheral or incidental stimuli. May seek solitude and then have some difficulty returning to a more stimulating environment.
5	S has moderately high sensory thresholds in most modalities. Only very strong central or focal stimuli would be bothersome. Peripheral and average range of light, sound, temperature, inner states would not be experienced as troublesome or offensive. When stimuli are bothersome, S tends to be aware of what the stimuli are.	A reasonably good balance between discharge and control patterns in the face of high levels of stimulus input. When there are motor-discharge reactions, they may be fairly even, or when more explosive, S is resilient and able to compose himself relatively soon after exposure to strong, potentially disruptive stimuli. Many adaptive activities can be carried out despite level of sensory stimulation. Appears to "ride the waves" somewhat comfortably, even in the middle of "5 o'clock mayhem" or a boisterous party.
6	Somewhat flexible and automatic fluctuations in thresholds to stimuli within a reasonably high range. Good "screening mechanism" to permit adequate input and avoid sensory overload (e.g., S is receptive to mild noises, unruffled by loud ones. Sensitivity to subliminal and peripheral stimuli varies adaptively with the situation.	Coping modes, including motor discharge patterns, are reasonably flexible. Sleeps well without need for oblivion and defensive withdrawal from stimuli.
7	Very flexible, automatic fluctuations in thresholds to stimuli. Thresholds appear to be high. There is an optimal "screening mechanism."	Flexible, automatic responses to all degrees of stimulation. There is an optimally smooth operation of responses. Person is reasonably comfortable with what to others is "sensory overload"; he sleeps well, adapts flexibly to all sensory impingements.

X. AUTONOMOUS FUNCTIONING

Instructions to Raters. Intrusion of conflict, ideation, affect, and/or impulse upon functioning is a major criterion for determining impairment of either the primary or the secondary autonomy.

The basic apparatuses and functions of primary autonomy are

perception	memory	language
intentionality	hearing	productivity
concentration	vision	motor development and
attention	speech	expression

Secondarily autonomous functions are more numerous and include most of the ego functions in this manual. We are therefore focusing the scoring of autonomous functioning on habit patterns, skills, routines, hobbies, and interests.

Autonomous Functioning

Stop	a	b
	Degree of freedom from impairment of apparatuses of primary autonomy (attention, concentration, memory, learning, perception, motor function, intention).	Degree of freedom from impairment of secondary autonomy (disturbances in habit patterns, learned complex skills, work routines, hobbies, and interests).
1	Severe interference with the functioning of one or more of the "apparatuses" of primary autonomy. Inability to concentrate or attend no matter how much effort is expended. Word use and pronunciation may be markedly impaired. Perceptually, there may be tunnel vision, loss of ability to estimate seen distances correctly. Motor coordination may be poor or interfered with. Efforts at willful performance are virtually ineffective.	Habit patterns, work habits, and/or learned skills of any kind are massively hampered so that person is unable to utilize most of these (e.g., a previously skilled worker who cannot carry out his job because the component activities have taken on sexual and aggressive meanings to a marked extent, showing minimal resistance to intrusions from instinctual drives or from the environment).
2	Interference with primary autonomous functions is significant. Examples may be selective visual scotoma; serious interference with intentionality or "will"; grave difficulties in motor coordination or in mobilizing one's self to exercise ordinary motor functions. Attention, concentration, and learning suffer considerable impairment.	Complex skills and habits are interfered with to a serious degree (e.g., a housewife's previously automatically accomplished routine tasks are no longer carried through effectively). Even with maximal effort, performance in learned, automatic tasks falls short of minimal adequacy. "Writer's cramp" might be another example if it is severe without being totally disabling. Experience of extreme lack of energy.
3	Interference with primary autonomous functions is moderately high. Illusory experiences may be fairly prominent in thinking and perception. There may be blurred vision when reading school assignments, novels with general sexual	Skills, habits, and automatic behavior are interfered with to a moderately high degree, so that much effort must be expended to perform tasks previously automatic and routine. Ongoing complex behavior may be easily disrupted when drive-related ideas,

Autonomous Functioning (Continued)

Stop	a	b
3 (Cont)	content, or whatever material may be upsetting to the particular individual concerned. Similarly, concentration and attention may be impaired while reading any emotionally charged material.	affects, or stimuli intrude. Work may be impaired by intruding sexual or aggressive fantasies. Some difficulty with routine activities like dressing or walking.
4	Disturbance of primary autonomous functions to a moderate degree. Vision, motor behavior, language, intention, etc., could suffer from the intrusion of circumscribed aggressive and sexual thoughts, feelings, and fantasies.	Secondary autonomous habits, patterns, and skills are interfered with to a moderately low degree. Greater than usual effort must be expended to carry out routine tasks and work only when these become associated with circumscribed conflict areas. Such conflict-related intrusions do not occur frequently. S may sometimes get tongue-tied, physically awkward.
5	Primary autonomous functions may be interfered with by drive derivatives to a mild, but noticeable, degree (e.g., occasional stuttering, mind-wandering, forgetting of names and some remote and recent events.	Moderate resistance to intrusions upon secondary autonomous habits and skills. When interferences do occur, some extra effort is required to perform work previously done with little strain. Occasionally, it may be hard just to "get going."
6	Structures of primary autonomy are interfered with rarely or only to a minor degree, as under extreme stress. Might stumble over words when in a hurry or under great pressure.	Habit patterns and skills are utilized with relative ease or with relatively minor interference except under extreme stress. Good resistance to intrusions upon skills and work patterns, when these intrusions have the potential to interfere with ongoing work. Energy level is reasonably high.
7	Minimal interference with structures of primary autonomy by drive interference or other intrusions. Attention, concentration, memory, perception, and will function optimally in accordance with the person's potential.	There is high resistance to intrusions from instinctual drives and environmental influences among secondary autonomous functions. Habits and skills are carried on with ease and flexibility despite inner and outer pressure. Great energy level and productivity

XI. SYNTHETIC-INTEGRATIVE FUNCTIONING

This ego function fulfills one of the major tasks of the ego as defined by Freud in terms of reconciling the often conflicting demands of the id, superego, and outside world, as well as the incongruities within the ego. We focus on the reconciling of areas that are in conflict and also on the extent of relating together areas that are not in conflict.

Synthetic-Integrative Functioning

Stop	a	b
	Degree of reconciliation or integration of discrepant or potentially contradictory attitudes, values, affects, behavior, and self-representations.	Degree of *active* relating together (i.e., integrating) of both intrapsychic and behavioral events. These events may or may not be conflict-ridden and are not necessarily limited to behavior.

1   S has minimal ability to reconcile contradictions (e.g., the content of his thought may remain opposite to the quality of the accompanying feeling, and S is at best puzzled by the discrepancy). Certain aspects of identity and self-feeling may be dissociated from others, as in multiple personality. Maximal intolerance for ambiguity or incongruity in external events might be seen in adopting extremist points of view that oversimplify, in accordance with the S's inability to grasp a unity underlying surface contradictions. May be large discrepancy between affect display and behavior or thoughts (e.g., laughing when telling bad news).

S cannot cope with more than one task at a time. He needs to stay on "one track." If he is absorbed in one simple task and a second is introduced, he cannot cope with the second: he might either cling rigidly to the first or become so disorganized that any active coping behavior is minimal. Active, adaptive connection-making among different aspects of experience is nil. For example, S is virtually unable to utilize relevant past experience toward the solution of current problems. The ability to first plan and then carry out activities according to that plan is nil, especially when that planning and activity involve the organization of two or more elements of behavior. There might be rapid fluctuation of moods due to poorly integrated sense of continuity about what produced one mood or another. Fragmentation in the extreme.

2   Only a slight degree of synthesis and integration of disparate aspects of experience, behavior and self-representations, S experiences most events as fragmented, ambiguous and contradictory. He may say that he opposes violence yet regularly engage in violent behavior. Apparent contradictions are experienced as very distressing.

Only a small degree of active effort can be expended in relating different aspects of experience. The relation of past experience and events to present experience and behavior is rarely used in solving current problems. Disorganization in daily living is typical. Life is a lot of bits and pieces and loose ends that S cannot tie together.

3   Significant indications of unintegrated ego functioning. May be no consistent life goals, very divergent sets of career and future plans. S is puzzled by apparent contradictions

Quite difficult to carry out more than one project or activity at a time—even simple ones. Not adequately organized in daily life, but simple activities can be carried out reliably enough. Organizational efforts show

Synthetic-Integrative Functioning (Continued)

Stop	a	b
3 (Cont)	and ambiguities. May belong to or support "extremist" political groups. May be breakthroughs of opposing attitudes and beliefs.	fragmented or piecemeal results (e.g., living from day to day rather than following an overall directional plan).
4	Some areas of potential contradiction are reconciled while others remain unintegrated (e.g., may be moderately difficult to tolerate feelings of love and hate directed at the same person or to integrate disparate aspects of his personality into a unified identity). Outbursts reflecting lack of integration may occur (e.g., uncontrollable laughing during a tragic time).	Active efforts to relate different aspects of experience are only moderately successful. Purposeful, planned activities can be carried out, but considerable trouble results in S's attempts to keep up with the demands of everyday life for organization. Because of a defect in carrying through, or in tolerating unexpected intrusions into routines, he may be chronically quite far behind in meeting obligations and deadlines. Things are often left undone, S may either not care or be extremely concerned because of his difficulties in getting them done.
5	Major areas of the personality show a fair degree of consistency (e.g., there may be reasonable harmony between behavior and affect), but there are periodic exceptions of inconsistent attitudes, values, affects, and behavior. The inconsistencies are occasionally experienced as troublesome (e.g., some conflict in adopting apparently contradictory roles: being a follower one day, a leader the next.	Active efforts to reconcile different areas of experience in the service of adaptation show periodic lapses, as does carrying out purposeful activities and meeting demands and commitments. May be thrown out of gear when unexpected demands for changes in routine occur but does eventually recover equilibrium.
6	Consistency and a fair degree of integration in the major sectors of the personality are found. There may be a few minor inconsistencies, as in behavior, affect, and thinking. Good tolerance for the inevitable inconsistencies and incongruities that may occur. Can retain sense of humor while doing serious work.	S shows effective, successful efforts to make causal connections between the different areas of his experiences. Behavior is generally well organized and S deals with integrative requirements with relatively little stress and strain. Social, sexual, and vocational areas are satisfactorily integrated. Can tie loose ends together but has no compulsion to do this, which may disrupt adaptation.
7	S shows high, but flexible, consistency and integration in thinking, feeling, and behavior. His attitudes and values cover a wide range of feeling and opinion, yet despite	S actively makes connections, causal or otherwise, between different aspects of his experience. He responds flexibly to complex problems and can cope with a great variety of tasks simultaneously, alternately and

Synthetic-Integrative Functioning (Continued)

Stop	a	b
7 (Cont)	apparent disparities, possess an underlying consistent unity.	automatically in both thought and behavior employed in the service of active problem-solving. He can easily shift "set" when required to do so. Plans are carried out with minimal stress, with the aid of rapid, automatic shifts in orientation (e.g., when things are not going according to a prearranged "blueprint". That is, when a second or unexpected "track" is introduced, the person can automatically incorporate its demands into goal-oriented behavior. He has a good sense of continuity about what caused one mood or another (e.g., he would stay in a bad mood for an appropriate time).

XII. MASTERY-COMPETENCE

Instructions to Raters. Raters are asked to score competence and sense of competence separately, since a number of different relationships between the two are possible: (1) they may be congruent; (2) actual performance may exceed the sense of competence; (3) sense of competence may exceed mastery-competence. In addition, score -, =, or + for discrepancy score.

The specific environment and the limitations it imposes on the *form* of a person's competence should be carefully considered. A highly intelligent minority group person, for example, from a truly restrictive environment who performs a menial task skillfully would receive a higher score than his counterpart from an "advantaged" group performing the same work. Similarly, a well-educated housewife, realistically restricted to the rearing of four young children, would be rated in the context of competence within that role.

(1) Component c, the discrepancy score, reflects an aspect of self-esteem: that which has relevance only to actively mastering and affecting the environment. Thus, it should not overlap with all the other aspects of self-esteem, which are scored under the appropriate component factor of the ego function, sense of reality.

(2) The scaling of this ego function does not involve the desired degree of independence of all components. While component factors a and b are independent in the same manner as all other ego function components, component c differs radically. Component c, by definition, is the degree of dependence and *interaction* between the other two components. It perhaps will be the best indicator, among the three components, of mastery-competence as a whole.

There will be no global rating for mastery-competence. Each component *must* be rated separately, in order to get a discrepancy score (component c).

Mastery-Competence

Stop	a	b	c
	Competence. How well S actually performs in relation to his existing capacity to interact with and *actively* master and affect his environment.	The subjective role, or S's feeling of competence with respect to actively mastering and affecting his environment. S's expectations of success or actual performance (How he feels about how he does and what he can do). Sense of competence is scored *at face value* (e.g., higher than actual competence if there is an exaggerated sense of competence).	The degree of discrepancy between component a and component b (i.e., between actual competence and sense of competence). It may be negative (−), as when actual competence exceeds sense of competence. It may be equal (=), when actual competence and sense of competence are congruent. It may be positive (+), when sense of competence exceeds actual competence, as in a grandiose, exaggerated sense of competence compared with performance.
1	S does almost nothing with respect to altering, affecting, or interacting with his environment, because he is largely unable to utilize abilities and capacities in relation to reality. What minimal apparently effective action might be seen results merely from passive reacting rather than active coping.	The sense of competence is almost nil, and S feels powerless to act effectively in most ways, independently of his actual performance.	Discrepancy score may be either −, =, or +. Minus or plus discrepancies would be extremely high. Where +, sense of competence is grossly overinflated.
2	S is able to make only minimal efforts in coping with the environment. Prototypically, he waits for things to happen, rather than take an active role in effecting their occurence	Sense of competence is only minimally or sporadically present, so that any realistic effectuality is experienced as "luck" or "fate."	Discrepancy score may be −, =, or +; when + or − it will be so to a very high degree.
3	Successful interactions with the environment	A rather low sense of competence, as among	Discrepancy score may be −, =, or +. When − or + it

Mastery Competence (Continued)

Stop	a	b	c
3	come primarily from passive mastery or passive manipulation of people. Typical might be the "underachieving" college student with very high aptitudes who has coasted along and then falls progressively **lower** in his achievements as more active efforts to master are actually required. Tools and skills have been poorly mastered.	severely masochistic people who suffer ego restrictions and the concomitantly low sense of effectuality (e.g., S may seek employment for which he is over-qualified).	will be so to a rather high degree.
4	Mastery is partial: sometimes passive, sometimes active. Active efforts, however, will probably be directed toward getting others to achieve the desired outcomes rather than through direct coping or altering. Other stumbling blocks to mastery might be caused by restricting activity due to fears of failure, rejection, risk-taking, etc.	Sense of competence may be somewhat low because S devaluates his own efforts, no matter how effective they actually are. This devaluation may be caused by low esteem, guilt, masochism, poor sense of reality, fear of envy.	Discrepancy score may be −, =, or +. When − or + it will be so to a somewhat high degree.
5	Performance level is high a good part of the time, but in limited areas there may be some underachievement and lapses in competence (e.g., S in psychotherapy might have achieved maximal insight about conflict areas but delays exerting his own energy to actually work through and resolve the conflicts). At this level might also be the exaggerated "do-it-yourself" person whose need for active mastery is inordinate	Sense of competence is somewhat more likely to be high than low.	Discrepancy score may be −, =, or +. More likely to be = at this level than at previous ones. When − or + it will be so to a small degree. When −, poor self-appraisal in relation to actual effectiveness.

Mastery Competence (Continued)

Stop	a	b	c
5 (Cont)	and who fears relinquishing overcompensated efforts because he feels the competing passive tendencies.		
6	Actual competence and efforts at active mastery of the environment are quite high with only occasional lapses.	Sense of competence is usually quite high. S is aware of the successes he achieves in altering the environment in his own interests.	Discrepancy score is most likely to be =. Any + or − score is very slight.
7	The prototype here is the "do-it-yourself" person who is unusually resourceful at actively coping with, mastering and altering the environment effectively in the service of adaptation. He performs appropriately in his environmental context, or in harmony with the facilities and limitations of his environment and constitutional endowment.	Subjective sense of competence is maximally high. S feels extraordinarily able to affect and master his environment.	Discrepancy score will be =.

SUPEREGO SCALES

General Considerations

Below you will find three sections relating to superego functioning:

(1) a listing of how superego factors may interfere with each of the ego functions;

(2) a description of the dimension inconsistency-consistency of superego functioning;

(3) a scale of overall superego adaptation (13-points with half stops).

The rating sheet will provide a 4-point scale for rating interference with ego functions; a 7-point scale for rating adaptation; and a 4-point scale for rating consistency.

It seemed important enough to rate interference with ego functions specifically and also to evaluate the dimension consistency-inconsistency.

The third scale represents superego adaptiveness-maladaptiveness from an overall viewpoint. Adaptiveness-maladaptiveness is for practical purposes identical with strength of the superego. It is important to keep in mind the difference between strength and severity in this context. An overly severe superego is often maladaptive and, from that standpoint, not better than a very weak superego (compare the fact that excessive defenses are as pathological as defective ones).

Rating interference of the superego with ego functions and consistency-inconsistency should make overall superego rating easier. A superego that interferes with ego functions and is inconsistent is hardly a strong or adaptive superego. In that sense, the overall rating should reflect the detailed ratings, above and beyond the specification in the rating stops provided for general guidance.

Interference of Superego Factors with Ego Functions

Reality Testing
Strong underlying hostility, in conjunction with a superego that "prevents" direct awareness of the hostility, can result in projection of the hostility and thereby interfere with reality testing.

Judgment
Judgment can be interfered with by a mechanism similar to that described above for reality testing, as when action is taken relevant to defective awareness.

Sense of Reality
(1) Feelings of depersonalization, an important disturbance in the sense of self, can result from underlying guilt over strong hostility. (2) Both guilt and shame can affect S's sense of self.

Object Relations
(1) Projection of severe superego attitudes — blaming, faultfinding, and so on — can vitally affect object relations. (2) A weak superego, associated with irresponsibility, unfairness, cheating, taking advantage of, and so on, also can be seen to vitally affect an individual's interpersonal relations. (3) A superego response-prohibition to experienced aggression can result in withdrawal from another person.

Thought Processes
(1) Obsessive thought mechanisms may be a result of superego prohibition of aggressive and/or sexual drive derivatives. (2) Indecisiveness or obsessive doubting can result from the unconscious idea that decisiveness constitutes destructive aggressive behavior.

ARISE
This function requires becoming aware of more primitive, sexual, aggressive, and

forbidden contents. Individuals with severe superego would be expected to have difficulty in controlled regressions.

Defensive Functioning

A severe superego will tend to be associated with excessive use of defensive operations. Some defensive maneuvers are directed primarily against superego contents.

Stimulus Barrier

(1) Strong voyeuristic trends, when "disapproved" by a superego, can result in disturbances in vision and headaches (Greenacre, 1947). The same appears to be true in the auditory sphere. (2) High hostility in conjunction with superego blocking can result in projection of hostility and consequent vigilance and sensitization. Depressives often manifest high sensitivity to noise, which may reflect the above mechanism. Insomniacs may also illustrate the above mechanism: fear of aggression and of being attacked at night is often found.

Autonomous Functioning

Reading disabilities may involve an invasion of voyeuristic trends. Writing cramp can occur where phallic or hostile trends intrude. The general formulation here is (1) the autonomous functioning becomes libidinized, (2) superego prohibitions ensue, and (3) ego functioning is interfered with or inhibited by superego prohibitions.

Synthetic-Integrative Functioning

Superego gaps will be manifest in low synthetic functioning.

Interference of superego factors with ego functions will be rated on a four-point scale: severe (1), moderate (2), mild (3), negligible (4).

Scale of Superego Adaptation

Stop	a	b
	Guilt and blame, including: 1. degree of self-directed punishment for aggressive and libidinal drive expression; 2. transformations and displacements of unconscious guilt; 3. degree of blame-avoidance; 4. degree to which talion principle (desire for revenge for wrongs) operates; 5. extent to which guilt feelings are reality-based.	Ego-ideal status, including: 1. extent of realistic evaluation of ego goals and strivings; 2. sense of worth; 3. self-esteem regulation.
1	Highest degree of self-punishment	Ego's goals are excessively disproportionate

Scale of Superego Adaptation

Stop	a	b

1
(Cont)

for aggressive and libidinal drive expression. Suicidal behavior may be associated with extreme depression. Transformations of guilt may be seen in extreme projection, reaction-formation, and denial of wishes. Placing and avoiding blame are paramount characteristics of life style.

Demands for strict conformity to rules may be as high for others as for self. Guilt is predominantly unrealistically based.

to S's abilities. Extreme self-criticism where S regards himself and his actions as bad and unworthy.

Standards for performance and achievement are archaic and ruthlessly primitive. Examples are strivings for ultimate perfection in all areas without regard for whether such maximal performance can be realistically expected of him or anyone.

2

For severe superego: Self directed punishment short of suicidal behavior. May be self-mutilation, conviction that he has an incurable disease. Real source of guilt may be masked by delusional guilt, as of chronic, undeserved persecution by others. Delusions about committing unpardonable sins.

For weak superego: No conscience or guilt feelings, whether realistic or not. Psychopathic personality or impulse ridden personality in the extreme. Lax or indulgent standards of responsibility to self and others.

For severe ego-ideal: Overly strict and unrealistic standards of goal achievement for self and others. Poor sense of worth may be manifest in great self-abnegation and denial.

For weak ego-ideal: Highly indifferent as to own performance, strivings and life goals.

3

For severe superego: Rigid, authoritarian attitudes about sex and aggression in self and others. Guilt may be transformed into experiences of fear and hate. Characteristically attributes blame to self and others, and tries to avoid inner and outer signs of it. May be over concerned with minutiae in assuming obligations in order to avoid blame and criticism.

For weak superego: Quite lax with respect to impulses and urges. May be concerned with consequences to self but not to others. More likely to see evidences of shame than guilt.

For severe ego-ideal: Unrealistically critical self-observations with respect to achievements and successes. Severe self-criticism could alternate with overinflated sense of worth. Generally hypercritical of others in areas of achievement and ideals.

For weak ego-ideal: Self-indulgence and careless self-evaluations. Overly lax and lenient about standards for self and others.

Superego Adaptation Scale (Continued)

Stop	a	b
4	*For severe superego:* Sizable "puritan" streak in moral judgments of self and others. May be "do-gooder" type of person as reaction-formation against opposite wishes. Overconscientious; seeks moderate infractions of rules and standards. Tendency to protest innocence and blamelessness too much. *For weak superego:* Happy-go-lucky type; overly glib when can't meet responsibilities. Somewhat too casual.	Perfectionism in many areas of self and self-goals often interferes with adaptation.
5	S overcautiously anticipates or offers criticism for mistakes. Some guilt feelings can be tolerated or lived with. Some occasional alteration of behavior or environment to eliminate the source of guilt feelings may occur. Occasional defensive behavior (e.g., compulsiveness, displacement, projection) to deal with guilt over impulses, wishes, and deeds. Or, can role play acceptable, responsible behavior without much internal pressure to do so.	Somewhat perfectionistic or somewhat lax in living up to ideals. Sense of worth may suffer only with respect to a feeling of falling short of own (and others') expectations in circumscribed areas. The areas may have to do either with work, certain social relationships, marriage, but never all of them.
6	Reasonably strong superego—neither too strict nor too lenient. Realistically based guilt feelings serve primarily as a signal to reinforce fair-minded behavior. Assertive behavior and sexual gratifications are rarely interfered with by guilt and remorse and are undertaken with a sense of responsibility toward self and others.	Reasonably realistic approval of ego's actions in terms of current and future consequences. Aspirations are harmonious with achievement capacity. Self-esteem regulation is internalized and not merely dependent on current feedback from others.
7	Guilt feelings, if any, are realistically based and do not impede adaptation. A realistic orientation toward rectifying errors where possible and tolerance of past mistakes is noted to the exclusion of blame, worrying, recriminations. No transformations	Ego-ideal corresponds closely to ego functioning potential. Self-evaluation and sense of worth are based on optimally reality-oriented self-observations.

Scale of Superego Adaptation (Continued)

Stop	a	b
7	or displacements are observed. S is flexibly accepting or rejecting of others, depending on considerations.	

Inconsistency-Consistency Ratings

The rater is also to rate the S on a four-point scale for integration and consistency of superego functioning:

1. Most maladaptive: extreme inconsistencies between behavior and standards, between standards, or between segments of behavior. "Swiss cheese" or corrupt, gap-ridden superego.
2. Tending toward maladaptive.
3. Tending toward adaptive.
4. Most adaptive: optimally unified superego. Relatively few contradictions between standards and behavior, between standards, or between different segments of behavior.

ID SCALES (DRIVE STRENGTH)

Instructions to Raters: Below are two scales: (A) rating strength of libidinal drive, and (B) rating strength of aggressive drive manifestations. We are attempting to rate instinctual drive derivatives and have used both behavioral and ideational reactions as criteria from which we can observe directly or make inferences about drive strength. A major difficulty with the scale is distinguishing behavior that is the result of high drive strength per se from apparent manifestations of drive strength that are a function of such various ego factors as lack of judgment about where drives are expressed or object-relations difficulties that determine maladaptive forms of drive expression. We shall attempt to take account of this source of unclarity by the specific scale-stop descriptions and by the way the id scales are constructed in relation to the regulation-and-control scale.

These two id scales differ specifically from the ego function scales in one important structural respect. Stop 3 in the scales for both libidinal and aggressive manifestations represents the highest drive strength, and stop -6 represents the lowest. Stop 0 would be considered as approaching "average." This ordering stands in obvious contrast to the ego scales in which stop 1 is low, 6 is average, and 7 is optimal. These are scales of drive strength, not ego adaptation.

On the rating sheet, an opportunity will also be provided to judge, on a 4-point scale, the extent to which libidinal and aggressive drives are sublimated and neutralized, 4 being optimal. For purposes of scaling, we will not differentiate between neutralization and sublimation. For a discussion of the concepts, see chapter on autonomous functioning.

A. Rating of Sublimation-Neutralization

One reflects minimal libidinal or aggressive sublimation-neutralization. There is behavioral evidence of any or many of the components, especially of pregenital, libidinal behavior, privately and (sometimes inappropriately) publicly. Perversions are the classical pathology of lack of sublimation. Psychotic behavior may involve smearing of feces, ingestion of any material, and so on. Classical lack of neutralization of aggression appears as major acting out in violent ways.

Two might represent unsuccessful ways of sublimation and neutralization as in primitive gratifications of oral drives, for instance, in gross obesity and anhedonia resulting from poor object relations, and poor neutralization of aggression in socially unacceptable voyeurism, such as spending much time in looking into apartment windows with a telescope.

Three would be consistent with isolated areas of failure of sublimation, such as inappropriate libidinization of flying and other customary activities resulting in anxieties that are troublesome but present in many people. Episodic failure of neutralization of aggression manifesting itself sometimes under stress in minor tics or frequent breakage of glassware or other accident-prone behavior might be suitable examples. Characterological manifestations might be, on the one hand, in the area of private indulgences in more pregenital behavior than is customary or, on the other, in such aggressive outlets as are not entirely socially accepted in some subcultures, as hunting or serving as a guard in a penal institution with chances for occasional breakthroughs of sadism.

Four represents a high degree of neutralization of aggression, as found in a surgeon, for instance, who treats his patients with utmost care, including their psychological sensitivities, without any breakthroughs of the original sadistic desires in any form of his behavior. A similar level of sublimation of voyeurism is attained professionally in well-functioning psychoanalysts or experimenters-for instance, microbiologists who might also have an interest in art.

B. Indications of Aggressive Drive Strength

This is a unipolar scale in which only presence-absence of aggressive drive manifestations is dimensionalized. Love, passivity, or any of the traditionally considered opposites do not here constitute the extremes indicating relative absence of aggressive drive.

Libidinal Drive Strength
(a,b,c,d,e = components)

Stop	a	b	c	d	e
	Overt sexual behavior: includes frequency and intensity of heterosexual contacts, intercourse, masturbation, pregenital behavior, homosexuality, perversions, etc. Only overt sexual *acts* are included in this category.	Associated and substitute sexual behavior: includes behavior short of overt sexual acts. Relevant behavior here would be voyeurism, exhibitionism, flirting, choice of occupation, hobbies and interests, and associated aspects of oral and anal and other pregenitally based behavior, as well as associated aspects of genital behavior.	Fantasies and other ideation: includes verbalization about sex; daydreams with overt or associated sexual content; sexualized ideational activities, such as reading pornography. Also includes inferences about unconscious fantasies other than dreams.	Dreams: includes frequency and intensity of any kind of sexual content in both the manifest dream and the latent dream thoughts.	Symptoms, defenses, and controls: this category is included only insofar as actual libidinal drive strength may be *inferred* from strength of counter-cathectic measures employed against it (e.g., impotence, frigidity or avoidance of sex would be strong indicators only if they reflect S's way of dealing with excessive sexual pushes). Repression would be a defense especially relevant to libidinal drive strength
+3	Overt sexual activity at its most excessive extreme. Sexual mode (e.g., intercourse, masturbation, fellatio, homosexuality) and selection of partner may be indiscriminate owing to *pressure of urges* (as opposed to a primary disturbance	Associated sexual activity at its most excessive extreme. May be public disrobing, exhibitionistic advances on subway, gluttony and obesity, drug addiction, and rituals like smearing feces, inappropriate rubbing of self and	Almost total preoccupation and/or fantasy about sexual matters; frequent reading of pornography, which nearly obliterates concern with other life issues.	Sexual themes in dreams extremely prominent — if not in manifest content, then in latent dream thoughts. Dreams contain almost no other content	Impotence, frigidity or blocking with respect to libidinal *issues in the extreme so that sexual behavior is markedly incapacitated.* When controls, defenses and symptoms are extreme, it is because of drive. With poor controls, may be symptoms of excessive sexual acting out.

Libidinal Drive Strength
(a,b,c,d,e, = components)

Stop	a	b	c	d	e
	in object relations or judgment). This pressure may, for example, be due to an excessive constitutional strength of the instincts. Activity is so frequent as to interfere markedly with other areas of functioning. Rape, etc., may lead to arrest.	others. Occupation may be stripteaser or other sexually oriented work, independent of the degree of primitivity or sublimation.			
+2	Excessive overt sexual activity. Frequent intercourse and masturbation, etc., where pressure of urges still makes it difficult to channel behavior appropriately.	Pronounced associated sexual behavior, such as concern with body preening, seductiveness, erotization of relatively nonsexual situations.	Very pronounced sexual preoccupation in *thoughts and fantasy*, except where very strong competing "pulls" prevent this.	Many dreams have sexual themes in manifest content and latent thoughts.	Symptoms, defenses and controls related to libidinal issues pronounced but not totally incapacitating.
+1	Intercourse, masturbation and other direct sexual activity more pronounced than	Associate or substitute behavior shows more than average concern with bodily functions,	Above average amount of sexual thought and fantasy.	More than average, but not excessive, number of "sex" dreams.	While not incapacitating or excessive specific symptoms, defenses or anxiety are elicited by

Libidinal Drive Strength
(a,b,c,d,e, = components)

Stop	a	b	c	d	e
	average. Pressure of urges greater than usual.	contact needs, enjoyment of food and excretory activity. Above average seductiveness, interest in appearance for sexual reasons. More than average sexual motivation can be ascribed to choice of occupation and hobbies.			libidinal issues. Symptom-formation only sometimes replaces overt sexual behavior.
0	Intercourse and masturbation, etc., are moderately frequent. Promiscuity more likely to come from object-relations problems than from extreme pressure of urges.	Some seductiveness and flirting, but could not be considered out of bounds.	Moderate amount of preoccupation and fantasy about sexual matters.	Some dreams with sexual content.	Anxiety, symptoms, defenses, etc., occur in circumscribed situations indicating moderate strength of drive in need of defending against;
-1	Intercourse and masturbation and other overt sexual activity occur with less than average intensity and less than average overall urge toward sexuality.	Associated behavior, such as interest in appearance, bodily contact, and seductiveness are less than would be expected as compared with others of his age and his	Sexual fantasies only occasionally intrude upon thought. When they do, they relate more to associated than direct sexual activities.	Very few dreams have sexual content.	No specific symptomatic reactions can be readily associated with sexual urges, but there may be some occasional defensive operations or diffuse anxiety about sexual matters.

Libidinal Drive Strength
(a,b,c,d,e = components)

Stop	a	b	c	d	e
		situations. There may be some remote libidinal motivation in choice of hobbies or occupation.			
-2	Overt sexual activity of any kind is rare, even under conditions extremely stimulating to the average person. S experiences very little spontaneous or induced stimulation.	Associated sexual behavior is also rare. Coolness verging on frigidity in social contacts is typical, as opposed to warmth and seductiveness, which characterize strong drive. Hobbies and occupation have little sexual relevance, even taking neutralization and sublimation into account.	Sexual fantasies almost never intrude upon thought and they are rarely volitionally entertained.	Sexual content in dreams almost never occurs.	No symptoms and almost no defensive operations, controls, or anxiety relevant to sexual matters from which we could infer pressure of sexual drive.
-3	Overt sexual activity of any sort is almost never observed, and would thus appear *burnt out or dead.* Actual and psychological celibacy.	Practically no associated sexual behavior is observed. Occupation interests and hobbies imply a bland or "dead" basis to libidinal motivations.	No clear evidence of sexual fantasies.	No evident sexual content in dreams.	No symptoms, defenses, or controls are present to suggest significant underlying libidinal urges.

Aggressive Drive Strength
(a,b,c,d,e = components)

Stop	a	b	c	d	e
	Overt aggressive behavior: includes prominence and intensity of direct physical acts of aggression toward self, others, and inanimate objects, resulting from *pressure of destructive urges*.	Associated and substitute aggressive behavior: includes verbal expressions; various forms of primitive or more developed behavior associated with aggressive drives; degree of aggression associated with interests, hobbies, and occupation; behavioral manifestations other than direct physical acts of violence.	Fantasies and other ideation: includes conscious and unconscious thoughts and fantasies with aggressive content of any sort.	Dreams: frequency and intensity of aggressive content of any sort in both manifest dream and latent dream thoughts.	Symptoms, defenses, and controls: this category is included only insofar as actual aggressive drive strength may be inferred from strength of counter-cathectic measures employed against it. Especially relevant would be defenses of projection and reaction-formation, and severe or rigid superego formation to deal with guilt where they reflect underlying aggression.
+3	Overt aggressive activity most prominent and intense. Attempts to assault, murder, and destroy. The most extreme degree and kind of self-mutilation. May incite riots and throw bombs.	At this stop we would also generally expect sexual drive-derivative behavior to be fused with aggression. Intense sadomasochism as a drive component of object-relations; verbal abuse accompanied by the most extreme rage:	Fantasies about aggressive acts at their most frequent and intense level. "Morbid" preoccupation with death, murder, cruelty and wish to violently inflict harm.	Aggressive themes in dreams extremely prominent in manifest content and latent dream thoughts.	Symptoms, controls, defenses imply the highest level of aggression; all-persuasive delusions of persecution; withdrawal in the extreme to avoid killing.

487

Aggressive Drive Strength
(a,b,c,d,e = components)

Stop	a	b	c	d	e
		interests in violence, torture, and genocide. Occupation may be professional hangman, career military man with expressed preference for hand-to-hand combat.			Symptoms, controls, defenses imply a very high level of aggression. Encapsulated delusions of persecution; extreme work or activity blocks; convulsive disorders with psychomotor rage equivalents.
+2	Excessive overt aggressive activity. Physical injury short of death inflicted on self and others results from pressure of destructive urges. Chronic suicide attempts. Arson and extreme assaultiveness may be common.	May talk about needs to destroy and devour. Interests may include hunting for the purpose of maiming; intense interest in offensive military strategy and tactics; all of these independent of the degree of adaptation but related only to strength of drive (not overlooking the fact that when drive strength is extreme, there may be little adaptation possible). Intense need to	Very pronounced aggressive thoughts and fantasies, often with others instead of the self, inflicting the harm.	Aggressive elements in dreams very prominent in manifest content and latent thoughts.	

488

Aggressive Drive Strength
(a,b,c,d,e = components)

Stop	a	b	c	d	e
		engage in competitive sports such as boxing, wrestling, Judo or karate to exclusion of other interests. May enjoy threatening strangers over the telephone.			While not incapacitating or excessive, specific symptoms, defenses, or anxiety are elicited by aggressive issues. Somewhat exaggerated forms of protest against war, such as compulsive participation in protest marches; fiery missionary zeal for helping oppressed people; hand-washing and cleaning compulsions. Some oversensitivity to hostility or rejection by others.
+1	Overt acts of aggression more frequently intense than average. Presence of physical assaultiveness with intent to harm but not kill. Suicide gestures. Pressures of urges strong.	Associated or substitute behavior shows more than average concern with destruction. Hostile punning, witty repartee, self-righteous preaching are favored modes of verbal communication. Occupational choice may be lawyer, policeman. Interests may include hunting, competitive sports such as sports-car racing, football.	Above average amount of hostile and aggressive thought and fantasy, but these not totally intrusive or persuasive. Enjoys reading pulp stories and seeing monster movies.	More than average but not excessive number of aggressive dreams.	

Aggressive Drive Strength
(a,b,c,d,e = components)

Step	a	b	c	d	e
0	May be angered or enraged when sufficiently provoked and express this anger within average limits. Occasional self-chastisement or other self-directed aggression, such as moral masochism.	Humor contains average amount of aggression. Occasional biting sarcasm. Interest and/or participation in competitive sports; enjoyment of skiing, tennis, racing. Competes actively for jobs. Would be good soldier if drafted to defend country. Other interests coexist with aggression-ridden ones.	Moderate amount of fantasy about aggressive matters.	Some dreams with aggressive content.	Anxiety, symptoms, and defenses, etc. are sporadic and limited to circumscribed areas of conflict over aggressive drives indicating lower strength of drive in need of defending against.
-1	Overt expressions of aggression toward self and others are less frequent and intense than average. S's general vitality might seem less than average.	S ignores (although does not "make a point" of staying away from) many activities with aggressive connotations. If a pacifist, would have no particular interest in speaking out against aggression or in proselytizing.	Less than average fantasy about aggressive matters. When they do occur, they are easily relinquished and never significantly intrude upon other thinking.	Very few dreams have aggressive content.	No specific symptomatic reactions can be readily associated with aggressive urges, but there may be some occasional defensive operations or diffuse anxiety about circumscribed aggressive matters.

Aggressive Drive Strength
(a,b,c,d,e = components)

Step	a	b	c	d	e
-2	Overt aggressive activity is very rare. There is a paucity of response even to severe provocations. Lethargy is characteristic.	Associated aggressive behavior is also very rare. Verbalizations are quite bland, choice of occupation indicates low aggressive drive level (e.g., sorting mail for post office). Competitive behavior is absent.	Aggressive fantasies almost never intrude upon thought, nor are they often volitionally entertained.	Aggressive content in dreams almost never occurs.	There are no symptoms and almost no defensive operations or diffuse anxiety relevant to aggression.
-3	No overt aggressive activity toward self, others, or inanimate objects is observed. S appears to have "no starch" in him at all.	No significant associated aggressive behavior is observed. Interests and hobbies convey blandness in the extreme, and occupations would be the least taxing possible, such as chronic loafing.	No important evidence of aggression in thought and fantasies.	No relevant aggressive content in dreams.	No significant symptoms, defenses or controls are present from which we could infer underlying aggressive urges.

APPENDIX C

Clinical Interview Rating Form

S Code_____
Rater _____

Date_____

CLINICAL INTERVIEW RATING FORM[a]

Please rate each Ego Function (and/or component factor), indicating the specific content used as the basis for the rating. Use mostly primary data. Inferences should be in parentheses.

I. REALITY TESTING

a. Distinction between inner and outer stimuli   Char
                                                  Cur

b. Accuracy of perception   Char
                             Cur

c. Reflective awareness and   inner reality testing   Char
                                                       Cur

LEVEL OF FUNCTIONING	
LOWEST	
HIGHEST	
CHARACTERISTIC	
CURRENT	

[a]For rating interviews from the *Manual for Rating Ego Functions From a Clinical Interview*

492

II. JUDGMENT

a. Anticipation of consequences   Char ☐
      Cur ☐

b. Manifest in behavior   Char ☐
      Cur ☐

c. Emotional appropriateness   Char ☐
      Cur ☐

LEVEL OF FUNCTIONING	
LOWEST	
HIGHEST	
CHARACTERISTIC	
CURRENT	

S Code _____

Rater _____

Date _____

III. SENSE OF REALITY

a. Extent of derealization   Char ☐
      Cur ☐

b. Extent of depersonalization   Char ☐
      Cur ☐

c. Self identity and self esteem   Char ☐
      Cur ☐

d. Clarity of boundaries between self and world   Char ☐
      Cur ☐

LEVEL OF FUNCTIONING	
LOWEST	
HIGHEST	
CHARACTERISTIC	
CURRENT	

IV. REGULATION AND CONTROL OF DRIVES, IMPULSES AND AFFECT

a. Directness of impulse expression   Char [   ]
                                                    Cur [   ]

b. Effectiveness of delay mechanisms   Char [   ]
                                                    Cur [   ]

LEVEL OF FUNCTIONING	
LOWEST	
HIGHEST	
CHARACTERISTIC	
CURRENT	

S Code _____
Rater _____
Date   _____

V. OBJECT RELATIONS

a. Degree and kind of relatedness   Char [   ]
                                                    Cur [   ]

b. Primitivity — Maturity   Char [   ]
                                                    Cur [   ]

c. Others perceived independently   Char [   ]
                                                    Cur [   ]

d. Object constancy   Char [   ]
                                                    Cur [   ]

LEVEL OF FUNCTIONING	
LOWEST	
HIGHEST	
CHARACTERISTIC	
CURRENT	

VI. THOUGHT PROCESSES

a. Memory, concentration, attention
Char
Cur

b. Ability to conceptualize
Char
Cur

c. Primary-secondary process
Char
Cur

LEVEL OF FUNCTIONING	
LOWEST	
HIGHEST	
CHARACTERISTIC	
CURRENT	

S Code _____

Rater _____

Date _____

VII. ADAPTIVE REGRESSION IN THE SERVICE OF THE EGO

a. Regressive relaxation of acuity
Char
Cur

b. New configurations
Char
Cur

LEVEL OF FUNCTIONING	
LOWEST	
HIGHEST	
CHARACTERISTIC	
CURRENT	

VIII. DEFENSIVE FUNCTIONING

a. Presence of defensive indicators   Char [＿＿＿]
Cur [＿＿＿]

b. Success and failure of defenses   Char [＿＿＿]
Cur [＿＿＿]

LEVEL OF FUNCTIONING	
LOWEST	
HIGHEST	
CHARACTERISTIC	
CURRENT	

S Code ＿＿＿＿＿＿
Rater ＿＿＿＿＿＿

Date ＿＿＿＿＿＿

IX. STIMULUS BARRIER

a. Threshold for stimuli   Char [＿＿＿]
Cur [＿＿＿]

b. Coping success   Char [＿＿＿]
Cur [＿＿＿]

LEVEL OF FUNCTIONING	
LOWEST	
HIGHEST	
CHARACTERISTIC	
CURRENT	

X. AUTONOMOUS FUNCTIONING

a. Degree of freedom from impairment   Char [＿＿＿]
of primary autonomy apparatuses   Cur [＿＿＿]

b. Degree of freedom from impairment   Char [＿＿＿]
of secondary autonomy   Cur [＿＿＿]

LEVEL OF FUNCTIONING
LOWEST
HIGHEST
CHARACTERISTIC
CURRENT

S Code _____

Rater _____

Date _____

XI. SYNTHETIC INTEGRATIVE FUNCTIONING

a. Degree of reconciliation of incongruities   Char [   ]
Cur [   ]

b. Degree of active relating together of events   Char [   ]
Cur [   ]

LEVEL OF FUNCTIONING
LOWEST
HIGHEST
CHARACTERISTIC
CURRENT

XII. MASTERY COMPETENCE

a. Actual competence   Char [   ]
Cur [   ]

b. Sense of competence   Char [   ]
Cur [   ]

c. Discrepancy between performance and self-   Char [   ]
feeling   Cur [   ]
Discrepancy Score (−, +, or =.)   Competence   _____
Sense of Competence _____
(Discrepancy)   _____

LEVEL OF FUNCTIONING	
LOWEST	
HIGHEST	
CHARACTERISTIC	
CURRENT	

S Code _____
Rater   _____

Date   _____

SUPEREGO SCALE

a. Guilt (self-directed punishment, unconscious
   sense of guilt, blame-avoidance, talion
   principle)   Char [   ]
                                                 Cur [   ]

c. Ego ideal (self evaluation, sense of worth
   self-esteem regulation)   Char [   ]
                                                 Cur [   ]

LEVEL OF FUNCTIONING	
LOWEST	
HIGHEST	
CHARACTERISTIC	
CURRENT	

SUPEREGO FACTORS

INTERFERENCE OF SUPEREGO FACTORS WITH EGO FUNCTIONS

Severe	Moderate	Mild	Negligible
1	2	3	4

CONSISTENCY OF SUPEREGO
Basis for Ratings:

Most Maladaptive	Tending Toward Maladaptive	Tending Toward Adaptive	Most Adaptive
1	2	3	4

S Code _____
Rater   _____
Date   _____

ID SCALE (Drive Strength)

Strength of:	+3	+2	+1	0	−1	−2	−3
Libidinal Drive							
Aggressive Drive							

Basis for ratings:
   Libidinal Drive:

Char [   ]
Cur [   ]

   Aggressive Drive: 1

Char [   ]
Cur [   ]

Extent to which you judge Libidinal and Aggressive Drives to be sublimated and/or neutralized.

	Negligible	Somewhat Low	Moderate	Well Neutralized
Libidinal	1	2	3	4

Basis for ratings:

Aggressive	1	2	3	4

Basis for ratings:

Leopold Bellak, M. D., Principal Investigator
MULTIDISCIPLINARY STUDY OF SCHIZOPHRENIA
RESEARCH PROJECT
N.I.M.H. Grant #18395

Subject # _____
Group # _____
Rater(s) ____ ____
Date ____ ____

	I	II	III	IV	V	VI	VII	VIII	IX	X	XI	XII	Superego			Id scales			
	Reality Testing	Judgment	Sense of Reality	Regulat. & Cont. of Drives	Object Relat.	Thought Process	ARISE	Defensive Functs.	Stimulus Barrier	Auton. Functs.	Synthet. Functs.	Mastery–Cmptnc.	Interference (w/ ego functions)	Consistency of Superego	Overall Superego Adaptiveness	Libidinal Drive	Aggressive Drive	Sublimation (libidinal drive)	Sublimation (aggressive drive)
13																			
12																			
11																			
10																			
9																			
8																			
7																			
6																			
5																			
4																			
3																			
2																			
1																			

Ego functions

Superego scale: 3, 2, 1, 0, −1, −2, −3

Id scales: 4, 3, 2, 1

BIBLIOGRAPHY *(See additional references, p. 535)*

Abraham, K. (1916, 1921, 1924, 1925). *Selected Papers on Psychoanalysis* (New York: Basic Books, 1953).

Abrams, S. The psychoanalytic unconscious. In *The Unconscious Today* (New York: International Universities, 1971).

Adler, A. *The Neurotic Constitution* (New York, Moffat, Yard, 1917).

_____. *Social Interest, A Challenge to Mankind* (New York: Putnam, 1939; repr. Capricorn, 1964).

_____. *The Problems of Neurosis (Book of Case Histories)* (New York: Cosmopolitan, 1939; repr. Harper and Row, 1964).

_____. *Understanding Human Nature*, 2nd ed. (New York: Greenberg, 1946).

_____. *The Practice and Theory of Individual Psychology*, 2nd ed. (New York: Humanities, 1951).

Aichhorn, A. *Wayward Youth.* With a preface by Sigmund Freud (New York: Viking, 1935).

Alexander, F. The castration complex in the formation of character. *International Journal of Psycho-Analysis*, **4** *(1923), 11-42.*

Alexander, F. and French T. *Studies in Psychosomatic Medicine* (New York: Ronald, 1948).

Allport, G. *Personality: A Psychological Interpretation* (New York: Holt, 1937).

Alpert, A., Neubauer, P., and Weil, A. Unusual variations in drive endowment. In *The Psychoanalytic Study of the Child*, Vol. II (New York: International Universities, 1956), pp. 125-163.

Altschul, S. Denial and ego arrest. *Journal of the American Psychoanalytic Association*, **16** (1968), 301-318.

Amacher, P. Freud's neurological education and its influence on psychoanalytic theory. *Psychological Issues*, Monograph 16 (1965).

American Psychoanalytic Association. Panel on the Concept of Psychic Energy. *Journal of the American Psychoanalytic Association*, **11** (1963).

Angel, K. Loss of identity and acting out. *Journal of the American Psychoanalytic Association* **13** (1965), 79-84.

Angyal, A. Disturbances of thinking in schizophrenia. (1944) In J. Kasanin (ed.) *Language and Thought in Schizophrenia* (New York: Norton, 1964), pp. 115-123.

Angyal, A., Hanfmann, E., and Jones, R. (eds.) *Neurosis and Treatment: A Holistic Theory* (New York: Wiley, 1965).

Anthony, J. Children of a schizophrenic parent. In *National Institute of Mental Health, Special Report on Schizophrenia* (1971).

Apfelbaum, B. Some problems in contemporary ego psychology. *Journal of the American Psychoanalytic Association*, **10** (1962), 526-537.

_____, On ego psychology: a critique of the structural approach to psycho-analytic theory. *International Journal of Psycho-Analysis,* **47** (1966), 451-475.

Arieti, S. *Interpretation of Schizophrenia* (New York: Brunner, 1955).

————. Studies of thought processes in contemporary psychiatry. *American Journal of Psychiatry*, **120** (1963), 58-64.

————. Conceptual and cognitive psychiatry. *American Journal of Psychiatry,* **122** (1965), 361-366.

————. *The Intrapsychic Self: Feeling, Cognition, and Creativity in Health and Mental Illness* (New York: Basic Books, 1967).

Arlow, J. Depersonalization and derealization. In R. Loewenstein, et al. (eds.), *Psychoanalysis − A General Psychology* (New York: International Universities, 1966).

————. Fantasy, memory and reality testing. *Psychoanalytic Quarterly,* **38** (1969), 28-51.

Arlow, J. and Brenner, C. *Psychoanalytic Concepts and the Structural Theory* (New York: International Universities, 1964).

Bak, R. The schizophrenic defense against aggression. *International Journal of Psycho-Analysis,* **35** (1954), 129-134.

————. Object relationships in schizophrenia and perversion. *Ibid.,* **52** (1971), 235-242.

Balint, M. (Early Development States of the Ego: Primary Object Love. (In) *Primary Love and Psychoanalytic Technique* (New York: Liveright, 1965).

————. Contributions to reality testing. *British Journal of Medical Psychology,* **19** (1942) 201-214.

————. Younger sister and prince charming. *International Journal of Psycho-Analysis,* **44** (1963), 226-227.

Bannister, D. and Salmon, P. Schizophrenic thought disorder: specific or diffuse? *British Journal of Medical Psychology,* **39** (1966), 215-219.

Bartemeir, L. Micropsia. *Psychoanalytic Quarterly,* **10** (1941), 573-582.

Bateson, G. Jackson, D., et al. Toward a theory of schizophrenia. *Behavioral Science,* **1** (1956), 251-264.

Beck, A. Reliability of psychiatric diagnoses: I. A critique of systematic studies. *American Journal of Psychiatry,* **119** (1962), 210-216.

Bellak, L. The concept of projection: an experimental investigation and study of the concept. *Psychiatry,* **7** (1944), 353-370.

————. A multiple-factor psychosomatic theory of schizophrenia. *Psychiatric Quarterly,* **23** (1949), 738-755.

————. The use of oral barbiturates in psychotherapy. *American Journal of Psychiatry,* **105** (1949), 849-850.

_____. On the problems of the concept of projection (1950). In L. Abt and L. Bellak (eds.), *Projective Psychology* (New York: Grove, 1959).

_____. Thematic apperception: failures and the defenses. *New York Academy Science Series II,* **12** (1950), 122-126.

_____. *Manic-Depressive Psychosis and Allied Disorders* (New York: Grune and Stratton, 1952).

_____. *The T.A.T. and C.A.T. in Clinical Use* (New York: Grune and Stratton, 1954), revised, second edition 1971.

_____. Toward a unified concept of schizophrenia. *Journal of Nervous and Mental Disease* **121** (1955), 60-66.

_____. Freud and projective techniques. *Journal of Projective Techniques,* **20** (1956), 5-13.

_____. *Schizophrenia: A Review of the Syndrome* (New York: Logos, 1958; now distributed by Grune and Stratton).

_____. Creativity: some random notes to a systematic consideration. *Journal of Projective Techniques,* **22** (1958), 363-380.

_____. Free association: conceptual and clinical aspects. *International Journal of Psycho-Analysis,* **42** (1961) 9-20.

_____. Acting out: some conceptual and therapeutic considerations. *American Journal of Psychotherapy,* **17** (1963) 375-389.

_____. Depersonalization as a variant of self-awareness. In A. Abrams (ed.), *Unfinished Tasks in the Behavioral Sciences* (Baltimore: Williams and Wilkins, 1964).

_____. Research on ego function patterns: a progress report. In L. Bellak and L. Loeb (eds.), *The Schizophrenic Syndrome* (New York: Grune and Stratton, 1969).

_____. The role of psychoanalysis in contemporary psychiatry. *American Journal of Psychotherapy,* **24** (1970), 3.

_____. *The Porcupine Dilemma,* New York: The Citadel Press, 1970.

_____. The need for public health laws for psychiatric illness. *American Journal of Public Health,* **61** (1971) 1.

_____. Ego function assessment and analyzability. Delivered before Westchester Psychoanalytic Society, 1972. To be published.

Bellak, L. and Berneman, N. A systematic view of depression. *American Journal of Psychotherapy,* **25** (1971) 385.

Bellak, L. and Black, B. Rehabilitation of the mentally ill through controlled transitional employment. *American Journal of Orthopsychiatry,* **26** (1956), 285-296.

_____. The rehabilitation of psychotics in the community. *Ibid.*, **30** *(1960)*, 346-355.

Bellak, L. and Chassan, J. An approach to the evaluation of drug effect during psychotherapy: a double-blind study of a single case. *Journal of Nervous and Mental Disease,* **139** (1964), 20-30.

Bellak, L., Chassan, J., Gediman, H., and Hurvich, M. The systematic assessment of ego functions in psychoanalytic psychotherapy combined with drug therapy. *Journal of Nervous and Mental Disease,* **157** (1973), 465-469.

Bellak, L. and Hurvich, M. A systematic study of ego functions. *Journal of Nervous and Mental Disease,* **148** (1969), 569-585.

Bellak, L., Hurvich, M., and Crawford, P. Psychotic egos. *Psychoanalytic Review,* **56** (1970), 526-542.

Bellak, L., Hurvich, M., Silvan, M., and Jacobs, D. Towards an ego psychological appraisal of drug effects. *American Journal of Psychiatry,* **125** (1968), 45-56.

Bellak, L. and Loeb, L. *The Schizophrenic Syndrome* (New York: Grune and Stratton, 1969).

Bellak, L. and Rosenberg, S. Effects of anti-depressant drugs on psychodynamics. *Psychosomatics,* **7** (1966), 106-114.

Bellak, L. and Small, L. *Emergency Psychotherapy and Brief Psychotherapy* (New York: Grune and Stratton, 1965).

Belmont, H. Remarks on the etiology and management of ego disturbance in children. *Bulletin of the Philadelphia Association for Psychoanalysis,* **85** (1955), 80-90.

Benedek, T. Adaptation to reality in early infancy. *Psychoanalytic Quarterly,* **7** (1938), 200-215.

Benjamin, J. A method for distinguishing and evaluating formal thinking disorders in schizophrenia (1939). In J. Kasanin (ed.), *Language and Thought in Schizophrenia* (New York: Norton, 1964).

_____. Prediction and psychopathological theory. In L. Jessner and E. Pavenstadt (eds.), *Dynamic Psychopathology in Childhood* (New York: Grune and Stratton, 1959).

_____. Some developmental observations relating to the theory of anxiety. *Journal of the American Psychoanalytic Association,* **9** (1961), 652-668.

_____. The innate and experiential in development. In H. Brosin (ed.), *Lectures in Experimental Psychiatry* (Pittsburgh: U. of Pittsburgh, 1961), pp. 19-42.

_____. Further comments on some developmental aspects of anxiety, in H. Gaskill (ed.), *Counterpoint: Libidinal Object and Subject* (New York: International Universities, (1963), pp. 121-153.

————. Developmental biology and psychoanalysis. In N. Greenfield and W. Lewis (eds.), *Psychoanalysis and Current Biological Thought* (Madison: U. of Wisconsin, 1965), pp. 57-80.

Beres, D. Ego deviation and the concept of schizophrenia. In R. Eissler et al. (eds.), *The Psychoanalytic Study of the Child*, Vol. XI (New York: International Universities, 1956).

————. Vicissitudes of superego functions and superego precursors in childhood. *Ibid.*, Vol. XIII (New York: International Universities, 1958).

————. Perception, imagination, and reality. *International Journal of Psycho-Analysis*, **41** (1960), 327-334.

————. The unconscious fantasy. *Psychoanalytic Quarterly*, **31** (1962), 309-328.

————. Structure and function in psychoanalysis. *International Journal of Psycho-analysis*, **46** (1965) 53-63.

————. The functions of the superego. In R. Litman (ed.), *Psychoanalysis in the Americas* (New York: International Universities, 1966).

Beres, D. and Arlow, J. Discussants in development and metapsychology of the defense organization of the ego, reported by R. Wallerstein. *Journal of the American Psychoanalytic Association*, **15** (1966), 130-149.

Beres, D. and Joseph, E. The concept of mental representation in psychoanalysis. *International Journal of Psycho-Analysis*, **51** (1970), 1-10.

Berezin, M. Some observations of art (music) and its relation to ego mastery. *Bulletin of the Philadelphia Association for Psychoanalysis*, **8** (1958), 49-65.

Berger, P. and Luckmann, T. *The Social Construction of Reality* (Garden City, N.Y.: Doubleday, 1966).

Bergler, E. Further studies on depersonalization, *Psychiatric Quarterly*, **24** (1950), 480-486.

Bergman, P. and Escalona, S. Unusual sensitivities in very young children. In *The Psychoanalytic Study of the Child*, Vols. III-IV (New York: International Universities, 1949), pp. 333-352.

Bergmann, M. The place of Paul Federn's ego psychology in psychoanalytic metapsychology. *Journal of the American Psychoanalytic Association*, **11** (1963), 97-116.

Berkowitz, L. *Aggression: A Social-Psychological Analysis* (New York: McGraw-Hill, 1962).

Bettelheim, B. *The Informed Heart* (New York: Free Press, 1960).

Bexton, W., Heron, W., and Scott, T. Effects of decreased variation in the sensory environment. *Canadian Journal of Psychology*, **8** (1954), 70-76.

Bibring, E. The development and problems of the theory of the instincts (1936). *International Journal of Psycho-Analysis*, 22 (1941), 102-131.

_____. The mechanism of depression. In P. Greenacre (ed.), *Affective Disorders* (New York: International Universities, 1953).

Bieri, J. et al. *Clinical and Social Judgment* (New York: Wiley, 1966).

Bird, B. Feelings of unreality. *International Journal of Psycho-Analysis*, 38 (1957), pp. 256-265.

Blanck, R. and Blanck, G. *Marriage and Personal Development* (New York: Columbia U., 1968).

Blank, H. Depression, hypomania, and depersonalizationn. *Psychoanalytic Quarterly*, 23 (1954), pp. 20-37.

Bleuler, E. *Dementia Praecox or the Group of Schizophrenias* (1911; repr., New York: International Universities, 1950).

Bleuler, E. *Textbook of Psychiatry* (New York: Macmillan, 1924).

Blos, P. The concept of acting out in relation to the adolescent process. Presented to the New York Psychoanalytic Society, September 25, 1962.

Bolland, J. & Sandler, J. *The Hampstead Psychoanalytic Index: A Study of the Psychoanalytic Case Material of a Two-Year-Old Child* (New York: International Universities, 1965).

Boorstein, S. Ego autonomy in psychiatric practice. *Bulletin of the Menninger Clinic*, 23 (1959), 148-156.

Bowlby, J. The child's tie to his mother. Review of the psychoanalytic literature (1958), in J. Bowlby (ed.), *Attachment* (New York: Basic Books, 1969).

_____. Separation anxiety. *International Journal of Psycho-analysis*, 41 (1960), 89-113.

_____. Pathological mourning and childhood mourning. *Journal of the American Psychoanalytic Association*, 11 (1963), 500-541.

_____. *Attachment* (New York: Basic Books, 1969).

Boyer, L. and Giovacchini, P. *Psychoanalytic Treatment of Characterological and Schizophrenic Disorders* (New York: Science House, 1967).

Brazelton, T. Observations of the neonate. *Journal of the American Academy of Child Psychiatry*, 1 (1962), 28-38.

Brenner, C. *An Elementary Textbook of Psychoanalysis* (New York: International Universities, 1955).

_____. The nature and development of the concept of repression in Freud's writings. In *The Psychoanalytic Study of the Child*, vol. XII (New York: International Universities, 1957), pp. 19-46.

_____. On aggression. *International Journal of Psycho-Analysis*, 52 (1971), p. 138-144.

Breuer, J. and Freud, S. *Studies in Hysteria* (1893-1895), repr. in Standard Edition, vol. II (London: Hogarth, 1955).

Bridger, W. Panel discussion: symposium on research in infancy and early childhood. *Journal of the American Academy of Child Psytry,* **1** (1962), 92-107.

Brody, S. and Axelrad, S. Anxiety, socialization and ego formation in infancy. *International Journal of Psycho-Analysis,* **47** (1966), 218-229.

————. *Anxiety and Ego Formation in Infancy* (New York: International Universities, 1970).

Brown, J. States in newborn infants. *Merrill-Palmer Quarterly* , **10** (1964).

Buerger-Prinz, H. and Kaila, M. Ueber die Struktur des anamnestischen symptomen complexes. *Zeitschrift der Neurologie und Psychiatrie,* **124** (1930), 553-595.

Bühler, K. *Kindheit und Jugend* (Leipzig: Hirzel, 1930).

Bush, M. Psychoanalysis and scientific creativity. *Journal of the American Psychoanalytic Association,* **17** (1969), 136-190.

Cameron, N. A study of thinking in senile deterioration and schizophrenic disorganization. *American Journal of Psychology,* **51** (1938), 650-665.

————. Experimental analysis of schizophrenic thinking. (1944) In J. Kasanin (ed.), *Language and Thought in Schizophrenia.* (New York: Norton, 1964), pp. 50-64.

————. *Personality Development and Psychopathology* (Boston: Houghton Mifflin, 1963).

Cancro, R. and Pruyser, P. A historical review of the development of the concept, in R. Cancro (ed.), *The Schizophrenic Reactions: A Critique of the Concept, Hospital Treatment, and Current Research,* (New York: Brunner/Mazel, 1969).

Caroll, E. Acting out and ego development. *Psychoanalytic Quarterly,* **23** (1954), 521-528.

Chassan, J. *Research Design in Clinical Psychology and Psychiatry.* (New York: Appleton-Century-Crofts, 1967).

Coppolilillo, H. Maturational aspects of the transitional phenomena, *International Journal of Psycho-Analysis,* **48** (1967), 237-246.

Corman, H., Escalona, S., and Reiser, M. Visual imagery and preconscious thought processes. *Archives of General Psychiatry,* **10** (1964), 160-172.

Dahl, H. Panel on psychoanalytic theory of instinctual drives in relation to recent developments, reported by Dahl. *Journal of the American Psychoanalytic Association,* **16** (1968), 613-637.

Dawson, G. The central control of sensory inflow. *Proceedings of the Royal Society of Medicine,* **51** (1958), 531-535.

_____. The effect of cortical stimulation on transmission through the cunate nucleus in the anaesthetized rat. *Journal of Physiology* **142** (1958), (London), 2P-3P.

Décarie, T. *Intelligence and Affectivity in Early Childhood: An Experimental Study of Jean Piaget's Object Concept and Object Relations* (New York: International Universities, 1965).

Delgado, J., Roberts, W., and Miller, N. Learning maturated by electrical stimulation of the brain. *American Journal of Physiology,* **179** (1954), 587-593.

de Monchaux, C. The psycho-analytic study of thinking. III. Thinking and negative hallucination. *International Journal of Psycho-Analysis,* **43** (1962), 311-314.

_____. The contribution of psychoanalysis to the psychology of thinking. In I. Sarason (ed.), *Psychoanalysis and the Study of Behavior* (New York: Van Nostrand, 1965), pp. 165-173.

de Saussure, J. Some complications in self-esteem regulation caused by using an archaic image of the self as an ideal. *International Journal of Psycho-Analysis,* **52** (1971), 87-97.

Despert, L. Dreams in children of preschool age. In *The Psychoanalytic Study of the Child,* Vols. III-IV. (New York: International Universities, 1949), pp. 141-180.

Deutsch, H. Some forms of emotional disturbances and their relationship to schizophrenia (1942). In *Neuroses and Character Types.* (New York: International Universities, 1965).

Dixon, W. and May, P. Methods of statistical analysis. In P. May (ed.), *Treatment of Schizophrenia* (New York: Science House, 1968).

Dorsey, M. Some considerations on psychic reality. *International Journal of Psycho-Analysis,* **24** (1943), 147-151.

Eagle, M. Personality correlates of sensitivity to subliminal stimulation. *Journal of Nervous and Mental Disease,* **134** (1962).

Edwards, A. *Experimental Design in Psychological Research,* rev. ed. (New York: Rinehart, 1960).

Eissler, K. *Searchlights on Delinquency: New Psychoanalytic Studies.* (New York: International Universities, 1949).

_____. Notes upon the emotionality of a schizophrenic patient and its relation to problems of technique, In *The Psychoanalytic Study of the Child,* Vol. VIII (New York: International Universities, 1953), pp. 199-251.

Ekstein, E. and Caruth, E. The relation of ego autonomy to activity and passivity in the psychotherapy of childhood schizophrenia. In R. Ekstein, *The Challenge: Despair and Hope in the Conquest of Inner Space* (New York: Brunner/Mazel, 1971).

Ellenberger, H. *The Discovery of the Unconscious* (New York: Basic Books, 1970).

Engel, G. *Psychological Development in Health and Disease* (Philadelphia: Saunders, 1962).

Epstein, S. Unconscious self-evaluation in a normal and a schizophrenic group. *Journal of Abnormal and Social Psychology,* **50** (1955).

Erikson E. *Childhood and Society* (New York: Norton, 1950).

———. The problem of ego identity. *Journal of the American Psychoanalytic Association,* **4** (1956), 56-121.

———. *Identity and the Life Cycle* (New York: International Universities, 1959).

———. Reality and actuality. *Journal of the American Psychoanalytic Association,* **10** (1962), 451-474.

Escalona, S. The study of individual differences and the problem of state. *Journal of Child Psychiatry.* **1** (1962).

Fairbairn, R. *An Object-Relations Theory of the Personality* (1952) (New York: Basic Books, 1954).

Federn, P. Some variations in ego feeling (1926). In E. Weiss (ed.), *Ego Psychology and the Psychoses* (New York: Basic Books, 1952).

———. Narcissism in the structure of the ego (1927), Ibid.

———. Psychoanalysis of psychoses (1943). Ibid.

———. Principles of psychotherapy in latent schizophrenia (1947) Ibid.

———. Mental hygiene of the ego in schizophrenia (1948). Ibid.

———. Depersonalization (1949). Ibid.

———. *Ego Psychology and the Psychoses.* E. Weiss (ed.) (New York: Basic Books, 1952).

Fenichel, O. Early stages of ego development (1937). In D. Rapaport and H. Fenichel (eds.), *The Collected Papers of Otto Fenichel* (New York: Norton, 1954).

———. Ego strength and ego weakness (1938). Ibid.

———. The study of defense mechanisms and its importance for psychoanalytic technique (1940) Ibid.

———. *The Psychoanalytic Theory of Neuroses* (New York: Norton, 1945).

———. Neurotic acting out. *Psychoanalytic Review,* **32** (1945), 197-206.

Ferenczi, S. Stages in the development of the sense of reality (1913, 1916, 1924). In *Sex in Psychoanalysis* (New York: Basic Books, 1950).

———. The problem of acceptance of unpleasant ideas – advances in knowledge of the sense of reality (1926). In *Further Contributions to the Theory and Technique of Psychoanalysis* (London: Hogarth, 1950).

———. Gulliver fantasies (1926). In M. Balint (ed.), *Final Contributions to the Problems and Methods of Psychoanalysis* (New York: Basic Books, 1955), pp. 41-60.

———. Each adaptation is preceded by an inhibited attempt at splitting (1930). Ibid. p. 220.

Fine, R. *Freud, A Critical Reevaluation* (New York: McKay, 1962).

Fisher, C. and Joseph E. Fugue with awareness of loss of personal identity. *Psychoanalytic Quarterly*, **18** (1949).

Fisher, S. and Cleveland, S. *Body Image and Personality* (New York: Dover, 1958).

————. Ibid., 2nd ed. (New York: Dover, 1968).

Fraiberg, S. *The Magic Years* (New York: Scribner's, 1959).

Frankl, L. Some observations on the development and disturbances of integration in childhood. In *The Psychoanalytic Study of the Child*, Vol. XVII (New York: International Universities, 1961), pp. 146-163.

Freeman, T. Symptomatology, diagnosis, and clinical course. In L. Bellak and L. Loeb (eds.) *The Schizophrenic Syndrome* (New York: Grune and Stratton, 1969).

————. The psychopathology of the psychoses: a reply to Arlow and Brenner. *International Journal of Psycho-Analysis*, **51** (1970), 407-415.

Freeman, T., Cameron, J., and McGhie, A. *Chronic Schizophrenia* (New York: International Universities, 1958).

————. *Studies on Psychosis* (New York: International Universities, 1966).

French, J. The reticular formation. In *Handbook of Physiology II*. (Washington, D.C.: American Physiological Society, 1960), pp. 1281-1305.

French, T. Goal, mechanism and integrative field. *Psychosomatic Medicine*, **3** (1941), 226-252.

————. The integration of social behavior. *Psychoanalytic Quarterly*, **14** (1945), 149-168.

————. *The Integration of Behavior* (Chicago: University of Chicago): Vol. I. *Basic Postulates* (1952); Vol. II. *The Integrative Process in Dreams* (1953); Vol. III. *The Reintegrative Process in a Psychoanalytic Treatment* (1958).

Freud, A. *The Ego and the Mechanisms of Defense* (New York: International Universities, 1936).

————. The mutual influences in the development of ego and id: introduction to the discussion. In *The Psychoanalytic Study of the Child*, Vol. VII (New York: International Universities, 1952), pp. 42-50.

————. Discussion of Dr. Bowlby's paper, Grief and mourning in infancy and early childhood. Ibid., Vol. XV (1960), pp. 53-62.

————. The concept of developmental lines. Ibid., Vol. XVIII (1963), pp. 245-265.

————. *Normality and Pathology in Childhood* (New York: International Universities, 1965).

————. Comments on trauma. In S. Furst (ed.), *Psychic Trauma* (New York: Basic Books, 1967).

Freud, A. and Dann, S. An experiment in group upbringing. In *The Psychoanalytic Study of the Child*, Vol. VI (New York: International Universities, 1951), pp. 127-168.

Freud, A., Nagera, H., and Freud,W.E. A metapsychological assessment of the adult personality: the adult profile. Ibid., Vol. XXII.

Freud, S. *The Standard Edition of the Complete Psychological Works of Sigmund Freud.* J. Strachey (ed.). 23 vols. (London: Hogarth, 1886-1957).

Fries, M. and Woolf, P. Some hypotheses on the role of the congenital activity type in personality development. In *The Psychoanalytic Study of the Child,* Vol. VIII (New York: International Universities, 1953), pp. 48-62.

Frosch, J. The psychotic character: clinical psychiatric considerations. *Psychiatric Quarterly,* **38** (1964), 81-96.

_____. A note on reality constancy, in R. Loewenstein et al. (eds.), *Psychoanalysis—A General Psychology: Essays in Honor of Heinz Hartmann* (New York: International Universities, 1966).

_____. Severe regressive states during analysis: summary. *Journal of the American Psychoanalytic Association,* **15** (1967), 3, 606-625.

_____. Delusional fixity, sense of conviction and the psychotic conflict. *International Journal of Psycho-Analysis,* **48** (1967), 475-495.

_____. Psychoanalytic considerations of the psychotic character. *Journal of the American Psychoanalytic Association,* **18** (1970), 24-50.

Frosch, J. and Wortis, S. A contribution to the nosology of the impulse disorders. *American Journal of Psychiatry,* **3** (1954), 132-138.

Furst, S. *Psychic Trauma* (New York: Basic Books, 1967).

Galambos, R. Suppression of auditory nerve activity by stimulation of efferent fibers to the cochlea. *Federal Procedures* **14** (1955), 53.

Galdston, I. On the etiology of depersonalization. *Journal of Nervous and Mental Disease,* **105** (1947).

Gardner, R., Holzman, P., Klein, G., Linton, H., and Spence, D. Cognitive control: a study of individual consistencies in cognitive behavior. *Psychological Issues,* **4** (1959).

Gardner, R. and Moriarty, A. *Personality Development at Pre-adolescence: Exploration of Structure Formation* (Seattle: U. of Washington, 1968).

Garma, A. Present thoughts on Freud's theory of dream hallucination. *International Journal of Psycho-Analysis,* **50** (1969), 4, 485-494.

Geleerd, E. Adolescence and adaptive regression. *Bulletin of the Menninger Clinic,* **28** (1964), 302-308.

_____. Two kinds of denial: neurotic denial and denial in the service of the need to survive. In R. Loewenstein (ed.), *Drives, Affects, Behavior* (New York: International Universities, 1965), pp. 118-127.

Gerö, G. The concept of defense. *Psychoanalytic Quarterly,* **20** (1951), 565-578.

Getzels, J. and Jackson, P. *Creativity and Intelligence* (New York: Wiley, 1962).

Gill, M. Topography and systems in psychoanalytic theory. *Psychological Issues,* Monograph 10. (New York: International Universities, 1963).

_____. The primary process. In R. Holt (ed.), *Motives and Thought. Psychoanalytic Essays in Hornor of David Rapaport* (New York: International Universities, 1967).

512   **Appendices**

Gill, M. and Brenman, M. *Hypnosis and Related States* (New York: International Universities, 1959).

Gill, M. and Klein, G. The structuring of drive and reality. *International Journal of Psycho-Analysis,* 45 (1964), 483-498.

Giovacchini, P. On scientific creativity. *Journal of the American Psychoanalytic Association,* 8 (1960), 407-426.

Glasner, S. Benign paralogical thinking. *Archives of General Psychiatry,* 14 (1966), 94-99.

Glauber, I. Dysautomatization: a disorder of preconscious ego functions. *International Journal of Psycho-Analysis,* 49 (1968), 1.

Glover, E. Grades of ego-differentiation (1930), In *On the Early Development of Mind* (New York: International Universities, 1956).

———. A psycho-analytic approach to the classification of mental disorders (1932). Ibid.

———. The relation of perversion-formation to the development of reality sense (1933). Ibid.

———. Contribution to symposium "Criteria of Success in Psycho-Analysis." British Psycho-Analytic Society, March 4, 1936.

———. The Concept of Dissociation (1943). In *On The Early Development of The Mind* (New York: International Universities, 1956).

———. The future development of psycho-analysis (1948). Ibid.

———. *The Technique of Psycho-analysis* (New York: International Universities, 1955).

Glueck, S. and Glueck, E. *Physique and Delinquency* (New York: Harper and Row, 1956).

Goffman, E. Characteristics of total institutions. In *Walter Reed Army Institute of Research Symposium on Preventive and Social Psychiatry, April 15-17, 1957.* (Washington, D. C.: U. S. Government Printing Office).

Goldfarb, W. *Childhood Schizophrenia* (Cambridge, Mass.: Harvard University, 1961).

———. Division into neurologically determined and environmentally determined groups. In NIMH *Special Report of the National Institute of Mental Health* (1971).

Goldstein, K. *The Organism* (New York: American Book, 1939).

Grand, S., Freedman, N. and Steingart, I. A study of the representation of objects in schizophrenia. *Journal of The American Psychoanalytic Association* (in press).

Granit, R. and Kadda, B. Influence of stimulation of central nervous structures on muscle spindles in cat. *Acta Physioligica Skandinavia,* 27 (1952), 130-160.

Grauer, D. How autonomous is the ego. *Journal of the American Psychoanalytic Association* 6 (1958), 502-518.

Green, S. The evaluation of ego adequacy. *Journal of Hillside Hospital,* **3** (1954), 199-203.

Greenacre, P. The predisposition to anxiety (1941). In *Trauma, Growth and Personality* (London: Hogarth, 1953).

———. Vision, headache and halo. *Psychoanalytic Quarterly,* **16** (1947), 177-194.

———. General problems of acting out. *Psychoanalytic Quarterly,* **19** (1950), 455-467.

———. *Trauma, Growth and Personality* (London: Hogarth, 195).

———. *Swift and Carroll: A Psychoanalytic Study of Two Lives* (New York: International Universities, 1955).

———. Early physical determinants in the development of the sense of reality. *Journal of the American Psychoanalytic Association,* **6** (1958).

———. The imposter. *Psychoanalytic Quarterly,* **27** (1958), 359-382.

———. Toward an understanding of the physical nucleus of some defense reactions. *International Journal of Psycho-Analysis,* **39** (1958), 69-76.

———. Considerations regarding the parent-infant relationship. *International Journal of Psycho-Analysis,* **41** (1960), 571-584.

Greenfield, N. and Lewis, W. *Psychoanalysis and Current Biological Thought* (Madison: U. of Wisconsin, 1965).

Greenson, R. The struggle against identification. *Journal of the American Psychoanalytic Association,* **2** (1954), 200-217.

Grinberg, L. The relationship between obsessive mechanisms and a state of self disturbance: depersonalization. *International Journal of Psycho-Analysis,* **47** (1966).

Grinker, R., Sr., Werble, B., and Drye, R. *The Borderline Syndrome: A Behavioral Study of Ego Functions* (New York: Basic Books, 1968).

Grinspoon, L., et al. *Schizophrenia: Pharmacotherapy and Psychotherapy* (Baltimore: Williams and Wilkins, 1972).

Groddeck, G. The Book of the Id; Psychoanalytic Letters to a Friend. New York, Washington: Nervous and Mental Disease Publishing Company, 1928. Monograph Series #49.

Groos, K. *The Play of Man* (New York: Appleton, 1901).

Guilford, J. *Psychometric Methods* (New York: McGraw-Hill, 1954).

———. *The Nature of Human Intelligence* (New York: McGraw-Hill, 1967).

Guntrip, H. *Personality Structure and Human Interaction* (New York: International Universities, (1961).

Hacker, F. Symbols and psychoanalysis. *Psychosomatics,* **11** (1957), 641-671.

———. The discriminating function of the ego. *International Journal of Psycho-Analysis,* **43** (1963), 395-405.

Hammerman, S. Conceptions of superego development. *Journal of the American Psychoanalytic Association,* **13** (1965), 320-355.

Hartmann, H. An experimental contribution to the psychology of obsessive-compulsive neurosis: on remembering completed and uncompleted tasks (1933). In *Essays on Ego Psychology* (New York: International Universities, 1964).

_____. *Ego Psychology and the Problem of Adaptation* (1939; repr., New York: International Universities, 1958).

_____. Psychoanalysis and the concept of health (1939). In *Essays and Ego Psychology* (New York: International Universities, Press, 1964).

_____. Psychoanalysis and sociology (1944). Ibid.

_____. On rational and irrational action (1947). Ibid.

_____. Comments on the psychoanalytic theory of instinctual drives (1948) . Ibid.

_____. Comments on the psychoanalytic theory of the ego (1950). Ibid.

_____. Technical implications of ego psychology (1951). Ibid.

_____. The mutual influences in the development of ego and id. (1952). Ibid.

_____. Contribution to the metapsychology of schizophrenia (1953). Ibid.

_____. Notes on the theory of sublimation. (1955). Ibid.

_____. Notes on the reality principle. (1956). Ibid.

Hartmann, H., Kris, E., and Loewenstein, R. Comments on the formation of psychic structure. *Psychological Issues,* (1946) **4, 14** (1964), 27-55.

_____. Notes on the theory of aggression. In Papers on Psychoanalytic Psychology. *Psychological Issues,* **14** (1949).

Hartmann, H. and Loewenstein, R. Notes on the superego. In *The Psychoanalytic Study of the Child* Vol.XVII pp. 42-81. (New York: International Universities, 1962).

Hemple, C. Fundamentals of concept formation in empirical science. *International Encyclopedia of Unified Science II,* Vol. VII (Chicago: U. of Chicago, 1952).

Henderson, D. and Gillespie, R. *A Textbook of Psychiatry.* 7th ed. (London: Oxford, 1950).

Hendrick, I. *Facts and Theories of Psychoanalysis* (New York: Knopf, 1934; repr. Dell, 1947).

Hoffer, E. *The True Believer* (New York: Harper and Row, 1951).

Hoffer, W. Mouth, hand, and ego integration. In *The Psychoanalytic Study of the Child,* Vols. III-IV (New York: International Universities, 1949). pp. 49-56.

_____. Development of the body ego. In *The Psychoanalytic Study of the Child,* Vol. V (New York: International Universities, 1950). pp. 18-23.

_____. Defensive process and defensive organization: their place in psychoanalytic technique. *International Journal of Psycho-Analysis,* **335** (1954), 194-198.

_____. Notes on the theory of defense. In *The Psychoanalytic Study of the Child*, Vol. XXIII (New York: International Universities, 1968), 178-188.

Hobarth, K. and Kerr, D. Central influences on spinal afferent conduction. *Journal of Neurophysiology*, **17** (1954), 295-307.

Holt, R. Some recent applications of Freud's concept of stimulus barrier to psychological research. Unpublished MS (1948).

_____. Gauging primary and secondary processes in Rorschach responses. *Journal of Projective Techniques*, **20** (1956), 14-25.

_____. A critical examination of Freud's concept of bound vs. free cathexis. *Journal of the American Psychoanalytic Association*, **10** (1962).

_____. A review of some of Freud's biological assumptions and their influence on his theories. In N. Greenfield and W. Lewis (eds.), *Psychoanalysis and Current Biological Thought* (Madison: U. of Wisconsin, 1965).

_____. Beyond vitalism and mechanism: Freud's concept of psychic energy. In J. Masserman (ed.), *The Ego, Science, and Psychoanalysis,* vol. XI (New York: Grune and Stratton, 1967).

_____. Motives and thought. *Psychological Issues,* **18/19** (1967).

Holt, R. and Luborsky, L. *Personality Patterns of Psychiatrists.* 2 vols. (New York: Basic Books, 1958).

Holzman, P. and Ekstein, R. Repetition-functions of transitory regressive thinking. *Psychoanalytic Quarterly,* **28** (1959), 228-235.

Holzman, P. and Klein, G. Motive and style in reality contact. *Bulletin of the Menninger Clinic,* **20** (1956), 181-191.

Hurvich, M. On the concept of reality testing. *International Journal of Psycho-Analysis,* **51** (1970), 299-312.

Hurvich, M. and Bellak, L. Ego function patterns in schizophrenics. *Psychological Reports,* **22** (1968), 299-308.

Huston, P. and Pepernick, M. Prognosis in schizophrenia. In L. Bellak (ed.), *Schizophrenia: A Review of the Syndrome* (New York: Grune and Stratton, 1958).

Isakower, O. A contribution to the pathopsychology of phenomena associated with falling asleep. *International Journal of Psycho-Analysis,* **19** (1938).

Jacobson, E. Contribution to the metapsychology of cyclothymic depression. In P. Greenacre (ed.), *Affective Disorders* (New York: International Universities, 1953).

_____. The affects and their pleasure-unpleasure qualities in relation to the psychic discharge process. In R. Loewenstein (ed.), *Drives, Affects, Behavior* (New York: International Universities, 1953).

_____. The self and the object world. In *The Psychoanalytic Study of the Child,* vol. XIX (New York: International Universities, 1954). pp. 75-127.

_____. Depersonalization. *Journal of the American Psychoanalytic Association,* **7** (1959).

_____. *The Self and the Object World* (New York: International Universities, 1964).

_____. Depression: Comparative Studies of Normal, Neurstic, and Psychotic Conditions (New York: International Universities, 1971).

Jahoda, M. *Current Concepts of Positive Mental Health* (New York: Basic Books, 1958).

Janis, I. *Psychological Stress* (New York: Wiley, 1958).

Joffe, W. and Sandler, J. Comments on the psychoanalytic psychology of adaptation, with special reference to the role of affects and the representational world. *International Journal of Psycho-Analysis,* **49** (1968), 445-453.

Johnson, A. Sanctions for superego lacunae of adolescents. In K. Eissler (ed.), *Searchlights on Delinquency* (New York: International Universities, 1949).

Jones, E. Fear, guilt and hate. *International Journal of Psycho-Analysis,* **10** (1929), 383-397.

Joseph, E. Regressive ego phenomena in psychoanalysis. *Monograph I of the Kris Study Group of the New York Psychoanalytic Institute* (New York: International Universities, 1965).

_____. Memory and conflict. *Psychoanalytic Quarterly,* **35** (1966), 1-17.

Kanzer, M. Acting out, sublimation and reality testing. *Journal of the American Psychoanalytic Association,* 5 (1957), 663-683.

Kaplan, R., Sand, W. and Whitman, R. Humiliation, mortification, and the negative ego ideal. Paper presented at the May, 1963 meeting of the American Psychoanalytic Association.

Kardiner, A. and Preble, E. *They Studied Man* (New York: World, 1961).

Kardos, E. and Peto, A. Contributions to the theory of play. *British Journal of Medical Psychology,* **29** (1956), 100-112.

Karush, A., Easser, B., Cooper, A., and Swerdloff, B. The evaluation of ego strength. I: A profile of adaptive balance. *Journal of Nervous and Mental Disease,* **139** (1964), 236-253.

Kasanin, J. The disturbance of conceptual thinking in schizophrenia (1939), in J. Kasanin (ed.), *Language and Thought in Schizophrenia* (New York: Norton, 1964), pp. 41-49.

Katan, M. Schreber's pre-psychotic phase. *International Journal of Psycho-Analysis,* **34** (1953), 43-51.

Katz, M., Cole, J., and Lowery, H. Studies of the diagnostic process: the influence of symptom perception, past experience, and ethnic background on diagnostic decisions. *American Journal of Psychiatry,* **125** (1969), 937-947.

Keiser, S. Body ego during orgasm. *Psychoanalytic Quarterly,* **21** (1952).

Kelly, L. and Fiske, D. *The Prediction of Performance in Clinical Psychology* (Ann Arbor: U. of Michigan, 1951).

Kernberg, O. Structural derivatives of object relationships. *International Journal of Psycho-Analysis,* **47** (1966), 236-253.

―――――. Borderline personality organization. *Journal of the American Psychoanalytic Association,* **15** (1967), 641-685.

―――――. Factors in the psychoanalytic treatment of narcissistic personalities. Ibid., **18** (1970), 51-84.

―――――, Barriers to being in love. Paper presented at meeting of the New York Society of Freudian Psychologists, 1971.

Kahn, M. The role of polymorph-perverse body-experiences and object relations in ego-integration. *British Journal of Medical Psychology,* **35** (1962) 245-261.

―――――. The concept of cumulative trauma. In *The Psychoanalytic Study of the Child,* Vol. XVIII (New York: International Universities, 1963), p. 286-306.

Kind, H. Prognosis. In L. Bellak and L. Loeb (eds.), *The Schizophrenic Syndrome* (New York: Grune and Stratton, 1969).

Klein, G. The personal world through perception. In R. Blake and C. Ramsey (eds.), *Perception: An Approach to Personality.* (New York: Ronald, 1951).

―――――. Peremptory ideation: structure and force in motivated ideas. In R. Holt (ed.), Motives and Thought: Psychoanalytic Essays in Honor of David Rapaport. *Psychological Issues.* **18/19** (1967).

―――――. The ego in psychoanalysis – a concept in search of identity. *Psychoanalytic Review,* **56** (1970), 511-525.

Klein, G. and Schlesinger, H. Where is the perceiver in perceptual theory? *Journal of Personality,* **18** (1949), 32-47.

Klein, M. The importance of symbol-formation in the development of the ego. *International Journal of Psycho-Analysis,* **11** (1930).

―――――. *The Psycho-Analysis of Children* (London: Hogarth, 1932; 3rd ed. New York: Evergreen, 1960).

―――――. Notes on some schizoid mechanisms. *International Journal of Psycho-Analysis,* **27** (1946), 99-110.

―――――. *Contribution to Psychoanalysis. 1921-1945.* (London: Hogarth, 1948).

―――――. *Developments in Psychoanalysis* (London: Hogarth, 1952).

Klein, M. et al. *New Directions in Psychoanalysis* (London: Tavistock, 1955).

Köhler, W. *The Mentality of Apes* (New York: Harcourt, Brace, 1926).

Kohut, H. Forms and transformations of narcissism. *Journal of the American Psychoanalytic Association,* **14** (1966), 243-272.

Kohut, H. *The Analysis of the Self.* Monograph series of *The Psychoanalytic Study of the Child* (New York: International Universities, 1971).

Kris, E. *Psychoanalytic Explorations in Art* (1936; repr., New York: International Universities, 1952).

―――――. The psychology of caricature (1936). In *Psychoanalytic Explorations in Art* (New York: International Universities, 1952).

_____. Preconscious mental processes. *Psychoanalytic Quarterly*, **19** (1950), 540-560.

_____. The development of ego psychology. *Samiksa*, **5** (1951).

_____. On preconscious mental processes. In *Psychoanalytic Explorations in Art* (New York: International Universities, 1952).

_____. On some viscissitudes of insight in psychoanalysis. *International Journal of Psycho-Analysis*, **41** (1956), 1-18.

_____. The personal myth. *Journal of the American Psychoanalytic Association*, **4** (1956).

_____. Decline and recovery in the life of a three-year-old; or: data in psychoanalytic perspective on the mother-child relationship. In *The Psychoanalytic Study of the Child*, Vol. XVII (New York: International Universities, 1962), pp. 175-215.

Kris, M. Discussion remarks: Symposium on Infantile Trauma. (Psychoanalytic Research and Development Fund, 1964).

Kubie, L. The fallacious use of quantitative concepts in dynamic psychology. *Psychoanalytic Quarterly*, **16** (1947), 507-518.

Kubie, L. Neurotic distortion of the creative process. In *Porter Lectures.* ser. 22 (Lawrence: U. of Kansas, 1958).

Kupper, H. Psychodynamics of the "intellectual." *International Journal of Psycho-Analysis*, **3** (1950), 85-94.

Laing, R. *The Divided Self* (Chicago: Quadrangle, 1960).

Lampl de Groot, J. On defense and development: normal and pathological. (1957). In *The Development of the Mind* (New York: International Universities, 1962).

_____. Ego ideal and superego. Ibid.

Lazarus, R. *Psychological Stress and the Coping Process* (New York: McGraw-Hill, 1966).

Lecky, P. Self-consistency (New York: Island Press, 1945).

Levin, S. Toward a clarification of external factors capable of inducing psychological stress. *International Journal of Psycho-Analysis,* **47** (1966), 546-551.

_____. Some metapsychological considerations on the differentiation between shame and guilt. *International Journal of Psycho-Analysis*, **48** (1967), 267-276.

Levita, D. On the psycho-analytic concept of identity. *International Journal of Psycho-Analysis,* **47** (1966).

Levy, L. and Orr, T. The social psychology of Rorschach validity research. *Journal of Abnormal and Social Psychology*, **58** (1959), 79-83.

Lewin, B. Sleep, the mouth, and the dream screen. *Psychoanalytic Quarterly,* **15** (1946), 419-434.

_____. Inferences from the dream screen. *International Journal of Psycho-Analysis*, **29** (1948), 224-231.

_____. *The Psychoanalysis of Elation* (New York: Norton, 1950).

Lewis, H. *Shame and Guilt in Neurosis* (New York: International Universities, 1971).

Lewis, H. Some observations relevant to early defenses and precursors. *International Journal of Psycho-Analysis* 44 (1963), 132-142.

_____. Structural aspects of the psychoanalytic theory of instinctual drives, affects and time. In N. Greenfield and W. Lewis (eds.). *Psychoanalysis and Current Biological Thought* (Madison: U. of Wisconsin, 1965).

Lewy, E. On micropsia. *International Journal of Psycho-Analysis,* 35 (1954).

Lichtenberg, J. and Slap, J. On the defensive organization. Ibid., 52 (1971), 451-458.

Lilly, J. Mental effects of reduction of ordinary levels of physical stimuli on intact, healthy persons. *Psychiatric Research Report,* 5 (1956), 1-9.

Linn, L. The discriminating function of the ego. *Psychoanalytic Quarterly,* 23 (1954), 38-47.

Livingston, R. Central control of afferent activity. In H. Jasper, et al. (eds.), *Reticular Formation of the Brain* (Boston: Little, Brown, 1958), p. 177-185.

Loevinger, J., Wessler, R., and Redmore, C. *Measuring Ego Development* (San Francisco: Jossey Bass, 1970).

Loewald, H. Ego and reality, *International Journal of Psycho-Analysis,* 32 (1951), 10-18.

Loewenstein, R. Some remarks on defenses, autonomous ego and psychoanalytic technique. *Ibid.,* 35 (1954) 188-193.

_____. On the theory of the superego: a discussion. In R. Lowenstein, L. Newman, M. Schur, and A. Solnit (eds.), *Psychoanalysis – A General Psychology* (New York: International Universities, 1966).

_____. Defensive organization and autonomous ego functions. *Journal of the American Psychoanalytic Association,* 15 (1967), 795-809.

_____. Ego autonomy and psychoanalytic technique. *Psychoanalytic Quarterly,* 41 (1972).

Lowenfeld, H. and Lowenfeld, Y. Our permissive society and the superego. *Ibid.,* 39 (1970), 4.

Luborsky, L. The patient's personality and psychotherapeutic change. In H. Strupp and L. Luborsky (eds.), *Research in Psychotherapy.* (Washington: American Psychological Assc. 1962).

Luborsky, L., Fabian, M., Hall, B., Ticho, E., and Ticho, G. Treatment variables. *Bulletin of the Menninger Clinic,* 22 (1958), 126-147.

Lustman, S. Impulse control, structure, and the synthetic function. In R. Loewenstein, L. Newman, M. Schur, and A. Solnit (eds.), *Psychoanalysis– A General Psychology. Essays in Honor of Heinz Hartmann* (New York: International Universities, 1966).

Macalpine, I. The development of the transference. *Psychoanalytic Quarterly*, **19** (1950), 501-539.

Magni, F., Melyak, R. Monizzi, G., and Smith, C. Direct pyramidal influences on the dorsal column nuclei. *Archives of Italian Biology*, **97** (1959), 357-377.

Magoun, H. Non-specific brain mechanisms. In H. Harlow and C. Woolsey (eds.), *Biological and Biochemical Bases of Behavior* (Madison: U. of Wisconsin, 1958), pp. 25-36.

Mahler, M. Thoughts about development and individuation. In *The Psychoanalytic Study of the Child*,Vol. XVIII (New York: International Universities, 1963), pp. 307-324.

Mahler, M. and Furer, M. *On Human Symbiosis and the Vicissitudes of Individuation* (New York: International Universities, 1968).

Mahler, M. and McDevitt, J. Observations on adaptation and defense in statu nascendi. *Psychoanalytic Quarterly*, **37** (1968), 1-21.

Malev, M. Use of the repetition compulsion by the ego. *Psychoanalytic Quarterly*, **38** (1969), 52-71.

Mannheim, K. *Ideology and Utopia* (London: Routledge and Kegan Paul, 1936).

Marcovitz, E. The concept of the id. *Journal of the American Psychoanalytic Association*, **11** (1963), 151-160.

Mason, R. *Internal Perception and Bodily Functioning* (New York: International Universities, 1961).

May, P. (ed.). *Treatment of Schizophrenia. A Comparative Study of Five Treatment Methods* (New York: Science House, 1968).

May, P. and Dixon, W. Methods of statistical analysis. Ibid.

May, P., Wexler, M., Salkan, J. and Schoop, T. Non-verbal techniques in the re-establishment of body image and self identity—a preliminary report. *Psychiatric Research Report 16* (1963), pp. 68-82.

May, R. The problem of will and intentionality in psychoanalysis. *Contemporary Psychoanalysis*, **3** (1966), 55-70.

————. *Love and Will* (New York: Norton, 1969).

Mayman, M. *Manual for Scoring the Form Level of Rorschach Responses* (Topeka, Kans.: Menninger Foundation, 1964).

McGhie, A. Psychological studies of schizophrenia. *British Journal of Medical Psychology*, **39** (1966), 281-288.

Mednick, S. A learning theory approach to research in schizophrenia. (1958) In: A. Buss and E. Buss (eds.) *Theories of Schizophrenia*. New York: Atherton Press, 1969.

————. The children of schizophrenics: serious difficulties in current research methodologies which suggest the use of the "high risk group" method. In J, Romano (ed.), *The Origins of Schizophrenia* (Amsterdam: Excerpta Medica Foundation, 1967).

Mednick, S. and Schulsinger, F. Some premorbid characteristics related to breakdown in children with schizophrenic mothers. In *The Transmission of Schizophrenia* (London: Pergamon, 1968).

Meissner, W. Freud's methodology. *Journal of the American Psychoanalytic Association,* **19** (1971), 265-309.

Menaker, E. The masochistic factor in the psychoanalytic situation. *Psychoanalytic Quarterly,* **11** (1942), 171-186.

Menaker, E. and Menaker, W. *Ego in Evolution* (New York: Grove, 1965).

Menninger, K. *The Vital Balance* (New York: Viking, 1963).

Meyer, J. Konzentrative Entspannungsubungen nach Elsa Gindler und ihre Grundlager. *Zeitschrift für Psychotherapie,* **11** (1961), 4.

Michaels, J. Character structure and character disorders. In S. Arieti (ed.), *American Handbook of Psychiatry,* vol. I (New York: Basic Books, 1959), pp. 353-377.

Miller, J., Isaacs, K., and Haggard, E. On the nature of the observing function of the ego. *British Journal of Medical Psychology,* **38** (1965), 161-169.

Miller, S. Ego-autonomy in sensory deprivation, isolation, and stress. *International Journal of Psycho-Analysis,* **43** (1962), 1-20.

Milner, M. Aspects of symbolism in comprehension of the not-self. Ibid., **33** (1952), 181-195.

Milner, M. *On Not Being Able To Paint* (London: Heinemann, 1957).

Mintz, E. On fostering development of some conflict-free ego functions. *Psychotherapy: Theory, Research, & Practice,* vol. II (1965), 2, 84-88.

Mittelman, B. Motility in infants, children, and adults: patterning and psychodynamics. In *The Psychoanalytic Study of the Child,* Vol. IX (New York: International Universities, 1954), p. 142.

Modell, A. The concept of psychic energy. *Journal of the American Psychoanalytic Association,* **11** (1963), 605-618.

————. *Object Love and Reality* (New York: International Universities, 1968).

Moore, B. and Fine, B. (eds.) *A Glossary of Psychoanalytic Terms and Concepts* (New York: American Psychoanalytic Assc., 1968).

Morgenstern, S. Psychoanalytic conception of depersonalization. *Journal of Nervous and Mental Disease,* **73** (1931).

Mosher, L. (ed.), *Special Report on Schizophrenia* (Washington, D.C.: National Institute of Mental Health, 1971).

Munroe, R. *Schools of Psychoanalytic Thought* (New York: Dryden, 1955).

Murphy, G. and Spohn, H. *Encounter with Reality: New Forms for an Old Quest* (Boston: Houghton, Mifflin, 1968).

Murphy, L. *The Widening World of Childhood.* New York: Basic Books, 1962.

————. Adaptational tasks in childhood in our culture. *Bulletin of the Menninger Clinic,* **28** (1964).

Murray, H. *The Assessment of Men* (New York: Rinehart, 1948).

Nacht, S. Psychoanalysis of today. *Psychoanalytic Quarterly,* **29** (1960), 401-402.

Nagera, H. The concepts of structure and structuralization: psychoanalytic usage and implications for a theory of learning and creativity. In *The Psychoanalytic Study of the Child,* Vol. XXII (New York: International Universities, 1967).

————. The concept of ego apparatus in psychoanalysis: including considerations concerning the somatic roots of the ego. Ibid., Vol. XXIII (1968).

Nagera, H. and Colonna, A. Aspects of the contribution of sight to ego and drive development. Ibid., Vol. XX (1965).

Nass, M. The superego and moral development in the theories of Freud and Piaget. Ibid., Vol. XXI (1966), pp. 51-68.

Novey, S. The role of the superego and ego ideal in character formation. *International Journal of Psycho-Analysis,* **36** (1955), 254-259.

————. The sense of reality and values of the analyst as a necessary factor in psycho-analysis. Ibid., **47** (1966), 492-501.

Nunberg, H. The sense of guilt and the need for punishment. Ibid., **7** (1926), 420-433.

————. The synthetic function of the ego (1930). In *The Practice and Theory of Psychoanalysis* Vol. I (New York: International Universities, 1960).

————. *Principles of Psychoanalysis,* Vol. I (New York: International Universities, 1932.

————. Ego Strength and ego weakness (1938). In *The Practice and Theory of Psychoanalysis,* vol. I (New York: International Universities, 1938).

————. Transference and reality. *International Journal of Psycho-Analysis,* **32** (1951), 1-9.

Oberndorf, C. On retaining the sense of reality in states of depersonalization. Ibid., **20** (1939).i,

————. The role of anxiety in depersonalization. Ibid., **31** (1950).

Offer, D. and Sabshin, M. *Normality* (New York: Basic Books, 1966).

Olds, J. and Milner, P. Positive reinforcement produced by electrical stimulation of septal area and other regions of rat brain. *Journal of Comparative Physiological Psychology,* **47** (1954), 419-427.

Ostow, M. The metapsychology of autoscopic phenomena. *International Journal of Psycho-Analysis,* **41** (1960).

————. *Drugs in Psychoanalysis and Psychotherapy* (New York: Basic Books, 1962).

Pacella, B. Early ego development and the déja vu. *Proceedings of the American Psychoanalytic Association,* December, 1971 (Abstract).

Paine, R. The contribution of developmental neurology to child psychiatry. *Journal of Child Psychiatry,* **4** (1965).

Parens, H. and Saul, L. *Dependence in Man* (New York: International Universities, 1971).

Payne, R. Thought disorder in schizophrenia and its implications for etiology and treatment. Paper presented at NIMH Conference on Schizophrenia, 1970.

Perl, E., Whitlock, D., and Gentry, J. Cutaneous projection to second-order neurons of the dorsal column system. *Journal of Neurophysiology,* **25** (1962), 337-358.

Peto, A. On so-called depersonalization. *International Journal of Psycho-Analysis,* **36** (1955).

Phillips, L. *Human Adaptation and its Failures* (New York: Academic, 1967).

Piaget, J. *The Moral Judgment of the Child* (New York: Harcourt, Brace, 1932).

————. *The Construction of Reality in the Child* (1937; repr. New York: Basic Books, 1954).

Piers, G. and Singer, M. *Shame and Guilt* Springfield, Ill.: Thomas. 1953).

Pine, F. and Holt, R. Creativity and primary process: a study of adaptive regression. *Journal of Abnormal and Social Psychology,* **61** (1960), 370-379.

Pollin, W. and Stabenau, J. Early characteristics of monozygotic twins discordant for schizophrenia. *Archives of General Psychiatry,* **17** (1967), 723-732.

Pollin, W., Stabenau, J., et al. Biological, psychological, and historical differences in a series of monozygotic twins discordant for schizophrenia. In D. Rosenthal and S. Kety (eds.), *The Transmission of Schizophrenia* (London: Pergamon, 1968).

Prelinger E. Identity diffusion and the synthetic function. In B. Wedge (ed.), *Psychosocial Problems of College Men* (New Haven, Conn.: Yale U., 1958).

Prelinger, E., Zimet, C. Schafer, R. and Levin, S. *An Ego Psychological Approach to Character Assessment* (New York: The Free Press of Glencoe, 1964).

Pribram, K. Freud's project: an open, biologically based mold for psychoanalysis. In N. Greenfield and W. Lewis (eds.), *Psychoanalysis and Current Biological Thought* (Madison: U. of Wisconsin, 1965). pp. 81-92.

Provence, S. Some aspects of early ego development: data from a longitudinal study. In R. Loewenstein, L. Newman, M. Schur, and A. Solnit (eds.), *Psychoanalysis—A General Psychology* (New York: International Universities, 1966).

Provence, S. and Lipton, R. *Infants in Institutions* (New York: International Universities, 1962).

Provence, S. and Ritvo, S. Effects of deprivation on institutionalized infants: disturbances in development of relationship to inanimate objects. In *The Psychoanalytic Study of the Child,* Vol. XVI (New York: International Universities, 1961).

Pumpian-Mindlin, E. Propositions concerning energic-economic aspects of libido theory: conceptual models of psychic energy and structure in psychoanalysis. In L. Bellak (ed.), *Conceptual and Methodological Problems in Psychoanalysis. Annals of the New York Academy of Science,* **76** (1959), p. 1038-1052.

_____. Defense organization of the ego and psychoanalytic technique. American Psychoanalytic Association Meeting, May, 1966. *Journal of the American Psychoanalytic Association,* **15** (1967), 150-165.

Rabin, A. Diagnostic use of intelligence tests. In B. Wolman (ed.), *Handbook of Clinical Psychology* (New York: McGraw-Hill, 1965).

Rado, S. The economic principle in psychoanalytic technique. *International Journal of Psycho-Analysis,* **6** (1925), 35.

Rado, S. and Daniels, G. (eds.), *Changing Concepts of Psychosomatic Medicine* (New York: Grune and Stratton, 1956).

Rangell, L. The metapsychology of psychic trauma. In S. Furst (eds.), *Psychic Trauma* (New York: Basic Books, 1967), pp. 51-84.

Rapaport, D. *Emotions and Memory* (New York: International Universities, 1942).

_____. On the psychoanalytic theory of thinking (1950). In M. Gill (ed.), *The Collected Papers of David Rapaport* (1950). (New York: Basic Books, 1967).

_____. The autonomy of the ego. *Bulletin of the Menninger Clinic,* **15** (1951), 113-123.

_____. *Organization and Pathology of Thought* (New York: Columbia U., 1951).

_____. On the psychoanalytic theory of affects. *International Journal of Psycho-Analysis* **34** (1953).

_____. The development and the concepts of psychoanalytic ego psychology. Twelve seminars given at the Western New England Institute for Psychoanalysis. S. Miller (ed.). Mimeographed (1955).

_____. Present-day ego psychology (1956). In M. Gill (ed.), *The Collected Papers of David Rapaport* (New York: Basic Books, 1967).

_____. Cognitive structures (1957). In M. Gill (ed.), *The Collected Papers of David Rapaport* (New York: Basic Books, 1967).

_____. In S. Miller (ed.). *Seminars in Advanced Metapsychology,* Vol. IV (Stockbridge, Mass: Austin Riggs Center, 1957).

_____. The theory of ego autonomy: a generalization. *Bulletin of the Menninger Clinic,* **22** (1958), 13-35.

_____. An historical survey of psychoanalytic ego psychology, In *Identity and the Life Cycle:* Selected Papers E. Erikson, Psychological Issues. Monograph 1 (New York: International Universities, 1959).

_____. The theory of attention cathexis (1959). In M. Gill (ed.). *The Collected Papers of David Rapaport* (New York: Basic Books, 1967).

_____. The Structure of Psychoanalytic Theory. Psychological Issues Mono-
graph 6 (New York: International Universities, 1960).

_____. On the psychoanalytic theory of motivation. In M. Jones (ed.),
Nebraska Symposium on Motivation Lincoln: U. of Nebraska, 1960), pp.
173-247.

Rapaport, D. and Gill, M. Points of view and assumptions of metapsychology.
International Journal of Psycho-Analysis **40** (1959), 153-162.

Rapaport, D., Gill, M., and Schafer, R. *Diagnostic Psychological Testing.* vols.
I-II (Chicago: Year Book, 1946).

_____.Ibid 2nd ed. R. Holt (ed.) (New York: International Universities,
1968).

Redl, F. and Wineman, I. *Children Who Hate* (Glencoe, Ill.: Free Press, 1951).

Reed, J. Schizophrenic thought disorder: a review and hypothesis. *Comprehensive Psychiatry,* **2** (1970), 5.

Reich, A. Early identification as archaic elements in the superego. *Journal of the
American Psychoanalytic Association,* **2** (1954), 218-238.

_____. Pathologic forms of self-esteem regulation, in *The Psychoanalytic Study
of the Child,* Vol. XV (New York; International Universities, 1960).

Reich, W. *Character Analysis* (1933; New York: Orgone Institute, 1945).

_____. Ibid. 3rd ed. (New York: Orgone Institute, 1949).

Reik, T. *The Compulsion to Confess* (New York: Farrar, Straus, and Cudahy,
1925).

Riviere, J. Hate, greed and aggression (1937), in M. Klein and J. Riviere (eds.)
Love, Hate and Reparation (New York: Norton, 1964).

Roazen, P. *Brother Animal* (New York: Knopf, 1969).

Robbins, L. and Wallerstein, R. The research strategy and tactics of the
psychotherapy research project of the Menninger Foundation and the
problem of controls. In E. Rubinstein and M. Lorr (eds.), *Research in
Psychotherapy,* vol. I (Washington, D.C. American Psychological Assc.
1959).

Rogers, C. *Counseling and Psychotherapy: Newer Concepts in Practice* (Boston:
Houghton Mifflin, 1942).

Roland, A. The reality of the psychoanalytic relationship and situation in the
handling of transference-resistance. *International Journal of Psycho-
Analysis,* **48** (1967), 504-510.

Romm, M. Influences determining types of regression. *Psychoanalytic Quarterly,*
28 (1959), 170-182.

Rose, G. Body ego and creative imagination. *Journal of the American
Psychoanalytic Association* **11** (1963), 775-789.

_____. Body ego and reality. *International Journal of Psycho-Analysis,* **47**
(1966), 502-509.

Rosen, J. *Direct Psychoanalytic Psychiatry* (New York: Grune and Stratton, 1962).

Rosen, V. On mathematical illumination and the mathematical thought process. In *The Psychoanalytic Study of the Child,* vol. VIII (New York: International Universities 1953), pp. 127-154.

————. Strephosymbolia: an intrasystemic disturbance of the synthetic function of the ego. Ibid. vol. X (1955), pp. 83-89.

————. Review of the id and the regulatory principles of mental functioning. *International Journal of Psycho-Analysis,* 49 (1968), 100-101.

Rosenblatt, A. and Thickstun, J. A study of the concept of psychic energy. Ibid, 51 (1970), 265-278.

Rosenfeld, H. Analysis of a schizophrenic state with depersonalization. Ibid., 28 (1947).

————. Notes on the psycho-analysis of the super-ego conflict of an acute schizophrenic patient. Ibid. 33 (1952).

————. *Psychotic States: A Psychoanalytic Approach* (New York: International Universities, 1965).

Rosenthal, D. *The Genain Quadruplets* (New York: Basic Books, 1963).

————, An historical and methodological review of genetic studies of schizophrenia. In J. Romano (ed.), *The Origins of Schizophrenia* (Amsterdam: Excerpta Medica Foundation, 1967).

————. In *Heredity and Schizophrenia. Crosscurrents of Psychiatric Thought* (Roche Laboratories, 1967).

————. *Genetic Theory and Abnormal Behavior* (New York: McGraw-Hill, 1970).

Rosenthal, D. et al. Schizophrenics' offspring reared in adoptive homes. In D. Rosenthal and S. Kety (eds.), *The Transmission of Schizophrenia* (London: Pergamon, 1968).

Rosenwald, G. Personality description from the viewpoint of adaptation. *Psychiatry,* 31 (1968), 16-31.

Roshco, M. Perception, denial, and depersonalization. *Journal of the American Psychoanalytic Association,* 15 (1967), 243-260.

Ross, N. The "as if" concept. *Journal of the American Psychoanalytic Association*, 15 (1967), 59-82.

Rothenberg, A. The iceman changeth. Ibid., 17 (1969), 549-607.

Rubinfine, D. Perception, reality testing, and symbolism. In *The Psychoanalytic Study of the Child,* vol. XVI (New York: International Universities, 1961).

————, Maternal stimulation, psychic structure, and early object relations; with special reference to aggression and denial. Ibid. vol. XVII (1962), pp. 265-282.

Rubinstein, B. Explanation and mere description: a metascientific examination of certain aspects of the psychoanalytic theory of motivation. In R. Holt (ed.). *Motives and Thought. Psychological Issues* 18/19 (1967).

Rycroft, C. An observation of the defensive function of schizophrenic thinking and delusion-formation. *International Journal of Psycho-Analysis*, **43** (1962), 32-39.

St. John, R. Regression as a defense in chronic schizophrenia. *Psychoanalytic Quarterly*, **35** (1966), 414-422.

Sachs, H. Metapsychological points of view in technique and theory. *International Journal of Psycho-Analysis*, **6** (1925), 5-12.

Sachs, W. *Black Hamlet* (London: Saunders, 1937).

Salzman, L., Goldstein, R., Atkins, R., and Babigian, H. Conceptual thinking in psychiatric patients. *Archives of General Psychiatry*, **14** (1966), 55-59.

Sandler, J. The background of safety. *International Journal of Psycho-Analysis*, **44** (1960), 352.

_____. The Hampstead Index as an instrument of psychoanalytic research. Ibid., **43** (1962), 287-291.

Sandler, J., Holder, A. and Meers, D. The ego ideal and the ideal self. In *The Psychoanalytic Study of the Child*, vol. XVIII (New York: International Universities, 1963), pp. 139-158.

Sandler, J. and Joffe, W. Notes on obsessional manifestations in children. Ibid., vol. XX (New York: International Universities, 1965).

_____. On skill and sublimation. *Journal of the American Psychoanalytic Association*, **14** (1966), 335-355.

Sandler, J. and Rosenblatt, B. The concept of the representational world. In *The Psychoanalytic Study of the Child*, vol. XVII (New York: International Universities, 1962).

Sanford, N., Webster, H., and Freedman, M. Impulse expression as a variable of personality. *Psychological Monograph*, **71** (11) (1957), pp. 1-21.

Sargent, H., Modlin, H., Faris, M., and Voth, H. The psychotherapy research project of the Menninger Foundation: situational variables. *Bulletin of the Menninger Foundation*, **22** (1958), 148-166.

Sarlin, C. Depersonalization and derealization. *Journal of the American Psychoanalytic Association*, **10** (1962).

Satterfield, J. Effect of sensorimotor cortical stimulation upon cunate nuclear output through medial lemniscus in cat. *Journal of Nervous and Mental Disease*, **135** (1962), 507-512.

Saul, L. *Emotional Maturity* (Philadelphia: Lippincott, 1947).

_____. The punishment fits the source. *Psychoanalytic Quarterly*, **19** (1950), 164-169.

Savage, C. Variation in ego feelings induced by D-lysergic acid diethylamide (LSD-25). *Psychoanalytic Review*, **42** (1955).

Savitt, R. Psychoanalytic studies on addiction: ego structure in narcotic addiction. *Psychoanalytic Quarterly*, **32** (1963), 43-57.

Schactel, E. *Metamorphosis: On the Development of Affect, Perception, Attention, and Memory* (New York: Basic Books, 1959).

Schafer, R. *The Clinical Application of Psychological Tests* (New York: International Universities, 1950).

――――. *Psychological Interpretation in Rorschach Testing* (New York: Grune and Stratton, 1954).

――――. Regression in the service of the ego: the relevance of a psychoanalytic concept for personality assessment. In G. Lindzey (ed.), *Assessment of Human Motives* (New York: Holt, Rinehart and Winston, 1958).

――――. The loving and beloved superego in Freud's structural theory. In *The Psychoanalytic Study of the Child*, vol. XV (New York: International Universities, 1960), pp. 163-188.

――――. *Aspects of Internalization* (New York: International Universities, 1968).

――――. An overview of Heinz Hartmann's Contributions to Psychoanalysis. *International Journal of Psycho-Analysis*, **51** (1970), 4, 425-446.

Scherrer, H. and Hernandez-Peon, R. Inhibitory influence of recticular formation upon synaptic transmission in gracilis nucleus. *Federal Procedures*, **14** (1955), 132.

Schilder, P. On encephalitis (1928). In P. Schilder (ed.), *Brain and Personality* (New York: International Universities, 1951)

――――. (1930). In D. Rapaport (ed.), *Organization and Pathology of Thought* (New York: Columbia U. 1951).

――――. *The Image and Appearance of the Human Body* (London: Kegan Paul, Trench, Trubner, 1935).

――――. *Brain and Personality* (New York: International Universities, 1951).

――――. *Medical Psychology* (New York: International Universities, 1953).

Schimek, J. Cognitive style and defenses: a longitudinal study of intellectualization and field independence. *Journal of Abnormal Psychology*, **73** (1968), 575-580.

Schmideberg, M. After the analysis. *Psychoanalytic Quarterly*, **7** (1938), 122-142.

Schnier, J. Restitution aspects of the creative process. *American Imago*, **14** (1957), 211-223.

Schopler, E. and Loftin, J. Thinking disorders in parents of young psychotic children. *Journal of Abnormal Psychology*, **74** (1969), 281-287.

――――. Thought disorders in parents of psychotic children. *Archives of General Psychiatry*, **20** (1969).

Schulsinger, F. and Achte, K. Decreased recidivism in Denmark and Finland. In *Special Report on Schizophrenia* (Washington, D.C.: National Institute of Mental Health, 1971).

Schupper, F. and Calogeras, R. Psycho-cultural shifts in ego defenses. *American Imago* 28 (1971), 1.

Schur, M. The ego in anxiety. In R. Loewenstein (ed.). *Drives, Affects, and Behavior* (New York: International Universities, 1953).

————. Discussion of Dr. Bowlby's paper, Grief and mourning in infancy and early childhood. In *The Psychoanalytic Study of the Child,* (New York: International Universities, 1960), vol. XV pp. 63-84.

————. *The Id and the Regulatory Principles of Mental Functioning* (New York: International Universities, 1966).

Scott, J. *On Aggression* (Chicago: U. of Chicago, 1958).

Scott, T. Effects of decreased variation in the sensory environment. *Canadian Journal of Psychology,* 8 (1954).

Searles, H. Integration and differentiation in schizophrenia (1959). In *Collected Papers on Schizophrenia and Related Subjects* (New York: International Universities, 1965).

————, *Collected Papers on Schizophrenia and Related Subjects* (New York: International Universities, 1965).

Sechehaye, M. *Symbolic Realization: A New Method of Psychotherapy Applied to a Case of Schizophrenia* (New York: International Universities, 1951).

Shevrin, H. and Toussieng, P. Conflict over tactile experiences in emotionally disturbed children. *Journal of the American Academy of Child Psychiatry,* 1 (1962), 564-590.

————. Vicissitudes of the need for tactile stimulation in instinctual development. In *The Psychoanalytic Study of the Child,* vol. XX (New York: International Universities, 1965), pp. 310-339.

Siegel, R. What are defense mechanisms? *Journal of the American Psychoanalytic Association,* 17 (1969), 785-807.

Silberman, I. Synthesis and fragmentation. In *The Psychoanalytic Study of the Child,* vol. XVI (New York: International Universities, 1961), 90-117.

Silverman, J. The problem of attention in research and theory in schizophrenia. *Psychological Review,* 71 (1964), 352-379.

Simon, J. The paradoxical effect of effort. *British Journal of Medical Psychology,* 40 (1967), 375.

Singer, M. and Wynne, L. Stylistic variables in family research. Presented at a symposium, Milwaukee Psychiatric Hospital and Marquette University, Wisconsin, Department of Psychiatry, 1964.

————, Thought disorder and family relations of schizophrenics: III. Methodology using projective techniques. *Archives of General Psychiatry,* 12 (1965), 187.

————. Thought disorder and family relations of schizophrenics: IV. Results and implications. Ibid., 12 (1965b), 201.

_____. Principles for scoring communication defects and deviances in parents of schizophrenics: Rorschach and T.A.T. scoring manuals. *Psychiatry,* **29** (1966), 260.

Solomon, P., et al. *Sensory Deprivation.* (Cambridge, Mass.: Harvard U., 1961).

Special Report on Schizophrenia L. Mosher (ed.), (Washington, D.C. National Institute of Mental Health, 1969).

Special Report on Schizophrenia L. Mosher (ed.), (Washington, D.C.: National Institute of Mental Health, 1971).

Sperling, S. On denial and the essential nature of defense. *International Journal of Psycho-Analysis,* **39** (1958), 25-38.

Spiegel, L. Acting out and defensive instinctual gratification. *Journal of the American Psychoanalytic Association* 2 (1954), 1, 107-119.

_____. Superego and the function of anticipation with comments on "anticipatory anxiety." In R. Loewenstein, L. Newman, M. Schur, and A. Solnit (eds.), *Psychoanalysis—A General Psychology. Essays in Honor of Heinz Hartmann* (New York: International Universities, 1966).

Spitz, R. Hospitalism. In R. Eissler, A. Freud, H. Hartmann, and E. Kris (eds.), *The Psychoanalytic Study of the Child* (New York: International Universities, 1945).

_____. Anxiety in infancy: a study of its manifestations in the first year of life. *International Journal of Psycho-Analysis* 31 (1950), 138-143.

_____. Relevancy of direct infant observation. In *The Psychoanalytic Study of the Child,* vol. V (New York: International Universities, 1950), pp. 66-73.

_____. The psychogenic diseases of infancy. Ibid., vol. VI (1951), pp. 255-278.

_____. The primal cavity. Ibid. vol. X (1955), pp. 215-240.

_____. *No and Yes* (New York: International Universities, 1957).

_____. On the genesis of superego components. In *The Psychoanalytic Study of the Child,* vol. XIII (New York: International Universities, 1958), pp. 375-404.

_____. *A Genetic Field Theory of Ego Formation* (New York: International Universities, 1959).

_____. Discussion of Dr. Bowlby's paper, Grief and mourning in infancy and early childhood. In *The Psychoanalytic Study of the Child,* (New York: International Universities, 1960), vol. XV pp. 85-94.

_____. Early prototypes of ego defenses. *Journal of the American Psychoanalytic Association,* **9** (1961).

_____. *The First Year of Life* (New York: International Universities, 1965).

Stamm, J. Altered ego states allied to depersonalization. *Journal of the American Psychoanalytic Association,* **10** (1962).

Stanton, A. Propositions concerning object choices. In L. Bellak (ed.), *Conceptual and Methodological Problems in Psychoanalysis* (New York Academy of Science, 1959).

Stein, M. Self observation, reality and the superego. In R. Loewenstein et al.

(eds.), *Psychoanalysis—A General Psychology: Essays in Honor of Heinz Hartmann* (New York: International Universities, 1966).

Steingart, I. and Freedman, N. A language construction approach for the examination of self/object representations in varying clinical states. In R. Holt and E. Peterfreund (eds.),*Psycho-Analysis Contemporary Science*, vol. I (New York: Macmillan, 1972).

Stengel, E. A re-evaluation of Freud's book *On Aphasia*. Its significance for psychoanalysis. Read at the 185th International Psychoanalytic Congress, London, July 27, 1953. *International Journal of Psycho-Analysis*, 35 (1954), 85-89.

Sterba, R. The fate of the ego in analytic theory. *International Journal of Psycho-Analysis*, 15 (1934), 117-126.

_____. *Introduction to the Psychoanalytic Theory of Libido* (New York: Nervous and Mental Disease Publ. 1942).

Stewart, W. Depersonalization. Panel report of the American Psychoanalytic Association, St. Louis, May, 1963, V. Rosen, Chairman. *Journal of the American Psychoanalytic Association*, 12 (1964).

Stone, L. Reflections on the psychoanalytic concept of aggression. *Psychoanalytic Quarterly*, 40 (1971), 2.

Storr, A. *Human Aggression* (New York: Atheneum, 1968).

Sutherland, J. Object relations theory and the conceptual model of psychoanalysis. *British Journal of Medical Psychology*, 36 (1963), 109-124.

Székely, L. Symposium: the psychoanalytic study of thinking. *International Journal of Psycho-Analysis*, (1962), 297,305.

Szurek, S. Notes on the genesis of psychopathic personality trends. *Psychiatry*, 43 9, (1942) 1--6.

Tabachnick, N. Three psychoanalytic views of identity. *International Journal of Psycho-Analysis*, 46 (1965), 467-474.

Taush, V. On the origin of the influencing machine in schizophrenia. *Psychoanalytic Quarterly*, 2 (1933).

Thurstone, L. *Primary Mental Abilities* (Chicago: U. of Chicago, 1938).

Valenstein, A. The defense mechanisms and activities of the ego: some aspects of a classificatory approach. In M. Kanzer (ed.), *The Unconscious Today: Essays in Honor of Max Schur* (New York: International Universities, 1972).

Varendonck, J. *The Psychology of Daydreams* (London: Allen and Unwin, 1921).

Visotsky, H., Hamburg, D., Goss, M., and Lebovits, B. Coping behavior under extreme stress: observations of patients with severe poliomyelitis. *Archives of General Psychiatry*, 5 (1961), 423-448.

von Domarus, E. The specific laws of logic in schizophrenia. (1944) In. J. Kasania (ed.), *Language and Thought in Schizophrenia* (New York: Norton, 1964), pp. 104-114.

Voth, H. Ego autonomy, autokinesis, and recovery from psychosis. *Archives of General Psychiatry,* 6 (1962), 288-293.

Waelder, R. The principle of multiple function: observations on over-determination (1930). *Psychoanalytic Quarterly,* 5 (1936), 45-62.

_____. The psychoanalytic theory of play. Ibid., 2 (1932), 208-224.

_____. The problem of freedom in psycho-analysis and the problem of reality-testing. *International Journal of Psycho-Analysis,* 17 (1936), 89-108.

_____. Notes on prejudice. *Vassar Alumni Magazine* (May 1949).

_____. The structure of paranoid ideas. *International Journal of Psycho-Analysis,* 32 (1951), 167-177.

_____. *Basic Theory of Psychoanalysis* (New York: International Universities, 1960).

Wallerstein, R. Development and metapsychology of the defense organization of the ego. Panel report, American Psychoanalytic Association Meeting, May 1966, Jacob Arlow, Chairman. *Journal of the American Psychoanalytic Association,* 15 (1967), 130-149.

_____. Reconstruction and mastery in the transference psychosis. *Journal of the American Psychoanalytic Association* 15 (1967), 551-583.

_____. The psychotherapy research project of the Menninger Foundation: A semifinal view. In J. Shlein, H. Hunt, J. Matarazzo, and C. Savage (eds.), *Research in Psychotherapy,* vol. III (Washington, D.C.: American Psychological Assc., 1968.

Wallerstein, R., Robbins, L., Sargent, H., and Luborsky, L. The psychotherapy research project of the Menninger Foundation; rationale, method and sample size. *Bulletin of the Menninger Foundation,* 20 (1956), 221-278.

Wangh, M. Panel: the scope of the contribution of psychoanalysis to the biography of the artist. *Journal of the American Psychoanalytic Association,* 5 (1957), 564-575.

Wechsler, D. *Manual for the Wechsler Adult Intelligence Scale* (New York: Psychological Corp. 1955).

Weil, A. The basic core. In *The Psychoanalytic Study of the Child* vol. XVIII (New York: International Universities, 1970), pp. 442-460.

Weiner, I. *Psychodiagnosis in Schizophrenia* (New York: Wiley, 1966).

Weisman, A. Reality sense and reality testing. *Behavioral Science,* 3 (1958), 228-261.

_____. *The Existential Core of Psychoanalysis* (Boston: Little Brown, 1965).

Weiss, E. Sense of reality and reality testing. *Samiksa,* 4 (1950), 171-180.

Weiss, J. The integration of defences. *International Journal of Psycho-Analysis,* 48 (1967), 520-524.

Weissman, P. Development and creativity in the actor and playwright. *Psychoanalytic Quarterly,* 30 (1961), 549-567.

———. Psychological concomitants of ego functioning in creativity. *International Journal of Psycho-Analysis,* **49** (1968), 464-469.

———. Creative fantasies and beyond the reality principle. *Psychoanalytic Quarterly,* **38** (1969).

Werner, H. *Comparative Psychology of Mental Development* (New York: International Universities, 1948).

Wheelis, A. Will and psychoanalysis. *Journal of the American Psychoanalytic Association,* **4** (1956), 285-303.

White, R. Motivation reconsidered: the concept of competence. *Psychological Review,* **66** (1959), 297-333.

———. Competence and the psychosexual stages of development. In *Nebraska Symposium on Motivation* (Lincoln: U. of Nebraska, 1960).

———. Ego and reality in psychoanalytic theory. *Psychological Issues* (New York: International Universities, 1963), 3.

———. Competence and the growth of personality. In *Science and Psychoanalysis, vol. XI, The Ego* (New York: Grune and Stratton, 1967).

Wild, C. Creativity and adaptive regression. *Journal of Personality and Social Psychology,* **2** (1965), 161-169.

Winnicott, D. Primary maternal preoccupation. In *Collected Papers* (New York: Basic Books, 1965), pp. 300-305.

———. *Collected Papers: Through Paediatrics to Psychoanalysis* (London: Tavistock; New York: Basic Books, 1958).

———. The theory of the parent-infant relationship (1960). In *The Maturational Processes and the Facilitating Environment.* (New York: International Universities, 1965), pp. 37-55.

———. From dependence toward independence in the development of the individual (1963) Ibid., pp. 83-92.

Witkin, H. Psychological differentiation and forms of pathology. *Journal of Abnormal Psychology,* **70** (1965).

Witkin, H., Dyk, R., Faterson, H., Goodenough, D., and Karp, S. *Psychological Differentiation* (New York: Wiley, 1962).

Wolff, P. The developmental psychologies of Jean Piaget and psychoanalysis. *Psychological Issues. Monograph 5* (New York: International Universities, 1960).

———. The causes, controls and organization of behavior in the neonate. *Psychological Issues,* **17** (1966).

Woodbury, M. Altered body-ego experiences: a contribution to the study of regression, perception, and early experiences. *Journal of the American Psychoanalytic Association* **14** (1966).

Wynne, L. Family transactions and schizophrenia: II. Conceptual considerations for a research strategy (1967). In J. Romano (ed.), *The Origins of Schizophrenia* (Amsterdam: Excerpta Medica Foundation, 1967), pp. 165-178.

Wynne, L. and Singer, M. Thought disorder and family relations of schizophrenics: I. A research strategy. *Archives of General Psychiatry,* **9** (1963a), 191.

_____. Thought disorder and family relations of schizophrenics: II, A classification of forms of thinking. Ibid. **9** (1963b), 199.

Yankelovich, D. and Barrett, W. *Ego and Instinct: The Psychoanalytic View of Human Nature.* Rev. ed. (New York: Random House, 1970).

Zetzel, E. Anxiety and the capacity to bear it. *International Journal of Psycho-Analysis,* **30** (1949), 1-12.

_____. The significance of the adaptive hypothesis for psychoanalytic theory and practice. *Journal of the American Psychoanalytic Association,* **11** (1963).

_____. The theory of therapy in relation to a developmental model of the psychic apparatus. *International Journal of Psycho-Analysis,* **46** (1965), 39-52.

Zilboorg, G. The sense of reality. *Psychoanalytic Quarterly,* **10** (1941), 183-210.

Zubin, J., Eron, L., and Schumer, F. *An Experimental Approach to Projective Techniques* (New York: Wiley, 1965).

Zuckerman, M. Albright, R., Marks, C., and Miller, G. Stress and hallucinating effects of perceptual isolation and confinement. *Psychological Monographs,* **76** (1962).

Zwerling, I. Community-based long term treatment of psychotic patients in the Bronx. Paper given in Paris, February, 1972, at the symposium organized by the Association for Mental Health and Control of Alcoholism in the 13th District.

Additional References

Bannister, D. and Salmon, P.   Schizophrenic thought disorder: specific or diffuse. *British Journal of Medical Psychology,* **39** (1966), 215-219.

Bychowski, G.   Patterns of anger. *Psychoanalytic Study of the Child,* XXI (1966), 172-192.

Dugas, L. "Un Cas de Dépersonnalisation." *Revue philosophie de la France et de l'étranger.* **23** (1898).

Heston, L.   Psychiatric disorder in foster-home reared children of schizophrenic mothers. *British Journal of Psychiatry,* **112** (1966), 819-825.

Krishaber, M.   De la Néuropathie Cerebrocardiaque. Paris, 1873.

Namnum, A.   Contribution to symposium on indications and contraindications for psychoanalytic treatment. *International Journal Psycho-Analysis,* **49** (1968), 271.

Reider, N.   Transference psychosis. *Journal Hillside Hospital,* **6**, (1957), 131-149.

Vigotsky, L.   Thought and speech in psychiatry. *Journal Biology. & Pathology of Interpersonal Relations,* **2** (1939).

Yolles, S. and Kramer, M.   Vital statistics.. In Bellak, L. & Loeb, L. (eds.), *The Schizophrenic Syndrome.* (New York: Grune and Stratton, 1969).

Author Index

Schachtel, E., 185
Schafer, Roy, 45, 46, 53, 55, 62, 63, 70,
83, 86, 94, 98, 103, 104, 144, 185, 186,
203, 240, 252, 253, 279, 327
Scherrer, H., 224
Schilder, P., 70, 91, 98, 103, 114, 118, 163,
202, 247, 254
Schimek, J., 275
Schlesinger, H., 205
Schmideberg, M., 140
Schneir, J., 188
Schoop, T., 359
Schopler, E., 172
Schulsinger, F., 401, 417, 418
Schumer, F., 295
Schupper, F., 199
Schur, M., 17, 20, 151
Scott, J., 19, 26
Scott, T., 122
Searles, H., 154, 254
Sechehaye, M., 340, 359
Sheldon, William, 140
Shevrin, H., 86, 219
Shields, J., 279
Siegel, R., 63, 70, 198, 201
Silvan, M., 75
Silverman, J., 95, 252
Silverman, Lloyd, 331
Simon, J., 233, 359
Singer, M., 37, 40, 166, 172, 178, 363
Slap, J., 199
Sloane, P., 161
Small, L., 354, 359, 401
Solomon, P., 213
Spearman, C., 271, 272, 302
Sperling, S., 198, 200, 204, 280
Spiegel, L., 103, 106, 277
Spitz, R., 14, 15, 43, 122, 147, 150, 151,
152, 158, 201, 214, 222, 248, 262, 264,
268, 280
Spohn, H., 122
Stabenau, J., 417
Stamm, J., 118
Stanton, A., 145
Steingart, I., 156
Stengel, E., 160
Sterba, R., 11, 25, 108, 114, 251
Stewart, W., 119, 123
Stone, L., 27
Storr, A., 27

Strachey, J., 23, 96, 102, 193, 243
Sullivan, H., 79, 115, 352
Sutherland, J., 150, 158
Swerdloff, B., 56
Székely, L., 162
Szurek, S., 136

Tabachnick, N., 234
Tausk, V., 51, 118
Thickstun, J., 240
Thurstone, L., 271
Ticho, E., 53
Ticho, G., 53
Tolman, Edward, 245
Toussieng, P., 86, 219

Valenstein, A., 206
Varendonck, J., 180, 181, 182
Vernon, M., 272
Visortsky, H., 262
Vigotsky, L., 171
von Domarus, E., 171
Voth, H., 53, 235

Waelder, R., 21, 27, 67, 85, 88, 89, 104,
188, 197, 206, 225, 259, 264, 269, 270
Wallerstein, R., 53, 54, 69, 214, 217, 220,
226, 268
Wangh, M., 187
Wechsler, D., 336
Weil, A., 16, 30
Weiner, I., 96
Weisman, A., 61, 113, 187, 270
Weiss, E., 83, 89, 270
Weiss, J., 199
Werble, B., 56
Werner, Heinz, 87, 177
Wessler, R., 16
Wheelis, A., 263
White, R. W., 36, 93, 239, 256, 259, 260,
262, 265, 275, 281
Wild, C., 186
Wineman, I., 130, 135, 137
Winnicott, D., 151, 212, 215, 216, 220
Witkin, H., 117, 206, 267
Wolff, P., 87, 213, 214
Woodbury, M., 109
Woolf, P., 30, 134, 140
Worth, L., 95
Wortis, S., 129

Subject Index

Fear, 124, 138, 202
of loss of love, 33
of rejection, 40
by others, 40
Feces, 149
Fetish, 142
Fetishism, 112, 128, 244
Field-dependence-independence, 58, 117
cognitive style dimension of, 41
Fight, 102
Figure-Drawings, 295, 331, 386
Fiji Islander's, 353
Finger Apposition Test, 298
Flight, 102
Fitting together, 246
Forensic psychiatry, 100
Forgetting, 50
Free association, 184
Fragmentation, 206, 250
Freud's ego concept, 9–13
Freud's instinct theory, 20
Frigidity, 138
Frustration, 125, 129, 134, 136, 139, 140,
148, 153, 157, 158, 300
anal, 150
oral, 42, 149
pleasure, see Pleasure-frustration
Frustration tolerance, 126, 130, 132, 133,
137, 139, 140, 162
Fugues, 370
Fugue states, 109, 122
Function, apparatus and, 59–62
change of, 65
coping, 226
defense, 210
discriminating, of the ego, 83
integrative, 204
motor, 78, 133
multiple, 104
principle of, 269
oscillating, 183
structure and, 59–62
Functioning, autonomous, see Autonomous
functioning
characteristic, 293
characteristic levels of, 291, 299
creative, 324
current, 294
current levels of, 291, 293, 299
defensive, 50, 76, 78, 125, 139, 192–207,
298, 366

disturbances of, treatment of, 366
highest level of, 291, 293, 294, 299
lowest level of, 291, 293, 294, 299
moral, 31
regressive, 93
synthetic, see Synthetic functioning
thoughts, 138
Function pleasure, 263, 264
Functions, autonomous, see Autonomous
functions
adaptive, 126
of the ego, 224
ego, see Ego functions
protective, 219, 223
receptive, 219, 223
self-regulating, 53
sexual, 138, 257
superego, see Superego functions
synthetic, see Synthetic functions
Fusion, 117, 153, 154, 155, 157, 158, 253
unconscious, 116

Gain, secondary, 70, 245
Gemini, 391
Genetic point of view, 115
Genetics, 133, 165; see also Heredity
Genital, 114, 150
Genitals, 128, 256
Genital organization, 145
Genital phase, 25, 143
Genital sexual impulses, 126
Genital stage, 146
of libidinal development, 66
Genogenic, 166, 351
German, 166
Gestalt, 160
Gestalten, 184
Global Ego Strength Scale, 57, 74
Goals, ego, see Ego goals
Gratifications, 125, 126, 127, 128, 130, 140,
148, 152, 161, 203, 256, 263, 264
drive, 147
impulse, 153
instinctual, 129, 259
need, 146, 153, 154
Ghandi, 236
Grief, 151
Group psychology, 144, 356
Guilt, 37, 56, 119, 128, 129, 130, 135, 137,
149, 196, 197, 202

anticipatory feelings of, 106
versus initiative, 25
Oedipal, *see* Oedipal guilt
sense of, 8, 32, 91
and shame, 39, 41
unconscious sense of, 31, 33, 34, 35, 202
"Gulliver Fantasies," 120

Habits, 78, 132, 227, 232
Halo effects, 75, 89, 304, 310, 327, 328
Hallucinations, 74, 76, 81, 82, 84, 109, 112,
    122, 127, 128, 134, 161, 167, 293,
    370, 391
  visual, 85
Hallucinatory images, 161
Hallucinatory psychoses, 192
Hamlet, 99
Hampstead Clinic, 56
Hand-mouth coordination,122
Hatching, 147, 148
Hate, 126, 143, 149, 157, 202
Health, mental, 74, 75
Health-Sickness Rating Scale, 57
Hebephrenic, 288
Helplessness, 142, 152, 153, 209
  sense of, 140, 258
Hereditary ego core, 239
Heredity, 136, 140; *see also* Genetics
Hierarchical layering, 202
  multiple synthetic functions and, 246
Hierarchy, 202
  defense, 201, 202
  of other ego functions, 224
Hippies, 200, 212
Hobbies, 78, 227
Hollingshead Index, 287, 305
Homeostasis, 147, 226
Homicide, 357
Homosexuality, 145
Homosexuals, 142, 155, 200
Hospitalism, 150, 214
Hospitalization, 291, 293, 295, 311
Hospitalized patients, 294
Hostility, 114, 136, 142, 158, 193
  inhibition of, 139
  projection of, 50
Humor, 188
Hunger, 213
  stimulus, 134, 211, 212, 213, 214, 367
Hurvich sorting test, 299

Hyperanmesias, 241
Hypercathexis, 122, 164, 218
Hypersensitivity, 219, 221, 225
Hypnagogic phenomena, 109, 119, 122, 123
Hypnagogic state, 118
Hypnoid states, 80, 250
Hypnopompic experiences, 109. 119, 123
Hypnosis, 109, 119
Hypochondriasis, 139, 140
Hypothesis, heuristic, 399
Hysteria, 80, 82, 133, 229, 250

Id, 105, 114, 125, 126, 138, 144, 196, 199,
    203, 237, 239, 243, 256, 259, 264,
    291
  and ego, relations between, 28–30
  ego and superego, relationships between,
    253
  and ego ideal, tension between, 40
Id concept, 17–30
Id derivative, 119
Id impulse, 195
Id strivings, 236
Id wish, 203
Ideal, ego, *see* Ego ideal
Ideal object representations, 38, 47
Ideals, 229
Ideal self-representations, 38, 47
Ideas, 60, 126, 192, 193, 198, 199
  delusional, 193
  and perceptions, distinction between, 84–
    88
  incompatible, 243
  overvalent, 103
Ideation, 77
  primary process, 45
Ideational signals, 237
Ideational styles, 55
Identifications, 9, 14, 32, 33, 42, 45–46,
    48, 60, 115, 116, 120, 134, 135,
    137, 140, 144, 151, 154, 155, 198,
    200, 201
  with the aggressor, 43
  projective, 162, 206
  psychotic, 86, 155
  secondary, 206
  superego, 155
Identity, 91, 108, 113, 114, 115, 116, 117,
    119, 120, 153, 234, 281
  ego, *see* Ego identity

Instinctual vicissitudes, 23
Institutionalized infants, 150
Intact residue, 271
Integration, 78, 132, 157, 227
  ego, 216
  of ego development, 250
  of libidinal development, 250
Integrative capacity, 263, 316
  of cognitive field, 245
Integrative ego functions, 152
Integrity, 136
Intellect, 221
Intellectual activities, 258
Intellectual development, 87
Intellectualization, 375
Intellectual level, 292
Intelligence, sensorimotor, 88
  social, 298
Intentionality, 84, 227, 238, 240, 241
Intentions, 78, 131, 228, 260
Interactions, organism-environment, 221
Interactive process, 223
Interests, ego, see Ego interests
Internal objects, 148
Internal stimuli, 122, 211, 212
Internal stimulus barrier, 103
Internalization, 42, 45–46, 77, 136, 153,
  155, 158, 186
  of self-criticism, 45
Interpersonal relations, 54, 225, 236
Interpretation, 355
Interrater reliabilities, see Reliabilities,
  interrater
Intersystemic tension, 126
Intervention, area of, 354
  methods of, 354
    sequence of, 354
Interview, 286, 288, 290, 291, 294, 299
  clinical, 291
  taped, 294
Interviewers, 291, 292, 294, 295
Interview material, 54
Interview raters, 301
Interview ratings, 324, 326
Interview scoring manual, 292, 295, 296
Interview training, 294
Intrapsychic, 78
Intrapsychic conflicts, see Conflicts,
  intrapsychic
Intrasystemic factors, 51

Intrasystemic tensions, 126
Introjections, 45–46, 86, 115, 136, 143, 144,
  148, 149, 155, 157, 193, 195, 198,
  204, 205, 206, 231
Introspective report, 293
Intrusion, 216
I.Q., 287, 310
Irradiation of values, 88
Isolation, 119, 193, 195, 196, 198, 203, 205,
  206
  in obsessional neuroses, 194
  perceptual, 359
  sensory, 83

Joking, 188
Judgment, 9, 14, 49, 54, 75, 76, 79, 81, 82,
  126, 132, 135, 261, 276, 293, 298
  disturbances in, 105
    treatment of, 356
  reality testing and, 98–99
    relationship between, 96–97
  sources of error in, 97
Judgments, of just noticeable differences, 100
Jurisprudence, 100

Kafka, 275
Kant, Immanuel, 99
King, Martin Luther, Jr., 236
Kleinians, 352
Knowledge, sociology of, 94–95
Kraepelin, 400
Kris Study Group, 68, 240

Laboratory approach, 288
Laboratory procedures experimental, 286,
  297, 299
Language, 77, 111, 133, 157, 228, 260
Language disturbances, 241
Latency phase, 25
Learning, 16, 112, 201, 227, 231, 259, 261,
  264
  in human adaptation, 65
Learning difficulties, 241, 371
Lesions, organic, 100
Leveling, 58, 205
Libidinal aims, 149
Libidinal cathexis, see Cathexis, libidinal
Libidinal development, 149
  genital stage of, 66
  integration of, 250